SEVENTEENT

CW01483750

TWO YEAR OLDS OF 2001

STEVE TAPLIN

ISBN 1 901570 25 8

Price £6.99

Printers &
Publishers

This Edition First Published in 2001
by Portway Press Limited

CONTENTS

Cover photographs

Noverre's victory in the July Stakes at Newmarket was one of three in Britain last year for Godolphin's French-based trainer David Loder whose operation will be based at Newmarket in 2001; the picture of the July Stakes was taken by Ed Byrne, the inset photo of David Loder by George Selwyn

Two Year Olds of 2001

Author Steve Taplin hears it from the horse's mouth at Godolphin Stables (inset, pictured with trainer David Loder)

FOREWORD

I am delighted to be asked to write this foreword for Steve Taplin's 2001 edition of 'Two Year Olds'. It is consistently one of the most interesting and informative guides for the forthcoming season. Steve's knowledge and enthusiasm for pedigrees is always evident in his annual interview. In fact, he usually knows more about my horses than I do.

I have always particularly enjoyed training two-year-olds, and this season we have over one hundred at Godolphin Stables. The excitement is palpable at this time of year as one identifies the future stars in their morning work, and one just hopes that they have the Ferrari engine to go with the Ferrari pedigree. Which is, of course, why the combination of Steve's well-researched pedigree guides, together with the views of the trainers, gives the reader the inside track on each season's new crop of juveniles.

I expect that you will enjoy reading 'Two Year Olds'—now in its seventeenth year—as much as I do, and that you will be rewarded with plenty of winners.

David Loder

INTRODUCTION

My family and I were on holiday in the United Arab Emirates for the Dubai World Cup last year. After watching the incredible exploits of Dubai Millennium, we were treated to another lovely holiday surprise. Sheikh Mohammed invited my daughter for an impromptu photo session with him which had all the locals – and us – staring in amazement. That lovely picture now adorns our living room wall!

The Sheikh's penchant for blue-blooded racehorses is known throughout the racing world. The return of the Godolphin two-year-olds to England this year may not be universally popular amongst other owners and trainers. I'm sure they must feel they could do without the competition! Speaking for myself however, I really am pleased that David Loder and the Maktoum two-year-olds are back. Quality racehorses on the racecourses of England will always be welcome as far as I'm concerned and I wish David and his team all the best for the coming season.

One of the benefits of writing this book is visiting the trainers in spring, just as their young horses are beginning to show their true potential. I particularly enjoy my visits to the Lambourn area and of course to Newmarket, as I am guaranteed a friendly welcome at so many famous racing stables. With so much mystery surrounding the Racing Game, it is refreshing to hear so many trainers willing to discuss their hopes and estimations on their two-year-olds. If only the ultra secretive Ballydoyle/Coolmore team would take a leaf out of the relatively open books of so many trainers whose frank opinions can be found within these pages!

Last year's edition of this book was once more a comprehensive success in terms of number of winners – and in terms of handsome starting prices! Here are just a handful of the pointers my readers were able to take advantage of. Rich Gift (25-1), CD Europe (25-1), Sayedah (25-1), Fromsong (16-1), Fair Question (14-1), Oreana (12-1) and Dora Carrington (12-1). In all, there were over 260 individual 2-y-o winners highlighted.

New to the book this year are my Star Ratings for the two-year-olds. Quite simply, I've given a star for each English or Irish trained 2-y-o with (a) a particularly glowing assessment from the trainer (b) positive encouragement from the bloodstock agent or stud manager (c) a pedigree which suggests a 2-y-o win is very much on the cards (d) a sire/damsire cross that has been significantly successful already, and (e) a provisional Timeform Rating of 100 or above. I've listed separately those 2-y-o's with at least three stars – and I can't wait to see how they get on!

Once again, the Provisional Timeform Ratings are printed for the information of readers. These ratings reflect the Timeform figure the horse is considered capable of running to based on its pedigree and other relevant factors. Crucially, they are compiled on the same scale as Timeform's form ratings, so the two are directly comparable. Lack of some of the necessary data means that provisional Timeform Ratings cannot be published for many of the overseas-based stables.

The "Fifty To Follow" section will hopefully show a healthy profit and a good many of those selections will be aiming for the top prizes next season as three-year-olds. Indeed, it's as 3-y-o's that many of my selections excel, like the recent classic winners Always Loyal, Bachir, Bosra Sham, Cape Verdi, Dance Design, Entrepreneur, Island Sands, King's Best, Love Divine, Mutafaweq, Oath, Reams of Verse, Saffron Walden, Sleepytime, Spinning World, Ta Rib, Wince and Winona.

As usual, in addition to the comprehensive index of two-year-olds, breeding pundits will find an index of dams, making it easy to search for the latest two-year-olds out of favourite broodmares.

The book is divided into the following sections :-

(a) Fifty To Follow. An elite group of two-year-olds particularly highly regarded by their trainers.

(b) Star Two-Year-Olds.

(c) The Bloodstock Experts Mark Your Card. Bloodstock agents and stud managers suggest potentially smart two-year-olds bought or raised by them last year.

(d) Two-Year-Olds. The main section of the book, with each two-year-old listed under the trainer. This year I have combined the 'Premier' and 'Early Type' sections found in previous editions. For those new to this book, you will find the trainers' comments (when given) in italics after the pedigree assessments.

(e) The Stallion Reference, detailing the racing and stud careers of the sires of each two-year-old in the book.

(f) Two-year-old Racing Trends. A statistical analysis of those juvenile events which regularly highlight the stars of the future.

(g) Timeform Statistical Review.

Readers should bear in mind that all the trainers' comments come from my interviews which took place throughout April.

Once again I would like to thank John Ingles and Claire Curry of Timeform for their considerable help, the trainers for their invaluable advice and the racing and stud secretaries for their kind assistance.

Researched and compiled by Steve Taplin BA.

**Statistical Review and Provisional Timeform Ratings
by the kind consent of Timeform.**

FIFTY TO FOLLOW

*A smooth victory on Timeform Charity Day at York for Chianti (top picture);
Saratov, pictured winning at Ascot, was also among last year's 'Fifty'*

The 'fifty' have given their trainers every encouragement for a good season.

BELEZA (IRE)
b.f. Revoque – La Alla Wa Asa (Alzao).
"This really is a very nice filly and I intend to give her just one outing before heading for the Cherry Hinton Stakes". Clive Brittain.

BRIGHTER FUTURE
b.f. Night Shift – Welsh Mist (Damister).
"A lovely filly, she's going to be a nice 2-y-o and will probably start off over six furlongs. She's so well-built that she looks like a colt and she goes really well. A nice filly that could be anything". Barry Hills.

BURNING SUN (USA)
b.c. Danzig – Media Nox (Lycius).
"A very likeable, strong colt and a good mover. He'll be a nice colt later on this season". Henry Cecil.

COOL STORM
b.f. Rainbow Quest – Classic Park (Robellino).
"A good deal more forward than you'd expect for a filly bred this way. She'll definitely make a 2-y-o and I think she's a really nice filly. I wouldn't be at all surprised if she started off at five furlongs, despite being by Rainbow Quest. A classic filly". Peter Harris

COPERNICAN (USA)
b.c. Kingmambo – Mysterial (Alleged).
"An extremely nice horse, he's going very well at the moment and may have the speed for six furlongs but could be better over seven". David Loder.

DANISH DECORUM
ch.c. Danehill Dancer – Dignified Air (Wolver Hollow).
"He's a nice horse and although he's big he could well make a mid-summer 2-y-o as he's done particularly well over the past few weeks. From being particularly backward he's pulled himself together and he looks as though he'll make a 2-y-o. He looks to have a bit of speed and should be suited by six or seven furlongs". Michael Jarvis.

DECEPTOR (USA)
b.c. Machiavellian – Satin Flower (Shadeed).
"He'll be one of our first runners. He's been here all winter so he's acclimatised earlier than his three-parts brother Lujain did.

Lujain had been in Dubai until May. This colt is tuned in and he goes very nicely. He's hopefully Ascot material as he's an obvious Coventry Stakes type horse". David Loder.

DERWENT (USA)
b.br.c. Distant View – Nothing Sweeter (Darby Creek Road).
"A very nice horse bought in America. He's good-looking, quite forward and should be ready to run by July time. I'd expect him to be good enough to win some races as a 2-y-o". Luca Cumani.

DIDDYMU (IRE)
b.f. Revoque – Family At War (Explodent).
"You won't see her out until mid-season but I think she's a really nice filly. One for the short-list, she's got bags of size and scope". Mick Channon.

DUPONT
b.c. Zafonic – June Moon (Sadler's Wells).
"This is the nicest one we've got. A nice pedigree, he goes well and I'm hopeful. He does everything very easily and the only other Zafonic I've had is Count Dubois who has done well for us. This colt would have more speed and I'm going to try to get him to Ascot – the races that is, not the Sales! A very solid-looking horse and a nice walker". William Haggas.

ELUTRAH
b.f. Darshaan – Balaabel (Sadler's Wells).
"A very good-looking filly. Her sister Sayedah is too, but in a way this filly seems to have even more scope. Anyone who bred a filly who looks like this would be absolutely thrilled – she's really nice and sensible just like her sister. She seems to be full of potential, is a nice mover and of all our fillies I'd pick her out – on looks anyway". Marcus Tregoning.

ESENIN
b.c. Danehill – Boojum (Mujtahid).
"A nice horse, he's very sharp and he'll make a sprint-type 2-y-o before mid-season. I'd say he was my best bet for a Group class 2-y-o". Neville Callaghan.

GENGHIS (IRE)

br.c. Persian Bold – Cindy's Baby (Bairn).

"Probably the pick of my 2-y-o's I would think. He looks a nice horse and although he's big, he's very much up-together and an early-maturing sort, so I don't think his size will bother him. He's a mid-season type of 2-y-o and finds everything easy. Very typical of his sire... and he has a nice temperament". Henry Candy.

GOOGOOSH (IRE)

b.f. Danehill – Literary (Woodman).

"A very nice Danehill filly. She's quite leggy, was fairly neat when we bought her but has done her growing. At the moment she looks to be amongst the best of the fillies and looks to be useful at this stage. A filly with a lot of scope about her and it's surprising to see how well she's going at this stage, so she has an outside chance of being an Ascot 2-y-o". Ed Dunlop.

HAPPY DREAMS (IRE)

b.f. Sadler's Wells – Flame Of Tara (Artaius).

"She's a gorgeous filly with a lot of quality about her. We'd be looking at the end of May or early June over six furlongs to begin with. She's very strong and is much more of a 2-y-o than the rest of the family have been...the nicest filly from the family since Salsabil". Michael Grassick.

HIDEAWAY HEROINE (IRE)

ch.f. Hernando – Dulcinea (Selkirk).

"I think she's gorgeous...She stands over a lot of ground and has a lot of Selkirk about her. She really does go up the gallops as well as anything but she's quite a big filly and I wouldn't expect her coming on stream before June...She goes really well and is very promising". John Hills.

KAHZIMA (USA)

b.br.f. Gulch – Gharayib (Nureyev).

"Not over-big and looks to be a 2-y-o type. I should imagine this is one for your short list!". Ed Dunlop.

KRUGERRAND (USA)

ch.c. Gulch – Nasers Pride (Al Nasr).

"A lovely, quality horse. Very athletic, he's a powerful mover with plenty of scope and size. He'll be a June or July 2-y-o and is a very handsome horse. We like him". Michael Bell.

LIPSTICK

b.f. Zamindar – Final Shot (Dalsaan).

"Lipstick will win the Queen Mary! A very nice filly that does everything right – she's very sharp and is a definite 2-y-o. She's got a great attitude and is certainly a winner". Mick Channon.

MADAME BOULANGERE

b.f. Royal Applause – Jazz (Sharrood).

"She goes really well and it won't be long before she's racing. As soon as we get some decent ground in fact". Richard's son added "I think this is the best filly we've got – as nice as I've seen here for a couple of years and she's such a lovely mover". Richard Hannon.

MANQUE NEUF

b.c. Cadeaux Genereux – Flying Squaw (Be My Chief).

"He's a very, very nice horse, quite tall and leggy but classy. He'd be my favourite at the moment and I would hope he'd be ready for around July time. He'll want six or seven furlongs this year". James Bethell.

MINE HOST

b.c. Elmaamul – Divina Mia (Dowsing).

"One of our most forward colts, he's very strong and will probably have run by the time this book is published. We like him and he may be alright over five furlongs but he's bred to be better over a bit further. His main aim will be the Fairyhouse Sales race and I'm hoping he's going to be at least listed class". Michael Bell.

MISTERAH

b.f. Alhaarth – Jasarah (Green Desert).

"When I first started on this filly I told Sheikh Hamdan that she'd be Alhaarth's first 2-y-o winner. She's just had one or two small hiccups since then but she's much better now. She's going to be speedy and for us will be an early 2-y-o – possibly late May. She's got the most marvellous, powerful quarters behind – she really pushes away well. We're really quite keen on her and hoping for the best". Marcus Tregoning.

MONSAL DALE (IRE).

ch.c. Desert King – Zanella (Nordico).

"He's a good, tough type of colt, I like him and hopefully he'll be ready to race in June over six furlongs. A fairly hardy sort, he'll

probably want plenty of work to stop him getting too above himself". James Toller.

MONTEX (USA)
ch.c. Royal Academy – Omara (Storm Cat).

"A good, strong type that moves well and I like him. He's a July type 2-y-o that seems to take more after the damsire Storm Cat than Royal Academy. He just seems to have those typical Storm Cat attributes of a great top line and plenty of strength. One to follow". Jeremy Noseda.

MOPPY MAY (IRE)
b.f. Alhaarth – Lacinia (Groom Dancer).

"She's very sharp indeed. We've just let her grow up and develop a bit but she'll be a sharp 2-y-o over five furlongs, maybe six furlongs at the most". Terry Mills.

OCTENNIAL
gr.c. Octagonal – Laune (Kenmare).

"I've got a lot of time for him – in fact I've got a quarter share in him. I like the mare and I think this is going to be a very nice horse. There's no reason why he shouldn't make it as a 2-y-o". Richard Hannon.

OFFICIAL FLAME (USA)
ch.c. Deputy Minister – Fire The Groom (Blushing Groom).

"A very nice horse. A strong, sprint type 2-y-o and he'll make a 3-y-o as well. He looks great and we'll see if he makes it to Ascot. If not, we'll be looking at something like the July meeting for him. He's an all-round, tough, nice horse". David Loder.

PACIFIC (USA)
b.c. Gulch – Wedding Of The Sea (Blushing Groom).

"A lovely horse this fellow, he's very well-forward and I like him. I had his half-brother last year and this is a better-looking horse. Hopefully he won't start to grow because at the moment he's going well and it looks like we can press on with him". John Oxx.

PASSING GLANCE
b.c. Polar Falcon – Spurned (Robellino).

"A lovely horse. If I had to make a choice right now he'd be my pick, but I'm slightly biased as we bred him. He'll be ready for mid-season and should have the speed for six furlongs. He's a lovely, big horse". Ian Balding.

PETER THE GREAT
b.c. Hector Protector – Perfect Alibi (Law Society).

"A very nice horse. He'll need a bit of time and I wouldn't expect him out until mid-season, probably over six furlongs, although he'll get seven later on. I like him a lot". Ralph Beckett.

PRIVILEGE (USA)
b.c. Foxhound – Pretty Miswaki (Miswaki).

"A powerful horse, he goes well and could be out relatively early if all goes well. I think I'll go for the first six furlong maiden with him". John Gosden.

QAZWEEN
b.c. Primo Dominie – Be My Lass (Be My Guest).

"He's a nice, good-topped colt and he'll be a 2-y-o. He goes well and he's certainly very nice. He should be out by early May and will be better over six furlongs than five". Mick Channon.

RAWABI
b.f. Sadler's Wells - Flying Melody (Auction Ring).

"Very nice. She's not over-big and so isn't particularly typical of Sadler's Wells – she looks like a sort of mini-version! A reasonably sharp filly, you would have to think that five furlongs might be too sharp although I'm not ruling it out at all. I'm looking forward to running her and she's a possible for the Queen Mary". David Loder.

REDBACK
ch.c. Mark Of Esteem – Patsy Western (Precocious).

"A good-looking horse from a good family…I can see why he cost as much as he did because he looks like being a good 2-y-o". Richard's son added – "this is the best colt we've got – a real tool I promise you! He's a really nice colt". Richard Hannon.

REHEARSAL HALL (USA)
ch.c. Diesis – Performing Arts (The Minstrel).

"Yes, he's working nicely and he's quite early. He should start off in May over five or six furlongs". John Gosden.

RISTRA (USA)
b.f. Kingmambo – Rhetorical Lass (Capote).

"A very athletic filly, the plan would be to run her when the six furlong races start after mid-May. I think she's a nice prospect". Jeremy Noseda.

RODOMONTADE (USA)

b.f. Machiavellian – Lajna (Be My Guest).

"She's a really nice filly, big and strong with a good attitude and she's a good mover. She came in a bit late so I don't expect her to be racing before June. A nice type of filly". Paul Cole.

SASARAN (IRE)

ch.c. Indian Ridge – Flaming June (Storm Bird).

"I liked him very much at the sales where it was hard to fault him and he's definitely shaping up nicely now. He's got a great length to his quarters and stands over a nice bit of ground. He moves extremely well, is quite a tall horse with an awful lot to like about him. I'm certainly looking forward to seeing him run, everyone who rides him likes him and I think he's certain to be a nice horse". Marcus Tregoning.

SECOND MINISTER

ch.c. Lion Cavern – Crime Of Passion (Dragonara Palace).

"A three-parts brother to Senior Minister, I like this colt a lot. He should be racing sometime during May over five furlongs and shows plenty of speed…He looks a real athlete and I'd say he was my best 2-y-o". James Eustace.

SHEILA BLIGE

ch.f. Zamindar – Stripanoora (Ahonoora).

"This is a really nice filly and she goes well, just like her half-sister Classy Act. She looks sharp and will be a decent 2-y-o". Alan Berry.

SOHAIB (USA)

b.c. Kingmambo – Fancy Ruler (Half A Year).

"Michael and Richard (Hills) both reckon he's a really nice horse and the best of our lot in Dubai, so we hope he'll be a decent 2-y-o". Barry Hills.

SOSUMI

br.f. Be My Chief – Princess Deya (Be My Guest).

"She's a very nice filly, could be an early 2-y-o and goes well. A filly with the right attitude, she's strong and is one to follow I should think". Mark Tompkins.

TIKKUN (IRE)

gr.c. Grand Lodge – Moon Festival (Be My Guest).

"Tikkun is a very nice horse and is one you could get running whenever you wanted him to – like most nice horses. Very strong and a good mover, we won't be in a hurry with him but I hope that he'll make a nice 2-y-o over seven furlongs or a mile in the autumn". Roger Charlton.

TORCH LIGHT (USA)

ch.c. Distant View – Flaming Torch (Rousillon).

"A medium-sized, active colt, he looks like a real 2-y-o and will hopefully be an Ascot type". Henry Cecil.

TWILIGHT BLUES (IRE)

ch.c. Bluebird – Pretty Sharp (Interrex).

"A lovely, big, imposing Bluebird colt. He's definitely got Royal Ascot potential and despite the high purchase price I'd give it for him again. A real corker and I'd hope to get him on the racetrack sometime in May. One of my nicest, I'd say". Brian Meehan.

WESTERN OVERTURE (USA)

ch.c. Gone West – Musical Bliss (The Minstrel).

"A nice, strong horse. Probably a stronger, tougher horse than his brother Raneem and we hope he makes a nice horse. I would say July over six or seven furlongs would be his starting point". David Loder.

WESTERN VERSE (USA)

b.c. Gone West – Reams Of Verse (Nureyev).

"A strong colt, he's very nice and will hopefully be an Ascot type". Henry Cecil.

WIXOE EXPRESS (IRE)

b.c. Anabaa – Esquiline (Gone West).

"A big horse but he'll run this year over seven furlongs or a mile and I like him a lot. He oozes a bit of class, I'm very happy with him and he seems to be coming on all the time". Sean Woods.

ZONE

b.c. Zilzal – Thea (Marju).

"A big, strong, attractive horse, he's coming along well in his work and will be suited by six furlongs plus in late May or June". Paul Cole.

STAR TWO YEAR OLDS

A new section for this year, the idea to give readers an instant appraisal of the regard in which a two-year-old is held. Each horse is rated according to the following criteria:

a)   A glowing assessment from the trainer

b)   Encouraging reports from the bloodstock agent or stud manager

c)   A pedigree that suggests a 2-y-o win is very much on the cards

d)   A sire/damsire cross that has been significantly successful already

e)   A provisional Timeform Rating of 100 or above

As you can see, the highest rating a horse can achieve is five stars and clearly this is a very firm statement of the high opinion in which the horse is held.

The following is a list of the two-year-olds for this year which have achieved three stars or more, with their reference number and the name of their trainer. Keep an eye on them!

ALBANIA
Trained by M. Channon (162)

ALLURING PARK (IRE)
Trained by J. Bolger (91)

ARROW
Trained by M. Bell (42)

ASAAFEER (USA)
Trained by M. Tregoning (994)

BELEZA (IRE)
Trained by C. Brittain (105)

BISHR
Trained by M. Tregoning (996)

BROKEN BARRICADES (IRE)
Trained by B. Hills (562)

BROWN EYES
Trained by B. Hills (563)

BURNING SUN (USA)
Trained by H. Cecil (135)

CHURCH CROSS (IRE)
Trained by D. Weld (1030)

COPERNICAN (USA)
Trained by D. Loder (687)

DANISH DECORUM (IRE)
Trained by M. Jarvis (618)

DECEPTOR (USA)
Trained by D. Loder (688)

DEMINI (IRE)
Trained by J. Oxx (842)

DERWENT (USA)
Trained by L. Cumani (249)

DISTINCTIVE STATE
Trained by D. Loder (689)

DIVINE STATUS (USA)
Trained by D. Loder (690)

DRAMATIC RING
Trained by I. Balding (10)

DUBAI EXCELLENCE
Trained by D. Loder (692)

EBARIYA (IRE)
Trained by J. Oxx (843)

ELUTRAH
Trained by M. Tregoning (998)

FARQAD (USA)
Trained by D. Loder (696)

FLORENTINE FLUTTER
Trained by J. Gosden (399)

FORTUNE (IRE)
Trained by J. Oxx (846)

GLAM ROCK
Trained by J. Gosden (401)

GOODWOOD PROMISE
Trained by J. Dunlop (305)

GOOGOOSH (IRE)
Trained by E. Dunlop (270)

HAPY DREAMS (IRE)
Trained by M. Grassick (445)

INDIAN COUNTRY
Trained by J. Noseda (792)

JOYOUS GIFT
Trained by D. Loder (699)

KAHZIMA (USA)
Trained by E. Dunlop (274)

KITALPHA (USA)
Trained by H. Cecil (143)

KRISKOVA (USA)
Trained by D. Loder (701)

KRUGERRAND (USA)
Trained by M. Bell (52)

LOLITA'S GOLD (USA)
Trained by J. Oxx (850)

MASSARRA
Trained by J. Dunlop (314)

MELLOW PARK (IRE)
Trained by J. Noseda (798)

MISTERAH
Trained by M. Tregoning (1005)

MOLLY ELLEN (IRE)
Trained by D. Weld (1041)

MOMENT
Trained by J. Gosden (410)

MOON'S WHISPER
Trained by J. Gosden (411)

MOSCOW
Trained by J. Gosden (412)

NAYYEL
Trained by J. Dunlop (316)

OCTENNIAL
Trained by R. Hannon (500)

OFFICIAL FLAME (USA)
Trained by D. Loder (705)

ON EDGE
Trained by D. Loder (706)

PACIFIC (USA)
Trained by J. Oxx (855)

PETER THE GREAT (IRE)
Trained by R. Beckett (39)

PIOUS
Trained by J. Fanshawe (378)

PRAIRIE DUNES (IRE)
Trained by J. Noseda (800)

RAWABI
Trained by D. Loder (709)

REDBACK
Trained by R. Hannon (508)

REHEARSAL HALL (USA)
Trained by J. Gosden (419)

RODOMONTADE (USA)
Trained by P. Cole (238)

RUM DESTINY (IRE)
Trained by A. Berry (75)

SASARAN (IRE)
Trained by M. Tregoning (1010)

SAXE
Trained by J. Oxx (859)

SCALADO (USA)
Trained by R. Charlton (214)

SECOND BURST (IRE)
Trained by J. Gosden (421)

SELWAN (USA)
Trained by D. Loder (713)

SHEILA BLIGE
Trained by A. Berry (76)

SILENCE IS GOLDEN
Trained by B. Meehan (749)

SILENT CRYSTAL (USA)
Trained by J. Noseda (805)

SOHAIB (USA)
Trained by B. Hills (592)

STORMY CHANNEL (USA)
Trained by H. Cecil (154)

SUNDRENCHED (IRE)
Trained by W. Haggas (468)

TAJRAASI (USA)
Trained by M. Channon (192)

TARAFAH
Trained by M. Tregoning (1014)

TIKKUN (IRE)
Trained by R. Charlton (217)

TREE PIPIT (USA)
Trained by B. Hills (596)

TRIPLE PLAY (IRE)
Trained by B. Meehan (750)

TURN OF PHRASE (IRE)
Trained by D. Weld (1052)

WESTERN OVERTURE (USA)
Trained by D. Loder (718)

WIXOE EXPRESS (IRE)
Trained by S. Woods (1060)

WOODLYON (USA)
Trained by J. Noseda (810)

XERAPHIN
Trained bty W. Jarvis (641)

XTRASENSORY
Trained by R. Hannon (515)

ZANANA
Trained by R. Hannon (517)

THE BLOODSTOCK EXPERTS MARK YOUR CARD

Following the successful introduction of this section last year, I have extended it to include, not only Bloodstock Agents, but also Stud Managers. All of them were asked to suggest a few 2-y-o's, which they had either raised themselves or bought as yearlings.

Bloodstock agent John Warren was the top of this particular class last year, as his inspired selection included the Gimcrack Stakes winner Bannister. We'll be sure to take a close look at your picks this year John!

PETER DOYLE

All three are in training with Richard Hannon.

UNNAMED
b.c. Barathea – Bold Fashion.
"A very nice, strong sort of colt with classic potential. He'll be out in the second half of the year".

GLENMORANGIE
gr.c. Danzig Connection – In The Highlands.
"A very nice individual and a sharp sort, he could easily make a good 2-y-o".

JUST A CARAT (IRE)
b.f. Distinctly North – Justice System.
"A very nice filly, Richard likes her and we're hoping she'll be the one for the Fairyhouse Sales race".

WILL EDMEADES

REDBACK
ch.c. Mark Of Esteem – Patsy Western.
"A lovely, strong horse with plenty of pedigree, whom I feel was remarkably cheap at 40,000 Guineas possibly because his sire is as yet unproven. Richard Hannon likes him a lot and he should be early".

SEROCKI (IRE)
ch.c. Danzig Connection – Mainly Sunset.
"Another very nice, correct colt who would have realised a lot higher price (he cost 50,000 Guineas) had he been by a more fashionable stallion. He too comes from a good female line and was bought to replace the useful Whyome with Michael Bell".

n.b. after Will had written to me, I was informed by Michael Bell that Serocki would sadly be out of action for the year, but added that he thought he was a really nice colt.

XTRASENSORY
b.f. Royal Applause – Song Of Hope.
"Also cost 50,000 Guineas coming from the impressive first crop of Royal Applause. An attractive, racy filly who has also caught Richard Hannon's eye, she should be out in May".

JOHN FERGUSON

All in training with David Loder.

COPERNICAN (USA)
b.c. Kingmambo – Mysterial.

"An outstanding individual and he's done well since the sales. I'd expect him to be racing over seven furlongs in the second half of the season. An exciting horse by a world-class stallion".

ON EDGE
b.c. Zafonic – Gull Nook.

"A half-brother to Pentire who was an old friend of mine, as I purchased him for the Mollers. This 2-y-o has an interesting pedigree, being by Zafonic (the sire of Xaar). The one thing I thought about this horse was that he had the athleticism of Pentire and also the look of Xaar. I wouldn't expect him to be out early but he'll be a nice horse in the second half of the year".

JOYOUS GIFT
ch.c. Cadeaux Genereux – Elfin Laughter.

"A similar type of 2-y-o to On Edge, he's a half-brother to David Elsworth's Smirk who won at the Craven meeting". As individuals go, this Cadeaux Genereux was as nice a yearling as there was at the October Sales. Straightforward, easy to like and athletic. He's a horse we should have some fun with this year".

OFFICIAL FLAME (USA)
ch.c. Deputy Minister – Fire The Groom.

"At the sales he was a neat butt of a horse. The question was whether or not he would develop. He's done extremely well and is a brother to an outstanding sprinter. He'll be a sprinter himself".

ANGUS GOLD (SHADWELL STUD)

KAHZIMA (USA)
b.br.f. Gulch – Gharayib.

"In Dubai until the end of April, she looks sharp, has a good attitude and looks a real 2-y-o type. With Ed Dunlop".

MOON'S WHISPER (USA)
b.f. Storm Cat – East Of The Moon.

"She looks tremendously well, has grown and strengthened and we like the way she goes at this stage. In training with John Gosden".

SOHAIB (USA)
b.c. Kingmambo – Fancy Ruler.

"I liked him very much when I was in Dubai. Kingmambo's are not usually early types and this colt is big and scopey – so he'll need a bit of time. He's with Barry Hills".

BISHR
b.c. Royal Applause – Hawayah.

"In training with Marcus Tregoning, this colt will be a nice sprinter in time. He's a big, powerful horse and he looks like he's going to be fast".

CHARLIE GORDON-WATSON

KING OF HAPPINESS (USA)
ch.c. Spinning World – Mystery Rays.

"Trained by Sir Michael Stoute, this is a very nice horse and he's a really athletic type".

WIXOE EXPRESS (IRE)
b.c. Anabaa – Esquiline.

"In training with Sean Woods, this colt is big and strong. He's a mid-season type 2-y-o and he looks the part".

TIKKUN (IRE)
gr.c. Grand Lodge – Moon Festival.

"With Roger Charlton, the great thing about this colt is that despite his pedigree suggesting he's much more of a 3-y-o, he really looks like making a nice 2-y-o also".

LESLIE HARRISON (PLANTATION STUD)

"Of the colts that we sold at last year's yearling sales, look out for the following horses" –

OCTENNIAL
gr.c. Octagonal – Laune.

"Sold at Tattersalls October Sale and now trained by Richard Hannon".

BANDSTAND
b.c. Spectrum – Licorne.
"Sold at Tattersalls Houghton Sales and now trained by David Loder".

"Of the fillies we retained" –

XERAPHIN
b.f. Zafonic – Rose Noble.
"Trained by William Jarvis, she has the look of a filly who could have far more precocity than her dam".

ZANANA
b.f. Zafonic – Divine Quest.
"Trained by Richard Hannon. At least has a speed pedigree and the trainer reports it as 'nippy'".

ANDREW MEAD (MEAD GOODBODY LTD)

"We purchased the following at the Tattersalls October Sales. Trained by Geoff Wragg, we have high hopes for them all".

JERPAHNI
b.f. Distant Relative – Oublier L'Ennui.
"This filly is owned by the delightful Mrs Claude Lilley, a long time owner with Geoff Wragg. A smooth-walking, well-grown filly, we hope she can fulfil the owner's ambition of having a runner at Royal Ascot – we have a strong feeling that this filly may well be good enough".

ELEGY (USA)
ch.f. Diesis – Affirmative Fable.
"A beautifully bred Diesis filly, out of an Affirmed half-sister to the dam of the Prix Jacques le Marois winner Muhtathir. Purchased for Irishman Trevor Stewart, a notoriously 'lucky' owner (Cassaandra Go, etc), this filly was a snip at 57,000 Guineas being worth that alone as a potential broodmare. She has improved considerably since she was purchased (being a May 16th foal), and Geoff Wragg will hopefully start her in the autumn".

CERTAINLY BRAVE
b.f. Indian Ridge – Dead Certain.
"Another well-bred filly for Trevor Stewart being out of the Cheveley Park and Lowther Stakes winner Dead Certain. A scopey filly,

her dam has already produced two black type horses. On paper and type, this 130,000 Guinea yearling could be capable of winning the Cheveley Park Stakes like her mother. The trainer must be hoping so!"

DAVID REDVERS (TWEENHILLS STUD)

RUM DESTINY (IRE)
b.c. Mujadil – Ruby River.
"Like Strange Destiny and Bouncing Bowdler, this colt is by Mujadil. Very typical of his sire and the image of Bouncing Bowdler, he cost 28,000 Irish Guineas and I'm hoping lightning can strike twice. Alan Berry trains this one for Chris and Antonia Deuters, and he loves him at the moment".

FALCON HILL
b.c. Polar Falcon – Branston Jewel.
"A 20,000 Guineas son of Polar Falcon and Branston Jewel. Very sharp and very athletic, he is trained by Mark Johnston for my new syndicate – Tweenhills Racing. Expect to see him out as soon as he has his second birthday in mid-April. The trainer is uncharacteristically positive about this one".

PETER THE GREAT (IRE)
b.c. Hector Protector – Perfect Alibi.
"At 25,000 Guineas the most expensive yearling I bought for Ralph Beckett. This colt is a gorgeous son of Hector Protector, he is oozing natural ability at home and could be a bit special. The trainer will not be rushing him and he will be out in June or July".

CHRIS RICHARDSON (CHEVELEY PARK STUD)

ARROW
b.c. Pivotal – Cremets.
"Very similar to Red Carpet in make and shape and a very athletic individual. Trained by Michael Bell".

PIOUS
b.f. Bishop Of Cashel – La Cabrilla.
"With James Fanshawe, she looks like a 2-y-o and should show plenty of speed. Her sire has got off to a good start at stud".

UNLEASH (USA)

ch.c. Benny the Dip – Lemhi Go.

"A very nice colt and a typical Benny The Dip, he's a good individual that could well prove a useful 2-y-o. Trained by Sir Mark Prescott".

LINDA SADLER

SILENCE IS GOLDEN

ch.f. Danehill Dancer – Silent Girl (Krayyan).

"I bought her at the December Sales and I know her family well. I worked for the stud who bred her dam Silent Girl and also Always Valiant who won the July Stakes. There is plenty of speed in the family and this filly has been entered up early. Trained by Brian Meehan, she promises to be an early type and looks ready to do her job now".

GENERAL AMNESTY

b.c. General Monash – Beautyofthepeace.

"I bought this colt as a foal, being a half-brother to the multiple winner Windshift. He is a scopey, attractive 2-y-o in training with Derek Shaw who will run over 6f and is being aimed at the Doncaster Breeze Up Stakes at Kempton in September".

DANISH DECORUM (IRE)

ch.c. Danehill Dancer – Dignified Air.

"Another Danehill Dancer! This is a big but well-balanced colt with plenty of scope and he is a half-brother to the listed winner Proud Titania. Trained by Michael Jarvis, he is doing well and should run around May or June time. I think he'll be a good 2-y-o and follow in his father's hoofprints".

ROBIN SHARP (COLLIN STUD)

GLENMORANGIE

gr.c. Danzig Connection – Highland Reel.

"Trained by Richard Hannon, he's a big, scopey horse with a good outlook. He'll be a nice horse at 2 yrs and is sure to go on and be a good 3-y-o".

It's interesting to note that this is Glenmorangie's second mention in this section.

UNNAMED

b.f. Alhaarth – Roxy Music.

"A filly I bought as a yearling for 9,000 Guineas and re-sold for 22,000. An early-looking filly, she's a great walker and is a sprint type 2-y-o. Trained by Alan Jarvis".

UNNAMED

b.c. Danzig Connection – Mo Stopher.

"Trained by Jon Akehurst, he's a good-looking horse with a great temperament. By all accounts he's a decent colt and he goes very well".

AMANDA SKIFFINGTON

DERWENT (USA)

b.br.c. Distant View – Nothing Sweeter.

"In training with Luca Cumani, this colt is well put-together and looks fairly sharp. Hopefully he'll be racing by July and he's moving well on the gallops".

HIDEAWAY HEROINE (IRE)

ch.f. Hernando – Dulcinea.

"A big filly trained by John Hills, she probably won't be out until August time but she's a lovely mover and they are very happy with her. The dam is by Selkirk and Hideaway Heroine very much takes after him, rather than Hernando".

SCALADO (USA)

ch.c. Mister Baileys – Lady Di Pomadora.

"This attractive colt is with Roger Charlton and he's a very sharp horse that should definitely make a 2-y-o.

SUNDRENCHED (IRE)

ch.f. Desert King – Utr.

"A big, scopey filly, she's very well-balanced and a beautiful mover. We've got our sights set quite high with her and with luck she'll make it to the Fillies Mile at Ascot in the autumn. Trained by Willie Haggas.

ANTHONY STROUD

PRAIRIE DUNES (IRE)

br.c. Indian Ridge – Ceide Dancer.

"In training with Jeremy Noseda, this is a nice colt purchased at Goffs Orby. He looks like he could be the type to run as a 2-y-o and has shown ability at home".

PRAYERS FOR RAIN (IRE)
b.f. Darshaan – Whispered Melody.

"In training with Michael Jarvis. Another Goffs purchase, this filly has been going well at home and looks like she could be early despite her pedigree".

LINDA TATE

MOLLY ELLEN (IRE)
b.f. Fayruz – Magic Melody.

"In training with Dermot Weld, the reason I went for this filly was the fact that she stood out at Goffs Challenge Sales when I purchased her. She has size, scope and a real athletic walk to her. She'll be running in May and Dermot is very hopeful that she will make up into a really nice 2-y-o. Let's face it, it's not every day you'd give 43,000 Irish punts for a filly by Fayruz. That shows just how nice she was".

SHEILA BLIGE
ch.f. Zamindar – Stripanoora.

"With Alan Berry, this filly has great character and all she wants to do is please you. I gave 27,000 Guineas for her from the Doncaster St Leger Sales and she strode around the sales ring with an air that said - "well look no further I'm the one you want". This is a quality filly with the right trainer so watch this space! We're just waiting for some good ground".

BELEZA (IRE)
b.f. Revoque – La Alla Wa Asa,

"Now let's move on to quality. This filly is not over big but she has the heart of a lion. She cost 30,000 Guineas from Newmarket October Sales and just walks for England and floats on the gallops. Her trainer, Clive Brittain, rates this filly very highly and there is no better man than Clive. We hope to see her out in May with a view to going on to quality races throughout the season".

JOHN WARREN

NATURE (IRE)
b.f. Bluebird – Nawaji.

"Should make up into a nice early summer 2-y-o. Trained by Richard Hannon and owned by the Royal Ascot Racing Club".

KRUGERRAND (USA)
ch.c. Gulch – Nasers Pride.

"A very nice late summer 2-y-o colt with the scope and class to train on. Trained by Michael Bell and owned by Highclere Thoroughbred Racing".

ZONE
b.c. Zilzal – Thea.

"A strong colt with class. Trained by Paul Cole and owned by Highclere Thoroughbred Racing".

TWO YEAR OLDS

Mick Channon (top) and Richard Hannon were the two most successful trainers of two-year-olds in Britain in 2000

E ALSTON

1 - INDIAN SHORES * [53] b.f. Forzando – Cottonwood (Teenoso).
April 22. 3,000Y. Tattersalls Autumn.
Half-sister to the modest 2000 2-y-o 5f winner White Star Lady (by So Factual), to a hurdles winner by First Trump and a minor winner abroad by Primo Dominie. The dam, a quite useful 10f winner, is a half-sister to 6 winners including the champion Italian 2-y-o and Group 2 1m Premio Regina Elena winner Arranvanna. The second dam, Smoke Creek (by Habitat), is a placed half-sister to 6 winners. (Paul Curry). *"Quite a tall filly, she's been growing and has yet to come in her coat but she's nice and can go a bit. Expect her to be out in mid-May".*

2 - ROCK STEADY * [44] b.f. Puissance – Just A Gem (Superlative).
January 31. 3,000Y. Tattersalls Autumn.
The dam is an unraced sister to the listed 7f Sweet Solera Stakes winner and subsequent US Grade 1 placed Pearl Angel and a half-sister to 5 other winners. The second dam, More Or Less (by Morston), won at 3 yrs and is a half-sister to 3 winners. (Burlington Partnership). *"She finished third in her first race at Doncaster and is a big, strong, well-made filly that should get further than five furlongs.*

D ARBUTHNOT

3 - ALI-PASHA ** [64] b.c. Ali-Royal – Edge Of Darkness (Vaigly Night).
February 14. Fourth foal. 25,000Y. Doncaster St Leger.
Half-brother to the fair 2000 2-y-o triple 6f winner Joint Instruction (by Forzando) and to the quite useful 12f, 14f and hurdles winner Salford Flyer (by Pharly). The dam, a modest winner of three races from 10f to 2m, is a half-sister to 3 winners including the fairly useful 2-y-o 5f winner Oh Boyar. The second dam, Atoka (by March Past), a fairly useful winner of 4 races from 6f to 15f, is a sister to the listed Windsor Castle Stakes winner Dawn Review and a half-sister to the dam of the Group 3 Meld Stakes winner Ulterior Motive. (Mr M J Peters). *"He's coming on very nicely and will be reasonably early. He'd probably want six furlongs to start with and will be aimed at the Doncaster St Leger Sales race. Not very big when he came in but he's grown and thickened".*

4 - BOUDICA (IRE) ** [65] b.f. Alhaarth – Supportive (Nashamaa).
April 8. Fifth foal. IR£62,000Y. Goffs Orby.
Half-sister to the quite useful Irish 2000 2-y-o 5f winner La Stellina (by Marju), to the 1999 Irish 2-y-o winner and Group 1 Phoenix Stakes fourth Galloway Boy, the useful 5f and 6f winner and Group 3 Cornwallis Stakes third Grand Lad and a winner in Germany by Last Tycoon. The dam won four races over 5f at 2 and 3 yrs in Ireland and is a half-sister to 3 winners including the Italian listed winner Arapiti. The second dam, Amiga Mia (by Be Friendly), won at 3 yrs and is a half-sister to 6 winners including the Sun Chariot Stakes second Sedra (herself dam of the St Leger third Samraan). (Mr D C Broomfield). *"She's potentially very nice and there are good vibes about her sire Alhaarth. She's a mid-season type 2-y-o, has some strengthening up to do, but goes nicely".*

5 - LIQUIDITY ** [62] b.f. Robellino – Faraway Waters (Pharly).
February 13. First foal. 35,000Y. Tattersalls October.
The dam, a useful 6f winner (at 2 yrs) and listed 10f Pretty Polly Stakes second, is a half-sister to the very useful 1m to 10.4f winner and Group-placed Prince Of Denial. The second dam, Gleaming Water (by Kalaglow), a quite useful 2-y-o 6f winner, is a sister to the Group 3 Solario Stakes winner Shining Water (herself dam of the Group 1 1m Grand Criterium winner Tenby) and a half-sister to 7 winners. (Mr A Haynes). *"I think she's a nice filly. I trained the dam and she had feet problems but it's a lovely family. This filly will be ready by mid-season, will start off at six furlongs and is a definite 2-y-o".*

6 - LONG TALL SALLY (IRE) ** [68] b.f. Danehill Dancer – Miss Galwegian
April 30. Twelfth foal.
Half-sister to the modest 2-y-o 7f winner Jubal Early, to the poor 2-y-o 6f winner A Bridge Too Far (both by The Noble Player), the modest 13f all-weather winner Western Rainbow (by Rainbows For Life), and a 2-y-o winner in Italy by Fayruz. The dam, placed over 6f at 2 yrs in Ireland, is a half-sister to 4 minor winners here and abroad. The second dam, Miss Brittain (by Tudor Melody), is an unplaced sister to the Group 3 Horris Hill Stakes winner Welsh Harmony. *"A nice, strong, early type 2-y-o. She'll be a sprinter and will be aimed at the Breeze Up Sales Stakes at Kempton in June".*

I BALDING

Although Ian is always kind enough to help me out with my book, I hadn't actually visited Kingsclere for a good number of years until this spring. My return prompted in me an instant recollection of the great character and beauty surrounding historic Park House Stables. The great days of Mill Reef may seem ages ago now, but the yard consistently sends out high-class winners and hopefully this year will be no exception.

---

7 - BORORA * [60]　　　　　　　　　　gr.c. Shareef Dancer – Bustling Nelly (Bustino).
January 20. Twelfth foal. 30,000Y. Tattersalls October.
Brother to the fairly useful 12f all-weather winner Shareef and half-brother to the very smart Yorkshire Cup winner Busy Flight (by Pharly), the Italian listed winner Joyeus Garde (by Never So Bold), the moderate 2m winner Silk Degrees (by Dunbeath), the poor 12f winner Passion And Mirth (by Known Fact), a winner in Germany by Kalaglow and a hurdles winner by Nishapour. The dam, a fairly useful middle-distance winner of 2 races, is a half-sister to the smart Doncaster Cup, Goodwood Cup and Jockey Club Cup winner Further Flight and a half-sister to the dam of the St Leger third The Fly. The second dam, Flying Nelly (by Nelcius), won 6 races including the Cambridgeshire. (Mr Robert Hitchins). *"Borora looks a lovely horse and I like him very much. We bought him relatively cheaply and we've had relations of his that looked nice. The type to start off at seven furlongs from the mid-season onwards".*

---

8 - CLIPPERTON * [78]　　　　　　　　　　b.c. Mister Baileys – Theresita (Surumu).
April 16. Tenth foal. 66,000Y. Tattersalls October.
Brother to the unraced 2000 2-y-o Mister Putt and half-brother to the US stakes-placed winner Robbin Banks (by Robin des Pins), the German winner of 7 races Thalasso (by Mining) and minor winners abroad by General Assembly, Northern Baby, Sportin' Life and Robin des Pins. The dam won once in Germany, was listed-placed over 6f and 1m and is a sister to the Group 1 German Derby winner Temporal. The second dam, Theresa (by Zeddaan), won twice in Germany and is a half-sister to 4 other winners there. (Mr Robert Hitchins). *"Yes, he's a nice horse. Both of our Mister Baileys 2-y-o's have high knee actions and both of them are very nice. I'd be very disappointed if he didn't win this year and he should be ready by mid-season".*

---

9 - COMTESSE NOIRE (CAN) * [76]　　　　　　b.f. Woodman – Faux Pas (Sadler's Wells).
February 3. First foal. $150,000Y. Saratoga August.
The dam, an Irish maiden who stayed 12f, is a half-sister to the smart performers Negligent (winner of the Rockfel Stakes and third in the One Thousand Guineas), Ala Hounak and Ala Mahlik. The second dam, Negligence (by Roan Rocket), was placed once over 10f at 3 yrs and is a half-sister to the dams of the very useful sprinter Governor General and the smart French 10f performer Galunpe. (Holistic Racing Ltd). *"Another I bought at Saratoga, she looks classy and although she's got a bit of a temperament, she's a lovely mover and will make a 2-y-o by mid-season".*

---

10 - DRAMATIC RING *** [75]　　　　　　b.c. Magic Ring – Dramatic Mood (Jalmood).
May 1. Seventh foal. 35,000Y. Tattersalls October.
Brother to the useful Group 3 6.5f Prix Eclipse winner and Group 3 Greenham Stakes third Merlin's Ring and half-brother to the 2000 unplaced 2-y-o Drama Premiere (by Emarati), the fair Irish 12f winner Lifesforliving and the modest 10f winner Absolutelystunning (both by Aragon). The dam is an unraced half-sister to 8 winners including the Moyglare Stud Stakes third Annie Laurie. The second dam, Drama School (by Young Generation), is an unplaced half-sister to 3 minor winners. (Mrs Ann Plummer). *"He looks a nice sort and I like him a lot. He's only just come in but he looks a proper little 2-y-o and he could be a five furlong type in May – that sort of thing".*
Significant sire/damsire crosses:- Merlin's Ring.

---

11 - DREAM GENIE * [68]　　　　　　　　b.f. Puissance – Aryaf (Vice Regent).
March 10. Eighth foal. 13,000F
Sister to the high-class sprinter Mind Games, winner of the Group 2 Temple Stakes (twice), the Norfolk Stakes and the Palace House Stakes, to the quite useful 7f winner Quiz Show (by Primo Dominie) and the fair 2-y-o 1m all-weather winner Able Fun (by Double Schwartz). The dam is an unplaced half-sister to 5 winners including the Group 2 Tripleprint Celebration Mile third Peartree House. The second dam, Fashion Front (by Habitat), is an unraced half-sister to the Horris Hill Stakes winner Long Row, the

Norfolk Stakes winner Colmore Row and the dam of the Irish Oaks winner Possessive Dancer. *"She looks OK, but she's coughing and is a bit backward now. She'll be fine once she's going again but wouldn't be one of my stars".*

12 - FIREBREAK ** [90]
b.c. Charnwood Forest – Breakaway (Song).
March 6. Seventh foal. 27,000Y. Tattersalls October.

Half-brother to the fairly useful 2-y-o 5f winner and listed 7f Sweet Solera Stakes second Stop Out (by Rudimentary), to the quite useful 1m winner Hippy, the Italian winner of 5 races Roma Caveau (both by Damister), the modest 2-y-o 7f all-weather winner Sirene (by Mystiko) and a winner in Switzerland by Superlative. The dam, a fairly useful 5f winner of 3 races, is a half-sister to 5 winners. The second dam, Catherine Howard (by Tower Walk), is a placed sister to the 2-y-o winner and Norfolk Stakes third My Dear Fellow and a half-sister to 11 winners. (Kennet Valley Thoroughbreds). *"He looks a nice horse – I like him. He should start off in the middle of the season and do well as a 2-y-o".*

13 - FLORIANA ** [79]
b.f. Selkirk – Mara River (Efisio).
February 14. First foal.

The dam, a quite useful 6f to 1m winner, is a half-sister to several winners. The second dam, Island Mill (by Mill Reef), was a fair stayer. (Kingsclere Stud). *"Very nice. She looks classy and you shouldn't leave her out of the book".*

14 - GOLDEN CHALICE (IRE) ** [92]
ch.c. Selkirk – Special Oasis (Green Desert).
April 22. First foal. 110,000Y. Tattersalls Houghton.

The dam is an unraced half-sister to the the Group 1 Juddmonte International winner One So Wonderful, the Group 3 7f Rockfel Stakes winner and Irish One Thousand Guineas third Relatively Special and the Group 2 Dante Stakes winner Alnasr Alwasheek. The second dam, Someone Special (by Habitat), a useful 3-y-o 7f winner, was third in the Coronation Stakes and is a half-sister to the top-class miler Milligram. (Holistic Racing Ltd). *"He was rather small and under-developed but he's done very well recently and is beginning to look like a nice horse. I like him and he's doing well at the moment. Should win this year".*
Significant sire/damsire crosses:- Trans Island.

15 - GOLDEN DIXIE (USA) * [87]
ch.c. Dixieland Band – Beyrouth (Alleged).
April 16. First foal. $80,000Y. Saratoga August.

The dam, a useful French 3-y-o 1m winner, was listed-placed over 1m and subsequently won 3 races in the USA, notably the Grade 2 9f All Along Stakes. She is a half-sister to the smart British/US performer at up to 10f Flame Valley. The second dam, Lightning Fire (by Kris), won the listed 7f Prix Imprudence and is a sister to the Group 1 7f Prix de la Salamandre winner and good sire Common Grounds and a half-sister to the Group 3 10f Prix de Psyche winner Angel In My Heart. (Holistic Racing Ltd). *"I bought him at Saratoga and he was bred by George Strawbridge. He looks a nice sort for the mid-season".*

16 - LASANGA ** [90]
ch.c. Zamindar – Shall We Run (Hotfoot).
April 26. Sixth foal. 55,000Y. Tattersalls October.

Half-brother to the 2000 Group 2 6f Gimcrack Stakes winner Bannister (by Inchinor), to the fairly useful 1999 5f and 6f 2-y-o winner Roo (by Rudimentary) and the modest all-weather 9.4f and 12f winner Absolute Majority (by Absalom). The dam was placed once over 5f at 2 yrs, is a sister to the useful 10f performer Fire Top and a half-sister to 7 winners including the Group 1 6f Cheveley Park Stakes winner Dead Certain. The second dam, Sirnelta (by Sir Tor), won from 1m to 10f in France. (Mr Robert Hitchins). *"I like Lasanga a lot. He has to have an operation to remove a testicle but he looks a very nice horse. He was lovely at the sales and has gone on – he's a big, strong boy. He'll be very nice by mid-season".*

17 - LISSOME (USA) * [76]
b.f. Lear Fan – Miss Otis (One For All).
April 2. Third foal.

The dam won 9 races in the USA, notably the Grade 3 8.5f Noble Damsel Stakes at 5 yrs. The second dam, Puzzlement (by Tentam), won twice in the USA and is a half-sister to the minor US stakes winner General Strike. (H Rathbun & J Miller). *"She looks very nice – very classy. She's home-bred by some Americans and I like her – she goes well".*

18 - LOCHRIDGE ** [79] ch.f. Indian Ridge – Lochsong (Song).
March 27. Third foal.

Half-sister to the unraced 2000 2-y-o Gift Of Speed and the unplaced 2000 3-y-o Loch Diamond (both by Cadeaux Genereux). The dam, a champion sprinter and winner of the Prix de l'Abbaye (twice), the Nunthorpe Stakes and the Kings Stand Stakes etc., is a half-sister to several winners including the very smart Nunthorpe Stakes winner Lochangel. The second dam, Peckitts Well (by Lochnager), was a fairly useful winner of five races at 2 and 3 yrs from 5f to 6f. (Mr J C Smith). *"The nicest foal yet out of Lochsong. She looks a nice filly, has a nice temperament and is a beautiful mover. She's fine although it's hard to say when she'll be ready to race".*

19 - PASSING GLANCE ** [85] b.c. Polar Falcon – Spurned (Robellino).
March 11. Seventh foal.

Half-brother to the smart Group 3 7f Prix de Palais-Royal and European Free Handicap winner Hidden Meadow, the smart 11f listed winner Scorned (both by Selkirk), the useful 6f (at 2 yrs) and listed 1m winner Kingsclere (by Fairy King), the fairly useful sprinter Overbrook (by Storm Cat) and the modest 9.7f winner Jona Holley (by Sharpo). The dam, a fairly useful 2-y-o 7f winner, later stayed 10f. The second dam, Refill (by Mill Reef), was placed over 6f here before winning over 11f in the USA. (Kingsclere Stud & Mr M W Wates). *"A lovely horse. If I had to make a choice right now he'd be my pick, but I'm slightly biased as we bred him. He's going to run in the Mellon colours which were left to me. Our home-bred horses will run in those colours. He'll be ready for mid-season and should have the speed for six furlongs. He's a lovely, big horse".*

20 - RISOTTO (USA) ** [94] b.f. Kris S – Routilante (Rousillon).
February 14.

Closely related to the fairly useful 1997 2-y-o 7f winner Amabel (by Silver Hawk) and half-sister to the quite useful 2000 2-y-o 8.5f winner Changing Scene (by Theatrical) and the US stakes-placed winner Wood Creek (by Lear Fan). The dam, a useful 2-y-o 6f winner, is a half-sister to several winners. The second dam, Danseuse Classique (by Northern Dancer), ran once and is a half-sister to the high-class Canadian colt Son Of Briarctic. (Mr G Strawbridge). *"She looks like being a really nice filly and looks to be the type to be racing by June or July".*

21 - RIVER MASTER ** [66] b.c. Most Welcome – River Spey (Mill Reef).
May 9. 13,000Y. Tattersalls October.

Half-brother to the fairly useful 2000 2-y-o 5f and 7f (all-weather) winner River Raven (by Efisio), to the smart winner of 10 races (including the Group 3 10f Royal Whip Stakes) Jahafil, the fairly useful 10f winner Mondschein, the minor French winner Merrow (all by Rainbow Quest), the fairly useful winner of 7 races from 7f to 1m, Dune River (by Green Desert), the minor French winner Kuriakin (by Belmez) and the modest 12.2f winner Rispoto (by Mtoto). The dam, a fairly useful 2-y-o 7f winner, stayed 12f and is closely related to the listed Glorious Stakes winner Spinning. The second dam, Strathspey (by Jimmy Reppin), a useful winner of 4 races from 6f to 1m including 2 listed events, is a sister to the One Thousand Guineas third Joking Apart. (David Watson & Duncan Lofts). *"A nice horse, I trained his dam who was pretty good and this colt goes very well. I can hardly believe he only cost 13,000 and I should think he'd start off at seven furlongs. I like him".*

22 - ROTUMA (IRE) * [70] b.c. Tagula – Cross Question (Alleged).
April 28. Third foal. 26,000Y. Doncaster St Leger.

Brother to the 3-y-o Lake Siria and half-brother to the fair 7f to 10f placed Bold Guest (by By My Guest). The dam, a quite useful Irish 9.6f and 10f winner at 4 yrs, is out of the listed 10f Virginia Stakes winner Rambushka (by Roberto), herself a half-sister to 9 winners including the Group 2 Laurent Perrier Champagne Stakes second Arokat. (Mr Robert Hitchins). *"We bought him at Doncaster and I like him a lot. He's a nice sort and should be one of the earlier ones. I would say he'd be ready by May or June".*

23 - SANTA ANA * [68] br.f. Robellino – Iota (Niniski).
February 14. Second foal. 28,000Y. Doncaster St Leger.

Half-sister to As Good As It Gets (by Alhijaz), unplaced in one start at 2 yrs in 2000. The dam, a quite useful staying winner of 9 races, is a half-sister to one winner. The second dam, Iosifa (by Top Ville), a very useful 2-y-o 7f winner, was second in the listed Lingfield Oaks Trial and is a full or half-sister to 3 winners. (Mr Robert Hitchins). *"Yes, she's as nice as anything we've got at this stage. She looks lovely and will be one of the earlier ones I think. She's in the Super Sprint at Newbury in July and the Watership Down Sales race at Ascot in September. Those are the races we'll probably aim for".*

24 - SEA PRINCE * [87]
ch.c. Bering – Gersey (Generous).
March 19. First foal. 30,000Y. Tattersalls Houghton.
The dam ran once unplaced and is a half-sister to 7 winners including the smart winner of 10 races (including the Group 3 10f Royal Whip Stakes) Jahafil, the 2-y-o 5f and 7f (all-weather) winner River Raven, the 10f winner Mondschein and the 7f to 1m winner of 7 races Dune River – all 3 fairly useful. The second dam, River Spey (by Mill Reef), a fairly useful 2-y-o 7f winner, stayed 12f and is closely related to the listed Glorious Stakes winner Spinning. (Holistic Racing Ltd). *"I like him a lot. He actually sustained a hairline fracture of a cannon bone early on so he's going steady. He's more likely to be an August/September type I think".*

25 - SKIES ARE BLUE * [86]
b.f. Unfuwain – Blue Birds Fly (Rainbow Quest).
March 3. Fourth foal. 220,000Y. Tattersalls October.
Half-sister to the fairly useful 2000 2-y-o dual 5f winner Strange Destiny (by Mujadil), to the fairly useful 2-y-o winner of 6 races at around 5f For Old Times Sake (by Efisio) and a winner in Italy by Ezzoud. The dam, a fair 10f winner, is a half-sister to 6 winners including the Irish listed 9f winner and Group 3 placed Golden Form. The second dam, Pale Gold (by New Chapter), won twice in France and is a half-sister to 10 winners including the Group 3 10.5f Prix Penelope winner Pale Ale. (Mr T Rootes). *"She failed her wind test after the sales so the owners decided to keep her and put her in training here. She's an absolutely lovely filly and up to now she hasn't made a noise so we're hopeful as she looks full of class. She'll be one for the late summer".*

26 - THUNDERGOD * [?]
b.c. Torrential – Reach The Wind (Relaunch).
February 26. Sixth foal. 32,000Y. Tattersalls October.
Half-brother to the 3-y-o Tea Leaves (by Twining), to a winner of 10 minor races in the USA by Gone West and a winner in Hong Kong by Affirmed. The dam, a dual 6f winner (including at 2 yrs) in Ireland, is a half-sister to the Group 2 5.5f Prix Robert Papin winner Ozone Friendly (herself dam of the Group 3 Prix du Bois winner Ozone Layer). The second dam, Kristana (by Kris), a fairly useful 10f winner, was fourth in the Group 2 10f Pretty Polly Stakes and is a half-sister to the dams of the good winners Ardkinglass, Reprimand, Wiorno and Soft Currency. (Miss A V Hill). *"I like Thundergod. He'll be ready by mid-season I think and he's a good-sized horse that goes well. He should win this year".*

27 - TOP EXECUTIVE (IRE) ** [81]
ch.c. Entrepreneur – Tout A Coup (Ela-Mana-Mou).
February 17. First foal. 100,000Y. Tattersalls Houghton.
The dam, a useful winner of 7 races here and in Ireland including over 7f at 2 yrs and the listed Cheshire Oaks, is a half-sister to 5 minor winners here and abroad. The second dam, Coupe d'Hebe (by Ile de Bourbon), was a quite useful 2-y-o 1m winner. (Holistic Racing Ltd). *"He had an injury early on and was blistered. He's going nicely now, is a quality horse and I like him. One for later in the season".*

28 - VANDERLIN ** [82]
ch.c. Halling – Massorah (Habitat).
May 11. Tenth foal. 38,000Y. Tattersalls October.
Half-brother to the unraced 2000 2-y-o La Yoram, to the fairly useful 1999 2-y-o 7f winner Miss Orah (both by Unfuwain), the quite useful 7f winner Wisham (by Be My Guest), the fairly useful winner of 4 races over 6f Massiba, the French 7.5f and 1m winner Monaiya (dam of the listed Pretty Polly Stakes winner Musetta), the French listed-placed winner Mashoura (all by Shareef Dancer) and a winner in Germany by Shadeed. The dam, a very useful winner of the Group 3 5f Premio Omenoni and second in the Group 3 5f Prix du Gros-Chene, is a half-sister to 4 minor winners abroad. The second dam, Marala (by Sir Khalito), won once in France. (Mr Robert Hitchins). *"Although he's a May foal he looks like being quite early. He's a nice colt and I'd be very disappointed if he didn't win races this year".*

29 - WOODLARK * [96]
b.c. Zilzal – Prima Volta (Primo Dominie).
February 1. Second foal. 64,000Y. Tattersalls October.
Half-brother to the useful 2000 2-y-o Bouncing Bowdler (by Mujadil), a winner of 3 races including the Group 2 6f Mill Reef Stakes. The dam, a quite useful 6f (at 2 yrs) and 9f winner, is a half-sister to 3 minor winners. The second dam, Femme Formidable (by Formidable), is an unplaced half-sister to one

winner. (Mr Robert Hitchins). *"He's a big, heavy horse by Zilzal but he looks OK and he'll hopefully make a 2-y-o at the back-end of the season".*

D BARRON

30 - DASHING BEAU (USA) * [67]
b.g. Beau Genius – Full O Cherries (Full Out). April 14. $10,000Y. Keeneland September.

Half-brother to 5 minor winners including the US winner of 19 races Princess Cherri (by Fighting Fit). The dam is a placed half-sister to 8 winners including the US Grade 1 Travers Stakes winner Willow Hour and the US Grade 3 winner Cherry Jubilee (herself dam of the US Grade 3 winner Traverse City). The second dam, Cherry Willow (by Pia Star), was unraced. *"A good sort of horse, he'll be racing in May and is showing us plenty at home".*

31 - MARCUS AURELIUS (IRE) * [83]
b.c. Alzao – Kaguyahime (Distant Relative). April 30. Third foal. 27,000Y. Tattersalls October.

Brother to the Irish trained 3-y-o Beauty. The dam won once in France at 3 yrs and is a half-sister to 7 winners including the Group 1 1m St James's Palace Stakes winner Bijou d'Inde. The second dam, Pushkar (by Northfields), is an unraced half-sister to the Group 3 1m Brownstown Stakes winner Red Chip. *"A nice horse, he'll be relatively early and is a very good-looking horse. He's working well at present".*

32 - WATER BABY (IRE) * [84]
b.c. Tagula – Flooding (Irish River). May 1. Ninth living foal. 23,000Y. Doncaster St Leger.

Half-brother to the fairly useful 1998 2-y-o 6f and 7f winner Lough Swilly (by Mukaddamah), to the Spanish listed winner over 1m and 11f Eowyn (by Distant Relative) and winners abroad by Damister, Unfuwain and Imp Society. The dam is an unraced half-sister to 4 winners including the US stakes winner and Grade 3 placed Swift Bird. The second dam, Flood Light (by Bold Lad, USA), is an unraced half-sister to several good stakes winners out of the champion 2-y-o filly High Voltage. *"A lovely horse to look at, he'll make a 2-y-o and shows us plenty at home but he won't be ready early".*

P BARY

33 - FORMALHAUT (USA)
b.c. Spinning World – Coup de Folie (Halo). April 10. Eleventh foal.

Closely related to the very useful Group 2 1m Prix d'Astarte winner and French One Thousand Guineas second Hydro Calido (by Nureyev) and half-brother to the very smart Group 1 Prix Jacques le Marois winner Exit to Nowhere (by Irish River), the 1999 2-y-o Group 3 1m Prix La Rochette winner Ocean Of Wisdom, the champion European 2-y-o and high-class sire Machiavellian, the smart Group 1 Prix Morny and Group 1 Prix de la Salamandre winner Coup de Genie, the quite useful 10f winner Houdini's Honey (all by Mr Prospector) and the unraced dam of the Group 1 1m Grand Criterium winner Way Of Light. The dam won four races from 6f to 10f including the Group 3 1m Prix d'Aumale and was stakes placed in the USA. The second dam, Raise the Standard (by Hoist the Flag), is an unraced half-sister to Northern Dancer.

34 - GLIA (USA)
b.f. A P Indy – Coup de Genie (Mr Prospector). March 8. Third foal.

The dam was a smart winner of the Group 1 6f Prix Morny and the Group 1 7f Prix de la Salamandre and was third in the One Thousand Guineas. She is a sister to the champion 2-y-o Machiavellian and a half-sister to the high-class miler Exit to Nowhere, the smart miler Hydro Calido and the unraced dam of the Grand Criterium winner Way Of Light. The second dam, Coup de Folie (by Halo), won the Group 3 1m Prix d'Aumale at 2 yrs and is out of an unraced half-sister to Northern Dancer.
Significant sire/damsire crosses:- Tomisue's Delight (Gr 1), Pulpit (Gr 2), Accelerator (Gr 3).

35 - SHWEGZIGON (IRE)
ch.c. Nashwan – Whakilyric (Miswaki). May 2.

Brother to the useful 2-y-o listed 10f Zetland Stakes winner Adnaan, closely related to the French middle-distance winner Res Judicata (by Rainbow Quest) and half-brother to the top-class middle-distance colt Hernando (by Niniski), a winner of seven races notably the Group 1 Prix du Jockey Club and Group 1 10.5f Prix Lupin and second in the Prix de l'Arc de Triomphe, the very useful Group 1 10.5f

Prix Lupin and US Grade 2 1m winner Johann Quatz and the smart French 10.5f to 13.5f listed winner Walter Willy (both by Sadlers Wells). The dam won over 5.5f and the Group 3 7f Prix du Calvados, was third in the Prix de la Salamandre (all at 2 yrs) and in the Group 1 7f Prix de la Foret and is a half-sister to the Prix Daphnis winner Bricassar. The second dam, Lyrism (by Lyphard), was an unraced daughter of the very useful miler and subsequent smart American middle-distance performer Pass a Glance.

---

36 - SEA OF SHOWERS (USA)　　　　　b.f. Seattle Slew – Chimes Of Freedom (Private Account).
April 23.

Closely related to a minor 1m stakes winner in the USA by A P Indy and half-sister to the extremely promising 2000 2-y-o 7f winner Aldebaran (by Mr Prospector) and a winner in the USA by Seeking The Gold. The dam, a smart filly, won the Group 1 6f Moyglare Stud Stakes and the Group 3 6f Cherry Hinton Stakes at 2 yrs, prior to winning the Group 1 1m Coronation Stakes and the Group 2 1m Child Stakes in her second season. She is a half-sister to the very useful 2-y-o 6f listed Firth of Clyde Stakes winner and Cheveley Park Stakes second Imperfect Circle (herself dam of the top-class miler Spinning World) and to the useful 3-y-o 10.3f winner Binkhaldoun. The second dam, Aviance (by Northfields), was a very useful winner of the Group 1 6f Heinz 57 Phoenix Stakes and is out of the 7f and 1m winner Minnie Hauk, herself a sister to the smart winners Gielgud, Malinowski and Monroe and a half-sister to the US Grade 1 Kentucky Oaks winner Blush With Pride and the top-class broodmare Sex Appeal - dam of El Gran Senor and Try My Best. (Niarchos Family).

---

37 - VINDEMIATRIX (IRE)　　　　　b.f. Nashwan – Vingt et Une (Sadler's Wells).
March 8. Second foal.

Half-sister to the unraced 2000 2-y-o Year Two Thousand (by Darshaan). The dam is a sister to the very useful Group 1 10.5f Prix Lupin and US Grade 2 1m winner Johann Quatz and to the smart French 10.5f to 13.5f listed winner Walter Willy and a half-sister to the top-class middle-distance colt Hernando (by Niniski), winner of seven races notably the Group 1 Prix du Jockey Club and Group 1 Prix Lupin and second in the Prix de l'Arc de Triomphe. The second dam, Whakilyric (by Miswaki), won over 5.5f and the Group 3 7f Prix du Calvados, was third in the Prix de la Salamandre (all at 2 yrs) and in the Group 1 7f Prix de la Foret. (Niarchos Family).
Significant sire/damsire crosses:- Bint Salsabil (Gr 3).

---

38 - UNNAMED　　　　　ch.f. Diesis – Allegretta (Lombard).
January 23. FF9,000,000Y.

Half-sister to 7 winners including the top-class filly Urban Sea (by Miswaki), winner of the Group 1 Prix de l'Arc de Triomphe and the Group 2 Prix d'Harcourt, the high-class Two Thousand Guineas winner King's Best (by Kingmambo), the smart Allez Les Trois (by Riverman), winner of the Group 3 10.5f Prix de Flore and the listed-placed Turbaine (by Trempolino). The dam, a useful 2-y-o 1m and 9f winner and second in the Lingfield Oaks Trial, is a sister to the German St Leger winner Anno and a half-sister to the German Group 2 winner Anatas. The second dam, Anatevka (by Espresso), was a listed winner in Germany.

R BECKETT

---

39 - PETER THE GREAT (IRE) *** [?]　　　　　b.c. Hector Protector – Perfect Alibi (Law Society).
March 23. Seventh foal. 25,000Y. Tattersalls October.

Half-brother to the unraced 2000 2-y-o Guilt Edged (by Kris), to the fairly useful 2-y-o 6f and listed 3-y-o 6f winner Likely Story (by Night Shift), the quite useful 7.7f and 1m winner Beggars Belief (by Common Grounds), the fair 1999 2-y-o 1m winner Saafend Boy (by Marju), the modest 11f winner Acquittal (by Danehill) and the modest 10f winner Final Trial (by Last Tycoon). The dam is an unraced half-sister to 8 winners including the Group 1 2m 4f Prix du Cadran winner Chief Contender and the 6f Heinz "57" Phoenix Stakes winner Aviance (herself dam of the Coronation Stakes winner Chimes of Freedom and grandam of the top-class miler Spinning World). The second dam, Minnie Hauk (by Sir Ivor), won over 7f and 1m and is a sister to Malinowski, Gielgud and Monroe (all at least smart) and a half-sister to the US Grade 1 winner Blush With Pride and the unraced Sex Appeal (dam of El Gran Senor and Try My Best). (Mr P Rosas) *"A very nice horse. He'll need a bit of time and I wouldn't expect him out until mid-season, probably over six furlongs, although he'll get seven later on. I like him a lot".*

40 - SPLENDID ROSE * [60] b.f. Prince Sabo – Little Emmeline (Emarati).
February 9. Third foal. 10,500Y. Doncaster St Leger.
Half-sister to the modest 2000 2-y-o 6f winner Spice Island (by Reprimand) and to the poor 11f all-weather winner Preposition (by Then Again). The dam, a moderate 2-y-o 5f winner, is a half-sister to 3 winners including the listed 5f Roses Stakes winner Dealers Wheels. The second dam, Hyacine (by High Line), is a placed sister to the smart middle-distance winner and Group 1 placed Capricorn Line and a half-sister to 4 winners. (Mr P Rosas). *"A good, hard-knocking type of filly, she's tough and will win her races. She'll start off at five furlongs and will get six in time. The type for a median auction event or a nursery".*

M BELL

41 - ANGEL COURT [69] b.g. Shareef Dancer – Nekhbet (Artaius).
April 19. Eleventh foal. IR£42,000Y. Goffs Orby.
Half-brother to the 3-y-o Janet's Pride (by Ezzoud), to the very useful 1m Lincoln Handicap winner and Group 2 Gallinule Stakes second Right Wing (by In The Wings), the French listed winner Tarquina (by Niniski), the useful 5f to 7f winner Cim Bom Bom (by Dowsing), the fair 5f and 6f winner Abu Hanifah (by Ahonoora) and the 2-y-o 8.2f seller winner Hillside Rose (by Beldale Flutter). The dam, a fair 5f to 7f placed 2-y-o, is a half-sister to 7 winners including the Irish St Leger winner M-Lolshan. The second dam, Supreme Lady (by Grey Sovereign), won once at 2 yrs. (Mr R P B Michaelson and Lord Blyth). *"He's just been gelded. The same thing was done to his half-brothers Right Wing and Cim Bom Bom who were both characters. He'll take a bit of time but I think he'll be alright this horse".*

42 - ARROW * [76] b.c. Pivotal – Cremets (Mummy's Pet).
April 15. Tenth foal. 28,000Y. Tattersalls October.
Half-brother to Brockhall Lad (by Primo Dominie), unplaced in 2 starts at 2 yrs in 2000, to the Italian winner of 13 races at up to 15f (including 2 listed events) My Irish (by Assert), the fair 1m winner Sejaal (by Persian Heights) and a 2-y-o winner in Italy by Unfuwain. The dam, a fairly useful 6f and 7f winner at 2 and 3 yrs, is a full or half-sister to 8 winners including the Group 2 Vernons Sprint Cup winner Runnett. The second dam, Rennet (by King's Bench) was a very useful winner of 7 races and stayed 10f. (Cheveley Park Stud). *"Arrow is a similar stamp to Red Carpet but not as precocious. He's a very good mover, has a very good temperament and we like him. A very tough, sound horse".*

43 - B BEAUTIFUL (IRE) * [54] ch.f. Be My Guest – Lady Donna (Dominion).
February 1. Tenth foal. IR£160,000Y. Goffs Orby.
Half-sister to the very smart Group 1 6f Heinz 57 Phoenix Stakes winner Lavery, to the quite useful dual 6f winner (including at 2 yrs) At Large (by Night Shift), the Australian and Hong Kong winner of 7 races Basic Instinct and the New Zealand winner Holly Hunter (both by Bakharoff). The dam, a fairly useful 2-y-o 5f winner, is a half-sister to the English and Irish Two Thousand Guineas winner Tirol and to the dam of the smart sprinter Eveningperformance. The second dam, Alpine Niece (by Great Nephew), was placed over 6f (at 2 yrs) and 12f and is a half-sister to the Group 3 Prix de Conde winner Minatzin. (Mrs Caroline Parker).

44 - BIRDIE * [64] b.f. Alhaarth - Fade (Persepolis).
February 25. Sixth foal.
Half-sister to the French middle-distance winner of 10 races (including 4 listed events) Faru (by Mtoto), to the fairly useful 1m and 10f winner Fickle (by Danehill), the quite useful winner of 3 races over 1m Eve (by Rainbow Quest) and the French winner of 3 races from 7.5f to 10f Flip Fantasia (by Batshoof). The dam is an unraced half-sister to Tom Seymour, a winner of five Group 3 events in Italy and fourth in the Queen's Vase. The second dam, One Over Parr (by Reform), won the Group 3 Lancashire Oaks and the Group 3 Cheshire Oaks and is a sister to the Oaks winner Polygamy. (Lady Caroline Warren). *"A very attractive filly. We've trained her two half-sisters who've done well and this filly would be far more precocious. She looks a quality filly in the making and if she's good enough I have the Fillies Mile at Ascot in mind for her".*

45 - BOGUS BALLET ** [88]

ch.f. Halling – Classic Ballet (Fabulous Dancer).
February 8. First foal. 27,000Y. Tattersalls October.

The dam, a fair 1m and 12f winner, is a sister to Ferdi, a champion miler in Spain, and to a French 2-y-o 7f winner and a half-sister to 4 minor winners. The second dam, Tyranesque (by Key To The Mint), won over 4.5f at 2 yrs in France. (Northmore Stud). *"A very nice filly, very active and athletic. More of a six or seven furlong type but a very easy mover and definitely a 2-y-o type".*

46 - FIZA (IRE) [69]

b.c. Revoque – Double Eight (Common Grounds).
February 3. First foal. IR£62,000Y. Goffs Orby.

The dam, a fair dual 12f winner, is a sister to the useful 2-y-o listed 6f Doncaster Stakes winner Proper Madam and a half-sister to 2 winners. The second dam, Boldabsa (by Persian Bold), won over 9f and 10f in Ireland and is a half-sister to 5 winners. (Mr Richard I Morris Jnr). *"He wouldn't be very early, but he's a nice, attractive, strong colt".*

47 - FLUENT ** [67]

b.f. Polar Falcon – Lady Barrister (Law Society).
May 7. Eighth foal.

Sister to the fairly useful 2-y-o 6f winner and listed 7f second Eloquent and half-sister to the Italian 2-y-o listed 1m winner Edipo Re (by Slip Anchor), the modest 2-y-o 7f winner Stately (by Be My Chief) and minor winners abroad by Rainbow Quest and Saddlers' Hall). The dam is an unraced half-sister to the Italian Group 3 winner Visto Si Stampi. The second dam, Jardiniere (by Nijinsky), is a placed sister to the top-class miler Kings Lake and a half-sister to the champion Irish 2-y-o Cloonlara and the very smart middle-distance colt Salmon Leap. (Cheveley Park Stud). *"A May foal, she looks like she'll make a 2-y-o from July onwards and is a nice filly".*

48 - FLYING FULMAR * [60]

ch.f. Bahamian Bounty – West Humble (Pharly).
February 5. First foal. 42,000Y. Tattersalls Autumn.

The dam, fairly useful 3-y-o 7f winner, is a half-sister to the Group 3 5f Premio Omenoni winner and Group 2 Diadem Stakes second Leap For Joy (by Sharpo). The second dam, Humble Pie (by Known Fact), a fairly useful 2-y-o 6f winner, is a half-sister to 4 winners including the high-class sprinter College Chapel. (Sir Thomas Pilkington). *"A very, very good-moving filly who will want fast ground and five or six furlongs. She'll be out in May or June, is a nice filly, a real 2-y-o and has plenty of speed. We like her".*

49 - INSTANT HIT * [78]

b.c. Indian Ridge – Pick Of The Pops (High Top).
April 28. Eighth foal. 100,000Y. Tattersalls Houghton.

Half-brother to the useful 1996 2-y-o 8.2f winner Fascinating Rhythm (by Slip Anchor), to the useful 10f to 11f winner of 5 races (including on the all-weather) Migwar (by Unfuwain) and a winner in Germany by Polish Precedent. The dam, a very useful 2-y-o 7f winner, was second in the Group 2 Hoover Fillies Mile and is a half-sister to 4 winners. The second dam, Rappa Tap Tap (by Tap on Wood), won the listed 6f Blue Seal Stakes and is a half-sister to the Prix de l'Opera winner Bella Colora (the dam of Stagecraft, Hyabella and Balalaika), the Irish Oaks winner Colorspin (the dam of Opera House and Kayf Tara) and the Irish Champion Stakes winner Cezanne. (Lancen Farm Partnership). *"I really like this horse. He's got a wonderful temperament and is a good,solid horse – more of a back-end of the season 2-y-o really, but he does everything very nicely at this stage".*

50 - IROQUOIS CHIEF (USA) * [73]

b.c. Known Fact – Celtic Shade (Lomond).
February 14. Third foal. $32,000Y. Keeneland September.

The dam was placed in France and is a half-sister to the Group 3 Rose Of Lancaster Stakes and subsequent Grade 1 Santa Anita Handicap winner Urgent Request. The second dam, Oscura (by Caro), won at 3 yrs in England and is a half-sister to the Grade 1 Washington D.C. International winner Johnny D and to the US Grade 2 winner Stardusk. (M L W Bell Racing Ltd). *"He's a nice, big, strong horse and is coming to hand earlier than I thought. He's probably more of a seven furlong type, but he may sharpen up more and have the speed for six".*

51 - JACK CARTER (IRE) * [65]   ch.c. Desert King – Miss Garuda (Persian Bold).

February 23. Seventh foal. 80,000Y. Tattersalls October.

Half-brother to the quite useful 7f winner (stays 10f), Bali Batik (by Barathea), to the quite useful 10f winner Indonesian (by Alzao) and the fair 2-y-o 8.5f winner Pampered Guest (by Be My Guest). The dam, a fairly useful 2-y-o 7f winner, stayed 10f and is a half-sister to 8 winners including the listed winners Bali Dancer and Miss Waterloo. The second dam, Miss Bali (by Crepello), won over 12f and is a half-sister to the Horris Hill Stakes winner Welsh Harmony. (Mr Wafic Said & Mr R P B Michaelson). *"On the burly side, he hasn't been here very long. He seems to have a very good temperament and I would say he's a June/July type of 2-y-o over six or seven furlongs. I trained two of his half-brothers and I'd be hopeful this one would win as a 2-y-o. He also seems to have more quality than they did".*

52 - KRUGERRAND (USA) * [76]   ch.c. Gulch – Nasers Pride (Al Nasr).

March 15. Fifth foal. $190,000Y. Keeneland September.

Closely related to a minor winner at 2 and 3 yrs in the USA by Woodman. The dam, a 2-y-o stakes winner in the USA, was second in the Grade 1 Las Virgenes Stakes and is a half-sister to the US stakes winner Caromine. The second dam, Screenland (by Silent Screen), won several minor stakes events in the USA. (Highclere Thoroughbred Racing Ltd). *"A lovely, quality horse. Very athletic, he's a powerful mover with plenty of scope and size. He'll be a June or July 2-y-o and is a very handsome horse. We like him".*

53 - LEOPOLD * [80]   b.c. Lion Cavern – Warning Star (Warning).

January 29. Second foal. 22,000Y. Tattersalls October.

Half-brother to the 2000 Italian 2-y-o winner Sele Alt (by Zafonic). The dam, a useful winner of 4 races over 5f and 6f, was third in the Group 2 6f Lowther Stakes and second in the Group 3 6f Prix de Meautry. The second dam, Blade Of Grass (by Kris), a fair 3-y-o 7f winner, is a half-sister to the French winner and Group 3 placed Brindle. (Cheveley Park Stud). *"A very strong, 2-y-o type who looks an out-and-out sprinter. From a fast family, he'll do the job".*

54 - MAGENTA (IRE) * [62]   b.br.f. Spectrum – Bird In My Hand (Bluebird).

January 20. First living foal. IR£34,000Y. Goffs Orby.

The dam is an unraced half-sister to 8 winners including the Group 1 Grand Prix de Paris and Group 1 Premio Roma winner Yawa, the 2-y-o Group 2 1m Beresford Stakes winner Euclid and the dam of the Group 1 Italian Oaks winner Lady Bentley. The second dam, Lucky For Me (by Appiani II), won the listed 12f Galtres Stakes and is a half-sister to the US Grade 1 winner and Irish Derby fourth Nor. (Highclere Thoroughbred Racing Ltd). *"She's a sharp 2-y-o type and she'll be on the track by the end of May. Maybe not from our top drawer at this stage but she's speedy".*

55 - MINE HOST * [66]   b.c. Elmaamul – Divina Mia (Dowsing).

April 2. Third foal. IR25,000Y. Tattersalls Fairyhouse.

Half-brother to the fair 2000 2-y-o 5f winner So Divine (by So Factual). The dam, a modest 2-y-o 6f winner, stayed 11f and is a half-sister to the dam of the Australian Grade 1 winner Markham. The second dam, Hardihostess (by Be My Guest), a useful winner of 2 races over 7f (at 2 yrs), is a half-sister to the Derby winner Shirley Heights and to the high-class broodmare Bempton (dam of numerous winners including Gull Nook - herself the dam of Pentire). (Mr Nick Hodges). *"One of our most forward colts, he's very strong and will probably have run by the time this book is published. We like him and he may be alright over five furlongs but he's bred to be better over a bit further. His main aim will be the Fairyhouse Sales race and I'm hoping he's going to be at least listed class".*

56 - MOUNT OLYMPUS * [63]   b.f. Primo Dominie – Penthouse Lady (Last Tycoon).

March 31. Third foal.

Sister the fairly useful 1999 triple 5f winner Dorchester (by Primo Dominie). The dam is an unraced half-sister to 6 winners including the US Grade 1 Mervyn Leroy Handicap winner and Group 1 Criterium de Saint-Cloud second Louis Cyphre and to the Group 2 Prix Robert Papin winner and French Two Thousand Guineas third Psychobabble. The second dam, Princesse Timide (by Blushing Groom), won twice in France and was listed placed four times. (Cheveley Park Stud). *"A sharp 2-y-o type, she's bred to be speedy and we'll know our fate by mid-summer".*

57 - NORWOOD ORIGO ** [66] ch.c. Elmaamul – Miller's Creek (Star de Naskra).

February 18. Tenth foal. 27,000Y. Tattersalls Autumn.

Half-brother to the useful 1994 2-y-o 6f winner and Group 1 5f Heinz 57 Phoenix Stakes placed Fast Eddy (by Sharpo), to the useful 6f (at 2 yrs) to 10.2f winner Stone Mill (by Caerleon), the modest 11.6f to 14f winner Dalby Of York (by Polar Falcon), the hurdles winner Sandro (by Niniski) and a winner in Italy by Pursuit Of Love. The dam, a modest 1m placed maiden, is a half-sister to 6 winners including the Italian St Leger winner Sierra Star. The second dam, New Chant (by New Providence), a 2-y-o 6f winner and Grade 1 placed in Canada, is a half-sister to the Canadian Grade 1 winner Giboulee. (Norwood Partition Systems Ltd). *"By Elmaamul, who I like, this colt is a lovely, easy mover. He wouldn't be in our early bracket but he really covers the ground and would be a sort of June 2-y-o".*

58 - ON STAGE (USA) * [71] b.c. In The Wings – Lady Thynn (Crystal Glitters).

April 2. Fifth foal. 160,000Y. Tattersalls October.

Half-brother to the 3-y-o Double Dipsea (by Fairy King) and to winners in France by Pistolet Bleu and Wolfhound. The dam won once at 3 yrs in France and was listed-placed. She is a half-sister to 7 winners including the US Grade 2 All Along Stakes and Group 3 12f Prix Minerve winner Lady Blessington, the French Group 3 11f winner Lowell and the US stakes winner Red Cat. The second dam, Lady Sharp (by Sharpman), won once in France and is a half-sister to the French Group 3 1m winner Prospero. (Mrs Evelyn Hankinson). *"A lovely horse and the most expensive In The Wings yearling last year. A very athletic horse and I like him. More of a 3-y-o prospect, but he'll do himself justice in the autumn".*

59 - PACHARA ** [59] b.c. Mind Games – Miss Mercy (Law Society).

April 1. Second living foal. 25,000Y. Doncaster St Leger.

Half-brother to the fair 2000 6f and 7f placed 2-y-o That's Jazz (by Cool Jazz). The dam, a modest 2-y-o 6f winner, is a half-sister to 2 minor winners. The second dam, Missing You (by Ahonoora), was second in the listed 6f Silver Flash Stakes and is a sister to listed Sceptre Stakes winner Arjuzah. (Mr Billy Maguire). *"One of our early types, he'll be running by the time this book is printed. He looks a ready made 2-y-o".*

60 - PSYCHIC (IRE) ** [67] b.f. Alhaarth – Mood Swings (Shirley Heights).

March 7. Second foal. IR£75,000Y. Goffs Orby.

Half-sister to the useful 2000 2-y-o 6f winner and Group 2 6f Gimcrack Stakes fourth Hurricane Floyd (by Pennekamp). The dam, a fair 2-y-o 6f winner, is a sister to the listed 2-y-o Sweet Solera Stakes winner Catwalk. The second dam, Moogie (by Young Generation), a useful 2-y-o 6f winner, was fourth in the Group 1 1m Coronation Stakes and is a half-sister to 6 winners. (Hon. Mrs C Corbett & Partners). *"An attractive filly and one of our quality types, she'll be out in mid-summer and is showing me all the right signs at the moment".*

61 - RED BRIAR (IRE) ** [63] b.c. Desert King – Rose Society (Caerleon).

March 30. Fifth foal. IR£40,000Y. Goffs Orby.

Half-brother to the useful 1m, 10f and subsequent US stakes winner Silverani (by High Estate) and to 2 minor 2-y-o winners in France (by Tirol) and Germany (by College Chapel). The dam, placed over middle-distances in Ireland, is a half-sister to 7 minor winners. The second dam, a middle-distance winner, is a half-sister to the good broodmare Centre Piece (dam of the Group 2 winners Red Sunset and Greenland Park). (Mr Terry Neill). *"A sharp, early 2-y-o type. He's active, precocious and ready to go".*

62 - SCHOOL DAYS [60] b.f. Slip Anchor – Cradle of Love (Roberto).

April 27. Sixth foal.

Sister to the fairly useful 1m to 12f winner Captain's Log and half-sister to the Italian 2 and 3-y-o winner Stracch (by Polish Precedent) and the quite useful Ivory Dawn (by Batshoof), a winner of 5 races over 6f. The dam, a quite useful 3-y-o 9f winner, is a sister to the Nassau Stakes winner Mamaluna and the US stakes winner Saucy Bobbie and a half-sister to 11 winners. The second dam, Kadesh (by Lucky Mel), won the 5f Nursery Stakes in the USA at 2 yrs and was second in the Grade 2 Hollywood Lassie Stakes. (Mr Chris Wright). *"Very much a 3-y-o prospect but I would envisage her being able to perform well as a 2-y-o over 1m at the back-end. She's a very easy mover and a nice filly in the making".*

63 - SHIRLEY COLLINS * [59]   b.f. Robellino – Kisumu (Damister).
April 19. Fourth foal. 46,000Y. Tattersalls October.

Half-sister to the 3-y-o Bobby's Pride and to the Group 1 Premio Presidente della Repubblica winner Timboroa (both by Salse). The dam is an unraced half-sister to 5 winners including the very smart Group 1 Premio Emilio Turati winner and good sire Efisio and the Grade 1 10f Santa Barbara Handicap and Grade 2 9f San Gorgonio Handicap winner Mountain Bear. The second dam, Eeldoret (by High Top), was a useful 6f and 1m winner and was second in the listed Virginia Stakes. (D G H Partnership). *"A lovely pedigree and she's a nice filly. A little bit on the burly side at the moment, but she definitely has the makings of a 2-y-o. Hopefully the type to start in a fillies maiden at Newmarket in July".*

---

64 - SOFTLY (IRE) * [59]   ch.f. Grand Lodge – Decrescendo (Polish Precedent).
April 29. Third foal. IR£25,000Y. Goffs Orby.

Half-sister to the unplaced 2000 2-y-o Shirley Fong (by Bluebird). The dam is an unraced half-sister to the smart 1998 2-y-o Calando, winner of the Group 3 May Hill Stakes. The second dam, Diminuendo (by Diesis), was a top class, game and genuine winner of the Hoover Fillies Mile, Cherry Hinton Stakes (both at 2 yrs), Epsom Oaks, Irish Oaks (in a dead-heat), Yorkshire Oaks and Musidora Stakes and was officially rated the top racehorse of her generation in the 11f+ category. (Mr Edward Kessly & Partner). *"One of our very early types. She goes well and, like her grandam, is not very big. What she lacks in scope is made up for in speed. I like her a lot".*

---

65 - TERFEL * [84]   ch.c. Lion Cavern – Montserrat (Aragon).
February 5. Second foal.

Half-brother to the moderate Renee (by Wolfhound), placed once over 5f at 2 yrs in 2000. The dam, a quite useful 5f (at 2 yrs) and 6f winner, is a half-sister to several winners. The second dam, Follow The Stars (by Sparkler), was a quite useful 8.5f and 10f winner. (Mrs Anne Yearley). *"A very good mover with plenty of scope and one that will be out around July time".*

---

66 - WING COMMANDER ** [70]   b.c. Royal Applause – Southern Psychic (Alwasmi).
April 9. Third foal. IR£180,000Y. Goffs Orby.

Half-brother to the extremely promising 2000 2-y-o 6f and Dubai Two Thousand Guineas Trial winner Rumpold (by Mister Baileys) and to a minor 2-y-o winner in the USA by Alydeed. The dam, a sprint winner at 4 yrs in the USA, is closely related to the Canadian dual 6f stakes winner Sing And Swing and a half-sister to the US 9f stakes winner Windansea and to the dam of the Group 2 Gimcrack Stakes winner Chilly Billy. The second dam, Sun And Snow (by Hawaii), won the Grade 2 9f Kentucky Oaks and the Grade 3 8.5f Ashland Stakes and is a half-sister to 7 winners. (Mr Mark Hawlin). *"A big, strong 2-y-o type, he's very attractive and will take a bit of time but should be a July 2-y-o I think. Really good-limbed, he's a very nice horse and he looks the part".*

---

67 - YALLAMBIE * [61]   b.f. Revoque – Tahnee (Cadeaux Genereux).
February 5. Third foal. 26,000Y. Tattersalls October.

The dam is an unraced half-sister to the Group 1 5f Heinz 57 Phoenix Stakes winner Princely Heir. The second dam, Meis-El-Reem (by Auction Ring), won the Group 3 1m Prix d'Astarte and the Group 3 1m Child Stakes. (Mr Peter Ward & Partners). *"A very attractive, easy-moving filly and her principal aim is the new Sales race at Ascot at the end of September. She's very well-in at the weights and her campaign will be heading towards that race. She won't be out until July at the earliest".*

A BERRY

68 - BONNIE LAD (IRE) ** [80]   b.c. Tagula – Sabonis (The Minstrel).
April 19. Seventh foal. 22,000Y. Doncaster St Leger.

Half-brother to the fairly useful 2000 2-y-o 5f winner and listed-placed Stregone (by Namaqualand) and to the fair 1997 2-y-o 1m winner Premium Quest (by Forzando). The dam, a fair 2-y-o 6f winner, is a half-sister to 7 winners including the US stakes winner Loft . The second dam, Journey (by What A Pleasure), is an unraced full or half-sister to 7 winners in the USA. (Owen Promotions). *"His owner Michael Owen will be looking forward to seeing him at Chester in May. He looks quite sharp and is a racy, compact horse. He's just getting the hang of things now and he seems like a nice 2-y-o, really sensible and with a good future ahead of him".*

69 - GALAXY SAM (USA) * [94]   ch.c. Royal Academy – Istiska (Irish Ruler).

January 18. Twelfth foal. $30,000Y. Keeneland September. 35,000Y. Tattersalls December.
Half-brother to the US winner of 12 races and Grade 1 Norfolk Stakes second Zurich (by Private Account), to the Irish 1m winner and Group 3 7f C L Weld Park Stakes third Fairy Water (by Warning), the quite useful 2-y-o 7f and 5-y-o 13f winner Noyan (by Northern Baby), the modest 7f winner Terdad (by Lomond) and minor winners in France by Cresta Rider and Fluorescent Light. The dam was placed 5 times in France and is a half-sister to 6 winners including the Prix de Flore and Prix Penelope winner Demia and the grandam of the Group 1 winners Ebadiyla, Enzeli and Edabiya. The second dam, Evisa (by Dan Cupid), was unraced. (Mr Simon Munir). *"He's by Royal Academy who isn't noted for getting many 2-y-o winners, but he's got every chance this year and is a big strong horse that just needs to fill out".*

70 - GALAXY THUNDERBIRD * [74]   ch.c. Bahamian Bounty – Milva (Jellaby).

February 9. Twelfth foal. 24,000Y. Tattersalls October.
Half-brother to the quite useful dual 6f winner Milagro (by King Of Spain), to the fair 1991 2-y-o 7f and subsequent Italian winner Miltiades (by Magic Mirror), the modest 5f and 6f winner Mill End Quest (by King's Signet), the modest 14f winner Serious Time (by Good Times), the modest 6f (at 2 yrs) and 12f winner Full Egalite (by Ezzoud), the Italian winner Belong To Me (by Squill) and the 1997 French 3-y-o winner Yucatan (by Saint Andrews). The dam, a modest 3-y-o 6f winner, is a half-sister to 4 winners. The second dam, Cornflower (by Vilmorin), won at 2 yrs and was a fairly useful sprinter. (Mr Simon Munir). *"He needs to furnish a little bit yet. My 2-y-o's seem to be a bit behind because of all the wet weather but he'll be OK".*

71 - JOYCE'S CHOICE ** [67]   b.c. Mind Games – Madrina (Waajib).

April 23. Second foal. 21,000Y. Doncaster St Leger.
Half-sister to the quite useful triple 5f winner (including at 2 yrs) Laurel Dawn (by Paris House). The dam, a modest 6f winner, is a half-sister to 4 winners including the quite useful 5f winner Antonia's Choice. The second dam, Mainly Sunset (by Red Sunset), raced only once due to an injury and is a half-sister to 8 winners including the high-class sprinter Bolshoi and the useful sprinters Tod and Great Chaddington. (Mr W Parker). *"A real angular, lean colt, but he'll fill out and is a half-brother to Laurel Dawn who won twice for us last year. Hopefully this fellow will be just as good. He's a good-looking horse, he shows a bit of speed and I think he'll be OK".*

72 - LADY ANSELL ** [72]   b.f. Puissance – Rare Indigo (Timeless Times).

April 10. First foal. 3,000Y. Tattersalls Autumn.
The dam, a quite useful 2-y-o dual 5f winner, is out of the modest 4-y-o 7f winner Miss Ritz (by Robellino). (Ansells of Watford). *"She was very cheap and has already won easily at Southwell. A grand, strong 2-y-o out of Rare Indigo who had bad knees, this filly is as sound as a bell. She goes really well and will be aimed at the Supersprint at Newbury as it's always a little filly like this carrying next to nothing that wins it".*

73 - PETRULA ** [71]   ch.c. Tagula – Bouffant (High Top).

February 17. Eighth foal. 24,000Y. Doncaster St Leger.
Closely related to the quite useful 10f winner Sahil and the plating-class 2-y-o 7f winner Fanfan (both by Taufan) and half-brother to the fairly useful 10f to 12f winner of 6 races High Tatra, the fair 5f (at 2 yrs) to 10f winner Smart Boy and the German winner Mutassariff (all by Polish Patriot). The dam was placed four times in Ireland over middle-distances at 3 yrs and is out of the Group 3 12f Lingfield Oaks Trial winner Lucent (by Irish Ball) - herself a daughter of the July Cup winner Lucasland. (Mr & Mrs Peter Foden). *"A really nice-looking colt, he'll be one for the end of May and has the right attitude. He's a five furlong 2-y-o type but he could well get further in time".*

74 - POLAR IMPACT ** [87]   br.c. Polar Falcon – Boozy (Absalom).

May 14. Seventh foal. 8,500Y. Doncaster St Leger.
Brother to the fair 5f (at 2 yrs) to 7f placed Skylark and half-brother to the quite useful 2000 6f placed 2-y-o Double Brew (by Primo Dominie) and the fair triple 5f winner (including at 2 yrs) Gwespyr (by Sharpo). The dam, a very useful winner of the Group 3 Phoenix Flying Five, is a half-sister to 2 winners. The second dam, The High Dancer (by High Line), is an unraced half-sister to 3 winners. (Mr R

Heathcote). *"He looks a really, big strong colt and unlike his mother he's a sensible colt. He has a laid-back attitude and does everything easily".*

75 - RUM DESTINY (IRE) *** [88]   b.c. Mujadil – Ruby River (Red God).
March 18. IR28,000Y. Tattersalls Fairyhouse.
Brother to the fair 1999 3-y-o 7f winner Riverbird and half-brother to the unplaced 2000 2-y-o Bolingbroke Castle (by Goldmark), the fairly useful 2-y-o dual 6f winner and Cherry Hinton Stakes third Rohita (by Waajib), the fairly useful 2-y-o 5f winner Super Zoom (by Ballad Rock), the quite useful 1m to 10f winner of 16 races Knock Knock (by Tap On Wood) and the fair winner of 3 races at around 1m Don't Jump (by Entitled). The dam ran once unplaced and is a half-sister to 6 winners here and abroad. The second dam, River Craft (by Reliance II), ran once unplaced and is a sister to the Group 3 Brigadier Gerard Stakes winner Rymer and a half-sister to the dam of the Group 3 winners Sayyaf and Impudent Miss. (Chris & Antonia Deuters). *"A bit disappointing on the heavy going on his first outing when he also missed the break. He looks the part and seems a real 2-y-o – he might get six furlongs but when you see him he's the finished article now".*

76 - SHEILA BLIGE *** [81]   ch.f. Zamindar – Stripanoora (Ahonoora).
April 5. Seventh foal. 27,000Y. Doncaster St Leger.
Half-sister to the fair 2000 2-y-o 6f and 7f winner Classy Act (by Lycius), to the very useful 1m (at 2 yrs) to 12f winner and Group 3 Gordon Richards Stakes third Naked Welcome, the fair 2-y-o 6f winner She's My Love, the Norwegian 2-y-o winner Salobre (all by Most Welcome) and the fairly useful 5f and 6f (at 2 yrs) and subsequent US winner Olympic Spirit (by Puissance). The dam was placed once at 3 yrs and stayed 1m and is a full or half-sister to 5 minor winners. The second dam, Strip Fast (by Virginia Bay), won 4 minor races. *"This is a really nice filly and she goes well, just like her half-sister Classy Act. She looks sharp and will be a decent 2-y-o".*

77 - STORMY PARKES ** [77]   ch.f. Zamindar – Lucky Parkes (Full Extent).
March 28. Second foal.
Half-sister to the fairly useful Charlie Parkes (by Pursuit Of Love), placed second over 5f in all three of his races at 2 yrs in 2000. The dam, a useful winner of 13 races over 5f, is a half-sister to several winners including the useful dual 5f winner and Moyglare, Lowther and Queen Mary Stakes placed My Melody Parkes. The second dam, Summerhill Spruce (by Windjammer), was a fair winner of a 6f seller at 3 yrs. (Mr J Heler). *"A half-sister to Charlie Parkes who was unlucky not to win last year. This filly isn't quite as big as him, she's compact and looks more like her mother than he does. The owner's been lucky with the ones he's bred and the Zamindar's seem sharp, so she'll be OK. I'd like to think she could go for the Queen Mary but she's got to win first".*

78 - TARRAGONA (IRE) ** [66]   b.f. Charnwood Forest – Limerick Princess (Polish Patriot).
March 26. Second foal. 25,000Y. Doncaster St Leger.
Sister to the Irish 3-y-o The Maigue. The dam, a modest winner of 4 races over 5f and 6f, is a half-sister to 6 winners including the 2-y-o listed winner Limerick Belle and the quite useful triple 2-y-o 6f winner and Group 3 Molecomb Stakes and Group 3 Queen Mary Stakes second It's All Academic. The second dam, Princess Of Nashua (by Crowned Prince), is an unraced half-sister to 5 minor winners. (Chris & Antonia Deuters). *"She'll come on a lot for her first outing at Southwell where she ran green. I like her and was a bit disappointed with her first effort, but she's a nice filly".*

79 - THE LEATHER WEDGE (IRE) ** [73]   b.c. Hamas – Wallflower (Polar Falcon).
February 13. First foal. 8,500Y. Doncaster October.
The dam ran once unplaced over 5f at 2 yrs and is a half-sister to several winners including the useful listed 7f Rockfel Stakes winner Fearless Revival (herself dam of the high-class sprinter Pivotal), the dual 1m winner Brave Revival and the 10f winner Revival – both fairly useful. The second dam, Stufida (by Bustino), won the 10f Premio Lydia Tesio. (Mr J L Young). *"A nice 2-y-o, he's a little bit straight in front but he's going really well".*

80 - BLUE CASCADE (IRE) [75]

b.c. Royal Academy – Blaine (Lyphard's Wish).
April 22. Seventh foal. IR£72,000Y. Goffs Orby.

Half-brother to the quite useful 1m and subsequent US winner St Blaine (by St Jovite) and to 2 minor winners in the USA by Relaunch and Wolf Power. The dam was placed in the USA and is a half-sister to 6 winners including the Fillies Mile third Alligatrix (herself dam of the Group 1 winner Croco Rouge and grandma of the Group 1 winners Ali-Royal, Sleepytime and Taipan). The second dam, Shore (by Round Table), won 6 races including a stakes event in the USA and is a half-sister to three good US stakes winners and to the dam of the Prix de l'Abbaye winner Polonia. (M J Dawson). *"I had thought he'd be reasonably early, but he's grown a bit and he'll take a bit more time. From what I've seen so far he looks quite nice and I would have thought he'd want seven furlongs to begin with".*

81 - MANQUE NEUF ** [73]

b.c. Cadeaux Genereux – Flying Squaw (Be My Chief).
April 30. Third foal. 67,000Y. Tattersalls October.

Half-brother to the fair 3-y-o 8.5f winner Flying Carpet (by Barathea). The dam, winner of the Group 2 6f Moet and Chandon Rennen winner Flying Squaw at 2 yrs, is a half-sister to numerous winners including the quite useful 5f and 6f winner Cauda Equina. The second dam, Sea Fret (by Habat), a fairly useful 2-y-o 6f winner, is a half-sister to the Lancashire Oaks placed fillies Main Sail and Sextant. The third dam, Fluke (by Grey Sovereign), won the Duke Of York Stakes and the Jersey Stakes and is a half-sister to the Oaks winner Bireme and the Coronation Cup winner Buoy. (M J Dawson). *"He's a very, very nice horse, quite tall and leggy but classy. He'd be my favourite at the moment and I would hope he'd be ready for around July time. He'll want six or seven furlongs this year".*

82 - MARRIFORTH * [73]

ch.f. Wolfhound – Ghassanah (Pas de Seul).
April 9. Ninth foal. 7,500Y. Tattersalls October.

Sister to the modest 6f (at 2 yrs) to 1m placed Alawar, closely related to the fair triple 7f all-weather winner Sand Hawk and the modest 3-y-o 7f winner Willisa (both by Polar Falcon) and half-sister to the useful 6f (at 3 yrs) and 7f (at 2 yrs) winner Return Of Amin (by Salse), the fairly useful 5f and 6f winner and Group 3 6f Prix de Meautry third Alzianah, the fairly useful 2-y-o 7f and 7.6f winner Amin (by Last Tycoon) and the quite useful 8.5f and 12f winner Little Amin (by Unfuwain). The dam, a fair 7f winner, is a half-sister to 10 winners including the Italian Derby winner Don Orazio and the Group 2 Premio Emilio Turati winner Les Boyer. The second dam, Debutante (by Silly Season), won once at 3 yrs and is a half-sister to 8 winners including the dam of the Champion Stakes winner Swiss Maid. (Clarendon Racing). *"I'm very pleased with her, she's a very nice little filly that goes well and will be an early type. Very much a sprint type 2-y-o, she's been entered in the Sales race at Ascot in September".*

83 - MARTIN HOUSE (IRE) [69]

b.c. Mujadil – Dolcezza (Lichine).
April 27. Sixth foal. 35,000Y. Tattersalls October.

Half-brother to the 3-y-o Sweet Golden (by Charnwood Forest), to the minor French 4-y-o winner Dairen (by Kaldoun) and a winner in Germany by Hernando. The dam is an unraced sister to the French 1m and 9f listed winner Bormio and a half-sister to the French listed winner Cortona and the Group 3 10.5f Prix Cleopatre winner Caprarola (herself dam of the Prix Hocquart winner Arbatax). The second dam, Olbia (by Mill Reef), is a placed half-sister to the Prix Ganay winner Romildo, the Prix de Conde winner Pevero and the dams of the Group/Graded stakes winners Golden Reef, Virginia Carnival and Muroto. (M J Dawson). *"He's a very big, leggy, backward horse for later on – probably August at the earliest. He moves very well and I would think he'd want at least seven furlongs".*

84 - THIRN * [72]

b.c. Piccolo – Midnight Owl (Ardross).
March 4. Sixth foal. 20,000Y. Tattersalls October.

Brother to the fair 2000 7f placed 2-y-o Floot and half-brother to the modest 1m winner Feathertime (by Puissance) and to the Irish 6-y-o 12f and hurdles winner Regency Rake (by Ti King). The dam ran twice unplaced and is a half-sister to 10 winners including the listed 1m Prix La Camargo winner Party Dol (herself dam of the French Group 2 winner Titus Livius) and the useful French 2-y-o 6.5f winner Microcosme. The second dam, Midnight Lady (by Mill Reef), won once at 2 yrs and is a half-sister to the US Grade 2 winner Regal Bearing and to the dams of the Grade 1 winners Metamorphose (in the USA) and Super Sheila (in South Africa). *"An extremely nice colt, he's a big horse but he's the most lovely mover and I would hope he'd be out by mid-summer. Doing everything right at the moment".*

M BLANSHARD

85 - EL RAYMONDO [67]
b.c. Night Shift – Alaraby (Caerleon).
March 22. First foal. 20,000Y. Tattersalls October.

The dam, a fair 14f winner, is a sister to the useful 10f winner and Craven Stakes third Circus and a half-sister to the quite useful sprint winner of 6 races Robin Lake. The second dam, Circe (by High Top), a fair 1m placed 2-y-o, is out of the Group 3 Hoover Fillies Mile winner Nepula.

86 - OPEN OUTCRY [60]
ch.c. Bluegrass Prince – Bowden Rose (Dashing Blade).
April 26. First foal. 21,000Y. Tattersalls Autumn.

The dam was a useful winner of 10 races from 5f to 6f and is a half-sister to a winner over hurdles. The second dam, Elegant Rose (by Noalto), a fair dual 6f winner (including on the all-weather), is a daughter of the Group 3 Fred Darling Stakes winner Shapina.

87 - PERFECT STORM [66]
b.c. Vettori – Gorgeous Dancer (Nordico).
May 8. Fourth foal. 32,000Y. Tattersalls October.

Half-brother to the useful 2000 2-y-o 5f and 7f winner Imperial Dancer (by Primo Dominie) and to the useful 10.4f listed winner Lafite (by Robellino). The dam, an Irish 3-y-o 1m winner and third in the listed Oaks Trial at the Curragh, is a half-sister to the Italian winner and Group 3 placed Campalto. The second dam, Simply Gorgeous (by Hello Gorgeous), is an unraced half-sister to the high-class middle-distance filly Give Thanks, winner of the Irish Oaks, the Musidora Stakes and the Lancashire Oaks (herself grandam of the One Thousand Guineas winner Harayir).

88 - RED CHINA [61]
ch.c. Inchinor – Little Tramp (Trempolino).
April 19. First foal. 22,000Y. Tattersalls October.

The dam is an unraced half-sister to the fairly useful 12f winner Aymara. The second dam, Chipaya (by Northern Prospect), was a smart winner of 6 races including the Racecall Gold Trophy (at 2 yrs) and the listed 1m October Stakes and is a half-sister to 4 winners including the Group 3 Prestige Stakes second Fernanda.

89 - JUST MY HOBBY [91]
b.f. Kris – Noble Peregrine (Lomond).
March 20. Fifth foal.

Half-sister to the quite useful 2000 7f placed 2-y-o Wannabe Around (by Primo Dominie), to the useful 7.5f to 10f winner and French Group 3 1m placed Nobelist (by Bering) and the fairly useful 7f (at 2 yrs) and 1m winner Noble Pursuit (by Pursuit Of Love). The dam, an Italian 10f winner, is closely related to the French 2-y-o listed 10f winner Noble Ballerina and a half-sister to 6 winners including the very useful Amrak Ajeeb. The second dam, Noble Dust (by Dust Commander), is an unraced half-sister to 6 winners.
Significant sire/damsire crosses:- Balisada, Ultimately Lucky.

90 - RHICONICH (IRE) [69]
gr.c. Ashkalani – Snowing (Tate Gallery).
April 26. Third foal.

Half-brother to the useful 2000 2-y-o dual 5f winner The Trader (by Selkirk). The dam, a quite useful dual 5f winner at 3 yrs, is a half-sister to 2 minor winners. The second dam, Biding (by Habat), a fairly useful dual 5f winner at 3 yrs, is a half-sister to 11 winners including the Group 3 5f Cornwallis Stakes winner Splashing (herself dam of the Group 1 Middle Park Stakes winner Bassenthwaite and the Group 3 Cornwallis Stakes winner Glancing) and the dams of the Group winners Hadeer, Bay Street and Monassib.

J BOLGER

91 - ALLURING PARK (IRE) ***
b.br.f. Green Desert – Park Express (Ahonoora).
April 30.

Sister to the Japanese stakes winner Shinko Forest and half-sister to the Group 3 1m Matron Stakes and listed 9f winner Dazzling Park (by Warning), the French 7f winner Lady Express (by Soviet Star) and the French 2-y-o 7f winner Tycoon King (by Last Tycoon). The dam won 5 races including the Group 1 10f Phoenix Champion Stakes, the Group 2 10f Nassau Stakes and the Group 3 12f Lancashire Oaks and is a half-sister to numerous winners including the listed 6f Firth of Clyde Stakes winner Myra's Best. The second dam, Matcher (by Match III), ran unplaced twice and was a half-sister to 4 winners

including a minor stakes winner in the USA. *"She's a strong filly that will make a nice 2-y-o by mid-season and she has the pedigree to do well over six furlongs or more this year".*
Significant sire/damsire crosses:- Cape Cross, Gabr, Shinko Forest.

92 - ALMOST FAMOUS (IRE) *

ch.c. Grand Lodge – Smouldering (Caerleon).
April 3. Fifth foal. 210,000Y. Tattersalls October.

Half-brother to Magic To Do (by Spectrum), unplaced in one start at 2 yrs in 2000, to the quite useful 1999 2-y-o 6f winner Camp Fire (by Lahib) and to 2 minor winners in Italy (by Cadeaux Genereux) and Japan (by Sanglamore). The dam ran once unplaced and is a half-sister to 8 winners including the Irish Two Thousand Guineas winner Flash Of Steel and the dam of the Group 3 10f Select Stakes winner Fahris. The second dam, Spark Of Fire (by Run The Gantlet), is an unplaced half-sister to the US Grade 1 winners Spark Of Life (herself dam of the Premio Roma winner Fire Of Life) and Musical Lark and to the French Group 3 Prix de la Grotte winner Hartebeest. *"Yes, he's a good type, has a good pedigree and he'll make a 2-y-o by the second half of the season".*

93 - CAPEL STREET (IRE)

b.c. Erin's Isle – Capellino (Imperial Frontier).
March 26. Second foal.

Half-brother to unplaced 2000 2-y-o Imperial Eye (by Eagle Eyed). The dam, a fair Irish 2-y-o 5f winner, is a half-sister to the useful Irish dual 6f listed winner (at 2 yrs) and Group 3 7f Concorde Stakes third Azra. The second dam, Easy To Please (by What A Guest), a useful Irish 2-y-o 1m winner, trained on to win the Queen Alexandra Stakes. *"A good model, but he's one for seven furlongs at the end of the season".*

94 - CELTIC DANCER (IRE)

b.c. Sadler's Wells – Noora Abu (Ahonoora).
April 19. Seventh foal.

The dam won 12 races including the Group 2 10f Pretty Polly Stakes and the listed 7f Ballycorus Stakes and is a half-sister to 6 winners including the dual Irish listed winner Condor Pan. The second dam, Ishtar Abu (by St Chad), won at 3 yrs. *"A good-looking colt with a good action but he's not going to be seen out until much later in the season".*

95 - DANELETA (IRE) **

b.f. Danehill – Zavaleta (Kahyasi).
April 13.

Half-sister to a winner in Japan by Caerleon. The dam, a useful winner of the listed 7f Athasi Stakes and the listed 1m Derrinstown Stud One Thousand Guineas Trial, is a half-sister to the useful 6f and 7f winner Nordic Fox and the fairly useful 2-y-o 5f winner and Molecomb Stakes second Raghida. The second dam, La Meilleure (by Lord Gayle), a quite useful 7f and 1m winner in Ireland, is from the family of Double Form and Scimitarra. *"A good-looking filly from a very 'live' family, she'll make a nice 2-y-o by mid-season and has the scope to go on at 3 yrs".*

96 - MARGARULA (IRE)

b.f. Doyoun – Mild Intrigue (Sir Ivor).
March 15. Eighth foal. IR£33,000Y. Goffs Orby.

Half-sister to the quite useful 2000 1m placed 2-y-o Conspire (by Turtle Island), to the 1998 Irish 2-y-o listed 9f winner Wild Heaven (by Darshaan), the Italian winner of 5 races at up to 11f Mild Dancer (by Fairy King), the fairly useful 13.4f to 2m winner High Intrigue (by Shirley Heights) and the 1998 French 3-y-o winner Suaverof (by Suave Dancer). The dam, a fairly useful 10f winner, is a half-sister to the useful listed 10f winner Grimesgill, the US stakes winner Determined Bidder and the dam of the South African Grade 1 winner Milleverof. The second dam, Mild Deception (by Buckpasser), won 3 races in the USA at up to 1m, is a half-sister to Arkadina (placed in 3 Irish classics and a high-class broodmare), to the Queen's Vase and Jockey Club Cup winner Blood Royal, the Group 1 Joe McGrath Memorial Stakes winner Gregorian and the Grade 3 Test Stakes winner Ivory Wand (dam of the Group 1 winner Gold And Ivory). *"She's backward at the moment but she'll make a 2-y-o later on and she's a good mover".*

97 - MARIONNAUD (IRE) **

b.f. Spectrum – Raghida (Nordico).
March 13. Third foal.

The dam, a fairly useful Irish 2-y-o dual 5f winner, was second in the Group 3 5f Curragh Stakes and the Group 3 Molecomb Stakes and is a sister to the useful 6f to 7f winner and Group 3 placed Nordic Fox and a half-sister to 3 winners including the useful dual listed 7f winner Zavaletta. The second dam,

La Meilleure (by Lord Gayle), was a quite useful listed 1m winner in Ireland at 3 yrs. *"She was beaten by a short head on her debut but she'll win her races and will stay a mile later on".*

98 - MARTIN GUNNE (IRE) *

b.c. Mark Of Esteem – Gradille (Home Guard).
April 22.

Half-brother to the Irish listed 1m winner and dam of numerous winners La Meilleure (by Lord Gayle), to the Irish 6f winner Canadian Patriot (by Polish Patriot), the Irish 9f winner Topsey's Tipple (by Hatim) and a winner in Belgium by Sallust. The dam, a fair 6f and 7f winner, is a half-sister to 3 winners including the Group 3 6f Goldene Peitsche third Nephrite - herself the dam of 6 winners. The second dam, Gradiva (by Lorenzaccio), was a very useful winner from 5f to 1m and a half-sister to the high-class sprinter Double Form and the Lupe Stakes winner Scimitarra. *"He'll be relatively early and I'd expect him to be fast enough for six furlongs".*

99 - UNNAMED

b.f. Sadler's Wells – Helianthus (Groom Dancer).
May 2. First foal. 100,000Y. Tattersalls Houghton.

The dam, a minor 4-y-o winner in France, is a half-sister to 5 winners including the Group 2 12f Princess Of Wales's Stakes winner Wagon Master. The second dam, Sunny Flower (by Dom Racine), was placed twice in France and is a half-sister to the dam of the good miler Then Again and to the top-class broodmare Sunny Valley (the dam of Sun Princess and Saddlers Hall). *"A good-actioned filly for the second half of the season".*

100 - STAGE CALL (IRE)

b.c. Sadler's Wells – Humble Eight (Seattle Battle).
April 6.

The dam, winner of the Grade 3 8.5f Honeybee Handicap in the USA, is a half-sister to the 2-y-o listed 6f Silver Flash Stakes winner April Starlight. The second dam, Alleged Devotion (by Alleged), is an unraced half-sister to the top-class Irish Derby and Epsom Oaks winner Balanchine, to the Group 2 Jockey Club Stakes winner Romanov and the Group 2 Sun Chariot Stakes winner Red Slippers. *"A good-moving colt with a good attitude, he'll make a 2-y-o in the second half of the season".*

101 - COLOURFAST (IRE) **

b.f. Spectrum – Sedulous (Tap On Wood).
May 11. Eighth foal. IR£100,000Y. Goffs Orby.

Half-sister to the unraced 2000 2-y-o Indaba (by Indian Ridge), to the useful dual 1m winner So Sedulous (by The Minstrel and herself dam of the German Group 3 winner Subiaco), the quite useful 2-y-o 6f winners Lady Diesis (by Diesis) and Hindaawee (by Zilzal) and the Irish 2-y-o 6f winner Adamant (by Lyphard). The dam, a very useful winner from 5f to 1m at 2 yrs in Ireland including the Group 3 Killavullen Stakes, subsequently won in the USA and is a sister to the listed Tyros Stakes winner Tapolite. The second dam, Pendulina (by Prince Tenderfoot), won the listed 1m Cornelscourt Stakes in Ireland and is a half-sister to the Moyglare Stud Stakes winner Gala Event. *"A sharp, strong filly and she'll make a 2-y-o by mid-season over six furlongs".*

C BRITTAIN

102 - AMPOULE ** [94]

b.c. Zamindar – Diamond Park (Alzao).
February 13. Fourth foal. 22,000Y. Tattersalls October.

Half-brother to the fair 2000 7f placed 2-y-o Park Hall (by Saddlers' Hall), to the fair 2-y-o 5f winners Key (by Midyan) and Pop Shop (by Owington). The dam, a quite useful if disappointing maiden, was placed five times at up to 10.2f and is a half-sister to 8 winners including the French listed winner Droiture and the dam of 2 stakes winners in the USA. The second dam, Diamond Spring (by Vaguely Noble), won over 1m in France and is a half-sister to the dams of the US Grade 1 winners Another Review, No Review and Urbane. *"A nice horse for July/August time. He's got a good action and will probably be suited by six furlongs to a mile, being out of an Alzao mare".*

103 - APPLE DUMPLING (IRE) * [68]

gr.f. Dr Devious – Safkana (Doyoun).
February 24. Third foal. 20,000Y. Tattersalls October.

Half-sister to the Spanish 1m and 10.5f winner Barakana (by Barathea) and to the Italian winner of 4 races at up to 9f Satrail (by Catrail). The dam, a 3-y-o 1m winner in Ireland, is a half-sister to 5 winners including the very useful listed 1m Heron Stakes winner and Group 1 7f Prix de la Salamandre third Speedfit Too. The second dam, Safka (by Irish River), a useful 2-y-o 5f winner, was third in the Group 3 5f Cornwallis Stakes and is a half-sister to 9 winners including the Group 2 1m Lockinge Stakes winner Safawan and the dam of the Group 2 12f Prix Hocquart winner Sayarshan. (Mrs R A Pledger). *"A very nice filly. She wasn't very big when I bought her but within two months you wouldn't have recognised her. A filly with a bit of speed and a good temperament, she's certainly going to win this year".*

104 - A VENDRE (FR) * [70]

b.c. Kendor – Waaria (Shareef Dancer).
April 5. Eighth foal. FF350,000. Deauville August.

Half-brother to 2 minor winners in the USA by Arctic Tern and Irish River. The dam is an unplaced sister to the high-class colt Rock Hopper, a winner of numerous Group races including the Princess of Wales's Stakes, the Hardwicke Stakes and the Jockey Club Stakes. The second dam, Cormorant Wood (by Home Guard), was a top-class winner of the Group 1 Champion Stakes and the Group 1 Benson and Hedges Gold Cup. (Mr A J Richards). *"A really nice horse, he moves well and shows nice speed. His temperament is fine and I expect him to start over six furlongs in May".*

105 - BELEZA (IRE) *** [67]

b.f. Revoque – La Alla Wa Asa (Alzao).
January 15. Third foal. 30,000Y. Tattersalls October.

Half-sister to the unraced 3-y-o Chloe's Return and to the Swedish 2-y-o winner Atout (both by Common Grounds). The dam ran unplaced twice at 3 yrs and is a sister to the very useful Aldbourne, a winner from 6f (at 2 yrs) to 8.5f and placed in the English and Irish One Thousand Guineas and to the useful 1993 2-y-o Group 3 1m Beresford Stakes winner Sheridan. The second dam, Steady The Buffs (by Balidar), was a modest 7f to 10f placed 3-y-o out of a sister to the One Thousand Guineas winner Abermaid. *"This really is a very nice filly and I intend to give her just one outing before heading for the Cherry Hinton Stakes".*

106 - ESPRIT D'ARTISTE (IRE) ** [88]

ch.c. Selkirk – Fracci (Raise A Cup).
April 21. Sixth foal. 45,000Y. Tattersalls Houghton.

Brother to the French trained 3-y-o Rocky Mountains and to the very smart Group 1 7f Prix de la Foret and Group 2 1m Prix d'Astarte winner Field Of Hope and half-brother to Stage Set (by Old Vic), a winner of 9 races from 7f to 10f in Italy. The dam, a winner of 4 races from 5f (at 2 yrs) to 7f, including a listed event in Italy, was Group 3 placed over 1m and is a half-sister to one winner. The second dam, Fancy Walk (by Tower Walk), won once at 3 yrs. (Abdullah Saeed Bel Hab). *"I bought this colt within three minutes of seeing him at the sales and I think he was well-bought. Not an early sort, particularly as Selkirks tend to be a bit on the leg. One for the back-end of the year".*
Significant sire/damsire crosses:- Field Of Hope.

107 - HAWAYIL (USA) * [80]

b.f. Halling – Avice Caro (Caro).
April 25. Fourth foal.

Half-sister to the useful French 1m winner Actoris (by Diesis) and the fairly useful 10f winner Anschluss (by Alzao). The dam, a quite useful 3-y-o dual 10f winner, is a half-sister to several winners including the smart Group 2 1m Falmouth Stakes winner Sensation and the US Grade 2 placed Outlasting. The second dam, Outstandingly (by Exclusive Native), a champion US 2-y-o filly, won the Grade 1 Breeders Cup Juvenile Fillies Stakes and the Grade 1 Hollywood Starlet Stakes. (Saeed Manana). *"She's a good mover and should make a 2-y-o. I'm pleased with my 2-y-o fillies this year and this one looks like making a 2-y-o from the mid-season onwards".*

108 - JAKARTA (IRE) * [85]

b.f. Machiavellian – Lunda (Soviet Star).
January 29. Second foal. 135,000Y. Tattersalls Houghton.

Half-sister to Dancing Tsar (by Salse), unplaced in one start at 2 yrs in 2000. The dam ran three times unplaced at 3 yrs and is a half-sister to the high-class middle-distance horse Luso, winner of the Aral-Pokal, the Italian Derby and the Hong Kong International Vase etc., the smart Group 3 7f Nell Gwyn Stakes winner and Prix Vermeille second Cloud Castle and the smart Group 3 12f Meld Stakes winner Needle Gun. The second dam, Lucayan Princess (by High Line), a very useful winner of the listed 6f Sweet Solera Stakes at 2 yrs, was third in the 12.3f Cheshire Oaks and is a half-sister to 7 winners. (Saeed Manana). *"Not over-big for an early foal, this filly looks to me like she'll be racing in May over six furlongs and she has a lot of buzz about her".*

109 - MAJBORAH (IRE) ** [64] b.f. Entrepreneur – Safka (Irish River).

March 14. Tenth foal. 20,000Y. Tattersalls October.

Half-sister to the unraced 2000 2-y-o Paradise Blue (by Bluebird), to the very useful listed 1m Heron Stakes winner and Group 1 7f Prix de la Salamandre third Speedfit Too (by Scenic), the 1999 Italian 2-y-o winner Lecamar (by Grand Lodge), the Irish 3-y-o 1m winner Safkana (by Doyoun), the Irish 2-y-o 7f winner Sannkaya (by Soviet Star), a winner in Scandinavia by Night Shift and a winner over the jumps by Darshaan. The dam, a useful 2-y-o 5f winner, was third in the Group 3 5f Cornwallis Stakes and is a half-sister to 9 winners including the Group 2 1m Lockinge Stakes winner Safawan and the dam of the Group 2 12f Prix Hocquart winner Sayarshan. The second dam, Safita (by Habitat), won the listed 1m Prix de la Calonne and was second in the French One Thousand Guineas. (Saeed Manana). *"Quite cheap considering her pedigree, she was a bit small at first but has done tremendously well. The type to start over seven furlongs around July time".*

110 - MAMEYUKI * [74] ch.f. Zafonic – Musetta (Cadeaux Genereux).

March 6. Second foal.

Half-sister to the fairly useful 2000 7f placed 2-y-o Mameha (by Rainbow Quest). The dam, a useful winner of the listed 10f Pretty Polly Stakes winner and fourth in the Oaks, is a half-sister to several winners including the fairly useful 6f winner Fiametta. The second dam, Monaiya (by Shareef Dancer), a French 7.5f and 1m winner, is a sister to a listed-placed winner in France out of the Group 3 5f Premio Omenoni winner Massorah (by Habitat). (Mr B H Voak). *"A very nice filly and she's every bit as nice as Mameha. Her temperament is very good and she'll make a 2-y-o by June or July. A filly with a bit of quality about her".*

111 - MOLAAF * [81] b.f. Shareef Dancer – Amber Fizz (Effervescing).

May 5.

Half-sister to several winners including the Group 3 Diadem Stakes winner Cool Jazz (by Lead On Time). The dam ran once unplaced and is a half-sister to 9 winners including the US stakes winner and Grade 1 placed Groton High. (Saeed Manana). *"Despite her pedigree she should be a factor as a 2-y-o over six furlongs or more. She shows an amazing amount of speed at the moment".*

112 - RUWAYA (USA) * [75] b.br.f. Red Ransom – Upper Class Lady (Upper Nile).

March 17. Sixth foal. $50,000Y. Keeneland September.

Half-sister to the moderate 2000 9.4f placed 2-y-o Ann Summers (by Dehere) and to the middle-distance placed Silver Wonder (by Silver Hawk). The dam is an unplaced half-sister to 7 winners including the Group 1 Prix de Diane winner Lady In Silver. The second dam, Lorn Lady (by Lorenzaccio), won at 3 yrs in Ireland and is a half-sister to 5 winners including the sire Double-U-Jay and the Prix de Royallieu winner Riverside (dam of the French One Thousand Guineas winner Riverqueen). (Saeed Manana). *"This is a very nice filly and she'll be worth waiting for. A well-grown 2-y-o that goes really well".*

113 - SHINY ** [76] b.f. Shambo – Abuzz (Absalom).

April 20. Eighth foal.

Brother to the quite useful 2000 2-y-o 5f and 6f winner Shush and half-brother to the listed Chesham Stakes and Brocklesby Stakes winner World Premier (by Shareef Dancer), the quite useful winner of 6 races at up to 10f Puzzlement, the modest 2-y-o 7f winner Mysticism (both by Mystiko) and the modest 7f winner Agoer (by Hadeer). The dam, a winner of 5 races including the Group 3 7.3f Hungerford Stakes, is a half-sister to the dams of the high-class 2-y-o Revoque and the Group 3 sprint winner Point Of Light. The second dam, Sorebelle (by Prince Tenderfoot), was a useful winner of three races at up to 1m and was placed in the listed Bunbury Cup. *"The best-looking filly in the yard. She'll be a 2-y-o from five to seven furlongs and is just like her dam". (Mrs C Brittain).*

114 - UNNAMED * [74] b.c. Pine Bluff – Cuando Quiere (Affirmed).

March 19. Sixth foal. $180,000Y. Keeneland September.

Half-brother to the US Grade 3 winner Cuando Puede, to the US stakes winner and Grade 2 placed Cuando (both by Lord At War) and the US winner and Grade 3 placed Cuanto Es (by Exbourne). The dam is a placed half-sister to 3 minor winners. The second dam, Quatre Saisons (by Court Recess), is a stakes winning half-sister to the US Grade 2 Kentucky Oaks winner Sun And Snow. (Saeed Manana).

"This colt was well worth the money he cost. He certainly looks a 2-y-o type and looks like he'll show speed when we ask him".

---

115 - UNNAMED ** [80]   b.f. Green Desert – Pripet (Alleged).
April 2.

Sister to the useful 1997 2-y-o Group 1 5.5f Prix Robert Papin winner Greenlander (by Green Desert) and half-sister to the modest 13.8f winner Priluki (by Lycius). The dam, a quite useful 3-y-o 2m winner, is a sister to the One Thousand Guineas and Oaks winner Midway Lady and to the very useful 11.8f listed winner Capias (both by Alleged). The second dam, Smooth Bore (by His Majesty), won 2 stakes events at around 1m at 4 yrs. (Sheikh Marwan Al-Maktoum). *"A bit on the small side but she moves well. One to look out for towards the back-end".*
Significant sire/damsire crosses:- Greenlander, Umniyatee.

---

116 - UNNAMED [69]   ch.f. Mark Of Esteem – Warning Shadows (Cadeaux Genereux).
April 2. Third foal.

Half-sister to the fairly useful 2000 6f to 1m placed 2-y-o Shadowless (by Alzao) and to the fair 1m all-weather winner Shady Point (by Unfuwain). The dam, a very useful filly and winner of the Group 2 10f Sun Chariot Stakes, was second in the Irish One Thousand Guineas. The second dam, Silent Movie (by Shirley Heights), was a poor half-sister to the very smart 7f to 10f performer Noalto. (Sheikh Marwan Al-Maktoum). *"Another very nice filly. Well-made, she has a fairly strong temperament and looks a quality filly".*

G BUTLER

---

117 - COMPTON DRAGON (USA) [94]   ch.c. Woodman – Vilikaia (Nureyev).
February 2. Twelfth foal. IR£75,000Y. Goffs Orby.

Brother to the unraced 2000 2-y-o Verasina, closely related to the fairly useful 1995 2-y-o 7f winner and Group 3 Prix de Saint-Georges third Vilayet (by Machiavellian) and half-brother to the 1989 2-y-o 5f winner and useful 3-y-o 7f and 1m winner Villeroi (by Kris) and the US stakes winner Legend of Russia (by Suave Dancer). The dam won 3 races at 7f and 1m including the listed Prix Imprudence, was second in the Irish One Thousand Guineas and the Prix de l'Abbaye and fourth in the English One Thousand Guineas. She is a sister to the listed Prix des Lilas winner Navratilovna and a half-sister to the good filly Maximova - herself dam of the Group 1 winners Septieme Ciel and Macoumba. The second dam, Baracala (by Swaps), is a winning half-sister to the top-class Two Thousand Guineas winner Nonoalco and the smart Whitehall Stakes winner Stradavinsky.
Significant sire/damsire crosses:- Gay Gallanta (Gr 1).

---

118 - KLOONLARA (IRE) * [106]   b.f. Green Desert – Diamond Quest (Rainbow Quest).
May 7. First foal. 90,000Y. Tattersalls Houghton.

The dam is an unraced half-sister to 5 winners including Kundalini, a champion 3-y-o filly in South Africa, the minor US stakes winner Pixie Spirit and the useful 7f (at 2 yrs) and 10.4f winner Ludgate. The second dam, Hatton Gardens (by Auction Ring), a fairly useful Irish 6f to 1m winner, won the listed Carna Fillies Stakes and was third in the Group 2 6f Premio Umbria. She is a half-sister to 5 winners including the Coronation Stakes, Eclipse Stakes and Irish One Thousand Guineas winner Kooyonga.

---

119 - ROS THE BOSS (IRE) * [104]   b.f. Danehill – Bella Vitessa (Thatching).
April 9. Third foal. FF750,000Y. Deauville August.

Half-sister to the quite useful 2-y-o 6f winner Bella Bellisimo (by Alzao). The dam is an unplaced half-sister to 6 winners including the German Group 1 12f Aral-Pokal and listed Pretty Polly Stakes winner Wind In Her Hair and the Grade 3 Vineland Handicap and Pretty Polly Stakes winner Capo di Monte. The second dam, Burghclere (by Busted), a quite useful 14f winner, is closely related to the Princess Of Wales's Stakes winner Height Of Fashion (the dam of Nashwan and Unfuwain).
Significant sire/damsire crosses:- Great Dane, Restructure.

---

120 - SHOLAY (IRE) [81]   b.c. Bluebird – Splicing (Sharpo).
March 10. Second foal. 60,000Y. Tattersalls October.

Half-brother to the quite useful 2000 2-y-o 6f winner Pairing (by Rudimentary). The dam, a quite useful 5f and 6f winner, is a sister to the useful listed 6f Abernant Stakes winner Splice and a half-sister to the fairly useful 1m winner and subsequent Italian winner Alfujairah. The second dam, Soluce (by Junius), won the Group 3 Irish One Thousand Guineas Trial and is a half-sister to 3 winners.

N CALLAGHAN

121 - BRUBEL (IRE) ** [84]
ch.c. Entrepreneur – Renzola (Dragonara Palace).
March 19. Tenth foal. 180,000Y. Tattersalls October.

Half-brother to the twice unplaced 2000 2-y-o Dr Strangelove (by Dr Devious), to the smart Group 2 Criterium des Deux Ans winner Deadly Dudley (by Great Commotion), the useful listed Harry Rosebery Challenge Trophy winner Miss Nosey Parker, the fair 2-y-o 5f winner Sober Lad, the fair 6f winner Rapier Point (all by Cyrano de Bergerac) and the modest 6f winner Petit Palais (by Paris House). The dam is an unraced half-sister to the dam of the Grand Prix de Paris, Prix Jean Prat and Man O'War Stakes winner Millkom. The second dam, Bright Brook (by Deep Diver), is an unplaced half-sister to 4 winners including the dams of the Group winners Hanu, End Of The Line and Reo Racine and the Irish Two Thousand Guineas third Parliament. (Mr M Tabor). *"A lovely horse by Entrepreneur. He'll be a six or seven furlong type 2-y-o and everything about him is good".*

122 - COP MY GATOR (IRE) ** [70]
b.c. Danehill Dancer – Delta Blues (Digamist).
April 9. Fourth foal. 28,000Y. Tattersalls October.

Half-brother to the Italian winner of 7 races (including at 2 yrs) and listed-placed Wild Bunch (by Distinctly North) and to a minor winner at 2 and 3 yrs in Italy by College Chapel. The dam ran once unplaced and is a half-sister to 5 winners, two of them listed-placed. The second dam, Spring Spray (by Silly Season), is an unraced half-sister to 6 winners including the Group 3 Prix de Meautry winner King Of Macedon. (Havana Horse UK Ltd). *"A nice horse in every way, he's similar to his sire, goes really well and he'll make a 2-y-o alright".*

123 - ESENIN ** [79]
b.c. Danehill – Boojum (Mujtahid).
February 25. First foal. 200,000Y. Tattersalls October.

The dam, a useful 2-y-o winner of the listed 7.3f Radley Stakes, is a half-sister to the useful 7f and 8.2f winner and listed-placed Abeyr. The second dam, Haboobti (by Habitat), is an unplaced half-sister to 6 winners including the US stakes winner and Grade 3 placed Aerturas and to the unplaced dam of the US Grade 2 winner Distinct Habit. (Mr M Tabor). *"A nice horse, he's very sharp and he'll make a sprint-type 2-y-o before mid-season. I'd say he was my best bet for a Group class 2-y-o".*

124 - GAVRILOV ** [69]
b.c. Danehill Dancer – Elminya (Sure Blade).
April 9. Sixth foal. IR£85,000Y. Goffs Orby.

Half-brother to the 3-y-o Diamond Joshua (by Mujadil), to the quite useful 1997 2-y-o 6f and 7f winner Belle de Nuit (by Statoblest), the fair 7f (at 2 yrs), 10f and 12f winner Soden (by Mujadil) and a winner over hurdles by Don't Forget Me. The dam is an unraced half-sister to 5 winners including the Ruby Tiger, a winner of 9 Group races including the Group 2 Nassau Stakes (twice), the Group 2 Pretty Polly Stakes and the E P Taylor Stakes. The second dam, Hayati (by Hotfoot), was a fairly useful 7f and 10f winner. (Mr M Tabor). *"As nice a horse as you could get. Big and strong - he's very much like his father and will be a mid-season 2-y-o".*

125 - SHOVE HA'PENNY (IRE) * [73]
b.c. Night Shift – Penny Fan (Nomination).
April 24. Fifth foal. 60,000Y. Tattersalls October.

Half-brother to City Of London (by Grand Lodge), unplaced in one start at 2 yrs in 2000 and to the fairly useful 1997 2-y-o listed 7.3f and 3-y-o 1m winner Ffestiniog (by Efisio). The dam was placed once over 5f at 3 yrs, is closely related to the listed 5f Scarborough Stakes winner and Group 2 5f Temple Stakes third Rivers Rhapsody and a half-sister to the Group 3 5f Prix d'Arenberg winner Regal Scintilla. The second dam, Trwyn Cilan (by Import), was a sprint winner of 3 races. *"A small, sharp 2-y-o, he'll have been out before the book is published and he'll win a maiden".*

H CANDY

126 - FOLLOW FLANDERS * [86]
b.f. Pursuit Of Love – Pretty Poppy (Song).
March 21. Seventh foal. 42,000Y. Doncaster St Leger.

Half-sister to the fairly useful 2000 2-y-o 5f winner Kyllachy (by Pivotal), to the very useful dual 3-y-o 5f winner Borders (by Selkirk), the useful 5f winner of 4 races Speed On, the quite useful 2-y-o 5f winner

Loving And Giving (both by Sharpo) and the fair dual 5f winner (including at 2 yrs) Poppy's Song (by Owington). The dam, a modest 2-y-o 5f winner, stayed 7.6f and is a half-sister to 4 winners. The second dam, Moonlight Serenade (by Crooner), is a placed sister to the winner and Group 3 5f Duke Of York Stakes third Blackbird. *"She's done nothing but cough since I got her back from the sales, but when we can get her healthy she'll be a five furlong specialist. She looks very sharp and is the sort of horse that will come to hand quickly once she's OK. Very much a sprinter to look at her".*

---

127 - GENGHIS (IRE) ** [73]   br.c. Persian Bold – Cindy's Baby (Bairn).
March 19. Fourth foal. 35,000Y. Doncaster St Leger.
Brother to the fair 7f to 10f winner Karakul and half-brother to a winner in Italy by Paris House. The dam, a poor placed 3-y-o, is a sister to the 5f Windsor Castle Stakes winner and Group 1 Phoenix Stakes third Gipsy Fiddler and a half-sister to 7 winners including the listed Doncaster Stakes winner Two Clubs. The second dam, Miss Cindy (by Mansingh), a fairly useful 5f to 7f winner, is a sister to the Vernons Sprint Cup winner and useful sire Petong. *"Probably the pick of my 2-y-o's I would think. He looks a nice horse and although he's big, he's very much up-together and an early-maturing sort, so I don't think his size will bother him. He's a mid-season type of 2-y-o and finds everything easy. An almost black horse, he's very typical of his sire (he has that roman nose that so many of the Persian Bold's have) and he has a nice temperament".*

---

128 - RINGING HILL * [70]   b.f. Charnwood Forest – Not Before Time (Polish Precedent).
March 3. Fifth foal. 55,000Y. Tattersalls October.
Half-sister to the very promising 2000 2-y-o 1m winner Time Away (by Darshaan), to the fairly useful 10f and 12.4f winner Original Spin (by Machiavellian) and the quite useful 10.2f winner Time Loss (by Kenmare). The dam is an unraced half-sister to the very useful Group 3 12f Jockey Club Stakes winner Zinaad and to the very useful Group 3 12f Princess Royal Stakes winner Time Allowed (by Sadlers Wells). The second dam, Time Charter (by Saritamer), was an exceptionally talented filly and winner of the Oaks, the King George VI and Queen Elizabeth Diamond Stakes, the Champion Stakes, the Coronation Cup, the Prix Foy and the Sun Chariot Stakes. *"Seven furlongs should suit her to start with. She's a big, well-grown, strong, easy-moving sort. There's no reason why she shouldn't make a 2-y-o and she has a great look of her grandmother Time Charter about her head".*

---

129 - ZARZU * [86]   b.c. Magic Ring – Rivers Rhapsody (Dominion).
April 12. Fifth foal. 27,000Y. Tattersalls Autumn.
Half-brother to the fair 2000 5f and 6f placed 2-y-o Upstream (by Prince Sabo), to the smart miler and listed-placed See You Later (by Emarati) and the fairly useful dual 5f winner (including at 2 yrs) For Your Eyes Only (by Pursuit Of Love). The dam, a useful winner of the listed 5f Scarborough Stakes and third in the Group 2 5f Temple Stakes, is a half-sister to the Group 3 5f Prix d'Arenberg winner Regal Scintilla. The second dam, Trwyn Cilan (by Import), was a sprint winner of 3 races. *"He's just about as broad as he's long, has slightly immature knees at the moment but will be at work by mid-May. I should think he'd train himself and he looks a pure five furlong horse. Apparently, if you go to see the film "The Lion King" you'll find a character in there called Zarzu!".*

---

130 - UNNAMED ** [81]   b.c. Robellino – Legend Of Aragon (Aragon).
March 223. First foal. 25,000Y. Tattersalls December.
The dam, a modest 2-y-o 5f winner, is a half-sister to 2 minor winners. The second dam, Legendary Dancer (by Shareef Dancer), was a fairly useful 12f winner and a half-sister to 7 winners including the dam of the smart middle-distance horse Midnight Legend. *"Very much on a par with another of my 2-y-o's, Ghengis. He's doing quite a bit and finds it all quite easy. A well-balanced horse and a good mover, he seems to enjoy life. I'd expect him to be a June type 2-y-o over six furlongs".*

H CECIL

On my two previous visits to Warren Place, Henry's assessment of the vast majority of his two-year-olds as being "backward 3-y-o types" proved to be spot on. This year however, things seem to be different. In our chat about his horses his optimism for the coming season was obvious and Henry expects more from his young horses than he has done for some time. I had planned on adding a few more 2-y-o's than the ones below, but as they weren't recommended by Henry I've left them out – with the exception of one. I couldn't bring myself to omit the 2-y-o out of Miesque. Henry's optimism for his 2-y-o's is carried over to his older horses. He really does feel that Warren Place has every chance of having a vintage year.

---

131 - ALLOVER (USA) *   [76]   b.c. Spinning World – Gossamer (Seattle Slew).
March 29. Third living foal. IR£540,000Y. Goffs Orby.
Half-brother to the Irish trained 3-y-o Translucid (by Woodman). The dam, a winner of 2 races in the USA, is a half-sister to 4 winners including the German Group 3 winner and Group 2 Prix Saint-Roman second Miss Tobacco and to the unraced dam of the listed winners White Gulch and Bodyguard. The second dam, Lisaleen (by Northern Dancer), won twice at 3 yrs, was third in the Group 3 1m Gilltown Stud Stakes and is a full or half-sister to 5 winners including the Group 1 National Stakes winner Fatherland, the Irish listed winners Yeats and Golden Dome and the dam of the US Grade 2 winner Sword Dance. (Thoroughbred Corporation). *"This is an attractive colt and an active one too. I'm hopeful for him".*

---

132 - BAGAN (FR)   [92]   b.c. Rainbow Quest – Maid Of Erin (Irish River).
February 25. Eleventh foal.
Half-sister to the Group 2 1m Premio Regina Elena winner Erin Bird, to a minor winner in France (both by Bluebird), the fair middle-distance staying winner Mizyan (by Nelyno) and minor winners abroad by Tate Gallery and Primo Dominie. The dam was unplaced in France and is a half-sister to the Group 3 12f Princess Royal Stakes winner Dancing Bloom, to the useful 10f winner Cloudy Sky and the good French 2-y-o 5f winner and One Thousand Guineas third River Dancer (herself dam of the Champion Stakes winner Spectrum). The second dam, Dancing Shadow (by Dancer's Image), a very useful filly, won over 1m and 10f including the Sean Graham Fillies Stakes and is a half-sister to the top-class Oaks winner Sun Princess and the high-class middle-distance colt Saddlers' Hall. (Niarchos Family). *"A big colt, he's backward at the moment and will need time but he's a nice mover".*

---

133 - BAHRQUEEN (USA) *   [76]   b.f. Bahri – April In Kentucky (Palace Music).
March 18. Third foal. IR£23,000Y. Goffs Orby.
Half-sister to a minor 2-y-o winner in the USA by Mr Greeley and to the 2000 2-y-o Frazzled (by Prized). The dam is an unplaced half-sister to 7 winners including the Grade 1 10f Santa Barbara Handicap and Grade 1 Santa Ana Handicap winner Reloy and the Group 2 Prix du Conseil de Paris winner En Calcat. The second dam, Rescousse (by Emerson),won the Group 1 10.5f Prix de Diane and was second in the Prix de l'Arc de Triomphe. (Raymond Tooth). *"A nice filly – she has a good 'low to the ground' action and I like her".*

---

134 - BOJANGLES (IRE) **   [83]   b.c. Danehill – Itching (Thatching).
April 16. Fifth reported foal.
Brother to the very smart Group 2 9f Budweiser International Stakes winner Great Dane and half-brother to the unraced 2000 2-y-o Itchington (by Royal Academy) and the fairly useful 2-y-o 6f winner Witching Hour (by Alzao). The dam is an unraced half-sister to Croco Rouge and to the outstanding broodmare Alidiva (dam of Sleepytime, Ali Royal and Taipan). The second dam, Alligatrix (by Alleged), was a very useful 2-y-o 7f winner, was third in the Group 1 Fillies Mile and is a half-sister to 6 winners. (Greenbay Stables Ltd). *"A tall colt, he needs time but is likeable".*
Significant sire/damsire crosses:- Great Dane, Restructure.

---

135 - BURNING SUN (USA) ***   [105]   b.c. Danzig – Media Nox (Lycius).
January 21. First foal.
The dam, a useful 2-y-o winner of the Group 3 5f Prix du Bois, is a half-sister to the very useful Bonash, a winner of 4 races in France from 1m to 12f including the Prix d'Aumale, the Prix Vanteaux and the Prix de Malleret. The second dam, Sky Love (by Nijinsky), a fairly useful 10f winner, is a half-sister to

the high-class Prix de la Cote Normande winner Raft. (Khalid Abdulla). *"A very likeable, strong colt and a good mover. He'll be a nice colt later on this season".*

136 - CONTINUOUSLY (USA) * [88]

b.c. Diesis – Play On And On (Stop The Music).
January 25.

Half-brother to the fairly useful dual 7f winner Neverending (by Sabona), the fairly useful 7f and 1m winner Joyeux Player (by St Jovite) and a minor winner in the USA by Trempolino. The dam won once at 5 yrs in the USA and is out of the unraced Heavenly Blue (by Raise A Native), herself a daughter of the champion US 3-y-o filly Our Mims. (Mr S Khaled). *"A very nice colt and a good mover, he could make a nice 2-y-o later on in the year".*

137 - FAMILY (USA) ** [93]

b.f. Danzig – Razyana (His Majesty).
May 9.

Sister to the extremely promising 2000 2-y-o 1m winner Quick To Please, to the top-class sprinter and sire Danehill, the US Grade 2 9f winner Eagle Eyed, the smart 2000 3-y-o 7f winner and St James's Palace Stakes fourth Shibboleth, the fairly useful 1999 3-y-o 1m winner Nuclear Freeze and the French 2-y-o 5f winner Anziyan and closely related to the smart French and US performer Euphonic (by The Minstrel). The dam, placed over 7f at 2 yrs and 10f at 3 yrs, is out of Spring Adieu (by Buckpasser), a winner of three small sprint races at 3 yrs and a half-sister to Northern Dancer. (Khalid Abdulla). *"A nice filly from a female line I know well, she needs time".*
Significant sire/damsire crosses:- Danehill, Tribulation (Gr 1).

138 - FIVE STARS ** [76]

ch.f. Bahamian Bounty – Star Ridge (Storm Bird).
February 12.

Half-sister to numerous winners including the very promising 2000 2-y-o 7f winner Jungle Lion (by Lion Cavern), the smart 7f and 1m winner On The Ridge (by Risk Me), the quite useful 2-y-o 5f winner Astrakan and the 1m and 10f winner Barrier Ridge (both by Lycius). The dam ran twice in France. (Buckram Oak Holdings). *"A well-grown type, Five Stars is a nice-moving filly".*

139 - GRANADILLA ** [81]

b.f. Zafonic – Epagris (Zalazl).
April 27. Third foal.

Half-sister to the unraced 2000 2-y-o Askri (by Lion Cavern) and to the fairly useful 10f winner Krantor (by Arazi). The dam, a useful 6f (at 2 yrs) and 7f listed winner, is a half-sister to several winners including the useful 10f winner Ismaros. The second dam, Trikymia (by Final Straw), was placed third over 5f at 2 yrs on her only outing and is a half-sister to the Irish Derby winner Tyrnavos, the champion 2-y-o Tromos, the Coronation Stakes winner Tolmi and the Middle Park Stakes winner Tachypous. (Mr L Marinopoulos). *"A medium-sized, good-moving filly, she'll hopefully be a nice 2-yo".*

140 - HANDA ISLAND (USA) * [75]

b.br.c. Pleasant Colony – Remote (Seattle Slew).
March 26. Second foal. $210,000Y. Keeneland September.

The dam was unplaced in two starts and is a half-sister to 7 winners including the Group 2 5f Kings Stand Stakes second Irish Shoal, the Group 3 10f Brigadier Gerard Stakes winner Hibernian Gold and the dam of the Group 1 Moyglare Stud Stakes winner Belle Genius. The second dam, Irish Wave (by Raise A Native), won 2 minor races in the USA and is a half-sister to 8 winners. (Khalid Abdulla). *"A big colt, he's improving all the time and is a nice mover that grows on me".*

141 - I WALKED BY NIGHT ** [75]

ch.c. Primo Dominie – Malwiya (Shahrastani).
March 20. Fifth foal. 28,000Y. Tattersalls October.

Half-brother to the 3-y-o Princess Anoushka (by Prince Sabo), to the German and Dutch 7f to 10f winner Maltayar (by Be My Chief) and a winner in Spain from 5f to 1m by Polish Patriot. The dam is an unraced daughter of the Group 3 10.5f Prix de Flore winner Masmouda (by Dalsaan), herself a half-sister to 8 winners including the Group 2 Prix Dollar winner Mourtazam. (Mr Colin Davey). *"This is a well-made colt and he's going to make a 2-y-o alright".*

142 - JAVA * [79]

b.f. Rainbow Quest – Island Jamboree (Explodent).
February 16. Fifth living foal.

Sister to the unraced 2000 2-y-o Barbuda and to the Grade 1 Yellow Ribbon Stakes and Grade 1 Gamely Breeders Cup Handicap winner Fiji and half-sister to the Group 2 Grand Prix de Deauville and Group 2 Cumberland Lodge Stakes winner Capri. The dam won 10 races in the USA at up to 8.5f including the listed Run For The Roses Stakes and was second in the Grade 1 Gamely Handicap. She is a half-sister to 4 winners. The second dam, Careless Virgin (by Wing Out), is a placed half-sister to the US Grade 1 winners Fabulous Notion (herself dam of the US Grade 1 winner Fabulously Fast) and Cacoethes placed in the King George and the Derby). (Prince Fahd Salman). *"A sister to Fiji, she's a tall, attractive filly and a good mover".*

---

143 - KITALPHA (USA) *** [116]
ch.c. Mr Prospector – Miesque (Nureyev).
March 31.

Brother to the top class miler Kingmambo, winner of the French Two Thousand Guineas, the St James's Palace Stakes and the Prix du Moulin and to the smart Group 3 6f Prix de Ris-Orangis winner Miesque's Son, closely related to the listed winner Moon Is Up (by Woodman) and half-brother to the high-class French One Thousand Guineas, Prix de Diane and Prix Jacques le Marois winner East of the Moon (by Private Account). The dam, a great filly and possibly the best miler of the eighties, won ten Group or Grade 1 events including the Breeders Cup Mile (twice), the Prix Jacques le Marois (twice), the One Thousand Guineas, the French One Thousand Guineas and the Prix du Moulin. The second dam, Pasadoble (by Prove Out), won 4 races in France over 1m including two stakes events, is a sister to the US Grade 1 Brooklyn Handicap winner Silver Supreme and is out of an unraced half-sister to the top class filly Comtesse de Loir.
Significant sire/damsire crosses:- Kingmambo (Gr 1), Dance Sequence, Shake Hand, Souvenir Copy (all Gr 2), Miesque's Son (Gr 3).

---

144 - LIFELONG (USA) ** [87]
b.f. Mr Prospector – Jolypha (Lyphard).
February 20. Fifth foal.

Half-sister to the very useful 1m and 10f winner Eaton Square (by Nureyev). The dam was a top-class winner of the Group 1 10.5f Prix de Diane and the Group 1 12f Prix Vermeille and was placed in the Grade 1 Breeders Cup Classic and the Grade 1 Beverly Hills Handicap. She is a sister to the great Dancing Brave, winner of the Prix de l'Arc de Triomphe, the King George VI and Queen Elizabeth Diamond Stakes and the Two Thousand Guineas etc., The second dam, Navajo Princess (by Drone), a good winner of 16 races at up to 1m including the Grade 2 Molly Pitcher Handicap and the Grade 3 Falls City Handicap, is a sister to the stakes winner Passamaquoddy (herself dam of 5 winners) and a half-sister to the Grade 3 winner Soldier Boy. (Khalid Abdulla). *"A nice filly although she does need some time to come to herself".*
Significant sire/damsire crosses:- Lycius, Tereshkova.

---

145 - NIGHT SKY ** [81]
ch.f. Zafonic – Felucca (Green Desert).
March 5. Third living foal.

The dam, a fairly useful 2-y-o 6f winner, was placed over 7f at 3 yrs and is a half-sister to the Group 2 10f Prix Eugene Adam winner Radevore. The second dam, Bloudan (by Damascus), is an unraced half-sister to the high-class Irish One Thousand Guineas and Coronation Stakes winner Al Bahathri, the US Grade 2 winner Geraldine's Store and the Cheshire Oaks winner Peplum. (Khalid Abdulla). *"A well-made filly and a nice size, she has the makings of a nice 2-y-o prospect when we get to six furlongs and over".*

---

146 - OVAL OFFICE ** [87]
ch.f. Pursuit Of Love – Pushy (Sharpen Up).
February 22.

Half-sister to the unraced 2000 2-y-o First (by Highest Honor), to the smart 6f (at 2 yrs) and Group 3 7f Nell Gwyn Stakes winner Myself, the quite useful 10f winner Nanda (both by Nashwan), the smart Group 3 6f Princess Margaret Stakes and Group 3 6f Prix de Seine et Oise winner Bluebook (by Secretariat), the useful 1m winner Phountzi (by Raise a Cup), the 2-y-o 6f winner Eye Drop (by Irish River), the 3-y-o 5f winner Pushoff (by Sauce Boat) and herself dam of the Nell Gwyn Stakes winner Thrilling Day) - both quite useful, the fair 12f all-weather winner Power (by Bustino) and a winner in Macau by Shadeed. The dam was a very useful 2-y-o winner of 4 races including the Group 2 Queen Mary Stakes and is a half-sister to the high-class 2-y-o Precocious, the Group 1 Japan Cup winner Jupiter Island, the good 2-y-o Krayyan and 6 other winners including the 2-y-o 5f winner Putupon (dam of the smart French sprinter Pole Position). The second dam, Mrs Moss (by Reform), won over 5f at 2 yrs (her only season to race). (Bloomsbury Stud). *"An attractive filly, she may need a little more time than her dam who won me my first Queen Mary Stakes".*

147 - REVEALING * [84]   ch.f. Halling – Rive (Riverman).

February 20. Fourth foal.

Half-sister to the 1998 French 2-y-o 1m winner Promote (by Linamix). The dam, a French 2-y-o 10f winner and fourth in the Group 3 12f Prix Minerve, is a half-sister to 5 winners including the US stakes winner Have Fun and the dam of the Royal Lodge Stakes winner Mons. The second dam, Arewehavingfunyet (by Sham), won the Grade 1 8.5f Oak Leaf Stakes and the Grade 2 7f Del Mar Debutante Stakes and is a half-sister to 6 winners. (Khalid Abdulla). *"This is a good-moving, tall filly that's grown a great deal lately".*

148 - SECRET DREAM (IRE) [75]   b.f. Zafonic – Sleepytime (Royal Academy).

April 22. First foal.

The dam, a very smart filly and winner of the One Thousand Guineas, is a sister to the high-class Group 1 1m Sussex Stakes winner Ali Royal and a half-sister to the high-class Group 1 12f Europa Preis and Group 1 10f Premio Roma winner Taipan. The second dam, Alidiva (by Chief Singer), was a useful winner of 3 races from 6f to 1m, including a listed event. *"She was in her paddock in Ireland when she got frightened by a pheasant and got loose, pulled up very sharp and cracked a bone. I think she's going to be alright but she's not here yet".*

149 - SENTIMENTAL VALUE (USA) * [89]   ch.f. Diesis – Stately Star (Deputy Minister).

April 10. Second foal.

The dam won 6 races from 21 starts in the USA including minor stakes events at 4 and 5 yrs and is a half-sister to the Grade 1 Oak Leaf Stakes third Stylish Talent. The second dam, Stylish Star (by Our Native), won 6 races including the Grade 3 Del Mar Oaks and the Grade 3 Dahlia Handicap and was Grade 1 placed. (Thoroughbred Corporation). *"A nice filly this, she's well-grown and moves nicely".*

150 - SHARPCUT (IRE) ** [95]   b.c. Alhaarth – Safiya (Riverman).

March 9. Seventh foal. IR£325,000Y. Goffs Orby.

Half-brother to the Group 2 5f Flying Childers Stakes winner and French Two Thousand Guineas fourth Cayman Kai, the useful 1997 2-y-o 6f winner Tajasur (both by Imperial Frontier) and a winner in Hong Kong by Marju. The dam is an unraced sister to the German Group 2 winner and Group 1 Premio Parioli third Sulaafah. The second dam, Celerity (by Dancer's Image), won twice in the USA. (Khalid Abdulla). *"A very likeable, attractive colt and a good mover".*

151 - SPARKLING WATER (USA) ** [90]   b.c. Woodman – Shirley Valentine (Shirley Heights).

April 9. Sixth foal.

Half-brother to the extremely promising 2000 2-y-o 7f winner Fully Invested (by Irish River), to the very useful 10f winner Valentine Band (by Dixieland Band) and the very useful 10f and Irish Group 3 14f winner Memorise (by Lyphard). The dam, a useful 11.8f winner, was fourth in the Park Hill Stakes and the Lancashire Oaks. She is a sister to the high class Irish Derby second Deploy and half-sister to several winners including the Derby and Irish Derby winner Commander in Chief, the champion 2-y-o and miler Warning and the Grade 1 10f Flower Bowl Invitational Handicap winner Yashmak. The second dam, Slightly Dangerous (by Roberto), a very smart filly and winner of the 7.3f Fred Darling Stakes, was second in the Oaks to Time Charter and is a half-sister to the dams of the Arc winner and top class sire Rainbow Quest and the Dewhurst Stakes dead-heater Scenic. (Khalid Abdulla). *"A very nice, strong colt and a good mover that should make a 2-y-o before training on next year".*

152 - STANCE [71]   b.c. Salse – De Stael (Nijinsky).

March 17.

Half-brother to the unraced 2000 2-y-o Anticipate, to the smart 12f listed Newmarket winner and subsequent Grade 1 Santa Ana Handicap and Grade 1 10f Santa Barbara Handicap winner Wandesta (both by Nashwan), the Group 2 12f Prix du Conseil de Paris winner De Quest, the useful 10.3f to 14f winner Source of Light (both by Rainbow Quest), the smart French 10f to 15f winner Turners Hill (by Top Ville) and the fairly useful 12f winner Fine Detail (by Shirley Heights). The dam, a fairly useful dual 7f winner at 2 yrs, is a sister to the high-class middle-distance colts Peacetime and Quiet Fling and a half-sister to the Cambridgeshire winner Intermission - herself dam of the good sprinter Interval. The second dam, Peace (by Klairon), won the 6f Blue Seal Stakes at 2 yrs and was second in the One Thousand Guineas Trial. (Khalid Abdulla). *"A nice mover and a good-looking colt".*

153 - STING LIKE A BEE (IRE) * [67]   b.c. Ali-Royal – Hidden Agenda (Machiavellian). February 9. First foal.

The dam, a modest maiden who stayed 11f, is a half-sister to 5 winners including the fairly useful 5f and 7f winner Present Laughter. The second dam, Ever Genial (by Brigadier Gerard), was a smart filly and a winner of 4 races at up to 1m including the Group 3 Hungerford Stakes and the Group 3 May Hill Stakes. (Greenbay Stables Ltd). *"A medium-sized colt, he's a nice mover and very likeable"*.

154 - STORMY CHANNEL (USA) *** [92]   ch.f. Storm Cat – All At Sea (Riverman). March 27. Fifth living foal.

Half-sister to the very promising 2000 1m placed 2-y-o Painted Room (by Woodman), to the useful listed 1m winner Insinuate (both by Mr Prospector) and the useful 6f and 7f winner and listed-placed Imroz (by Nureyev). The dam was a high-class winner of 5 races from 1m to 10.4f including the Group 1 Prix du Moulin, the Musidora Stakes and the Pretty Polly Stakes and was second in the Oaks, the Juddmonte International and the Nassau Stakes. She is a half-sister to the Free Handicap winner Over the Ocean, the listed 10f winner Quandary and the US stakes winner Full Virtue. The second dam, Lost Virtue (by Cloudy Dawn), an unraced half-sister to the US Grade 2 Shuvee Handicap winner Anti-Lib, is out of a half-sister to Damascus. (Khalid Abdulla). *"Stormy Channel is another nice Abdulla horse I have with a touch of class"*.
Significant sire/damsire crosses:- Three Wonders.

155 - STREAM * [76]   b.f. Unfuwain – Fleet River (Riverman). January 21. First foal.

The dam, a fairly useful 2-y-o 7f winner, is a half-sister to the very smart Eltish (by Cox's Ridge), winner of the 7f Lanson Champagne Stakes and the 1m Royal Lodge Stakes and runner-up in the Grade 1 8.5f Breeders Cup Juvenile, to the useful 8.3f winner Yamuna, the useful 5f and 6f winner Forest Gazelle and the French listed 10f winner Souplesse. The second dam, Nimble Feet (by Danzig), a quite useful 2-y-o 5f winner, is a sister to the Grade 1 Washington Lassie Stakes winner Contredance and to the listed Roses Stakes winner Old Alliance and a half-sister to the Group winners Shotiche and Skimble and to the dam of the One Thousand Guineas winner Wince. (Khalid Abdulla). *"A tall, backward filly, she's a good mover and is very likeable"*.

156 - SUCCINCT * [75]   ch.f. Hector Protector – Pitcroy (Unfuwain). April 13. Second foal.

Half-sister to the 3-y-o Exuberant (by Exit To Nowhere). The dam, a useful 10f winner, is a half-sister to the very useful Group 3 7f Jersey Stakes winner Ardkinglass, the useful dual 7f winner Darnaway and the useful 10f winners Kinlochewe and Jura. The second dam, Reuval (by Sharpen Up), a useful winner of 2 races over 1m at 3 yrs, is closely related to Kristana (dam of the Prix Robert Papin winner Ozone Friendly) and a half-sister to Just You Wait (dam of the Group 2 winners Reprimand and Wiorno) and Little Loch Broom (dam of the very useful colts Fawzi and Soft Currency). *"A well-grown 2-y-o, she'll need some time but is a nice filly and a good mover"*.

157 - SURPLUS (IRE) ** [91]   b.c. Sadler's Wells – Puck's Castle (Shirley Heights). April 19. Third foal. IR£400,000Y. Goffs Orby.

Brother to the unraced 2000 2-y-o Major Drive and half-brother to the useful 5f winner and Group 2 5f Flying Childers Stakes second Emerald Peace (by Green Desert). The dam, a fairly useful 2-y-o 1m winner and third in the listed 10f Zetland Stakes, is a half-sister to the champion 2-y-o filly and Cheveley Park Stakes winner Embassy. The second dam, Pass The Peace (by Alzao), won the Cheveley Park Stakes, was second in the French One Thousand Guineas and is a half-sister to 3 winners. (Thoroughbred Corporation). *"He takes after his dam a bit and is from a quite precocious family. You never know, he could make a Chesham Stakes horse"*.

158 - TORCH LIGHT (USA) ** [82]   ch.c. Distant View – Flaming Torch (Rousillon). January 25. Fourth foal.

Half-sister to the 2-y-o 7f winner Flaming West (by Gone West) and the 3-y-o 1m winner Flame Cutter (by Miswaki) – both quite useful. The dam, a winner over 1m at 2 yrs in France, subsequently won a Grade 3 11f event at 4 yrs in the USA and is a half-sister to the fair 1m and 12f winner Peace King. The second dam, Flaming Peace (by Lyphard), was a disappointing half-sister to numerous winners including the good middle distance performers Peacetime and Quiet Fling and the Cambridgeshire winner Intermission - herself dam of the very useful filly Interval. (Khalid Abdulla). *"A medium-sized, active colt, he looks like a real 2-y-o and will hopefully be an Ascot type".*

---

159 - UP MARKET * [74] b.f. Mark Of Esteem – Top Shop (Nashwan).
February 10. Second foal.
Half-sister to the 3-y-o Cut Price (by Diesis). The dam, a fair 12f winner, is a half-sister to the Group 2 12f King Edward VII Stakes winner Private Tender. The second dam, Select Sale (by Auction Ring), is an unraced half-sister to 5 winners including the Group 2 Ribblesdale Stakes winner Queen Midas and the Scandinavian Group 1 winner Etoile des Indes. (Cliveden Stud). *"A very active filly, Up Market is a good mover with plenty of character about her".*

---

160 - WESTERN VERSE (USA) ** [91] b.c. Gone West – Reams Of Verse (Nureyev).
February 3. First foal.
The dam, a very smart winner of the Oaks, the Fillies Mile, the Musidora Stakes and the May Hill Stakes, is a half-sister to numerous winners including the high-class Group 1 10f Coral Eclipse Stakes and Group 1 10f Phoenix Champion Stakes winner Elmaamul. The second dam, Modena (by Roberto), is an unraced half-sister to the smart 2-y-o 7f winner and Queen Elizabeth II Stakes third Zaizafon - herself the dam of Zafonic. The second dam, Mofida (by Right Tack), won 8 races at up to 7f and was placed in the Duke of York Stakes. (Khalid Abdulla). *"A strong colt, he's very nice and will hopefully be an Ascot type".*

M CHANNON

---

161 - ADDEYLL * [74] ch.c. Efisio – Rohita (Waajib).
February 15. Fourth foal. 130,000Y. Tattersalls October.
Brother to the useful 5f (at 2 yrs) and listed 7f winner Kalindi and half-brother to the unraced 2000 2-y-o Makara (by Lion Cavern). The dam, a fairly useful 2-y-o 5f and 6f winner, was third in the Group 3 6f Cherry Hinton Stakes and is a half-sister to 4 minor winners. The second dam, Ruby River (by Red God), ran once unplaced and is a half-sister to 6 minor winners and to the unplaced dam of the Group 3 Ballyogan Stakes winner Anzio. (Sheikh Ahmed Al-Maktoum). *"This is a horse I like for the middle of the season. A brother to Kalindi, but he's totally different and has a great attitude. A colt that loves galloping, he'll probably be a really nice horse over six or seven furlongs".*

---

162 - ALBANIA * [104] ch.c. Selkirk – Elaine's Honor (Chief's Crown).
January 30. Fourth foal. 82,000Y. Tattersalls October.
Brother to Ishaam, unplaced in one start over 7f at 2 yrs in 2000 and half-brother to fairly useful the 1999 2-y-o 5f winner Areydha (by Cadeaux Genereux) and a 1m winner in Japan by Indian Ridge. The dam, a winner of 2 races at around 8.5f in France, is a half-sister to the Group 3 7f Prix du Calvados winner and subsequent US Grade 1 9f La Canada Stakes third Savannah's Honor and to the French listed 12f winner Anna's Honor. The second dam, Honor To Her (by Sir Ivor), is an unraced full or half-sister to 12 winners out of the US stakes winner of 16 races Frederick Street. (Sheikh Ahmed Al-Maktoum). *"He'll be a 2-y-o and is a very nice half-brother to a filly I had last year called Areydha. He goes well and will be an early sort I should think".*

---

163 - ALDAFRA [75] b.f. Spectrum – Abeyr (Unfuwain).
March 20. Second foal.
Half-sister to Raheibb (by Lion Cavern), unplaced in 2 starts at 2 yrs in 2000. The dam, a useful 3-y-o 7f and 8.2f winner, was listed-placed over 1m and is a half-sister to the useful 2-y-o 7.3f Radley Stakes winner Boojum and the fairly useful 1999 2-y-o 7f winner Shaibani. The second dam, Haboobti (by Habitat), is an unplaced half-sister to 6 winners including the US stakes winner and Grade 3 placed Aerturas and to the unplaced dam of the US Grade 2 winner Distinct Habit. (Sheikh Ahmed Al-Maktoum). *"A nice filly but she's backward and will need time".*

---

164 - ANNA WALHAAN (IRE) * [90] b.c. Green Desert – Queen's Music (Dixieland Band).
February 3. Second foal. 70,000Y. Tattersalls Houghton.
Closely related to the Irish trained 3-y-o Anabaa's Music (by Anabaa). The dam, a minor Irish 13f winner, is a half-sister to 6 winners including the Gimcrack Stakes winner Splendent and the Princess Elizabeth Stakes winner Aim For The Top. The second dam, Sticky Habit (by Habitat), a quite useful 1m

and 10f winner, was a half-sister to 7 winners including the Group 3 Mulcahy Stakes winner I've a Bee. *"He's a nice horse that's just starting to go the right way. He was very backward but he gives the impression he might be a very nice horse".*

---

165 - ANNIVERSARY GUEST (IRE) * [66]   b.br.f. Desert King – Polynesian Goddess (Salmon Leap).
April 20. Sixth foal. IR£60,000Y. Goffs Orby.
Half-sister to the 3-y-o Top Of The Right (by Topanoora), to the quite useful dual 1m winner Sea Squirt (by Fourstars Allstar), the fairly useful 2-y-o dual 6f winner Jay Gee (by Second Set) and a winner in Germany over 11f by Law Society. The dam was placed once over 7f in Ireland and is a half-sister to 10 winners and to the dam of the Kentucky Derby winner Charismatic. The second dam, Polynesian Charm (by What A Pleasure), is an unplaced half-sister to 11 winners. (Mr J Guest). *"A nice filly that's gone the right way. I'd be very hopeful for her from the mid- season onwards, she's done really well".*

---

166 - ASHGAR SAYYAD (USA) * [93]   b.c. Kingmambo – Quelle Affaire (Riverman).
February 3. Third foal. 60,000Y. Tattersalls Houghton.
Half-brother to the useful 1999 2-y-o Ma Yoram (by Dayjur), a winner over 5f and placed in both the Group 2 6f Gimcrack Stakes and the Group 2 6f Mill Reef Stakes. The dam is a French placed sister to the Group 3 7f Concorde Stakes winner and Queen Anne Stakes second Rami and a half-sister to the Group 3 6.5f Prix Eclipse winner Crack Regiment and the listed Prix Yacowlef winner La Grand Epoque. The second dam, Ancient Regime (by Olden Times), won the Group 1 Prix Morny and is a half-sister to the Prix Maurice de Gheest winner Cricket Ball. (Mr Jaber Abdullah). *"A bonny little horse, although he wouldn't be among the best in the yard".*

---

167 - CHANCIT * [67]   b.f. Piccolo – Polly Worth (Wolver Hollow).
April 5. 9,000Y. Doncaster St Leger.
Half-sister to the modest 2-y-o 7f winner Sizzling Symphony (by Sizzling Melody), to the modest 2-y-o 5f and 6f winner Culsyth Flyer (by Nomination) and to the poor 7f winner Aragona (by Aragon). The dam, a modest maiden, was placed once and stayed 1m. She is a half-sister to 9 minor winners out of the placed Parez (by Pardao). *"She didn't cost much but she'll be alright once we get some decent ground".*

---

168 - COUNTESS MILETRIAN (IRE) ** [88]   b.f. Barathea – Sweet Alma (Alzao).
February 25. Seventh foal. IR£120,000Y. Goffs Orby.
Half-sister to the 1996 Irish 2-y-o 6f winner Mubadara (by Lahib) and a winner abroad by Marju. The dam, a minor Irish 3-y-o winner, is a half-sister to 5 winners including Montekin (Group 2 Waterford Crystal Mile). The second dam, Sweet Relations (by Skymaster), ran unplaced twice and is a half-sister to the Group 3 Prix d'Astarte winner Madame's Share. *"As with quite a number of my 2-y-o's, she won't be ready until the middle of the year but she'll be OK".*

---

169 - DIDDYMU (IRE) ** [87]   b.f. Revoque – Family At War (Explodent).
April 6. Sixth foal. IR£100,000Y. Goffs Orby.
Half-sister to the 3-y-o Gone With The Wind, to the very useful 5f Windsor Castle Stakes winner and 5.2f Weatherby Super Sprint winner and Group 2 Kings Stand Stakes second Flanders, the quite useful 6f winner Disputed and a 5f winner in Macau (all by Common Grounds). The dam, a fair 2-y-o 5f winner, is a half-sister to 4 minor winners in the USA. The second dam, Sometimes Perfect (by Bold Bidder), a minor 2-y-o 6f winner in the USA, is a half-sister to 6 winners including the French listed winner and Group 1 Grand Prix de Saint-Cloud third Gain and the US Grade 3 winner Krotz. (Mr Derek & Mrs Jean Clee). *"You won't see her out until mid-season but I think she's a really nice filly. One for the short-list, she's got bags of size and scope".*

---

170 - DILEER (IRE) ** [97]   b.c. Barathea – Stay Sharpe (Sharpen Up).
March 23. Ninth foal. 80,000Y. Tattersalls October.
Half-brother to the 2000 Irish 2-y-o 7f winner Allez La Classe (by Mujadil), to the useful 7f and 1m winner Jalaab, the quite useful 5f and 6f winner Ishtiyak, the fair 7f and 10f winner Fawz (all by Green Desert), the fairly useful 10f winner Manazil (by Generous) and the modest 10f winner Khuchn (by Unfuwain). The dam is an unraced half-sister to the dams of the top-class filly Indian Skimmer, the US Grade 1 winner Missy's Mirage and the US Grade 2 winners Country Pine and Classy Mirage. The second dam, Gray Mirage (by Bold Bidder), won 4 races including a stakes event in the USA and was

Grade 1 placed. (Sheikh Mohammed Obaid Al-Maktoum). *"A nice colt for the mid-season onwards. I'm happy with him and he'll be OK".*

171 - FIRE MOON (IRE) ** [87] b.c. Royal Applause – Welwyn (Welsh Saint).
February 3. Tenth foal. 57,000Y. Tattersalls October.
Half-brother to the useful Welsh Mist (by Damister), a winner of 4 races over 5f and 6f including a listed event, to the poor 3-y-o 7f winner Bashaq (by Jalmood) and a 2-y-o winner in Italy by Lion Cavern. The dam, a fairly useful sprint winner of 5 races, is a sister to the Cheveley Park Stakes second Welshwyn and a half-sister to 4 other winners. The second dam, Takawin (by Takawalk II), won the listed Acorn Stakes and was Group 3 placed on three occasions at 2 yrs. (Mr Salem Suhail). *"He's going the right way and we might see him out in late April or early May. He's just starting to show all the right signs and he might just fit the bill".*

172 - FOR EVVA SILCA * [63] ch.f. Piccolo – Silca-Cisa (Hallgate).
April 15. Fifth reported foal.
Half-sister to the quite useful 2000 2-y-o dual 6f winner Silca Legend (by Efisio), to the smart Group 2 6f Mill Reef Stakes and German Group 2 winner and Group 1 placed Golden Silca (by Inchinor) and to the Italian 2-y-o 5f winner Muso Corto (by Reprimand). The dam, a fairly useful dual 5f winner, was listed placed over 5f at 4 yrs. The second dam, Princess Silca-Key (by Grundy), was a modest 7f winner. (Aldridge Racing and McDowell Racing). *"I need some decent ground before I can assess this Piccolo half-sister to Golden Silca".*

173 - GOLD GUEST * [82] ch.c. Vettori – Cassilis (Persian Bold).
February 8. First foal. 44,000Y. Tattersalls October.
The dam is an unraced half-sister to 5 winners including the German Group 3 1m winner Sinyar and to the unraced dam of the US Grade 2 winner Ventiquattrofogli. The second dam, Place Of Honour (by Be My Guest), won once at 3 yrs and is out of the Coronation Stakes winner Sutton Place. (Mr J Guest). *"He's a sharp colt and he'll be running soon – probably in May – and will prefer further than five furlongs and decent ground".*

174 - GRAND MADAM * [92] ch.f. Grand Lodge – Vax Lady (Millfontaine).
March 5. Sixth foal. Doncaster October. 35,000Y.
Half-sister to the fairly useful 2-y-o 5f listed winner Vax Star (by Petong), to the quite useful 2-y-o 5f winner Vax Rapide (by Sharpo) and the fair 2-y-o 6f winner Lord Bergerac (by Cyrano de Bergerac). The dam, a fairly useful listed sprint winner of 4 races, is a half-sister to 2 minor winners. The second dam, Opinebo, won once at 3 yrs. (Mr A and Mrs L Brazier). *"She's a nice filly but she's just started to grow all of a sudden".*

175 - HAIRY NIGHT (IRE) ** [80] b.f. Night Shift – Snowcap (Snow Chief).
February 25. First foal. 20,000Y. Tattersalls October.
The dam is an unplaced half-sister to 3 winners including the US Grade 2 placed Dianehill. The second dam, Very Subtle (by Hoist The Silver), won four races including the 6f Breeders Cup Sprint, the 1m Hollywood Starlet Stakes and the 8.5f Fantasy Stakes (all Grade 1 events) and is a half-sister to the stakes winner Schematic. (Lewis Caterers). *"She's sharp and will be an early type. There's nothing wrong with her and she's quite a nice filly".*

176 - HARNOUR * [83] ch.c. Desert King – Irish Light (Irish River).
February 5. First foal. 90,000Y. Tattersalls October.
The dam, a fairly useful dual 1m winner, is a half-sister to the US stakes winner and Grade 3 placed Solar Bound. The second dam, Solar Star (by Lear Fan), a fairly useful 2-y-o 6f winner, is a half-sister to 5 winners including Gold Land, a winner of three Grade 3 stakes in the USA. (Sheikh Ahmed Al-Maktoum). *"He'll be alright when the six furlong races arrive. A nice horse that will definitely be a 2-y-o, he moves well and will probably be racing in May. He just gives me the impression he needs six or seven furlongs now".*

177 - HIGHDOWN (IRE) ** [97] b.c. Selkirk – Rispoto (Mtoto).
April 2. Fourth foal. 34,000Y. Tattersalls October.
Half-brother to the unplaced 2000 Irish 2-y-o Sweet Surrender (by Pennekamp) and to the 1999 Irish 2-y-o winner Mitsubishi Trium (by Formidable). The dam, a modest 12f winner, is a half-sister to 6

winners including the Group 3 10f Royal Whip Stakes winner Jahafil. The second dam, River Spey (by Mill Reef), a fairly useful 2-y-o 7f winner, stayed 12f and is closely related to the listed Glorious Stakes winner Spinning. (Mrs W Fleming). *"A very nice colt by Selkirk. He'll be ready by the beginning of May and he certainly shows me enough. A nice, big horse that does everything right".*

---

178 - HI HO SILCA ** [65]

b.f. Atraf – You Make Me Real (Give Me Strength).
February 17. Sixth foal. 52,000Y. Tattersalls October.

Half-sister to the Group 3 6f Railway Stakes and subsequent US winner Camargo (by Brief Truce), to the Irish 7f and 1m winner Forget About It and the Irish 9f, 14f and hurdles winner Real Guest (both by Be My Guest). The dam, a sprint winner of 4 races in the USA, is a half-sister to 6 winners including the US stakes winner Wonderloaf. The second dam, Icy Dial (by Banderilla), won 11 races in the USA including a minor stakes and is a half-sister to the dam of the US Grade 3 winners Gala Spinaway and Power Play. *"A nice filly that's just starting to go the right way".*

---

179 - KULACHI (IRE) * [83]

b.c. Royal Applause – Silly View (Scenic).
February 24. Second foal. 110,000Y. Tattersalls October.

Half-brother to a winner in Sweden by Mujtahid. The dam, a minor 4-y-o 9f winner in Ireland, is a half-sister to 7 winners including the dams of Seattle Rhyme (Group 1 Racing Post Trophy winner) and Dairine's Delight (dual listed sprint winner). The second dam, Silly Song (by Silly Season), won once at 3 yrs and was a half-sister to the William Hill Gold Cup winner Aliante and the White Rose Stakes winner Juggernaut. (Sheikh Ahmed Al-Maktoum). *"A very nice horse. One for the middle of the year, he'll be alright over six furlongs or more and is going well now".*

---

180 - LIPSTICK ** [88]

b.f. Zamindar – Final Shot (Dalsaan).
March 13. Seventh foal. 95,000Y. Tattersalls October.

Half-sister to the fairly useful 2000 2-y-o 5.7f winner Final Pursuit (by Pursuit Of Love), to the smart 5f (at 2 yrs) and 6f winner and Ayr Gold Cup second Double Action (by Reprimand), the very useful dual 6f winner (including at 2 yrs) Sir Nicholas (by Cadeaux Genereux), the fair 8.5f all-weather winner Magical Shot (by Magic Ring) and the fair 2-y-o 6f winner Miss Waterline (by Rock City). The dam, a quite useful filly, won 3 races including the Ayr Gold Cup. The second dam, Isadora Duncan (by Primera), is a placed half-sister to the dam of the Yorkshire Oaks and Nassau Stakes winner Connaught Bridge. (Mr J Breslin). *"Lipstick will win the Queen Mary! A very nice filly that does everything right – she's very sharp and is a definite 2-y-o. She's got a great attitude and is certainly a winner".*

---

181 - LORD LAHAR ** [72]

b.c. Fraam – Brigadier's Bird (Mujadil).
April 1. Second foal.

Brother to the useful 2000 2-y-o Lady Lahar, winner of the Group 3 7f Futurity Stakes at the Curragh. The dam was unraced. *"This full-brother to Lady Lahar would be worth mentioning. He's by Fraam – a proper stallion".*

---

182 - MARTHA DALY ** [89]

b.f. Royal Applause – Primulette (Mummy's Pet).
February 18. Tenth foal. 15,000Y. Tattersalls Autumn.

Half-brother to the 2000 6f placed 2-y-o Proletariat (by Petong), to the 1996 2-y-o 6f winner Makhbar (by Rudimentary), the 2-y-o 6f winner Bring On The Choir (by Chief Singer) – all quite useful, the fair 2-y-o 6f winner Diminuet (by Dominion), the fair 7f (at 2 yrs) and 12f winner Boogy Woogy, the modest 1m all-weather winner Rockette (both by Rock Hopper) and the modest 2-y-o 6f winners Premium (by Dominion) and Primost (by Most Welcome) The dam, a quite useful 5f (at 2 yrs) and 1m winner, is a half-sister to one winner on the flat and two over jumps. The second dam, Primrolla (by Relko), was a modest 10f winner and a useful hurdler. (Ridgeway Downs Racing). *"A sharp runner, she won't win much but she'll win a race early on".*

---

183 - MASTER ROBBIE * [80]

b.c. Piccolo – Victoria's Secret (Law Society).
April 14. Third foal.

Brother to the Italian 7f and 1m winner Small Secret. The dam, a fair 12f winner, is a half-sister to several winners. The second dam, Organdy (by Blakeney), was a quite useful 3-y-o 1m winner. *"He's definitely alright, but being by Piccolo he'll need good ground – I've got some good 2-y-o's by that sire".*

184 - PRINCESS MILETRIAN (IRE) ** [89]   b.f. Danehill – Place Of Honour (Be My Guest).
February 19. Tenth foal. IR£110,000Y. Goffs Orby.
Half-sister to 5 winners including the German Group 3 1m winner Sinyar and the fair 1998 2-y-o 7f winner Ski Lodge (by Persian Bold) and to the unraced dam of the US Grade 2 winner Ventiquattrofogli. The dam won once at 3 yrs and is a half-sister to the Group 3 Ferrans Futurity Stakes winner Sunstart out of the Coronation Stakes winner Sutton Place (by Tyrant). (Miletrian plc). *"A lovely filly for the middle of the season, she's an Ascot/Goodwood type. She goes really nicely and I like her".*

185 - QAZWEEN ** [81]   b.c. Primo Dominie – Be My Lass (Be My Guest).
February 10. Fifth foal. 72,000Y. Tattersalls October.
Half-brother to the 3-y-o Belief (by Polar Falcon), to the fairly useful 1997 2-y-o 6f winner Behold (by Prince Sabo) and the quite useful 12f winner My Lass (by Elmaamul). The dam won once at 4 yrs in France and is a half-sister to the Grade 1 Yellow Ribbon Invitational winner Bonne Ile, the Group 3 Cumberland Lodge Stakes winner Ile de Nisky and the Group 3 Prix Gladiateur winner Hi Lass. The second dam, Good Lass (by Reform), won once in France. (Sheikh Ahmed Al-Maktoum). *"He's a nice, good-topped colt and he'll be a 2-y-o. He goes well and he's certainly very nice. He should be out by early May and will be better over six furlongs than five".*

186 - QUEEN'S LOGIC (IRE) * [69]   ch.f. Grand Lodge – Lagrion (Diesis).
February 21. Fifth foal. FF1,000,000. Deauville August.
Half-sister to the 3-y-o Kilkenny (by Namaqualand), to the poor 10f all-weather winner Tulsa (by Priolo) and a winner in Italy by Lahib. The dam was placed 5 times in Ireland and stayed 12f and is a sister to the Group 1 Middle Park Stakes second Pure Genius. The second dam, Wrap It Up (by Mount Hagen), is a placed half-sister to 6 winners including the Oaks Trial winner Gift Wrapped. (Mr Jaber Abdullah). *"A very nice filly. She does everything right but won't be that early".*

187 - RIDGEWAY SUNSET (IRE) [72]   b.f. Alhaarth – Floralia (Auction Ring).
April 17. Fifth living foal. IR£35,000Y. Goffs Challenge.
Half-sister to the fair dual 1m winner Dorissio (by Efisio) and the minor French 3-y-o winner Flavinia (by Cadeaux Genereux). The dam, a quite useful 3-y-o 7f and 9f winner, is a half-sister to 4 winners including the listed 1m Easter Stakes winner Ultimo Imperatore and the smart dual Group 3 winner Sugarfoot. The second dam, Norpella (by Northfields), was a fairly useful 10f and 12f winner and a daughter of a half-sister to Teenoso. (Ridgeway Downs Racing). *"A filly that will need plenty of time".*

188 - SPEEDFIT BLUE (IRE) * [97]   b.c. Bluebird – She's The Tops (Shernazar).
February 13. Seventh foal. 85,000Y. Tattersalls October.
Half-brother to the smart Group 2 10f Pretty Polly Stakes winner Lady Upstage (by Alzao), to the useful 6f (at 2 yrs) winner and 1m listed second Lycility (by Lycius) and the fairly useful 17.2f winner The Blues Academy (by Royal Academy). The dam, a quite useful 12f winner, is a half-sister to the winner and listed-placed Nayland out of the modest 10f winner Troytops (by Troy), herself a half-sister to the Lockinge Stakes winner and Derby second Most Welcome and the listed winners Bourbon Topsy and Top Guest. (Mr J Guest). *"Quite backward at the moment but he'll be worth following by mid-season".*

189 - STICKY GREEN * [76]   b.f. Lion Cavern – Creme de Menthe (Green Desert).
February 12. Third foal.
Half-sister to the fair 2000 2-y-o 5f winner Piccled (by Piccolo) and to the fairly useful 1999 5f and 6f placed 2-y-o Bee Eight (by Mujtahid). The dam is an unraced half-sister to 6 winners including the top class filly In the Groove, winner of the Champion Stakes, Juddmonte International Stakes, Irish One Thousand Guineas and Coronation Cup, the useful 5f to 1m winner Spanish Pine (by King of Spain) and the quite useful 3-y-o 7f winner Awesome Venture (by Formidable). The second dam, Pine Ridge (by High Top), won two minor races at 3 yrs over 12f. (Capt. J Macdonald-Buchanan). *"A nice filly but backward, so she needs time".*

190 - STRAW DOGS (IRE) * [76]   b.c. Thatching – La Duse (Junius).
February 8. Eighth foal. IR20,000Y. Tattersalls Fairyhouse.
Brother to a winner at 4 yrs in Kuwait and half-brother to the 3-y-o M N L Princess (by Tirol), the modest 8.2f winner Cindy's Star (by Dancing Dissident) and the modest winner of 10 races at around 6f

Blushing Grenadier (by Salt Dome). The dam, a modest 12f placed 3-y-o, is a half-sister to 4 winners including the Group 3 Chester Vase fourth Stetchworth and to the placed dam of the Middle Park Stakes winner Creag-An-Sgor. The second dam, Grenadiere (by Right Royal V), won twice and was second in the Lancashire Oaks. (Ridgeway Downs Racing). *"A nice horse, he'll be running in May and he goes well"*.

191 - SUMMERSON ** [74]
b.c. Whittingham – Summer Sky (Skyliner).
May 6. Ninth foal. 9,000Y. Doncaster St Leger.
Half-brother to the fair 6f (at 2 yrs) to 9f winner Whispering Dawn (by Then Again), to the fair sprint winner of 5 races Lord Sky (by Emarati) and the hurdles winner River Orchid (by Mashhor Dancer). The dam, a fair 2-y-o dual 5f winner, is a half-sister to 3 winners including the US stakes winner and Group 3 Diomed Stakes second Lucky Scott. The second dam, Soft Pedal (by Hotfoot), was a fairly useful winner of 5 races at around 6f. (Mr W H Ponsonby). *"A nice colt, he'll be running by May time and he goes real well. Henry Ponsonby likes this family and this colt goes alright"*.

192 - TAJRAASI (USA) *** [89]
b.c. Trempolino – Inca Princess (Big Spruce).
April 22. Tenth living foal.
Brother to the unraced 2000 2-y-o Yanaseeni and to the German-trained middle-distance dual Group 1 winner Germany and half-brother to 4 minor winners in the USA by Fly Till Dawn, Sovereign Dancer, Gone West and Storm Bird. The dam won over 6f in Ireland and is a half-sister to the US Graded stakes winners Exile King, Hail Bold King and Metfield and to the dam of the US Grade 1 winner Catinca. The second dam, Inca Queen (by Hail To Reason), won 4 stakes races in the USA. (Mr Jaber Abdullah). *"A really nice colt that needs time to mature but I'm hoping he's going to be a good 2-y-o later on"*. Significant sire/damsire crosses:- Germany.

193 - TICKIT (IRE) ** [85]
b.c. Alhaarth – Pericolo (Kris).
April 28. Fifth foal.
Half-brother to the fair 2-y-o 5f winner Nantucket (by Turtle Island), to the modest 2-y-o 6f all-weather winner Lady Caroline (by Hamas) and a 3-y-o 1m winner in Norway by Royal Academy. The dam, a fairly useful 7f placed 2-y-o on her only start, is a half-sister to 4 minor winners here and abroad. The second dam, Wild Abandon (by Graustark), ran once unplaced and is a half-sister to 7 winners including the Group/listed winners Lady Roberta, Tursanah, Mangayah and Worood. (Mr Tim Corby). *"An Alhaarth colt that shows all the right signs – he'll be OK by mid-season and is worth a mention in the book"*.

194 - TRAVERSE (IRE) [79]
b.c. Fayruz – Travel Magic (Henbit).
April 3. Sixth foal. IR£22,000Y. Goffs Challenge.
Half-brother to minor winners at 3 yrs and upwards by Celestial Storm (in Germany) and Be My Chief (in Italy). The dam, a quite useful dual 7f winner, is a sister to one winner and a half-sister to 6 winners including the listed winners Cutting Reef and Jazz Ballet. The second dam, Quiet Harbour (by Mill Reef), is an unplaced half-sister to the Group winning middle-distance horses Armistice Day, Peacetime and Quiet Fling and to the dams of the Group winners Wandesta, De Quest, Interval and Bon Point. (Queensberry Thoroughbreds). *"A nice enough colt for the middle of the season onwards"*.

195 - WASHINGTON PINK (IRE) ** [83]
b.c. Tagula – Little Red Rose (Precocious).
May 6. Seventh living foal.
Half-brother to the 2000 2-y-o 6f seller winner Presentofarose (by Presenting), to the fairly useful 1998 2-y-o 6f winner Maple and the Italian winner at up to 7.5f Soviet Rose (both by Soviet Lad). The dam was unraced. The second dam, Relfo, won the Ribblesdale Stakes. *"Washington Pink is a sharp horse and he's doing everything well at the minute. He's certainly alright"*.

196 - YA HAJAR ** [66]
b.f. Lycius – Shy Lady (Kaldoun).
February 26. First foal.
The dam, winner of a listed event over 6f in Germany, was fourth in the Group 2 6f Moet and Chandon Rennen. The second dam, the minor French 3-y-o winner Shy Danceuse (by Groom Dancer), is a half-sister to the very smart colt Diffident, winner of the Group 3 6f Diadem Stakes, the Group 3 6f Prix de Ris-Orangis and the listed 7f European Free Handicap. The third dam, Shy Princess (by Irish River), a smart French 2-y-o 7f winner and second in the Group 1 Prix Morny, is a half-sister to the Breeders Cup

Mile winner and Eclipse Stakes second Opening Verse and the US Grade 3 winner So She Sleeps. (Mr Jaber Abdullah). *"Ya Hajar is a nice 2-y-o filly and she definitely goes alright".*

197 - ZEEBA (IRE) * [84]

b.f. Green Desert – Liffey's Secret (Riverman). March 25. Fourth foal. IR£55,000Y. Goffs Orby.

Half-sister to the French 3-y-o Cascina (by Cadeaux Genereux). The dam won twice over 10f in Ireland and is a half-sister to 6 winners including the US Grade 3 winner Lady Roberta, the Irish Group 3 winner Tursanah and the French listed winners Mangayah and Worood. The second dam, Farouche (by Northern Dancer), a dual winner in the USA and second in the Grade 3 Pageant Handicap, is closely related to the US Grade 2 winner Dancing Champ and a half-sister to the Grade 2 Kentucky Oaks winner Sweet Alliance (herself the dam of Shareef Dancer). (Sheikh Mohammed Obaid Al-Maktoum). *"A very nice filly, she's just growing on us at present but she'll be alright this year".*

198 - UNNAMED ** [81]

b.br.c. Primo Dominie – Pericardia (Petong). April 20. Fourth foal. 60,000Y. Tattersalls October.

Half-brother to the fairly useful 5f and 6f winner (including at 2 yrs) Card Games (by First Trump) and to a winner in Italy by Deploy. The dam is an unplaced half-sister to 4 winners including Prince Ferdinand, winner of the Group 3 7f Jersey Stakes. The second dam, Greensward Blaze (by Sagaro), won a 1m seller and is a half-sister to 2 minor winners. *"A very nice colt that goes well, he'll be out in May and will be one to watch".*

R CHARLTON

199 - ABSOLUTE CHARMER (IRE) ** [69]

ch.f. Entrepreneur – Diavolina (Lear Fan). March 12.

Half-sister to the quite useful 2000 2-y-o 7f winner Breakfast Bay (by Charnwood Forest), to the fairly useful 2000 3-y-o 10.5f winner Golden Way (by Cadeaux Genereux), the French listed 11f winner Go Boldly (by Sadler's Wells), the useful Polish Spring (by Polish Precedent), a winner here and in the USA from 6f (at 2 yrs) to 8.5f including a stakes event, the quite useful 2-y-o 6f and 7f winner The Rich Man (by Last Tycoon) and the 1999 Irish 3-y-o winner Canaletto (by Royal Academy). The dam, a French 10f winner at 3 yrs, is a half-sister to 7 winners including the French listed winner Droiture. The second dam, Diamond Spring (by Vaguely Noble), won once in France and is a half-sister to the dams of the US Graded stakes winners Another Review, No Review and Urbane. (Lady Richard Wellesley). *"A neat, attractive filly and a good mover. She'll hopefully make a 2-y-o from May onwards. Goes quite nicely".*

200 - BALERNO * [94]

b.c. Machiavellian – Balabina (Nijinsky). March 29.

Half-sister to the smart dual 12f winner Bequeath, the French listed 10f winner Binary, the French 12f winner Balabac, the fairly useful 9f and 10.8f winner Balnibarbi (all by Rainbow Quest), the very useful 7f (at 2 yrs) and triple 10f winner Bal Harbour, the very useful dual 10f winner Bina Gardens (both by Shirley Heights) and the fairly useful 9f winner Bina Ridge (by Indian Ridge). The dam was a very useful winner over 10f at 3 yrs, was fourth in the Sun Chariot Stakes, is a sister to the Coronation Cup winner Quiet Fling and the Guardian Classic Trial winner Peacetime and a half-sister to the Cambridgeshire winner Intermission (herself dam of the good 6f filly Interval) and the good middle-distance stayers Armistice Day and Peaceful. The second dam, Peace (by Klairon), won the 6f Blue Seal Stakes. (Khalid Abdulla). *"He's an attractive, strong horse that moves well. He could make a 2-y-o over seven furlongs from July onwards".*

201 - BARINGO (USA) * [74]

b.c. Miswaki – Galega (Sure Blade). April 13. Fourth living foal.

Half-brother to the quite useful 8.5f to 10f all-weather winner Burning Truth (by Known Fact). The dam won twice over 9f at 3 yrs in France and was listed placed. She is a half-sister to the Grade 3 Athenia Handicap winner Flaming Torch. The second dam, Flaming Peace by Lyphard), is a placed half-sister to numerous winners including the good middle distance performers Peacetime and Quiet Fling and to the dams of the Group/Graded stakes winners Wandesta, De Quest, Interim and Interval. (Khalid Abdulla). *"He looks an attractive, strong, good-moving horse. His coat looks good, he looks very forward and he should prove worth watching – especially over seven furlongs or more".*

202 - BIRTHDAY PRESENT *   [71]   ch.f. Cadeaux Genereux – Topicality (Topsider).
May 23. Fourth living foal.

Half-brother to the fairly useful 3-y-o 7f and 8.3f winner Border Subject (by Selkirk). The dam, a winner over 1m in France at 3 yrs, is a sister to the very smart filly Top Socialite (winner of the Cherry Hinton Stakes and the Fred Darling Stakes and placed in both the French and Irish One Thousand Guineas) and a half-sister to 7 winners including the Two Thousand Guineas second and subsequent US Grade 1 winner Exbourne. The second dam, Social Lesson (by Forum), won 3 minor sprint races and is a half-sister to the US stakes winner Cherry Pop. (Khalid Abdulla). *"She's nice, very strong and powerfully built. I'd hope she'll make a 2-y-o from July onwards".*

203 - BLAGOVEST   [79]   b.c. Singspiel – Tass (Soviet Star).
March 14. Fourth foal.

The dam is an unraced half-sister to the smart middle-distance colts Alleging, Monastery and Nomrood and to the dam of the 2000 2-y-o Group 1 1m Racing Post Trophy winner Dilshaan. The second dam, Sweet Habit (by Habitat), is an unraced half-sister to the Group 2 10f Pretty Polly Stakes winner and Irish Oaks second Fleur Royale. (D Bromilow/C Coleridge Cole). *"I would hope we'll see him out this year but we'll have an eye on his 3-y-o career for him really. A nice horse, he could be anything although the dam has been disappointing".*

204 - CAP HORN *   [91]   b.c. Mtoto – Tabyan (Topsider).
April 7. Sixth foal.

Brother to the smart 1m to 10f winner (including the Cambridgeshire Handicap) Cap Juluca (by Mtoto) and half-brother to Curtsey (by Mark Of Esteem), unplaced in one start over 5.7f at 2 yrs in 2000. The dam, a modest 6f winner, is out of the useful 6f winner Wink (by Forli), herself a half-sister to the smart US colt Glow. (Mountgrange Stud). *"He will need time, but he's quite a nice horse and is one for the autumn".*
Significant sire/damsire crosses:- Cap Juluca.

205 - CLIMATE CONTROL (USA) **   [91]   ch.f. Mt Livermore – Descant (Nureyev).
January 24. Second foal.

Half-sister to the unraced 2000 2-y-o Far Note (by Distant View). The dam is inbred 2x3 to Northern Dancer and is an unraced half-sister to the champion 2-y-o and 3-y-o Zafonic, winner of the Two Thousand Guineas, the Dewhurst Stakes, the Prix de la Salamandre and the Prix Morny and to the smart Group 3 Prix de Cobourg winner and Prix Morny second Zamindar. The second dam, Zaizafon (by The Minstrel), won twice over 7f at 2 yrs and was a smart 3-y-o, being placed in the Group 1 1m Queen Elizabeth II Stakes and the Group 3 1m Child Stakes. She is a half-sister to the unraced Modena, herself dam of the high-class Group 1 winners Reams Of Verse and Elmaamul. (Khalid Abdulla). *"She's very small and very neat. A typical Mt Livermore in that she's short-backed and short-legged. A bit of a character and it would appear that she ought to make an earlyish 2-y-o".*

206 - COMMISSAR (IRE) *   [74]   b.c. Common Grounds – Trescalini (Sadler's Wells).
March 23. Fourth foal. IR£220,000Y. Goffs Orby.

Half-brother to the useful 10f and 11f winner and listed-placed Fantazia (by Zafonic) and to the fairly useful Irish 7f and 1m winner Machalini (by Machiavellian). The dam, an Irish 2-y-o 10f winner, is a half-sister to 4 winners. The second dam, Noble Treasure (by Vaguely Noble), is an unraced half-sister to the Group 3 winners Kanz and Diomedia (dam of the Group 3 winner Media Starguest) and to the dam of the high-class middle-distance horses Glint Of Gold and Diamond Shoal. (Mr Michael Pescod). *"Commissar is an attractive horse. He looks more like Sadler's Wells than Common Grounds but whether that's a good thing or not, I don't know. He had a bit of a setback in the spring but will hopefully be running this summer. He belongs to a lucky owner so that must count for something!".*

207 - DUNE   [72]   b.c. Desert King – Flamands (Sadler's Wells).
April 4. Second foal. IR£55,000Y. Goffs Orby.

Half-brother to the 3-y-o Pomme de Flanders. The dam, a fairly useful 12.3f and 14f winner, is a sister to several winners including the Irish listed 10f winner Casey Tibbs. The second dam, Fleur Royale (by Mill Reef), a very useful winner of the Group 2 10f Pretty Polly Stakes, was second in the Irish Oaks and is a half-sister to the dam of the smart colts Nomrood, Alleging and Monastery. (Mountgrange Stud

Ltd). *"A big colt, he slightly reminds me of Danehill when he was at this stage in that he's rather plain and laid-back. It's difficult to know what sort of distance a son of Desert King will need and this colt is backward at the moment".*

208 - GLADE RUNNER (USA) * [88]

b.f. Woodman – Maid Of Camelot (Caerleon).
February 18. First foal.

The dam was a useful winner of the listed 10f Lupe Stakes. The second dam, Waterfowl Creek (by Be My Guest), a quite useful 3-y-o dual 1m winner, is a sister to the very useful dual 1m winner Guest Artiste, closely related to the very useful Inchmurrin (a winner of 6 races including the Group 2 Child Stakes and herself dam of the very smart colt Inchinor) and a half-sister to numerous winners including the very useful 2-y-o Group 2 6f Mill Reef Stakes winner Welney. (Mr A E Oppenheimer). *"At the moment she looks to be more forward than her dam was at this stage. She's very deep and strong and hopefully she'll be a six or seven furlong filly from July onwards".*

209 - INCORPORATION * [71]

b.c. In The Wings – Danishkada (Thatch).
May 25. Ninth foal. 150,000Y. Tattersalls October.

Half-brother to the 3-y-o Najda (by Halling), to the French winner and Group 2 6.5f Prix Maurice de Gheest second Danakal (by Diesis) and a winner of 10 minor races in the USA by Lyphard. The dam won the Group 1 1m Grand Criterium and is a half-sister to 7 winners. The second dam, Demo (by Abdos), won once in France. (Mountgrange Stud Ltd). *"An attractive horse from a fast mare. He's a late foal but is quite mature looking and I expect him to make a 2-y-o from mid-summer".*

210 - IRISH VALE * [74]

ch.c. Wolfhound – Valencia (Kenmare).
March 27. First foal.

The dam, placed over 1m at 2 yrs on her only start, is a half-sister to numerous winners including the Grade 1 Santa Ana Handicap and Grade 1 10f Santa Barbara Handicap winner Wandesta, the Group 2 12f Prix du Conseil de Paris winner De Quest and the smart French 10f to 15f winner Turners Hill. The second dam, De Stael (by Nijinsky), a fairly useful dual 7f winner at 2 yrs, is a sister to the high-class middle-distance colts Peacetime and Quiet Fling and a half-sister to the Cambridgeshire winner Intermission - herself dam of the good sprinter Interval. (Khalid Abdulla). *"Very small, he looks quite sharp and this is the first foal of Valencia. Rather surprisingly for this family, he looks like being an early 2-y-o and as he's so small I think we'd better 'go to the well' as soon as we can".*

211 - MACKENZIE'S FRIEND [82]

ch.f. Selkirk – Always Friendly (High Line).
May 5. Third foal. 210,000Y. Tattersalls October.

Half-sister to the unraced 2000 2-y-o Arabie (by Polish Precedent) and to Dane Friendly (by Danehill), a winner in Italy at 4 yrs and third in the Group 2 Premio Emilio Turati. The dam, a very useful filly, won 3 races including the Group 3 12f Princess Royal Stakes and was placed in the Prix Royal-Oak and Gran Premio de Milano. The second dam, Wise Speculation (by Mr Prospector), was unplaced and bred four other minor winners. (Mountgrange Stud). *"A late foal and with a staying pedigree, she's done very well but I wouldn't expect to see her until later in the year. An attractive filly that will hopefully make a better horse next year".*

212 - MASTER RATTLE ** [90]

b.c. Sabrehill – Miss Primula (Dominion).
March 17. Ninth living foal. 32,000Y. Tattersalls October.

Half-brother to the fair sprint winner of 6 races Tinker Osmaston (by Dunbeath), to the modest sprint winner of 8 races Primula Bairn (by Bairn), the listed-placed winners Tinker Amelia (by Damister) and Magic Grey (by Petong) and a winner in Belgium by Rudimentary. The dam was a quite useful sprint winner of 5 races at 2 and 4 yrs. The second dam, Pasha (by Dicta Drake), won twice at 2 and 3 yrs. (Mrs Caroline Parker). *"He's taken very much after the dam's side. They've all been five or six furlong types and this colt looks like he'll be running in May".*

213 - MASTER SUN (IRE) [88]

b.c. Grand Lodge – Mersada (Heraldiste).
March 20. Fourth foal. IR£25,000Y. Goffs Orby.

Half-brother to the minor Irish 2000 4-y-o winner One For The Money (by Doubletour). The dam is an unplaced half-sister to 3 minor winners. The second dam, Marchesana (by March Past), won twice at 3 yrs. (Mr Michael Pescod). *"A small horse and a good mover, he's still a bit on the weak side but hopefully we'll get going fairly soon with him".*

214 - SCALADO (USA) *** [79]   ch.c. Mister Baileys – Lady Di Pomadora (Danzig Connection).

January 31. Fourth foal. 46,000Y. Tattersalls December.

Half-brother to the unraced 2000 2-y-o Twice A Lady, to a minor winner in France (both by Exbourne) and to the useful 7f (at 2 yrs) and 1m winner Trident (by Red Ransom). The dam won 3 minor races at up to 9f in the USA and is a half-sister to 4 minor winners. The second dam, Hope And Charity (by Powder Horn), won at 3 yrs in the USA and is a half-sister to 2 stakes winners including the dam of Najavo Princess - herself the dam of Dancing Brave and the French Oaks winner Jolypha. (Hippodrome Racing). *"A very strong, good-moving colt that looks like he'll make a 2-y-o. I think the sire is slightly underrated as a stallion".*

215 - SUMMER RECLUSE (USA) * [81]   b.c. Cozzene – Summer Retreat (Gone West).

March 11. Second foal.

Half-brother to High Pasture (by El Gran Senor), unplaced in 2 starts at 2 yrs in 2000. The dam, a fair 3-y-o 7f winner, is a sister to the smart sprinter Western Approach and a half-sister to the US Grade 1 10f winner Tinner's Way. The second dam, Devon Diva (by The Minstrel), won over 9f at 4 yrs in the USA. (Khalid Abdulla). *"He looks to be pretty sharp. A little bit hot maybe, but he looks like an early 2-y-o. His half-sister certainly wasn't early but he looks pretty nippy and he comes from the speedy family of Devon Ditty".*

216 - THE MAGIC KEY * [93]   ch.f. Unfuwain – Anchorage (Slip Anchor).

March 23. Fifth foal. 44,000Y. Tattersalls October.

Half-sister to the quite useful 2000 triple 2m winner Lord Alaska (by Sir Harry Lewis) and closely related to the quite useful 7f winner Red Leggings (by Shareef Dancer). The dam, a quite useful dual 12.3f winner, is a half-sister to 6 winners including the Ormonde Stakes winner Brunico. The second dam, Cartridge (by Jim French), was a useful 6f and 7f winner and a half-sister to the dam of the German Group 2 winner Sulaafah. (Mrs & Mrs Orton). *"A very attractive filly and a very good mover and although she has a pedigree full of late-maturing types I would expect her to make a 2-y-o in the second half of the season. She goes nicely and she has a very similar head to Petrushka".*

217 - TIKKUN (IRE) *** [89]   gr.c. Grand Lodge – Moon Festival (Be My Guest).

April 15. Fifth living foal. IR£260,000Y. Goffs Orby.

Half-brother to the Sita (by Indian Ridge), placed third over 7f on her only start at 2 yrs in Ireland in 2000, to the fairly useful Irish 14f winner Lunasa (by Don't Forget Me) and the fairly useful dual 1m winner Silver Apple (by Danehill). The dam, a fair 10f and 12f placed maiden, is a sister to the fair middle-distance winner Moon Carnival and a half-sister to 6 winners including Moon Madness (St Leger and Grand Prix de Saint-Cloud), Sheriff's Star (Coronation Cup and Grand Prix de Saint-Cloud) and Lucky Moon (Goodwood Cup). The second dam, Castle Moon (by Kalamoun), won from 1m to 13f, is a sister to the very smart middle-distance stayer Castle Keep and a half-sister to the Ascot Gold Cup winner Ragstone. (Mountgrange Stud Ltd). *"Tikkun is a very nice horse and is one you could get running whenever you wanted him to – like most nice horses. Very strong and a good mover, we won't be in a hurry with him but I hope that he'll make a nice 2-y-o over seven furlongs or a mile in the autumn".*

218 - TREKKING (USA) ** [84]   ch.f. Gone West – Didina (Nashwan).

January 16. First living foal.

The dam, a winner over 6f at 2 yrs here, subsequently won the Grade 2 8.5f Dahlia Handicap in the USA and is a half-sister to the French listed 10f winner Espionage. The second dam, Didicoy (by Danzig), a useful winner of 3 races over 6f, is closely related to 3 winners including the Group 3 1m Prix Quincey winner Masterclass and a half-sister to the champion 2-y-o Xaar and the Group 3 10.5f Prix Corrida winner Diese. The third dam, Monroe (by Sir Ivor), a useful Irish 5f and 6f winner, is a sister to the good 2-y-o Gielgud and to the very smart Malinowski and a half-sister to the dual Grade 1 winner Blush With Pride and to Sex Appeal - the dam of El Gran Senor and Try My Best. (Khalid Abdulla). *"A very nice, big filly out of a mare I trained. She had a little setback in late winter but I would hope that she'd be a 2-y-o from the mid-summer onwards".*

P COLE

219 - BALLYBUNION (IRE) ** [90]   ch.c. Entrepreneur – Clarentia (Ballad Rock).
February 12. Seventh foal. IR£230,000Y. Goffs Orby.
Half-brother to the very smart 1996 2-y-o Bahamian Bounty, winner of the Group 1 6f Prix Morny and the Group 1 6f Middle Park Stakes (by Cadeaux Genereux) and to the fairly useful 2-y-o 5f winner Forentia (by Formidable). The dam, a very useful winner of 5 races at up to 6f and third in the Group 3 Cornwallis Stakes, is out of the unraced Laharden (by Mount Hagen), an unraced half-sister to 2 winners and to the dam of the Group 3 winner Hawkins. (Mr John Poynton). *"Ballybunion had a few moderate scrapes over the winter and so hasn't done any serious work yet but he looks marvellous and moves well. He looks precocious and should make a 2-y-o".*

220 - CALA DI VOLPE (USA) ** [89]   ch.c. Mt Livermore – Frenchman's Cove (Caerleon).
January 26. Fourth foal. $50,000Y. Keeneland September.
The dam, a winner of 6 races in France and the USA and Grade 3 placed is a half-sister to numerous winners including the very useful 1986 2-y-o Group 3 1m Prix la Rochette winner Grand Chelem, the smart 2-y-o Group 3 1m winner and French Two Thousand Guineas fourth Splendid Moment, the useful French 7f and 1m winner Flushing Meadow and the dual French 1m handicap winner Evening Kiss (herself the dam of 2 stakes winners in Germany). The second dam, Racquette (by Ballymore), was a smart Irish 3-y-o 7f and 10f winning half-sister to the Irish One Thousand Guineas winner Arctique Royale and to the dam of Ardross. (Mr Chris Wright). *"A sharp, early type, he may well have run before your book comes out".*

221 - CHERRY HILLS (IRE) ** [86]   b.f. Anabaa – Fernanda (Be My Chief).
January 28. First foal. IR£220,000Y. Goffs Orby.
The dam, a useful 2-y-o dual 6f winner, was second in the Group 3 Prestige Stakes and won once in France at 3 yrs. She is a half-sister to 4 winners including the smart listed 2-y-o 1m winner Chipaya. The second dam, Flaming Rose (by Upper Nile), was placed five times in the USA and is a half-sister to 6 winners including the Queen Mary Stakes winner Gwydion (herself dam of the Greenham Stakes winner Enrique). (Mr John Poynton). *"She came in late and isn't very big, but she looks a nice filly. She won't be that early but she should be a 2-y-o".*

222 - CONSTABLE ** [74]   gr.g. Efisio – Tagiki (Doyoun).
May 4. Fourth foal. 45,000Y. Tattersalls October.
Half-brother to the quite useful 2000 2-y-o dual 6f winner Barathiki (by Barathea) and to the useful Peacock Alley (by Salse), a winner of 3 races at around 7f. The dam won once over 7f at 2 yrs in Italy and is a half-sister to 6 winners including the listed Ulster Harp Derby winner Tijara. The second dam, Tibriza (by Nishapour), is a placed half-sister to 8 minor winners out of the Prix de l'Abbaye winner Texanita. (Richard Green, Fine Paintings). *"He was a bit colty so he's been gelded and he's going to be ready for racing around late May. A small, sharp, 2-y-o type".*

223 - CORTON (IRE) ** [94]   b.c. Definite Article – Limpopo (Green Desert).
April 25. Seventh foal.
Brother to the 2001 3-y-o 7f all-weather winner Smoothie and half-brother to the very smart Group 1 6f Haydock Park Sprint Cup and Group 3 5f Palace House Stakes winner Pipalong (by Pips Pride), the fairly useful 1999 2-y-o 6f to 7f winner Out Of Africa and the minor US winner of 2 races Henry Kitchener (both by Common Grounds). The dam, a poor 5f placed 2-y-o, is a half-sister to 4 winners here and abroad. The second dam, Grey Goddess (by Godswalk), was a smart winner of 5 races in Ireland from 7f to 8.5f including the Group 3 Gladness Stakes and the Group 3 Matron Stakes. (Mr J Harvey). *"A big horse, he won't be early but he's a horse with more scope than his brother Smoothie".*

224 - DESERT AIR (JPN) ** [81]   ch.c. Desert King – Greek Air (Ela-Mana-Mou).
April 4. Second foal. FF800,000Y. Deauville August.
Half-brother to the unraced 2000 2-y-o Real Chief (by Caerleon). The dam won 3 races including the listed Prix Solitude and was second in the Group 3 1m Prix des Chenes. She is a sister to the Group 2 7f Criterium de Maisons-Laffitte winner and Prix du Moulin and Prix Saint-Alary third Grecian Urn (herself dam of the listed winners Dark Shell and Grecian Dart). The second dam, Sea Singer (by Sea Bird II), won once and was third in the Group 1 12f Yorkshire Oaks. (Mrs Belinda Harvey). *"A fine,*

athletic kind of horse, he'll be racing from June onwards over six or seven furlongs. An attractive horse and a very good mover".

225 - FULL HOUSE (IRE) [83]

b.c. King's Theatre – Nirvavita (Highest Honor).
February 14. Second foal. 37,000Y. Tattersalls October.

Half-brother to the unraced 2000 2-y-o Yorkshire Grey (by Royal Abjar). The dam, a winner of 3 races in France and listed-placed over 7.5f and 1m, is a half-sister to 4 winners. The second dam, Neomeris (by Pharly), won twice in France and is a half-sister to the Group 3 Prix Edmond Blanc winner Nikos and the dual listed winner No Attention (both Group 1 placed in France). (The Blandford Partnership). *"A big, strong horse but he's quite backward at the moment. He'll be racing over six or seven furlongs in the summer".*

226 - GUYS AND DOLLS ** [75]

ch.c. Efisio – Dime Bag (High Line).
May 1. Fourth foal. 58,000Y. Tattersalls October.

Half-brother to the useful 2000 dual 7f 2-y-o winner Blushing Bride (by Distant Relative), to the smart 1m (at 2 yrs) to 11f listed winner Pawn Broker (by Selkirk) and the fairly useful Irish 7f winner Blushing Melody (by Never So Bold). The dam, a quite useful winner of 4 races at up to 2m (including on the all-weather), is a half-sister to 4 minor winners. The second dam, Blue Guitar (by Cure The Blues), a fairly useful winner of 2 races over 1m and 8.3f, is a half-sister to the listed Somerville Tattersalls Stakes winner Polished Silver and the listed Tipperary Stakes winner Melody (dam of the Group 3 Kiveton Park Stakes winner Guest Performer and the US Grade 3 winner Sojourn). (Mr Anthony Speelman). *"He shouldn't be that late and he's a nice type of horse. Strong and active, he's pleased me so far and should be ready by mid-season".*

227 - HENRI LEBASQUE (IRE) * [83]

b.c. Sri Pekan – Almost A Lady (Entitled).
April 5. Fourth foal. 30,000Y. Tattersalls October.

Half-brother to the modest 2000 2-y-o 6f winner Thanks Max (by Goldmark). The dam was placed over 7f and 1m at 2 yrs in Ireland and is a half-sister to the high-class colt Insatiable, winner of the Prix Dollar and the Brigadier Gerard Stakes and second in the Champion Stakes, and to the dam of the Criterion Stakes winner Pipe Major. The second dam, Petit Eclair (by Major Portion), a fairly useful 7f (at 2 yrs) and 10.8f winner, is a half-sister to the Prix Foy winner Beeshi and the John Smith's Magnet Cup winner Chaumiere. (Richard Green, Fine Paintings). *"He needs a bit of time but he's done nothing wrong as yet and he'll make a 2-y-o later on.".*

228 - INVESTOR (IRE) ** [89]

b.c. Marju – Shine On Me (Machiavellian).
March 11. First foal. FF400,000. Deauville August.

The dam won twice and was listed-placed in France and is a half-sister to 3 winners including the listed winner Sardamati and the dam of the US Grade 2 winner Shanawi. The second dam, Shapaara (by Rheingold), is a winning half-sister to Shergar and the Group 2 Geoffrey Freer Stakes winner Shernazar. (Mr A Smith & Mr G Seidler). *"This is a nice horse and he looks like he"ll be ready by the summer over six or seven furlongs".*

229 - JAN BREUGHEL (USA) * [71]

ch.c. Phone Trick – Sunk (Polish Navy).
February 9. Second foal. 70,000Y. Tattersalls October.

The dam, a minor 3-y-o winner in the USA, is a half-sister to 8 winners including the Group 3 7f Rockfel Stakes winner At Risk and the dam of the US Grade 1 placed Wheelaway. The second dam, Misgivings (by Cyane), won 8 races in the USA including the Grade 3 Chrysanthemum Handicap, was Grade 1 placed and is a half-sister to the high-class broodmare Nimble Folly (dam and grandam of numerous Group/Graded stakes winners including the US Grade 1 winner Contredance). (Richard Green, Fine Paintings). *"This colt is in full work and is a 2-y-o type although he hasn't quite come in his coat yet. He could be quite early".*

230 - KOOL (IRE) ** [78]

b.c. Danehill Dancer – New Rochelle (Lafontaine).
February 5. Third foal. 72,000Y. Doncaster St Leger.

Half-brother to the fair 2000 2-y-o 1m all-weather winner Tower Of Song (by Perugino). The dam, a minor 14f winner at 5 yrs in Ireland, is a sister to the Geoffrey Freer Stakes and Ormonde Stakes winner Shambo. The second dam, Lucky Appeal (by Star Appeal), is an unplaced half-sister to the Chesham Stakes and European Free Handicap winner Lapierre. (Mr A Smith & Mr G Seidler). *"Kool will have started his career in April. I think he was the top-priced horse at the St Leger Sales and he's made good progress through the winter".*

231 - LONG GOODBYE (IRE) [82]

ch.c. Dr Devious – Lady Nessa (Al Nasr).
March 25. Fourth foal. IR£65,000Y. Goffs Orby.

Half-brother to the 2000 4-y-o listed 10f Prix d'Automne winner Pretty (by Darshaan). The dam, placed three times over 12f at 3 yrs in Ireland, is a half-sister to 9 winners including the US Grade 1 Matchmaker Stakes winner Dancers Countess (dam of the US Grade 2 winner Paris Prince). The second dam, Countess Belvane (by Ribot), was a minor winner of 2 races at 3 yrs in the USA. (Mr Luciano Gaucci). *"Dr Devious horses seem to be taking their time to come to hand. This colt moves well and is a nice type of horse for the seven furlong races onwards".*

232 - MAN FROM HAVANA (USA) * [87]

b.c. Green Dancer – Charmie Carmie (Lyphard).
May 29.

Brother to the fair 1998 2-y-o 6f winner Sundae Girl (by Green Dancer) and half-brother to the quite useful 6f and 7f winner Himmah (by Habitat) and the Peruvian champion Faaz (by Fappiano). The dam was placed 9 times in the USA and is a half-sister to numerous winners including the triple Grade 1 winner Chris Evert (the grandam of Chief's Crown) and All Rainbows (dam of the Kentucky Derby winner Winning Colors). The second dam, Miss Carmie (by T.V. Lark), won 3 races in the USA including a stakes event over 6f at 2 yrs. (Mr Chris Wright). *"Another backward sort that would want seven furlongs plus later on this season. He's a medium-sized, good-moving, slightly plain horse that will keep developing".*

233 - MY BAYARD ** [90]

ch.c. Efisio – Bay Bay (Bay Express).
April 21. Ninth foal. 42,000Y. Tattersalls October.

Half-brother to the useful 5f and 6f winner Boast (by Most Welcome), to the fairly useful 2-y-o 5f and 4-y-o 1m winner Great Bear (by Dominion), the fair 6f and 7f winner Butrinto (by Anshan) and the fair 2-y-o 5f winner Baskerville (by Night Shift). The dam, a useful 7.6f winner, was listed-placed twice and is a half-sister to 7 winners. The second dam, Lambay (by Lorenzaccio), was a quite useful 2-y-o 7f winner. (Viscountess Portman). *"He's not very big but he's a nice, strong horse and he should be out by June at the latest".*

234 - ORINOCOVSKY (IRE) * [92]

ch.c. Grand Lodge – Brillantina (Crystal Glitters).
March 31. Fourth foal. 45,000Y. Tattersalls October.

Half-brother to 2 winners at 2 yrs in Italy by Dashing Blade and Law Society. The dam won once in Germany and is a half-sister to the German listed winner Bandira. The second dam, Brigantin (by Arratos), won 3 listed events in Germany. (Mr Andy J Smith). *"A very big, backward horse but you couldn't say anything against him and he should be racing from mid-season onwards".*

235 - PIETER BREUGHEL (USA) * [80]

b.c. Citidancer – Smart Tally (Smarten).
February 9. First foal. 62,000Y. Tattersalls October.

The dam won 2 races in the USA at 3 yrs. The second dam, She Can Add (by Robellino), won 5 races on the flat and over jumps in the USA and is a half-sister to the Grade 2 Diana Handicap winner Ratings. (Richard Green, Fine Paintings). *"This is a nice horse – he's a good mover and will probably start over six furlongs. He's working well".*

236 - PUREPLEASURESEEKER (IRE) ** [65]

ch.f. Grand Lodge – Bianca Cappello (Glenstal).
March 9. Second foal. 50,000Y. Tattersalls October.

Half-sister to the useful 2000 2-y-o Group 3 6.5f Prix Eclipse winner Potaro (by Catrail). The dam is an unplaced half-sister to Idris, a winner of four Group 3 events in Ireland at up to 12f and to the winner and US Grade 3 placed Sweet Mazarine. The second dam, Idara (by Top Ville), was a very useful winner over 11f and 12f at 3 yrs and was third in the Group 2 Prix de Pomone. (Mr C Wright & the Hon Mrs J M Corbett). *"She's a nice, rangy filly and a very good mover. I'd say she probably wants six furlongs and I like her".*

237 - RIVELLI (IRE) * [86]

b.f. Lure – Kama Tashoof (Mtoto).
January 25. Second living foal. 100,000Y. Tattersalls Houghton.

Half-sister to the fairly useful 1m winner Judicious (by Fairy King). The dam, a fair middle-distance placed maiden, is a half-sister to 5 winners including the useful listed 1m winner Pfalz. The second dam, Leipzig (by Relkino), a useful listed winner over 1m, was second in the Nell Gwyn Stakes and is a half-sister to the dams of the Group winners Adam Smith, Braashee, Careafolie, Ghariba, Gouriev and Run And Gun. (Mr Faisal Salman). *"A very nice filly but she's been a bit slow in her coat and I've done nothing with her yet. An attractive filly though".*

238 - RODOMONTADE (USA) *** [99]

b.f. Machiavellian – Lajna (Be My Guest). February 28.

Half-sister to numerous winners including the triple US Grade 3 winner Gold Land and the fairly useful 2-y-o 6f winner Solar Star (by Lear Fan). The dam is an unraced half-sister to the high-class dual Group 1 1m Lockinge Stakes winner Soviet Line and the useful middle-distance winners Mamdooh and South Shore. The second dam, Shore Line (by High Line), a very useful 7f winner, was fourth in the Oaks and is a sister to the Group 2 winners Ancholia and Quay Line (grandam of the Oaks winner Pure Grain). (H R H Prince Fahd Salman). *"She's a really nice filly, big and strong with a good attitude and she's a good mover. She came in a bit late so I don't expect her to be racing before June. A nice type of filly".* Significant sire/damsire crosses:- Don Michelotto, Titus Livius, Sinyar.

239 - SIGNED AND DATED (USA) * [90]

b.c. Red Ransom – Libeccio (Danzatore). May 7. Fifth foal. $40,000Y. Keeneland September.

Half-brother to the fair 8.5f all-weather winner Hollow Haze (by Woodman). The dam is an unraced daughter of the US stakes winner Windy Triple K (by Jaklin Klugman), herself a half-sister to the top-class Derby, Irish Derby and King George VI and Queen Elizabeth Stakes winner Generous, the Irish One Thousand Guineas second Strawberry Roan and the Irish Group 3 winner Wedding Bouquet. (Richard Green, Fine Paintings). *"A nice, big, strong horse. Again, he won't be early but he's a good mover".*

240 - SPANISH JOHN (USA) * [81]

b.br.c. Dynaformer – Esprit d'Escalier (Diesis). February 23. Fourth foal. IR£95,000Y. Goffs Orby.

Half-brother to the US Grade 3 winner and Grade 1 placed Gastronomical and to a minor US 4-y-o winner (both by Sunshine Forever). The dam was placed at 3 yrs in the USA and is a half-sister to 2 minor winners. The second dam, Nonchalance (by Native Charger), won 5 minor races in the USA. (Mr Anthony Speelman). *"This is a nice 2-y-o. He'll probably be suited by six or seven furlongs as a 2-y-o and is a very nice type of horse".*

241 - STARZAAN (IRE) * [86]

b.c. Darshaan – Stellina (Caerleon). April 9. Fifth living foal. 220,000Y. Tattersalls Houghton.

Closely related to the French listed winner and French Derby third Sestino (by Shirley Heights) and half-brother to 2 minor winners in France by Machiavellian and High Estate. The dam, a minor 2-y-o winner in France, is a sister to the Group 3 1m Prix d'Aumale winner Mackla and a half-sister to 5 winners including the French listed winner Delimara. The second dam, Mariella (by Sir Gaylord), won the Group 1 Premio Roma and is a half-sister to the dual Ascot Gold Cup winner Sagaro and the Italian Group 1 winner Scorpio. (Mr M Arbib). *"I think he's my most expensive 2-y-o, but he's a 3-y-o type and has done nothing except basic work. A big, powerful horse but he'll take time".* Significant sire/damsire crosses:- Mutamam, Truly A Dream.

242 - THIN CLIENT (USA) ** [86]

ch.c. Atticus – Aliata (Mr Prospector). May 19. Ninth foal. $27,000Y. Keeneland September.

Half-brother to 3 winners including the US stakes-placed winner of 4 races Storm Boot (by Storm Cat) and a minor US winner of 6 races by Chief's Crown. The dam, a fairly useful 2-y-o 5f and 6f winner, is a half-sister to 7 winners including the very useful US sprinter and sire Topsider, the US 2-y-o stakes winner War Of Words and the Group 3 winning stayer and Italian Derby second Brogan. The second dam, Drumtop (by Round Table), was a top-class US middle-distance winner of 17 races and a sister to the Group 1 Observer Gold Cup winner Take Your Place. (W J Smith & M D Dudley). *"Yes, he's nice and he'll be ready to race as soon as the ground improves. He'll make a nice 2-y-o and we like him".*

243 - TITCHFIELD (USA) [90]

b.br.c. Mt Livermore – Morning Colors (Raise A Native). February 24. Second foal. $65,000Y. Keeneland September.

The dam, a stakes-placed winner in the USA, is a half-sister to 8 winners including the US Grade 2 La Prevoyante Handicap winner Lemhi Go. The second dam, Midnight Rapture (by Giboulee), won at 2 yrs in the USA, was third in the Grade 1 6f Spinaway Stakes and is a half-sister to the US Grade 3 winner Refinish. (Sir George Meyrick). *"A big, tall, extremely good-moving colt but he'll take a bit of time".*

---

244 - TOTAL TURTLE (IRE) ** [91]   b.c. Turtle Island – Chagrin d'Amour (Last Tycoon).
March 23. Third foal. 34,000Y. Tattersalls October.
Brother to the French 3-y-o winner Verlaine and half-brother to the 2000 French 2-y-o winner Nerval (by Common Grounds). The dam won once at 3 yrs in France and is a half-sister to 4 winners including the French listed 1m winner and US Grade 2 placed Wedding Ring. The second dam, Fleur d'Oranger (by Northfields), won the listed 12f Prix de la Ville de Trouville and is a half-sister to the German Group 3 winner and French Oaks third Premier Amour. (W J Smith & M D Dudley). *"He's very big but there's nothing weak about him and he's a very, very good mover. A nice type of horse, I can see him racing before mid-season".*

---

245 - ZANDOMENEGHI (IRE) [86]   ch.c. College Chapel – Fire Of London (Shirley Heights).
March 25. Third foal. 55,000Y. Tattersalls October.
Brother to the modest 1999 6f and 7f placed 2-y-o Pudding Lane and half-brother to the unraced 2000 2-y-o Bluewatch. The dam, a fair 10f placed 3-y-o, is a sister to the useful 7f (at 2 yrs) and 10f winner and Group 2 placed Spitfire and a half-sister to 8 winners here and abroad. The second dam, Home Fire (by Firestreak), was a useful sprint winner of 2 races at 2 yrs. (Richard Green, Fine Paintings). *"A strong horse with a slightly lazy attitude. He's quite fit at the moment so when we get a bit of fast ground and he does a bit of work he could run".*

---

246 - ZONE * [88]   b.c. Zilzal – Thea (Marju).
March 7. Second foal. 72,000Y. Tattersalls October.
The dam was a fairly useful 3-y-o 7f winner. The second dam, Switched On (by Known Fact), a quite useful 9f winner, is a half-sister to the listed winners Laughter, Special Leave and Spring To Action and to the unplaced dam of the Group 1 Lockinge Stakes winner Fly To The Stars. *"A big, strong, attractive horse, he's coming along well in his work and will probably want six furlongs plus in late May or June".*

L CUMANI

---

247 - CAMELOT [92]   br.c. Machiavellian – Bombazine (Generous).
February 14.
The dam, a useful 10f winner, is a half-sister to the high-class Breeders Cup Mile, Irish Two Thousand Guineas and Queen Anne Stakes winner Barathea, to the smart Prix du Chemin de Fer du Nord, Prix du Muguet and Prix Perth winner Zabar and the very useful 2-y-o 7f Somerville Tattersall Stakes winner and US stakes winner Free at Last. The second dam, Brocade (by Habitat), was a high-class filly at up to 1m, winning five races including the Group 1 7f Prix de la Foret and the Group 3 7f Bisquit Cognac Challenge Stakes. (Mr Gerald Leigh). *"A nice horse but more for the future, rather than early in his career. A good-looking horse from a lovely family, he'll want seven furlongs to start with".*

---

248 - CERVARO (USA) ** [75]   b.f. Red Ransom – Star Pastures (Northfields).
March 28. Twelfth foal. $60,000Y. Keeneland September.
Half-sister to the fair 2000 1m placed 2-y-o Western Edge, to the smart 10.3f to 12.4f winner Marcus Maximus, the useful 2-y-o 7f winner Monza (all by Woodman), the minor Canadian stakes winner and Grade 2 placed Stellarina (by Pleasant Colony), the useful Irish 7f to 13f winner Esprit d'Etoile (by Spectacular Bid), the fairly useful 10f winner Lord Justice (by Alleged), the fair 3-y-o 7f winner Turbulent River (by Riverman), the minor French winner of 3 races at 4 yrs Emir Albadou (by Bering) and the 1996 German 3-y-o winner Rassoul Al Arab (by Risen Star). The dam was a high-class filly at up to 10f, winning 5 races including the Group 3 Child Stakes and is a half-sister to 6 winners including the very useful 7f to 10f winner Pixie Erin and the smart middle-distance colt Skaramanga. The second dam, Spirit in the Sky (by Tudor Melody), won 3 races from 6f to 12f and was third in the Group 2 Nassau Stakes. (Mr Chris Wright). *"A very well-bred filly that was bought quite cheaply considering her pedigree. She goes quite well and all being well she should be running by July time".*

249 - DERWENT (USA) * [74]**   b.br.c. Distant View – Nothing Sweeter (Darby Creek Road).
March 17. Eleventh foal. $105,000Y. Keeneland September.
Half-brother to 8 winners including the Group 2 6f Premio Melton winner Secret Thing (by Secreto) and minor US winners by Known Fact, Relaunch and Twining. The dam, a stakes winner of 11 races in the USA, was second in the Grade 3 Riggs Handicap and is a half-sister to 7 winners. The second dam, Sweet Nothings (by Promised Land), was a stakes-placed winner of 3 races in the USA. (Mr M J Dawson). *"A very nice horse I bought in America. He's good-looking, quite forward and should be ready to run by July time. I'd expect him to be good enough to win some races as a 2-y-o".*

250 - EMANANT ** [56]   b.f. Emarati – Reamur (Top Ville).
March 31.
Half-sister to the very smart middle-distance winner and Group 3 12f St Simon Stakes third Boreas (by In The Wings) and to the French 2-y-o 6f to 9f winner Redeem (by Doyoun). The dam, a modest maiden, stayed 12f. (Aston House). *"A half-sister to Boreas, she's much more precocious than he was and looks like being OK".*

251 - GOSSAMER ** [73]   b.f. Sadler's Wells – Brocade (Habitat).
February 20.
Sister to the high-class Breeders Cup Mile, Irish Two Thousand Guineas and Queen Anne Stakes winner Barathea and half-sister to the smart colt Zabar (by Dancing Brave), winner of the Prix du Chemin de Fer du Nord, the Prix du Muguet and the Prix Perth - all Group 3 1m events, the very useful 2-y-o 7f Somerville Tattersall Stakes winner and One Thousand Guineas fourth Free at Last (by Shirley Heights) - subsequently winner of an 8.5f stakes event in the USA and the useful 10f winner Bombazine (by Generous). The dam was a high-class filly at up to 1m, winning five races including the Group 1 7f Prix de la Foret and the Group 3 7f Bisquit Cognac Challenge Stakes. She is a sister to the very useful 2-y-o Cause Celebre and a half-sister to 5 winners. The second dam, Canton Silk (by Runnymede), was a useful winner of 4 races over 5f. (Mr Gerald Leigh). *"She doesn't look like her brother Barathea – she's a smaller type. A bit late coming in, she's a bit behind the others and is difficult to assess at this stage. All being well she should be ready to have a run by September".*
Significant sire/damsire crosses:- Alnasr Alwasheek, Barathea, Batshoof, Dance Design, King Of Kings, Kirov Premiere.

252 - GRAMPIAN * [87]   b.c. Selkirk – Gryada (Shirley Heights).
February 15. Second foal. 200,000Y. Tattersalls October.
Half-brother to the quite useful 2000 1m placed 2-y-o Guaranda (by Acatenango). The dam, a fairly useful 2-y-o 7f and 8.3f winner, was third in the Group 3 1m Premio Dormello, is a full or half-sister to numerous middle-distance winners and to the useful stayer Gondolier. The second dam, Grimpola (by Windwurf), won over 6f and 1m in Germany including the Group 2 German One Thousand Guineas and stayed 12f. (Mr M J Dawson). *"A good-looking horse, he takes a bit more after Shirley Heights than Selkirk. He's a nice colt and goes well. One to see in the late summer".*

253 - LOOKALIKE ** [70]   b.f. Rainbow Quest – Balalaika (Sadler's Wells).
February 2. First foal.
The dam, a useful 4-y-o listed 9f winner, is a sister to the high-class Group 2 10f Prince of Wales's Stakes and Group 3 10f Brigadier Gerard Stakes winner Stagecraft and a half-sister to the very useful dual 1m listed winner Hyabella. The second dam, Bella Colora (by Bellypha), is from an excellent family and won four races including the Group 2, 9.2f Prix de l'Opera and the Group 3, 7f Waterford Candelabra Stakes and was a very close third in the One Thousand Guineas. She is a half-sister to the Irish Oaks winner Colorspin, herself dam of the top-class middle-distance colt Opera House, to the Irish Champion Stakes winner Cezanne and to the very useful filly Rappa Tap Tap. (Helena Springfield Ltd). *"A very nice, good-looking filly. She's bred to want at least ten furlongs next year and so will be a seven furlong/mile 2-y-o in late summer. A very correct filly – she looks wonderful".*
Significant sire/damsire crosses:- Happy Valentine.

254 - LUDYNOSA (USA) * [79] b.f. Cadeaux Genereux – Boubskaia (Niniski).
April 23. Seventh foal. FF2,100,000. Deauville August.
Half-sister to the 3-y-o Bourgeoisie (by Ashkalani) and to 5 winners including the Group 2 1m Prix d'Astarte winner and Group 1 1m Prix du Moulin fourth Daneskaya (by Danehill) and the Group 3 9f Prix Saint-Roman third Mumtaz (by Kaldoun). The dam, a winner at Maisons-Laffitte and listed-placed twice in France, is closely related to the Group 1 1m Gran Criterium winner Will Dancer and the US stakes winner Wind Symbol and a half-sister to 4 winners including the Group 2 6f Premio Umbria winner Dancing Eagle. The second dam, Frenetique (by Tyrant), won 3 listed events in France from 1m to 10f and is a half-sister to the dam of the US Grade 2 winner Talloires. (Mrs M Schulthess). *"A nice, strong filly. Although by Cadeaux Genereux she's out of a Niniski mare and has stamina in her blood. She's not going to be a sprinter (as a proper Cadeaux Genereux would be) but she'll be running by June or July. A good-looking filly and I like her".*

255 - OOPS (IRE) [75] b.c. In The Wings – Atsuko (Mtoto).
February 25. Fourth foal. IR£190,000Y. Goffs Orby.
Half-brother to the unraced 2000 2-y-o Triphenia (by Ashkalani), to the fair 1999 2-y-o 5f winner Night Shifter (by Night Shift) and the Irish 4-y-o winner and 9f listed placed Atacat (by Catrail). The dam, placed once at 2 yrs over 1m at Leopardstown, is closely related to the Group 3 10f Prix Gontaut-Biron winner Muroto, to the listed 10f Prix d'Automne winner Vanya and to the dam of the Italian Group 2 and listed Haydock Park July Stakes winner Ivan Luis. The second dam, Maresca (by Mill Reef), is a placed half-sister to the Group 1 Prix Ganay winner Romildo and the Group 3 9f Prix de Conde winner Pevero. (Mr M J Dawson). *"A very nice horse but he's more of a twelve furlong type so won't be out until the seven furlong or mile races in late summer or autumn. He goes very well and seems nice".*

256 - PARSIFAL * [89] b.c. Sadler's Wells – Moss (Woodman).
March 23. Third foal. IR£160,000Y. Goffs Orby.
Brother to the fairly useful 2000 2-y-o 7f winner Elrehaan and half-brother to the quite useful 10f winner Rousing Thunder (by Theatrical). The dam ran once unplaced in the USA and is a half-sister to 6 winners including the William Hill Sprint Championship and Prix de l'Abbaye winner Committed (by Theatrical and herself dam of the US Grade 1 winner Pharma) and the dam of the Cherry Hinton Stakes winner Musicale. The second dam, Mistinguette (by Boldnesian), ran once unplaced and is a half-sister to the US Grade 1 winner and good broodmare Miss Toshiba. (Mr Geoff Howard-Spink and Partners). *"Quite backward but a nice horse, Parsifal is tall and still a bit weak. He's a good mover and could be OK towards the back-end of the season".*

257 - PLATONIC [83] b.f. Zafonic – Puce (Darshaan).
February 6. First foal.
The dam, a very useful 12f listed winner, is a half-sister to the fairly useful 12f winner Seek and to the fairly useful 10.5f winner Shouk. The second dam, Souk (by Ahonoora), a fairly useful 7f winner, was listed placed over 1m and is out of an unraced half-sister to the French One Thousand Guineas winner Dumka (dam of the Group winners Doyoun, Dalsaan, Dolpour and Dafayna). (Fittocks Stud). *"A nice filly that will take a little time. Her family tends to develop as 3-y-o's but she should be running later on this year".*

258 - ROSA PARKS * [85] b.f. Sadler's Wells – Free At Last (Shirley Heights).
May 10. Fourth foal.
Sister to Freedom Now, unplaced over 7f on his only outing at 2 yrs in 2000 and half-sister to the fairly useful 10f winner and 12f listed-placed Coretta (by Caerleon) and the very useful 10f winner and listed-placed Trumpet Sound (by Theatrical). The dam, a very useful winner of three 7f events at 2 yrs including the listed Somerville Tattersall Stakes, was fourth in the One Thousand Guineas and won the Grade 3 8.5f Countess Fager Handicap in the USA. She is a half-sister to the high-class miler Barathea (winner of the Breeders Cup Mile and the Irish Two Thousand Guineas) and to the French and German Group 3 winner Zabar. The second dam, Brocade (by Habitat), was a high-class filly at up to 1m, winning five races including the Group 1 7f Prix de la Foret and the Group 3 7f Bisquit Cognac Challenge Stakes and is a half-sister to 7 winners including the dam of the dual Irish Group 3 winner Desert Style. (Mr G Leigh). *"This is a nice, good-looking filly. She was late coming into the yard (she*

was only broken in February) but she's catching up nicely and will be a filly to run this year. The best of her will come next year though".

Significant sire/damsire crosses:- In The Wings, Hawker's News, Hunting Hawk, Legend Maker, Subtle Power.

---

259 - ROYAL EAGLE (GER) *   [69]

ch.c. Eagle Eyed – Royal Rivalry (Sir Ivor).
February 21. Fourth foal. 18,000Y. Tattersalls October.

Closely related to the German 3-y-o winner Rivara (by Polish Precedent). The dam won 2 minor races at 3 yrs in France and is a half-sister to the Australian Grade 1 and Group 3 Prix Gladiateur winner Always Aloof. The second dam, Miranda (by Forli), won once at 2 yrs and is a half-sister to the useful 2-y-o 9f and subsequent Italian 12f winner River Jig (herself dam of the Group/Graded stakes winners Dance Parade and Ocean Queen). (Mr L Marinopoulos). *"A well-developed horse and quite strong, I'm hopeful that he'll be racing by July or August and that he'll prove OK".*

---

260 - SHIFTY *   [71]

b.c. Night Shift – Crodelle (Formidable).
March 2. Fifth foal. 155,000Y. Tattersalls Houghton.

Half-brother to the high-class Ela Athena (by Ezzoud), winner of the Group 3 Lancashire Oaks and placed in the Yorkshire Oaks, Man O'War Stakes and Turf Classic. The dam, a French 3-y-o 9.5f winner, is a half-sister to 6 winners including the US Grade 2 second Ianomami and the French listed winner Danish Field. The second dam, Pizziri (by Artaius), won 3 races in Italy and is a daughter of the Group 2 7f Premio Chiusura winner Croda Alta. (Mr M J Dawson). *"A good-looking colt for June/July time, he goes quite well and is a likeable horse".*

---

261 - TUNSTALL (USA) **   [80]

b.c. Bahri – Princess West (Gone West).
February 18. First foal. $190,000Y. Keeneland September.

The dam won at 3 yrs in Germany and is a half-sister to 2 winners including the Group 3 Grosser Preis von Dusseldorf winner Page's King. The second dam, Page Bleue (by Sadler's Wells), won at 2 yrs in France and is a half-sister to 3 winners. (Mr M J Dawson). *"Tunstall is another nice horse – again very good-looking and he should be running by July time over six furlongs before moving up to seven. I like him a lot".*

---

262 - VICIOUS PRINCE (IRE) *   [88]

b.c. Sadler's Wells – Sunny Flower (Dom Racine).
March 9. Ninth foal. 130,000Y. Tattersalls Houghton.

Half-brother to the high-class Group 2 12f Princess of Wales's Stakes, Group 3 12f Cumberland Lodge Stakes and Group 3 11f September Stakes winner Wagon Master (by Rainbow Quest), to a 2-y-o winner in Japan by Lammtarra and four minor winners in France by Groom Dancer (2), Darshaan and Kris. The dam was placed twice in France and is a half-sister to the dam of the good miler Then Again and to the top-class broodmare Sunny Valley (the dam of Sun Princess and Saddlers' Hall). The second dam, Sunland (by Charlottesville), won once at 3 yrs, was third in the Park Hill Stakes and is a half-sister to 6 winners including Sunny Cove (Park Hill Stakes). (Mrs C Samuel). *"Vicious Prince is a nice horse. He's quite big and despite the fact that he's from a slow-maturing family he's quite a strong horse so I wouldn't be surprised if he does more as a 2-y-o than the rest of the family have done. He'll hopefully have two or three runs this year over seven furlongs or a mile starting in August".*

---

263 - XCEL (IRE)   [73]

b.c. Revoque – Myran (In The Wings).
March 19. First foal. IRE70,000Y. Goffs Orby.

The dam was placed over 12f in Ireland and is a half-sister to 3 winners including the useful 2-y-o 1m listed Premio Novella winner Silent Tribute. The second dam, Tribal Rite (by Be My Native), was a fairly useful 6f (at 2 yrs) to 10f winner of 3 races including the listed 6f Silver Flash Stakes and is a half-sister to the Group 1 Middle Park Stakes winner Balla Cove, the Irish listed winner Blasted Heath and the US stakes winner Burning Issue. (Mr M J Dawson). *"A nice, good-looking horse, he's fairly mature if a bit on the small side and he should be on the racetrack by May or June. He's the only Revoque that I have but there were some quite good-looking ones at the Sales last year. It's difficult to predict, but potentially he's a nice stallion".*

P D'ARCY

264 - LADY HIGH HAVENS (IRE) * [62]   b.f. Bluebird – Blanche Dubois (Nashwan).
February 18. First foal. 50,000Y. Tattersalls October.

The dam is an unraced half-sister to several winners including the useful listed placed Place de l'Opera and the smart 2000 2-y-o Count Dubois. The second dam, Madame Dubois (by Legend Of France), was a very smart winner of five of her seven starts at 3 yrs from 9f to 14.6f including the Group 2 Park Hill Stakes, the Group 2 Prix de Royallieu and the 12f Galtres Stakes and is a half-sister to the dam of the very smart 2-y-o Daggers Drawn. The third dam, Shadywood (by Habitat), a useful 10f winner, was second in the Lancashire Oaks and is a half-sister to the very useful fillies Kashmir Lass, Overdrive (dam of the Queens Vase winner Endorsement) and Mill on the Floss (dam of the useful winners Hatta's Mill, Milly Ha Ha and Yeltsin). (Mrs A Lovat). *"A nice filly with a good pedigree that includes Count Dubois, it looks like she'll make a 2-y-o alright".*

265 - UNNAMED [79]   ch.c. Lion Cavern – Val d'Erica (Ashmore).
April 23 . Twelfth foal.

Half-brother to the unplaced 2000 2-y-o Astral Prince (by Efisio) and to 8 winners including the Group 3 10f Premio Ambrosiano winner Veradi (by Mill Reef) and Italian winners by Shirley Heights, Pharly, Soviet Star, Warning and Priolo. The dam won the Group 1 1m Premio Regina Elena and the Group 1 11f Italian Oaks. The second dam, Laconia (by Great Nephew), is an unplaced half-sister to 11 winners. (Musaed Al Salem). *"A very nice, scopey individual, he'll probably make his debut sometime during May".*

E DUNLOP

266 - BALDOUR (IRE) * [79]   b.c. Green Desert – Baldemara (Sanglamore).
March 11. First foal.

The dam is an unraced to 5 winners including the Group 1 5.5f Prix Robert Papin winner Balbonella (herself dam of the top-class sprinter Anabaa and the French One Thousand Guineas winner Always Loyal) and the French listed 12f winner Bamwhite. The second dam, Bamieres (by Riverman), was placed fourth twice in France and is out of the French middle-distance winner Bergamasque (by Kashmir II). (Maktoum Al-Maktoum). *"A nice, attractive colt. He was going well until he had a minor setback but he seems to have settled down well now. We haven't done much with him - he's grown and lengthened a bit but prior to that he seemed an obvious 2-y-o type".*

267 - CLASSIC EXAMPLE ** [72]   ch.c. Mark Of Esteem – Classic Form (Alzao).
January 11. First foal. 95,000Y. Tattersalls Houghton.

The dam, a modest 7f and 10f placed 3-y-o, is a sister to the 1998 Oaks winner and One Thousand Guineas second Shahtoush and a half-sister to the Group 2 10f Pretty Polly Stakes winner and Epsom Oaks second Game Plan (by Darshaan). The second dam, Formulate (by Reform), was a very smart filly and a winner of 4 races including the Group 3 Hoover Fillies Mile. (Mr Khalifa Sultan). *"A neat, powerful, attractive colt and an early foal. He looks a very obvious 2-y-o type that would be suited by six furlongs to begin with. He's working nicely and his temperament looks good. One of my more forward 2-y-o's, he looks nice this horse".*

268 - DALAL ** [74]   b.f. Cadeaux Genereux – Proudfoot (Shareef Dancer).
March 5. Seventh foal. 55,000Y. Tattersalls October.

Half-sister to the fairly useful 1996 2-y-o listed 5.2f winner Head Over Heels (by Pursuit Of Love), to the fairly useful 1m winner Harlequin Dancer (by Distant Relative), the French 10f winner Tiriana (by Common Grounds) and the Italian 7.5f and 1m winner Second Barrage (by Royal Academy). The dam won over 14f in Ireland and is a sister to the listed Prix Isonomy winner Noble Ballerina and a half-sister to the very useful winner of 6 races Amrak Ajeeb. The second dam, Noble Dust (by Dust Commander), is an unraced half-sister to 6 winners. (Mr Mohammed Jaber). *"A beautiful walker when we bought her, she's now a typical Cadeaux Genereux filly, strong, quite tall and slightly coarse-looking. She's tough and moves well at this stage and I'm pleased with her".*

269 - FAIR TIME (USA) ** [75]　　　　　　　　　　　　b.f. Woodman – Anakid (Danzig).
April 1. First foal. $80,000Y. Keeneland September.
The dam is an unraced half-sister to the listed Oh So Sharp Stakes winner and Group 3 1m May Hill Stakes third Ruznama and to the minor US stakes winner Precious Feather. The second dam, Last Feather (by Vaguely Noble), won the Group 3 Musidora Stakes, was third in the Oaks and is a half-sister to the Irish St Leger winner Caucasus and the US stakes winner of 13 races One For All. (Mr Abdullah Ali). *"An attractive filly, she looks to have a good temperament at this stage for a Woodman. She moves nicely and will be one for the middle of the season onwards I should think".*
Significant sire/damsire crosses:- Hula Angel (Gr 1), Raise Suzuran (Gr 3).

270 - GOOGOOSH (IRE) * [75]**　　　　　　　　　b.f. Danehill – Literary (Woodman).
February 10. First foal. FF1,300,000. Deauville August.
The dam, a fair 3-y-o 1m winner and placed over 6f at 2 yrs, is a sister to the quite useful 1m winner Bibliotheque and is closely related to the French winner of 3 races Fortieth (by Forty Niner). The second dam, Book Collector (by Irish River), won 4 races here and in the USA including a stakes event, is closely related to the US Grade 2 Dixie Handicap winner Akabir and a half-sister to the Group 1 Middle Park Stakes winner Lycius and the Group 3 Prix de Cobourg winner Tereshkova. (Mr Mohammed Jaber). *"A very nice Danehill filly. She's quite leggy, was fairly neat when we bought her but has done her growing. At the moment she looks to be amongst the best of the fillies and looks to be useful at this stage. A filly with a lot of scope about her and it's surprising to see how well she's going at this stage, so she has an outside chance of being an Ascot 2-y-o".*

271 - GRIZEDALE (IRE) ** [83]　　　　　　　　ch.c. Lake Coniston – Zabeta (Diesis).
January 29. Fifth foal. 36,000Y. Tattersalls October.
Half-brother to the fair 1999 2-y-o 7f winner Lady Of Honour (by Bigstone) and the fair 5f (at 2 yrs) and 7f winner Turtle's Rising (by Turtle Island). The dam won over 1m in France and is a half-sister to 4 winners including the Prix Eugene Adam third Hecquet. The second dam, Haidee (by Irish River), won 2 listed events over 1m in France and is a half-sister to the Prix de Diane and Prix Saint-Alary winner Harbour. (Queensberry Thoroughbreds). *"I thought he was going to be earlyish, he went well but then just started to grow a little. Hopefully he'll fill out, he appears to possess quite a lot of speed and has done his growing now. He's been coming along well recently".*

272 - HELLOIMUSTBEGOING (USA) * [79]　　　　　b.f. Red Ransom – Arsaan (Nureyev).
April 4. Seventh living foal.
Half-sister to the US winner of 7 races and dual US Grade 3 placed Hanarsaan (by Hansel), to the fairly useful 1m winner Musical Tones (by Diesis) and the quite useful 10f winner Allgrit (by Shadeed). The dam, a useful winner of the 7f Oh So Sharp Stakes (at 2 yrs) and the listed 1m Venus Stakes, is a half-sister to the Hollywood Gold Cup, Charles H. Strub Stakes and Californian Stakes winner Desert Wine, to the US dual Grade 1 winner Menifee and to the dam of Fasliyev. The second dam, Anne Campbell (by Never Bend), a stakes winner of 3 races in the USA, is a half-sister to the Prix d'Arenberg winner Repercussionist and the US stakes winners Royal North and Boomer's Luck. (Maktoum Al-Maktoum). *"A half-sister to a colt I trained called Allgrit who was a very big horse and this filly would be very much the same. She was a very attractive filly but she's grown and grown and she's now a very big filly. She moves well, has a good temperament and is an end of season type 2-y-o, building up to be a 3-y-o".*

273 - IZMAIL (IRE) ** [72]　　　　　　　　b.c. Bluebird – My-Lorraine (Mac's Imp).
February 20. First foal. IR£150,000Y. Goffs Orby.
The dam, a minor Irish 3-y-o 5f and 6.5f winner, is a half-sister to 5 winners including the Group 3 5f Ballyogan Stakes winner and Group 1 Haydock Park Sprint Cup third Catch The Blues. The second dam, Dear Lorraine (by Nonoalco), won over 10f in France and is a half-sister to 4 winners. (Mohammed Ali). *"A nice horse by Bluebird and he looks an obvious 2-y-o type. He's neat and attractive, does everything asked of him, has a good temperament and is a straightforward horse. He could be OK".*

274 - KAHZIMA (USA) * [85]**   b.br.f. Gulch – Gharayib (Nureyev).
March 16. First foal.

The dam won over 8.5f in the USA. The second dam, Lazer Show, won 14 races in the USA, notably the Grade 2 5f Sorority Stakes at 2 yrs. (Hamdan Al-Maktoum). *"Again, she's still in Dubai but apparently she's not over-big and looks to be a 2-y-o type. I should imagine this is one for your short list!".*

275 - KING'S ENVOY (USA) * [79]   b.c. Royal Academy – Island Of Silver (Forty Niner).
April 30. Third foal.

Half-brother to the unraced 2000 2-y-o I Need A Holiday (by Nureyev) and to a minor winner in Dubai by Danzig. The dam, a very useful winner of 6 races from 1m to 10.2f, is a half-sister to 9 winners including the US Grade 2 winner Seattle Dawn (herself dam of the US Grade 3 winner Gold Sunrise). The third dam, Embellished (by Seattle Slew), won over 6f at 3 yrs in the USA and is a half-sister to the champion American 2-y-o filly of 1983 Althea, to the US Grade 1 winners Ketoh and Ali Oop, the Grade 2 winners Aishah, Aquilegia and Twining and to the unraced dam of Green Desert. (Maktoum Al-Maktoum). *"He's a horse that's turned himself inside out. He was narrow and not a particularly attractive horse when he came in but he's done his growing, he's beginning to fill out and he's done well. He has a little bit of a knee action if one wants to be critical but his temperament is pretty good for a Royal Academy. Again he looks to move well and is cantering and finding things quite easy".*

276 - KING'S THOUGHT * [84]   b.c. King's Theatre – Lora's Guest (Be My Guest).
May 28. Seventh foal. 110,000Y. Tattersalls Houghton.

Half-brother to the very useful 7f (at 2 yrs) and 1m listed winner Centre Stalls (by In The Wings), to the useful 1999 2-y-o 6f and 7f winner and listed Free Handicap second Catchy Word (by Cadeaux Genereux) and the quite useful 14.6f winner Nawahil (by Shirley Heights). The dam, a useful 3-y-o 7f winner, is a sister to the One Thousand Guineas and Sussex Stakes winner On The House and to the dam of the listed Grand Metropolitan Handicap winner Nuryana. The second dam, the unplaced Lora (by Lorenzaccio), was closely related to the good sprinter D'Urberville and a half-sister to the dam of the champion sprinter Habibti. (Mr Abdullah Ali). *"A horse that I've always liked but he's a late foal and we've done nothing with him. He's a good-looking, big stamp of a horse that moves well but is very much one for next year".*

277 - LENGAI (USA) ** [93]   b.c. Dixieland Band – La Pepite (Mr Prospector).
February 2. Fifth foal. $60,000Y. Keeneland September.

Half-brother to the very useful 2000 1m and 10f winner Asly (by Riverman), to the US stakes-placed winner Patriot Strike (by General Assembly) and 2 minor winners by Boundary (at 2 yrs in Japan) and Slew O'Gold (in the USA). The dam is a placed half-sister to the Canadian champions L'Enjoleur, La Voyageuse and Medaille d'Or and to the Grade 2 winner D'Accord. The second dam, Fanfreluche (by Northern Dancer), was a champion filly in Canada and the USA. (Khalid Ali). *"I like this horse. He's tough, strong and mature. He looks to be going OK, has a little bit of a knee action perhaps, but he looks alright. He could be nice".*

Significant sire/damsire crosses:- Chimes Band (Gr 2), Didyme (Gr 2), Love That Jazz (Gr 3), Southern Rhythm (Gr 3), Jazz Club (Gr 3).

278 - LOBOS (SWI) * [75]   ch.c. Rainbow Quest – Lady Of Silver (Caerleon).
February 10. Second foal. 100,000Y. Tattersalls Houghton.

Half-sister to the French 2-y-o winner Lady Dadar (by Dadarissime). The dam won once at 2 yrs in France and is a sister to a listed-placed winner of 5 races in France and a half-sister to 11 winners including the listed winners Papermoon, Jolie Zaza and Lavender Mist (herself dam of the Italian Group 1 winner Steamer Duck). The second dam, Bold Lady (by Bold Lad, USA), won 3 races and was listed-placed in France. (Mr Khalifa Sultan). *"He had a setback early on which has prevented him from doing anything but has always attracted. He moves very well and is now back cantering so he hasn't done an enormous amount yet, but he'd be the type of horse that's bred to do more next year. He could be OK".*

279 - LUNA MOTH (USA) *   [74]   b.f. Silver Hawk – Night And Dreams (Fappiano).
January 4. Third foal.

Half-sister to Deep Sleep (by Rahy), placed in France at 2 and 3 yrs. The dam, a winner of 3 minor races in the USA over 6f, is a half-sister to 5 winners including the US champion sprinter and triple Grade 1 winner Housebuster. The second dam, Big Dreams (by Great Above), won 11 races including four stakes events in the USA. (Maktoum Al-Maktoum). *"A big, strong, mature filly. She's more colty than feminine and moves well. We've brought her along fairly gently, she looks tough and is one for later in the season".*

---

280 - MR PITZ **   [72]   ch.c. Hector Protector – Moogie (Young Generation).
April 28. Ninth foal. 30,000Y. Tattersalls October.

Half-brother to the fairly useful 2-y-o listed 7f Sweet Solera Stakes winner Catwalk, to the fair 2-y-o 6f winner Mood Swings (both by Shirley Heights) and the modest 6f all-weather winner Pup's Pride (by Efisio). The dam, a useful 2-y-o listed 5f winner, was fourth in the Group 1 Coronation Stakes and is a half-sister to 6 winners including the French listed winner Dazzling Heights. The second dam, Cape Chestnut (by Bustino), was a quite useful 3-y-o 1m winner and a half-sister to the US Grade 2 winner Colway Rally. (Mr John D Pitt). *"A neat little horse, he hasn't grown an awful lot since we bought him and he looks an obvious 2-y-o type. We gave him some time and blistered him, but again he's always cantered very well. He has a good temperament and I like him".*

---

281 - MUBKERA (IRE) *   [85]   ch.f. Nashwan – Na-Ayim (Shirley Heights).
May 5. Fifth foal.

Sister to the fair 1999 3-y-o 7.6f winner Hishmah and half-sister to Wa-Naam (by Cadeaux Genereux), unplaced in one start over 6f at 2 yrs in 2000 and the quite useful 10f winner Tajawuz (by Kris). The dam was a modest 2-y-o 6f winner, is closely related to a winner by Slip Anchor and a half-sister to 2 winners by Nashwan (the sire of this filly). The second dam, Christabelle (by Northern Dancer), was placed at 2 yrs in Ireland and is a half-sister to the outstanding broodmare Slightly Dangerous (dam of Commander In Chief, Warning, Dushyantor, Deploy and Yashmak) and to the dams of Rainbow Quest and Scenic. (Hamdan Al-Maktoum). *"Still in Dubai in early April".*

---

282 - MULABEE (USA) **   [79]   b.br.c. Gulch – Shir Dar (Lead On Time).
January 5. Second foal. $120,000Y. Keeneland September.

The dam won 6 races in France (at 2 and 3 yrs) and the USA including the Grade 2 Palomar Handicap and is a half-sister 6 minor winners. The second dam, Irish Sea (by Irish River), is a placed half-sister to 9 winners including the Group 3 12f Meld Stakes winner Sailor's Mate (the dam of 2 listed winners) and Grecian Sea (dam of the Yorkshire Oaks and Ribblesdale Stakes winner Hellenic). (Mr Mohammed Jaber). *"He was a small horse but he's grown, thickened out and done well. He'll never be over-big and is beginning to look like a seven furlong/mile horse as he doesn't possess the sort of speed as some of the others, but he looks a 2-y-o type".*

---

283 - NIGHT AURORA **   [81]   ch.c. Pennekamp – India Atlanta (Ahonoora).
February 17. Eighth foal. 180,000Y. Tattersalls October.

Half-brother to the modest 2000 6f placed 2-y-o Big John (by Cadeaux Genereux), to the smart English 2-y-o and subsequent US Grade 2 1m and German Group 3 1m winner Ventiquattrofogli (by Persian Bold), the German 6f to 11f listed winner Irish Fighter (by Persian Heights), the French and Italian winner Fairy Hoof (by Fairy King) and the Italian 2-y-o winner and listed-placed Suspiria (by Glenstal). The dam is an unraced half-sister to 5 winners including the German Group 3 1m winner Sinyar. The second dam, Place Of Honour (by Be My Guest), won once at 3 yrs and is out of the Coronation Stakes winner Sutton Place. (Mr Saeed Suhail). *"Nice. We paid a lot of money for this colt. He was a neat little horse when we bought him, then just grew and just looked a bit weak. But he's filling out well and has tremendous hind quarters. He'll be relatively well-forward and looks an obvious 2-y-o type from the mid-season onwards. He goes well and I'm pleased with him".*

---

284 - POWERFUL GAZE (IRE) *   [74]   ch.c. Nashwan – Hiwaayati (Shadeed).
April 2. Fifth foal.

Half-brother to Twilight Haze (by Darshaan), unplaced in one start over 1m at 2 yrs in 2000 and to the useful 1m winner and 1m listed placed Sweet Emotion (by Bering). The dam is an unraced half-sister

to the very smart colt Great Commotion (winner of the Group 3 6f Cork and Orrery Stakes and the Group 3 7f Beeswing Stakes and second in both the July Cup and the Irish Two Thousand Guineas) and to the smart performer Lead on Time (winner of the Group 2 7f Criterium de Maisons-Laffitte and the Group 2 6.5f Prix Maurice de Gheest). The second dam, Alathea (by Lorenzaccio), showed no form but is a half-sister to the good 2-y-o R.B.Chesne and is out of Vive la Reine - a winning half-sister to Vaguely Noble. *"Still in Dubai in early April"*.
Significant sire/damsire crosses:- Bint Shadayid.

285 - SWEET BAND (USA) ** [93]

b.c. Dixieland Band – Sweetheart (Mr Prospector).
March 16. First foal. $190,000Y.

The dam won at 2 yrs in France and at 3 yrs in the USA. The second dam, Gorgeous (by Slew O'Gold), won 8 races in the USA including three Grade 1 events and is a half-sister to the Grade 1 Kentucky Oaks winner Seaside Attraction (herself dam of the US Grade 1 winners Golden Attraction and Cape Town), the Canadian dual Grade 3 winner Key to the Moon, the Group 3 Princess Margaret Stakes winner Hiamm and the dam of the Hong Kong Cup and Man O'War Stakes winner Fantastic Light. (Mr Abdullah Ali). *"A lovely horse but not an early type. He moves well, has a good temperament and covers the ground nicely but he's not one of the more forward 2-y-o's. We'll be looking to introduce him towards the back-end"*.
Significant sire/damsire crosses:- Chimes Band (Gr 2), Didyme (Gr 2), Love That Jazz (Gr 3), Southern Rhythm (Gr 3), Jazz Club (Gr 3).

286 - TOLCEA (IRE) * [83]

ch.c. Barathea – Mosaique Bleue (Shirley Heights).
April 16. Sixth foal. IR£60,000Y. Goffs Orby.

Closely related to the Group 2 King Edward VII Stakes and subsequent US Graded stakes winner Subtle Power (by Sadler's Wells) and half-brother to the promising 2000 6f placed 2-y-o Arhaaf (by Danehill), the fairly useful Irish 7f to 9f winner Almazhar (by Last Tycoon) and the quite useful 9f winner Poker School (by Night Shift). The dam is an unraced half-sister to the Prix Royal-Oak winner Mersey, to the 10f Prix Saint-Alary winner Muncie and to the dam of the Irish Group 3 winner Morcote and the Irish listed winner Miami Sands (subsequently Grade 1 placed in the USA). The second dam, Martingale (by Luthier), won twice over 1m at 3 yrs and is a half-sister to the Prix du Moulin winner Mount Hagen and to the French One Thousand Guineas and Prix de Diane winner Madelia (herself dam of the Prix Saint-Alary winner Moonlight Dance). (Mohammed Ali). *"A colt that's grown and changed and has had niggling little problems doing that. He's cantering now and the penny is beginning to drop. He's done his growing but it's too early to tell"*.
Significant sire/damsire crosses:- Barafamy, Barathea Guest.

287 - WAHCHI (IRE) ** [96]

ch.c. Nashwan – Nafhaat (Roberto).
February 26. Eighth foal.

Closely related to the quite useful 2000 7f and 1m placed 2-y-o Ranin (by Unfuwain) and half-brother to the very useful 7f and 1m winner Ghalib (by Soviet Star), the useful 1998 2-y-o 6.5f and 7f winner Qhazeenah (by Marju), the quite useful 6f (at 2 yrs) and 1m winner Mihnah (by Lahib) and the quite useful 7.6f and 10f winner Hadeel (by Polish Precedent). The dam, a fairly useful 12f winner, stayed 15f. The second dam, Distant Horizon (by Exclusive Native), was a lightly raced sister to Sisterhood, a US Grade 1 turf winner over 12f and a half-sister to the smart French middle-distance filly Sweet Rhapsody. *"Not yet arrived from Dubai but I've seen him, I like him and he seems to move well. They certainly speak highly of him over there and he's one to keep a close eye on"*.

288 - WELL CHOSEN * [87]

b.c. Sadler's Wells – Hawajiss (Kris).
February 11. Third foal.

Half-brother to Royal Kiss (by Royal Academy), unplaced in 2 starts at 2 yrs in 2000. The dam was a smart winner of 4 races including the Group 3 1m May Hill Stakes (at 2 yrs), the Group 2 10f Nassau Stakes and the Group 3 10.4f Musidora Stakes. The second dam, Canadian Mill (by Mill Reef), was a smart 2-y-o 6f winner and was second in the Group 1 6f Cheveley Park Stakes but failed to train on at 3 yrs. (Maktoum Al-Maktoum). *"Not yet in training in early April"*.
Significant sire/damsire crosses:- Moonshell, Samsaam.

289 - UNNAMED * [78] b.c. Revoque – Forelino (Trempolino).
April 16. Fifth foal. 17,000Y. Tattersalls October.
Half-brother to the quite useful 12f and hurdles winner Tough Act (by Be My Chief) and to the modest dual 12f seller winner Maiella (by Salse). The dam was a modest 3-y-o 10.5f winner and is a half-sister to one winner. The second dam, Forelie (by Formidable), a quite useful 2-y-o 6f winner, is a half-sister to the Italian Derby winner My Top and to the dam of the German Grade 2 winner Baroon and the Group 3 Prix de Saint-Georges winner Struggler. (Stars and Stripes). *"A good-looking horse, he's done well and will be a seven furlong type 2-y-o. I haven't done that much with him but he moves well and I like him".*

290 - UNNAMED * [81] ch.c. Diesis – Golden Vale (Slew O'Gold).
February 19. First foal. $70,000Y. Keeneland September.
The dam, a stakes-placed winner in the USA, is out of the US stakes winner and Grade 1 Arlington-Washington Lassie Stakes second Maniches (by Val de l'Orne). (Saeed Abdullah Humaid). *"A horse we bought in America, he's a very attractive colt although he's just grown a bit and has gone a bit leggy. He'll probably take a bit longer but he's very athletic, he moves well and is a fairly typical Diesis. I'm happy with him".*

291 - UNNAMED * [68] b.br.c. Atticus – No Rego (Riverman).
January 28. Second foal. $130,000Y. Keeneland September.
The dam is an unplaced half-sister to 5 winners including the useful Free Thinker, a 1m winner in England and Italy and second in the listed Derrinstown Stud One Thousand Guineas Trial. The second dam, Top Hope (by High Top), a very useful 2-y-o 7f winner and second in the Group 3 12f Lancashire Oaks, is a half-sister to the smart colt Wylfa and to the Italian Group 3 winner Pretty Pol - herself dam of the listed winner Polka Dancer. (Saeed Abdullah Humaid). *"I thought he was going to be earlier than he's proved to be. He always moved well but he's just gone leggy and a little bit light on us. With time he'll fill out, his temperament looks good and he's doing everything asked of him at the moment".*

J DUNLOP

292 - AJEEL (IRE) * [89] b.c. Green Desert – Samheh (Private Account).
February 17. Third foal. IR£38,000Y. Goffs Orby.
Half-brother to the fairly useful 1999 2-y-o 7f winner Marah (by Unfuwain). The dam, a modest 7f placed 2-y-o, stayed 10f and is a half-sister to 4 winners. The second dam, Lucky Lucky Lucky (by Chieftain), won the Grade 1 Kentucky Oaks and the Grade 1 Matron Stakes in the USA and is a half-sister to the US stakes winner and Grade 1 placed Fast Forward. (Hamdan Al-Maktoum). *"Still in Dubai until the end of April".*

293 - ANGEL OF THE GWAUN (IRE) * [83] b.f. Sadler's Wells – Ballerina (Dancing Brave).
May 15. Fourth foal.
The dam, a quite useful 2-y-o 7f winner, is a half-sister to the very useful 6f (at 2 yrs) and Group 3 12f Princess Royal Stakes winner Dancing Bloom, to the useful 10f winner Cloudy Sky (both by Sadler's Wells) and the good French 2-y-o 5f winner and One Thousand Guineas third River Dancer (herself dam of the Champion Stakes winner Spectrum). The second dam, Dancing Shadow (by Dancer's Image), a very useful filly, won over 1m and 10f including the Sean Graham Fillies Stakes and is a half-sister to the top-class Oaks winner Sun Princess and the high-class middle-distance colt Saddlers Hall. (Mr L Neil Jones). *"Very nice, but she's a late foal and a backward 2-y-o".*
Significant sire/damsire crosses:- Beat Hollow (Gr 1).

294 - ATARAMA (IRE) ** [74] b.f. Sadler's Wells – Regal Portrait (Royal Academy).
February 5. Third foal. 400,000Y. Tattersalls Houghton.
Half-sister to the Italian winner of 5 races (including at 2 yrs) and listed-placed King's Ivory (by Lake Coniston). The dam, a moderate maiden, is a half-sister to the top-class colt King's Theatre (by Sadler's Wells), winner of the Group 1 Racing Post Trophy, the Group 1 King George VI and Queen Elizabeth Diamond Stakes and second in both the Epsom Derby and the Irish Derby and to the champion 2-y-o colt High Estate. The second dam, Regal Beauty (by Princely Native), was unplaced in two starts and is a half-sister to 8 minor winners. (The Thoroughbred Corporation). *"This is a very good-looking filly and she'll make a 2-y-o by mid-summer".*

295 - BELLBOTTOM * [71]   b.c. Mtoto – Satin Bell (Midyan).
April 8. Second foal.

The dam, a useful 7f winner, is a half-sister to several winners including the useful listed 6f winner Star Tulip. The second dam, Silk Petal (by Petorius), a useful German listed 1m winner and third in the Group 3 10.5f Prix de Flore, is a half-sister to numerous winners including the dam of the Group 2 12f Ribblesdale Stakes winner Fairy Queen. (Mr Nicholas Jones). *"A small, sharp colt, he'll be racing from July or August".*

296 - DAANA * [76]   b.f. Green Desert – Shining Water (Riverman).
February 25. Sixth foal. 50,000Y. Tattersalls October.

Closely related to the fair 10f all-weather winner Bold Precedent (by Polish Precedent) and half-sister to the French listed 12f winner and Group 3 10.5f Prix de Flore third Blue Water and the French middle-distance winner of 5 races and Group 3 Prix la Force third Norton Sound (both by Bering). The dam won once over 10f in France at 3 yrs and is a half-sister to the French Group-placed winner Shimmer. The second dam, Radiance (by Blakeney), won the Group 3 10.5f Prix Corrida and is out of the Prix de Royallieu winner Sybarite. (Kuwait Racing Syndicate). *"Daana will be a relatively early 2-y-o, expect her to be racing by the end of May or early June".*

297 - DUSTY ANSWER * [78]   b.f. Zafonic – Dust Dancer (Suave Dancer).
March 13. First foal. 120,000Y. Tattersalls Houghton.

The dam won 4 races including the Group 3 10f Prix de la Nonette and is a half-sister to 5 winners including the Group 3 7.3f Fred Darling Stakes winner Bulaxie (herself dam of the listed winner Claxon) and the dual French listed winner Zimzalabim. The second dam, Galaxie Dust (by Blushing Groom, a quite useful 2-y-o 6f winner, is a half-sister to 2 minor winners. (Hesmonds Stud). *"This is a very nice filly and I'd expect her to be ready for mid-season".*

298 - EB AAD (USA) * [93]   b.f. Gone West – Oumaldaaya (Nureyev).
May 6. Sixth foal.

Closely related to the 2000 unraced 2-y-o Moondafa (by Gulch) and to the fair 6f (at 2yrs) to 8.2f placed Intizaa (both by Mr Prospector) and half-brother to the smart 7f (at 2 yrs) and 9f listed winner Haami and the fairly useful 1996 2-y-o 1m winner Asas (both by Nashwan). The dam, a very useful filly, won over 7f at 2yrs and the Group 2 10f Premio Lydia Tesio and listed 10f Lupe Stakes at 3 yrs. She is a half-sister to the 1994 Derby winner Erhaab out of the French 10.5f winner Histoire (by Riverman), herself a half-sister to the smart Group 3 Prix de la Porte Maillot winner Hamanda. (Hamdan Al-Maktoum). *"Still in Dubai until late April".*

299 - ENCORE MY LOVE ** [64]   b.f. Royal Applause – Lady Be Mine (Sir Ivor).
February 11.

Half-sister to the top-class 1989 2-y-o Be My Chief, winner of the Group 1 1m Racing Post Trophy, the Solario Stakes and the Lanson Champagne Stakes etc., to the fairly useful 9f to 14.6f winner Chief Bee (both by Chief's Crown), the 2-y-o 5f winner Run Little Lady (by J O Tobin), the 1m winner Albemine (by Al Nasr) and the 11.8f winner Kota (by Kris) – all fair winners. The dam, a minor 3-y-o 1m winner at Yarmouth, is a half-sister to Mixed Applause, dam of the high-class miler Shavian and the Gold Cup winner Paean. The second dam, My Advantage (by Princely Gift), won over 5f at 2 yrs and is a half-sister to the dam of Marwell. (Mrs Mark Burrell). *"One of my earliest 2-y-o's, she'll be racing in May".*

300 - ESGRIMA (IRE) [82]   b.f. Sadler's Wells – Lavinia Fontana (Sharpo).
May 23. Second foal.

Half-sister to the very promising 2000 2-y-o 6f winner Oreana (by Anabaa). The dam was a very smart sprinter and winner of the Group 1 6f Haydock Sprint Cup, the Group 2 6f Premio Umbria, the Group 3 5f Prix du Petit-Couvert and the Group 3 7f Premio Chiusura. The second dam, Belle Origine (by Exclusive Native), a minor winner over 9.5f at 3 yrs in France, is a half-sister to the French listed stakes winners Bel Sorel and My Volga Boatman. (Mr Cyril Humphris). *"A very late foal, she's turned out at the moment".*

301 - FAYDAH (USA) * [82]   b.f. Bahri – Lady Cutlass (Cutlass).
February 25.

Closely related to the top-class Group 1 1m Queen Elizabeth II Stakes and Group 2 1m Queen Anne Stakes winner Lahib and to the useful 1997 10f winner Eshtiaal (both by Riverman) and half-sister to the smart 1994 2-y-o 6f winner and Group 3 1m Craven Stakes third Nwaamis, the useful 7f (at 2 yrs) and listed 1m winner Hawriyah (both by Dayjur), the very useful US miler Maceo (by Nodouble), the fairly useful 7f and 1m winner Sajjaya (by Blushing Groom) and minor winners by Halo and Northern Baby. The dam won three races from 5f to 7f in the USA and was stakes placed. She is a half-sister to 10 winners including the high-class French middle distance colt General Holme, the Del Mar Oaks and Vanity Handicap winner Commisary and General Store - grandam of Al Bahathri. (Hamdan Al-Maktoum). *"Still in Dubai until late April".*

302 - FOLIE DE GRANDEUR (USA) * [75]   ch.f. Hennessy – Shameem (Nureyev).
February 16. Fourth foal.

Half-sister to a minor US winner by Warning and a winner in Barbados by Groom Dancer. The dam is an unplaced half-sister to 8 winners including Lucky Lucky Lucky, winner of the Grade 1 Kentucky Oaks and the Grade 1 Matron Stakes and the US stakes winner and Grade 1 placed Fast Forward. The second dam, Just One More Time (by Raise A Native), won 3 races in the USA. (Mr Robin F Scully). *"This is a good-looking filly that will make a 2-y-o by mid-season".*

303 - GOLDTHROAT (IRE) ** [78]   b.f. Zafonic – Winger (In The Wings).
March 24. Second foal. IR£100,000Y. Goffs Orby.

Half-sister to the quite useful 2000 2-y-o 5f winner Warrior Wings (by Indian Ridge). The dam, a fair Irish 9f winner, is a half-sister to several winners including the smart 1m winner Killer Instinct and the very useful 2-y-o 7f winner and Group 1 Hoover Fillies Mile second Pick of the Pops. The second dam, Rappa Tap Tap (by Tap On Wood), was a useful winner of 3 races from 6f to 1m including the Blue Seal Stakes and is a half-sister to the Irish Oaks winner Colorspin (herself dam of the top-class colt Opera House and the Ascot Gold Cup winner Kayf Tara), the Group 2 Prix de l'Opera winner Bella Colora (dam of the high-class colt Stagecraft) and the Irish Champion Stakes winner Cezanne. (Mrs Sonia Rogers). *"A nice filly that should make a 2-y-o by the summer".*

304 - GOODWOOD HOUSE (IRE) * [61]   ch.f. Grand Lodge – Business Centre (Digamist).
March 16. Third foal. 25,000Y. Tattersalls October.

Half-sister to the modest 2000 5f and 6f placed 2-y-o Alexander Star (by Inzar). The dam was placed 4 times at up to 7f in Ireland and is a half-sister to 4 winners including the listed-placed Souk (herself dam of the listed winner Puce). The second dam, Soumana (by Pharly), is an unraced half-sister to the top-class broodmare Dumka, winner of the French One Thousand Guineas and dam of the Group winners Doyoun, Dalsaan, Dafayna and Dolpour. (Goodwood Racehorse Owners Group). *"This filly is quite forward and should be racing from mid-May onwards".*

305 - GOODWOOD PROMISE *** [83]   b.c. Primo Dominie – Noble Destiny (Dancing Brave).
March 24. Seventh foal. 20,000Y. Tattersalls October.

Brother to the useful dual 5f winner (including at 2 yrs) Noble One and half-brother to the unraced 2000 2-y-o Sunsu Desura (by Rainbow Quest), the fairly useful 10f winner Maiden Castle (by Darshaan), the 1m all-weather and German 10f winner Noble Investment (by Shirley Heights) and a winner in Dubai by Lion Cavern. The dam was a fairly useful 2-y-o 7f winner. The second dam, Tender Loving Care (by Final Straw), a useful winner over 7f at 2 yrs, was second in the Group 3 1m May Hill Stakes and a half-sister to 9 winners including the May Hill Stakes winner Satinette. (Goodwood Racehorse Owners Group). *"An early 2-y-o type, he'll be racing from May onwards".*
Significant sire/damsire crosses:- Primo Valentino.

306 - HAKAM (USA) * [81]   ch.c. Woodman – Haniya (Caerleon).
March 16. Third foal.

Brother to the quite useful 1999 2-y-o 7f winner Atwaar and half-brother to the promising 2000 2-y-o 7.6f winner Zulfaa (by Bahri). The dam, a fairly useful 12f winner, is a half-sister to the very smart US Grade 2 Bernard Baruch Handicap winner and Grade 1 Rothmans International and Group 1 Prix de la Salamandre placed Volochine, to the stayer Mawared, the 1m (at 2 yrs) and listed 14.8f winner Kahtan, the middle-distance winner Ghataas and the sprinter Sakha - all very useful. The second dam, Harmless Albatross (by Pas de Seul), a very useful French filly, won the Group 3 1m Prix des Chenes at 2 yrs and a 1m listed event at 3 yrs and is a half-sister to the Group 2 10f Prix d'Harcourt winner Fortune's Wheel and the very useful French 5.5f (at 2 yrs) and 1m winner Libertine. (Hamdan Al-Maktoum). *"Still in Dubai until the end of April".*

307 - HIM OF DISTINCTION * [81]   br.c. Rainbow Quest – Air Of Distinction (Distinctly North).
April 19. Second foal.

Closely related to the quite useful 2000 2-y-o 6f winner Man Of Distinction (by Spectrum). The dam, a useful 2-y-o winner of the Group 3 6.3f Anglesey Stakes at the Curragh, is a sister to the French listed winner Rabican and a half-sister to 5 winners including the very useful Kayfa, a winner of 4 listed events in Ireland from 1m to 10f. The second dam, Kaysama (by Kenmare), a winning French sprinter, is a half-sister to 3 listed winners. (Normandie Stud). *"This is a very nice colt that won't be seen out until the second half of the season".*

308 - IN DISGUISE ** [88]   ch.c. Nashwan – Conspiracy (Rudimentary).
January 23. First foal.

The dam, a useful 2-y-o listed 5f winner, is a half-sister to the smart Group 2 10f Sun Chariot Stakes winner Ristna, to the 6f Sandy Lane Stakes and 7f Oak Tree Stakes winner Gayane and the 7f Beeswing Stakes winner Shahid. The second dam, Roussalka (by Habitat), won 7 races at up to 10f including the Coronation Stakes and the Nassau Stakes (twice) and is a half-sister to the Fillies Triple Crown winner Oh So Sharp (herself dam of the Prix Saint Alary winner Rosefinch). (The Earl Cadogan). *"A very nice colt by Nashwan, he should be running in the second half of the season".*

309 - I SWEAR * [74]   b.c. Barathea – Karlafsha (Top Ville).
January 30. Seventh foal. 875,000Y. Tattersalls Houghton.

Half-brother to the French winner of 4 races and listed 1m and 10f placed Karliyka (by Last Tycoon), the unraced 2000 2-y-o Kalimar (by Bigstone) and 2 minor winners in France by Darshaan and Doyoun. The dam won twice in France including the listed 1m Prix des Lilas, was fourth in the Group 2 9.2f Prix de l'Opera and is a half-sister to the US stakes winner Kanatiyr, the German listed winner Dream For Future and to the dams of the Group or listed winners Air Of Distinction, Kayfa, Rabican, Proud Native and Karikata. The second dam, Karosa (by Caro), won once in France and was second in the Group 3 5f Prix d'Arenberg. (The Thoroughbred Corporation). *"A big colt I expect will be out sometime from the mid-season onwards".*

310 - ITHRAIR (IRE) * [88]   ch.c. Machiavellian – Saleemah (Storm Bird).
February 27. Second foal.

Brother to the 2000 2-y-o Medraar, unplaced in one start over 7f. The dam, a useful winner of 3 races at around 1m at 3 yrs, is a half-sister to 2 winners in the USA. The second dam, Retire (by Secretariat), was unplaced twice. (Hamdan Al-Maktoum). *"Still in Dubai until the end of April".*
Significant sire/damsire crosses:- Medicean (Gr 2).

311 - KARAMAH * [84]   b.f. Unfuwain – Azdihaar (Mr Prospector).
March 15. Third foal.

Half-sister to the quite useful 2000 7f placed 2-y-o Mosaaim (by Nashwan) and to the useful 6.5f winner Sand Pigeon (by Lammtarra). The dam, a quite useful dual 7f at 3 yrs is a half-sister to the high-class and genuine filly Shadayid, winner of the One Thousand Guineas and the Prix Marcel Boussac and placed in the Coronation Stakes, the Sussex Stakes and the Queen Elizabeth II Stakes and to the very useful listed 7f winner and Jersey Stakes third Dumaani (by Danzig). The second dam, Desirable (by Lord Gayle), won the Group 1 6f Cheveley Park Stakes and the 6f Princess Margaret Stakes, was third in the One Thousand Guineas and is a half-sister to the Irish Oaks winner Alydaress, the Cheveley Park winner Park Appeal and the very useful middle-distance colt Nashamaa. (Hamdan Al-Maktoum). *"In Dubai until late April".*
Significant sire/damsire crosses:- Lahan.

312 - LOVE APPEAL (IRE) [65]   ch.f. Singspiel – Royale (Royal Academy).
March 27. First foal. 45,000Y. Tattersalls Houghton.

The dam, an Irish 3-y-o 7f and 1m (listed) winner, is a half-sister to 3 winners. The second dam, Societe Royale (by Milford), is an unraced half-sister to the Prix de l'Abbaye and Kings Stand Stakes winner

Double Form and the Lupe Stakes winner Scimitarra. (The Thoroughbred Corporation). *"A lightly-made 2-y-o filly, she'll be racing from June or July onwards".*

---

313 - MAID TO PERFECTION **   [81]   b.f. Sadler's Wells – Maid For The Hills (Indian Ridge).
March 31. Second foal.
Half-sister to the quite useful 2000 2-y-o 6f winner Green Tambourine (by Green Desert). The dam was a useful 2-y-o and won twice over 6f including the listed Empress Stakes. She is a half-sister to 3 winners including the Group 3 6f Princess Margaret Stakes second Maid For Walking and to the placed dam of the Empress Stakes winner and Nassau Stakes second Lady In Waiting. The second dam, Stinging Nettle (by Sharpen Up), was a fairly useful 2-y-o listed 6f winner and a half-sister to the smart miler Whistlefield and the Group 2 1m Royal Lodge Stakes winner Gairloch. (Normandie Stud). *"A very nice filly for September onwards".*

---

314 - MASSARRA ***   [94]   b.f. Danehill – Rafha (Kris).
April 9.
Closely related to the smart 1999 2-y-o listed 6f winner Invincible Spirit (by Green Desert) and half-sister to Aquarius (by Royal Academy), unplaced in one start at 2 yrs in 2000, to the smart 7.6f (at 2 yrs) to 14f winner and St Leger fourth Sadian (by Shirley Heights), the useful 14f and 2m winner Fnan (by Generous) and the useful dual 1m (at 2 yrs) and 11.8f winner Al Widyan (by Slip Anchor). The dam, a very smart winner from 6f (at 2 yrs) to 11.5f including the Group 1 10.5f Prix de Diane, the Group 3 Lingfield Oaks Trial and the Group 3 May Hill Stakes, is a half-sister to the 2-y-o 7f winner Fayfa and to the middle-distance winners Alkhafji and Sarawat - all fairly useful. The second dam, Eljazzi (by Artaius), a fairly useful 2-y-o 7f winner, is a half-sister to the good miler Pitcairn and to Dingle Bay (dam of the smart stayer Assessor) out of the Yorkshire Oaks and Park Hill Stakes second Border Bounty. (Prince A A Faisal). *"This filly should make a 2-y-o by May or early June".*
Significant sire/damsire crosses:- Kissing Cousin (Gr 1).

---

315 - NAJAYEB (USA) *   [89]   b.f. Bahri - Thawakib (Sadler's Wells).
February 8. Fifth foal.
Sister to the unraced 2000 2-y-o Khazayin and to the high-class 1m (at 2 yrs), Group 3 10f Thresher Classic Trial and Group 3 10.4f Dante Stakes winner and Derby second Sakhee. Closely related to the useful 7f (at 2 yrs) and 10f winner Nasheed (by Riverman) and half-sister to the fairly useful 1997 2-y-o 7f winner Alharir (by Zafonic). The dam, a useful filly, won twice over 7f (at 2 yrs) and the Group 2 12f Ribblesdale Stakes. She is a half-sister to numerous winners including the top-class middle-distance colt Celestial Storm (winner of the Group 2 Princess of Wales's Stakes) and to the placed dam of the Group 1 Rothmans International winner River Memories. The second dam, Tobira Celeste (by Ribot), won twice at up to 9f in France, was third in the Group 3 12f Prix de Minerve and is a half-sister to the smart French filly A Thousand Stars. (Hamdan Al-Maktoum). *"Still in Dubai until the end of April".*

---

316 - NAYYEL ***   [104]   b.c. Zafonic – The Perfect Life (Try My Best).
January 29.
Half-brother to the very smart 7f (at 2 yrs) and Group 3 12f Gordon Stakes winner Rabah, to the useful 2-y-o 6f winner and Group 1 Cheveley Park Stakes third Najiya and the fairly useful 1m winner Muhtafel (all by Nashwan). The dam won the Group 3 5f Prix du Bois and the listed 7f Prix Imprudence and was second in the Group 2 Prix Robert Papin. She is a full sister to the top-class colt Last Tycoon (winner of the Grade 1 Breeders Cup Mile, the Group 1 Kings Stand Stakes and the Group 1 William Hill Sprint Championship) and is closely related to the very useful Group 2 6f Premio Melton and Group 3 6f Goldene Peitsche winner Astronef. The second dam, Mill Princess (by Mill Reef), won over 10f at 3 yrs in France and is a half-sister to the Irish Sweeps Derby winner Irish Ball and to the top-class broodmare Irish Bird (dam of the classic winners Assert, Bikala and Eurobird). (Hamdan Al-Maktoum). *"Nayyel is a very strong colt and a nice 2-y-o. Watch out for him in June or July".*

---

317 - OLD CALIFORNIA (IRE)   [96]   b.c. Sadler's Wells – Turban (Glint Of Gold).
May 9. Eighth foal.
Closely related to the quite useful Irish 10f winner First Son (by Barathea), to the useful 1m and 8.5f winner Barboukh and the fair 1m and 11.8f winner Lovely Lyca (both by Night Shift) and half-brother to the fairly useful 2-y-o 6f winner Tricorne and the useful 8.5f winner Papaha (both by Green Desert). The dam, a fair 10f and 11.7f winner at 3 yrs, is a half-sister to the top-class French and Irish Derby

winner Old Vic and to the smart Group 3 Prix Foy winner Splash of Colour. The second dam, Cockade (by Derring Do), won over 1m at 3 yrs and is a sister to the Two Thousand Guineas winner and high-class sire High Top. (Mr L Neil Jones). *"A very backward 2-y-o, he won't appear on a racecourse until September at the earliest".*

---

318 - OLDER BROTHER * [80]   b.c. Dynaformer – Love And Affection (Exclusive Era).
May 1. Seventh foal. 85,000Y. Tattersalls Houghton.

Half-brother to the useful 2000 dual 7f 2-y-o winner Londoner (by Sky Classic) and to 4 minor winners in the USA including the 5.5f winner My Tru Luv (by Bolger) and the 9f winner My Affection (by Flying Paster). The dam, a winner from 5f to 1m including a minor stakes at 3 yrs, was previously second in the Grade 1 6f Spinaway Stakes at 2 yrs and is closely related to the 9.3f Prix d'Ispahan and Budweiser International Stakes winner Zoman. (The Thoroughbred Corporation). *"A very nice colt, he's a staying type but will be racing from the mid-season onwards".*

---

319 - PHOTO FLASH (IRE) * ** [86]   ch.f. Bahamian Bounty – Zoom Lens (Caerleon).
February 15. Fourth living foal.

Half-sister to the fairly useful 2-y-o dual 1m winner Close Up (by Cadeaux Genereux) and the fair 2-y-o 5f winner Blue Movie (by Bluebird). The dam, placed once over 7f at 2 yrs, is a half-sister to 4 winners including the useful sprinter Quick Snap and the middle-distance winner Itqan (herself dam of the Group 1 Gran Criterium and US Grade 3 winner Hello). The second dam, Photo (by Blakeney), a quite useful 1m and 9f winner, is a half-sister to 8 winners and to the unplaced dam of the Australian Grade 1 winner Nick's Joy. (Mr D Jamison). *"This filly is quite forward and she'll be racing in May or soon after".*

---

320 - PLYMSOLE (USA) * ** [82]   ch.f. Diesis – Pump (Forli).
March 15.

Sister to the very smart Group 2 1m Berlin Brandenburg Trophy and the Grade 2 1m Hong Kong Vase winner Docksider and half-sister to the Irish listed middle-distance winner Classic Sport (by Nijinsky), the French winner and listed 1m placed Filao Beach (by Alysheba) and minor US winners by Alleged and Nijinsky. The dam is an unraced daughter of the US 8.3f stakes winner Espadrille (by Damascus), herself a half-sister to Thatch, to the US Grade 1 winner King Pellinore and to the dams of Nureyev and the Group 1 National Stakes winner Fatherland. (Mrs Sonia Rogers). *"A nice 2-y-o filly to look out for from June onwards".*

Significant sire/damsire crosses:- Docksider.

---

321 - RA-BOOB (IRE) * [79]   b.f. Alhaarth - Harmless Albatross (Pas de Seul).
March 17.

Half-sister to the useful 1998 2-y-o dual 6f winner Sakha (by Wolfhound), to the very smart French 6f (at 2 yrs) to 10f winner and Grade 1 Rothmans International and Group 1 Prix de la Salamandre placed Volochine (by Soviet Star), the very useful stayer Mawared, the very useful 1m (at 2 yrs) and listed 14.8f winner Kahtan (both by Nashwan), the very useful middle-distance winner Ghataas (by Sadler's Wells) and the fairly useful 12f winner Haniya (by Caerleon). The dam, a very useful French filly, won the Group 3 1m Prix des Chenes at 2 yrs and a 1m listed event at 3 yrs. She is a half-sister to the Group 2 10f Prix d'Harcourt winner Fortune's Wheel and the very useful French 5.5f (at 2 yrs) and 1m winner Libertine. The second dam, North Forland (by Northfields), a useful 3-y-o 10f winner and second in the Ribblesdale Stakes, is a half-sister to the Prix Ganay winner Infra Green (herself dam of 4 good winners and grandam of the St Leger winner Toulon). (Hamdan Al-Maktoum). *"A nicely-bred filly but turned-out at the moment (mid-April)".*

---

322 - RED LIASON (IRE) * [78]   ch.f. Selkirk – Red Affair (Generous).
March 30. First foal.

The dam, an Irish listed 10f winner, is a half-sister to the smart 7.6f to 10f winner Brilliant Red and to the useful 12f to 14f winner and Group 3 2m Queens Vase third Kassab (by Caerleon). The second dam, Red Comes Up (by Blushing Groom), was placed 6 times in France and is a sister to Rainbow Quest. (Lady Clague). *"Keep an eye out for her from the mid-season onwards, she's a nice 2-y-o filly".*

323 - ROBE CHINOISE [68] b.f. Robellino – Kiliniski (Niniski).
March 15. Ninth foal.

Half-sister to the 3-y-o Kiruna (by Northern Park), to the fair 11.8f winner Kilshanny (by Groom Dancer) and the Belgian winner Green Kilt (by Green Desert). The dam was a very smart winner of the Group 3 12f Lingfield Oaks Trial, was second in the Epsom Oaks and was fourth in the Epsom Oaks and is a half-sister to 5 winners including the dam of the US Grade 2 winner Bienamado. The second dam, Kilavea (by Hawaii), a winner on her only start at 2 yrs over 5f at Goodwood, is a half-sister to Nureyev and to the dam of Sadlers Wells. (Miss K Rausing). *"A nice, backward filly, she's one for September time onwards".*

324 - SHAGRAAN [81] b.c. Darshaan – L'Ideale (Alysheba).
February 20. Third living foal. 500,000Y. Tattersalls Houghton.

Half-brother to the fairly useful 8.5f and 9f winner Aegean Dream (by Royal Academy). The dam, unplaced twice in France, is a half-sister to the Group 1 Grand Criterium winner Loup Solitaire and to the 9.3f Prix d'Ispahan winner Loup Sauvage. The second dam, Louveterie (by Nureyev), won the Group 3 9.5f Prix Vanteaux, was second in the 10.5f Prix de Diane and the 10f Prix Saint-Alary and is a half-sister to the French Group 2 winner Lascaux and the Group 3 winners Leonardo da Vinci, L'ile du Reve and Legend Of France. (The Thoroughbred Corporation). *"This is a very nice horse, but he won't be racing until the autumn".*

**325 - SNOWFIRE ** ** [92] b.f. Machiavellian – Hill Of Snow (Reference Point).
March 27. Third foal.

Half-sister to the unraced Irish 2000 2-y-o Valley Of Song and to the smart 1999 2-y-o Group 1 7f Moyglare Stud Stakes winner Preseli (both by Caerleon). The dam, an Irish 10f winner, is a half-sister to the smart Group 2 Prix de Pomone winner Whitehaven. The second dam, White Star Line (by Northern Dancer), won the Alabama Stakes, the Delaware Oaks and the Kentucky Oaks (all Grade 1 events) and is a half-sister to the Prix Morny winner Filiberto and to the dam of the US Grade 1 winner On The Sly and the 10.5f Prix de Diane and 12f Prix Vermeille winner Northern Trick. (Mr L Neil Jones). *"Snowfire is a very nice filly and one to look out for from mid-season onwards".*

326 - SNOW LEOPARD (IRE) * [80] gr.c. Highest Honor – Leopardess (Ela-Mana-Mou).
March 5. Third foal. IRE33,000Y. Goffs Orby.

Half-brother to the 2000 Irish placed 2-y-o Madaama (by Alzao). The dam, a quite useful 3-y-o 10f winner, is a sister to the Irish listed 14f winner Na-Ammah and a half-sister to the Group 2 Queen Anne Stakes and the Group 2 Sea World International Stakes winner Alflora. The second dam, Adrana (by Bold Lad, Ire), won over 5f at 2 yrs on her only start and is a half-sister to the top-class middle-distance stayer Ardross, the Prix de Flore winner Gesedeh and the 12f Galtres Stakes winner Larrocha. (Susan Abbott Syndicate). *"This colt will be a nice 2-y-o from around June or July".*

327 - SPIELSONG (FR) [69] b.f. Singspiel – Germane (Distant Relative).
April 19. Third foal. FF480,000Y. Deauville August.

Half-sister to the useful 1m and 8.3f winner and listed placed Granted (by Cadeaux Genereux). The dam, a useful winner of the Group 3 7f Rockfel Stakes and placed in 2 listed events, is a half-sister to 5 winners including the very useful German 10f winner Fabriano. The second dam, Fraulein Tobin (by J O Tobin), a fair 1m winner, is a half-sister to the very smart 10f performer Running Stag out of the French One Thousand Guineas second Fruhlingstag. (Mrs Maria Mai Goransson). *"A backward filly at the moment, but she should be racing by mid-season".*

328 - TASHAWAK (IRE) * [75] b.f. Night Shift – Dedicated Lady (Pennine Walk).
February 7. Sixth foal. 200,000Y. Tattersalls October.

Half-sister to the 3-y-o Lady Emmaline (by Charnwood Forest), to the smart Group 2 12f Ribblesdale Stakes winner Fairy Queen (by Fairy King) and the fair 6f (at 2 yrs) and 1m winner Speedfit Too (by Scenic). The dam, a useful Irish 2-y-o 5f and 6f winner, is a half-sister to 4 winners including the German listed winner and Group 3 10.5f Prix de Flore third Silk Petal (herself dam of the listed Sandy Lane Stakes winner Star Tulip). The second dam, Salabella (by Sallust), is a placed half-sister to M-Lolshan, winner of the Irish St Leger and the Grosser Preis von Baden and placed in numerous Group races. (Hamdan Al-Maktoum). *"A backward filly but she should be racing towards the end of the season"*.

---

329 - THAQIB (IRE) * [88]
b.c. Sadler's Wells – Temple (Shirley Heights).
March 3. First foal. 320,000Y. Tattersalls Houghton.
The dam is an unraced half-sister to the quite useful 1992 2-y-o 5f to 6.5f winner Falsoola. The second dam, Favoridge (by Riva Ridge), won four races from 5f to 1m including the Group 3 Nell Gwyn Stakes and is a half-sister to the Queen Mary Stakes winner Amaranda. (Hamdan Al-Maktoum).
Significant sire/damsire crosses:- Hawker's News, Hunting Hawk, In The Wings, Legend Maker, Subtle Power. (Hamdan Al-Maktoum). *"Thaqib is a small, strong colt that will be racing this year from July onwards"*.

**330 - WAYLAAH ** ** [74]
b.f. Common Grounds – Inonder (Belfort).
April 13. Fifth foal. 36,000Y. Tattersalls October.
Sister to the fairly useful 1997 2-y-o Chips, a winner over 5f and 6f here and a German listed event over 7.5f, to the fairly useful 2-y-o 6f winner Aretino and the quite useful 3-y-o 5.7f winner Democracy and half-sister to the unraced 2000 2-y-o Black Rainbow (by Definite Article). The dam is an unplaced daughter of the fairly useful 12f to 2m winner Rainfall (by Relko), herself a half-sister to the John Smiths Magnet Cup winner Air Trooper and to the dam of the French Group 3 6f winner Three For Fantasy. (Kuwait Racing Syndicate). *"A relatively early filly and a 2-y-o type"*.
Significant sire/damsire crosses:- Rich Ground.

---

331 - WHAT A VIEW * [89]
b.c. Sadler's Wells – Ocean View (Gone West).
February 20. First foal. 400,000Y. Tattersalls Houghton.
The dam won 2 races in the USA, was second in the Grade 1 Oak Leaf Stakes and third in the Grade 1 Hollywood Oaks. She is a half-sister to the US stakes winner and multiple Graded stakes placed Jacksonport. The second dam, On The Brink (by Cox's Ridge), won twice in the USA and is a half-sister to the dams of numerous minor stakes winners. (The Thoroughbred Corporation). *"This colt will be a nice 2-y-o from June or July onwards"*.

---

332 - WHITE BRIDLE (IRE) * [80]
ch.f. Singspiel – Samira (Rainbow Quest).
February 23. First foal. 400,000Y. Tattersalls Houghton.
The dam, a minor 12f winner in Ireland, is a half-sister to 4 winners including the Group 3 12f Princess Royal Stakes winner Cunning. The second dam, Vice Vixen (by Vice Regent), is an unraced half-sister to 4 winners including the Group 2 10f Gallinule Stakes second Baltic Fox. (The Thoroughbred Corporation). *"A very nice filly, she'll make a 2-y-o by mid-season"*.

**333 - WISSAL (USA) ** ** [100]
b.f. Woodman – Wasnah (Nijinsky).
April 18. Fifth foal.
Half-sister to the top-class colt Bahri (by Riverman), a winner over 6f (at 2 yrs) and the Group 1 1m St James's Palace Stakes and Group 1 1m Queen Elizabeth II Stakes, to the fair 12f winner Winsa (both by Riverman) and to the very smart Bahhare (by Dayjur), winner of the Group 2 7f Laurent Perrier Champagne Stakes and third in the Champion Stakes. The dam, a fairly useful maiden, was placed five times from 7f (at 2 yrs) to 10.5f. She is closely related to the Group 3 Tetrarch Stakes winners Dance Bid and Northern Plain and a half-sister to the US Grade 2 winner Winglet. The second dam, Highest Trump (by Bold Bidder), won the Group 2 5f Queen Mary Stakes at Royal Ascot. (Hamdan Al-Maktoum). *"Still in Dubai until the end of April"*.

**334 - UNNAMED ** ** [100]
b.c. Sadler's Wells – Rain Queen (Rainbow Quest).
March 6. Second foal. 240,000Y. Tattersalls Houghton.
Brother to the 2000 Irish 3-y-o 2m 1f winner Mutahamis. The dam is an unraced half-sister to the Grade 2 E P Taylor Stakes and Group 3 Prix de Royaumont winner Truly A Dream. The second dam, Truly Special (by Caerleon), won the Prix de Royaumont, was placed in five Group events in France and is a half-sister to the French Group 2 winners Modhish and Russian Snows. (Mrs Michael Watt). *"A good-looking colt, he's by Sadler's Wells and out of a Rainbow Quest mare, but nonetheless I'd say he was a 2-y-o type"*.

335 - ARTIE * [60]   b.c. Whittingham – Calamanco (Clantime).
March 31. Third foal. 8,000Y. Doncaster St Leger.
Brother to the fair 2000 5f placed 3-y-o Worsted and half-brother to Kingscross (by King's Signet), unplaced in two starts at 2 yrs in 2000. The dam, a fair 5f winner at 3 and 4 yrs, is a sister to the sprint winner Cape Merino. The second dam, Laena (by Roman Warrior), is a placed half-sister to one minor winner. (Mr A Arton). *"Second at Doncaster on his first outing, he's very fast and he'll make a nice horse. I like him".*

336 - AUNTY MARY [57]   b.f. Common Grounds – Flirtation (Pursuit Of Love).
February 11. First foal. 31,000Y. Doncaster St Leger.
The dam ran unplaced once over 7f at 3 yrs and is a half-sister to 4 winners including the French listed winner and Group 2 placed Carmita and the useful 10f winner Ruscino. The second dam, Eastern Shore (by Sun Prince), was placed four times and stayed 12f and is a full or half-sister to 6 winners including the dams of the listed winners Airfield and Upper Strata (herself dam of the Prix de la Salamandre winner Lord Of Men). (Mr & Mrs J Cotton). *"She should make a 2-y-o but she's backward in her coat and needs some sun on her back".*

337 - BARTON BEAU (IRE) [54]   b.c. Kylian – Hetty Green (Bay Express).
February 11. Seventh foal. IR£30,000Y. Goffs Challenge.
Half-brother to the fairly useful 9.2f winner Barton Sands (by Tenby), to the Irish 2-y-o 6f winner Cohete (by Sallust), subsequently a winner in Hong Kong and the Irish 10f winner Sesame Heights (by High Estate). The dam, a minor 12f and hurdles winner in Ireland, is a half-sister to 6 winners including the Group 3 Princess Elizabeth Stakes winner Persian Market and the dam of the German Group 3 winner Last Midnight. The second dam, Londonderry Air (by Ballymoss), won at 2 yrs and is a half-sister to 9 winners here and abroad. (Sir Stanley Clarke). *"The sort to need seven furlongs this year, he's a nice type of colt".*

338 - CLASSIC CALVADOS (FR) ** [67]   b.c. Thatching – Mountain Stage (Pennine Walk).
April 18. Fifth foal. 19,000Y. Tattersalls October.
Brother to the quite useful 2000 2-y-o 5f winner Mountain Greenery and half-brother to the Italian 1m winner Alcatraz Jail (by Fayruz). The dam won over 10f and over hurdles in Ireland and is a half-sister to 2 winners. The second dam, Stage Lights (by Connaught), ran once unplaced and is a half-sister to 6 winners including the Lincoln Handicap winner King's Glory and the Group 1 Racing Post Trophy third Marcham. (Mr David Hilton Cox). *"A big horse, he's a nice type and looks like he'll be alright. Should make a 2-y-o".*

339 - DAISY BUTTONS (IRE) [71]   b.f. Bluebird – Centella (Thatching).
February 21. Fourth foal. IR£35,000Y. Goffs Challenge.
Half-sister to the modest 5f all-weather winner Cameo (by Statoblest). The dam was placed over 6f at 2 yrs in Ireland and is a half-sister to the Hong Kong Stewards Cup and Sha Tin Trophy winner Almante. The second dam, All Ashore (by Nureyev), is an unplaced half-sister to the Grade 1 National Stakes winner El Prado and the Group 3 Desmond Stakes winner Entitled. The third dam, Lady Capulet (by Sir Ivor), won the Irish One Thousand Guineas. (Mrs Jean P Connew). *"A nice sort of filly, but very backward in her coat at the moment".*

340 - DUSTY WUGG (IRE) * [58]   b.f. General Monash – Welsh Berry (Sir Ivor).
April 25. Ninth foal. IR£25,000Y. Goffs Challenge.
Half-sister to the moderate 7.5f to 9.2f winner Zahran (by Groom Dancer), to the 1998 Irish 3-y-o winner Hallucination (by Last Tycoon) and minor winners in Italy (by Fairy King) and the USA (by Law Society). The dam ran twice unplaced in France and is a half-sister to 13 winners including the US Grade 1 winners Avatar and Unconscious, the French Derby winner Hours After and the Group 2 Prix d'Harcourt winner Monseigneur. The second dam, Brown Berry (by Mount Marcy), won 6 races in the USA. (Mrs J Houghton). *"A nice filly, she looks like making a decent 2-y-o over five or six furlongs".*

341 - HAILWOOD (USA) * [76] b.c. Twining – Beat (Nijinsky).

March 7. Seventh foal. IR£42,000Y. Goffs Orby.

Half-brother to 3 winners including the quite useful 1995 3-y-o 10.5f winner Merry Festival (by Private Account), subsequently a winner over 11f in Dubai and a winner in France by Woodman. The dam, a winner of 4 races from 1m to 9f and Grade 3 placed in the USA, is a half-sister to the smart 7f and 1m winner and Group 1 St James's Palace Stakes third Lord Florey and to the US Grade 1 Maskette Stakes winner Too Chic (herself dam of the US Grade 1 winners Chic Shirine and Queena). The second dam, Remedia (by Dr Fager), won 4 races at 3 and 4 yrs in the USA at up to 1m and is a half-sister to the dam of the dual Ascot Gold Cup winner Sadeem. (Mr M Dawson). *"A beautiful looking colt, I hope he's as good as he looks. I'd expect him to make a 2-y-o by the middle of the year".*

---

342 - MISSING [74] b.f. Singspiel – Misbelief (Shirley Heights).

March 23. Second reported foal. 77,000Y. Tattersalls October.

Half-sister to the 3-y-o Far Into Night (by Polar Falcon). The dam won 5 races from 9.7f to 14f and is a half-sister to 5 winners. The second dam, Misguided (by Homing), was a useful sprint winner of 3 races and a half-sister to the listed Duke Of Edinburgh Stakes winner and Group 3 Hungerford Stakes third Missed Blessing (herself dam of the Group 3 winner Unblest). (Mr & Mrs J D Cotton). *"A very nice filly for seven furlongs or a mile at the back-end".*

---

343 - PASTICHIO MEDLEY * [68] b.c. Celtic Swing – Blue Nile (Bluebird).

March 24. Third foal. 23,000Y. Tattersalls October.

Half-brother to the fair 2000 2-y-o 7f winner Gone Too Far (by Reprimand). The dam, a fair 10f winner, is a half-sister to the Group 2 10f Prix Eugene Adam winner Revelation. The second dam, Angelus Chimes (by Northfields), a quite useful Irish 4-y-o 12f winner, is a half-sister to 4 winners. (Mr Ron George). *"A nice, seven furlong type 2-y-o".*

---

344 - RIDICULE * [66] b.c. Piccolo – Mockingbird (Sharpo).

February 23. Second foal. 34,000Y. Doncaster St Leger.

The dam, a modest 2-y-o 6f winner, is a half-sister to 2 winners including the French Group 2 third Anchor Clever. The second dam, Mountain Bluebird (by Clever Trick), a quite useful middle-distance winner, is a half-sister to 4 winners here and abroad. (Queensberry Thoroughbreds 1). *"A nice type of colt, he's biggish but should make a nice 2-y-o alright".*

---

345 - SANDERSTEAD ** [57] b.c. So Factual – Charnwood Queen (Cadeaux Genereux).

January 27. Second foal. 26,000Y. Doncaster St Leger.

Half-brother to the fairly useful 2000 2-y-o 6f winner Greenwood (by Emarati). The dam, a modest dual 6f winner at 3 yrs, is a half-sister to 3 winners including the Group 3 Beeswing Stakes third Sunstreak. The second dam, Florentynna Bay (by Aragon), a modest 2-y-o 5f winner, is a half-sister to the Group 1 5f Heinz 57Phoenix Stakes winner Superpower. (Chris & Antonia Deuters). *"He'll make a nice 2-y-o colt over six or seven furlongs".*

---

346 - SECRET SPOOF ** [66] b.c. Mind Games – Silver Blessings (Statoblest).

January 12. Third foal. 22,000Y. Doncaster St Leger.

The dam is an unraced half-sister to 5 winners including the Group 3 6f Cork And Orrery Stakes winner Sylvan Barbarosa. The second dam, The Silver Darling (by John Splendid), is a placed half-sister to 5 winners. (David & Steven Dudley). *"A nice little horse, he looks alright, will be suited by five or six furlongs and I quite like him".*

---

347 - TOUGH LOVE ** [86] ch.c. Pursuit Of Love – Food Of Love (Music Boy).

February 4. Fourth living foal. 22,000Y. Doncaster St Leger.

Half-brother to the quite useful 5f and 6.5f winner Branston Berry (by Mukaddamah) and the quite useful dual 5f winner Price Of Passion (by Dolphin Street). The dam, a very useful sprinter, won 6 races and was placed in the Group 3 King George Stakes and is a half-sister to 4 winners. The second dam, Shortbread (by Crisp And Even), was a useful 7f winner here and later won over 12f in Norway. (The Gordon Partnership). *"A very nice horse, I like him a lot and he'll be a decent 2-y-o".*

348 - VERONICA WARD (USA) [70]
b.f. Tinners Way – Ranales (Majestic Light).
January 23. Third foal. 40,000Y. Tattersalls October.
Half-sister to the fairly useful 1999 2-y-o 7f winner Fame At Last (by Quest For Fame). The dam, a minor 2-y-o 1m winner in the USA, is a half-sister to 9 winners including the listed 10f Virginia Stakes winner Rambushka and the Group 2 7f Laurent Perrier Champagne Stakes second Arokat. The second dam, Katsura (by Northern Dancer), won twice and was second in the Group 3 1m Brownstown Stakes and is a half-sister to 7 winners. (Jim McGrath & Reg Griffin). *"Despite her early foaling date, seven furlongs would be the minimum trip for her".*

349 - SILVER BAND * [75]
ch.f. Zilzal – Silver Braid (Miswaki).
March 5. Sixth foal. 21,000Y. Tattersalls October.
Half-sister to the unraced 2000 2-y-o Intrepidous (by Polar Falcon), to the fair 2000 3-y-o 1m winner Beading (by Polish Precedent) and to Kass Alhawa (by Shirley Heights), a fair winner of 7 races at up to 8.5f. The dam, a useful 2-y-o 7f winner, was second in the Group 3 7.3f Fred Darling Stakes and is a half-sister to 4 winners here and abroad. The second dam, Chalice Of Silver (by Graustark), is a placed half-sister to the Group 1 Premio Jockey Club e Coppa d'Oro winner Silvernesian and the US stakes winner and Grade 1 placed Native Plunder. (Mr G Pritchard-Gordon). *"A very good-looking filly, she'll definitely make a 2-y-o".*

C EGERTON

350 - CATCH FIRE (IRE) * [65]
b.f. Entrepreneur – Lyric Theatre (Seeking The Gold).
January 28. First foal. IR30,000Y. Tattersalls Fairyhouse.
The dam is an unraced daughter of the champion European 2-y-o of 1992 Lyric Fantasy (by Tate Gallery), a winner of 6 races including the Group 1 Keeneland Nunthorpe Stakes and the Group 3 Queen Mary Stakes. Lyric Fantasy is closely related to the Group 1 Dewhurst Stakes winner In Command and a half-sister to the Group 1 Middle Park Stakes and Group 1 Haydock Sprint Cup winner Royal Applause. (Mrs R F Lowe). *"Small as a yearling but growing now, she's a sharp filly and will come to hand quickly once she's through her growing stage. Not a big 2-y-o, she'll be suited by five or six furlongs this year".*

351 - FOOTNOTES (IRE) [73]
b.f. Alzao – Annotate (Groom Dancer).
February 20. First foal. IR22,000Y. Tattersalls Fairyhouse.
The dam is an unraced half-sister to one winner. The second dam, Sudeley (by Dancing Brave), won once at 3 yrs and is a half-sister to the high-class middle-distance colts Peacetime and Quiet Fling, to the Cambridgeshire winner Intermission (herself dam of the good sprinter Interval) and to the dams of the Group/Graded stakes winners Wandesta, De Quest and Flaming Torch. The third dam, Peace (by Klairon), won the 6f Blue Seal Stakes at 2 yrs and was second in the One Thousand Guineas Trial. (Mr C R Egerton). *"She's pulled a muscle and so won't be racing until late summer, but she's a nice filly and looks a typical Alzao".*

352 - UNNAMED * [75]
b.c. Revoque – Al Corniche (Bluebird).
April 6. First foal. 38,000Y. Tattersalls October.
Half-brother to the fair 2000 2-y-o 6f winner Lady Kinvarragh (by Brief Truce) and to the useful 1999 2-y-o 6f and 1m winner and Group 1 1m Gran Criterium second Whyome (by Owington). The dam, a modest 2-y-o 5f winner, stayed 1m 6f at 3 yrs and is a half-sister to the Irish 1m winner Noble Choice and the 11f to 1m 6f winner Nornax Lad - both fairly useful. The second dam, Naxos (by Big Spruce), won twice in the USA and is a half-sister to the Irish One Thousand Guineas winner Nicer and to the dam of the Italian Derby winner Passing Sale. (Chaddleworth partnership). *"A nice horse with scope and a bit of quality, he's just cantering at the moment and should be ready by mid-summer".*

353 - UNNAMED * [64]
ch.c. Efisio – Superspring (Superlative).
March 1. Second foal. 32,000Y. Tattersalls October.
Half-brother to the fair 2000 2-y-o 6f winner Our Destiny (by Mujadil). The dam is an unraced sister to the Group 1 5f Heinz 57 Phoenix Stakes winner Superpower and a half-sister to 4 winners. The second dam, Champ d'Avril (by Northfields), a fairly useful sprint winner of 2 races, is a half-sister to 2 minor winners. (Chaddleworth Partnership). *"He'll be ready in May and is a very tough, typical 2-y-o. I expect he'll be suited by six furlongs".*

354 - BOOBALA (IRE) ** [62]   b.f. General Monash – Best Swinger (Ela-Mana-Mou). April 21. Sixth foal. IR£40,000Y. Goffs Challenge.

Half-sister to the modest 2000 6f placed 2-y-o Scarteen Sister (by Eagle Eyed), to the useful 2-y-o 7f listed Somerville Tattersall Stakes winner Scarteen Fox (by Foxhound), the modest 2-y-o 7f seller winner Mari-ela and a winner in Norway (both by River Falls). The dam won over 7f in Ireland at 3 yrs and is a half-sister to 5 winners including the French listed winner Bellefan and the Chester Vase third Maralinga. The second dam, Bellinzona (by Northfields), won at 3 yrs in France. *"This will be an earlyish 2-y-o. I haven't done much with her, but she has a grand temperament and she looks a nippy little thing. A nice little filly and I like her".*

355 - CHAPEAU [76]   ch.f. Zafonic – Barboukh (Night Shift). February 19. Fifth foal.

Half-sister to the moderate 2000 1m placed 2-y-o Red Deer (by Cadeaux Genereux), to the Group 3 10f Prix Exbury winner and Group 1 Premio Presidente della Repubblica third Barbola (by Diesis), the fairly useful 10f winner Tarboush (by Polish Precedent). The dam, a fairly useful winner of the 1m listed Fern Hill Stakes, is a half-sister to 3 winners. The second dam, Turban (by Glint Of Gold), a fair 10f and 11.7f winner at 3 yrs, is a half-sister to the top-class French and Irish Derby winner Old Vic and the smart Group 3 Prix Foy winner Splash of Colour. *"She's going to take a bit of time and is one for the second half of the season over seven furlongs to start with".*

356 - GROOVY WILLOW (IRE) ** [71]   b.f. Night Shift – Miss Willow Bend (Willow Hour). February 2. Fifth foal. 40,000Y. Tattersalls October.

Half-sister to the unplaced 2000 2-y-o Century Star, to a minor winner in Japan (both by Bigstone), the quite useful 5f and 6f winner of 5 races Willow Dale (by Danehill) and a 1m winner in Denmark by Lycius. The dam won 2 races at up to 7f in the USA and is a half-sister to 11 winners. The second dam, Bend An Oar (by Never Bend), won 3 races in the USA. (Racing Certainty Partnership). *"She'll be alright and should be one for the first half of the season and I like her".*

357 - LIGHT OF THE WORLD (IRE) ** [74]   b.c. Revoque – Moonlight Partner (Red Sunset). April 5. Fourth foal. 40,000Y. Tattersalls October.

Half-brother to the fair 1997 2-y-o 1m winner and subsequent US Grade 3 placed Apache Red (by Indian Ridge). The dam, an Irish 3-y-o 5f winner, is a half-sister to 5 winners including the Group 3 10f Royal Whip Stakes winner Dancing Sunset. The second dam, Dance Partner (by Graustark), a stakes-placed winner in the USA, is a sister to the Grade 1 Santa Anita Derby winner Jim French and the French Group 3 winner Don't Sulk and a half-sister to the top-class broodmare Native Partner (dam of the Group 1 winners Ajdal, Formidable and Flying Partner). (McDowell Racing). *"I've hardly worked any of my 2-y-o's but at this stage he's the one that's giving me the best signals. A nice, big colt and I trained his half-brother. He'll be suited by five or six furlongs early on and I'll start him off at the end of May. He might just make it to Royal Ascot".*

358 - STRIKE MIDNIGHT (USA) * [90]   b.c. Silver Hawk – Fleur de Nuit (Woodman). February 22. First foal. 90,000Y. Tattersalls Houghton.

The dam won 4 races in the USA including the Grade 3 Matchmaker Stakes and is a half-sister to 3 winners. The second dam, Pearl Bracelet (by Lyphard), won the French One Thousand Guineas and is a full or half-sister to 6 winners. (Bill & Shirley Robins). *"A nice little colt and he'll one of my earlier 2-y-o runners. I like him, he's very active and enthusiastic and I see him starting over six furlongs".*

359 - UNNAMED ** [70]   b.f. King's Theatre – Solar Crystal (Alzao). March 24. Second foal.

Half-sister to the useful 2000 2-y-o 7f winner and listed placed Lunar Crystal (by Shirley Heights). The dam, a smart 2-y-o, won the Group 3 1m May Hill Stakes, was third in the Group 1 1m Prix Marcel Boussac and is a half-sister to the Group 3 12f Lancashire Oaks winner State Crystal and the Irish Derby third Tchaikovsky. The second dam, Crystal Spray (by Beldale Flutter), a minor Irish 4-y-o 14f winner, is out of a half-sister to Royal Palace and Glass Slipper (dam of the classic winners Fairy Footsteps and Light Cavalry). (Mr Michael Poland). *"She's a nice filly and will follow a similar pattern to her half-brother. Not very big, but I'm sure she'll do well and she's very active".*

J EUSTACE

360 - LIGHT BRIGADE [80]
b.c. Kris – Mafatin (Sadler's Wells).
March 4. Fourth foal. 5,000Y. Tattersalls October.

Half-brother to a 2-y-o winner abroad by Bahri. The dam, a fair 3-y-o 10f winner, is a half-sister to the One Thousand Guineas winner Fairy Footsteps and the St Leger winner Light Cavalry. The second dam, Glass Slipper (by Relko), a useful 13f winner, was second in the Musidora Stakes and is a half-sister to Royal Palace. (Mr C Curtis & Mr James Eustace). *"Not very forward, he's an ugly duckling turning into a swan at the moment. He looks like he'll make a racehorse by the second half of the season though and would want seven furlongs to start with".*

361 - SECOND MINISTER ** [87]
ch.c. Lion Cavern – Crime Of Passion (Dragonara Palace).
April 8. Ninth living foal. 22,000Y. Tattersalls October.

Half-brother to 5 winners including the useful 1991 2-y-o 5f and 6f winner Master Of Passion (by Primo Dominie), the quite useful dual 5f winner Crime ofthe Century (by Pharly and herself dam of the useful 2000 2-y-o 5f winner and listed 5f second Senior Minister) and the quite useful 2000 dual 5f all-weather winner Licence To Thrill (by Wolfhound) . The dam, a smart winner of the Group 3 Cherry Hinton Stakes, was third in the Group 1 Prix Robert Papin and is a half-sister to the Ayr Gold Cup winner Primula Boy. The second dam, Catriona (by Sing Sing), was a fairly useful 2-y-o winner of 3 races over 5f and a half-sister to 6 winners including the Dee Stakes winner Playboy Jubilee. (Mr R Carstairs). *"A three-parts brother to Senior Minister, I like this colt a lot. He should be racing sometime during May over five furlongs and shows plenty of speed. I've had three from this family and reckon that although this colt could get six furlongs, he probably won't. I went to see him at the stud as a yearling and was unimpressed, but at the sales he was completely different. He looks a real athlete and I'd say he was my best 2-y-o".*

362 - SIR DON (IRE) ** [76]
b.c. Lake Coniston – New Sensitive (Wattlefield).
April 3. Fifth foal. 34,000Y. Tattersalls October.

Half-brother to the fair dual 3-y-o 7f winner Anthemion (by Night Shift) and to 2 minor winners abroad by Eagle Eyed (at 2 yrs in Turkey) and Tom Boat (in Belgium). The dam won 9 races in Belgium from 2 to 5 yrs and is a half-sister to 8 winners including the Group 1 5f Prix de l'Abbaye winner Hever Golf Rose. The second dam, Sweet Rosina (by Sweet Revenge), was placed twice over sprint distances. (Mr Michael Scott & Mr J C Smith). *"From side on he looks very precocious but he's had sore shins and still has open knees. He has a great attitude though and I like him. Certainly capable of winning".*

363 - BLORENGE ** [67]
b.f. Prince Sabo – Sistabelle (Bellypha).
April 30.

Half-sister to the very useful Torch Rouge (by Warning), a winner from 5f to 1m here and the Grade 2 1m Arlington Handicap in the USA, to the quite useful 10f winner Filmore West (by In The Wings) and the hurdles winner Volunteer (by Midyan). The dam is an unraced sister to the Group 2 Prix de l'Opera and Group 3 Waterford Candelabra Stakes winner Bella Colora - herself dam of the high-class Prince of Wales's Stakes winner Stagecraft - and a half-sister to the Irish Champion Stakes winner Cezanne and the Irish Oaks winner Colorspin (dam of the King George winner Opera House). The second dam, Reprocolor (by Jimmy Reppin), won the Lingfield Oaks Trial, Lancashire Oaks and Pretty Polly Stakes. (Usk Valley Stud). *"Very good on pedigree but she came in very late. She looks very much like her sire with her great big backside and will make a 2-y-o by the mid-summer".*

A FABRE

364 - GULF NEWS (USA)
ch.c. Woodman – Balanchine (Storm Bird).
March 29. Third foal.

Half-brother to the 2000 French trained 2-y-o Dorothy's Shoes (by Rainbow Quest). The dam was a top-class filly and winner of 4 races from 7f (at 2 yrs) to 12f including the Epsom Oaks and the Irish Derby. She is closely related to the smart Jockey Club Stakes and Rose Of Lancaster Stakes winner Romanov and the very useful Sun Chariot Stakes winner Red Slippers (both by Nureyev). The second dam, Morning Devotion (by Affirmed), a useful winner over 6f at 2 yrs and third in the Fillies Mile, was fourth in the 12f Lancashire Oaks. (Maktoum Al-Maktoum).

365 - LOUVETEAU (USA) b.c. Bahri – Louveterie (Nureyev).

Closely related to the very smart Group 1 9.3f Prix d'Ispahan and Group 3 10f Prix du Prince d'Orange winner Loup Sauvage (also placed in the Dubai World Cup and the Irish Derby) and to the 1997 French 2-y-o 7.5f winner Loudeac (both by Riverman) and half-brother to the Group 1 1m Grand Criterium winner Loup Solitaire (by Lear Fan). The dam won the Group 3 8.2f Prix Vanteaux and was second in the Prix de Diane. She is closely related to the good miler Legend of France and a half-sister to the good winners Leonardo de Vinci, Louve Bleue and Louve Romaine. The second dam, Lupe (by Primera), won the Oaks, the Coronation Cup and the Yorkshire Oaks. (Mr D Wildenstein).

366 - MER DE CORAIL (IRE) b.f. Sadler's Wells – Miss Tahiti (Tirol).
February 23. Second foal.

Sister to the Andre Fabre trained 3-y-o Maximum Security. The dam won the Group 1 1m Prix Marcel Boussac at 2 yrs and was placed in the 10.5f Prix de Diane, the 12f Prix Vermeille and the 10f Prix Saint-Alary. The second dam, Mini Luthe (by Luthier), was a minor winner in France over 15f at 3 yrs. (Mr D Wildenstein).

367 - PISTOLERO (IRE) b.c. Sadler's Wells – Pampa Bella (Armos).
February 16.

Brother to the 1997 Group 3 10.5f Prix de Flore winner Palme d'Or, and half-brother to the top-class colt Pistolet Bleu (by Top Ville), winner of the Group 1 Criterium de Saint-Cloud (at 2 yrs), the Group 1 Grand Prix de Saint-Cloud, Group 2 Prix Hocquart, Group 2 Prix Noailles and Group 2 Grand Prix d'Evry. The dam, a very useful filly, won the Group 3 10.5f Prix Penelope and was third in both the 10.5f Prix de Diane and the Prix Saint Alary. The second dam, Kendie (by Klairon), won a small race in France.
Significant sire/damsire crosses:- Palme d'Or.

368 - SAGA D'OUILLY (FR) b.f. Linamix – Saganeca (Sagace).
Fifth foal.

Sister to the high-class colt Sagamix, winner of the Prix de l'Arc de Triomphe and the Prix Niel and the Group 3 1½m Prix de Malleret winner Sage Et Jolie and half-sister to the 2000 Group 1 1¼m Criterium de Saint-Cloud winner Sagacity (by Highest Honor). The dam was a very smart winner of the Group 3 12.5f Prix de Royallieu. The second dam, Haglette (by Hagley), won 3 races in the USA and is a half-sister to the smart French 7f and 1m winner Round Top.

J FANSHAWE

369 - CALAMINT * [79] b.br.c. Kaldoun – Coigach (Niniski).
January 13.

Half-brother to Motto (by Mtoto), unplaced in one start at 2 yrs in 2000 and to the quite useful 1999 2-y-o 7f winner Aston Mara (by Bering). The dam, a very useful 1m (at 2 yrs) and Group 3 Park Hill Stakes winner, is a half-sister to the listed Cheshire Oaks winner Kyle Rhea and to the Park Hill Stakes second Applecross. The second dam, Rynechra (by Blakeney), was a useful 3-y-o 12f winner and a half-sister to 6 winners. (Dr Catherine Wills). *"A nice, strong colt and he should have a 2-y-o career later in the season".*

370 - CASHMERE [98] ch.f. Barathea – Wanton (Robellino).
February 2.

Half-sister to 8 winners including the Irish One Thousand Guineas winner Classic Park (by Robellino) and the US Grade 2 winner Rumpipumpy (by Shirley Heights). The dam, a useful 2-y-o 5f winner and third in the Group 2 Flying Childers Stakes, is a half-sister to the listed 5f St Hugh's Stakes winner and Group 2 5f Prix du Gros-Chene second Easy Option. The second dam, Brazen Faced (by Bold And Free), a quite useful 2-y-o 5f winner, is a half-sister to 8 winners including the Musidora Stakes winner Lovers Lane and the City And Suburban Handicap winner Belper. (Lord Halifax). *"A nice, strong filly, she hasn't been in that long and is another one for the second half of the season".*

371 - DEFINING * [79] b.c. Definite Article – Gooseberry Pie (Green Desert). April 27. Second foal. 25,000Y. Tattersalls October.

Half-brother to the fair 2000 2-y-o 1m winner Siena Star (by Brief Truce). The dam, a modest maiden, was placed once and stayed 1m. She is a half-sister to 8 winners including the Group 3 12f John Porter Stakes winner Rakaposhi King. The second dam, Supper Time (by Shantung), won once at 3 yrs. (Mrs V Shelton). *"A nice moving colt by Definite Article who had quite a good year last year as a first season sire and this is going to be a second half of the season colt".*

372 - EXHIBITOR (USA) [76] b.f. Royal Academy – Akadya (Akarad). February 23. Sixth foal. $70,000Y. Keeneland September.

Half-sister to 3 winners including the listed Prix Petite Etoile winner Aka Lady (by Sanglamore). The dam, winner of the listed 12.5f Prix de Thiberville, is a half-sister to another French listed winner in Ken Sauce. The second dam, Sauce Royale (by Royal Palace), is an unplaced half-sister to the Child Stakes winner Sauceboat (herself dam of the Group 2 winners Dusty Dollar and Kind Of Hush). (Cheveley Park Stud). *"An immature filly but she has a nice pedigree and is one for later in the year".*

373 - HECTIC TINA * [86] ch.f. Hector Protector – Tinashaan (Darshaan). April 19. First foal.

The dam, a useful 12f winner, is a half-sister to several winners including the useful staying winner Life Of Riley. The second dam, Catina (by Nureyev), a useful Irish 2-y-o 6f winner, is a half-sister to the Premio Regina Elena winner Rosananti and to the very useful performer Claddagh. (Mr Bruce McAllister). *"Hectic Tina is out of a useful mare that I trained and she's a nice strong filly. The family take a bit of time but she's got plenty of strength and is a nice type".*

374 - JUDGE DAVIDSON [85] b.c. Royal Applause – Without Warning (Warning). March 9. Second foal. 22,000Y. Tattersalls October.

Half-brother to the unraced 2000 2-y-o Battraa (by Lion Cavern). The dam ran once unplaced in France and is a half-sister to 6 winners including the minor US stakes winner and Grade 3 placed Berillon. The second dam, Obertura (by Roberto), won 3 races at 3 yrs. (Mr Mark Fisch). *"He rather fell apart after the sales but he's gone back to the stud now and when he comes back he'll have a 2-y-o career".*

375 - KIRTLE * [80] b.f. Hector Protector – Kyle Rhea (In The Wings). January 16. First foal.

The dam, winner of the listed Cheshire Oaks, is a half-sister to several winners including the Group 3 Park Hill Stakes winner Coigach and the Park Hill Stakes second Applecross. The second dam, Rynechra (by Blakeney), was a useful 3-y-o 12f winner and a half-sister to 6 winners. (Lady Wills). *"Although her dam won a Cheshire Oaks this is not a big filly, in fact she's quite neat and she'll be a seven furlong /mile 2-y-o".*

376 - MISTRESS ELLIE ** [73] b.f. Royal Applause – Ellie Ardensky (Slip Anchor). April 27. Second foal.

Half-sister to the very promising 2000 7f and 1m placed 2-y-o Pole Star (by Polar Falcon). The dam, a fairly useful 10f listed winner, is a half-sister to the very useful listed 10f Lupe Stakes winner Lady Shipley, to the fairly useful 2-y-o 6f winner Finger Of Light and to the unraced dam of the Group 3 Solario Stakes and US Grade 3 winner Brave Act. The second dam, Circus Ring (by High Top), was a joint-champion 2-y-o filly and won 3 races at 2 yrs including the Group 2 Lowther Stakes. (Peter & Noreen Hodgson). *"I've got a couple of Royal Applause's and they both go OK. This filly would be more precocious than her dam and she should be OK this season".*

377 - OOPSIE DAISY [72] b.f. Singspiel – Oops Pettie (Machiavellian). April 22. First foal. 47,000Y. Tattersalls October.

The dam, a fairly useful winner of 3 races over an extended 10f, is a half-sister to 5 minor winners. The second dam, Miquette (by Fabulous Dancer), won over 12f and 13.5f in France including a listed event and is a half-sister to 6 winners including the Group 3 Prix de Pomone winner Moquerie (herself the dam of 4 listed winners) and the listed winner Rivermaid (dam of the Group 3 winners Movieland and Only Star). (Mrs M Slater). *"This filly is from the first crop of Singspiel and she'll be racing over seven furlongs later on. It would be nice to aim for the TBA fillies race at Ascot at the end of September".*

378 - PIOUS * [65]**   b.f. Bishop Of Cashel – La Cabrilla (Carwhite).
April 6.
Half-sister to 4 winners including the fair 7f, 8.5f and hurdles winner Mister RM (by Dominion) and the French 12f, 15f and useful British hurdles winner Teaatral (by Saddlers' Hall). The dam, a fairly useful 2-y-o 5f and 6f winner, was third in the Group 3 Princess Margaret Stakes and is a half-sister to 6 winners including the Group 1 Nunthorpe Stakes winner Ya Malak. The second dam, La Tuerta (by Hot Spark), a fairly useful sprint winner of 3 races, is a half-sister to 7 winners including Cadeaux Genereux. (Cheveley Park Stud). *"Bishop Of Cashel was the sire of two 2-y-o winners for me last year and this is a good, strong sort of filly from a very fast family. She'll probably need six furlongs and a bit of give in the ground but she should have a 2-y-o career".*

379 - RAJASTHAN (IRE) [79]   b.c. Spectrum – Sherkova (State Dinner).
February 3.
Half-brother to the fair 3-y-o 1m winner Russian Party (by Lycius) and to the fair 2m winner Norma's Lady (by Unfuwain). The dam is an unraced half-sister to numerous winners including the Group 1 Prix de Diane winner and Grade 1 Arlington Million second Lady In Silver (by Silver Hawk). The second dam, Lorn Lady (by Lorenzaccio), won once at 3 yrs and is a half-sister to the Prix de Royallieu winner Riverside - herself the dam of the Grand Prix de Saint-Cloud, French One Thousand Guineas and Prix Saint-Alary winner Riverqueen. (The Moguls). *"He's a nice, strong colt for later on".*

380 - REVEILLEZ [69]   br.c. First Trump – Amalancher (Alleged).
April 10. Ninth foal. 20,000Y. Tattersalls October.
Half-brother to the useful Irish middle-distance winner and Group 3 placed Dimancher (by Damister), to the fairly useful 6f and 8.5f winner Ysatirous (by Ahonoora), the fair dual 6f winner (including at 2 yrs) Arantxa (by Sharpo), the modest 12f winner Eurythmic (by Pharly) and a winner of 7 races in Italy by Kings Lake. The dam, a quite useful French 2-y-o 1m winner, is a sister to the Group 3 placed Alliston and a half-sister to the South African Grade 1 winner Icona and the Group 1 William Hill Futurity Stakes second Cock Robin. The second dam, Flyingtrip (by Vaguely Noble), won 4 races in Italy and is a half-sister to the US stakes winner Canvasser and to the unraced dam of three US stakes winners. (Miss A Church). *"Not a typical First Trump and I think he'll be more of a seven furlong/miler rather than a sprinter. But he's a nice, strong colt with a bit of scope".*

381 - THE SADLER (USA) [88]   b.c. Sadler's Wells – Carpet Of Leaves (Green Forest).
January 31. First foal.
The dam is a half-sister to the smart French middle-distance stayer Glorify, the Prix d'Arenberg winner Doree and the dam of the Group 1 Prix Marcel Boussac and triple US Grade 1 winner Ryafan. The second dam, Autumn Glory (by Graustark), won from 6f to 9f in the USA and was placed in the Grade 1 Acorn Stakes. (Car Colston Hall Stud). *"He's a nice strong colt by Sadler's Wells for later on in the season".*

J GIVEN

382 - ALLY McBEAL (IRE) * [62]   b.f. Ali-Royal – Vian (Far Out East).
April 20. 9,000Y. Tattersalls October.
Half-sister to the fair 2000 2-y-o 5f winner Blue Forest (by Charnwood Forest), to the useful 2-y-o dual 5f winner Wavian (by Warning), the minor French winner Chocolate (by Brief Truce), the 2-y-o 8.3f winner Hindsight (by Don't Forget Me) and the 2-y-o 1m winner Ansillo (by Rousillon) - all three fair performers. The dam is an unraced half-sister to 10 winners including the Nassau Stakes and Musidora Stakes winner Optimistic Lass (herself dam of the Coronation Stakes winner Golden Opinion). The second dam, Loveliest (by Tibaldo), a half-sister to the US Grade 1 stakes winner Arbees Boy, was a very useful winner at up to 10.5f in France and 9f in the USA. (Ally McBeal Partnership). *"A bit backward at the moment, she's slowly coming to hand but once she's fit I expect her to be OK. A mid to back-end type of 2-y-o".*

383 - SIOUXSIE SIOUX ** [72]   b.f. Pivotal – Tres Sage (Reprimand).
March 31. First reported foal. 28,000Y. Tattersalls October.
The dam, a minor 3-y-o winner in France, is a half-sister to 9 winners including the Group 3 Prix de la Jonchere winner and useful sire Aragon and the US Grade 3 winner Sun And Shine. The second dam,

Ica (by Great Nephew), is an unraced half-sister to 7 winners including the Kings Stand Stakes winner and very smart sire Song. (Mr A Clarke). *"This filly has grown but she's well-balanced, well-proportioned and does everything easily. I haven't pressed any buttons just yet but she gives every indication that she's going to be a lovely horse. The sort to be a nice 2-y-o and even better next year".*

384 - VOLITANT * [69]
ch.f. Ashkalani – Musianica (Music Boy).
March 2. Sixth foal. 30,000Y. Tattersalls Autumn.

Half-sister to the promising 2000 2-y-o 6f winner Volata (by Flying Spur), to the very useful 9f winner and Group 3 1m Craven Stakes fourth Mensa (by Rudimentary), the fairly useful 7f winner of 4 races Dime Time (by Midyan), the quite useful 6f to 9.4f winner at 2 to 4 yrs Barrel Of Hope (by Distant Relative) and the modest 1997 3-y-o 5f winner Pizzicato (by Statoblest). The dam, a fairly useful 2-y-o 6f winner, is out of the Italian winner of 7 races Penny Bianca (by My Swallow). (Mr J Ellis). *"He's just taking a little time maturing but he has an exciting pedigree and will make a mid-to-late 2-y-o over six and seven furlongs".*

385 - UNNAMED ** [85]
ch.c. Selkirk – Amazing Bay (Mazilier).
March 17. First foal. 33,000 Guineas. Doncaster Breeze Up Sale.

The dam, a useful winner of the listed 5f St Hugh's Stakes and second in the listed 5f Scarborough Stakes, is a half-sister to 2 winners. The second dam, Petriece (by Mummy's Pet), a modest 7f winner, stayed 1m and is a half-sister to 5 winners including the dam of both the champion sprinter and triple Group 1 winner Lochsong and the Group 1 Nunthorpe Stakes winner Lochspring. *"A lovely horse and to my mind the pick of the first day of Doncaster's Breeze Up Sale. As he'd been quickly tuned up for the Breeze Ups I'll be letting him down for a month before we set off. He'll make a 2-y-o by mid-season and will probably want six furlongs to start".*

J GOSDEN

386 - BEN HUR ** [92]
b.c. Zafonic – Gayane (Nureyev).
March 13.

Half-brother to the useful 1m winner Maramba (by Rainbow Quest), to the quite useful 6f winner Duel at Dawn (by Nashwan) and the fair 7f to 9f winner Giko (by Arazi). The dam, a very smart winner of the 6f Sandy Lane Stakes and 7f Oak Tree Stakes, is a half-sister to the Group 2 10f Sun Chariot Stakes winner Ristna. The second dam, Roussalka (by Habitat), won the Nassau Stakes (twice) and the Coronation Stakes and is a half-sister to the Fillies Triple Crown winner Oh So Sharp - herself dam of the Prix Saint-Alary winner Rosefinch. *"A rather backward colt that will take a bit of time".*
Significant sire/damsire crosses:- Kareymah.

387 - BRIANZA (USA) * [76]
b.f. Thunder Gulch – Las Meninas (Glenstal).
March 6. Third foal. IR£100,000Y. Goffs Orby.

Half-sister to the fair 10f all-weather winner Swinging Trio (by Woodman). The dam won the One Thousand Guineas and a listed event in Ireland and was second in the Irish One Thousand Guineas and the Heinz 57 Phoenix Stakes. She is a sister to Head Of The Abbey (a winner of 7 races in Ireland and the USA) and a half-sister to 3 winners. The second dam, Spanish Habit (by Habitat), is an unraced half-sister to 5 winners out of the Group 2 Player-Wills Stakes winner Donna Cressida. *"Yes, she's alright. A big, strong filly that goes nicely. One that should start over seven furlongs in August".*

388 - CATATONIC ** [93]
b.f. Zafonic – Circus Act (Shirley Heights).
March 17.

Half-sister to the unraced 2000 2-y-o Contour (by Indian Ridge), to the very useful 2-y-o Group 3 Solario Stakes winner Brave Act (by Persian Bold), the fair 1m (at 2 yrs) and 4-y-o 10f seller winner Tightrope (by Alzao), the useful 12f and 2-runner 14f listed winner Jellaby Askhir (by Salse) and the fair 10f winner Circus Star (by Soviet Star). The dam is an unraced sister to the listed 10f Lupe Stakes winner Lady Shipley and a half-sister to the listed 10f Upavon Stakes winner Ellie Ardensky. The second dam, Circus Ring (by High Top), won the Group 2 6f Lowther Stakes and the listed 6f Princess Margaret Stakes at 2 yrs and is a half-sister to 7 winners including the smart 2-y-o Great Paul. *"Yes, she goes fine – a little bit nervous – but she'll be alright. I'll probably start her over seven furlongs".*

389 - CHAPTER HOUSE (USA) ** [78]   c. Pulpit – Lilian Bayliss (Sadler's Wells).

Half-brother to the useful 1998 2-y-o 6f to 1m winner (including two listed events in Italy) Strike A Blow (by Red Ransom) and to a winner in Italy by Alleged. The dam, a useful 7f (at 2 yrs) and 9f winner, was third in the Group 3 Nell Gwyn Stakes, is a sister to the very useful French 2-y-o 6f winner Ernani and a half-sister to 12 winners including the high-class Prix Eclipse and Prix Quincey winner Phydilla (by Lyphard) and the Irish Derby second Observation Post (by Shirley Heights). The second dam, Godzilla (by Gyr), a useful winner of 5 races in Italy at up to 7.5f, is a half-sister to 8 winners including the dam of the Group 1 Gran Criterium winner Grease. *"Yes, he's a grand horse that goes nicely. He'll be racing in June or July and he goes alright this fellow"*.

390 - CHARLEY BATES (USA) * [72]   b.br.c. Benny The Dip – Vouch (Halo).
May 1. Fifth foal. $280,000Y. Keenland September.

Half-brother to a minor 3-y-o winner in the USA by Distant View. The dam, also a minor 3-y-o winner, is a half-sister to the Grade 2 Sapling Stakes winner Bio and to the US winner and Grade 1 Demoiselle Stakes second Bookkeeper. The second dam, Resume (by Reviewer), a minor 2-y-o winner in the USA, is a sister to the US triple Grade 1 winner Revidere. *"A nice sort of horse and one for the mid-season onwards"*.

391 - CODE SIGN (USA) * [86]   b.c. Gulch – Karasavina (Sadler's Wells).
First foal.

The dam is an unraced sister to the very useful 10f winner and St Leger fourth In Camera, to the very useful 11.5f winner and Yorkshire Oaks second Bineyah and the useful 1992 Group 2 1m Royal Lodge Stakes winner Desert Secret and a half-sister to numerous other winners. The second dam, Clandestina (by Secretariat), an Irish 3-y-o 10f winner, is a half-sister to the great Seattle Slew, to the Two Thousand Guineas winner Lomond and to the Gallinule Stakes winner Seattle Dancer. *"A strong horse, he goes well and is a solid citizen"*.

392 - COZY MARIE (USA) * [79]   gr.f. Cozzene – Mariamme (Verbatim).
March 8. Third foal. $300,000Y. Keeneland September.

Half-sister to the minor US 3-y-o winner Cushina (by Holy Bull). The dam, a minor winner of 2 races at 3 yrs in the USA, is a half-sister to the high-class filly Miss Alleged, winner of the Grade 1 12f Breeders Cup Turf, the Grade 1 Hollywood Turf Cup Handicap and the Group 2 12f Prix de Malleret and to the US stakes winners Bold Josh and Nancy's Champion. The second dam, Miss Tusculum (by Boldnesian), is an unraced half-sister to 2 stakes winners. *"A sweet filly that will make a 2-y-o. She's grand and goes really well"*.

393 - CRYSTAL MELODY (USA) ** [98]   b.f. Nureyev – Crystal Spray (Beldale Flutter).
February 15.

Sister to the smart 2000 2-y-o Group 1 Fillies Mile winner Crystal Music, closely related to the smart 7f (at 2 yrs) and 10f winner Tchaikovsky (by Sadler's Wells) and half-sister to the 1995 2-y-o Group 3 8f May Hill Stakes winner and Cheshire Oaks second Solar Crystal (by Alzao), the Group 3 12f Lancashire Oaks winner and Yorkshire Oaks and Prix Vermeille placed State Crystal (by High Estate) and the fairly useful 12f and 14f winner Star Crystal (by Brief Truce). The dam, a minor Irish 4-y-o 14f winner, is out of the unplaced - in one start - Crystal Fountain (by Great Nephew), herself a half-sister to Royal Palace and Glass Slipper (dam of the classic winners Fairy Footsteps and Light Cavalry). *"A very backward filly at the moment"*.
Significant sire/damsire crosses:- Crystal Music.

394 - DEPTH (USA) ** [102]   b.c. Danzig – Quinpool (Alydar).
Second living foal.

The dam, a winner of 3 races in the USA and third in the Grade 1 Kentucky Oaks, is a half-sister to 3 winners. The second dam, Squan Song (by Exceller), won the Grade 3 8.5f Affectionately Handicap, was Grade 1 placed and is a half-sister to the Group 3 7f Larkspur Stakes winner Heron Bay. *"A strong colt, he does everything alright at the moment but wouldn't want to be rushed. He might be racing by the middle of the season"*.

395 - DISCOVOLANTE ** [83] b.f. Sadler's Wells – Divine Danse (Kris).
April 4. Sixth foal.
Closely related to the very smart 6f winner (at 2 yrs) and French Two Thousand Guineas and St James's Palace Stakes placed Valentino and to the minor French winner Divin Danseur (both by Nureyev) and half-sister to the minor French and US winner Djinn (by Mr Prospector). The dam was a smart sprinter and winner of 5 races including the Group 2 Prix du Gros Chene, the Group 2 Prix du Ris-Orangis, the Group 3 Prix de Seine et Oise and the Group 3 5.5f Prix d'Arenberg. She is a half-sister to the high-class colt Pursuit of Love, winner of the Group 2 Prix Maurice de Gheest and second in the July Cup. The second dam, Dance Quest (by Green Dancer), was smart winner of 3 sprint races and a half-sister to the Prix de la Salamandre winner Noblequest. *"A tall filly with plenty of scope, she's attractive and is one for August onwards and seven furlongs plus. A good sort and she goes nicely"*.

396 - DOCK LEAF (USA) ** [78] ch.f. Woodman – Dokki (Northern Dancer).
March 5.
Half-sister to the Grade 1 9f Hollywood Oaks winner Sleep Easy (by Seattle Slew), to the smart US 6f (at 2 yrs) to 8.5f winner Electrify (by Warning) and the fair 1998 2-y-o 7f winner Shoogle (by A P Indy),. The dam is an unraced half-sister to the champion US colt Slew O'Gold - winner of seven Grade 1 events - and Coastal, winner of the Belmont Stakes. The second dam, Alluvial (by Buckpasser), is an unraced daughter of the champion US 3-y-o filly Bayou and a half-sister to the Santa Margarita Handicap winner Batteur. (Khalid Abdulla). *"She's a neat, racy little filly and she should be early"*.

397 - ENVIRONMENTALIST ** [81] b.c. Danehill – Way O'Gold (Slew O'Gold).
February 13. First foal. 220,000Y. Tattersalls Houghton.
The dam was placed twice at 2 yrs in France and is a half-sister to 5 winners including the Group 3 6f Prix de Cabourg winner Secrage (herself dam of the Group 2 Royal Lodge Stakes winner Teapot Row). The second dam, Wayage (by Mr Prospector), is a placed half-sister to 8 winners including the US Grade 3 winner De Niro and the Italian Group 3 winner Vidalia. The third dam, Waya, won four Grade 1 events in the USA. *"He goes well and is a nice sort of horse with a big action for the mid-season onwards"*.

398 - EPICENTRE (USA) ** [91] b.c. Kris S – Carya (Northern Dancer).
March 13.
Closely related to the Group 1 Prix Marcel Boussac, Grade 1 Queen Elizabeth II Challenge Cup, Grade 1 Yellow Ribbon Stakes and Grade 1 Flower Bowl Invitational winner Ryafan (by Lear Fan), and half-brother to the quite useful 10.5f winner Stage Direction (by Theatrical) and the Italian 9f winner Hong Kong King (by Rousillon). The dam was placed over 9.5f in France, is closely related to the smart French middle-distance stayer Glorify and a half-sister to the Prix d'Arenberg winner Doree. The second dam, Autumn Glory (by Graustark), won from 6f to 9f in the USA and was placed in the Grade 1 Acorn Stakes. (Khalid Abdulla). *"A nice sort of colt, he'll be a September 2-y-o but he goes well and does everything right"*.

399 - FLORENTINE FLUTTER * [95]** b.c. Machiavellian – Party Doll (Be My Guest).
February 3. Seventh foal. 280,000Y. Tattersalls Houghton.
Brother to the Group 2 6.5f Criterium des 2 Ans and Group 2 5f Prix du Gros-Chene winner Titus Livius and to the minor French winner Bahama Dream and half-brother to the 2-y-o winner and listed-placed Party Zane (by Zafonic) and the fairly useful 2-y-o 5f and subsequent US winner Shegardi (by Primo Dominie). The dam was a very useful winner of 4 races in France including 3 listed events from 5f to 1m, was Group 3 placed twice and is a half-sister to 9 winners. The second dam, Midnight Lady (by Mill Reef), won once at 2 yrs and is a half-sister to the US Grade 2 winner Regal Bearing and the dam of the US Grade 1 winner Metamorphose. *"A grand colt with a quick action, he wants top of the ground and he's a nice type. He'll definitely make a 2-y-o over six furlongs"*.
Significant sire/damsire crosses:- Titus Livius, Sinyar, Don Michelotto.

400 - FOREIGN ACCENT ** [98] b.c. Machiavellian – Rappa Tap Tap (Tap On Wood).
March 25. Eleventh foal. 270,000Y. Tattersalls Houghton.
Half-brother to the 3-y-o Rapacki (by Polish Precedent), to the very useful 1m winner and Group 1 St James's Palace Stakes fourth Killer Instinct (by Zafonic), the very useful 1988 2-y-o 7f winner and Group

1 Hoover Fillies Mile second Pick of the Pops (by High Top), the Irish 1m winner and listed-placed Oriane (by Nashwan), the fairly useful dual 10f winner Tap on Air (by Caerleon) and the fair Irish 9f winner Winger (by In the Wings). The dam was a useful winner of 3 races from 6f to 1m including the Blue Seal Stakes and is a half-sister to the Irish Oaks winner Colorspin (herself dam of the top-class colt Opera House and the Ascot Gold Cup winner Kayf Tara), to the Group 2 Prix de l'Opera winner Bella Colora (dam of the high-class colt Stagecraft) and the Irish Champion Stakes winner Cezanne. The second dam, Reprocolor (by Jimmy Reppin), won the Lingfield Oaks Trial and the Lancashire Oaks in 1979. *"A grand horse, he's a powerful type that does everything right and he'll be out by mid-season".*

---

401 - GLAM ROCK * [102]**   ch.f. Nashwan – Band (Northern Dancer).

March 28. Fifth foal.

Closely related to the unraced 2000 2-y-o Sauterne (by Rainbow Quest), to the very useful Group 3 6f Cherry Hinton Stakes winner Applaud and the useful 2-y-o 7f winner Houston Time (both by Rahy). The dam is a placed half-sister to 5 winners including the US Grade 3 9f New Orleans Handicap winner Festive. The second dam, Swingtime (by Buckpasser), won 9 races here and in the USA including the Grade 2 8.5f Santa Maria Handicap, the Group 3 6f Cork And Orrery Stakes, the Group 3 6f Diadem Stakes and the Grade 3 Las Palmas Handicap. Swingtime is a half-sister to 5 winners including the Grade 2 Kentucky Oaks winner Bag Of Tunes (herself dam of the Lancashire Oaks winner Prophecy) and Song Sparrow (dam of the US Grade 1 winner Cormorant). *"Yes, she goes fine, is a good mover and does everything right. She'll make a 2-y-o".*

---

402 - HAREER * [83]   b.f. Anabaa – On The Tide (Slip Anchor).

April 11. Third foal. 240,000Y. Tattersalls October.

Half-sister to the useful 1m and 10f winner Tier Worker (by Tenby). The dam, a fair 3-y-o 1m winner, is a half-sister to 8 winners including the high-class Gimcrack Stakes winner Rock City and the smart Cherry Hinton Stakes winner Kerrera. The second dam, Rimosa's Pet (by Petingo), was a very useful winner from 6f to 10.5f including the Group 3 Musidora Stakes and the Group 3 Princess Elizabeth Stakes. (Hamdan Al-Maktoum). *"A very powerful filly, she goes really nicely".*

---

403 - HAWKWIND (USA) * [74]   b.c. El Prado – Pleasantly Quick (Roanoke).

February 7. First foal. $160,000Y. Keeneland September.

The dam, a minor 2-y-o winner in the USA, is a half-sister to the US Grade 3 winner and dual Grade 1 placed Forcing Bid and to the dam of the dual US Grade 3 winner Mil Kilates. The second dam, Quick Honors (by To The Quick), won at 3 yrs in the USA. *"Yes, he'll just take some time and I'll probably want to start him off in a seven furlong or mile maiden in September".*

---

404 - IMPERIAL THEATRE (IRE) ** [85]   b.c. Sadler's Wells – Aunt Pearl (Seattle Slew).

February 4.

Brother to the unraced 2000 2-y-o Social Order and closely related to the fairly useful 1997 2-y-o dual 6f winner Social Charter (by Nureyev). The dam, a winner at up to 7f in the USA, is out of a sister to Prospector's Fire (dam of the Vernon's Sprint Cup winner Dowsing) and a half-sister to the smart US colts Royal And Regal and Regal And Royal. *"He's a strong, good-looking, well-balanced colt that should be out by July time and he goes well. He'll make a 2-y-o and is a nice colt".*

---

405 - LOWESWATER (USA) ** [94]   b.c. Nureyev – River Empress (Riverman).

March 23. First reported foal. 330,000Y. Tattersalls Houghton.

The dam was unplaced in the USA and is a half-sister to 9 winners, three of them stakes-placed. The second dam, Call The Queen (by Hail To Reason), won once in the USA and is a half-sister to 6 winners including the dam of the Prix de l'Abbaye winner Silver Fling. *"A neat horse, he goes well and will make a 2-y-o by June. A nice sort of horse".*
Significant sire/damsire crosses:- Spinning World.

---

406 - MACAW (IRE) ** [86]   b.c. Bluebird – No Quest (Rainbow Quest).

January 27. Second foal. IR£160,000Y. Goffs Challenge.

The dam was placed once in France and is a half-sister to 8 winners including the French Two Thousand Guineas winner No Pass No Sale and the Group 3 1m Prix de Sandringham winner Once In My Life. The second dam, No Disgrace (by Djakao), won once in France at 2 yrs over 7.5f, was fourth in the Prix de Flore, the Prix Chloe and the Prix Cleopatre (all Group 3 events) and is a half-sister to the

99

dam of the US Grade 2 San Bernardino Handicap and Group 2 Supreme Stakes winner Anshan. *"A neat colt that goes fine, he should be an early 2-y-o"*.

407 - MANANAN McLIR (USA) ** [84]
b.c. Royal Academy – St Lucinda (St Jovite).
January 28. First foal.

The dam, a fair 2-y-o 6f winner here, subsequently won and was stakes-placed in the USA. She is a half-sister to 5 winners including the US stakes-placed winners Magic Carr and Majestico and the French 2-y-o 1m winner Gypsy Trail. The second dam, Majestic Nature (by Majestic Prince), won at up to 1m in the USA and is a sister to US Grade 3 2-y-o 6.5f winner Royal Suite. *"A well-built, well-balanced colt that should be racing sometime in June"*.

408 - MAWAWEEL (USA) * [74]
b.f. Theatrical – Sweet Soul Dream (Conquistador Cielo).
February 26. Sixth foal. $190,000Y. Keeneland September.

Half-sister to 2 winners in Japan by Capote and Night Shift and to the quite useful 2000 Irish 6f and 7f placed 2-y-o Marseille Express (by Caerleon). The dam was a poor 5f (at 2 yrs) and 7f placed maiden and is a half-sister to 6 winners including the top-class sprinter Committed (winner of the Prix de l'Abbaye and the William Hill Sprint Championship and herself dam of the US Grade 1 winner Pharma). The second dam, Mistinguette (by Boldnesian), ran once unplaced and is a half-sister to the Grade 1 Vanity Handicap winner Miss Toshiba. *"Yes, she goes fine, she's quite strong and should make a 2-y-o. A nice type of filly"*.

409 - MIST OF TIME (IRE) * [80]
b.f. Danehill – Lothlorien (Woodman).
February 23. Second foal.

The dam, a quite useful 3-y-o 1m winner, is a sister to the useful 1m (at 2 yrs) to 10f winner Monsajem and to the US 2-y-o winner Mellifont and a half-sister to 5 winners. The second dam, Fairy Dancer (by Nijinsky), a winner over 6f in Ireland at 2 yrs, is closely related to 4 winners by Northern Dancer, notably the top-class racehorse and sire Sadler's Wells, the high-class sire Fairy King and the 2-y-o Group 1 winner Tate Gallery. The third dam, Fairy Bridge (by Bold Reason), was a good 2-y-o 5f and 6f winner and a half-sister to Nureyev. *"Yes, she's an attractive filly that moves nicely and is well-balanced. One for the mid-season"*.

410 - MOMENT *** [80]
ch.f. Nashwan – Well Away (Sadler's Wells).
January 30. Fifth foal.

Half-sister to the smart 2000 Group 2 6f Richmond Stakes winner Endless Summer (by Zafonic). The dam, a minor winner over 1m in France at 2 yrs, is a sister to the very smart colt Scenic, winner of the Group 1 7f Dewhurst Stakes (in a dead-heat) and the Group 3 10f William Hill Classic at Ayr and a half-sister to the Group 3 9f Prix Daphnis winner Silent Warrior. The second dam, Idyllic (by Foolish Pleasure), is an unraced half-sister to the Oaks second Slightly Dangerous (herself the dam of Commander in Chief, Warning, Deploy, Dushyantor and Yashmak) and I Will Follow (the dam of Rainbow Quest). (Khalid Abdulla). *"Yes, she's a nice filly and she goes well. I'd expect her to be ready by June or July and she's a similar type to another Nashwan 2-y-o of mine, Glam Rock"*.
Significant sire/damsire crosses:- Bint Salsabil (Gr 3).

411 - MOON'S WHISPER (USA) **** [85]
b.f. Storm Cat – East Of The Moon (Private Account).
May 1. Fourth foal. $4,400,000Y. Keeneland September.

Half-sister to the French-trained 3-y-o North Of Neptune, to the 1999 2-y-o Group 3 5.5f Prix d'Arenberg winner Moon Driver and the US winner and Grade 2 Californian Stakes second Mojave Moon (all by Mr Prospector). The dam was a high-class winner of the French One Thousand Guineas, the 10.5f Prix de Diane and the Prix Jacques le Marois and is a half-sister to the top class miler Kingmambo, winner of the French Two Thousand Guineas, the St James's Palace Stakes and the Prix du Moulin and to the smart Group 3 6f Prix de Ris-Oranges winner Miesque's Son. The second dam, Miesque (by Nureyev), was a great filly and possibly the best miler of the eighties, winning ten Group or Grade 1 events including the Breeders Cup Mile (twice), the Prix Jacques le Marois (twice), the One Thousand Guineas, the French One Thousand Guineas and the Prix du Moulin. (Hamdan Al-Maktoum). *"Still in Dubai until the end of April, she's quite a neat filly that should make a 2-y-o"*.
Significant sire/damsire crosses:- Sir Cat, Vision And Verse (US Grade 2 winners).

412 - MOSCOW (IRE) * [94]** ch.c. Cadeaux Genereux – Madame Nureyev (Nureyev).
April 8. Ninth foal. IR£290,000Y. Goffs Orby.
Half-brother to the 3-y-o Under Construction (by Pennekamp), to the US Grade 3 Yerba Buena
Handicap winner Miss Universal (by Lycius), the fairly useful dual 10f winner Cloak Of Darkness (by
Thatching), the fairly useful 7.6f and 1m winner Bernard Seven (by Taufan) and the modest dual 15f
winner Fen Dance (by Trojan Fen). The dam, a 2-y-o 6f winner in France, is a half-sister to 4 minor
winners. The second dam, Miss Derby (by Master Derby), won 3 races in the USA and is a half-sister
to the US stakes winner Jetta J. *"A grand horse with a good attitude and he moves well. One for the
mid-season and he probably takes more after the sire than the damsire".*
Significant sire/damsire crosses:- Touch Of The Blues (Gr 2).

413 - NAZEEH (USA) ** [76] b.br.c. Benny The Dip – Falconese (Imperial Falcon).
May 2. Third foal. $75,000Y. Keeneland September.
Half-brother to the 1999 US 2-y-o winner and Grade 3 Miss Grillo Stakes second Windsong (by
Unbridled). The dam, a minor US stakes winner of 6 races, is out of the minor US winner Winnowing
Wind (by Super Moment). *"Yes, he's fine. A nice sort of horse and well-balanced, he goes alright".*

414 - ON VIEW (USA) * [75] ch.f. Distant View – Wandesta (Nashwan).
April 1. Second foal.
Sister to Greek Dream, unplaced in one start over 7f at 2 yrs in 2000. The dam, a smart 12f listed winner
here and subsequently winner of the Grade 1 9f Santa Ana Handicap and Grade 1 10f Santa Barbara
Handicap in the USA, is closely related to the Group 2 12f Prix du Conseil de Paris winner De Quest
and the useful 10.3f to 14f winner Source of Light and a half-sister to the smart French 10f to 15f winner
Turners Hill (by Top Ville). The second dam, De Stael (by Nijinsky), a fairly useful dual 7f winner at 2
yrs, is a sister to the high-class middle-distance colts Peacetime and Quiet Fling and a half-sister to the
Cambridgeshire winner Intermission - herself dam of the good sprinter Interval. *"She's a neat filly,
she'll make a 2-y-o over seven furlongs and she's fine".*

415 - PERIGEO (IRE) * [90] b.c. Sadler's Wells – Lacandona (Septieme Ciel).
February 11. First foal.
The dam is a half-sister to the US stakes winner Smackover Creek and to the dams of the Australian
triple Grade 1 winner Flying Spur, the US Grade 2 winner Fit To Lead and the Grade 1 Yellow Ribbon
Invitational winner Aube Indienne. The second dam, Grand Luxe (by Sir Ivor), is a stakes winner of 10
races in Canada and the USA and a half-sister to the Grade 1 winners L'Enjoleur, La Voyageuse and
Medaille d'Or. *"He's a nice horse that goes well and he should make a 2-y-o".*

416 - PRIVILEGE (USA) ** [75] b.c. Foxhound – Pretty Miswaki (Miswaki).
March 17. Third foal. 150,000Y. Tattersalls October.
Brother to the unraced 2000 2-y-o My Foxy Way. The dam ran once unplaced in the USA and is a half-
sister to 2 minor winners there. The second dam, Pretty Sham (by Sham), was a stakes winner of 6
races in the USA and a half-sister to 9 winners. *"A powerful horse, he goes well and could be out
relatively early if all goes well. I think I'll go for the first six furlong maiden with him".*

417 - RAVENGLASS (USA) ** [87] b.c. Miswaki – Urus (Kris S).
March 23. Third foal. $250,000Y. Keeneland September.
Half-brother to the smart winner of 3 races at around 10f Happy Diamond (by Diesis). The dam won 7
races at up to 10f in the USA including a minor stakes and is a half-sister to the stakes winner Vilhelm.
The second dam, Erstwhile (by Arts And Letters), won the Florida Oaks. *"He's working well at the
moment and he'll be racing in May".*

418 - RAWYAAN * [93] b.c. Machiavellian – Raheefa.
February 25. First foal.
The dam was a fair 3-y-o 10f winner. The second dam, Oogie Poogie (by Storm Bird), was placed at
up to 10f here before winning in the USA and is a daughter of the champion mare Cascapedia.
(Hamdan Al-Maktoum). *"He goes fine, is a sharpish horse and should be out in May or June".*

419 - REHEARSAL HALL (USA) **** [102]   ch.c. Diesis – Performing Arts (The Minstrel).

Brother to the useful 1997 2-y-o listed 6f winner Dance Trick and half-brother to the very useful 1995 2-y-o Woodborough (by Woodman), winner of the Group 3 Anglesey Stakes and placed in the Prix de la Salamandre, the Phoenix Stakes and the Middle Park Stakes, to the useful 1999 2-y-o 5f and 1m winner Performing Magic and the US stakes-placed Perfect Mandate (both by Gone West). The dam was a useful 2-y-o 5f and 6f winner and was third in the Irish One Thousand Guineas. She is a sister to the smart Heron Stakes and subsequent US winner The Noble Player and a half-sister to 9 winners. The second dam, Noble Mark (by On Your Mark), was a smart winner of the 6f Duke of York Stakes and was third in the Kings Stand Stakes. *"Yes, he's working nicely and he's quite early. He should start off in May over five or six furlongs".*
Significant sire/damsire crosses:- Jahid (Gr 3).

420 - RHETORIC (IRE) [69]   b.c. Desert King – Squaw Talk (Gulch).
March 21. Second reported foal. 160,000Y. Tattersalls October.
Half-brother to a minor winner in the USA by Clever Trick. The dam won 3 races and was stakes-placed in the USA and is a half-sister to 3 winners. The second dam, Indian Romance (by Raja Baba), a minor stakes winner of 8 races in the USA, is a half-sister to the Group 2 Nassau Stakes winner Optimistic Lass (dam of the Coronation Stakes winner Golden Opinion) and to the listed Athasi Stakes winner Dangerous Diva. *"A backward colt but he does everything alright".*

421 - SECOND BURST (IRE) *** [97]   b.f. Sadler's Wells – Kanmary (Kenmare).
March 2.
Sister to the 1998 2-y-o Group 1 1m Racing Post Trophy winner Commander Collins and closely related to Lit de Justice, winner of the 1996 Grade 1 Breeders Cup Sprint, the very smart 7f Washington Singer Stakes winner and Two Thousand Guineas, Derby and Irish Derby placed Colonel Collins, the useful 6f and 7f winner Captain Collins (all by El Gran Senor) and the fair 2-y-o 5f winner Stormswept (by Storm Bird). The dam, a smart French 2-y-o 5f winner, was third in the Group 1 Prix Robert Papin and stayed 9f. She is a half-sister to 11 winners including the Prix de Royallieu winner Passionaria. The second dam, Djallybrook (by Djakao), was a minor French 11f winner and a half-sister to the dam of the Prix du Cadran winner Trebrook. *"A nice filly, she's light on her feet but she'll take a bit of time and won't be out until around September".*
Significant sire/damsire crosses:- Commander Collins.

422 - SECRET EXPLORER (IRE) ** [70]   br.c. Blues Traveller – Mystery Bid (Auction Ring).
March 3. Ninth foal. 42,000Y. Tattersalls October.
Half-brother to the quite useful 2-y-o 7f winner Spy, to the fair 2-y-o 5f winner Keep Tapping (both by Mac's Imp), the fair 12f winner Secret Service (by Classic Secret) and the modest 1m and 10f winner Contract Bridge (by Contract Law). The dam was placed twice and stayed 12f and is a half-sister to 4 winners including the listed Ben Marshall Stakes winner Cresta Auction. The second dam, Baby Clair (by Gulf Pearl), won once at 2 yrs. *"He goes very nicely, I'll start him off over six furlongs and he's a nice horse".*

423 - SHAHM (IRE) * [92]   b.c. Marju – Istibshar (Mr Prospector).
March 29. Fourth living foal.
Half-brother to Mostabshir (by Unfuwain), unplaced over 7f on his only start at 2 yrs in 2000. The dam, a fair 3-y-o 6f winner, is a half-sister to the French 2-y-o and US 3-y-o Grade 3 8.5f Lamplighter Handicap winner Namaqualand. The second dam, Namaqua (by Storm Bird), a minor winner at 3 yrs in the USA, is a half-sister to the champion US 2-y-o filly Althea (herself dam of the champion Japanese 2-y-o filly Yamanin Paradise), to the Grade 1 winners Ali Oop and Ketoh, the US graded stakes winners Aishah, Aquilegia, Native Courier and Twining, and to the dams of Green Desert, the US Grade 2 winner Seattle Dawn and the November Handicap winner Azzaam. (Hamdan Al-Maktoum). *"Still in Dubai until the end of April".*
Significant sire/damsire crosses:- Oriental Fashion.

**424 - SHALLOWS ** ** [83]   b.f. Sadler's Wells – Cutting Reef (Kris).
                                                                        April 13. Fourth foal.

Closely related to the quite useful 10.5f winner Bedara (by Barathea) and half-sister to the 1998 German 3-y-o 10f winner Sampa Coeur (by Caerleon). The dam, a staying winner of 2 races in France including a listed event at Maisons-Laffitte, is a half-sister to 7 winners including the Irish listed winner Jazz Ballet. The second dam, Quiet Harbour (by Mill Reef), is an unplaced half-sister to 10 winners including Quiet Fling (Coronation Cup), Peacetime (Guardian Classic Trial), Armistice Day (Prix Exbury) and the dams of the Group/Graded stakes winners De Quest, Flaming Torch, Interim, Interval and Wandesta. *"She's a neat sort of filly that moves well and she should be out in mid-summer".*
Significant sire/damsire crosses:- Moonshell, Samsaam.

**425 - SHATARAH ** * [89]   ch.f. Gulch – Arjuzah (Ahonoora).
                                                                        April 30.

The dam, a useful winner of the listed 7f Sceptre Stakes, is a half-sister to the Irish listed winner Ormsby out of the useful 1m Lincoln Handicap winner Saving Mercy (by Lord Gayle). (Hamdan Al-Maktoum). *"Still in Dubai until the end of April".*

**426 - SILVER YEN (USA) ** [86]   b.f. Silver Hawk – Yenda (Dancing Brave).
                                                                        Third foal.

The dam won the Grade 2 Long Island Handicap, was second in the Prix Vermeille and is a half-sister to the 1990 Derby winner Quest For Fame, to the very useful 14f winner and 2m Queens Vase second Silver Rainbow and the useful 11f winner Air Quest. The second dam, Aryenne (by Green Dancer), was a high-class winner of the French One Thousand Guineas and is a half-sister to Apachee, herself dam of the Group winners Antheus and Alexandrie. (Khalid Abdulla). *"A nice type of filly, she has a big stride and will want a mile around September time to start with".*

**427 - SPECIALI (IRE) ** ** [75]   b.c. Bluebird – Fille Dansante (Dancing Dissident).
                                              January 30. Third foal. 140,000Y. Tattersalls October.

Half-brother to a 3-y-o winner in Austria by Shalford. The dam is an unraced half-sister to 4 winners including the useful sire Cyrano de Bergerac. The second dam, Miss St Cyr (by Brigadier Gerard), won once at 2 yrs, was fourth in the Nell Gwyn Stakes and is a half-sister to 5 winners including the dam of the Ascot Gold Cup winner Arcadian Heights. *"A colt who should appear by mid-season and he's a good, strong horse".*

**428 - SULK (IRE) ** * [85]   ch.f. Selkirk – Masskana (Darshaan).
                                                                        February 15. Fourth foal.

Half-sister to the very smart 1m listed winner Wallace (by Royal Academy) and to the modest 9f winner Twilight World (by Night Shift). The dam, a minor 9f and 10f winner in France, is a half-sister to the US Grade 3 Arcadia Handicap winner Madjaristan and the Group 2 Gallinule Stakes winner Massyar. The second dam, Masarika (by Thatch), won the French One Thousand Guineas and the Prix Robert Papin. *"A nice, attractive filly, she's very light on her feet and has a bit of class about her".*

**429 - SUNDARI (IRE) ** * [74]   b.f. Danehill – My Ballerina (Sir Ivor).
                                                                        February 10.

The dam, a fairly useful 10f and 12f winner, is a half-sister to the very useful dual 6f winner and Group 1 1m Coronation Stakes third Zarani Sidi Anna. The second dam, Emmaline (by Affirmed), won twice at up to 9f in the USA including a stakes event and is a half-sister to the Grade 1 winners Bates Motel and Hatim. *"A powerful filly that goes very nicely".*

**430 - SUVRETTA (USA) ** ** [81]   b.f. Nureyev – Naughty Nana (Houston).
                                                                        January 17. Second foal.

The dam, a stakes-placed winner of 2 races at 3 yrs in the USA, is a half-sister to 4 winners including the US stakes winner and Grade 2 placed Nantahela. The second dam, Georgia Power (by Our Native), is a placed sister to the champion US 2-y-o colt Rockhill Native. *"A powerful, quick filly, she shows plenty of speed and will want top of the ground".*

431 - TANGO FANDANGO (IRE) * [60]   b.f. Be My Guest – Green Belt (Tirol).

February 22. First foal. IR£22,000Y. Goffs Orby.

The dam is an unraced half-sister to 3 winners including the French listed-placed Hill Reef. The second dam, Green Reef (by Mill Reef), won the Group 3 Prix de Psyche and is a half-sister to 7 winners including Infrasonic (Queens Vase), Ecologist (Prix Berteux) and the dam of the St Leger winner Toulon. *"A strong, neat little filly that goes nicely and has a good attitude".*

432 - THE PLAYER * [84]   b.c. Octagonal – Patria (Mr Prospector).

February 7. Second foal. 70,000Y. Tattersalls October.

Half-brother to the quite useful 2000 2-y-o 6f winner Parvenue (by Ezzoud). The dam, a fair 2-y-o 7.6f winner, is a sister to Lycius, winner of the Group 1 6f Middle Park Stakes and placed in the Two Thousand Guineas, the Irish Two Thousand Guineas, July Cup, Prix Jacques le Marois and Prix du Moulin and to Tereshkova, winner of the Group 3 6f Prix de Cabourg and second in the Moyglare Stud Stakes. The second dam, Lypatia (by Lyphard), won over 6.5f in France and 1m in the USA. *"A nice backward horse, he's one for September time and he goes well".*

433 - THRASHER ** [83]   b.f. Hector Protector – Thracian (Green Desert).

April 23. Second foal.

Half-sister to the unraced 2000 2-y-o Zhdanov (by Zafonic). The dam, a fairly useful 2-y-o 6f and 7f winner, is a half-sister to 12 winners including the very useful Group 2 12f Ribblesdale Stakes winner Third Watch, the high-class Prix Foy winner Richard of York, the Group 2 Premio Dormello winner Three Tails (herself dam of the high-class colts Tamure and Sea Wave), the Group 3 Fred Darling Stakes winner Maysoon and the dams of the Group winners Lend A Hand and Talented. The second dam, Triple First (by High Top), won 7 races including the Sun Chariot Stakes, the Nassau Stakes and the Musidora Stakes. *"A neat filly, she goes fine and will make a 2-y-o".*

434 - TRILOGY * [87]   ch.c. Grand Lodge – Three More (Sanglamore).

January 23. Second foal.

The dam is a half-sister to the very smart 9f Feilden Stakes and 10f Mecca Bookmakers' Classic winner Kefaah, to the smart 2-y-o 7f Somerville Tattersall Stakes winner and Group 2 Criterium de Maisons Laffitte second Tertian and the useful Tote-Ebor Handicap winner Primary. The second dam, Tertiary (by Vaguely Noble), was second over 10.5f in France, is a sister to the Prix Saint-Alary and Washington DC International winner Nobiliary and a half-sister to the Prix de la Foret and Prix Jacques le Marois winner and top class sire Lyphard. *"A neat colt, he should be fairly early and he's working OK".*

435 - VOLCANIC ** [95]   b.c. Zafonic – Ryafan (Lear Fan).

February 3. First foal.

The dam was a high-class winner of the Group 1 Prix Marcel Boussac, the Grade 1 Queen Elizabeth II Challenge Cup, the Grade 1 Yellow Ribbon Stakes, the Grade 1 Flower Bowl Invitational and the Group 2 Nassau Stakes. The second dam, Carya (by Northern Dancer), was placed over 9.5f in France , is closely related to the smart French middle-distance stayer Glorify and a half-sister to the Group 3 5.5f Prix d'Arenberg winner Doree. *"A nice horse out of Ryafan who sadly died foaling the other week. This colt is a powerful looking 2-y-o that goes well and is the type to start over six furlongs".*

436 - ZENDA ** [69]   b.f. Zamindar – Hope (Dancing Brave).

February 18. Third foal.

Half-sister to the very useful 2-y-o 7f and 3-y-o dual listed 1m winner Hopeful Light (by Warning). The dam is an unraced sister to the very smart filly Wemyss Bight, a winner of five races from 9f (at 2 yrs) to 12f including the Group 1 Irish Oaks and the Group 2 Prix de Malleret. The second dam, Bahamian (by Mill Reef), was a very useful winner of the Group 3 12f Lingfield Oaks Trial and was placed in the Prix de l'Esperance (disqualified from first place), Prix de Pomone, Park Hill Stakes and Princess Royal Stakes. She is a half-sister to the very useful winners Captivator, Eileen Jenny and Kasmayo. *"A good, powerful sort of filly and a good mover that does everything right".*

437 - UNNAMED ** [84] b.f. Southern Halo – Glaze (Mr Prospector).
April 4. Ninth foal. $130,000Y. Keeneland September.
Half-sister to the smart 1998 2-y-o 7f winner and Group 1 1m Grand Criterium third Glamis, to the minor US winner Verreaux (both by Silver Hawk) and to Glassine (by Assert), a minor winner of 5 races in the USA. The dam, a winner of 3 races in the USA at up to 7f and second in a 6f stakes event at 2 yrs, is a half-sister to 4 winners including the dam of the US Graded stakes winners Vivid Angel, Fine N' Majestic and Electric Flash. The second dam, Round Pearl (by Round Table), won 10 races including a stakes event in the USA. *"She goes fine, is a neat filly and fairly racy. She'll make a 2-y-o".*

438 - UNNAMED ** [80] b.c. Benny The Dip – Night Fax (Known Fact).
February 17. Second foal. 150,000Y. Tattersalls October.
Half-brother to a minor 2-y-o winner in the USA by Thunder Gulch. The dam won 7 races including the Grade 2 10f Delaware Handicap and is a half-sister to 4 winners. The second dam, Night Letter (by Marduk), won 3 races in Germany. *"He goes well and would be one for July or August over seven furlongs".*

439 - UNNAMED * [80] ch.c. Spinning World – Northern Gulch (Gulch).
March 10. First foal. $375,000Y. Keeneland September.
The dam, a minor US placed 3-y-o, is a half-sister to 7 winners including the Grade 3 Del Mar Oaks and Grade 3 Dahlia Handicap winner Stylish Star. The second dam, Northern Style (by Ack Ack), was a stakes winner of 3 races and Grade 3 placed in the USA. *"He should be an early 2-y-o and he works well".*

440 - UNNAMED ** [76] ch.c. Distant View – Polly Adler (Housebuster).
March 4. Second foal. $160,000Y. Keeneland September.
The dam is an unraced half-sister to the champion US 2-y-o filly Epitome, winner of the Group 1 Breeders Cup Juvenile. The second dam, Honest And True (by Mr Leader), a stakes winner of 6 races, was third in the Grade 1 Fantasy Stakes and the Grade 1 Kentucky Oaks and is a half-sister to the high-class 2-y-o and miler Green Forest. *"A grand horse, he's alright at this stage but will just take a little time".*

441 - UNNAMED ** [76] b.br.f. Zafonic – Silver Lane (Silver Hawk).
March 13. Sixth living foal.
Half-sister to the useful Irish listed 10f winner Shakespeare (by Rainbow Quest), to the Japanese 1m stakes winner Black Hawk (by Nureyev) and the useful French 7f (at 2 yrs) and 1m winner and Group 2 placed Starmaniac (by Septieme Ciel). The dam, a very useful winner of three races including the Group 3 1m Prix de la Grotte, was third in the Irish Oaks and is a sister to the high-class middle-distance colt Hawkster (three Grade 1 wins) and the French listed winner Silver Kite. The second dam, Strait Lane (by Chieftain), is an unraced half-sister to 9 winners. *"A nice filly and she's going well at the moment".*

N GRAHAM

442 - TARAYIB * [71] br.f. Hamas – Enaya (Caerleon).
April 11.
Sister to Hata, placed fourth over 6f on her only start at 2 yrs in 2000 and to the quite useful but unreliable 6f winner Sulalat and half-sister to the useful Jila (by Kris), a winner from 6f to 7f, including at 2 yrs. The dam, a useful 2-y-o 6f winner, is a half-sister to the very smart 7f and 1m performer Gabr and to the smart middle-distance horse Kutta. The second dam, Ardassine (by Ahonoora), won over 12f in Ireland and was fourth in the Group 3 North Ridge Farm One Thousand Guineas Trial. (Hamdan Al-Maktoum). *"Still in Dubai until late April, but Angus Gold tells me they like her a lot. Apparently, even more so than they did her half-sister Hata last year and she's showing good form over there now".*

443 - UNNAMED * [59] gr.f. Alhaarth – Shakamiyn (Nishapour).
March 2. Fifth foal. 41,000Y. Tattersalls October.
Half-sister to the fair Shakiyr (by Lashkari), a winner of 6 races at up to 2m including on the all-weather and to a winner over the jumps by Kahyasi. The dam is an unraced half-sister to the Group 1 Grand

Prix de Saint-Cloud winner Shakapour, the Grade 1 Bowling Green Handicap winner Sharannpour and the dams of the Derby winner Shahrastani and the French Oaks winner Shemaka. The second dam, Shamim (by Le Haar), won over 1m at 2 yrs and is a half-sister to the high-class middle-distance stayer Kamaraan. *"A lovely, big, rangy filly. I like her very much and she'll make a 2-y-o later in the season. A beautiful mover with a lovely temperament."*

M GRASSICK

444 - ALEXANDER BALLET **

b.f. Mind Games – Dayville (Dayjur).
March 15. First foal. 66,000Y. Tattersalls October.

The dam, a quite useful triple 6f winner, is a half-sister to 3 winners including the Grade 1 Yellow Ribbon Handicap winner Spanish Fern. The second dam, Chain Fern (by Blushing Groom), is an unraced sister to the Irish One Thousand Guineas and Coronation Stakes winner Al Bahathri and a half-sister to Geraldine's Store, an American stakes-winning filly at up to 10f, and to the Cheshire Oaks winner Peplum. (Fenpark Syndicate). *"A small filly when we bought her but she's done so much developing it's unreal. I thought she was going to be early but now we're talking about July or August before she'd be on the track. She's a five or six furlong type".*

445 - HAPPY DREAMS (IRE) ***

b.f. Sadler's Wells – Flame Of Tara (Artaius).
February 16.

Sister to numerous winners including the brilliant filly Salsabil, winner of the One Thousand Guineas, Oaks, Irish Derby and Prix Vermeille, the smart dual 12f winner Song of Tara and the very useful 10f and 10.5f winner Nearctic Flame and half-sister to the high-class Group 1 St James's Palace Stakes winner Marju (by Last Tycoon) and the 1995 2-y-o Group 3 6f Railway Stakes winner Flame of Athens (by Royal Academy). The dam won 8 races including the Group 2 1m Coronation Stakes and the Group 2 Pretty Polly Stakes and was second in the Champion Stakes. She is a half-sister to the useful dual 2-y-o 7f winner Blaze of Tara and to Fruition - dam of both the Breeders Cup Turf winner Northern Spur and the high-class stayer Kneller. The second dam, Welsh Flame (by Welsh Pageant), won 4 races at up to 1m and is a half-sister to the Musidora Stakes second Sofala - herself dam of the good stayer Bourbon Boy. (Miss P F O'Kelly). *"This is the nicest one from the family I've had. She's a gorgeous filly with a lot of quality about her. We'd be looking at the end of May or early June over six furlongs to begin with. She's very strong and is much more of a 2-y-o than the rest of the family have been. The owner/breeder Miss O'Kelly agrees that this is the nicest filly from the family since Salsabil".*
Significant sire/damsire crosses:- Salsabil (Gr 1), Chiang Mai (Gr 3).

446 - ST AYE (USA) *

b.f. Nureyev – Montage (Alydar).
April 24. Tenth foal.

Closely related to a Japanese winner of 6 races by Lyphard and to the useful 2000 Irish 2-y-o 6f winner and Group 2 Gimcrack Stakes third Juniper (by Danzig) and half-sister to the very useful Group 2 12f Blandford Stakes winner Andros Bay (by Alleged), the fairly useful 3-y-o 1m winner Mahrah (by Ela-Mana-Mou), the minor US 3-y-o winner Attractive Missile (by Relaunch) and the Japanese winner of 3 races Sweet Hikko (by Buckaroo). The dam, a winner at around 1m at 3 yrs in the USA, is closely related to the US triple Grade 2 winner Give Me Strength and a half-sister to the Grade 2 winner Talakeno. The second dam, Katonka (by Minnesota Mac), a half-sister to three US stakes winners, was a US Grade 3 winner. (Mr K Knellman). *"I thought she'd be early but she's done a lot of developing in the last two months and is a good-sized filly with a lot of quality. She'll probably start off in a six or seven furlong fillies maiden in mid-summer".*

447 - SWEET DEIMOS *

b.f. Green Desert – Bint Zamayem (Rainbow Quest).
February 15. Third foal. 50,000Y. Tattersalls Houghton.

Half-sister to Queenie (by Indian Ridge), unplaced in one start over 7f at 2 yrs in 2000. The dam, a fairly useful 3-y-o 10f winner, was listed-placed over 10f and is a half-sister to the Group 3 Prix Chloe winner Rouquette and the US listed winner Moody's Cat. The second dam, Zamayem (by Sadler's Wells), is an unraced half-sister to 4 winners. (Mr J Higgins). *"A strong individual and a nice filly with a lot of quality. She took a lot of time to break but she's settled in well now and I'd expect her to start in a six furlong fillies maiden at the end of May or in June".*

448 - UNNAMED * b.c. Danehill – Miss Arizona (Sure Blade).
April 26. Fourth foal.
Half-brother to the 3-y-o Tunstall (by Salse) and the quite useful 6f (at 2 yrs) and 9f winner Manhattan (by Fairy King). The dam, a winner of 2 races in Germany at 3 yrs, is a half-sister to the very smart Tattersalls Rogers Gold Cup and Prince Of Wales's Stakes winner Batshoof and to Regular Guest (a champion miler in Hong Kong). The second dam, Steel Habit (by Habitat), won two races in Italy and is a sister to the Irish dual Group 3 and US Grade 3 winner Ancestral and to the dam of the Two Thousand Guineas winner King Of Kings. (Mr Mervyn Stewkesbury). *"A big, tall, backward horse but he has a nice action and will probably start over seven furlongs in August or September".*

449 - UNNAMED * ch.f. Diesis – Sombreffe (Polish Precedent).
February 26. Third foal.
Half-sister to the unraced Irish-trained 2000 2-y-o Uliana (by Darshaan). The dam, a fair 7f all-weather winner, is closely related to the Group 2 Mill Reef Stakes winner Russian Bond and the Group 2 Temple Stakes winner Snaadee and a half-sister to the Group 3 Prix de Conde winner Cristofori. The second dam, Somfas (by What A Pleasure), won 4 races at up to 7f in the USA and is a half-sister to the Canadian Horse of the Year Fanfreluche (dam of three Canadian Grade 1 winners). (Mr J Higgins). *"She's a lovely, quality filly and you're looking at seven furlongs in July or August. A good-sized, very athletic filly".*

450 - UNNAMED * b.c. Seeking The Gold – Shapiro's Mistress (Unpredictable).
February 17. Eighth foal.
Half-brother to 5 winners including the US stakes winner and Grade 2 Astarita Stakes third Mistress S and the US winner and Grade 1 Hollwood Starlet Stakes third Viz (both by Kris S). The dam, a stakes winner at 2 yrs in the USA, is a half-sister to the Grade 1 Breeders Cup Juvenile and Santa Anita Derby winner Brocco. (Mr K Knellman). *"There's a lot of quality about this colt. He's a big, strong 2-y-o for the second half of the season".*

R GUEST

451 - CAROLLAN (IRE) [68] b.f. Marju – Caroline Lady (Caro).
April 4. Fifth foal. IR£30,000Y. Goffs Orby.
Sister to the quite useful 2000 7f and 1m placed 2-y-o Starry Lady and half-sister to the quite useful 10f winner Forest Heath (by Common Grounds), the Irish 10f winner Sandholes (by Tirol) and a winner of 3 races in Japan by Generous. The dam, a French 12f winner, is a half-sister to 5 winners including the US Grade 3 winner Lord Sreva. The second dam, Lyphard's Lady (by Lyphard), won 2 races in France and the USA, was second in the listed 1m Prix de Saint-Cyr and is a half-sister to 7 winners. (Davies, Moss, Vaessen). *"A nice, athletic filly, she's not too big but has some scope. She won't be ready until the seven furlong races come along".*

452 - FIRST EXHIBIT [82] b.f. Machiavellian – My Emma (Marju).
March 14.
The dam, a smart winner of the Group 1 12f Prix Vermeille, is a half-sister to the Group 1 St Leger and Group 1 Ascot Gold Cup winner Classic Cliché. The second dam, Pato (by High Top), a fairly useful 2-y-o 7f and triple 4-y-o 10f winner, is a sister to the very smart sprinter Crews Hill. (Matthes Breeding & Racing). *"Being out of My Emma, this filly is obviously close to everyone's heart here. She looks like her dam, although a bit slighter at the moment, but the family is a late-maturing sort and she won't be anything until next year".*

453 - NAZARETH (IRE) * [69] b.c. Woodborough – Tinos Island (Alzao).
March 11. First foal. 8,000Y Ir gns. Tattersalls Fairyhouse.
The dam was unplaced in three starts at 2 yrs. The second dam, Lady Windley (by Baillamont), an 11f winner of 3 races in France, is a half-sister to 3 winners and to the placed dam of the Group 1 Tattersalls Gold Cup winner Shiva and the Group 2 Prix Jean du Chaudenay winner Limnos. The third dam, Northern Trick (by Northern Dancer), won the 10.5f Prix de Diane and the 12f Prix Vermeille, was second in the Prix de l'Arc de Triomphe and is a half-sister to the US Grade 1 Jockey Club Gold Cup winner On The Sly. (The Rae Guest Racing Partnership). *"A neat, active colt, he should be ready by*

early May and be the yard's first 2-y-o runner. He's going well but needs some decent ground and he'll be effective at five or six furlongs this year".

454 - VILLANELLE (USA) [76]   b.f. Cozzene – Elvia (Roberto).
May 5. Eleventh foal. $50,000Y. Keeneland September.
Sister to the fair 2000 10f placed 3-y-o Brady Boys and half-sister to the 1992 2-y-o dual 1m winner Elkhart (by Gone West), subsequently a winner of 5 races and Grade 3 placed in the USA and to minor winners in the USA by Alleged, Gone West and Known Fact. The dam, a minor winner at 4 yrs in the USA, is a half-sister to the Italian winner and Group 2 third Brace Blu. The second dam, Chain Bracelet (by Lyphard), won 9 races including the Grade 1 9f Top Flight Handicap and the Grade 2 Shuvee Handicap and is a half-sister to the US Grade 3 winner Dancing Slippers. (Kirsten Rausing). *"She only came into the yard late and so is difficult to assess. The pedigree doesn't suggest that she'll be particularly early, but she'll make a 2-y-o later on".*

W HAGGAS

455 - ALNAJA (USA) ** [85]   b.c. Woodman – Cursory Look (Nijinsky).
February 22. Sixth foal. 82,000Y. Tattersalls Houghton.
Brother to the 3-y-o Admiring and half-brother to the fairly useful 12f winner Glance (by Ela-Mana-Mou). The dam ran once unplaced and is a full or half-sister to 6 winners and to the unplaced dam of Whakilyric (herself dam of Hernando and Johann Quatz). (Mr J Caplan). *"He's doing very well and should start off at the July meeting – that sort of time. He should be a seven furlong horse and is a nice, powerful type that's got a chance. He's particularly well at the moment and is a nice horse. I'm looking at him now thinking – has this got a chance of being a proper horse?"*
Significant sire/damsire crosses:- Bahhare, Ciro, Way Of Light.

456 - BEAT TIME * [93]   gr.f. Lion Cavern – Brilliant Timing (The Minstrel).
February 23.
Half-sister to Pendulum (by Pursuit Of Love), unplaced on her only start at 2 yrs in 2000, to the fairly useful 2-y-o 6f and 7.5f winner Watch The Clock (by Mtoto), the fair 2-y-o 6f winner Bold Timing (by Never So Bold) and the fair 1996 2-y-o Perpetual (by Prince Sabo), a winner of 3 races from 5f to 6f - including on the all-weather. The dam ran once, being placed over 6f at 2 yrs, is a sister to the Irish 1m to 10f winner Minstrel's Assertion and a half-sister to Timely Writer (four Grade 1 wins in the USA) and Timely Assertion (Grade 1 Santa Anita Oaks winner). The second dam, Timely Roman (by Sette Bello), was unraced. (Cheveley Park Stud). *"She was as narrow as anything but had a break for a couple of months and has come back looking terrific. She's not doing much at the moment (early April) and is one for later in the year".*

457 - CHORIST * [90]   ch.f. Pivotal – Choir Mistress (Chief Singer).
February 11. Fifth foal.
Half-sister to the unraced 2000 2-y-o Choir School, to the very useful 2-y-o 7f winner and Group 3 7f Prestige Stakes second Choirgirl (both by Unfuwain) and the fair 7f (at 2 yrs) and 14.8f all-weather winner Operatic (by Goofalik). The dam is an unraced half-sister to 4 winners including the smart Group 2 11.9f Great Voltigeur Stakes winner Sacrament. The second dam, Blessed Event (by Kings Lake), a very useful winner of the listed 10f Ballymacoll Stud Stakes at 3 yrs, was second in the Yorkshire Oaks and fourth in the Champion Stakes. (Cheveley Park Stud). *"A huge filly but she has a nice pedigree and would have a chance. She's had a setback and was difficult to break. I won't get her back until May".*

458 - DUPONT **** [101]   b.c. Zafonic – June Moon (Sadler's Wells).
April 10. Fifth foal.
Brother to the Japanese 7f and 1m winner (including at 2 yrs) Zachariah and to the German Group 2 winner Pacino and half-brother to the quite useful 7f (at 2 yrs) to 12f winner Winsome George (by Marju). The dam is an unraced daughter of the smart Group 3 Cherry Hinton Stakes winner and One Thousand Guineas second Kerrera (by Diesis), herself a half-sister to the high-class 2-y-o Rock City. (Wentworth Racing & Mr P Bader). *"This is the nicest one we've got. A nice pedigree, he goes well and I'm hopeful. He does everything very easily and the only other Zafonic I've had is Count Dubois who has done well for us. This colt would have more speed and I'm going to try to get him to Ascot – the races that is, not the Sales! A very solid-looking horse and a nice walker".*

Significant sire/damsire crosses:- Endless Summer, Pacino.

459 - ENTRAP (USA) * [63] b.f. Phone Trick – Mystic Lure (Green Desert).
March 13. Second foal. $150,000Y. Keeneland September.
The dam, a fair 5f and 6f placed 2-y-o, is a half-sister to 5 winners including the Grade 1 Hollywood Derby and Group 3 Prix Daphnis winner Thrill Show and the Grade 3 Pilgrim Stakes winner David's Bird. The second dam, Splendid Girl (by Golden Eagle II), was a stakes winner of 7 races in the USA at up to 1m. (Cheveley Park Stud). *"A nice, attractive filly. She's quite tall and I haven't asked much of her yet so we shall see – but she's a pretty nice filly".*

460 - FIRST ALERT * [86] ch.f. Miswaki – First Amendment (Caerleon).
February 28. Second foal.
The dam was placed over 7f (at 2 yrs) and 12f here before winning a minor event in the USA and is a half-sister to 2 winners including the quite useful 10f winner Verdigris. The second dam, Penultimate (by Roberto), is an unraced half-sister to the listed Oh So Sharp Stakes winner Ruznama out of the Musidora Stakes winner Last Feather. (Cheveley Park Stud). *"I quite like her – she's a funny little thing but she doesn't half go nicely. Home-bred by Cheveley Park who have been very good to me, she's one of the horses you don't really notice is there because she's so uncomplicated. She has a good temperament and anyone can ride her. I'm not saying 'she could be anything', but she could win two races and that would be nice".*

461 - HOROSCOPE (IRE) * [91] b.g. Eagle Eyed – Council Rock (General Assembly).
March 10.
Half-brother to the very smart 2000 2-y-o Superstar Leo, winner of the Group 2 5f Flying Childers Stakes and the Weatherbys Super Sprint, to the quite useful 5f and 6f winner Chiquita (both by College Chapel), the fair 7f all-weather winner Royal Artist (by Royal Academy) and minor winners abroad by Keen, Anshan and Royal Academy. The dam, a fair 9f and 10f placed 3-y-o, is a half-sister to 6 winners including the Group 3 Prestige Stakes winner Glatisant and the listed Virginia Stakes winner Gai Bulga. The second dam, Dancing Rocks (by Green Dancer), was a very smart filly and winner of the Group 2 10f Nassau Stakes. (Horoscope Partnership). *"A half-brother to Superstar Leo, we had to geld him as a yearling. Lester went to see him but the horse wrapped his legs around a chap that was leading him up the field! He's going to be a racehorse – not a stallion. He'll be out in mid-summer, isn't very big and is pretty uncomplicated at the moment. A nice, kind little horse that will start at five furlongs".*

462 - LA PERLA ** [74] gr.f. Royal Applause – Lammastide (Martinmas).
April 1. Tenth foal. 25,000Y. Tattersalls October.
Half-sister to the unplaced 2000 2-y-o Dominion Prince (by First Trump), to the quite useful winner of 5 races over 7f Amber Fort (by Indian Ridge), the fair 2-y-o 6f winner Musabiq (by Superlative), the modest 2-y-o 5f winner Tribal Mischief (by Be My Chief), the moderate 5f and 6f winner Ganeshaya (by Formidable) and a winner in Germany by Pharly. The dam, a fairly useful 2-y-o 5f winner, is a half-sister to 6 winners including the listed 1m Easter Stakes winner Regiment. The second dam, Rossaldene (by Mummy's Pet), was a quite useful 2-y-o 5f winner and a half-sister to 6 winners. (Mr D Scott). *"A family I know very well. All the good ones are grey like her and she's quite a nice filly. She'll run early and if she wins her maiden she'll go to Royal Ascot".*

463 - NAILBITER [78] b.g. Night Shift – Scylla (Rock City).
January 29. First foal. 24,000Y. Tattersalls October.
The dam is an unplaced half-sister to 8 winners including the Group 3 Phoenix Sprint Stakes winner Northern Goddess (herself dam of the US Grade 3 winner Northern Quest). The second dam, Hearten (by Hittite Glory), is an unraced half-sister to 7 winners. (Mr B Haggas). *"I've just gelded him because if he was a human being he'd have green hair and earrings all over the place – a real yob! So we cut him to quieten him down – but he's a tough horse".*

464 - PRIMA DIVA ** [80] ch.f. Primo Dominie – Sylvan Song (Song).
May 1. Eighth foal. 28,000Y. Tattersalls October.
Half-sister to the 2001 all-weather 3-y-o winner Bravura (by Never So Bold), to the very useful 6f and 7f winner (including on the all-weather) Chewit (by Beveled) and a winner over jumps by Presidium. The dam is an unplaced sister to the useful listed-placed winners Band On The Run and Shark Song. The second dam, Sylvanecte (by Silver Shark), a fair 3-y-o 10f winner, is a half-sister to 7 winners. (Mr

A Hirschfeld). *"She has a nice pedigree and is a bit behind but she's alright. She shows a willingness to get on with it and I like chestnut Primo Dominie's. We've put her in the Super Sprint at Newbury even though she's a May foal".*
Significant sire/damsire crosses:- Millyant (Gr 2).

**465 - REDISHAM ** ** [84]   ch.f. Hector Protector – Barsham (Be My Guest).
February 8. Tenth foal. 26,000Y. Tattersalls October.
Half-sister to the very useful 1996 2-y-o listed 1m winner Falkenham (by Polar Falcon), to the fairly useful 2-y-o dual 5f winner Bemuse (by Forzando), the fairly useful 10f and 10.3f winner Jameel Asmar (by Rock City), the quite useful dual 1m winner Redisham (by Persian Bold) and the modest 15.4f winner Guestwick (by Blakeney). The dam, a fairly useful 10f winner, is a half-sister to 7 minor winners out of the 3-y-o 12f and 13.3f winner Bodham (by Bustino) - herself a daughter of a half-sister to Blakeney and Morston. (Cheveley Park Stud). *"Bought by Cheveley Park at the Sales and the owner Mr Thompson is a big fan of Hector Protector. A mid-season type of filly and quite strong, I should think she'll start over six furlongs".*

**466 - SALVINO (USA) ** ** [86]   b.c. Lear Fan – Fairy Fable (Fairy King).
May 2. Sixth foal. $120,000Y. Keeneland September.
Half-brother to 2 minor winners including the Irish and US winner Fabricate (by Crafty Prospector). The dam, an Irish 2-y-o winner, is a half-sister to 4 winners out of the unraced Gentle Freedom (by Wolver Hollow), herself a half-sister to the dams of Riviera Charm (multiple Australasian Grade 1 winner), La Grange Music (Group 3 Criterion Stakes) and Great Vintage (Australian Grade 2 winner). (Mr G Biszantz). *"This is a nice horse. Quite tall and backward at the moment, he's a September type 2-y-o but is a gorgeous mover. I've had a couple of Lear Fan's that have been temperamental – including Idle Hound who was called that because he was one! But this colt is a different matter. I should think he'd start off at around seven furlongs".*

**467 - SOCIETY (IRE) ** ** [89]   b.f. Barathea – Lobmille (Mill Reef).
February 19. Ninth foal. 120,000Y. Tattersalls Houghton.
Half-sister to the 2000 2-y-o triple 7f and Group 3 7f Nell Gwyn Stakes winner Lil's Jessy (by Kris), to the smart French 1m listed winner Lone Bid (by Priolo), the fairly useful Italian 7.5f and 1m winner Hurricane Louis (by Fabulous Dancer) and the 1m to 12f winner Lobbyist (by Mtoto). The dam is an unraced half-sister to 4 winners. The second dam, Light O'Battle (by Queen's Hussar), won at 2 yrs and is a sister to the One Thousand Guineas and French Oaks winner Highclere (the grandam of Nashwan and Unfuwain). (Highclere Thoroughbred Racing Ltd). *"A nice filly that's done really well. She was very temperamental when she came but she's really come good mentally. A nice mover, she's a solid filly. She's in the Houghton Sales race and should be running over seven furlongs in late August or September".*

---

468 - SUNDRENCHED (IRE) * *** [72]   ch.f. Desert King – Utr (Mr Prospector).
March 26. Third foal. 175,000Y. Tattersalls Houghton.
Half-sister to the smart 2000 6f winner and Group 1 1m Racing Post Trophy third Bonnard (by Nureyev) and to the quite useful 10f and 12.3f winner Andromedes (by Sadler's Wells). The dam is an unplaced daughter of the very useful listed 1m winner and Coronation Stakes second Hasbah (by Kris), herself a half-sister to the dam of the very useful sprinter Almaty out of the Irish One Thousand Guineas and Coronation Stakes winner Al Bahathri. (Lael Stables Partnership). *"A lovely, scopey filly with a good backside on her and a nice pedigree. I'd expect her to start shaping up in July and be racing shortly after. A filly with a lot of presence, I was keen for Amanda Skiffington to buy her and I haven't gone off her yet".*

**469 - WHITE CLIFFS ** ** [81]   ch.c. Bluebird – Preening (Persian Bold).
February 7.
Half-brother to the fair 1998 2-y-o 5f winner Alpha (by Primo Dominie). The dam, a modest 12f winner, is a half-sister to the snart 7f and 1m winner Hadeer. The second dam, Glinting (by by Crepello), won over 6f at 2 yrs, was placed in the Nell Gwyn Stakes and is a half-sister to the dams and grandams of numerous good winners including Bassenthwaite, Braashee, Ghariba and Keen Hunter. (Guy Reed). *"A strong horse, he's medium-sized with a great big backside and he looks a runner. A really nice colt".*

470 - UNNAMED * [66]   b.f. Efisio – Waypoint (Cadeaux Genereux).
March 9. First foal. 24,000Y. Doncaster St Leger.

The dam, a fairly useful 6f and 7f winner at 3 and 4 yrs (including on the all-weather), is a half-sister to the quite useful 2-y-o 5f winner Kissing Time. The second dam, Princess Athena (by Ahonoora), a very smart winner of the Group 3 5f Queen Mary Stakes, was placed in numerous Group events over sprint distances and is a half-sister to 4 winners. (Mr & Mrs G Middlebrook). *"I bought her because she's the spitting image of an Efisio filly I had called Riberac who won a listed race for Mark Johnston last year. She's exactly the same. She looks the same, is just as lazy, just as bad a mover and is as tough as old boots. I expect her to just wake up to it all one day".*

R HANNON

471 - ALEXANDER ACADEMY (USA) [78]   b.f. Royal Academy – Fantastic Bid (Auction Ring).
February 23. Sixth foal. IR£40,000Y. Goffs Orby.

Half-sister to the fair 3-y-o 7f winner Fantastic Dance (by Imperial Ballet) and the 1999 7f placed 2-y-o Formal Bid (by Dynaformer). The dam, winner of the listed 1m Prix de Saint-Cyr, is a half-sister to the French 1m to 10f winner and subsequent US stakes winner Fantastic Don (by Sovereign Dancer) and the smart Group 3 10f Gordon Richards Stakes winner Germano. The second dam, Gay Fantastic (by Ela-Mana-Mou), is an unraced sister to the Group 3 Prix de Flore winner Gay Hellene and a half-sister to the grandam of Pilsudski. *"A nice, tall filly but a bit backward at the moment. She's only just arrived from Ireland so I don't know an awful lot about her but she looks nice".*

472 - APPROVAL ** [80]   b.c. Royal Applause – Gentle Persuasion (Bustino).
April 24.

Half-brother to the very useful Group 2 6f Moet and Chandon Rennen winner and Group 2 Mill Reef Stakes third Sharp Prod and to the fair 2-y-o 5f winner Prompting (by Primo Dominie and herself dam of the German 2-y-o winner and Group 2 second Sharp Domino). The dam, a fairly useful 2-y-o 6f winner, was placed in the Princess Margaret Stakes and the Rockfel Stakes. (The Queen). *"We've got three very nice Royal Applause 2-y-o's. This one is the Queen's and he goes very, very well".*

473 - BIG BOPPER (IRE) ** [82]   b.c. Danehill Dancer – Apocalypse (Auction Ring).
March 23. Fourteenth foal. 35,000Y. Doncaster St Leger.

Half-brother to the modest 5f and 8.2f winner Lars Porsena (by Trojan Fen) and the modest 5f all-weather winner Cellito (by Flash of Steel). The dam, a minor French 1m winner, is a sister to one winner and a half-sister to 8 winners including King's Company (Irish Two Thousand Guineas) and Deep Diver (Nunthorpe Stakes). The second dam, Miss Stephen (by Stephen Paul), was unraced. (Speedlith Group). *"A nice, big horse, he'll make a 2-y-o from June onwards and be suited by six furlongs I should think".*

474 - CLIMATE (IRE) ** [78]   ch.c. Catrail – Burishki (Chilibang).
February 24. Fourth foal. IR22,000Y. Tattersalls Fairyhouse.

Brother to the modest 2000 6f placed 2-y-o Winfield and half-brother to a 2-y-o 5f winner in Italy by Indian Ridge. The dam, a moderate dual 6f winner, is a half-sister to 3 minor winners. The second dam, Hunza Water (by Relko), was a fair 11.5f winner and a half-sister to 11 winners. (Mr Louis Stalder). *"Yes, he's a nice horse and he goes very well. He'll be a six furlong horse".*

475 - COMMUNARD (IRE) ** [95]   b.c. Sri Pekan – Broadway Rosie (Absalom).
April 28. Seventh foal. IR£50,000Y. Goffs Orby.

Half-brother to the smart Group 3 6f Greenlands Stakes and listed 6f Sandy Lane Stakes winner Eastern Purple (by Petorius), to the quite useful sprint winner of 12 races Double Oscar (by Royal Academy) and the minor French 10f winner Mo's Main Man (by Taufan). The dam, a useful Irish listed winner of 4 races from 5f to 7f, is a half-sister to the Irish listed winner Mora. The second dam, Broadway Royal (by Royal Match), is an unraced half-sister to the Kings Stand Stakes winner African Song. (Mr Michael Pescod). *"A fine, big, strong horse. He'll be one of our earlier 2-y-o's".*

476 - DIAMOND MILL (IRE) ** [72]　　　　ch.f. Desert King – Euromill (Shirley Heights).
April 28.

Half-sister to the useful Tadwiga, winner of the 6.3f Goffs £100,000 Challenge and the listed 1m Masaka Stakes and to the useful Irish 2-y-o listed 7f Orby Stakes winner and Group 2 Premio Ribot fourth Bartok (both by Fairy King). The dam, a middle-distance stayer, won twice in Ireland and is a half-sister to 7 winners including the Group 2 Jockey Club Stakes second and Group 2 Prince Of Wales's Stakes second Luchiroverte. The second dam, Green Lucia (by Green Dancer), won a listed race in Ireland, was placed in the Yorkshire Oaks and the Irish Oaks and is a half-sister to the top-class middle-distance colt Old Vic. *"Very nice. She should be early and she's a sharp filly that works well".*

477 - EAGLES HIGH (IRE) * [82]　　　　ch.c. Eagle Eyed – Bint Al Balad (Ahonoora).
February 17. Third foal. IR£30,000Y. Goffs Challenge.

The dam, a modest 7f placed 3-y-o, is a sister to the useful Group 3 7f Nell Gwyn Stakes winner and Irish One Thousand Guineas fourth A-To-Z. The second dam, Zenga (by Try My Best), won 4 races in Italy, was listed-placed and is a half-sister to 7 winners. *"A colt that goes well, he'll be an early 2-y-o that should win races for us".*

478 - EXTREMIST (USA) [98]　　　　b.c. Dynaformer – Strumming (Ballad Rock).
April 5. Second foal. $95,000Y. Keeneland September.

The dam, a fair 3-y-o 1m winner here, subsequently won in the USA at 4 yrs and is a half-sister to a winner in Italy. The second dam, Casla (by Lomond), a minor Irish winner, is a half-sister to the useful 6f and 1m winner Nordica (herself dam of the Fred Darling Stakes winner Sueboog) and to the dam of the useful listed winner Recondite. (Highclere Thoroughbreds Ltd). *"A backward horse, he's going all right at the moment but I think he'll need seven furlongs this season".*

479 - FAIR KAI (IRE) ** [55]　　　　b.f. Fayruz – Raja Moulana (Raja Baba).
April 20. Eighth foal. 23,000Y. Doncaster St Leger.

Half-sister to the quite useful 2000 2-y-o 5f winner Sing A Song (by Blues Traveller) and to the useful 6f to 9f (at 2 yrs) and subsequent Italian listed winner Futurballa (by Taufan). The dam, a fair 7f winner, is a half-sister to one winner. The second dam, Gallatin Valley (by Apalachee), won 3 races at up to 1m and is a half-sister to 9 winners, mainly in the USA. (I A N Wight & D M Wight). *"A half-sister to Sing-A-Song, she's another nice, sharp, early sort".*

480 - GLENMORANGIE ** [78]　　　　gr.c. Danzig Connection – In The Highlands (Petong).
February 5. Second foal. IR13,500Y.

Half-brother to the moderate 2000 5f placed 2-y-o Highland Flight (by Missed Flight). The dam is an unplaced half-sister to 4 winners including the listed Heron Stakes second In Like Flynn. The second dam, Thevetia (by Mummy's Pet), is a placed half-sister to 7 winners including the Group 1 Coronation Stakes fourth Moogie and the French listed winner Dazzling Heights. *"I've been waiting for some decent ground for him but he may well have started his career before your book's published. He's a nice type of horse and he's working well".*

481 - GOLDEN BOUNTY ** [83]　　　　b.c. Bahamian Bounty – Cumbrian Melody (Petong).
February 20. Eighth foal. 65,000Y. Tattersalls October.

Half-brother to the moderate 1999 2-y-o 6f winner Cumbrian Princess (by Mtoto), to the 1996 German 3-y-o 6f winner and listed placed Woodfighter (by Ballad Rock) and the modest 1995 7f all-weather winner Titanium Honda (by Doulab). The dam, a quite useful 2-y-o 5f and 6f winner, is a half-sister to 5 winners including the dam of the Group 3 Beeswing Stakes winner Savahra Sound. The second dam, Avahra (by Sahib), was a useful winner of 3 races over sprint distances. *"A very nice six furlong 2-y-o. He's worked very well and will win races".*

482 - GOLDEN SPECTRUM (IRE) ** [81]　　　　ch.c. Spectrum – Plessaya (Nureyev).
May 8. Seventh foal. 28,000Y. Tattersalls October.

Brother to the fair 2000 2-y-o 7f winner Smart Dancer and half-brother to the Scandinavian winner of 4 races and listed-placed Parthe and the German/UAE 7f to 10f winner Paris Sport (both by Highest Honor). The dam is an unraced half-sister to the Group 1 Prix Lupin winner and Derby fourth Persepolis and to the listed Haydock Park Spring Trophy winner Chaddleworth. The second dam, Perlita (by

Baldric II), is a placed half-sister to the dam of the Group 1 winners Vayrann and Yashgar out of the French One Thousand Guineas and Prix du Moulin winner Pola Bella. (Mr George E K Teo). *"A big, strong, good-looking horse although he won't be an early 2-y-o".*

483 - GOLD HEART (IRE) ** [87]

b.f. Entrepreneur – Soha (Dancing Brave).
April 26. Fifth foal. 75,000Y. Tattersalls Houghton.

Half-sister to Tara Gold, a fair 6f and 7f placed 2-y-o in 2000, to the smart listed 9f Strensall Stakes winner Gold Academy (both by Royal Academy), placed third in the Group 1 1m St James's Palace Stakes and the Group 1 1m Queen Elizabeth II Stakes and the fair 1996 2-y-o 5f and 6f winner Without Friends (by Thatching). The dam, a modest 12f placed 3-y-o, is out of the Italian Oaks winner Paris Royal (by Mill Reef), herself a half-sister to the Irish Two Thousand Guineas winner Northern Treasure and the Athasi Stakes winner Etoile de Paris (dam of the Yorkshire Oaks winner Only Royale). (The Queen). *"A very nice filly – there's nothing wrong with her! She not done a lot of work but I'm pleased with the work she has done. A good mover and she could be sharp".*

484 - GRAND HARBOUR (IRE) * [96]

b.c. Grand Lodge – Port Isaac (Seattle Song).
April 24. Fifth foal. IR£60,000Y. Goffs Orby.

Half-brother to Greenborough (by Dr Devious), unplaced on one start at 2 yrs in 2000, to the fair dual 6f winner (including at 2 yrs) Howard's Lad and the Italian winner of 10 races at up to 1m Ambra Luciani (both by Reprimand). The dam was placed once over 7f at 2 yrs and is a half-sister to 10 minor winners in the USA. The second dam, Key Link (by Bold Ruler), ran twice unplaced, is a sister to the US Grade 3 winner Key To The Kingdom and a half-sister to 6 winners including the top-class US horses Fort Marcy and Key To The Mint. *"He's a smasher but you won't see him out until towards the back-end of the season".*

485 - HAMEEDA * [76]

b.f. Hector Protector – Habibti (Habitat).
March 2.

Half-sister to the Irish 2-y-o 5f winner Desert Lily (by Green Desert) and several disappointing animals. The dam, a brilliant sprinter, won the July Cup, William Hill Sprint Championship, Prix de l'Abbaye and Kings Stand Stakes (all Group 1 events) and the Group 2 Vernons Sprint Cup. She also finished fourth, promoted to third, in the One Thousand Guineas and is a half-sister to the useful Irish sprinter Knesset and to Eight Carat, dam of two Grade 1 winners in Australia and New Zealand. The second dam, Klairessa (by Klairon), won once at just under 6f, is a sister to the good sprinter D'Urberville and is closely related to Lora, herself dam of the 1,000 Guineas winner On the House. (Sussex Stud Ltd). *"A very sharp filly, I know the mare's been disappointing but we may have found the right one here as she looks a speedy type".*

486 - HANNON (FR) * [96]

b.c. Exit To Nowhere – Delphania (Fabulous Dancer).
February 27. Third foal. FF140,000. Deauville August.

Half-sister to a placed filly in France by Kaldoun. The dam, a minor winner in France, is a half-sister to 3 minor winners abroad. The second dam, Delphinskaia (by Green Dancer), won 3 races and was Group placed over 10f and 12f in France and is a half-sister to the dual French Group 3 winner Darly. *"A smashing colt, I like him and expect him to start over six furlongs but to get a mile. A very nice horse but I think the owner was taking the mickey when he named him!".*

487 - HIGH GODDESS [76]

ch.f. Singspiel – Severa (Kendor).
January 19. First foal. IR£45,000Y. Goffs Orby.

The dam won twice in Germany at 3 yrs and is a half-sister to 8 winners. The second dam, Santina (by Gimont), won in Germany and was third in the Group 2 German Oaks. (Mrs D Mort). *"A January foal, but she's very immature physically so we've left her alone for now".*

488 - INNOVATOR (IRE) * [82]

b.c. Entrepreneur – Midnight Angel (Machiavellian).
February 8. First foal. 30,000Y. Tattersalls October.

The dam is an unraced half-sister to 5 minor winners. The second dam, Night At Sea (by Night Shift), was a sprint winner of 3 races including the listed Trafalgar House Stakes and is a half-sister to 6 winners. (Highclere Thoroughbred Racing Ltd). *"A very nice horse. I was concerned he might be a bit soft but he's pleasing me more now".*

489 - IN THE FRAME (IRE) * [85]   b.c. Definite Article – Victorian Flower (Tate Gallery).
March 21. Fifth foal. IR£20,000Y. Goffs Challenge.
Brother to the modest 2000 5f to 7f placed 2-y-o Je'thame and half-brother to the minor 8.5f and 11.5f Italian winner Queen Of Belot (by Common Grounds) and a minor US winner by Silver Kite. The dam ran twice unplaced and is a half-sister to 3 winners and to the unraced dam of the US Grade 2 winners Yearly Tour and Victor Avenue. The second dam, Sir Ivor's Sorrow (by Sir Ivor), won 4 races in the USA and was fourth in the Grade 1 Mother Goose Stakes. (Mr P Lathom & Partners). *"One of the nicest-looking horses we've got. He won't be early and he should stay a mile easily. I'm very pleased with him. If he went back to the sales now he'd make three times the amount he cost as a yearling".*

490 - LADY DEVIKA ** [84]   b.f. Sri Pekan – The Frog Lady (Al Hareb).
April 26. Third foal. 36,000Y. Tattersalls October.
Half-sister to the useful 2000 2-y-o triple 6f winner Piccolo Player (by Piccolo) and to the modest 1999 2-y-o 7f all-weather winner The Frog Queen (by Bin Ajwaad). The dam, a moderate middle-distance placed maiden, is a half-sister to 3 minor winners. The second dam, Lady Bettina (by Bustino), ran once unplaced and is a half-sister to 3 minor winners. (Waney Racing Group Inc). *"She was a little bit ill for a while so she won't be early but she's a nice 2-y-o".*

491 - LADY LINKS * [62]   b.f. Bahamian Bounty – Sparky's Song (Electric).
February 22. Second foal. 22,000Y. Tattersalls October.
Half-sister to the unraced 2000 2-y-o Saariya (by Shaamit). The dam, a moderate 10.2f and 12f winner, is a half-sister to the very smart Group 1 6.5f winner Bold Edge (by Beveled) and to the listed winner and Group 3 5f Temple Stakes second Brave Edge. The second dam, Daring Ditty (by Daring March), ran unplaced twice and is a half-sister to 4 winners. (Coriolan Partnership). *"This really does look a very nice filly and a good mover but because of the state of the ground I've done very little with her as yet".*

492 - MADAME BOULANGERE ** [75]   b.f. Royal Applause – Jazz (Sharrood).
March 27. Fourth living foal. 29,000Y. Doncaster St Leger.
Half-sister to the hurdles winner Pebble Moon (by Efisio). The dam, a fair 7f (at 2 yrs) and 10f placed maiden, is a half-sister to 12 winners including the fairly useful 2-y-o 5f winner Chasing Moonbeams, the Italian Group 2 placed Finian's Rainbow and the French Group 2 placed Carmot. The second dam, Rainbow's End (by My Swallow), won once at 2 yrs. (Colin Baker). *"She goes really well and it won't be long before she's racing. As soon as we get some decent ground in fact".* Richard's son added *"I think this is the best filly we've got – as nice as I've seen here for a couple of years and she's such a lovely mover".*

493 - MOJO MAN * [73]   b.c. Millkom – Prima Sinfonia (Fairy King).
February 15. Third living foal. 35,000Y. Doncaster St Leger.
Half-brother to a winner in Japan by Tragic Role. The dam, a modest 7f and 8.2f placed maiden, is a half-sister to 4 winners including the Italian listed winners Louis' Queen and Golden Agos. The second dam, Bourbon Queen (by Ile de Bourbon), was a fair 7.6f placed 2-y-o. (Speedlith Group). *"He's a lovely, big horse that goes well. A five-to-six furlong type and a sharp, early colt – he'll make a nice 2-y-o".*

494 - MOTEN SWING * [86]   b.c. Kris – Lady Bankes (Alzao).
April 28. Second foal. FF200,000. Deauville August.
The dam, a fair 3-y-o 10f winner, is a half-sister to the Group 3 Prestige Stakes winner Circle Of Gold and to the listed Rose Bowl Stakes winner Crystal Crossing. The second dam, Never So Fair (by Never So Bold), is an unplaced half-sister to the Queen Mary Stakes winner Amaranda and the Nell Gwyn Stakes winner Favoridge. (Mr Bob Lalemant). *"A big, strong horse, he's working upsides and doing well. He looks a tidy colt".*

495 - MY DANCER (IRE) * [75]   b.f. Alhaarth – Dance Land (Nordance).
April 15. Fifth foal. 24,000Y. Doncaster St Leger.
Half-sister to the 3-y-o Jitterbug (by Marju) and to the minor Irish 3-y-o winner Dariole (by Priolo). The dam is an unraced sister to the Italian listed 10f winner Lifting and a half-sister to the listed Kingsclere Stakes winner and Queen Mary Stakes third Easy Landing and to the dam of the Zetland Stakes winner

Upper Strata (herself dam of the Prix de la Salamandre winner Lord Of Men). The second dam, Land Ho (by Primera), is an unplaced half-sister to the Group 3 Oaks Trial winner Lucent and to the grandam of Sonic Lady. (The Jubert Family). *"A very nice filly, she'll definitely make a 2-y-o. She's sharp, looks great in her coat and will be racing soon".*

---

496 - NATIONAL PARK * [78]   gr.c. Common Grounds – Success Story (Sharrood).
February 15. Fourth foal.
Half-brother to the useful 10f to 12f listed winner Film Script (by Unfuwain) and to the 8.5f and 10f winner Champagne (by Efisio). The dam, a modest 10f winner, is a half-sister to the Group 2 13.5f Prix de Pomone winner Interlude. The second dam, Starlet, was a smart 10f and 12f performer. (The Queen). *"A very nice colt owned by the Queen. He's working well".*

---

497 - NATURE (IRE) ** [62]   b.f. Bluebird – Nawaji (Trempolino).
February 10. Second foal. IR£30,000Y. Goffs Orby.
Half-sister to Brand New Day (by Robellino), unplaced in 2 starts at 2 yrs in 2000. The dam, a poor placed maiden at up to 13f, is a sister to the Group 3 10f Select Stakes winner Triarius and a half-sister to the listed Fred Archer Stakes winner Sharp Noble and the unraced dam of the Group 3 Prix des Reservoirs winner Bint Alnasr. The second dam, Noble Decretum (by Noble Decree), is an unraced half-sister to the US dual Grade 3 winner Vodka Time. (The Royal Ascot Racing Club). *"She's working nicely but just needs to come in her coat. She looks a speedy sort although the fact that her dam is by Trempolino may set her back a bit. A very nice filly".*

---

498 - NEMO FUGAT (IRE) * [57]   b.c. Danehill Dancer – Do The Right Thing (Busted).
February 21. Second reported foal. 34,000Y. Tattersalls October.
The dam, a fair 3-y-o 12f winner, is a half-sister to 4 winners including the useful 2000 2-y-o 5f and 6f winner and Coventry Stakes second Bram Stoker. The second dam, Taniokey (by Grundy), won once over 1m at 3 yrs in Ireland and is a half-sister to 5 winners including the Lowther Stakes winner Kittyhawk. (Dr A Haloute). *"A nice, big horse and good-looking, he'll be one for the mid-season onwards".*

---

499 - NOBLE ACADEMY (USA) ** [82]   ch.c. Royal Applause – Aristocratique (Cadeaux Genereux).
March 20. First foal. 25,000Y. Doncaster St Leger.
The dam was placed over 5f and 6.5f at 3 yrs in Ireland and is a half-sister to 9 winners including the Belgian Group 1 winner Sharpset and the listed Oak Tree Stakes winner Royal Loft. The second dam, Well Off (by Welsh Pageant), is an unplaced half-sister to the Swedish Group 1 and listed Clarence House Stakes winner Doc Marten. (Mrs Toni Tipper). *"A nice colt that will make a six or seven furlong type 2-y-o".*

---

500 - OCTENNIAL *** [85]   gr.c. Octagonal – Laune (Kenmare).
February 9. Fourth foal. 26,000Y. Tattersalls October.
Half-brother to Killarney (by Pursuit Of Love), unplaced in one start at 2 yrs in 2000 and to the fairly useful 1999 2-y-o 5f winner Launfal (by Rudimentary). The dam, a fair 5.3f winner at 2 yrs, is a half-sister to 6 winners including the Audtralian Grade 2 winner Hockney. The second dam, Artistic Princess (by Luskin Star), was a sprint winner of 7 races in Australia. (I A N Wight & D M Wight). *"I've got a lot of time for him – in fact I've got a quarter share in him. I like the mare and I think this is going to be a very nice horse. There's no reason why he shouldn't make it as a 2-y-o".*

---

501 - PARTYTIME (IRE) * [79]   ch.f. Tagula – Camarat (Ahonoora).
February 26. IR25,000Y. Tattersalls Fairyhouse.
Half-sister to the fair 1996 2-y-o 6f winner Columbia (by Mujtahid) and to the Austrian 6f winner Polish Bear (by Polish Patriot). The dam, a fair 9f winner, is a half-sister to 7 winners including the Group 2 Park Hill Stakes winner Trampship and the Lancashire Oaks second Cruising Height (herself dam of the St Leger and Yorkshire Oaks second High And Low). The second dam, Nomadic Pleasure (by Habitat), was a fairly useful 9f winner and a half-sister to the Prix Vermeille winner Paulista. (Lady Davis, J Perry & J Leek). *"Goes very well, we're just waiting for her coat to come. She'll be aimed at the Fairyhouse race".*

502 - PENNE DANCER (IRE) * [92]   gr.c. Pennekamp – Talama (Shakapour).
February 27. Fifth foal. 34,000Y. Tattersalls October.

Half-brother to 2 minor winners abroad by Kahyasi (in the UAE) and Second Set (in Sweden). The dam won once at 3 yrs in France and was listed-placed. The second dam, Talosca (by Abdos), won twice in France. *"He was fairly expensive but well-worth the money. He's the tallest 2-y-o we've got and I haven't done a lot with him but he's working really nicely and is a very nice colt".*

503 - PLAYBACK (IRE) * [89]   b.c. Revoque – Sound Tap (Warning).
February 1. First foal. IR£30,000Y. Goffs Orby.

The dam won 7 races in France from 2 to 5 yrs and is a half-sister to 4 minor winners in Europe. The second dam, Butterfly Rose (by Iron Ruler), a champion filly in Norway, is a half-sister to 6 winners including the dam of the US multiple Graded stakes winner Rare Blend. (Mr Luciano Gaucci). *"He's not the best of movers at the moment – I'm waiting for him to come to himself. But other than that he's a smashing colt".*

504 - PRINCE DAYJUR (USA) * [92]   b.c. Dayjur – Distinct Beauty (Phone Trick).
March 16. Second foal. IR£55,000Y. Goffs Challenge.

Half-brother to the 3-y-o Fancy Beauty (by Lear Fan). The dam, a minor 3-y-o winner in the USA, is a half-sister to 1 winner. The second dam, Wellomond (by Lomond), won at 3 yrs in France and is a half-sister to the Group 3 Blue Riband Trial Stakes winner Last Fandango. (Major A M Everett & Lucayan Stud). *"He goes very well and is a nice horse. There's no reason why he shouldn't be a 2-y-o as the work he's done up to now has been good".*

505 - PRINCE DOMINO ** [88]   b.c. Primo Dominie – Danzig Harbour (Private Account).
April 9. Seventh foal. 24,000Y. Tattersalls October.

Brother to the quite useful 2-y-o 5f winner Lord Lieutenant and to the poor 5-y-o 5f winner Allstars Dancer and half-brother to the fair 2-y-o 6f all-weather winner Puppet Master (by Prince Sabo). The dam, an Irish 7f winner, is a half-sister to the US stakes-placed winner Look See. The second dam, Ship N' Shore (by Danzig), was a stakes-placed winner in the USA and a half-sister to the US Grade 2 Cowdin Stakes winner Sail To Rome. *"A smashing horse, he's one to watch out for from the end of May onwards I guess and I like him a lot".*

506 - PRINCESS PETARDIA (IRE) ** [62]   b.br.f. Petardia – Coolrain Lady (Common Grounds).
March 17. Third foal. 23,000Y. Tattersalls October.

Half-sister to the useful 2000 2-y-o listed 1m winner La Vita E Bella (by Definite Article) and the fairly useful 1998 2-y-o dual 5f winner Light The Rocket (by Pips Pride). The dam was placed 12 times in Ireland from 1m to 10f and is a half-sister to 4 minor winners. The second dam, Moneycashen (by Hook Money), won once at 3 yrs and over hurdles. (Major A M Everett). *"This is a very nice filly – a half-sister to Light The Rocket. She's lovely, moves brilliant and is working really well".*

507 - RAVE ON (ITY) * [86]   b.f. Barathea – Kalliopina (Arctic Tern).
April 13. Fifth foal. FF300,000. Deauville August.

Half-sister to the 3-y-o Sopran Kalli, to the Italian listed winner Lady Bi (both by Alzao) and the Italian winner of 9 races Ritmo de la Noche (by Danehill). The dam won twice in Italy and is a half-sister to 6 winners including the German Group 2 11.5f winner Goofalik and the French-placed dam of the Group 3 Prix de Flore winner Oxava. The second dam, Alik (by Targowice), a very useful winner of the Group 3 1m Prix de Sandringham, is a half-sister to 4 winners and to the placed dam of the French Group 3 winner Belka. *"A small, sharp filly and she's very nice. I don't know what sort of trip she'll need but she's bonny. I haven't done much with her yet though".*

508 - REDBACK ** [101]   ch.c. Mark Of Esteem – Patsy Western (Precocious).
April 7. Seventh foal. 40,000Y. Tattersalls October.

Half-brother to Zoudie (by Ezzoud), unplaced in one start at 2 yrs in 2000, to the useful 2-y-o 5f winner Granny's Pet (by Selkirk), the Italian listed winner of 4 races Abe (by Barathea), the fairly useful 14f winner Way Out Yonder (by Shirley Heights), the quite useful triple 1m winner Western General (by Cadeaux Genereux) and the fair 10f and 12f winner Western Sal (by Salse). The dam, a quite useful 3-y-o 6f winner, is a half-sister to 7 winners including the Queen Anne Stakes winner Mr Fluorocarbon and to the Cornwallis Stakes winner Western Jewel. The second dam, Western Air (by Sound Track), won three races at 2 yrs and is is a half-sister to the grandam of Lyric Fantasy, Royal Applause and In Command. (Waney Racing Group Inc). *"A good-looking horse from a good family, we've got him marked down as one of the earlier ones. I can see why he cost as much as he did because he looks like being a good 2-y-o". Richard's son added – "this is the best colt we've got – a real tool I promise you! I was the underbidder on him but fortunately the horse came to the yard anyway. He's a really nice colt".*

509 - RED HALO ** [72]
b.c. Be My Guest – Pray (Priolo).
January 16. First foal. IR£100,000Y. Goffs Orby.

The dam is an unraced half-sister to the Grade 2 San Bernadino Handicap and Group 3 7f Supreme Stakes winner Anshan. The second dam, Lady Zi (by Manado), won once over 12f and is a half-sister to the dam of the French Two Thousand Guineas winner No Pass No Sale. (Mr Terry Neill). *"He'll be one of our better 2-y-o's. He's working very well and is as good a Be My Guest as I've seen. I could have him out early, but I'm hanging on to him because of his pedigree. A sound horse".*

510 - RED OPAL (IRE) * [83]
b.f. Flying Spur – Tamaya (Darshaan).
March 18. Fifth foal. FF500,000. Deauville August.

Half-sister to 2 minor winners in Germany by Saumarez and Lomitas. The dam, a French placed maiden, is a half-sister to 6 winners including the German Grade 2 placed Silvestro. The second dam, Kahara (by Habitat), was a listed-placed winner in France. (Mr Terry Neill). *"A smashing filly. Big, strong and sharp – she's working well at the moment".*

511 - ROUNDTREE (IRE) ** [81]
b.f. Night Shift – Island Desert (Green Desert).
March 1. Fourth foal. IR£39,000Y. Goffs Challenge.

Half-sister to the fair 1997 5.7f 2-y-o winner Brandon Frank (by Beveled), subsequently a winner in Macau. The dam, a poor 11f and 12f placed maiden, was unraced at 2 yrs and is a half-sister to 8 winners on the flat and over jumps. The second dam, Salote (by Forli), a very useful 3-y-o winner, was suited by 12f. (Echo Pond Stables Inc). *"On the small side but very well-built, she's very tough and I'd say she'll be a 2-y-o alright. A nice filly and I like her. Her target will be the Goffs Challenge race".*

512 - SANDY LADY (IRE) ** [67]
b.f. Desert King – Mamma's Too (Skyliner).
May 5. Fourth foal. IR£58,000Y. Goffs Orby.

Half-sister to 2 winners in Germany by Platini. The dam won 8 races here and in Germany including the listed 5f St Hugh's Stakes and the listed 5f Firth of Clyde Stakes and is a half-sister to 4 minor winners. The second dam, Maple Syrup (by Charlottown), is a placed half-sister to 5 winners including the Prix Vanteaux winner Bon Appetit (herself the grandam of the top-class miler Bigstone). (Thurloe Thoroughbreds VII). *"A very nice, big filly, she's all there and despite being a May foal looks sharp. She just needs to come in her coat a bit better, but she's working quite well".*

513 - STORM CLEAR (IRE) ** [96]
b.c. Mujadil – Escape Path (Wolver Hollow).
March 7. Fifth foal.

Half-brother to the very useful Group 3 7f Jersey Stakes winner Sergeyev and the Irish 1m winner Sea Fisher (both by Mulhollande). The dam, placed once over the jumps, is a half-sister to the Group 1 William Hill Futurity Stakes winner Sandy Creek. The second dam, Keep Right (by Klairon), is an unraced half-sister to 4 winners. (Mr D Boocock). *"A very nice horse. A little bit 'on the leg' and light of body, he seems to take after his damsire Wolver Hollow. But he's a real athlete and a very sharp 2-y-o".*

514 - WHASS URRP (IRE) * [75]
b.c. Desert King – Blue Burgee (Lyphard's Wish).
February 20. Second foal. IR£30,000Y. Goffs Orby.

Half-brother to the 3-y-o Napeta (by Woodman). The dam won once in France and once in the USA and was third in the Group 3 7f Prix du Calvados. She is a half-sister to 3 minor winners out of the French 3-y-o winner Bronislava (by Nonoalco), herself a half-sister to the Prix Saint-Alary winner Comtesse de Loir and to the grandam of Miesque. (Mr James Horgan). *"A really nice, big horse that goes well. He'll want six furlongs to start with".*

515 - XTRASENSORY * [84]**   b.f. Royal Applause – Song Of Hope (Chief Singer).
May 11. Seventh foal. 50,000Y. Tattersalls October.
Half-sister to the unraced 2000 2-y-o Premier Guest (by Primo Dominie), to the quite useful 5.2f (at 2 yrs) and 7f winner Song Of Skye (by Warning), the fair 2-y-o 6f winner Stolen Melody (by Robellino), the fair 7f and 1m all-weather winner Kingdom Princess and the modest dual 5f winner Miriam (both by Forzando). The dam, a useful 2-y-o 5f winner and second in the listed Firth of Clyde Stakes, is a half-sister to 10 minor winners. The second dam, Penny Blessing (by So Blessed), won twice at 2 yrs, was fourth in the Cheveley Park Stakes and is out of a winning half-sister to Mummy's Pet. (Waney Racing Group Inc). *"A smashing filly. I haven't done a lot with her but she's well-made and a good mover".*

516 - YOU GOT ME * [74]   gr.c. First Trump – Simply Sooty (Absalom).
March 15. Fifth foal. 20,000Y. Tattersalls October.
Brother to a winner in Denmark and half-brother to the unraced 2000 2-y-o Pie In The Sky (by Bishop Of Cashel) and to the very smart Group 3 7.3f Horris Hill Stakes and Group 3 7f Craven Stakes winner Umistim (by Inchinor). The dam, a fair 2-y-o dual 5f winner, is a half-sister to 2 minor winners. The second dam, Classical Vintage (by Stradavinsky), won once at 2 yrs and is a half-sister to 11 minor winners. (The South-Western Partnership II). *"A very nice horse but backward at this point in the season".*

517 - ZANANA * [88]**   b.f. Zafonic – Divine Quest (Kris).
April 5. Second foal.
Half-sister to the quite useful 2000 2-y-o 6f winner Ecstatic (by Nashwan). The dam, a quite useful 7f winner, is a sister to the smart Prix d'Arenberg, Prix de Ris-Orangis and Prix du Gros Chene winner Divine Danse and a half-sister to the high-class Free Handicap, Prix Maurice de Gheest and Kiveton Park Stakes winner Pursuit of Love. The second dam, Dance Quest (by Green Dancer), was a smart French 2-y-o sprinter and a half-sister to the high class 2-y-o Noblequest, winner of the Prix de la Salamandre. (Lady Howard de Walden). *"A narrow filly but she's quite sharp and is starting to improve every day. She runs a little bit on her nerves at times (I suppose that's Zafonic) but I like her and she can gallop"*

518 - ZANDICULAR * [81]   b.c. Forzando – Perdicula (Persian Heights).
February 14. Third foal. 54,000Y. Doncaster St Leger.
The dam is an unraced half-sister to 5 winners including the Derby winner High-Rise and to the placed dam of the Italian Oaks and E P Taylor Stakes winner Zomaradah. The second dam, High Tern (by High Line), a fairly useful winning stayer, is a half-sister to the Group 1 Premio Roma and Group 2 Ribblesdale Stakes winner High Hawk (herself dam of the Breeders Cup Turf winner In The Wings and the Group 2 winners Hunting Hawk and Hawker's News) and to Seriema (dam of the Rothmans International and Sun Chariot Stakes winner Infamy). (Mr Nicholas R Hodges). *"A big horse, he'd want six or seven furlongs to be seen at his best this year and he's a nice colt".*

519 - UNNAMED ** [99]   b.c. Barathea – Bold Fashion (Nashwan).
February 14. Third foal. 65,000Y. Tattersalls October.
The dam, a minor French 3-y-o winner, is a half-sister to 7 winners including La Groupie, a winner of 5 listed events in France. The second dam, L'Irlandaise (by Irish River), won the listed Prix de Honfleur. (Mr B T Stewart-Brown). *"This is a very nice, big, tall horse. One for the mid-summer".*

520 - UNNAMED ** [76]   gr.c. Vettori – Dolly Bevan (Another Realm).
March 11. Eighth foal. 76,000Y. Tattersalls October.
Half-brother to the useful Oggi, a winner of 6 races at up to 6f and to the fairly useful Pengamon (both by Efisio), a winner of 4 races at up to 1m and the fair 7f winner Avanti (by Reprimand). The dam a 2-y-o 6f seller winner, is a half-sister to Pips Pride, a winner of 6 races including the Group 1 6f Heinz "57" Phoenix Stakes. The second dam, Elkie Brooks (by Relkino), was a quite useful 6f placed 2-y-o. (Mr B T Stewart-Brown). *"A lovely colt and a 2-y-o type, he's a good mover and has been working upsides. He'll be alright this year".*

521 - TYPHOON TODD ** [82]   ch.c. Entrepreneur – Petite Liqueurelle (Shernazar).
May 18. Seventh foal. 45,000Y. Tattersalls October.

Half-brother to the useful 5f (at 2 yrs) and 1m winner Caviar Royale, to the fair 2-y-o 7f winner Vocation (both by Royal Academy), the Irish 11f winner Dancing Bluebell (by Bluebird), the Irish 2-y-o 1m winner Federico (by Waajib) and the 2000 Irish 3-y-o winner Petite Ville (by Bigstone). The dam is an unraced half-sister to 2 minor winners. The second dam, Luperca (by Dan Cupid), was placed in France and is a half-sister to the French One Thousand Guineas and French Oaks winner Apollonia and the Ascot Gold Cup and Prix Royal-Oak winner Macip. (Lucayan Stud & Major A M Everett). *"A smashing horse – not over-big but very nice. I'll try and get him towards a big meeting because he can step and he's a good mover. I like him and he'll be quite nice".*

P HARRIS

522 - BAROLO ** [98]   b.c. Danehill – Lydia Maria (Dancing Brave).
May 10.

Half-brother to the 3-y-o Kroisos (by Kris), to the fairly useful 6f (at 2 yrs) and 10.4f winner Premier Bay (by Primo Dominie) and the quite useful 7f (at 2 yrs) and 14f winner Taufan Boy (by Taufan). The dam, a fair 1m and 10.2f placed maiden, is a half-sister to the dam of both the Middle Park Stakes winner Primo Valentino and the Cherry Hinton Stakes winner Dora Carrington. The second dam, the high-class filly Connaught Bridge (by Connaught), won the Yorkshire Oaks and the Nassau Stakes. *"I think he's a really nice colt. He won't be an early sort and I wouldn't expect him to be out until August".*

523 - COOL STORM (IRE) ** [72]   b.f. Rainbow Quest – Classic Park (Robellino).
February 1. First foal. 120,000Y. Tattersalls Houghton.

The dam won 3 races including her first 2-y-o start over 5f and the Irish One Thousand Guineas and is a half-sister to 7 winners including the US Grade 2 winner Rumpipumpy. The second dam, Wanton (by Kris), a useful 2-y-o 5f winner and third in the Group 2 Flying Childers Stakes, is a half-sister to the listed 5f St Hugh's Stakes winner and Group 2 5f Prix du Gros-Chene second Easy Option. *"A good deal more forward than you'd expect for a filly bred this way. She'll definitely make a 2-y-o and I think she's a really nice filly. I wouldn't be at all surprised if she started off at five furlongs, despite being by Rainbow Quest. A classic filly".*

524 - HONOR ROUGE (IRE) [69]   ch.f. Highest Honor – Ayers Rock (In The Wings).
April 11. First foal. IR£25,000Y. Goffs Orby.

The dam, a winner over 10f and 12f in Ireland, is a half-sister to 2 winners including the US Grade 2 placed Hanuman Highway. The second dam, Cherry Ridge (by Riva Ridge), won the listed Sceptre Stakes, was fourth in the Group 3 Nell Gwyn Stakes and is a half-sister to the Group 2 Dante Stakes winner Red Glow. *"Unlikely to be out before the end of August and over seven furlongs minimum. She's a nicely made filly and if she was sprint-bred I'd expect her to be early – she just looks that way. But her pedigree tells me otherwise".*

525 - JAYCEER ** [69]   b.c. Green Desert – Centaine (Royal Academy).
May 6. Third foal. 40,000Y. Tattersalls Houghton.

Half-brother to the German 2000 2-y-o winner Vicchio (by Cadeaux Genereux). The dam, a winner of 3 races in Germany including the Group 2 11f Preis der Diana, is a half-sister to 3 winners. The second dam, Hi Lass (by Shirley Heights), won the Group 3 Prix Gladiateur and is a half-sister to the Grade 1 Yellow Ribbon Invitational Handicap winner Bonne Ile and the Group 3 Cumberland Lodge Stakes winner Ile de Nisky. *"Again, he's a nice sort that should start off over six furlongs".*

526 - LOTTIE BERK (IRE) * [74]   b.f. Danehill – Kinlochewe (Old Vic).
April 9. Second foal. 8,000Y. Tattersalls October.

Half-sister to the fair 2000 2-y-o 6f winner Statue Gallery (by Cadeaux Genereux). The dam, a useful 10f winner, was placed over 12f and is a half-sister to the very useful Group 3 7f Jersey Stakes winner Ardkinglass, the useful dual 7f winner Darnaway and the useful 10f winners Pitcroy and Jura. The second dam, Reuval (by Sharpen Up), a useful winner of 2 races over 1m at 3 yrs, is closely related to Kristana (dam of the Group 2 Prix Robert Papin winner Ozone Friendly) and a half-sister to Just You Wait (dam of the Group 2 winners Reprimand and Wiorno) and Little Loch Broom (dam of the very useful colts Fawzi and Soft Currency). *"A cheap yearling purchase but you couldn't buy her for 8,000*

Guineas now. Very small and weak as a yearling, she's come on nicely and will be a 2-y-o although not particularly early. Even if she does nothing, she was a bargain as a potential broodmare".

527 - LYRICAL LAD ** [70]

b.c. Primo Dominie – Lyrical Bid (Lyphard).
February 21. First foal. 22,000Y. Tattersalls October.

The dam, a fair winner of her only start, over 7.5f at 2 yrs, is a half-sister to the Irish listed winner and Group 3 Park Hill Stakes third On Call and to the fairly useful sprint winner Doctor's Glory. The second dam, Doctor Bid (by Spectacular Bid), is an unraced half-sister to 9 winners including the Group 3 Prix Thomas Bryon winner Glory Forever and the dam of the Coventry Stakes winner Verglas. *"A typical Primo Dominie in that he's not over-big and I should think he'll make a 2-y-o by June over six furlongs".*

528 - PALAMEDES * [87]

b.c. Sadler's Wells – Kristal Bridge (Kris).
January 25. First foal.

The dam, a fair 11f all-weather placed maiden, is a half-sister to the dam of both the Middle Park Stakes winner Primo Valentino and the Cherry Hinton Stakes winner Dora Carrington. The second dam, the high-class filly Connaught Bridge (by Connaught), won the Yorkshire Oaks and the Nassau Stakes. *"A nice colt and quite backward without being desperately so. He's got every chance of being a good horse as he's well-bred and is a very good-looking horse. More of a 3-y-o however".*
Significant sire/damsire crosses:- Moonshell, Samsaam.

529 - PERSIAN LASS (IRE) [52]

ch.f. Grand Lodge – Noble Tiara (Vaguely Noble).
April 30. Eleventh foal. 100,000Y. Tattersalls Houghton.

Half-sister to the French winner of 3 races and Group 3 10.5f Prix Fille de l'Air second On Credit (herself dam of the Group 2 Great Voltigeur Stakes winner Stowaway), to the French listed-placed winners Melisandra and High Tetra (both by Highest Honor) and minor winners in France and Italy by Fabulous Dancer, Highest Honor, Bellypha and Akarad. The dam won twice in France and was fourth in both the Group 3 10.5f Prix de Flore and the Group 3 12.5f Prix de Royallieu. The second dam, Tayyara (by Targowice), won the Group 3 1m Prix de la Grotte. *"A really nice type, she's likely to be a middle-distance filly next year. As a 2-y-o she'll be out around August or September time".*

530 - RAINBOW SPECTRUM (FR) ** [74]

b.f. Spectrum – Iguassu (Fabulous Dancer).
March 25. Third foal. FF480,000. Deauville August.

Half-sister to the listed 1m Prix Herod winner Radhwa (by Shining Steel). The dam was placed in the listed Prix des Yearlings at 2 yrs and is a half-sister to 7 winners including the US Grade 2 Palomar Handicap winner Shir Dar. The second dam, Irish Sea (by Irish River), won once and is a half-sister to 8 winners including the Group 3 12f Meld Stakes winner Sailor's Mate (the dam of 3 listed winners) and the dam of the Yorkshire Oaks winner Hellenic. *"I think she'll need seven furlongs to start with and she should be out in July. A really nice filly, she'll do some good as a 2-y-o and is of my nicest fillies".*

531 - RESPLENDENT CEE (IRE) * [72]

ch.c. Polar Falcon – Western Friend (Gone West).
March 3. Third living foal. 30,000Y. Tattersalls October.

Brother to the German 2-y-o winner and listed-placed Wild Woman and half-brother to the fair 11f to 14f all-weather winner Western Command (by Saddlers' Hall). The dam ran once unplaced and is a sister to the US triple Grade 3 winner Gold Land. The second dam, Lajna (by Be My Guest), is an unplaced half-sister to the dual Group 1 1m Lockinge Stakes winner Soviet Line. *"A nice colt and quite big, I think he'll make a 2-y-o by mid-season".*

532 - SEAMSTRESS (IRE) ** [92]

b.f. Barathea – Petite Epaulette (Night Shift).
January 21. Fourth foal. IR£14,000Y. Goffs Orby.

Sister to the quite useful 2000 2-y-o 5f winner Dress Code and half-sister to the fairly useful 1999 2-y-o dual 5f winner Lady Sarka (by Lake Coniston) and the quite useful 1997 2-y-o 5f winner Shalford's Honour (by Shalford). The dam, a fair 5f winner at 2 yrs, is a sister to the Sweet Solera Stakes second The Jotter and a half-sister to the Group 1 1m Gran Criterium second Line Dancer. The second dam, Note Book (by Mummy's Pet), a fairly useful 6f winner, is a sister to the Norfolk Stakes winner Colmore Row and a half-sister to the Horris Hill Stakes winner Long Row and the dam of the Irish Oaks winner Possessive Dancer. *"A very neat filly, she's really nice. The family all win at 2 yrs and I see no reason why she should be different. Very free-going and well forward, I wouldn't be surprised if she started off at five furlongs".*

533 - SHAMARCO (IRE) ** [65] b.f. Common Grounds – Fanciful (Mujtahid).
March 13. Second foal. 20,000Y. Doncaster St Leger.
Half-sister to the modest 2000 7.5f 2-y-o winner The Fancy Man (by Definite Article). The dam ran once unplaced over 7f at 2 yrs and is a half-sister to 3 winners. The second dam, Try My Rosie (by Try My Best), won once and was second in the Group 3 1m Killavullen Stakes in Ireland at 2 yrs and is a half-sister to 8 winners here and abroad. *"I've got a lot of Common Grounds horses and in my experience they mostly need good going or faster. She seems typical of the sire and has done everything asked of her nicely".*

534 - TRAVELLER'S TALE [84] b.c. Selkirk – Chere Amie (Mr Prospector).
January 26. Second foal.
Half-brother to the 2000 French trained 2-y-o Pistoia (by Alzao). The dam, placed over 6f and 7f at 2 yrs in Ireland and a winner at 3 yrs in France, is a half-sister to 6 winners including the US Grade 2 winner Esteemed Friend, the French listed 12f winner Red Monsoon and the dam of the US Grade 2 winner Yarrow Brae. The second dam, Charlotte Amalie (by Gay Mecene), won the listed 10.5f Prix de Strasbourg, was second in the Group 3 10f Prix de Psyche and is a half-sister to 7 winners. *"Much more of a 3-y-o, he's likely to have just the one run at the back-end".*

535 - UNNAMED ** [76] b.c. Danehill – Hever Golf Rose (Efisio).
March 6. First foal. FF1,200,000. Deauville August.
The dam won 17 races over sprint distances including the Group 1 Prix de l'Abbaye, the Group 2 Goldene Peitsche and the Group 2 6f Premio Melton. She is a full or half-sister to 8 winners including 2 listed winners in Belgium out of the sprint-placed Sweet Rosina (by Sweet Revenge). *"Quite a backward colt, we X-ray all our 2-y-o's in February and certainly his knees at that stage were one of the most backward. He's catching up and doing good canters now, is on the small side and I find that the best Danehill horses are that size. Big ones don't seem to be any good in my experience".*

536 - UNNAMED * [79] b.c. Zilzal – Sakura Queen (Woodman).
January 6. Fourth foal. 32,000Y. Tattersalls October.
Half-brother to the unraced 2000 2-y-o Chiu Chow Kid, to the fair 1999 2-y-o 7f winner Seeking Utopia (both by Wolfhound), the fair 12f winner Reine Cerise and a winner in Italy (both by Shareef Dancer). The dam, a modest Irish maiden, was placed three times and stayed 10f. She is a half-sister to 5 winners including the Irish listed winner Outside Pressure and the Group 1 Gran Criterium third Winning Venture. The second dam, Push A Button (by Bold Lad, Ire), won once at 2 yrs and is a half-sister to the French Two Thousand Guineas winner and top-class sire Riverman. *"Yes, he's a nice colt and for a Zilzal he's not at all 'hot'. He's doing good canters, is a nice-looking horse and I think he'll be out by July".*

P HASLAM

537 - ARGOSTOLI [57] b.f. Marju – Barque Bleue (Steinlen).
February 17. Second foal. 22,000Y. Doncaster St Leger.
The dam is an unraced half-sister to the Group 3 7f Prix du Palais Royal winner Bon Vent and to the French listed winners Ballerine and Bleu Roi. The second dam, Blithe Spirit (by Luthier), was a listed-placed winner in France and a half-sister to 4 winners including the dam of the top-class miler Bigstone. (John Roundtree). *"She gives me the impression that she'll need seven furlongs to start with in mid-summer and she's a nice 2-y-o filly".*

538 - BORN SPECIAL (IRE) ** [61] b.c. Bluebird – Dixie Eyes Blazing (Gone West).
February 25. Second foal. 12,000Y. Tattersalls October.
Half-brother to the fair 2000 5f placed 2-y-o Johnny Reb (by Danehill). The dam ran just twice and was placed once over 7f an the all-weather. She is a half-sister to the useful 5f (at 2 yrs) and 1m winner Well Beyond (herself dam of the Cherry Hinton Stakes third Well Warned). The second dam, Mariakova (by The Minstrel), was placed over 6f at 2 yrs and 1m at 3 yrs, is a sister to the smart filly Zaizafon (the dam of Zafonic) and a half-sister to the unraced Modena (dam of Elmaamul and Reams of Verse). The third dam, Mofida (by Right Tack), won 8 races at up to 7f and was placed in the Duke of York Stakes. (Les Buckley). *"A colt that's been pleasing us on the gallops, he'll be an early 2-y-o but he has the scope to go on. A big, strong horse that should do well this year and the next".*

539 - DAZZLING RIO (IRE) [55]   b.c. Ashkalani – Dazzling Fire (Bluebird).
February 14. Fifth foal. 32,000Y. Tattersalls October.
Half-brother to the 3-y-o O-Henry (by Cadeaux Genereux) and to the fair 1998 3-y-o 6f winner Mohawk (by Indian Ridge) – subsequently a winner in Norway. The dam, a modest 3-y-o 11.7f winner, is a half-sister to 7 winners including the fairly useful dual 2-y-o 6f winner Sotoboy. The second dam, Fire Flash (by Bustino), is a placed half-sister to the Lincoln Handicap winner King's Glory. (Rio Stainless Engineering Ltd). *"He's been cantering all winter and is a nice-looking colt that will make a 2-y-o over seven furlongs in mid-summer. A nice colt and I think he's going to be alright".*

540 - NATIAIN ** [67]   ch.c. Danzig Connection – Fen Princess (Trojan Fen).
April 6. Fifth foal. 10,000Y. Tattersalls October.
Half-brother to the 3-y-o Chacka Dancer (by Dancing Spree), to the 1996 2-y-o 7f and subsequent US 1m stakes winner Ben's Ridge (by Indian Ridge), the fairly useful 9.2f to 15f winner Fiori, and the fair 9.4f winner Prince Ashleigh (both by Anshan). The dam, a modest 15f winner at 4 yrs, is a half-sister to 5 minor winners in France. The second dam, Cenerentola (by Caro), a very useful winner of the Group 3 1m Prix de Sandringham, is a full or half-sister to 6 winners. *"A colt from a family I know well, he was bred next door to us here in Middleham by Mrs Peacock. He's a colt with a very nice temperament that falls into the category of a mid-summer, seven furlong type 2-y-o. I've trained three from this dam and they've all either won as 2-y-o's or been unlucky not to".*

541 - TUSCARORA (IRE) * [56]   b.f. Revoque – Fresh Look (Alzao).
January 8. Second foal. 20,000Y. Doncaster St Leger.
Half-sister to Major Review (by Definite Article), unplaced in one start over 7f at 2 yrs in 2000. The dam, a modest 11.5f winner, is a half-sister to 6 minor winners here and abroad. The second dam, Bag Lady (by Be My Guest), a quite useful placed maiden, stayed 1m and is a half-sister to 3 winners out of a winning half-sister to numerous good horses including the dams of Xaar, Aviance, Try My Best and El Gran Senor. (John Roundtree). *"She's a nice filly, I like her and it looks like she'll do the business for us somewhere. I can see her coming to hand sometime in May and she's a workmanlike 2-y-o type".*

MME C HEAD-MAAREK

542 - AMAZING KRISKEN (USA)   b.f. Kris S – Magic Gleam (Danzig).

Half-sister to the quite useful 1995 3-y-o 1m winner Touch a Million (by Mr Prospector). The dam was a very smart winner of the Group 2 1m Child Stakes and was placed in the Coronation Stakes, the Prix Jacques le Marois and the Juddmonte International (all Group 1 events). She is a half-sister to several winners including the South African Grade 1 winner Flying Snowdrop. The second dam, All Agleam (by Gleaming), is a half-sister to the top class CCA Oaks winner Davona Dale (herself dam of the good colt Le Voyageur). (Maktoum Al-Maktoum).
Significant sire/damsire crosses:- Arch (Gr 1).

543 - BUCK ASPEN (USA)   b.f. Seeking The Gold – Only Seule (Lyphard).

Half-sister to the high-class Group 1 7f Prix de la Foret and Group 1 6.5f Prix Maurice de Gheest winner Occupandiste (by Kaldoun), to the useful French 2-y-o 7.5f winner Lonely Tycoon (by Last Tycoon) and the French winner and listed Prix Djebel second Onlyman (by Woodman). The dam, a winner over 7.5f in France at 2 yrs, is closely related to the Irish One Thousand Guineas and Tripleprint Celebration Mile winner Mehthaaf, to the high-class July Cup and Diadem Stakes winner Elnadim and the listed Sceptre Stakes winner Ashraakat. The second dam, Elle Seule (by Exclusive Native), won 3 races including the Group 3 1m Prix d'Astarte and is a half-sister to the Group/Grade 1 winners Fort Wood, Hamas and Timber Country and to the Group winners Northern Aspen, Colorado Dancer and Mazzacano.

544 - DEMONIUS   ch.c. Dr Devious – Born Gold (Blushing Groom).
May 4. Third foal.
Half-brother to the 2000 Group 3 10.5f Prix Cleopatre winner Gold Round (by Caerleon) and to the French 11.5f winner Glamadour (by Sanglamore). The dam won over 8.3f and is a sister to the smart filly Gold Splash (by Blushing Groom), winner of the Group 1 1m Prix Marcel Boussac and the Group 1 1m Coronation Stakes. The second dam, Riviere d'Or (by Lyphard), was also a smart filly and winner

of the Group 1 10f Prix Saint-Alary, the Group 3 1m Prix d'Aumale and the Group 3 9.2f Prix Vanteaux, is closely related to the Group 3 Prix du Lys winner Chercheur d'Or and the French Two Thousand Guineas second Goldneyev. The third dam, Gold River (by Riverman), won the Prix de l'Arc de Triomphe, the Prix Jean Prat, the Prix du Cadran and the Prix Royal-Oak.

545 - GOLD SPHINX (USA)

b.c. Storm Cat – Gold Splash (Blushing Groom).

Half-brother to the French 3-y-o Goldzig (by Danzig). The dam, a very smart filly, won the Group 1 1m Prix Marcel Boussac and the Group 1 1m Coronation Stakes. The second dam, Riviere d'Or (by Lyphard), won the Group 1 Prix Saint-Alary, the Group 3 Prix d'Aumale and the Group 3 Prix Vanteaux. The third dam, Gold River (by Riverman), won the Prix de l'Arc de Triomphe. (Wertheimer et Frere).

546 - MAID OF HONOUR (IRE)

b.f. Bering – Fellwah (Sadler's Wells).
January 25. First foal.

The dam, placed fourth on her only outing, is closely related to the top-class Two Thousand Guineas and Queen Elizabeth II Stakes winner Shadeed. The second dam, Continual (by Damascus), won twice at up to 7f and is a half-sister to 4 winners. The third dam, Continuation (by Forli), also a dual winner at up to 7f, is a sister to Tuerta, dam of the Kentucky Derby and Belmont Stakes winner Swale and a half-sister to File, dam of the champion American 2-y-o colt Forty Niner. (Maktoum Al-Maktoum).

547 - MILLER'S PRIDE (JPN)

b.f. Lammtarra – Canadian Mill (Mill Reef).
February 12. Sixth living foal.

Half-sister to the smart Group 2 10f Nassau Stakes, Group 3 1m May Hill Stakes and Group 3 10.4f Musidora Stakes winner Hawajiss (by Kris), to the Irish 7f to 10.5f winner Mountain Rocket (by Nashwan) and the fair 7f winner Weaver Of Words (by Danehill). The dam, a 2-y-o 6f winner, was second the Group 1 Cheveley Park Stakes but did not train on. She is a half-sister to the Royal Lodge Stakes second Khozaam out of the champion Canadian 2-y-o and 3-y-o filly Par Excellance (by L'Enjoleur). (Maktoum Al-Maktoum).

548 - OFF YOU GO (USA)

b.f. Seattle Slew – Set In Motion (Mr Prospector).
January 14. Second foal.

Half-sister to the David Loder trained 2000 2-y-o Devine Task (by Irish River). The dam, a French 11f winner, is a half-sister to the Champion Stakes and One Thousand Guineas winner Hatoof, to the dual 10f listed winner Insijaam and the 12f listed winner Fasateen. The second dam, Cadeaux d'Amie (by Lyphard), a winner over 1m at 2 yrs and 10f at 3 yrs in France, was third in the Group 3 1m Prix d'Aumale and is a half-sister to the champion 2-y-o filly and Prix Vermeille and 10.5f Prix de Diane winner Mrs Penny. (Maktoum Al-Maktoum).
Significant sire/damsire crosses:- Event Of The Year (Gr 2), Bitooh (Gr 2), Nelson (Gr 3).

549 - PAS DE BRUIT (USA)

b.c. Danzig – Soundings (Mr Prospector).

Brother to the 1996 2-y-o Group 1 6f Cheveley Park Stakes winner Pas de Reponse, closely related to the very useful 1992 Group 1 5.5f Prix Robert Papin winner Didyme (by Dixieland Band) and half-brother to the high-class French Two Thousand Guineas and Prix d'Ispahan winner and St James's Palace Stakes and Prix du Moulin placed Green Tune (by Green Dancer), and the 1m listed winner Ecoute (by Manila). The dam won two races in the USA, is a sister to the very useful 5f and 6f winner Al Zawbaah and a half-sister to 5 other winners. The second dam, Ocean's Answer (by Northern Answer), won the Natalma Stakes and is closely related to Storm Bird.
Significant sire/damsire crosses:- Dayjur (Gr 1), Pas de Reponse (Gr 1).

550 - PORRETTA (IRE)

ch.f. Indian Ridge – Lambada (Lyphard).
March 21.

The dam, a French 3-y-o winner, was listed-placed and is a half-sister to the high-class 2000 2-y-o Tobougg and the French listed winner Otavalo. The second dam, Lacovia (by Majestic Light), winner of the Group 1 10.5f Prix de Diane and the Group 1 10f Prix Saint-Alary, is out of a half-sister to Miswaki.

551 - SPHINXY (USA)   b.c. Kingmambo – Egyptown (Top Ville).

Half-brother to the high-class Group 1 10.5f Prix de Diane winner Egyptown (by Dixieland Band), to the Group 3 15f Prix du Lutece winner Northerntown (by Manila) and the 2000 2-y-o 8.5f winner Topdown (by Dare And Go). The dam, a very useful French middle-distance stayer, won at up to 15f and is a half-sister to the smart French listed 10f winner Sand Reef. The second dam, Reine d'Egypte (by Val de l'Orne), a very useful filly, won the listed 10f Prix des Tuileries and the listed 12f Prix de la Porte Passy and is out of the high-class Prix de Diane and Prix Saint Alary winner Reine de Saba (by Lyphard).

552 - TWINKLE IN HER EYE (USA)   b.f. Hansel – Ville d'Amour (Irish River).
April 18 . Sixth foal.
Sister to the Group 1 1m Prix Marcel Boussac winner and Group 1 10f Prix Saint-Alary second Loving Claim and half-sister to the Group 3 6f July Stakes winner City On A Hill (by Rahy), the unraced 2000 2-y-o Aslaaf (by Quiet American) and a minor 2-y-o winner in France by Shadeed. The dam won 3 races including 2 listed events in France over 1m at 3 yrs. The second dam, Hanoof (by Northern Dancer), a quite useful 11f winner, is out of the very smart US Grade 2 winner and Irish Oaks second Little Bonny.
Significant sire/damsire crosses:- Loving Claim.

553 - WILLAMINA (USA)   b.f. Sadler's Wells – Animatrice (Alleged).

The dam, a very useful winner of the 1989 Group 2 12f Prix de Malleret and the Group 3 10f Prix de la Nonette, was third in the Oaks and is a half-sister to numerous winners including the Group 1 10f Criterium de Saint-Cloud and Group 2 10f Grand Prix d'Evry winner Poliglote. The second dam, Alexandrie (by Val de l'Orne), a very useful French filly, won the Group 3 10.5f Prix Cleopatre and is a half-sister to 8 winners including the high-class French middle-distance colt Antheus.
Significant sire/damsire crosses:- Dream Well (Gr 1), Camporese (Gr 3), Royal Court (Gr 3), Sadler's Flag (Gr 3).

B HILLS

Once again, I'm indebted to Barry's Assistant, Kevin Mooney, for discussing the South Bank two-year-olds with me.

554 - ALEXANDER THREE D (IRE) *   [89]   b.f. Pennekamp – Loon (Kaldoun).
May 6. Ninth living foal. IRE35,000Y. Goffs Orby.
Half-sister to the 3-y-o Golden Apples (by Pivotal), to the French 2-y-o 7.5f winner and US 1m stakes winner La Piaf, the French listed-placed winner Legendary (both by Fabulous Dancer) and 2 minor winners in France by General Holme. The dam won 4 races in France including the listed 12f Prix de la Porte de Passy and is a half-sister to 3 minor winners. The second dam, La Java (by Rapace), won twice in France and was third in the Prix de Royallieu. *"A big, scopey filly. She'll want some sun on her back but she'll be alright in time".*

555 - AMOURE KING (IRE) *   [73]   b.c. Desert King – Ange Rouge (Priolo).
February 15. First foal. IRE175,000Y. Goffs Orby.
The dam won once at 3 yrs in France and is a half-sister to 4 winners including the Group 3 1m Premio Bagutta winner Ardane and the French Group 3 placed Always On Time. The second dam, Arriance (by Gay Mecene), a listed-placed winner in France, is a half-sister to 7 winners. *"A lightly-made colt, a good mover and very active, he'll be a 2-y-o and is a straightforward horse. He'll be alright".*

556 - ANNE TUDOR (IRE) **   [85]   b.f. Anabaa – Alikhlas (Lahib).
February 1. First foal. IRE70,000Y. Goffs Orby.
The dam was a fair 3-y-o 1m winner. The second dam, Mathaayl (by Lahib), a quite useful 6f and 10f winner, is a half-sister to the Group 3 Princess Margaret Stakes winner Muhbubh (herself dam of the US Grade 2 winner Kayrawan) and to the dam of the Group 2 Cherry Hinton Stakes winner Asfurah. *"Quite a nice filly and well-made, she's a bit backward at the minute but she'll be a 2-y-o alright. Although she hasn't done any real work yet she'll be a nice filly".*

557 - A VIEW INDEED (USA) * [78] b.f. Distant View – A Shadeed Indeed (Shadeed).
April 26. Second foal. IR£72,000Y. Goffs Orby.

The dam is an unraced half-sister to the US Grade 3 California Jockey Club Handicap winner and Group 3 15f Prix du Lutece third Jo Knows. The second dam, Vidor (by Vaguely Noble), won the Group 3 10.5f Prix de Royaumont and was third in the French One Thousand Guineas. *"A nice, quality filly but backward and I can see her being ready for the seven furlong events".*

558 - BALLET FAME (USA) * [75] br.f. Quest For Fame – Bold Ballerina (Sadler's Wells).
May 10. Fourth foal.

Sister to the French-trained 3-y-o Bold For Fame and half-sister to the French 1998 2-y-o placed Ballerina Gold (by Slew O'Gold). The dam was placed four times at up to 10f in France and is a half-sister to 9 winners including the smart Group 2 6f Lowther Stakes winner and Group 1 Cheveley Park Stakes second Kingscote (herself dam of the smart Group 3 1m Prix de Fontainebleu winner and French Two Thousand Guineas second Rainbow Corner). The second dam, Bold Fantasy (by Bold Lad, Ire), won 2 races including the Group 3 Mulcahy Stakes, was second in the Irish One Thousand Guineas and the Cork and Orrery Stakes and is a sister to the top class colt Ragusa and the foundation mare Ela Marita (ancestress of such high-class horses as Princess Pati, Seymour Hicks and Crofter). (Khalid Abdulla). *"Another nice filly of Khalid Abdulla's, she'll be alright for the middle of the season".*

559 - BAMALKO (IRE) ** [81] b.c. Royal Applause – Shadowglow (Shaadi).
March 7. Second foal. IR£40,000Y. Goffs Orby.

Half-brother to Holy Orders (by Unblest), a quite useful winner in Ireland at 2 yrs and over 10f at 3 yrs. The dam ran once unplaced and is a half-sister to the US stakes winner and Group 1 Italian Oaks second Attire, to the US stakes winner Silca Key Service and the useful 7f winners Please Suzanne and Alpenglow. The second dam, Aquaglow (by Caerleon), a quite useful 7f and 1m winner, is a half-sister to 7 winners including the Italian listed winners Spend A Penny and Life On Light. *"Probably the most backward of our Royal Applause 2-y-o's, but he's got a nice way of going and is a nice colt that will win as a 2-y-o".*

560 - BRIGHT AND CLEAR ** [96] b.f. Danehill – Shining Water (Kalaglow).
April 24.

Half-sister to Indian File (by Indian Ridge), unplaced in one start at 2 yrs in 2000, to the high-class Group 1 1m Grand Criterium and Group 2 10.4f Dante Stakes winner Tenby, the very useful 1m (at 2 yrs) and 10f winner Bright Water, the fair 11.5f winner Maya Cove, the useful 2-y-o 7f and 1m winner River Usk, the fair 12.3f winner Bayswater (all by Caerleon), the very useful 1m (at 2 yrs), 11.5f listed and 12f listed winner Bristol Channel (by Generous), the very useful 2-y-o 7f winner and Group 1 1m Racing Post Trophy second Bude (by Dancing Brave) and the quite useful 9f and 10f winner Reflecting (by Ahonoora). The dam was a very useful winner of the Group 3 7f Solario Stakes and was placed in the Group 2 Park Hill Stakes. The second dam, Idle Waters (by Mill Reef), was a smart winner of 3 races including the Park Hill Stakes. (Khalid Abdulla). *"A lovely filly with a good attitude, she has a bit of class about her and she'll win as a 2-y-o".*

561 - BRIGHTER FUTURE ** [78] b.f. Night Shift – Welsh Mist (Damister).
February 19. Second foal. 60,000Y. Tattersalls October.

Half-sister to the fair 2000 2-y-o 6f winner Early Morning Mist (by Alzao). The dam, a useful winner of 4 races over 5f and 6f including a listed event, is a half-sister to 2 minor winners abroad. The second dam, Welwyn (by Welsh Saint), a fairly useful sprint winner of 5 races, is a sister to the Cheveley Park Stakes second Welshwyn and a half-sister to 4 other winners. *"A lovely filly, she's going to be a nice 2-y-o and will probably start off over six furlongs. She's so well-built that she looks like a colt and she goes really well. A nice filly that could be anything".*

562 - BROKEN BARRICADES (IRE) *** [95] gr.c. Common Grounds – Gratclo (Belfort).
April 12. Seventh foal. 50,000Y. Doncaster St Leger.

Brother to the useful 1996 2-y-o Group 3 6f July Stakes winner Rich Ground and half-brother to the unraced 2000 2-y-o Cheeney Basin (by King's Signet), the fairly useful 5f and 6f winner Bandanna (by Bandmaster) and a winner in Sweden by Presidium. The dam, a modest winner of 5 races over 6f and 7f, is a half-sister to 3 minor winners. The second dam, Shagra (by Sallust), is an unplaced full or half-

sister to 5 winners. *"A nice horse that's grown a lot and has filled into himself. He'll be a 2-y-o and will probably set off at six. A lovely-balanced horse that goes well and I can see him being OK".*
Significant sire/damsire crosses:- Rich Ground.

---

563 - BROWN EYES * [89]**   b.f. Danehill – La Belle Otero (Nureyev).
January 18. First foal. 165,000Y. Tattersalls Houghton.
The dam, unplaced in one start at 3 yrs, is a half-sister to 8 winners including the US Grade 3 Gardenia Stakes winner and Grade 2 placed Summer Matinee and the minor US stakes winners Pinecutter and Full Time Friend (herself dam of a stakes winner). The second dam, Part Time Lover (by Proud Clarion), won 3 minor races in the USA and is a half-sister to 7 winners. *"A lovely filly, not over-big, she goes really well and is a well-balanced filly. She'll definitely win as a 2-y-o and is really nice".*
Significant sire/damsire crosses:- Desert King.

---

564 - CEREUS (USA) ** [86]   ch.c. Gilded Time – Dayflower (Majestic Light).
March 8. Fourth foal.
Half-brother to the useful 2-y-o dual 6f winner Day Journey (by Dayjur). The dam was a useful winner of 4 races here and in the USA from 7f (at 2 yrs) to 10.4f, was fifth in the One Thousand Guineas and is a half-sister to 3 minor winners. The second dam, Equate (by Raja Baba), won 3 races in the USA and is a half-sister to the John Of Gaunt Stakes winner Weldnaas and to the dam of the Solario Stakes winner Raise A Grand. (Maktoum Al-Maktoum). *"If we've only got one 2-y-o type this is him. A lovely horse with a lovely action. Big and strong, he goes well and everyone who rides him likes him. He could be a nice horse and may want six furlongs to start with".*

---

565 - CHANGING GUARD (IRE) ** [95]   b.c. Royal Applause – Milne's Way (The Noble Player).
April 24. Sixth foal. IR£20,000Y. Goffs Challenge.
Half-brother to the fair 1999 2-y-o 5f winner Magical Millie (by Muhtarram), to the fair dual 5f winner That Man Again (by Prince Sabo), the modest dual 10f winner Who's That Man and the Irish winner of 5 races Crown Point (both by Mystiko). The dam, a quite useful 5.8f (at 2 yrs) to 1m winner of 4 races, is a half-sister to 6 winners abroad. The second dam, Daring Way (by Alydar), won at 3 yrs and is a half-sister to 7 winners including the US stakes winners and Grade 1 placed Introductivo and Robalea. *"A lovely mover – a good goer. By May he'll be back on song and I'd expect him to want at least six furlongs this year. He has a bit more making-up to do than our other Royal Applause 2-y-o's".*

---

566 - CRAIOVA (IRE) ** [90]   b.c. Turtle Island – Velvet Appeal (Petorius).
February 6. First foal. 130,000Y. Tattersalls Houghton.
The dam, a minor Irish 3-y-o 7.8f winner, is a sister to the 2-y-o Group 3 Horris Hill Stakes and subsequent South African Group 1 winner Sapieha and a half-sister to 4 winners including the Group 2 15f Prix Hubert de Chaudennay winner Dajrann. The second dam, Sugarbird (by Star Appeal), won once at 2 yrs and is a half-sister to 6 winners. *"A lovely, big, strong, strapping colt. He won't take much time to get ready and I'd say he'll start off at six furlongs. A nice horse".*

---

567 - DARK FLOWER (IRE) ** [89]   b.f. Sadler's Wells – Marino Casino (Alleged).
April 27. Fifth living foal. 120,000Y. Tattersalls Houghton.
The dam ran once unplaced and is a half-sister to the top-class miler Posse, to the US Grade 3 winner Late As Usual, the German Group 3 winner Hot Rodder, the US Grade 2 placed In Full Cry and the dam of the Italian Group 2 winner Lonely Bird. The second dam, In Hot Pursuit (by Bold Ruler), was a top 2-y-o filly in the USA in 1973 and won 3 races including the Grade 3 Fashion Stakes at Belmont Park. *"Not very big but she's all there. She'll need seven furlongs to start and is a nice filly with plenty to like about her. She'll be fine".*
Significant sire/damsire crosses:- Camporese, Dream Well, Royal Court, Sadler's Flag.

---

568 - DEAR BRIDIE (IRE) * [71]   ch.f. Entrepreneur – Shebasis (General Holme).
February 18. Seventh living foal. IR£25,000Y. Goffs Orby.
Half-sister to the useful 8.3f and 10f winner Sheba Spring (by Brief Truce), to the US winner of 2 races and stakes-placed Busheto (by Be My Guest), the modest 6f winner Bank House (by Zafonic) and a winner in Sweden by Bluebird. The dam is an unraced half-sister to 6 minor winners in the USA. The second dam, Annie Aaron (by Buffalo Lark), won twice in the USA and is a half-sister to the outstanding colt Alysheba (11 wins including nine Grade 1 stakes). *"She's growing and is a lovely-looking filly but still quite green at the moment. She'll be alright though and will win".*

569 - DONEGAL SHORE (IRE) * [81] ch.c. Mujadil – Distant Shore (Jareer).

April 11. Second foal. 35,000Y. Doncaster St Leger.

Half-brother to the 3-y-o So Saintly (by Petorius). The dam was placed once in Ireland at 3 yrs and is a half-sister to 6 winners including the Group 3 Greenlands Stakes winner Nautical Pet. The second dam, Sea Mistress (by Habitat), is an unraced half-sister to 2 minor winners. *"Quite a nice horse, he should be ready by May or June and there's a lot to like about him. He's growing all the time and isn't all-together at the minute, so we wouldn't know quite how good he'll be".*

570 - EXPECTED BONUS (USA) ** [92] br.c. Kris S – Nidd (Known Fact).

March 14. Third foal.

The dam won 3 races in France and the USA including the Group 3 7f Prix de la Porte Maillot and is a half-sister to 8 winners including the Breeders Cup Classic winner Skywalker, the US Grade 2 7f Malibu Stakes Pac Mania and the French listed 6.5f winner and US Grade 2 placed Danzante. The second dam, Bold Captive (by Boldnesian), won 10 races in the USA including a 9f stakes event. (Khalid Abdulla). *"A big horse but he'll have some speed. We're just giving him a bit more to do now. A nice horse and he'll be alright".*

571 - FAR LANE (USA) ** [86] b.c. Lear Fan – Pattimech (Nureyev).

March 11. Sixth foal. 75,000Y. Goffs Orby.

Half-brother to the 3-y-o Riverina (by Irish River), to the quite useful 8.2f winner Lamanka Lass and the 1999 US 3-y-o winner Pine Ridge Road (by Cox's Ridge). The dam won at up to 7f in the USA, is a sister to Annoconnor, winner of the Santa Ana Handicap, the Vanity Handicap and the Ramona Handicap (all Grade 1 9f events) and a half-sister to the Group 1 2m Grand Prix de Paris and the Grade 1 Melbourne Cup winner At Talaq and to the dam of the Group 3 Gordon Richards Stakes winner Scribe. The second dam, My Nord (by Vent du Nord), won twice at 3 yrs in the USA over sprint distances and is a half-sister to 11 winners including the US stakes winner Biller. *"A great big colt, he'll have speed but he's on the back-burner at the moment because he's too precocious for his size. But he's a lovely horse".* Significant sire/damsire crosses:- Loup Solitaire, Fantastic Fellow, Verveine.

572 - GRAFT ** [84] b.c. Entrepreneur – Mariakova (The Minstrel).

April 19. Thirteenth foal. 95,000Y. Tattersalls Houghton.

Half-brother to the useful 5f (at 2 yrs) and 1m winner Well Beyond (by Don't Forget Me), to the fairly useful 10f winner Krispin (by Kris) and the fair 12f all-weather winner Society Ball (by Law Society). The dam was placed over 6f at 2 yrs and 1m at 3 yrs, is a sister to the smart filly Zaizafon (the dam of Zafonic) and a half-sister to the unraced Modena (the dam of Elmaamul and Reams of Verse). The second dam, Mofida (by Right Tack), won 8 races at up to 7f and was placed in the Duke of York Stakes. *"A horse that's grown a lot. He's a nice individual that strengthens up every week and is sure to have a future in the middle part of the year and the back-end. A really nice horse – I like him a lot".*

573 - IMTIHAN (IRE) * [85] ch.c. Unfuwain – Azyaa (Kris).

April 8.

Brother to the useful 6f (at 2 yrs) to 11f winner Yarob and half-brother to the useful 7f to 11f winner Ihtiraz, the quite useful 1m winner Mukhatab (both by Soviet Star), the quite useful 8.5f winner Hadith (by Nashwan) and the 10.5f winner Shafi (by Reference Point). The dam, a useful 7.5f winner, is out of the 2-y-o 7f winner Milly Lass (by Bold Lad, USA). (Hamdan Al-Maktoum). *"Still in Dubai until the end of April".*

574 - INISHOWEN (IRE) * [81] b.c. Alhaarth – Naaman (Marju).

March 9. First foal. 30,000Y. Tattersalls October.

The dam is an unplaced half-sister to 3 minor winners including the Irish 10f winner Hopesville. The second dam, the fair 1m winner Shaiybaniyda (by He Loves Me), is a half-sister to 9 winners including Shaikiya, a listed winner over 1m and placed in numerous Group events including the Cheveley Park Stakes and the Coronation Stakes. *"A nice horse but he's gone backward on us. He's in two halves at the minute so it'll be the middle of the year before he's ready. But he's a nice horse, he goes well and is sure to win his races".*

575 - LADY'S SECRET (IRE) ** [86]   b.f. Alzao – Kaaba (Darshaan).

March 28. First foal. IR£68,000Y. Goffs Orby.

The dam is an unraced half-sister to 3 winners including the listed Glorious Stakes third Konigsberg. The second dam, Konigsalpen (by Priamos), a listed winner of 3 races in Germany, was fourth in the Group 2 German Oaks. *"A lovely, quality filly that will win races, she won't be ready until mid-season at the earliest. A big filly, she's grown and filled her frame".*
Significant sire/damsire crosses:- Alborada.

576 - LAHBERHORN (USA) [85]   ch.c. Affirmed – Skiable (Niniski).

January 26. Third foal.

Half-brother to Back Pass, unplaced in one start at 2 yrs in 2000 and to the French 12f winner Grail (both by Quest For Fame). The dam won four times at up to 9f in France and the USA and is out of a half-sister to the smart sprinter So Factual. (Khalid Abdulla). *"A horse for the middle to back-end of the season. He's backward now and growing but he's a nice-looking horse and will be alright".*

577 - LATINO L'AMOUR (IRE) * [89]   b.f. Diesis – Nuit Chaud (Woodman).

April 4. Second foal. IR£160,000Y. Goffs Orby.

Half-sister to the 3-y-o Nelson Street (by Fastness). The dam is an unplaced half-sister to the listed 7f John of Gaunt Stakes winner Swordsmith and to the dam of the dual Group 1 2-y-o winner Danehill Dancer. The second dam, Lettre d'Amour (by Caro), is an unraced daughter of the top-class filly Lianga, winner of the Prix de l'Abbaye, the July Cup and the Prix Jacques le Marois. *"On the back-burner at the minute, she's just growing but she's a nice filly. She has a wall-eye otherwise she'd have probably cost more".*

578 - MAFRUZ * [86]   ch.c. Hamas – Braari (Gulch).

February 14. Fourth foal.

Closely related to the very useful 2000 2-y-o listed 6f winner and Group 3 7f Lanson Champagne Vintage Stakes third Shaard (by Anabaa) and to the quite useful 1m winner Kareeb (by Green Desert). The dam, a fairly useful 2-y-o 6f winner, is a sister to a useful 2-y-o winner in the USA and a half-sister to several winners including the Italian Derby placed Saudi Desert. The second dam, So Cozy (by Lyphard), won twice at 2 yrs in the USA. (Hamdan Al-Maktoum). *"Still in Dubai until the end of April".*

579 - MAGIC TRICK ** [73]   b.c. Magic Ring – Les Amis (Alzao).

January 11. Fifth foal. 22,000Y. Doncaster St Leger.

Half-brother to a 2-y-o 1m winner in Italy by Never So Bold. The dam, a fair 6f (at 2 yrs) and 1m winner, is a half-sister to 3 winners including the Group 3 5f Curragh Stakes second Quel Esprit. The second dam, Les Sylphides (by Kashmir II), won once at 3 yrs and is a half-sister to 7 winners including the French Two Thousand Guineas winner Moulines. *"He was third in the Brocklesby Stakes but was a bit immature mentally and the race has done him good. A big, well-grown colt and he'll win his races".*

580 - MITAWA (IRE) ** [75]   b.f. Alhaarth – Susquehanna Days (Chief's Crown).

April 15. Fifth foal.

Closely related to the fairly useful 1999 2-y-o 6f winner and 7f listed-placed Tioga (by Unfuwain) and half-sister to the unplaced 2000 2-y-o Conquering Love (by Pursuit Of Love), the fairly useful dual 6f winner Clef Of Silver (by Indian Ridge) and the useful 9f winner and 12f placed Balladonia (by Primo Dominie). The dam, a fair 1m and 8.2f winner, is a half-sister to 6 winners including Clare Bridge (Group 3 Gilltown Stud Stakes), Song Of Sixpence (listed Winter Hill Stakes) and Early Rising (dam of the St Leger winner Silver Patriarch). The second dam, Gliding By (by Tom Rolfe), won over 6f on her only start, is closely related to Key To The Mint (four Grade 1 wins in the USA) and a half-sister to the US Horse Of The Year Fort Marcy and the Grade 1 winner Key To Content. *"She's going to be a 2-y-o and should be ready to run in May. She's got plenty of speed and is a big filly with a bit of making up to do but she's precocious".*

581 - MOUNT JOY * [83]   b.c. Mtoto – Nightitude (Night Shift).

January 31. Fourth foal. 45,000Y. Tattersalls October.

Half-brother to the 3-y-o Gingilla (by Cadeaux Genereux) and to the Italian winner of 4 races at 2 and 3 yrs and listed-placed Golden Cavern (by Lion Cavern). The dam, a fairly useful 2-y-o 5f winner and placed over 6f, became unreliable at 3 yrs. She is a half-sister to 7 winners including the useful 1985 2-y-o 7f winner Normanby Lass. The second dam, Rectitude (by Runnymede), was a useful winner of 3 races at up to 8.5f. *"A big horse belonging to Jack Hanson. All the Mtoto's we've had have needed time. He'd probably start off at six furlongs and he's a nice horse with plenty of scope".*

582 - NEGLIGEE ** [79]

gr.f. Night Shift – Vax Star (Petong).
February 14. First foal. 55,000Y. Tattersalls October.

The dam, a fairly useful 2-y-o 5f listed winner, is a half-sister to two 2-y-o sprint winners out of the fairly useful listed sprint winner Vax Lady (by Millfontaine). *"A grey filly belonging to Mrs Corbett, she'll be a 2-y-o. She goes well, is as straight as a gun barrel and won't take much educating. She should be racing in May".*

583 - NIGHT DRIVER (IRE) * [78]

b.c. Night Shift – Highshaan (Pistolet Bleu).
February 5. First foal. FF400,000. Deauville August.

The dam, a winner of 2 races in France at 3 yrs, is a half-sister to 2 other minor winners. The second dam, Renashaan (by Darshaan), won a listed race in France and was third in the Group 3 9.5f Prix Vanteaux. *"This big, strong, strapping colt is worth mentioning. A lovely horse, he'll set off over six furlongs and he'll be alright".*

584 - NOBLE VIEW (USA) ** [81]

ch.f. Distant View – Proud Lou (Proud Clarion).
April 26.

Half-sister to the French One Thousand Guineas and Prix de la Grotte winner Houseproud (by Riverman), to the French 1m winner Proud Fact and the fairly useful 10f winner Modus Operandi (both by Known Fact). The dam, winner of the Grade 1 1m Frizette Stakes at 2 yrs in the USA, is a half-sister to 5 winners. The second dam, Baby Louise (by Exclusive Native), won a 2-y-o stakes event in the USA. *"This filly will be a 2-y-o. Very light-framed and active, she goes really well and will probably start off at six furlongs".* (Khalid Abdulla).

585 - OCEAN SOUND (IRE) ** [81]

b.c. Mujadil – Ossana (Tejano).
April 3. First foal. IR50,000Y. Tattersalls Fairyhouse.

The dam won in Germany at 2 yrs and is a half-sister to a winner in France. The second dam, Orminda (by Bellypha), is a placed half-sister to the dual Group 3 winner Gaelic Bird and the dam of the Group 1 winners Gabina and Galetto. *"A horse that's done really well. He'll be a 2-y-o and will win his races. I wouldn't think it would be long before he's out and he's a nice horse".*

586 - OUR GLENARD ** [81]

b.c. Royal Applause – Loucoum (Iron Duke).
February 14. Ninth foal. 35,000Y. Tattersalls October.

Half-brother to the fair 2000 2-y-o 7f winner Brilliantrio, to the Hong Kong sprint winner Triple Expresso (both by Selkirk), the quite useful 1m winner Iktasab (by Cadeaux Genereux), the modest 2m winner Rigadoon (by Be My Chief), the moderate 2-y-o 6f all-weather winner Always Baileys (by Al Nasr), the moderate 12f all-weather winner Ajdar (Slip Anchor) and a winner in the UAE by Thatching. The dam, winner of 7 races in the USA at around 1m including a minor stakes, was third in the Group 3 Prix d'Arenberg, is a half-sister to 9 winners including the Group 3 5f Prix du Bois and the Group 3 5f Prix d'Arenberg winner Rich And Famous and the dam of the Group 3 Curragh Stakes winner Leading Time. The second dam, Paraxelle (by Poleax), won twice in France and was listed placed over 12f. *"This horse has turned himself inside out. He's thrived and shows plenty of speed and will be relatively early. I like him for how much he's improved and he goes along really well".*

587 - PHASED * [71]

b.f. Zamindar – Ypha (Lyphard).
February 6.

Closely related to the French trained 3-y-o Enhancer (by Gone West). The dam, a French 3-y-o 9f listed winner, is a sister to the Grade 2 American Derby, Group 3 Prix de la Jonchere and Group 3 Prix la Force placed Standiford, closely related to the very useful 2-y-o 7f Acomb Stakes and 3-y-o 8.5f winner Concordial and a half-sister to the US Grade 1 10f Carleton F Burke Handicap winner Louis le Grand and the US Grade 3 8.5f Bay Meadows Derby winner Le Belvedere. The second dam, Louisville (by Val de l'Orne), won over 1m in France and is a half-sister to the French stakes winner Laurius. (Khalid Abdulla). *"A nice, big filly with a good action. She's all there and I think she'll make a 2-y-o alright but would want a bit of time. A bit flighty, she needs the kidgloves treatment".*

588 - ROUGH SEAS (IRE) ** [81] b.c. Royal Applause – Hebrides (Gone West).
March 11. First foal. 60,000Y. Tattersalls October.
The dam is an unraced half-sister to 4 winners including the useful all-weather 7f to 10f winner Threadneedle. The second dam, Sleeping Beauty (by Mill Reef), a quite useful 1m winner, is a half-sister to the listed 12f Galtres Stakes winners Deadly Serious (herself dam of the Australian Grade 1 winner Runyon) and Sans Blague. *"All our Royal Applause 2-y-o's were precocious at the yearling stage but have gone back a little bit so we're giving them a bit of a break. This is a lovely horse that's going to be a 2-y-o. Very well put-together, he's a good mannered horse and a good mover. He'll do well".*

589 - SARABANDE * [89] ch.f. Nashwan – Western Reel (Gone West).
February 16.
The dam, a fairly useful 1m winner, is a sister to the very useful Group 3 5f Queen Mary Stakes and Group 3 7.3f Fred Darling Stakes winner Dance Parade and a half-sister to the Grade 3 9f Bay Meadows Derby winner Ocean Queen (by Zilzal). The second dam, River Jig (by Irish River), a useful 2-y-o 9f winner here, later won over 12f in Italy and is a half-sister to 5 winners including the dam of the Prix Gladiateur winner Always Aloof. (Fahd Salman). *"A lovely filly in the making and with a lovely attitude, she growing and backward now. One for the back-end of the season and next year. Hopefully she can win in the autumn".*

590 - SEA MUSIC * [63] b.f. Inchinor – Braissim (Dancing Brave).
March 9. Third foal. 54,000Y. Tattersalls October.
Half-sister to the Italian winner of 4 races at 3 and 4 yrs Lord Cavern (by Lion Cavern). The dam is an unraced half-sister to 6 winners including the listed Doncaster Mile winner White Heart and the useful 6f to 7.5f winner Green Barries. The second dam, Barari (by Blushing Groom), is an unraced half-sister to 9 winners including the Canadian Grade 1 winner Rainbows For Life and to the Group 2 Prix de l'Opera winner Colour Chart. *"She belongs to Mrs Roberts and is a nice, big filly that will need a lot of time but she has potential. A lovely filly".*

591 - SERIEUX ** [86] b.c. Cadeaux Genereux – Seranda (Petoski).
February 26. Fourth foal. 180,000Y. Tattersalls Houghton.
Half-brother to the French winner (including at 2 yrs) and listed-placed Shine On Me (by Machiavellian) and to 2 minor French winners by Efisio and Green Desert. The dam won once at 3 yrs and was listed-placed in France. She is a half-sister to 6 winners including the dam of the Group 1 Criterium de Saint-Cloud winner Shaka. The second dam, Servia (by Le Marmot), won twice in France and is a half-sister to 7 winners including the Group 2 Prix de l'Opera winner Secret Form. *"A big, backward horse, but a nice horse in the making. He'll be alright and will probably start off at seven furlongs. He'll make a 2-y-o".*

592 - SOHAIB (USA) * [92]** b.c. Kingmambo – Fancy Ruler (Half A Year).
April 8. First foal. $425,000Y. Keeneland September.
The dam ran unplaced twice and is a half-sister to the US stakes winner and Grade 3 placed American Odyssey. The second dam, Bittersweet Hour (by Seattle Slew), ran unplaced once and is a half-sister to the Grade 1 Breeders Cup Juvenile winner Success Express, the Grade 1 Champagne Stakes winner Greenwood Lake and the triple Grade 3 winner Charlie Barley. (Hamdan Al-Maktoum). *"Still in Dubai, but Michael and Richard (Hills) both reckon he's a really nice horse and the best of our lot over there, so we hope he'll be a decent 2-y-o".*

593 - STANDS TO REASON (USA) ** [88] b.f. Gulch – Sheer Reason (Danzig).
April 1. First foal.
The dam, winner of the listed 2-y-o 6f Criterium d'Evry and second in the Group 2 6.5f Criterium des Deux Ans, is closely related to the useful Group 3 12f Lingfield Oaks Trial winner Munnaya (by Nijinsky) and a half-sister to 4 winners including the listed 2-y-o 5f Prix Yacowlef winner Mall Queen. The second dam, Hiaam (by Alydar), was a very useful winner of the Group 3 6f Princess Margaret Stakes at 2 yrs and listed events over 7.6f and 1m at 3 yrs. She is a half-sister to the champion Canadian 3-y-o Key to the Moon, the triple US grade 1 winner Gorgeous, the Grade 1 Kentucky Oaks winner Seaside Attraction (herself dam of the Cherry Hinton winner Red Carnival and the US Grade 1 winners Cape

Town and Golden Attraction) and to the dam of the Hong Kong Cup and Man O'War Stakes winner Fantastic Light. (Maktoum Al-Maktoum). *"Definitely a 2-y-o, she's not over-big but she's precocious so I can see her setting off at six furlongs. A nice filly, it's all there and she won't take any educating at all".*

---

594 - STORM SEEKER * [89]   b.c. Rainbow Quest – Siwaayib (Green Desert).
February 27. Fourth foal.

Brother to the smart middle-distance stayer and Group 2 Yorkshire Cup second Rainbow Ways. The dam, a fairly useful winner of 3 races over 6f, is a half-sister to 6 winners here and abroad. The second dam, Ma Petite Cherie (by Caro), won 3 races in France and is a half-sister to 8 winners out of the US stakes winner Lady B. Gay (by Sir Gaylord). (Maktoum Al-Maktoum). *"He's a lovely horse. Not over-big and well put-together, despite his pedigree I can see him starting off at six furlongs and I think he'll be a 2-y-o alright".*

---

595 - SUNDIAL ** [74]   ch.f. Cadeaux Genereux – Ruby Setting (Gorytus).
March 30. Sixth foal.

Half-sister to the fair 2000 6f placed 2-y-o Sundown (by Polish Precedent) and to two winners in Japan by Fairy King and Woodman. The dam, a fairly useful 10f winner at 3 yrs, is a half-sister to 6 winners including the high-class 1989 2-y-o Prince Of Dance, winner of the Dewhurst Stakes (in a dead-heat) and to the unraced dam of the Japanese Derby winner Fusaichi Concorde. The second dam, Sun Princess (by English Prince), was a top-class winner of the Oaks, St Leger and Yorkshire Oaks and was placed in both the Prix de l'Arc de Triomphe and the King George. She is a half-sister to the high-class middle distance colt Saddlers Hall and to the Sean Graham Fillies Stakes winner Dancing Shadow - herself dam of the very useful fillies Dancing Bloom and River Dancer and thus grandam of the Champion Stakes winner Spectrum. *"A lovely filly belonging to Mr McCreery, she's probably the best of all those he's got with us. She's quite a big filly that should start off at five furlongs and progress to six. Probably one of the best Cadeaux Genereux's we've had".*

---

596 - TREE PIPIT (USA) *** [92]   ch.f. Woodman – Skimble (Lyphard).
April 22.

Closely related to the quite useful 10f winner Cloud Hopping (by Mr Prospector) and half-sister to the unraced 2000 2-y-o West Sound (by Irish River) and the very smart 2000 4-y-o Skimming (by Nureyev), a winner of 5 races from 1m to 10f here and in the USA including the Grade 1 Pacific Classic at Del Mar. The dam, a fairly useful 6f (at 2 yrs) and 10.4f winner here, subsequently won 7 stakes events in the USA. She is a sister to the fair 10f winner Flit (dam of the One Thousand Guineas winner Wince) and is closely related to the Grade 1 Washington Lassie Stakes winner Contredance, the listed Roses Stakes winner Old Alliance and to the dam of the Lanson Champagne Stakes winner Eltish. The second dam, Nimble Folly (by Cyane), is an unraced sister to the very useful 2-y-o Group 3 winner and Group 1 third Misgivings. (Khalid Abdulla). *"Not very big but precocious and will be an early, speedy 2-y-o. We had the half-brother Skimming who was a good horse".*
Significant sire/damsire crosses:- Fleur de Nuit (Gr 3).

---

597 - TRUE COURAGE ** [90]   b.c. Machiavellian – Try To Catch Me (Shareef Dancer).
March 18. Sixth foal.

Brother to the useful 2000 2-y-o 7f winner and Group 3 Solario Stakes second Storming Home and half-brother to the fairly useful 12.3f winner Follow That Dream (by Darshaan), the fairly useful 11f to 13f winner Desert Frolic (by Persian Bold) and the fair 2-y-o 7f winner Nawafell (by Kris). The dam won once over 1m at 3 yrs in France, is closely related to the US stakes winner Air Dancer and a half-sister to the Group 2 Criterium de Maisons-Laffitte winner Bitooh and the listed Virginia Stakes winner Monaassabaat. The second dam, It's In The Air (by Mr Prospector), was a Champion 2-y-o filly and winner of the Vanity Handicap (twice), the Ruffian Handicap, the Alabama Stakes and the Delaware Oaks (all Grade 1 events). (Maktoum Al-Maktoum). *"He's a lovely horse but he'll take quite a while to get ready. It took some time for the penny to drop for his brother Storming Home last year and this horse seems much the same. He'll be alright".*

598 - AZILLION (IRE) * [84]   b.c. Alzao – Olivia (Ela-Mana-Mou).
February 2. Second living foal. 21,000Y. Tattersalls October.

The dam, a minor Irish 10f winner, is a half-sister to 4 minor winners here and abroad. The second dam, Yankee Lady (by Lord Gayle), won once at 3 yrs and is a half-sister to the Group 2 Ballymoss Stakes winner Yankee Gold and the Group 2 Pretty Polly Stakes winner Lady Singer. (Mr R Bolam & Team). *"He goes well – better than he should do at this stage really. He's a big, scopey horse and yet he goes as well as the sharper types. To look at him and his pedigree you'd think of middle-distances, but to watch him go – he's got speed. He'll hopefully be out by June or July over seven furlongs and he's a very likeable colt".*

599 - BOLD ENTERPRISE (IRE) * [78]   b.c. Entrepreneur – Phylella (Persian Bold).
February 28. Ninth foal. IR£35,000Y. Goffs Orby.

Half-brother to the 2000 6f placed 2-y-o Speed Of Light (by Spectrum), to the very useful Group 3 7f Nell Gwyn Stakes winner Reunion (by Be My Guest), the fair 1m to 12.3f winner of 8 races Mono Lady (by Polish Patriot), the Irish 2-y-o 6f winner Foravella (by Cadeaux Genereux) and the 1999 Italian 2-y-o winner Avrai (by Rainbows For Life). The dam won in France (over 10f) and in the USA, is a sister to the US stakes winner Karman Girl and a half-sister to 4 winners. The second dam, Tumblella (by Tumble Wind), won the listed 1m Gilltown Stud Stakes and is a half-sister to 7 winners. (Mr N Browne & Partners). *"A very likeable but backward colt. I have a feeling that Entrepreneur has as good a chance as any of making the right kind of first season sire. This colt was quite big and plain at the yearling sales – but his half-sister Reunion was just the same, so we thought this colt was worth taking a chance with".*

600 - BOUNDLESS PROSPECT (USA) * [82]   b.br.c. Boundary – Cape (Mr Prospector).
May 14. Fifth foal. $39,000Y. Keeneland September.

Half-brother to 2 minor 3-y-o winners by Demons Begone (in the USA) and Time For A Change (in France). The dam is an unraced half-sister to 4 minor winners. The second dam, Cope Of Flowers (by Tom Rolfe), won 4 races and was third in the Grade 1 Flower Bowl Handicap and is a half-sister to the Grade 1 winner Great Neck. (M Wauchope, Sir S Dunning & R Cottam). *"He's a late foal from a sire who had a good year in 2000. A classy-looking colt and a very good mover, he should make a 2-y-o from July onwards. He goes as well as everything else right now but because of his late foaling I haven't really done too much with him. I think he's a real 'could be' and that he has a classy look about him".*

601 - DANEMERE (IRE) * [78]   b.f. Danehill – Kentmere (Galetto).
April 2. Third foal. IR£60,000Y. Goffs Orby.

Half-sister to the unplaced 2000 2-y-o Love (by Royal Academy) and to the minor French 13f winner Love Bitten (by Darshaan). The dam, a French 1m (at 2yrs) and 11f winner, is a half-sister to 4 winners including the French Oaks winner and Prix Vermeille fourth Lypharita. The second dam, Gracefully (by Lyphard), won over 10f in France and is a half-sister to the dams of the King George VI and Queen Elizabeth Diamond Stakes winner Belmez and the French Group 3 winners Arousal and River Test. (Wyck Hall Stud Ltd). *"Danemere's a nice filly and she goes particularly well. She's a bit unfurnished at this stage but she's got natural speed and will make a 2-y-o for sure. She's got a bit of quality about her and I think she's very nice".*

602 - DYNAMO MINSK (IRE) ** [80]   b.f. Polish Precedent – Blazing Glory (Glow).
May 17. Sixth foal. 22,000Y. Tattersalls October.

Half-sister to the 3-y-o Arboreta (by Charnwood Forest), to the fairly useful 5f and 6f winner La Piazza (by Polish Patriot), the quite useful 5f and 6f winner Prince Dome (by Prince Sabo) and the quite useful 5f winner (at 2 yrs) Brimstone (by Ballad Rock). The dam won 3 races over 5f and is a full or half-sister to 6 winners. The second dam, Salvationist (by Mill Reef), won 4 races at 3 yrs in France and is a half-sister to 8 winners including the Group 2 King Edward VII Stakes winner Marquis de Sade. (Chris & Antonia Deuters). *"The first one I've trained for these owners and she's a really nice filly that's done particularly well over the past couple of months. She moves well, has grown a lot and being a mid-May foal we'll have to be a bit easy on her for now. Despite that, I still think she'll make a 2-y-o from July onwards".*

603 - HIDEAWAY HEROINE (IRE) ** [74]   ch.f. Hernando – Dulcinea (Selkirk).
March 8. First foal. 40,000Y. Tattersalls October.
The dam, a fair 3-y-o 7f and 1m winner, is a half-sister to 5 winners includng the French listed winner Amato. The second dam, Ahohoney (by Ahonoora), won the Group 3 10.5f Prix Fille de l'Air (twice) and is a half-sister to 5 winners. (M Kerr Dineen & Partners). *"I think she's gorgeous. Amanda Skiffington bought her for the same team that owned Tempting Fate last year. She stands over a lot of ground and has a lot of Selkirk about her. She really does go up the gallops as well as anything but she's quite a big filly and I wouldn't expect her coming on stream before June. Also you'd be swimming against the tide to think that a Hernando 2-y-o was going to come any earlier. She goes really well and is very promising".*

604 - HIGH DIVA ** [61]   b.f. Piccolo – Gifted (Shareef Dancer).
March 15. Third foal. 10,000Y. Tattersalls October.
Half-sister to Abbot (by Bishop Of Cashel), unplaced over 6f on his only start at 2 yrs in 2000 and to a 2-y-o 5f winner in Poland by Tirol. The dam, a poor 12f placed maiden, is a half-sister to 5 winners including the Italian St Leger and Goodwood Cup winner Sergeyevich and the Park Hill Stakes second Princess Sobieska. The second dam, Rekana (by Relko), won over 1m and 12f in France including a listed event. (Sir J Robb & J W Hills). *"She's a gorgeous filly and I love her. We didn't pay a lot for her and I can see her starting off at six furlongs but she's such a good mover and will be better over a bit further. She should hopefully be ready to run in mid-June, is very well-balanced and does everything easily".*

605 - MOLOKO (USA) ** [76]   b.br.f. Boundary – Future Starlet (Theatrical).
April 9. Fourth foal. $60,000Y. Keeneland September.
Half-sister to a minor 3-y-o winner in the USA by Rubiano. The dam won 4 races in the USA (including at 2 yrs), was third in the Grade 3 Pucker Up Stakes and is a half-sister to 9 winners including the dual US Grade 3 winner Spring Beauty. The second dam, Necessity (by Sir Gaylord), was a minor winner in the USA. (Chris Wright). *"She's been going through a very backward stage and hasn't done an awful lot just yet. But she's well-balanced and has a bit of quality about her. An uncomplicated type of filly, the way she moves you'd expect her to have a bit of speed about her and I think she'll make a 2-y-o alright".*

606 - NOBLE PENNY [83]   b.f. Pennekamp – Noble Form (Double Form).
May 16. Sixth living foal. 32,000Y. Tattersalls December.
Half-sister to the modest 9.4f all-weather winner Golden Rod (by Rainbows For Life), to the modest 5f and 6f winner Noble Patriot and to a winner of 6 races in Italy from 2 to 4 yrs (both by Polish Patriot). The dam, a French 1m and 10.5f winner, is a half-sister to 5 winners including the Group 3 10.5f Prix Fille de l'Air winner Darine (herself dam of the Group 2 Gardner Merchant Mile winner Penny Drops). The second dam, Be Noble (by Vaguely Noble), ran once unplaced and is a half-sister to 8 winners including the Nell Gwyn Stakes winner Gently (herself dam of the listed winners and good broodmares Greedy Of Gain and Godzilla). (Queensberry Thoroughbreds). *"Although I like Noble Penny, I know very little about her as she's been coughing and I've done less with her than most of the others up to now".*

607 - QUITE A NIGHT * [72]   b.c. Night Shift – Ellebanna (Tina's Pet).
May 13. Sixth foal. 35,000Y. Tattersalls October.
Half-brother to the fair 2000 6f placed 2-y-o Mine (by Primo Dominie), to the useful 1999 3-y-o 7f winner King Midas (by Bluebird) and the fairly useful 7f winner of 4 races Gift Of Gold (by Statoblest). The dam, a fair winner of 3 races over 5f, is a half-sister to 7 winners including the high-class sprinter Bolshoi, winner of the Group 2 King's Stand Stakes and the Group 2 Temple Stakes. The second dam, Mainly Dry (by The Brianstan), is an unraced half-sister to 4 winners including the dam of the Portland Handicap winner Swelter and the French triple listed winner The Nub. (Mr L Godfrey & Partners). *"A well-balanced horse that moves well and he should make a 2-y-o. He's not going to be a five furlong performer though. Six or seven will suit him better and he should be ready for June or July".*

608 - RUISSEC (USA) ** [76]   b.br.f. Woodman – Jadana (Pharly).

March 5. Twelfth foal. $120,000Y. Keeneland September.

Closely related to the US Grade 1 9f and Grade 1 10f winner Jade Hunter (by Mr Prospector), to the very useful 5f (at 2 yrs) to 1m winner L'Ami Louis (by Easy Goer) and the unraced Jade Jewel (dam of the US stakes winner and Grade 2 third Green Light). The dam won 3 races including a minor stakes in the USA and is closely related to the champion 2-y-o and Group 1 Dewhurst Stakes winner Monteverdi. The second dam, Janina (by Match II), won at 3 yrs in France and is a half-sister to the Coronation Cup winner Nagami. (Wood Hall Stud Ltd). *"A good model, she moves well and will make a 2-y-o from June onwards. When she pulls herself together she's going to be quite a strong 2-y-o I think. I like her".*

609 - SADLER'S LAW (IRE) ** [90]   b.c. Sadler's Wells – Dathiyna (Kris).

March 9. First foal. 200,000Y. Tattersalls Houghton.

The dam is an unraced half-sister to the minor Irish 7f winner Daftari (by Soviet Star) and to the Irish 7f and 1m winner Darayna (by Shernazar). The second dam, Dafayna (by Habitat), was a smart winner of the Group 3 Cork and Orrery Stakes and the Salisbury One Thousand Guineas Trial and was placed in the July Cup, the Vernons Sprint Cup and the Diadem Stakes. She is a sister to the high-class 7f colt Dalsaan and a half-sister to the Two Thousand Guineas winner Doyoun, the high-class Champion Stakes second Dolpour and the very useful French winner at up to 10.5f Dayzaan. (Mr George Tong & Partners). *"For a Sadler's Wells he's not on the big side. A likeable horse, he's pleasing me but he's very much a horse for September onwards. He's rather immature looking, although when I bought him I did think he'd come to hand a bit sooner than some of the other Sadler's Wells horses I've had".* Significant sire/damsire crosses:- Moonshell, Samsaam.

610 - STAR PROTECTOR (FR) * [76]   b.c. Hector Protector – Frustration (Salse).

April 21. First living foal. 40,000Y. Tattersalls October.

The dam, a useful 10.2f listed winner, was placed in a German Group 3 event and in the listed 12f Galtres Stakes and is a half-sister to the US Grade 1 9f American Handicap winner Mister Wonderful and to the Italian listed winner Kavir. The second dam, Baffle (by Petingo), a quite useful 13.3f winner, is a half-sister to 5 winners including the 12f Princess Royal Stakes winner Predicament. (Mr G Tong). *"A really bonny colt bred by Lady Herries. He's a thoroughly likeable, well-balanced colt and I think he could make a 2-y-o over six or seven furlongs. I'd be disappointed if he didn't make some impact this year".*

611 - STARS IN HER EYES (IRE) ** [81]   b.f. Woodman – Wind In Her Hair (Alzao).

March 8. Fourth foal.

Half-sister to the useful dual 6f and 7f winner (including at 2 yrs) and listed placed Veil Of Avalon (by Thunder Gulch). The dam won the Group 1 12f Aral-Pokal and two listed events, was second in the Oaks and is a half-sister to the US Grade 3 and listed Pretty Polly Stakes winner Capo di Monte. The second dam, Burghclere (by Busted), won over 14f and is a half-sister to the Princess Of Wales's Stakes winners Milford and Height Of Fashion (the dam of Nashwan and Unfuwain). (Mrs D Nagle & Mrs S Magnier). *"I like this filly. She looks very racy and I'd say she looks like making a 2-y-o. She has a bit of the spirit that her mother had and is starting to thicken up through her neck and shoulder now. She's on the small side and I think she's going to make a 2-y-o. In one respect she isn't typical of the dam in that the family are mainly big and scopey".*

612 - THUNDERCLAP ** [75]   b.c. Royal Applause – Gloriana (Formidable).

March 12. First living foal. 10,000Y. Doncaster St Leger.

The dam, a fair 1m and 9f winner, is a daughter of the modest 7f winner Tudor Pilgrim (by Welsh Pageant), herself a half-sister to 3 winners. (J W Hills). *"This was a very plain, backward-looking yearling but he's transformed himself over the winter and I would see him as being a very early 2-y-o – possibly as early as May. He's just got something about him".*

613 - WATERSIDE (IRE) ** [87]   b.c. Lake Coniston – Classic Ring (Auction Ring).

April 6. Sixth foal. 16,000Y. Doncaster St Leger.

Half-brother to Poppaea (by Definite Article), placed fourth over 6f on her only outing at 2 yrs in 2000, to the useful 1999 2-y-o 5f and 6f winner Seven No Trumps (by Pips Pride) and a winner in Denmark by Silver Kite. The dam, a 2-y-o 7f seller winner, was placed 7 times and is a half-sister to 4 minor winners here and abroad. The second dam, Classic Choice (by Patch), is an unraced half-sister to 8 winners including the Group 3 White Rose Stakes third River Beauty. (Sir John Robb). *"This colt is going particularly well right now. He's quite a big, strong horse and I was tempted to run him very early but I think we're going to wait until the Guineas meeting".*

M JARVIS

614 - BRITANNIA HOUSE (USA) ** [96] ch.f. Diesis – Refill (Mill Reef).
April 18.
Sister to a winner in Japan and half-sister to the fairly useful 2-y-o 7f winner Spurned (by Robellino) and herself dam of the Group winners Hidden Meadow and Scorned), to the 1995 German champion 2-y-o and subsequent US Grade 2 placed Winter Quarters, the quite useful 2-y-o 6f winner Jumilla (both by El Gran Senor) and the fair 7f and 10f winner Shaffaaf (by Shadeed). The dam, placed fourth in the Group 3 6f Cherry Hinton Stakes at 2 yrs, subsequently won 4 races at up to 11f in the USA and is a half-sister to 9 winners including the dam of the Group 2 5f Kings Stand Stakes winner Don't Worry Me. The second dam, Regal Twin (by Majestic Prince), won at 3 yrs and is a half-sister to the US stakes winner and Grade 1 second Heisanative and to the dams of the US Grade 1 winner My Gallant and the Group/Graded stakes winners Cost Control, Tobin Lad and La Jalouse. (Mr M P Burke). *"She's nice. A medium-sized, lovely-balanced filly from a good family, we'd be looking for seven furlongs in mid to late summer to start her off. There's plenty of stamina on the dam's side so she should make up into a nice, staying filly. I like her a lot".*

615 - CALALOO KATIE * [68] b.f. Charnwood Forest – Calaloo Sioux (Our Native).
February 15. Tenth foal. IR£20,000Y. Goffs Orby.
Half-sister to the very useful Irish 1m winner and Group 2 Sea World International Stakes third Master Tribe (by Master Willie), to the fairly useful 1997 2-y-o 10f winner and Group 3 Derby Trial third Dashing Chief (by Darshaan), the listed Norwegian One Thousand Guineas winner Helensville (by Horage), the modest 6f winner Thatcham (by Thatching), the Irish 10f winner Double Colour (by Doyoun) and the placed dam of the Group 3 6f Prix de Cabourg winner Hunan. The dam, a useful 7.6f winner, is out of the unplaced Roshanndra (by Mill Reef), herself a half-sister to the champion French 2-y-o filly Mange Tout and the champion English 2-y-o filly Rose Dubarry. (Mr M McDonagh). *"A very tall filly and slightly 'on the leg', but she's out of a useful mare that produces winners. She looks a winner too, but as I say she is biggish so she won't be early. She'll make an autumn 2-y-o".*

616 - COSHOCTON (USA) * [89] b.c. Silver Hawk – Tribulation (Danzig).
Second foal.
Half-brother to a maiden in USA by Seeking The Gold. The dam won 5 races in the USA, notably the Grade 1 9f Queen Elizabeth II Invitational Challenge Cup, and is a half-sister to Graceful Darby, winner of 4 Grade 3 events. The second dam, Graceful Touch (by His Majesty) won 4 races in the USA. *"A home-bred from Darby Dan Farm in Kentucky, he's a lovely, big colt. He's only been here a short while but I already feel he's very nice and that he'll be ready to run by July time".*

617 - CRANMER [97] ch.c. Machiavellian – True Glory (In The Wings).
February 5.
The dam, a quite useful 11f winner, is a half-sister to the very smart Grade 2 10f E P Taylor Stakes winner Truly A Dream (by Darshaan). The second dam, Truly Special (by Caerleon), a very smart winner of the Group 3 10.5f Prix de Royaumont at 3 yrs after winning over 1m at 2 yrs, is a half-sister to the Group 2 13.5f Grand Prix de Deauville winner Modhish and the Prix de Royallieu winner Russian Snows. The third dam, Arctique Royale (by Royal and Regal), won the Irish One Thousand Guineas and the Moyglare Stud Stakes and is a half-sister to the dam of Ardross. (Mr Saif Ali). *"Quite a nice horse. He's very well-grown like most of the Machiavellians (they're biggish horses mostly) and he goes quite nicely. Again, you'd be looking at the autumn for him as he's a 3-y-o type".*

618 - DANISH DECORUM (IRE) *** [90] ch.c. Danehill Dancer – Dignified Air (Wolver Hollow).
March 21. Twelfth foal. 37,000Y. Doncaster St Leger.
Half-brother to the modest 2000 5f and 6f placed 2-y-o Regal Air (by Distinctly North), to the useful listed 7f Athasi Stakes winner Proud Titania (by Fairy King), the quite useful 2-y-o 7f and subsequent hurdles and jumps winner Regal Aura (by Glow) and winners abroad and over hurdles by Wassl,

Caerleon, Dancing Dissident and Marju. The dam, a fair 4-y-o 6f winner, is a half-sister to 4 minor winners. The second dam, Dismantle (by Aureole), a fair 2-y-o 7f winner, is a half-sister to the listed 9f Strensall Stakes winner and One Thousand Guineas third Joking Apart. (Mrs Christine Stevenson). *"He's a nice horse and although he's big he could well make a mid-summer 2-y-o as he's done particularly well over the past few weeks. From being particularly backward he's pulled himself together and he looks as though he'll make a 2-y-o. He looks to have a bit of speed and should be suited by six or seven furlongs".*

619 - HI TECH   [81]
b.c. Polar Falcon – Just Speculation (Ahonoora).
March 30. Third foal. 48,000Y. Tattersalls October.
Half-brother to The Judge (by Polish Precedent), unplaced in one start over 7f at 2 yrs in 2000 and to the Turkish 1m and 9f winner of 7 races Ezergecer (by Sharpo). The dam, an Irish 2-y-o 6f winner, was third in the Group 3 1m Killavullen Stakes and is a half-sister to 4 winners including Tyrone Bridge, a winner of 9 races on the flat and over hurdles and second in the Ascot Gold Cup and the Irish St Leger. The second dam, Rhein Bridge (by Rheingold), won the Group 3 12f Lancashire Oaks and is a half-sister to the Group 1 Yorkshire Oaks winner Connaught Bridge. *"A nice-actioned colt, he's medium sized and looks as though he'll be a summer 2-y-o over six and seven furlongs".*
Significant sire/damsire crosses:- Icicle.

620 - KAYSERI (IRE) *   [78]
b.c. Alzao – Ms Calera (Diesis).
March 16. Second foal. IR£105,000Y. Goffs Orby.
The dam is a US placed half-sister to 5 winners including the Group 1 Irish St Leger and Australian Grade 1 winner Authaal. The second dam, Galletto (by Nijinsky), won the listed 12f Galtres Stakes. (Sheikh Ahmed Al-Maktoum). *"A nice horse we bought at Goffs, he's a really nice, big, strong colt. One of our better horses I'd say and we rather think he'll start at seven furlongs this year and then take it from there".*

621 - KING NICHOLAS (USA) *   [67]
b.c. Nicholas – Lifetime Honour (Kingmambo).
April 25. First foal. 25,000Y. Tattersalls October.
The dam is an unraced half-sister to the US Grade 2 9f Jim Dandy Stakes winner Composer and to the US stakes winner Colonial Power. The second dam, Honoria (by Danzig), won the Group 3 6f Railway Stakes and was second in the Group 1 Moyglare Stud Stakes. She is a sister to the Irish One Thousand Guineas Trial winner Gdansk's Honour and a half-sister to 9 winners including the Irish St Leger second Father Rooney and the good broodmare Royalivor (dam of the Group/Graded stakes winners King Ivor, Linney Head and Snake Eyes). *"A horse for the first half of the season, he looked as though he'll be very early but he's grown quite a bit. Quite a nice horse".*

622 - MAIMANA (IRE) **   [64]
b.br.f. Desert King – Staff Approved (Teenoso).
February 23. Sixth living foal. IR£230,000Y. Goffs Orby.
Half-sister to the unraced 2000 2-y-o Zenita (by Zieten), to the very smart Group 1 10f Premio Presidente della Repubblica and Group 3 8.5f Diomed Stakes winner Polar Prince (by Distinctly North) and the fairly useful 7f (at 2 yrs), 1m and subsequent US winner Housekeeper (by Common Grounds). The dam, a fairly useful 2-y-o 1m winner, is a half-sister to 11 winners including the US Grade 2 Jockey Club Cup winner Irish Heart and to the unraced dam of the US Grade 2 winner Golden Klair. The second dam, Klairlone (by Klairon), won the listed Mulcahy Stakes and was placed in the Irish One Thousand Guineas and the Irish Oaks. (Sheikh Ahmed Al-Maktoum). *"A very nice, well-grown filly, she has a lot of her half-brother Polar Prince about her. She goes really nicely and is a promising filly. I'd expect her to be a middle-distance filly next year so I should think it unlikely that she'd start over six furlongs as a 2-y-o. Having said all that, she will make a 2-y-o alright".*

623 - MALMAND (USA)   [80]
ch.c. Distant View – Bidski (Explosive Bid).
March 16. Fourth foal. 47,000Y. Tattersalls October.
Half-brother to 2 minor winners in the USA by My Memoirs and Halissee. The dam, a minor 3-y-o winner in the USA, is a half-sister to 5 winners. The second dam, Mornin' Jig (by Jig Time), won once in the USA and is a half-sister to 9 winners. (Sheikh Ahmed Al-Maktoum). *"We bought him as an individual, rather than for his pedigree, although he is by a popular sire. He's a horse for August onwards and will want seven furlongs to begin with".*

624 - MIDNIGHT PARKES ** [96] b.br.c. Polar Falcon – Summerhill Spruce (Windjammer).
April 11.
Half-brother to Summerhill Parkes (by Zafonic), placed third over 6f on her only outing at 2 yrs in 2000, to the useful 1998 2-y-o 5f and 6f winner Ace Of Parkes, the useful dual 5f winner and Moyglare, Lowther and Queen Mary Stakes placed My Melody Parkes (both by Teenoso), the useful mare Lucky Parkes (by Full Extent), a winner of 13 races over 5f, the 4-y-o 6f winner Bella Parkes (by Tina's Pet) and a winner in Holland by Jupiter Island. The dam, a fair winner of a 6f seller at 3 yrs, is out of the unraced Sharper Still (by Sharpen Up). (Mr J Heler). *"Quite a well-grown horse, he's a bit immature just now both physically and mentally but I'd hope that he'd be ready for mid-summer. A colt with quite a lot of Polar Falcon about him".*

625 - MILLENNIUM DRAGON [79] b.c. Mark Of Esteem – Feather Bride (Groom Dancer).
January 29. Third foal. 25,000Y. Tattersalls October.
Closely related to the fair 10.2f winner Bless The Bride (by Darshaan) and half-brother to the 3-y-o Bride In Blue (by Bluebird). The dam, a minor 10.5f winner at 3 yrs in France, is a half-sister to 2 other winners there. The second dam, Bubbling Danseuse (by Arctic Tern), won once and was second in the Group 3 1m Prix de Sandringham and is a half-sister to 6 winners including the dam of Kotashaan, winner of five Grade 1 events in the USA and second in the Japan Cup. (Mr N S Yong). *"Another big horse, he came in quite late and he's a bit behind the others at the moment. He canters along nicely but I haven't really come to an opinion of him just yet".*

626 - MYSTIC MILE (IRE) ** [93] gr.f. Sadler's Wells – Delage (Bellypha).
May 22. Third living foal. IR£300,000Y. Goffs Orby.
Half-sister to a winner in Germany by Classic Music. The dam is an unraced half-sister to 5 winners including the Group 2 Prix Maurice de Gheest winner and July Cup second College Chapel and the very useful 6f and 7f winner Breadcrumb. The second dam, Scarcely Blessed (by So Blessed), won 3 races including the Group 3 King George Stakes and is out of the July Cup winner Parsimony (by Parthia). (Mr R N A Springer). *"A very nice filly, she's a late foal and pretty immature at the moment. I would think she's been bought with a view of making a decent 3-y-o. A nice, correct filly for later in the year".*
Significant sire/damsire crosses:- Stagecraft.

627 - PEKAN KU (USA) * [99] b.br.c. Kingmambo – Star Of Albion (Ajdal).
February 25. Third foal. 120,000Y. Tattersalls October.
The dam, a modest 2-y-o 7f winner, is closely related to the dual US Grade 1 winning filly Sabin, the useful 10.5f and 12f winner Fire Worshipper and the fair 10f winner Nadma and a half-sister to the smart 10.5f Musidora Stakes winner Fatah Flare and the very useful 2-y-o 6f winner Soughaan. The second dam, Beaconaire (by Vaguely Noble), a stakes winner of 3 races at up to 10f in France, is a half-sister to the high-class filly Kittiwake (herself dam of the Prix Jean Prat winner Kitwood and the excellent American filly Miss Oceana) and to the stakes winner Oilfield. (HRH Sultan Ahmad Shah). *"Very much a baby at the moment, he's quite a nice colt. Not over-big, I would hope he'd be ready for mid to late summer".*

628 - PRAYERS FOR RAIN (IRE) ** [87] b.f. Darshaan – Whispered Melody (Primo Dominie).
March 18. First foal. IR£300,000Y. Goffs Orby.
The dam, a modest 7f and 1m winner (including on the all-weather), is a half-sister to 4 winners including the very useful listed 10f all-weather Winter Derby winner Supreme Sound. The second dam, Sing Softly (by Luthier), won the Group 3 12f Lancashire Oaks. (Mr N R A Springer). *"A nice filly, she's on the small side and very active. There's a lot of Primo Dominie about her – in fact if you didn't know otherwise you'd say she was by that stallion. She looks speedy and would appear to be capable of starting over six furlongs. Quite forward in her coat and disposition, she should be an early runner for the yard".*

629 - SALADIM (IRE) * [84] b.c. Lahib – Wathbat Mtoto (Mtoto).
January 27.
Half-brother to the 7f placed 2-y-o Wathbat Mujtahid (by Mujtahid). The dam, a quite useful dual 10f winner, is a half-sister to the quite useful 10.5f winner Wathbat Nashwan. The second dam, Alwathba

(by Lyphard), a useful 2-y-o 6f winner of the Blue Seal Stakes and listed-placed over 1m at 3 yrs, is a sister to the smart 7f performer Dreams To Reality. The third dam, D'Arqueangel (by Raise A Native), won over 6f in the USA and is closely related to the Kentucky Oaks winner Native Street (herself dam of the good US colts Regal And Royal and Royal And Regal). (Sheikh Ahmed Al-Maktoum). *"A well-grown, nicely-balanced horse, he's a good mover and a nice colt with quality. I'd be looking for him to be running by July time over seven furlongs".*

630 - SEQUIN (IRE) ** [84]
b.f. Green Desert – Sans Escale (Diesis). March 25. Fifth foal.

Sister to the modest 2-y-o 7f placed Escalade and half-sister to the unraced 2000 2-y-o Without Words (by Lion Cavern) and the fairly useful 1m winner West Escape (by Gone West). The dam, a French 11f winner, was listed-placed and is a half-sister to numerous winners including the listed 12f Prix de l'Avre winner Arabian King. The second dam, Escaline (by Arctic Tern), a high-class winner of four races including the Group 1 10.5f Prix de Diane, is a half-sister to the Group 3 Premio Carla Porta winner Esdale and to the dam of the German Group 2 winner Royal Abjar. (Mr Mohammed Bin Hendi). *"A small, sharp-looking filly, she should be on the racecourse in the first half of the season certainly".* Significant sire/damsire crosses:- Strike Hard (Gr 3).

631 - TIOMAN (IRE) * [80]
b.br.c. Dr Devious – Tochar Ban (Assert). April 2. Fourth foal. 190,000Y. Tattersalls October.

Half-brother to the French 2-y-o 1m winner and subsequent US Grade 2 San Clemente Handicap winner Uncharted Haven (by Turtle Island) and to the fair 2000 5f and 6f placed 2-y-o Amber Tide (by Pursuit Of Love). The dam, a quite useful 10f winner, is a half-sister to 6 winners including the listed Italian winner Isticanna. The second dam, Guest Night (by Sir Ivor), a very useful 7f and 9f winner, was third in the Group 3 Fred Darling Stakes and is a half-sister to 4 winners and to the placed dam of Galaxy Libra (Grade 1 Man O'War Stakes) and Garden Of Heaven (Group 2 Prix du Conseil de Paris). (HRH Sultan Ahmad Shah). *"A very nice, scopey type, he looks more of a 3-y-o really but he's quite active and we'd hope to run him later in the year over six furlongs. Probably an autumn 2-y-o".*

632 - UNNAMED ** [78]
b.c. Key Of Luck – Lingering Melody (Nordico). March 26. Third foal. IR£50,000Y. Goffs Orby.

Half-brother to the unraced 2000 2-y-o Indian Prince (by Indian Lodge) and to the quite useful 1999 2-y-o 7f winner Rainbow Melody (by Rainbows For Life). The dam was placed at up to 1m in Ireland and is a half-sister to the Group 2 Queen Anne Stakes and the Group 2 Sea World International Stakes winner Alflora and the Irish listed 14f winner Na-Ammah. The second dam, Adrana (by Bold Lad, Ire), won over 5f at 2 yrs on her only start and is a half-sister to the top-class middle-distance stayer Ardross, the Prix de Flore winner Gesedeh and the 12f Galtres Stakes winner Larrocha. (Mr & Mrs Raymond Anderson Green). *"A medium-sized colt, he's just about as forward in condition as any of our colts. He looks like a 2-y-o type, is quite a strong horse and we like him. The sire won over five furlongs and this looks like a speed horse too".*

W JARVIS

633 - ALRIDA (IRE) ** [68]
b.c. Ali-Royal – Ride Bold (J O Tobin). April 6. Tenth foal. 50,000Y. Tattersalls October.

Half-brother to the very useful Irish sprinter Petite Fantasy (by Mansooj), winner of the listed Belgrave Stakes, to the fair 6f winner Beldray Park (by Superpower) and a winner in Japan by Astronef. The dam is an unraced half-sister to the Group 3 10.5f Prix de Royaumont winner and French One Thousand Guineas third Vidor (herself dam of the US Grade 3 winner Jo Knows). The second dam, Prestissimo (by Bold Reasoning), a stakes-placed winner of 3 races in the USA, is a half-sister to the Group 1 Premio Presidente della Repubblica winner Jalmood. (Mr Nigel Rich & Partners). *"He shows me an awful lot of speed but has had a touch of sore shins. Previously I thought he'd be my first 2-y-o runner and he's definitely got an engine. One for around May or June time I should think".*

634 - BALAKIREF ** [71]
b.c. Royal Applause – Pluck (Never So Bold). February 7. Third living foal. 25,000Y. Tattersalls October.

Half-brother to a winner of 6 races at 2 to 4 yrs in Sweden by Be My Chief. The dam, a fair 5.7f and 6f winner at 2 and 3 yrs, is a half-sister to 3 winners. The second dam, the very useful Tahilla (by Moorestyle), won 7 races including the listed 1m Atalanta Stakes and the listed 1m Sceptre Stakes and is a half-sister to the Group 1 Keeneland Nunthorpe Stakes winner Piccolo. (David Heath & Tim Hedin). *"Yes, I like this colt. He's quite a good-looking horse, will make a 2-y-o over six furlongs and is strong and well-made".*

---

635 - FUNKSOULBOROUGH (IRE) ** [75] b.c. Woodborough – White Paper (Marignan). March 3. First foal. 25,000Y. Tattersalls October.

The dam is an unraced half-sister to 4 winners including the Group 3 Prix d'Arenberg second Park Rapids. The second dam, Page Blanche (by Caro), a useful 3-y-o 1m winner, is a half-sister to the Group 1 1m William Hill Futurity Stakes winner Paradis Terrestre, to Premier Ministre (winner of four Grade 3 events in the USA) and to the dam of the Prix de la Foret winner Poplar Bluff. *"A very strong horse, he'll be a 2-y-o over six furlongs in June and I like him".*

---

636 - GEORGIANNA (IRE) ** [62] b.f. Petardia – Age Of Elegance (Troy). January 30. Tenth foal. 85,000Y. Tattersalls October.

Half-sister to the very useful 7f to 10f winner Sheer Precocity (by Precocious), to the quite useful 10f to 14f winner Netta Rufina (by Night Shift) and 2 minor winners in Italy and France by Auction Ring and Priolo. The dam, a French middle-distance winner of 2 races, is closely related to the listed winner Nemesia and a half-sister to numerous winners including the Tattersalls Rogers Gold Cup, Horris Hill Stakes and Westbury Stakes winner Elegant Air. The second dam, Elegant Tern (by Sea Bird II), won 3 times at around a mile inclusing the Group 3 Princess Elizabeth Stakes and was third in the Ribblesdale Stakes. (Sales Race 2001 Syndicate). *"I quite like her, she's fairly sharp and has a sound temperament. I expect her to be quite early and she would have been earlier still but for the particularly poor weather this year".*

---

637 - LORI'S DANCER * [85] ch.f. Zilzal – Brush Away (Ahonoora). May 12. Twelfth foal. 15,000Y. Tattersalls October.

Half-sister to Ribbon Of Light (by Spectrum), unplaced over 7f in one start at 2 yrs in 2000, to the useful 1997 2-y-o 6f winner Bintang (by Soviet Star), the fairly useful 7.5f winner Glanwydden (by Grand Lodge), the fairly useful Irish 7f listed winner Takwim (by Taufan), the German listed winner Capwell (by Celestial Storm), the fair 6f and 1m winner Mr Vincent (by Nishapour), the modest 2-y-o dual 5f winner Go Tally-Ho (by Gorytus) and a winner in Italy by Thatching. The dam is an unraced half-sister to 10 winners including the US stakes winner Fawlty Towers and the Musidora Stakes third Princess Genista. The second dam, Queen Of The Brush (by Averof), won at 3 yrs and is a half-sister to the Italian Derby winner Old Country. (Mr Stephen Purner). *"A late foal but a very good moving filly and from what we've seen so far we like her. A September 2-y-o for distances up to a mile".*

---

638 - MILLENNIUM KING * [75] b.c. Piccolo – Zabelina (Diesis). February 22. Fourth foal. 36,000Y. Tattersalls October.

Half-brother to the modest 9.2f to 11f winner Zorba (by Shareef Dancer) and to a winner in France by Soviet Star. The dam is an unplaced half-sister to 5 winners including the Dance Teacher (Grade 1 Ladies Handicap), Gold Mover (Grade 2 Schuylerville Stakes) and the dual 1m listed winner Lunar Mover. The second dam, Intentional Move (by Tentam), won twice in the USA and is a half-sister to 4 winners. (Mr N S Yong & Partners). *"Yes, he's a straightforward, well-made, decent type and I like him".*

---

639 - OZ [93] ch.c. Kris – Arletty (Rainbow Quest). February 9. First foal. 22,000Y. Tattersalls October.

The dam, a modest middle-distance placed maiden, is a sister to 4 winners including the high-class St James's Palace Stakes and Beefeater Gin Celebration Mile winner Shavian (by Kris), the 2-y-o 8.2f winner Censor and the 3-y-o 10f winner Tempering (both fairly useful) and a half-sister to 5 winners including the high-class Ascot Gold Cup winner Paean (by Bustino). The second dam, Mixed Applause (by Nijinsky), a useful winner of the 2-y-o 6f Sweet Solera Stakes, is a half-sister to the dam of the champion 2-y-o Be My Chief. (Mr J H Slade & Partners). *"A backward sort that won't be coming into his own until the autumn. A straightforward colt, he's a three-parts brother to Shavian and I like the horse".*

---

640 - STRATHCLYDE (IRE) * [54] b.c. Petong – It's Academic (Royal Academy). February 23. Third foal. IR£26,000Y. Goffs Challenge.

Half-brother to Greycoat (by Lion Cavern), unplaced in 2 starts at 2 yrs in 2000. The dam, a fair 3-y-o 6f and 7f winner, is a half-sister to 8 winners including a listed winner in Italy. The second dam, It's

Terrific (by Vaguely Noble), won 3 races. (Sales Race 2001 Syndicate). *"He looks a real nice horse but he's had a setback. He's just coming back now and will still make it this year. I like him".*

641 - XERAPHIN * *** [71]   b.f. Zafonic – Rose Noble (Vaguely Noble).
April 10. Fifth foal.

Half-sister to the unraced 2000 2-y-o Guinea (by Sillery) and to the useful 1m (at 2 yrs) and 10f winner Dower House (by Groom Dancer). The dam, a modest 3-y-o 11.5f winner, is a half-sister to the champion two-year-old and high-class sire Grand Lodge, winner of the St James's Palace Stakes and the Dewhurst Stakes and to the listed winner Papabile. The second dam, La Papagena (by Habitat), is an unraced half-sister to the listed Scottish Derby winner Eagling and to the Gallinule Stakes second and South African listed winner Lost Chord. (Lady Howard de Walden). *"This is a nice filly for the mid-season onwards. A powerful looking filly, she might well do something this year but is bred to be more of a 3-y-o".*

R F JOHNSON-HOUGHTON

642 - BANNING * [81]   b.c. Anabaa – Sea Wedding (Groom Dancer).
April 10. Third foal. 26,000Y. Tattersalls October.

Half-brother to the quite useful 9.4f all-weather winner Shakakhan (by Night Shift). The dam, a fair 10f placed maiden, is a half-sister to the listed Cheshire Oaks winner and St Leger second High And Low. The second dam, Cruising Height (by Shirley Heights), a very useful middle-distance winner and second in the Group 3 Lancashire Oaks, is a half-sister to the Group 3 Park Hill Stakes winner Trampship. (Mr Anthony Pye-Jeary & Mr Mel Smith). *"A bit more backward than I thought when I bought him. He's still a nice horse and he'll be alright although I'm not quite sure when he'll come to hand. Definitely one to make a 2-y-o and is a nice-sized colt".*

643 - DANCING WATER ** * [98]   ch.c. Halling – Gleaming Water (Kalaglow).
March 10. Seventh foal.

Half-brother to the very useful 1m to 10.4f winner Prince Of Denial (by Soviet Star), to the useful 2-y-o 6f winner and listed 10f Pretty Polly Stakes second Faraway Waters (by Pharly) and the fair 7f (at 2 yrs) and 11.6f winner Paradise Waters (by Celestial Storm). The dam, a quite useful 2-y-o 6f winner, is a sister to the Group 3 Solario Stakes winner Shining Water - herself dam of the Group 1 Grand Criterium winner Tenby - and a half-sister to 7 winners. The second dam, Idle Waters (by Mill Reef), won the Group 2 Park Hill Stakes. (Mr R Crutchley). *"He's a nice horse but he'll take a bit of time as he's from quite a staying family. I wouldn't think we see him racing until July or August and he's quite a big, tall horse that would probably need seven furlongs".*

644 - EXPLORING (IRE) *** [85]   br.c. Charnwood Forest – Caribbean Quest (Rainbow Quest).
April 20. Second foal. IR£18,000Y. Goffs Orby.

Half-brother to the French-trained 3-y-o Hispaniola (by Barathea). The dam, a quite useful 2-y-o 1m winner, is out of Jammayil (by Lomond), herself a quite useful 2-y-o 7f winner and a half-sister to 9 winners including the Nassau Stakes winner Optimistic Lass (dam of the Coronation Stakes winner Golden Opinion). (Mr Anthony Pye-Jeary & Mr Mel Smith). *"He's done some bits of work, goes nicely and will make a 2-y-o over five or six furlongs. A nice, strong horse, he's a bit backward in his coat yet but he'll be alright".*

645 - FIG LEAF (FR) * [62]   b.f. Distant Relative – Shady Leaf (Glint Of Gold).
May 1.

Half-sister to the unplaced 2000 2-y-o Cloudy (by Ashkalani) and to Academy House (by Sadler's Wells), a winner over 2m at the Curragh at 3 yrs. The dam, a poor middle-distance maiden, is a half-sister to the very useful Group 3 12f Princess Royal Stakes winner Dancing Bloom and to the One Thousand Guineas third River Dancer (herself dam of the Champion Stakes winner Spectrum). The second dam, Dancing Shadow (by Dancer's Image), a very useful winner over 1m and 10f including the Sean Graham Fillies Stakes, is a half-sister to the top-class Oaks winner Sun Princess and the high-class middle-distance colt Saddlers' Hall. (Lady Rothschild). *"I like her and she's a nice filly that will be racing sometime in May".*

646 - HOAX (IRE) ** [70]　　　　　　b.c. Robellino – Hocus (High Top).
April 3. Eighth foal. IR£22,000Y. Goffs Orby.

Half-brother to the Irish trained 3-y-o American Gothic, to the fair all-weather 8.5f and 9.4f winner High Noon, the fair 10f winner Trick (all by Shirley Heights), the modest 2-y-o 5f all-weather winner Hali (by Rousillon), the minor 1999 Irish 2-y-o winner Jamieson (by Be My Chief) and a winner in Brazil by Doyoun. The dam, a quite useful 3-y-o 7f winner, is a half-sister to 10 winners including the Group 1 5f Flying Childers and Group 1 6f Middle Park Stakes winner Hittite Glory. The second dam, Hazy Idea (by Hethersett), was a very smart winner of 5 races from 6f to 10f. *"He's going the right way and is a nice little horse that should already have run before your book is published. A sharp sort, I think he'll win races and he'll get six furlongs alright later on".*

647 - IMBIBING (IRE) ** [84]　　　　　ch.c. Halling – Polar Fizz (Polar Falcon).
April 28. Third foal. IR£40,000Y. Goffs Orby.

Half-brother to the unraced 2000 2-y-o Bucks Fizz (by Kris) and to the quite useful 1999 2-y-o 5f winner Saffizz (by Safawan). The dam is an unraced half-sister to 4 winners including the very smart very smart Group 1 1m Premio Vittorio di Capua and Group 2 8.5f Grosser Preis von Dusseldorf winner Port Lucaya (by Sharpo). The second dam, Sister Sophie (by Effervescing), a 10f winner in the USA, is a half-sister to the top-class filly Diminuendo, winner of the Oaks, the Irish Oaks and the Yorkshire Oaks (herself dam of the Group 3 1m May Hill Stakes winner Calando) and to the Pretty Polly Stakes winner and Oaks second Pricket. (Mr Anthony Pye-Jeary & Mr Mel Smith). *"A nice type of colt that will make a mid-season type of 2-y-o".*

648 - LUCKY ROMANCE * [74]　　　　b.f. Key of Luck – In Love Again (Prince Rupert).
May 2. Third foal. 23,000Y. Doncaster St Leger.

Closely related to the fair 2000 triple 7f 2-y-o winner Forever My Lord (by Be My Chief). The dam was a fairly useful winner of 4 races at around 5f at 2 yrs and is a half-sister to the high-class sprinter Hallgate (winner of the Cornwallis Stakes, the Diadem Stakes and the Palace House Stakes) and to the dam of the smart sprinter Mistertopogigo. The second dam, Beloved Mistress (by Rarity), was a quite useful 2-y-o 5f winner and a half-sister to 3 winners including the Group-placed sprinter Petrovich. (Mr W H Ponsonby). *"Only just about to enter the yard, I haven't seen her for a while but she was a nice filly when I last saw her. A bit leggy, she looks as though she'll do the business and is a half sister to Forever My Lord who did well for me last year".*

649 - UNNAMED ** [83]　　　　　　b.c. Lear Fan – River City Moon (Riverman).
March 27. First foal. IR£35,000Y. Goffs Orby.

The dam, a minor 2-y-o winner in the USA, is a half-sister to 3 winners including the listed Doncaster Mile winner Airport. The second dam, Vague Prospect (by Vaguely Noble), was placed once in the USA and is a half-sister to the Group 1 6f Vernons Sprint Cup winner Dowsing and the Grade 1 Beverly D Stakes winner Fire The Groom (herself dam of the Nunthorpe Stakes and July Cup winner Stravinsky). (Mr C W Sumner). *"A nice, sharp little colt that wouldn't be far off a run once the owner names him. He probably wouldn't mind any ground conditions and is a five or six furlong type 2-y-o".*

M JOHNSTON

650 - ATLANTIC QUEST (87)　　　　b.c. Woodman – Pleasant Pat (Pleasant Colony).
April 29. Fourth foal. $50,000Y. Keeneland September.

Half-brother to the US winner of 4 races and Grade 2 San Vicente Stakes third Pleasant Drive (by Salem Drive) and to the minor US winner of 5 races Civil Sultan (by Southern Sultan). The dam is an unraced sister to a stakes-placed winner and a half-sister to 11 winners including the Grade 3 Athenia Handicap winner Middle Stage and the California Oaks winner Northern Meteor. The second dam, Patelin (by Cornish Prince), won three good stakes events in the USA.

651 - BEACON WOOD (IRE) [90]　　　b.c. Woodman – Catch The Blues (Bluebird).
March 20. First foal. IR£60,000Y. Goffs Orby.

The dam, a smart 5f to 7f winner of 3 races including the Group 3 5f Ballyogan Stakes, was third in the Group 1 Haydock Park Sprint Cup. She is a half-sister to 5 winners including the Ballyogan Stakes third Sharp Catch. The second dam, Dear Lorraine (by Nonoalco), won over 10f in France and is a half-sister to 4 winners.

652 - BEER AND DONUTS (USA)   [75]   b.c. Carson City – Danzig's Bride (Danzig).

March 16. Seventh foal. $60,000Y. Keeneland September.

Closely related to the US stakes-placed winner of 7 races Ideal State (by Crafty Prospector) and half-brother to the minor US stakes winner Babai Danzig (by Cure The Blues). The dam, a stakes-placed winner of 6 races in the USA, is a half-sister to the US Grade 3 winner Arctic Honeymoon, to the minor US stakes winner Dr David Nathan and the US winner and Grade 2 placed Audacious Fool. The second dam, Misty Bride (by Hethersett), won in the USA and is a half-sister to the Cesarewitch winner Grey Of Falloden.

653 - BORU BORU (IRE   [91]   b.c. Bluebird – Tudor Loom (Sallust).

March 25. Sixth foal. IR£30,000Y. Goffs Orby.

Brother to the 2-y-o listed 6f winner, Irish Two Thousand Guineas second and US Grade 2 9f Del Mar Derby winner Rainbow Blues and half-brother to the fairly useful 2-y-o triple 6f winner Kashra (by Dancing Dissident) and the fairly useful dual 6f winner Midhish Two (by Midhish). The dam, an Irish placed maiden, is a half-sister to 2 minor winners. The second dam, Weavers Wand (by Weavers Hall), was unplaced twice and is a half-sister to the 2-y-o Group 3 New Stakes winner Cade's County. Significant sire/damsire crosses:- Rainbow Blues (Gr 2).

654 - BRANSTON TIGER   [96]   b.c. Mark Of Esteem – Tuxford Hideaway (Cawston's Clown).

May 14. Eleventh foal.

Half-brother to the unraced 2000 2-y-o Desert Deer (by Cadeaux Genereux), to the very useful and tough mare Branston Abby (by Risk Me), a winner of 24 races at up to 7f including numerous listed events, the fairly useful 2-y-o dual 5f winner Branston Jewel (by Prince Sabo), the fairly useful 2-y-o 6f and 7f winner Big Blow (by Last Tycoon), the fair 6f (all-weather) and 7f winner Branston Fizz (by Efisio) and minor winners by Glow, Risk Me and Shalford. The dam, a useful sprinter, won two races at 2 yrs and is a half-sister to 4 winners out of the minor 3-y-o winner Late Idea (by Tumble Wind). (Jaber Abdullah).

655 - BRIGHT AND EARLY (FR)   [78]   ch.f. Cadeaux Genereux – Light Fresh Air (Rahy).

April 25.

Half-sister to the 2000 2-y-o Swirl (by Halling) and to the fairly useful 12.4f winner Almost Free (by Darshaan). The dam won a 1m listed event in France at 2 yrs. The second dam. Worood (by Vaguely Noble), won three races in France at 3 and 4 yrs from 1m to 12f including the listed Prix Joubert and is a half-sister to the Group 3 winners Lady Roberta and Tursanah. (Maktoum Al-Maktoum).

656 - CELTIC SILHOUETTE (FR)   [71]   b.c. Celtic Swing – Smart 'n Noble (Smarten).

March 12. Second foal.

Sister to the very promising 2000 2-y-o 7f Chesham Stakes winner Celtic Silence. The dam won 12 races in the USA including the Grade 2 7f Barbara Fritchie Handicap and is a half-sister to 7 winners. The second dam, Noble Station (by Executioner), won 3 races in the USA and is a half-sister to the Grade 3 winner Dihela (herself the grandam of the US Grade 1 winner Share The Fantasy).

657 - DEVILSBEINBAD (USA)   [87]   b.f. Devil's Bag – En Cachette (Danehill).

May 8. Fourth foal. $70,000Y. Keeneland September.

The dam, a fair 2-y-o 6f winner, is a half-sister to the useful 10f winner and St Leger fourth In Camera, the very useful 11.5f winner and Yorkshire Oaks second Bineyah and the useful Royal Lodge Stakes winner Desert Secret (all by Sadler's Wells). The second dam, Clandestina (by Secretariat), an Irish 3-y-o 10f winner, is a half-sister to the great Seattle Slew, to the Two Thousand Guineas winner Lomond and to the Gallinule Stakes winner Seattle Dancer.

658 - DUNE SAFARI (IRE)   [84]   br.f. Key Of Luck – Zafaaf (Kris).

January 28. Fourth foal.

Half-sister to the unraced 2000 2-y-o Exciting Hero (by Catrail), to the 1999 2-y-o 5f and 7f winner Queen's Bench (by Wolfhound) and the 1999 3-y-o 5f and 6f winner Ashover Amber (by Green Desert) – both fairly useful. The dam, a useful 7f and 1m winner, is a half-sister to the useful 6f winner Siwaayib (dam of the smart middle-distance stayer Rainbow Ways). The second dam, Ma Petite Cherie (by Caro), won over 1m and 10f in France and is a half-sister to 8 winners. (Abdullah Ali).

659 - ENCHANTED OCEAN (USA) [82]

b.f. Royal Academy – Ocean Jewel (Alleged).
April 21. Tenth foal. IR£20,000Y. Goffs Orby

Half-sister to the 3-y-o Tjinouska (by Cozzene), to the German listed winner and Group 1 German Derby fourth Ocean Sea (by Bering), the US winner and Grade 3 third Dixie Splash (by Dixieland Band) and minor winners in Japan (by Hansel) and the USA (by Chimes Band). The dam is an unraced half-sister to 6 minor winners. The second dam, Lady Offshore (by Sir Ivor), won a stakes event over 9f in the USA and is a half-sister to 6 winners including the 7f Matron Stakes winner Bonnie And Gay (herself dam of the French Group 3 winner Look Fast).

660 - FALCON HILL [82]

b.c. Polar Falcon – Branston Jewel (Prince Sabo).
April 16. Second foal. 20,000Y. Tattersalls Autumn.

Half-brother to the modest 2000 5f placed Branston Gem (by So Factual). The dam, a fairly useful 2-y-o dual 5f winner, was second in the Group 3 5.5f Prix d'Arenberg and is a half-sister to the very useful and tough mare Branston Abby, a winner of 24 races at up to 7f including numerous listed events and the fairly useful 2-y-o 6f and 7f winner Big Blow. The second dam, Tuxford Hideaway (by Cawston's Clown), a useful sprint winner of two races at 2 yrs, is a half-sister to 4 winners.

661 - FRAGRANT STORM (USA) [85]

b.f. Storm Bird – Subtle Fragrance (Crafty Prospector).
February 10. First foal. $30,000Y. Keeneland September.

The dam, a minor 2-y-o winner in the USA, is a half-sister to 5 winners including the Grade 2 placed Perdition's Son. The second dam, My Red Wing (by Wing Out), won 7 minor races in the USA and is a half-sister to the US dual Grade 2 winner Bet Big.

662 - GALA GOLD [82]

b.f. Green Desert – Melting Gold (Cadeaux Genereux).
March 19. Fourth foal.

Half-brother to the French trained 2000 2-y-o Golden Days (by Mark Of Esteem). The dam, a very useful French 2-y-o 7f winner, was second in the Group 3 1m Prix de Sandringham at 3 yrs. The second dam, a fair 3-y-o 9f winner at Ayr, is a half-sister to the Two Thousand Guineas and Queen Elizabeth II Stakes winner Shadeed. The second dam, Continual (by Damascus), won twice at up to 7f in the USA and is a sister to the dam of the outstanding Kentucky Derby and Belmont Stakes winner Swale. (Maktoum Al-Maktoum).

663 - HAPPY REFERENCE (USA) [90]

ch.c. Diesis – Sabeline (Caerleon).
January 29. First foal. $150,000. Keeneland September.

The dam is an unraced half-sister to the high-class sprinter Tamarisk, winner of the Group 1 6f Stanley Leisure Sprint Cup at Haydock Park and second in the Dewhurst Stakes and the July Cup. The second dam, Sine Labe (by Vaguely Noble), is an unplaced half-sister to the Group 1 10f Prix Saint-Alary winner Treble out of a half-sister to Triptych. (Jaber Abdullah).

664 - HEARTHSTEAD PRIDE [90]

ch.c. Dr Devious – Western Heights (Shirley Heights).
April 27. Sixth foal. 27,000Y. Tattersalls October.

Half-brother to the very smart Group 3 7f Greenham Stakes winner and Two Thousand Guineas third Barathea Guest (by Barathea), to the fairly useful 1998 2-y-o 1m winner Dollar Law (by Selkirk), the quite useful 1m (at 2) to 10.4f winner Pinchincha (by Priolo) and the fair dual 7f winner Lionel Edwards (by Polish Patriot). The dam is an unraced half-sister to the listed Galtres Stakes winner Startino. The second dam, Western Star (by Alcide), won the 10f Lupe Stakes and is a half-sister to the Queen Anne Stakes winner Mr Fluorocarbon and the Cornwallis Stakes winner Western Jewel.

665 - IMPAVIDO (IRE) [96]

b.c. Sadler's Wells – Tis Juliet (Alydar).
May 25. Sixth foal. IR£35,000Y. Goffs Orby.

Half-brother to 2 minor winners in Japan (by Wild Again) and the USA (by Dayjur). The dam won the Grade 1 8.5f Shuvee Handicap and is a sister to Stella Madrid, a winner of four Grade 1 events from 6f to 1m in the USA. The second dam, My Juliet (by Gallant Romeo), won 24 races including six Graded stakes, notably the Grade 2 Vosburgh Handicap, the Grade 2 Test Stakes and the Grade 2 Michigan Mile and One Eighth Handicap. She is a half-sister to the September Stakes winner Lyphard's Special and to the dam of the Irish Oaks winner Winona.
Significant sire/damsire crosses:- Allurement (Gr 3).

666 - KATINA (USA)   [94]   b.f. Danzig – Alisidora (Nashwan).
January 8. First foal. IR£290,000Y. Goffs Orby.
The dam, a 12f winner and 10f listed-placed in Ireland, is a sister to the Japanese listed-placed winner Shinko Nobby and a half-sister to 4 winners. The second dam, Christabelle (by Northern Dancer), was placed at 2 yrs in Ireland and is a half-sister to the outstanding broodmare Slightly Dangerous (dam of Commander In Chief, Warning, Dushyantor, Deploy and Yashmak) and to the dams of Rainbow Quest and Scenic.

667 - LEGAL APPROACH   [98]   b.c. Zafonic – Legaya (Shirley Heights).
April 9. First foal.
The dam, a fairly useful Irish 12f winner, is a half-sister to the useful 12f winner Lucky Lady. The second dam, Jet Ski Lady (by Vaguely Noble), an Irish 6f, 7f (at 2 yrs) and listed 10f winner, won the Group 1 12f Epsom Oaks. The third dam, Bemissed (by Nijinsky), a good American filly, won the Grade 1 Selima Stakes at 2 yrs, was third in the Kentucky Oaks and is a half-sister to the very useful Group 2 12f Princess of Wales's Stakes winner Desert Team. (Maktoum Al-Maktoum).

668 - LEO'S LUCKYMAN (USA)   [82]   b.c. Woodman – Leo's Lucky Lady (Seattle Slew).
February 15. Fifth foal. $50,000Y. Keeneland September.
Half-brother to Asarari (by Seattle Slew), unplaced in one start at 2 yrs in 2000 and to a minor winner in the USA by Deputy Minister. The dam won twice at up to 6f, was stakes-placed over 9f in the USA and is a half-sister to to the outstanding broodmare Korveya (dam of the classic winners Bosra Sham, Hector Protector and Shanghai), to the Group 2 Premio Umbria winner Proskona, the Group 3 Prix de Seine-et-Oise winner Keos and the minor US stakes winner Carnet Solaire. The second dam, Konafa (by Damascus) won over 7f at 2 yrs, was second in the One Thousand Guineas and is a half-sister to the Yorkshire Oaks winner Awaasif (herself dam of the Oaks winner Snow Bride and thus grandam of Lammtarra).
Significant sire/damsire crosses:- Hishi Akebono (Gr 1), Patience Game (Gr 3), Rey Seattle (Gr 3).

669 - LOVE REGARDLESS (USA)   [99]   b.c. Storm Bird – Circus Toons (Wild Again).
February 10. First foal. IR£60,000Y. Goffs Orby.
The dam, a minor stakes winner of 8 races in the USA, is a half-sister to 3 stakes winners. The second dam, Circus Poster (by Crimson Satan), won 3 minor races in the USA.

670 - MONTESSORI MIO (FR)   [75]   b.c. Robellino – Child's Play (Sharpen Up).
February 22. Fourth foal. 75,000Y. Tattersalls October.
Half-brother to the very useful 7f to 9f winner (including the Swiss Two Thousand Guineas) Sharp Play (by Robellino) and to the quite useful 1999 2-y-o 6f winner Pax (by Brief Truce). The dam, a winner over 10.5f in France, is a half-sister to 3 winners. The second dam, Picnicing (by Good Times), a useful sprint winner of 3 races, is a half-sister to numerous winners including Jupiter Island (Japan Cup), Precocious (Gimcrack Stakes) and Pushy (Queen Mary Stakes and dam of the Group 3 winners Myself and Bluebook).
Significant sire/damsire crosses:- Mister Bailey's.

671 - PERFECT PICTURE   [?]   b.c. Octagonal – Greenvera (Riverman).
April 9. Fifth foal. 45,000Y. Tattersalls October.
Half-brother to the 3-y-o Greenfire (by Ashkalani) and to the very smart Group 2 2m Goodwood Cup and Irish listed 14f winner Royal Rebel (by Robellino). The dam was placed once in France and is a half-sister to the French listed 6.5f winner and Group 2 5f Prix du Gros-Chene third Way West (by Gone West). The second dam, Greenway (by Targowice), won the Group 3 5f Prix d'Arenberg and the Group 3 Prix du Petit-Couvert and is a half-sister to the Group 3 Prix Messidor winner Gay Minstrel and the dam of the Group 1 Prix de la Salamandre winners Oczy Czarnie and Glaieul.

672 - RAISED THE BAR (USA)   [90]   ch.f. Royal Academy – Barari (Blushing Groom).
February 24. Eighth living foal.
Half-sister to the very useful 9.2f to 12f winner Kind Regards (by Unfuwain), the very useful Group 3 1m Oettingen-Rennen and listed Doncaster Mile winner White Heart, the useful 2-y-o 7f and 1m winner Fair Flight, the useful 6f to 7.5f winner Green Barries (all by Green Desert), the fairly useful 12f winner

Generous Gift (by Generous) and the Belgian winner Zahabi (by Jareer). The dam is an unraced half-sister to the Canadian Grade 1 winner Rainbows For Life and the Group 2 Prix de l'Opera winner Colour Chart. The second dam, Rainbow Connection (by Halo), a Champion 2-y-o and 3-y-o filly in Canada, is a half-sister to 3 stakes winners including the Canadian Grade 1 winners Archdeacon and Hangin' on a Star. (Maktoum Al-Maktoum).

673 - RHEINPARK [87]
ch.c. Cadeaux Genereux – Marina Park (Local Suitor).
March 17. Second foal. 24,000Y. Tattersalls October.

Half-brother to the unraced 2000 2-y-o Super Canyon (by Gulch). The dam, a smart winner of 8 races here and in the USA including the Group 3 6f Princess Margaret Stakes and the Grade 3 6.5f Las Cienegas Breeders Cup Handicap, is a half-sister to 8 winners. The second dam, Mary Martin (by Be My Guest), is an unraced half-sister to the Coventry Stakes winner Red Sunset and to the Molecomb, Queen Mary and Cornwallis Stakes winner Greenland Park - herself dam of the high class French filly Fitnah.

674 - ROSHEEN DONN (IRE) [76]
b.f. Revoque – Mashoura (Shareef Dancer).
March 21. First living foal. IR£24,000Y. Goffs Challenge.

The dam, a 3-y-o winner and listed-placed in France, is a half-sister to 5 winners including the dam of the listed 10f Pretty Polly Stakes winner Musetta. The second dam, Massorah (by Habitat), a very useful winner of the Group 3 5f Premio Omenoni and second in the Group 3 5f Prix du Gros-Chene, is a half-sister to 4 minor winners abroad.

675 - SAME LOUBNA (IRE) [78]
b.f. Revoque – Kaweah Maid (General Assembly).
January 14. Eleventh foal. 41,000Y. Doncaster St Leger.

Half-sister to the modest 2000 2-y-o 7f winner Miss Progressive (by Common Grounds), to the Italian listed winner Classem Ducere, the Italian 1m (at 2 yrs) to 12f winner Skywasser (both by Suave Dancer), a minor winner in Italy by Polish Precedent and the modest 7f winner Edgeaway (by Ajdal). The dam is an unplaced half-sister to 7 winners including the champion 2-y-o and Group 1 Dewhurst Stakes winner Monteverdi. The second dam, Janina II (by Match III), won at 3 yrs in France and is a half-sister to the Coronation Cup winner Nagami. (Jaber Abdullah).

676 - SCOTTISH FLOWER (USA) [88]
ch.f. Woodman – Sultry Secret (Nijinsky).
May 5. Eighth foal. $37,000Y. Keeneland September.

Closely related to a minor 2-y-o winner in the USA by Forty Niner and half-sister to 2 minor winners. The dam won 3 races in North America at 3 yrs and is a half-sister to Sultry Song (three Grade 1 wins in the USA including the Hollywood Gold Cup Handicap) and Solar Splendor (two Grade 1 wins including the Turf Classic). The second dam, Sultry Sun (by Buckfinder), won 9 races including the Grade 2 Molly Pitcher Handicap.
Significant sire/damsire crosses:- Bahhare, Ciro, Way Of Light.

677 - SCOTTISH RIVER [83]
b.c. Thunder Gulch – Overbrook (Storm Cat).
March 30. Third foal. $42,000Y. Keeneland September.

Half-brother to a minor 2-y-o winner in the USA by Gulch. The dam, a fairly useful 5.7f (at 2 yrs) and 6f winner, was second in the Group 3 5f Cornwallis Stakes and is a half-sister to the smart Group 3 7f Prix du Palais-Royal and European Free Handicap winner Hidden Meadow, the smart 11f listed winner Scorned and the useful 6f (at 2 yrs) and listed 1m winner Kingsclere. The second dam, Spurned (by Robellino), a fairly useful 2-y-o 7f winner, later stayed 10f.

678 - SCOTT'S VIEW [94]
b.c. Selkirk – Milly Of The Vally (Caerleon).
February 5. First foal. 21,000Y. Tattersalls October.

The dam, a fairly useful 12f winner, is a half-sister to 5 winners including the very useful 10f winner Milly Ha Ha, the useful 7f (at 2 yrs) and 10.3f winner Yeltsin and the useful 10.2f winner Hatta's Mill. The second dam, Mill On The Floss (by Mill Reef), a winner over 7f at 2 yrs and the Group 3 12f Lingfield Oaks Trial at 3 yrs, was second in the Ribblesdale Stakes, the Princess Royal Stakes and the Lancashire Oaks, is closely related to the useful Queen Alexandra Stakes winner Overdrive (herself dam of the Queens Vase winner Endorsement) and a half-sister to the very useful Sun Chariot Stakes second Kashmir Lass and the Lancashire Oaks second Shadywood (dam of the Park Hill Stakes winner Madame Dubois).

679 - SOVEREIGN MAGIC [87]   b.f. Sadler's Wells – Jural (Kris).
March 21. Second foal.
Closely related to the quite useful 2000 6f and 6.8f 2-y-o winner Silk Law (by Barathea). The dam, a useful winner of the Group 3 1m Curragh Futurity Stakes and the 7f Sweet Solera Stakes, was second in the Group 1 Fillies Mile and is a half-sister to the useful 6f to 9.5f winner Committal. The second dam, Just Cause (by Law Society), is an unraced daughter of a half-sister to the One Thousand Guineas winner Nocturnal Spree. (Maktoum Al-Maktoum).
Significant sire/damsire crosses:- Moonshell, Samsaam.

680 - SYSTEMATIC [86]   b.c. Rainbow Quest – Sensation (Soviet Star).
January 31. First foal.
The dam, a smart winner of the Group 2 1m Falmouth Stakes and the Group 3 1m Prix de Sandringham, is a half-sister to 5 winners including the US Grade 2 8.5f placed Outlasting (herself dam of the US Grade 3 winner Fortitude). The second dam, Outstandingly (by Exclusive Native), was the champion American 2-y-o filly of 1984 and won the Grade 1 Breeders Cup Juvenile Fillies Stakes and the Grade 1 8.5f Hollywood Starlet Stakes. She is closely related to the Grade 3 9f Miss Grillo Stakes winner Loveliest and to the dam of the Group/Grade 3 winners Bernstein, Caress and Country Cat. (Maktoum Al-Maktoum).

681 - THUNDER KING (USA) [78]   b.br.c. Thunder Gulch – Savannah's Honor (Storm Bird).
March 21. Seventh foal. $12,000Y. Keeneland September.
Half-brother to the US winner and Grade 2 Breeders' Futurity third Blushing Jim and to the minor US winner of 7 races Fraley (both by Blushing John). The dam won the Group 3 7f Prix du Calvados, was Grade 2 placed in the USA and is a half-sister to the French listed winner and Group 3 Prix Thomas Bryon second Anna's Honor. The second dam, Honor To Her (by Sir Ivor), is an unraced sister to the winner and Grade 1 Caulfield Cup second Ivory Way.

682 - VERSAILLES [82]   b.c. Bluegrass Prince – Fabulous Pet (Somethingfabulous).
April 29. Seventh foal. 31,000Y. Doncaster St Leger.
Half-brother to the smart Group 2 13.3f Geoffrey Freer Stakes winner Murghem, to the fair 2-y-o 1m and hurdles winner Baisse d'Argent (both by Common Grounds), the Irish 7f and subsequent Hong Kong 5f to 9f winner Something Super (by Superpower), the moderate 1994 2-y-o 8.5f all-weather winner Something Speedy (by Sayf El Arab) and a winner over hurdles and jumps by Silver Kite. The dam, a winner over 12f in Ireland at 3 yrs, is a half-sister to 8 winners including the Group 2 Haydock Sprint Cup winner Orojoya and the US stakes winner Bywayofchicago. The second dam, Jemarjo Pet (by Peter Peter), won three races at up to 9f in the USA.

683 - ZABAT [96]   ch.c. Zamindar – Pluvial (Habat).
May 8. Seventeenth foal. 30,000Y. Tattersalls October.
Half-brother to 8 winners including the fair 2000 2-y-o 5f to 1m winner Flummox (by Rudimentary), the very smart Group 3 6f Benazet-Rennen and Group 3 6f Prix de Ris-Orangis winner Monaassib (by Cadeaux Genereux), the smart listed-placed miler Rain Burst (by Tolomeo), the fairly useful 1999 2-y-o dual 6f winner Awake (by Primo Dominie) and the useful winner of 19 races here and in Italy, Plymouth Hoe (by Busted). The dam, a fairly useful sprint winner of 2 races, is a half-sister to 11 winners including the Cornwallis Stakes winner Splashing (dam of the Group winners Bassenthwaite and Glancing) and the dams of the Group winners Hadeer, Bay Street and Rose Of Montreaux.

D LODER

Not surprisingly, I very much enjoyed my visit to Godolphin Stables in Newmarket where David was kind enough to discuss the two-year-olds with me at some length. It is well-documented that Godolphin have brought their 2-y-o's back to England after a couple of years in the doldrums at Evry and David's penchant for training young horses is unquestionable. He feels that this is a very much sharper bunch than in the previous two years and I've urged him to take on the O'Brien battalions at every possible opportunity! Let's hope this is the year the Godolphin two-year-olds really attack the Group races and make it a memorable season for high-class juvenile racing. David explained that he has a number of other 2-y-o's he'd expect to win, but that the following are the ones most likely to reach the top.

684 - AL MOULATHAM * [93]   b.c. Rainbow Quest – High Standard (Kris).

May 3. Second foal.

Closely related to the unraced 2000 2-y-o Comfortable Call (by Nashwan). The dam, a fairly useful 2-y-o 8.2f winner, stayed 12f at 3 yrs and is a half-sister to the fairly useful 10f winner Mowlaie (by Nashwan). The second dam, Durrah (by Nijinsky), a fairly useful French 2-y-o 1m winner, is a sister to the Grade 2 stakes winner Number (dam of the very smart 1989 2-y-o Jade Robbery), is closely related to the top-class sire Nureyev and a half-sister to Fairy Bridge (the dam of Sadlers Wells, Fairy King and Tate Gallery) and Kilavea (the dam of Kiliniski). (Maktoum Al-Maktoum). *"A nice horse and a nice model for a Rainbow Quest but he's more of a back-end of the season type and would want at least seven furlongs".*

685 - ANTIQUARY (IRE) ** [82]   ch.f. Polish Precedent – Anna Matrushka (Mill Reef).

February 1.

Half-sister to the very smart Group 2 12.5f Prix de Royallieu and Group 2 12f Prix du Conseil de Paris winner Annaba (by In The Wings), to the very useful Group 2 12f Park Hill Stakes winner Anna of Saxony (by Ela-Mana-Mou), the fairly useful Andrassy (by Ahonoora) a winner of 6 races here and in the USA, the fair Irish 12f winner Ancelin (by Sadler's Wells) and the minor 1995 German 3-y-o winner Anna d'Autriche. The dam is an unraced half-sister to the German Group 3 winner Anno Luce and to the dam of the very smart middle-distance colt Annus Mirabilis. The second dam, Anna Paola (by Prince Ippi), won the German Oaks. *"A nice filly but still quite backward and she'll want at least seven furlongs later in the year".*

Significant sire/damsire crosses:- Pure Grain.

686 - BANDSTAND ** [86]   b.c. Spectrum – Licorne (Sadler's Wells).

January 31. Fourth living foal. 270,000Y. Tattersalls Houghton.

Half-brother to the fairly useful 10f and hurdles winner Dabus (by Kris). The dam, a fairly useful 10f and 12f winner, is a half-sister to 4 winners including the Yorkshire Oaks winner Catchascatchcan. The second dam, Catawba (by Reform), a fairly useful 10.5f winner, is a half-sister to 7 winners including the Ribblesdale Stakes winner Strigida. *"A nice horse, Bandstand is going well at the moment but he'll need seven furlongs and is one for the second half of the season".*

687 - COPERNICAN (USA) *** [97]   b.c. Kingmambo – Mysterial (Alleged).

February 10. First foal. $1,500,000Y. Keeneland July.

The dam ran unplaced twice and is a half-sister to the top-class sprinter Agnes World (by Danzig), to the champion Japanese sprinter/miler Hishi Akebono and the US stakes winner My Sea Castles. The second dam, Mysteries (by Seattle Slew), was third in the Group 3 Musidora Stakes and is out of the Group 3 Prix Quincey winner Phydilla. *"An extremely nice horse, he's going very well at the moment and may have the speed for six furlongs but could be better over seven".*

688 - DECEPTOR (USA) *** [101]   b.c. Machiavellian – Satin Flower (Shadeed).

April 17. Sixth foal.

Closely related to the very smart 1998 2-y-o Group 1 6f Middle Park Stakes winner Lujain (by Seeking The Gold) and half-brother to the very promising 2000 2-y-o 7f listed winner Lilium (by Nashwan). The dam, a smart winner of the Group 3 7f Jersey Stakes and second in the Grade 1 9f Queen Elizabeth II Challenge Cup, is a half-sister to 7 winners including the US Grade 1 10f Santa Anita Handicap winner Martial Law. The second dam, Sateen (by Round Table), won two 6f stakes events in the USA. *"He'll be one of our first runners. He's been here all winter so he's acclimatised earlier than his three-parts brother Lujain did. Lujain had been in Dubai until May. This colt is tuned in and he goes very nicely. He's hopefully Ascot material as he's an obvious Coventry Stakes type horse".*

689 - DISTINCTIVE STATE *** [101]   ch.c. Halling – Avila (Ajdal).

March 29. Sixth foal. 130,000Y. Tattersalls Houghton.

Half-brother to the very smart 2000 2-y-o Group 1 1m Racing Post Trophy winner Dilshaan (by Darshaan), to the modest 10.5f winner Mama-San (by Doyoun) and a winner in Austria by Shirley Heights. The dam, a fair 7f placed maiden, is a half-sister to the smart middle-distance colts Alleging, Monastery and Nomrood. The second dam, Sweet Habit (by Habitat), is an unraced half-sister to the

Group 2 Pretty Polly Stakes winner Fleur Royale. *"A nice horse that should hopefully be ready to run over seven furlongs in July"*.

---

690 - DIVINE STATUS (USA) **[104]** b.c. Seeking The Gold – Possibly Perfect (Northern Baby).
January 31. Second foal. $700,000Y. Keeneland July.
Closely related to the US stakes-placed winner (including at 2 yrs) Promontory Gold (by Gone West). The dam was a champion turf mare in the USA, winning six Grade 1 stakes. The second dam, Avasand (by Avatar), won 2 minor races in the USA at 3 yrs and is a half-sister to the US Grade 3 winner Window Seat. *"I would hope that he'd have the speed for six furlongs, but he's more likely to want seven. A nice horse you shouldn't leave out"*. n.b. John Ferguson later told me he felt this colt was one of his picks from the Keeneland July Sales.

---

691 - DUBAI BELLE (USA) ** [97] b.f. Mr Prospector – Flagbird (Nureyev).
April 4. Second foal.
Sister to the 2000 2-y-o Marhoob. The dam, winner of the Group 1 Premio Presidente della Repubblica, is a half-sister to the Grade 1 Acorn Stakes and the Grade 1 8.5f Ashland Stakes winner Prospector's Delite (herself dam of the US Grade 1 Ruffian Handicap winner Tomisue's Delight), the US Grade 1 winner Runup The Colors and the US Grade 2 winner Top Account. The second dam, Up The Flagpole (by Hoist The Flag), won the Grade 2 Delaware Oaks. *"A very nice filly. She'll probably want seven furlongs to start with. She's in Dubai until the end of April and looks very well at the moment. I would be hoping that she'd start off over seven furlongs in July and I have quite high hopes for her"*.
Significant sire/damsire crosses:- Kingmambo (Gr 1), Dance Sequence, Shake Hand, Souvenir Copy (all Gr 2), Miesque's Son (Gr 3).

---

692 - DUBAI EXCELLENCE * [98]** gr.c. Highest Honor – Colorado Dancer (Shareef Dancer).
April 2.
Half-brother to the outstanding Dubai Millennium (by Seeking The Gold), winner of the Dubai World Cup, the Prix Jacques le Marois, the Prince Of Wales's Stakes and the Queen Elizabeth II Stakes (all Group 1 events), to the 1995 Group 2 10.5f Prix Greffulhe second Denver County (by Mr Prospector) and the useful French 12f winner Fort Morgan (by Pleasant Colony). The dam was a very smart winner of the Group 2 13.5f Prix de Pomone and the Group 3 12f Prix de Minerve and was placed in the Group 1 12f Prix Vermeille and two Grade 1 events in the USA. She is closely related to the very useful Grade 1 Gamely Handicap and Group 2 Prix d'Astarte winner Northern Aspen, to the Group 1 July Cup winner Hamas and the Group 1 Grand Prix de Paris winner Fort Wood and a half-sister to the Prix d'Astarte winner Elle Seule (herself dam of the Irish One Thousand Guineas winner Mehthaaf), the champion 1994 American 2-y-o colt Timber Country and the Goodwood Cup winner Mazzacano. The second dam, Fall Aspen (by Pretense) - clearly one of the finest broodmares of recent times - won 8 races notably the Grade 1 7f Matron Stakes. *"This is a very nice horse. On looks and performance at the moment he lives right up to his pedigree, so we'll see how he gets on. He's in Dubai and has just been cantering. When we get him home we'll see how he goes, but I would hope that he might run around July time. If everything goes smoothly for him I'm hoping that he might go all the way. He's certainly a nice horse and more mature than his half-brother Dubai Millennium was at this stage"*

---

693 - DUBAI FUJI (JPN) * [89] b.br.c. Sunday Silence – Millracer (Le Fabuleux).
May 16. Twelfth foal.
Brother to the champion Japanese 2-y-o colt Fuji Kiseki and to 2 other Japanese 2-y-o winners and half-brother to 3 minor winners in Japan by Dr Devious, Mining and Northern Taste. The dam, a quite useful 3-y-o 7.2f winner here before winning in the USA and finishing fourth in the Grade 1 Beldame Stakes, is a half-sister to 4 winners. The second dam, (Marston's Mill (by In Reality), a stakes-placed winner of 4 races at up to 1m, is a half-sister to the Flying Childers Stakes winner Peterhof and the Irish Group 3 winning 2-y-o's Western Symphony and Moscow Ballet. *"A colt that will probably want seven furlongs in mid-season and he's a really nice 2-y-o"*.

---

694 - EGYPTIAN MOMMY (USA) ** [96] b.f. Mt Livermore – Phantom Creek (Mr Prospector).
April 11. Second foal.
Closely related to the unraced 2000 2-y-o Unknownwaters (by Rahy). The dam, a 5f winner in Dubai at 3 yrs, is a half-sister to the outstanding 1991 2-y-o Arazi, winner of the Breeders Cup Juvenile, the Prix Robert Papin, the Prix Morny, the Prix de la Salamandre and the Ciga 1m Grand Criterium (all Group 1 events between 5f and 8.5f). The second dam, Danseur Fabuleux (by Northern Dancer), was placed in

the Group 3 12f Prix de Minerve and is closely related to the US Grade 1 winner Joyeux Danseur and the very useful 12f winner Fabulous Dancer. *"A filly in Dubai and with Royal Ascot potential. She's a very nice filly and I hope she makes it to the Queen Mary"*.

695 - ELITE DUBAI (IRE) ** [85]   ch.c. Grand Lodge – Kafayef (Secreto).

January 12. Fourth foal. 575,000Y. Tattersalls Houghton.

Half-brother to Gardrum (by Lycius), unplaced in one start over 6f at 2 yrs in 2000 and to the Italian 7.5f (at 2 yrs) and 10.5f winner Persian Filly (by Persian Bold). The dam is an unplaced half-sister to 7 winners including the US stakes winners Dysham and Queen's Gray Bee and the Group 1 5f Phoenix Stakes second Shahik. The second dam, Sham Street (by Sham), won 4 races in the USA, is a sister to an Italian Group 3 winner and a half-sister to 6 winners including the very useful listed winners Indian Trail and Palace Street. *"A nice, athletic horse and a January foal. He's in Dubai and looks very well although he's had one or two minor setbacks. I would hope that he'd be ready to run in June sometime and have enough speed to run over six furlongs"*.

696 - FARQAD (USA) *** [112]   b.c. Danzig – Futuh (Diesis).

April 1.

Closely related to the smart 1997 2-y-o Group 1 6f Middle Park Stakes winner Hayil and to the useful 1998 2-y-o dual 6f winner Mizhar (both by Dayjur) and half-brother to the very promising 2000 2-y-o 7f and 7.6f winner Elnahaar (by Storm Cat) and the fairly useful 1995 2-y-o dual 6f and subsequent Dubai 10f winner Tamhid (by Gulch). The dam, a fairly useful 2-y-o 6f winner, is a half-sister to the Canadian Selene Stakes winner Rose Park (herself the dam of the smart US Grade 2 winner Wild Rush). The second dam, Hardship (by Drone), won 4 races at up to 1m and was third in the Grade 1 Frizette Stakes. *"A very nice, strong, 2-y-o type and the July meeting at Newmarket might be a realistic target for him. A mature horse and he's ready to go"*.

697 - FOREST PEARL (USA) ** [80]   b.f. Woodman – Moonshell (Sadler's Wells).

March 7. Second foal.

Half-sister to the 2000 David Loder trained 2-y-o Alunissage (by Rainbow Quest). The dam, winner of the 1995 Oaks and second in the One Thousand Guineas, is a half-sister to the French listed 11f winner and Group 2 placed Ocean Of Storms. The second dam, Moon Cactus (by Kris), was a smart winner of the 7f Sweet Solera Stakes at 2 yrs and the 10f Lupe Stakes at 3 yrs, was placed in the Group 1 10.5f Prix de Diane and Group 2 Nassau Stakes and is a sister to the very smart 8.5f Diomed Stakes winner Shining Steel. *"A very nice, well put-together filly. You'd hope she'd be of classic potential and I can see her starting off at seven furlongs. She'll make a 2-y-o but not an early one and I should think July will be plenty early enough for her"*.

698 - IMTIYAZ (USA) ** [98]   gr.c. Woodman – Shadayid (Shadeed).

March 14. Sixth foal.

Closely related to the fairly useful 7f winner Shawaf (by Mr Prospector) and half-brother to the very promising 2000 2-y-o 6f winner Alshadiyah (by Danzig), the fair 1999 2-y-o 7f winner Ashjaan (by Silver Hawk) and the very useful Bint Shadayid (both by Nashwan), winner of the Group 3 7f Prestige Stakes and placed in the One Thousand Guineas and the Fillies Mile. The dam, a very smart filly, won the One Thousand Guineas, the Prix Marcel Boussac and the Fred Darling Stakes and was placed in the Oaks, the Coronation Stakes, the Queen Elizabeth II Stakes, the Sussex Stakes and the Haydock Park Ladbroke Sprint Cup. She is a half-sister to several winners including the very useful dual 7f winner and Jersey Stakes third Dumaani. The second dam, Desirable (by Lord Gayle), won the Group 1 6f Cheveley Park Stakes, was third in the One Thousand Guineas and is a half-sister to the Irish Oaks and Ribblesdale Stakes winner Alydaress and the Cheveley Park Stakes winner Park Appeal. *"You would expect him to want seven furlongs to start with. He's wintered in Dubai and looks very well. July would be realistic for him and he's a very nice colt"*.

699 - JOYOUS GIFT **** [86]   ch.c. Cadeaux Genereux – Elfin Laughter (Alzao).

February 8. Third foal. 220,000Y. Tattersalls October.

Brother to the fair 1999 5f and 7f placed 2-y-o Fantasy and half-brother to the 2001 Newmarket 3-y-o winner Smirk (by Selkirk). The dam, a fair 2-y-o 7.5f and 1m winner, is a half-sister to 11 winners including the very useful 2-y-o 6f and 7f winner Carmot, the useful 6f and 7.6f winner Finian's Rainbow and the quite useful the 2-y-o 5f winner Chasing Moonbeams. The second dam, Rainbow's End (by My Swallow), a quite useful 2-y-o 6f winner, is out of Pantomime (by Silly Season), a useful winner of

3 races at up to 1m. *"He's a nice horse and he will make a 2-y-o – probably around July time I should think. He should have the speed for six furlongs but he will go further".*
Significant sire/damsire crosses:- Embassy.

---

700 - KHAMS-ALHAWAS (IRE) ** [75] gr.f. Marju – Bint Shadayid (Nashwan).
February 12. First foal.

The dam, a very useful winner of the Group 3 7f Prestige Stakes and placed in the One Thousand Guineas and the Fillies Mile, is a half-sister to the fairly useful 7f winner Shawaf. The second dam, Shadayid (by Shadeed), was a very smart winner of the One Thousand Guineas, the Prix Marcel Boussac and the Fred Darling Stakes and was placed in the Oaks, the Coronation Stakes, the Queen Elizabeth II Stakes, the Sussex Stakes and the Haydock Park Ladbroke Sprint Cup. She is a half-sister to several winners including the very useful dual 7f winner and Jersey Stakes third Dumaani. *"A nice filly, she's due in from Dubai at the end of April and is doing very well at the moment. She could have the speed for six furlongs but is more likely to want seven in the second half of the season".*

---

701 - KRISKOVA (USA) * [97]** b.c. Kris S – Tereshkova (Mr Prospector).
April 3. Second foal.

Half-brother to the French trained 2000 2-y-o Russian Range (by St Jovite). The dam, a winner of 6 races including the Group 3 6f Prix de Cabourg, was second in the Group 1 7f Moyglare Stud Stakes and third in the Group 1 6f Prix Morny. She is a sister to the Group 1 6f Middle Park Stakes and multiple Group 1 placed Lycius and a half-sister to the US dual Grade 2 winner Akabir. The second dam, Lypatia (by Lyphard), won over 6.5f in France and 1m in the USA. *"He's wintered in Dubai and looks great at the moment. A very nice horse, I would think he'd want seven furlongs in mid-season. A nice prospect".*
Significant sire/damsire crosses:- Hollywood Wildcat (Gr 1).

---

702 - MINGORA (USA) ** [74] b.f. Mtoto – Silk Braid (Danzig).
Sixth foal.

Sister to Saleyma, unplaced in one start over 7f at 2 yrs in 2000 and to the useful 2-y-o 7f winner Velour and half-sister to the very useful listed 7f Oak Tree Stakes winner Beraysim (by Lion Cavern) and the UAE 1m winner Modelliste (by Bering). The dam, a useful winner of a 3-y-o 9f York maiden and a 12f Italian listed event and is a half-sister to the Belmont and Preakness Stakes winner and champion 3-y-o colt Risen Star. The second dam, Ribbon (by His Majesty), won 9 races from 6f to 11f in the USA including the Grade 3 Pucker Up Stakes and is a half-sister to the very useful 1m to 10f winner Polar Gap. *"A nice filly, she's cantering and goes very well. She may have enough speed to run over six furlongs and is a filly with some potential. I'm pleased with her".*

---

703 - MOON BALLAD (IRE) ** [84] ch.c. Singspiel – Velvet Moon (Shaadi).
March 4. Third foal. Tattersalls October. 350,000Y.

Half-brother to the unraced 2000 2-y-o Syria (by Halling) and to the useful 2000 3-y-o 1m winner Velvet Lady (by Nashwan). The dam, a very useful Group 2 6f Lowther Stakes and listed 10f winner, is a half-sister to the Group 1 12f Italian Derby, Group 2 7f Lanson Champagne Stakes and German Group 2 12f winner Central Park. The second dam, Park Special (by Relkino), won over 10f at 3 yrs in Ireland and is a half-sister to the useful 2-y-o winners Careafolie and Gouriev and the smart French 2-y-o winner Pantile. *"A very interesting horse. He's a very athletic, light-framed, well-balanced horse that goes nicely. I would think he'd want seven furlongs and he's an interesting prospect".*

---

704 - MOON SERENADE ** [79] br.f. Key Of Luck – Moonlight Saunter (Woodman).
April 1. Third foal.

Half-sister to the 2000 2-y-o Easy Enigma (by Selkirk), unplaced in 2 starts. The dam, a quite useful 7f winner, is a half-sister to the French dual 1m listed winner Bint Lariaff. The second dam, Etoile d'Amour (by The Minstrel), a quite useful 3-y-o 7f winner, is a sister to the dam of the US Grade 2 winner Topicount and a half-sister to the German Group 3 6f Benazet-Rennen winner Elnawaagi. The third dam, Gurkha's Band (by Lurullah), was a high-class US sprint winner of 22 races. *"An interesting one. She's in full training at the moment and might be our first filly to run. She looks sharp and goes quite nicely so it will be interesting to see how she gets on".*

705 - OFFICIAL FLAME (USA) **** [79] ch.c. Deputy Minister – Fire The Groom (Blushing Groom).
January 8. Fifth foal.
Half-brother to the top-class sprinter Stravinsky (by Nureyev), winner of the July Cup and the Nunthorpe Stakes. The dam, a smart winner of five races here at around 1m, subsequently won four times in the USA including the Grade 1 9.5f Beverly D Stakes and the Grade 2 Wilshire Handicap. She is a half-sister to the Group 1 6f Vernons Sprint Cup winner and useful sire Dowsing. The second dam, Prospector's Fire (by Mr Prospector), is a placed half-sister to the US stakes winners Royal And Regal (Grade 1 Florida Derby) and Regal And Royal. *"A very nice horse. A strong, sprint type 2-y-o and he'll make a 3-y-o as well. He looks great and we'll see if he makes it to Ascot. If not, we'll be looking at something like the July meeting for him. He's an all-round, tough, nice horse".*
Significant sire/damsire crosses:- Turnberry Isle (Gr 3).

706 - ON EDGE *** [93] b.c. Zafonic – Gull Nook (Mill Reef).
May 26. Eleventh foal. 220,000Y. Tattersalls October.
Half-brother to Panna (by Polish Precedent), placed over 7f on her only run at 2 yrs in 2000, to the top-class colt Pentire (by Be My Guest), winner of the King George VI and Queen Elizabeth Diamond Stakes and the Irish Champion Stakes etc., the very useful Group 3 14f Premio Roma winner and Group 1 Yorkshire Oaks fourth Spring, the minor 12.2f winner Tanz (both by Sadlers Wells), the fairly useful 10f winner and listed Kittiwake (by Barathea) and the fairly useful 1m to 10f winner Smart Generation (by Cadeaux Genereux). The dam, a smart filly, won over 10.5f at 3 yrs and was second in the Group 2 12f Ribblesdale Stakes. She is a sister to the useful 12f winner Primrose Valley, closely related to the Group 3 12f Princess Royal Stakes winner Banket and a half-sister to the Group 3 13.5f Ormonde Stakes winner Mr Pintips. The second dam, Bempton (by Blakeney), was placed four times at up to 11f and is a half-sister to Shirley Heights. *"A very nice horse and a late May foal but he doesn't look it. We'll nonetheless give him some time and probably look to run him in June. Certainly a horse we like very much, he's got a lot of quality and he may have enough speed to start over six furlongs".*

707 - PRIDE OF DUBAI (USA) ** [89] b.c. Seeking The Gold – Bint Baladee (Nashwan).
February 11. First foal.
The dam was a useful 1m and 10f winner at 3 yrs and is a half-sister to 3 winners. The second dam, Sahara Baladee (by Shadeed), is a placed half-sister to the high-class miler Thrill Show and to the US Grade 3 winner David's Bird. *"He's a nice, well-balanced, compact horse and I'm hopeful he'll be a potential Royal Ascot 2-y-o. He's doing a bit more now with a view towards running by the end of May".*

708 - PROFITEER (IRE) ** [86] b.c. Entrepreneur – Champagne Girl (Robellino).
February 22. Fourth foal. 160,000Y. Tattersalls October.
Half-brother to the fairly useful 2000 2-y-o 5f winner Speedy Gee and to the smart Group 3 5f Cornwallis Stakes and dual 6f listed winner Halmahera (both by Petardia) and half-brother to a winner in Sweden by Forest Wind. The dam, a modest 2-y-o 5f winner, is a half-sister to 3 winners including the useful sprinter Deep Finesse. The second dam, Babycham Sparkle (by So Blessed), a quite useful 5f and 6f winner, is a half-sister to the smart French middle-distance winner El Famoso and to the dams of the Gimcrack Stakes winner River Falls and the German Group 2 winning sprinter Premiere Cuvee. *"He's very precocious and I would hope he'll make it to Royal Ascot. He's a five furlong horse, so if he's good enough you'd be thinking of the Norfolk Stakes or Windsor Castle, but at this time of the year it's just a case of getting them fit and seeing what they can do. He's a very nice, straightforward, uncomplicated horse and I'm very pleased with him".*

709 - RAWABI *** [94] b.f. Sadler's Wells - Flying Melody (Auction Ring).
February 28.
Sister to the smart 1994 Group 1 7f Dewhurst Stakes winner In Command, closely related to the brilliantly speedy 1992 2-y-o Group 1 5f Keeneland Nunthorpe Stakes winner Lyric Fantasy (by Tate Gallery) and half-sister to the high-class 1995 2-y-o Royal Applause (by Waajib), winner of the Group 1 6f Middle Park Stakes, Group 2 Coventry Stakes and Group 2 Gimcrack Stakes, to the quite useful 5f and 6f winner (at 2 yrs) Mere Melody (by Dunphy), the five time Italian winner Flying Monarch (by Tender King) and the quite useful 8.5f winner Lucayan Cay (by Al Hareb). The dam won twice in France over sprint distances and is a half-sister to the listed stakes winners Pearl Star, Portese and Seadiver

and to the smart sprinter Blue Star. The second dam, Whispering Star (by Sound Track), won over 5f on her only start. *"Very nice. She's not over-big and so isn't particularly typical of Sadler's Wells – she looks like a sort of mini-version! A reasonably sharp filly, you would have to think that five furlongs might be too sharp although I'm not ruling it out at all. I'm looking forward to running her and she's a possible for the Queen Mary".*
Significant sire/damsire crosses:- In Command.

---

710 - SAMHARI (USA) * [93]

ch.c. Indian Ridge – Cambara (Dancing Brave). April 21. Fifth foal.

Half-brother to the unraced 2000 2-y-o Helaali (by Halling). The dam was a useful winner of three 1m events at 3 yrs and is a half-sister to the good French 6f to 1m winner Pluralisme, the very useful 10f Virginia Stakes winner Singletta, the very useful 11f Grand Prix Prince Rose winner Classic Tale, the useful 1m winners Only and Cambrian and to the 10f winner Ghislaine - herself dam of the high-class miler Markofdistinction. The second dam, Cambretta (by Roberto), won over 9f in Ireland at 3 yrs, is a sister to the high-class middle-distance colt Critique and a half-sister to the dam of the 1992 Derby winner Dr Devious. (Sheikh Ahmed Al-Maktoum). *"He's going quite nicely and has just started to do more serious work. Although he didn't seem like an obvious candidate to run early when he came in, he's up in the front group at the moment. We'll see how he gets on because he may show that he's not quite ready, so we'll give him a chance in the meantime. If everything goes smoothly for him he'll start over five furlongs".*

---

711 - SANABEL ** [70]

b.c. Royal Applause – Sabayik (Unfuwain). February 16. Fourth foal. 150,000Y. Tattersalls October.

Half-brother to the useful Khibrah (by Lahib), a winner of 7 races at 3 yrs from 1m to 10f in 1999 including a listed event. The dam was a fairly useful 3-y-o 1m winner and stayed 10f. She is a half-sister to 6 winners including the Doncaster Cup third Haitham out of the fairly useful Group 3 6f Premio Primi Passi winner Balqis (by Advocator), herself a half-sister to the dam of the Hollywood Derby winner Slew The Dragon. *"He looks quite precocious and is likely to run at the end of April or in early May. He'll possibly have the speed for five furlongs and the Royal Applause yearlings at the Sales looked like they'd be able to do their job.*

---

712 - SEBA ** [73]

b.f. Alzao – Persian Secret (Persian Heights). February 7. Second foal.

The dam, a fairly useful 2-y-o 6f winner here, subsequently won in France and is a half-sister to the smart Group 3 6f Coventry Stakes winner and Irish Two Thousand Guineas second Verglas (by Highest Honor). The second dam, Rahaam (by Secreto), a fairly useful 3-y-o 7f winner, is a half-sister to 8 winners including the Prix Thomas Bryon winner and French Two Thousand Guineas third Glory Forever. *"A nice, strong filly that's due to do more work now, she's got quite a precocious pedigree and may have already run by the time of the Newmarket Guineas meeting".*

---

713 - SELWAN (USA) *** [102]

b.f. Mt Livermore – Dubian (High Line). April 23. Eleventh foal.

Half-sister to the unraced 2000 2-y-o Dubianstar, to the top-class filly Sayyedati, winner of the Cheveley Park Stakes and Moyglare Stud Stakes at 2 yrs, the One Thousand Guineas and Prix Jacques le Marois at 3 yrs and the Sussex Stakes at 5 yrs, the 2-y-o 6f winner Shimaha (all by Shadeed), the very smart Group 1 9f and 12f winner Golden Snake (by Danzig) and the smart 7f (at 2 yrs) and 1m listed winner Race Leader (by Gone West). The dam, a smart filly, won over 7f at 2 yrs, 12f at 3 yrs and the Group 1 10f Premio Lydia Tesio at 4 yrs. She was also placed in the Epsom Oaks and Irish Oaks and is a half-sister to the triple champion hurdler See You Then. The second dam, Melodina (by Tudor Melody), won the 5f Seaton Delaval Stakes at 2 yrs, a 10f event at 3 yrs when she was placed in the Ribblesdale Stakes and the Musidora Stakes, and was a half-sister to the Irish Oaks winner Celina. *"She's in Dubai and she's a very nice filly. I'm hoping that she might be a Royal Ascot candidate, she's just cantering and looks very well. A mature type of 2-y-o".*

---

714 - SHAMI ** [80]

ch.c. Rainbow Quest – Bosra Sham (Woodman). January 30. First foal. 1,000,000Y. Tattersalls Houghton.

The dam was a top-class filly and winner of 7 races including the One Thousand Guineas, the Dubai Champion Stakes and the Fillies Mile (all Group 1 events). She is a sister to the champion European 2-y-o and French Two Thousand Guineas and Prix Jacques le Marois winner Hector Protector and a half-sister to the 1992 French Two Thousand Guineas winner Shanghai the dam of the 1m Grand Criterium and 10.5f Prix Lupin winner Ciro. The second dam, Korveya (by Riverman), won the Group 3 9f Prix Chloe and is a half-sister to the high-class 6f to 7f filly Proskona and the German Group 2 winner Keos. The third dam, Konafa (by Damascus), was second in the One Thousand Guineas and is a half-sister to the Yorkshire Oaks winner Awaasif - herself dam of the Oaks winner Snow Bride and thus grandam of Derby winner Lammtarra. *"A very nice horse. He'll want at least seven furlongs and will probably be more of a back-end type horse – or certainly second half of the season. For a Rainbow Quest he's very strong and he should do well".*

---

715 - SILENT HONOR (IRE) ** [85] ch.f. Sunday Silence – Wood Vine (Woodman).
February 25. First foal.

The dam is an unraced daughter of the French 3-y-o 7f listed winner Massaraat (by Nureyev) - a sister to the great filly Miesque, winner of ten Group/Grade 1 races including the Breeders Cup Mile (twice), the One Thousand Guineas, the Prix Jacques le Marois (twice) and the Prix du Moulin. *"She'll probably want seven furlongs to start with and is a really nice filly. I could see her racing by mid-summer. John Ferguson is very keen on Sunday Silence and we've got two in the string".*

---

716 - STEADFAST AND TRUE (USA) ** [98] b.c. Danzig – Always Loyal (Zilzal).
April 14. First foal.

The dam won 3 races including the French One Thousand Guineas and the Group 3 1m Prix de la Grotte and is a half-sister to the top-class sprinter Anabaa and the Group 3 Prix d'Arenberg winner Key Of Luck. The second dam, Balbonella (by Gay Mecene), won the Group 1 5.5f Prix Robert Papin and is a half-sister to the French listed 12f winner Bamwhite. *"He's a nice horse and one would hope he'd have the speed for six furlongs any time from July onwards I should think".*

---

717 - TAYIBAH (IRE) ** [85] b.f. Sadler's Wells – Wijdan (Riverman).
March 9.

The dam, a useful 1m and 10.4f winner, is a sister to the 7f (at 2 yrs) and 1m listed winner Sarayir and the 1m winner Bashayer (both useful) and a half-sister to several winners including the brilliant Nashwan, winner of the Two Thousand Guineas, the Derby, the Eclipse Stakes and the King George VI and Queen Elizabeth Diamond Stakes and the high-class middle distance colt Unfuwain. The second dam, Height of Fashion (by Bustino), a high-class winner of 5 races from 7f to 12f including the Group 2 Princess of Wales's Stakes, is a half-sister to the good middle-distance colt Milford. *"She's wintered in Dubai and she goes very nicely. An interesting filly that will want at least seven furlongs – I wouldn't expect her to be ready until the end of August at the earliest".*
Significant sire/damsire crosses:- Carnegie (Gr 1).

---

718 - WESTERN OVERTURE (USA) * [92]** ch.c. Gone West – Musical Bliss (The Minstrel).
February 14. Sixth foal.

Brother to the very promising 2000 French 2-y-o winner Raneem, closely related to the fair 13.8f winner Corelli (by Machiavellian) and half-brother to the French listed 10f winner Muscadel (by Nashwan) and the very useful 7f and 1m winner Hammerstein (by Kris). The dam, a very useful filly, won the 7f Rockfel Stakes at 2 yrs and the One Thousand Guineas. She is a half-sister to the Grade 1 La Canada Stakes winner Safe Play (herself dam of the Grade 1 Man O'War Stakes winner Defensive Play). The second dam, Bori (by Quadrangle), is a placed half-sister to the Grade 3 winner Bob's Majesty and to the Dewhurst Stakes second Draw the Line. *"A nice, strong horse. Probably a stronger, tougher horse than his brother Raneem and we hope he makes a nice horse. I would say July over six or seven furlongs would be his starting point".*
Significant sire/damsire crosses:- Dazzle, Muqtarib, Performing Magic, Tamayaz, Zafonic, Zamindar.

G MARGARSON

---

719 - INTERNATIONALGUEST (IRE) * [65] b.c. Petardia – Banco Solo (Distant Relative).
March 27. First foal. 24,000Y. Tattersalls October.
The dam is an unraced sister to the dual listed winner and Irish One Thousand Guineas third My Branch. The second dam, Pay The Bank (by High Top), a quite useful 2-y-o 1m winner, stayed 10f. (Mr J Guest). *"He should be ready to run in late May or early June, is a precocious colt and very laid back for a son of Petardia. He's still improving and will win as a 2-y-o but has plenty of scope and size for a first foal. He has the speed for five furlongs but he should get six alright".*

720 - MY ONLY SUNSHINE * [72]   b.c. First Trump – Fiveofive (Fairy King).
February 15. Fourth foal.

Half-brother to the fair 12f winner Sweet Angeline (by Deploy). The dam, a modest 5f (at 2 yrs) and 1m winner, is a half-sister to 4 winners including the Group 3 6f July Stakes third The Old Firm. The second dam, North Hut (by Northfields), ran twice unplaced and is a half-sister to 4 winners. (Mrs Forman). *"The owner usually sells the colts and keeps the fillies, so I had to beg her to keep this fellow! An out-and-out sprinter, he should win over five furlongs but I prefer to train them to get six to begin with. It teaches them to relax a bit more instead of burning up and you can always come back a furlong if necessary. A big, powerful horse with strong quarters".*

721 - STAR GUEST (IRE) [69]   b.f. Alhaarth – Lady's Vision (Vision).
March 30. Third foal. IR20,000Y. Tattersalls Fairyhouse.

Half-sister to the unraced 2000 2-y-o Shiraz Dancer (by Common Grounds) and to a winner in Hong Kong by Desert Style. The dam won 3 minor races at up to 11f in Ireland. The second dam, Lady's Prerogative (by General Assembly), is an unraced half-sister to 7 winners including the Italian Derby winner In A Tiff, the Tattersalls Gold Cup winner Perfect Imposter and the Queen Anne Stakes winner Pennine Walk. (Mr J Guest). *"Quite a big filly with plenty of size and scope about her, she's an easy mover and has a good temperament. A nice type, she'll be out around late June over six furlongs".*

B MEEHAN

722 - ABERCORN (IRE) ** [75]   b.g. Woodborough – Ravensdale Rose (Henbit).
March 19. Fifth foal. 38,000Y. Tattersalls October.

Half-brother to the quite useful 2000 2-y-o dual 7f winner Mamore Gap (by General Monash), to the fair 1999 3-y-o 9.2f winner Floorso'theforest (by Forest Wind) and to a minor winner abroad by Balla Cove. The dam ran twice unplaced in Ireland and is a half-sister to 6 minor winners here and abroad. The second dam, Organdy (by Blakeney), won once at 3 yrs and is a half-sister to 9 winners including the Group 3 1m May Hill Stakes winner Satinette. *"The most expensive Woodborough at the Sales, he's nice and very straightforward. He's a very thick-set, heavy horse and we've gelded him. A lovely attitude and temperament – I'd say six or seven furlongs for him. A good nursery type horse".*

723 - ALPINE RACER ** [92]   b.c. Lake Coniston – Cut No Ice (Great Nephew).
April 9. Sixth foal. IR£26,000Y. Goffs Challenge.

Half-brother to the fair 2-y-o 1m and hurdles winner Pietro Bembo (by Midyan), to the poor 1m winner Polar Refrain (by Polar Falcon) and 2 winners abroad by Thatching and Suave Dancer. The dam, a fairly useful 7f winner here, later stayed 10f and won a listed event in France. The second dam, Foiled Again (by Bold Lad, Ire), won the listed Sandleford Priory Stakes and was placed in the Prix Saint-Alary, the Nassau Stakes and the Ribblesdale Stakes. *"A colt for the mid-season onwards and a nice horse".*

724 - ANGELUS SUNSET (USA) ** [82]   b.c. Numerous – Angelic Note (The Minstrel).
January 29. Seventh foal. 42,000Y. Tattersalls October.

Half-brother to the minor US stakes winner Grand Forks (by Quiet American) and a minor winner in the USA by Unbridled. The dam, a fairly useful 2-y-o 7f winner, is a half-sister to 7 winners including the Grade 1 Santa Anita Derby winner Martial Law and the Group 3 Jersey Stakes winner Satin Flower (herself dam of the Middle Park Stakes winner Lujain). The second dam, Sateen (by Round Table), won 7 races including two 6f stakes events in the USA. *"A very nice horse that we're just starting to get on with. He's a big, hardy lad so we didn't dive in too early, but he's a lovely colt – hopefully he'll be a Royal Ascot type".*

725 - BORDER MINSTRAL (IRE) ** [96]   b.br.f. Sri Pekan – Persian Song (Persian Bold).
May 9. Fifth foal.

Sister to the fair 10f winner Zagaleta and half-sister to the unplaced 2000 2-y-o Zandeed (by Inchinor), the very useful 7f (at 2 yrs) to 10f winner and Group 1 National Stakes third Mountain Song and the fairly useful 2-y-o 6f winner and Group 3 6f Princess Margaret Stakes third Raindancing (both by Tirol). The dam is an unplaced sister to the Solario Stakes winner Bold Arrangement (placed in seven Group/Grade 1 races including the Kentucky Derby). The second dam, Arrangement (by Floribunda), is a placed half-sister to the Cheveley Park Stakes winner Lindsay. *"A very nice filly, the Sri Pekan fillies definitely seem to be better than the colts in my experience. She's typical of the sire – a brown filly, very tough and hardy. She's only just starting to come to herself really because she's a May foal. So it would certainly be the end of May before she's ready".*

726 - CABALLO NOBILE (USA) ** [81]

b.f. Kris S – Serene Nobility. March 2. Fifth foal.

Half-sister to 2 winners including the Group 2 1m Royal Lodge Stakes winner Mutaahab (by Dixieland Band). The dam, a stakes winner of 9 races in the USA, is a half-sister to the US stakes winner Corax. The second dam, Peaceful Snow (by Hold Your Peace), won at 3 yrs in the USA and is a sister to the US Grade 2 winner Hold Your Tricks. *"A lovely American-bred filly with a European pedigree. We've done a bit with her and I've laid off her a bit. She'll probably start more serious work in early May and she could be anything. I think she'll live up to her pedigree which means she may be more of a back-end filly".*

727 - CASTAIGNE (FR) ** [71]

ch.f. Pivotal – Storm Warning (Tumble Wind). April 28. Eighth living foal. FF280,000. Deauville August.

Half-sister to the fair 2-y-o 6f winner Bulletin (by Prince Sabo), to the modest dual 1m all-weather winner Dust (by Green Desert) and to Present Situation (by Cadeaux Genereux), a fair winner of 9 races at up to 8.5f, including on the all-weather. The dam, a very smart sprinter, won 4 races including the Group 3 Premio Omenoni and the listed Scarborough Stakes and is a half-sister to 7 winners. The second dam, Maggie Mine (by Native Prince), was a quite useful 2-y-o 5f winner and a half-sister to the Italian Group 3 winner Henghel. *"A mid-season sort of filly. A nice, straightforward filly with a lovely attitude. She has a lot of quality about her and she came from Deauville so she might do a bit of French racing".*

728 - CATERHAM COMMON ** [69]

b.c. Common Grounds – Pennine Pink (Pennine Walk). January 20. Third foal. 22,000Y. Doncaster St Leger.

Half-brother to the quite useful 5f (at 2 yrs) and 10f winner Never Diss Miss (by Owington). The dam, a winner of 4 races from 1m to 10f, is a half-sister to the fair 10f and 12f winner Lady Rachel. The second dam, Alpine Stream (by Head For Heights), a fairly useful Irish 2-y-o 7f winner, is a half-sister to the Group 2 Mill Reef Stakes winner Showbrook and the very useful 1m to 10f performer Smarginato. *"Another early horse that had a little setback and he probably wouldn't run until early May. He's nice and I think he's the type to run at the Royal meeting".*

729 - DELGADO ** [83]

b.c. Alhaarth – Nur (Diesis). February 3. Sixth foal. 26,000Y. Doncaster St Leger.

Half-brother to the 3-y-o Kanelinos (by Lycius), to the quite useful 1999 2-y-o 6f winner Kamareyah, the fairly useful Irish 2-y-o 7f and subsequent US winner Hamouse (both by Hamas) and the 5f winners Kawafil (by Warning) and Hajat (by Mujtahid). The dam, a fair 2-y-o 5f and 6f winner, is a sister to the useful sprinter Ra'a and to the listed Roses Stakes winner Janib and a half-sister to the very useful Group 2 6f Richmond Stakes winner Muqtarib (by Gone West). The second dam, Shicklah (by The Minstrel), a useful 2-y-o 5f and 6f winner, is out of the 2-y-o winner Logette - herself a half-sister to the grandam of Suave Dancer. *"He was due to go for the Brocklesby but he got a temperature. He's back in action now and should be racing before the book comes out. A real 2-y-o, he has the potential to go to Royal Ascot without necessarily having a great deal of scope for next year".*

730 - DOC HOLIDAY (IRE) * [80]

ch.c. Dr Devious – Easter Heroine (Exactly Sharp). March 24. Second foal. IR£28,000Y. Goffs Challenge.

Half-brother to the Irish trained 3-y-o Cabo Salinas (by Hamas). The dam was placed over 7f (at 2 yrs) and 10f in Ireland and is a half-sister to 3 winners including the useful 5f and 6f winner Ocker. The second dam, Violet Somers (by Will Somers), is an unraced sister to the smart sprinters Balidar (winner of the Prix de l'Abbaye) and Balliol (winner of the Cork and Orrery Stakes). *"He was going along very early there but I just dropped him back because he wanted a bit of time. I'd still expect him to be racing by the end of May. A grand, straightforward sort".*

731 - DOUBLE HELIX ** [91]

b.c. Marju – Totham (Shernazar). March 1. Sixth foal. 170,000Y. Tattersalls October.

Half-brother to the US Grade 2 9f Honeymoon Handicap winner Country Garden (by Selkirk), to the fairly useful 1998 2-y-o 6f winner Greensand and the modest 5f (at 2 yrs) to 10.2f winner Cherokee Flight (both by Green Desert). The dam, a quite useful 12f winner, is a half-sister to 6 winners including the Hoover Fillies Mile fourth Sue Grundy. The second dam, Susanna (by Nijinsky), is a placed half-sister to 4 winners including the dam of the Group 2 Mecca-Dante Stakes winner Hot Touch. *"A lovely colt – by the look of him you wouldn't think he'd take a lot of time, but I think he may be a June/July type. Certainly one very nice horse".*

732 - DRAMRAIRE MIST   [82]

gr.f. Darshaan – Marie Dora (Kendor).
March 6. First foal. 120,000Y. Tattersalls October.

The dam, a quite useful 3-y-o 1m winner, is a sister to the Group 3 10.5f Prix Fille de l'Air winner Marie de Ken and a half-sister to 5 winners. The second dam, Marie de Vez (by Crystal Palace), was a French 9f winner and a half-sister to 8 winners including the Group 2 13.5f Grand Prix de Deauville winner Dom Alaric. *"A lovely, quality filly and a typical Darshaan – she'll have her time mid-season and at the back-end".*

733 - FAIRY MONARCH (IRE) **   [67]

b.c. Ali-Royal – Cookawara (Fairy King).
March 25. Third foal. IRE40,000Y. Goffs Challenge.

The dam, an Irish 2-y-o 6f winner and listed 6f Debutante Stakes third, is a half-sister to the Irish Group-placed winner Erraruriz. The second dam, Miss Lee Ann (by Tumble Wind), was unraced. *"An early 2-y-o, he'll be out before the book is published and although he might be better over six furlongs he knows his game and has a lovely attitude".*

734 - GOBLET OF FIRE (USA)   [93]

b.c. Green Desert – Laurentine (Private Account).
February 23. First foal. 82,000Y. Tattersalls Houghton.

The dam, a listed-placed 3-y-o winner in France, is a half-sister to the Oaks and Lupe Stakes winner Love Divine. The second dam, La Sky (by Law Society), a useful 10f winner and second in the Lancashire Oaks, is closely related to the Champion Stakes winner Legal Case. *"A very nice, very strong colt for the back-end of the season".*
Significant sire/damsire crosses:- Desert Sky, Thourios.

735 - GREAT VIEW (IRE) **   [83]

b.c. Great Commotion – Tara View (Wassl).
April 2. Fourth foal. IRE23,000Y. Goffs Challenge

Half-brother to the modest 1998 2-y-o 5f winner Wind In Winnipeg (by Midhish). The dam is an unraced half-sister to 2 winners in Italy. The second dam, Julie Blake (by Blakeney), ran once unplaced and is a half-sister to the Two Thousand Guineas winner Roland Gardens and to the dam of the top-class filly Kooyonga. *"Very nice and I'd love to target him for the Goffs Challenge race. He looks just the type – he has a bit of size and scope about him. He's had an injury so he's resting at the moment but he's coming on very well".*

736 - GRIZEL**   [72]

b.f. Lion Cavern – Polska (Danzig).
January 31. Second foal. 45,000Y. Tattersalls October.

Half-sister to the 3-y-o Policy (by Nashwan). The dam, a useful winner of the 2-y-o listed 6f Blue Seal Stakes, was listed-placed over 7f at 3 yrs and is closely related to the useful filly Millstream, a winner of five races over 5f including the Group 3 Ballyogan Stakes and the Group 3 Cornwallis Stakes. The second dam, Aquaba (by Damascus), a Grade 3 stakes winner of 7 races in the USA, won from 7f to 9f and is a half-sister to 6 winners from the Northern Dancer line. *"A lovely filly – she's a cracker and although she's an early sort I may delay her start until early May because she could be an Ascot type. A filly with a lovely way about her and she's working like she's got plenty of toe".*

737 - HIDDENDALE (IRE) *   [82]

br.f. Indian Ridge – That'll Be The Day (Thatching).
April 4. Fourth foal. 180,000Y. Tattersalls Houghton.

Half-sister to the Italian listed winner and Group 3 placed That's The Way (by Hamas) and to the fairly useful 14f and 2m winner Majestic Bay (by Unfuwain). The dam, a modest 2-y-o 5f winner here, won 3 races at up to 7.5f in Italy at 3 yrs including a listed event. She is a half-sister to the very smart Group 1 Gran Criterium winner Candy Glen and to the Group 3 Derrinstown Stud Derby Trial winner Ashley Park. The second dam, Maiden Concert (by Condorcet), ran once unplaced and is a half-sister to 2 winners and to the dams of the Irish One Thousand Guineas winner More So and the Waterford Candelabra Stakes winner Obeah. *"She's come up a bit behind, so she's just going to take a bit of time, but she's really smart looking and I have a lot of high hopes for her. A very nice filly".*

738 - ITALIAN MIST (FR) * [76]   b.c. Forzando – Digamist Girl (Digamist).
February 26. Second foal. 13,000Y. Doncaster St Leger.
Half-brother to the quite useful Chispa (by Imperial Frontier), a dual 5f winner at 2 yrs in 2000. The dam, a sprint winner of 8 races in Belgium, is a half-sister to 5 winners in France and one in Switzerland. The second dam, Cupids Hill (Sallust), is an unraced half-sister to the Queen Anne Stakes and Hungerford Stakes winner Ardoon. *"A very nice colt, we're just starting to get into him a bit now. A big horse, but the way he's going at the moment he could easily be quite an early type".*

739 - MADAME MAXINE (USA) ** [87]   b.br.f. Dayjur – Political Parody (Doonesbury).
March 23. Sixth foal. IR£90,000Y. Goffs Orby.
Half-sister to the 2000 French 2-y-o winner and Group 3 6f Prix de Cabourg fourth Panis (by Miswaki) and to the US stakes winner of 12 races Political Whit (by Line Of Power). The dam, a stakes-placed winner in the USA, is a half-sister to 5 minor US winners. The second dam, Urakawa (by Roberto), is an unraced sister to the US stakes winner and Grade 2 placed Endicotta. *"A very nice filly - she probably won't be racing until mid-summer as she's just come up a little behind. So we're going to give her a bit of time".*

740 - MARK OF RESPECT ** [74]   b.f. Mark Of Esteem – Bassmaat (Cadeaux Genereux).
March 2. Third foal. Doncaster St Leger. 20,000Y.
Half-sister to the 2000 Irish 2-y-o winner El-Libaab (by Unfuwain). The dam, a fair 3-y-o 7f winner, is a half-sister to 2 minor winners abroad. The second dam, Mangayah (by Spectacular Bid), a smart French listed 12f winner, is a half-sister to the Group 3 winners Lady Roberta and Tursanah. *"A nice, sharp sort of filly, she should be racing sometime in May".*

741 - OCTINA (FR) * [82]   b.f. Octagonal – Anastina (Thatching).
April 5. Second foal. FF260,000Y. Deauville August.
The dam, a quite useful 4-y-o 7f (all-weather) and 1m winner, is a half-sister to 5 winners including the dam of the 12f Galtres Stakes winner Rambling Rose. The second dam, Nikitina (by Nijinsky), a useful Irish 10f winner, is a daughter of the Group 1 Criterium des Pouliches winner Vela III. *"One for the middle of the season, she's a nice, quality filly".*

742 - OMEY STRAND (IRE) * [75]   b.c. Desert Style – Ex-Imager (Exhibitioner).
April 1. Eighth foal. IR£28,000Y. Goffs Challenge.
Brother to a 3-y-o in Italy and half-brother to the Norwegian winner of 8 races Demon Dancer (by Gallic League) and the minor French and Belgian winner Dissidentia (by Dancing Dissident). The dam is an unraced half-sister to 2 winners including the fair 5f to 7f handicapper Ballad Dancer. The second dam, Manx Image (by Dancer's Image), is a placed half-sister to the Chester Cup winner Attivo. *"He was going to be one of my earliest but he had a little setback. He should be on the track by May and is very nice. He could be a Royal Ascot type".*

743 - PASOFINO (IRE) * [82]   b.c. Alzao – Kentucky Fall (Lead On Time).
February 21. First foal. IR£40,000Y. Goffs Orby.
The dam, a fair 4-y-o 6f winner, is a half-sister to 3 winners including the French listed winner and Group 3 Prix Penelope second Welsh Autumn. The second dam, Autumn Tint (by Roberto), won over 12f in France and is a half-sister to the French Group 3 winners Doree and Glorify and to the dam of the top-class middle-distance filly Ryafan. *"A lovely horse and a real Alzao. One I'd expect to be ready by mid-summer. A nice, well-balanced colt".*

744 - PRINCESS GISELLE (USA) ** [84]   b.f. Nureyev – Humble Fifteen (Feather Ridge).
May 17. Second foal.
The dam, a minor US 2-y-o stakes-placed winner, is a half-sister to the US Grade 3 8.5f Honeybee Stakes winner Humble Eight, the 2-y-o listed 7f winner Thady Quill (by Nureyev) and the 2-y-o listed 6f winner April Starlight. The second dam, Alleged Devotion (by Alleged), is an unraced half-sister to the top-class Irish Derby and Epsom Oaks winner Balanchine, to the Group 2 Jockey Club Stakes winner Romanov and the Group 2 Sun Chariot Stakes winner Red Slippers. *"We bought her in the States privately. A lovely filly and being by Nureyev she's a collector's item. Real quality – she's likely to be out in either June or July".*

745 - PRINCESS SERENA (USA) * [74] gr.f. Unbridled's Song – Serena's Sister (Rahy). February 11. Second foal.

The dam, unplaced in both her starts, is a sister to the outstanding US filly Serena's Song (a winner of eleven Grade 1 events) and a half-sister to the US Grade 3 Golden Rod Stakes winner Vivid Imagination. The second dam, Imagining (by Northfields), won 2 minor races in the USA and is a half-sister to the US Grade 3 First Flight Handicap winner and Grade 1 placed Alabama Nana. *"You really ought to give her a mention – she looks an outstanding filly. We bought her privately in the States last year and I see her as a real back end of the season filly. She's not very big but she's rather weak at the moment".*

746 - RAPADASH (IRE) ** [81] ch.c. Boundary – Imelda (Manila). January 31. First foal. IR£80,000Y. Goffs Orby.

The dam ran once unplaced at 2 yrs and is a half-sister to 6 winners including Kraemer, a winner of 4 races in France and the USA including the listed 8.5f Bay Meadows Oaks and the high-class Group 2 Prix du Rond-Point and Group 2 Prix d'Astarte winner Shaanxi. The second dam, Rich And Riotous (by Empery), won once over 1m in France and is a half-sister to 6 winners out of the Italian Oaks winner Carnauba. *"A real sharp sort. Definitely an early type, except that the other day he got a temperature and so he's missed the kick a little bit. But I'd like to think we'd be making some plans for him for May".*

747 - SAVANNAH BAY ** [87] ch.c. In The Wings – High Savannah (Rousillon). April 9. Sixth foal. 92,000Y. Tattersalls October.

Half-brother to the unraced 2000 2-y-o Maid For Romance (by Pursuit Of Love), to the very useful listed 6f Empress Stakes (at 2 yrs) and Group 2 10f Sun Chariot Stakes winner Lady In Waiting (by Kylian), the useful 7f (at 2 yrs) and 1m winner Smart Savannah (by Primo Dominie) and the quite useful 2-y-o 5.7f winner Sabina (by Prince Sabo). The dam, a fair middle-distance placed maiden, is a half-sister to the useful sprinters Maid For The Hills and Maid For Walking. The second dam, Stinging Nettle (by Sharpen Up), won the listed 6f Duke Of Edinburgh Stakes at 2 yrs and is a half-sister to the Royal Lodge Stakes winner Gairloch. *"A lovely, quality horse. He's a bit immature mentally at the moment and is one for the middle of the year".*

Significant sire/damsire crosses:- In Waiting (Gr 3 placed LW).

748 - SHORT CHANGE (IRE) ** [75] b.c. Revoque – Maafi Esm (Polish Precedent). January 21. Third foal. 24,000Y. Doncaster St Leger.

Half-brother to the modest 2000 2-y-o 7f seller winner Sawbo Lad (by Namaqualand). The dam is an unraced half-sister to a listed winner in Scandinavia. The second dam, Hayya (by Shergar), is an unraced half-sister to 8 winners including the French Group 3 second Luderic. *"A big, imposing horse who would hopefully be racing in May. He does it all easily and I don't think he'll take too long".*

749 - SILENCE IS GOLDEN *** [67] ch.f. Danehill Dancer – Silent Girl (Krayyan). February 5. Sixth foal. 7,500Y. Tattersalls December.

Half-sister to 2 minor winners abroad by Law Society and Shalford. The dam, a fair 1m (at 2 yrs) to 12f winner of 5 races, is a half-sister to 3 winners including the Group 3 July Stakes winner Always Valiant. The second dam, Silent Pearl (by Silent Screen), won twice in the USA at up to 7f and is a half-sister to the US Grade 2 winner Gallant Pearl. *"A grand filly and an early type, she's straightforward and will win her races over five and six furlongs this year.*

750 - TRIPLE PLAY (IRE) *** [75] br.c. Tagula – Shiyra (Darshaan). April 15. Sixth living foal. 70,000Y. Doncaster St Leger.

Brother to the 2000 German 2-y-o Group 2 winner Tagshira and half-brother to the Italian 5f and 6f winner of 5 races Flaming Soul (by Mac's Imp). The dam, a minor Irish 1m and 10f winner, is a half-sister to 3 winners. The second dam, Sharya (by Lord Gayle), won once at 3 yrs in France and is a half-sister to 9 winners. *"A lovely colt I plan to start at Newmarket in April. He's done a lot of work and has kept his condition really well. I'm very fond of him and he'll probably be better over six furlongs than five".*

Significant sire/damsire crosses:- Tagshira (Gr 2).

751 - TUMBLEWEED CHARM (IRE) ** [99]   b.c. Zafonic – Vienna Charm (Sadler's Wells).
March 22. Third foal. 62,000Y. Tattersalls October.
Half-brother to the unraced 2000 2-y-o Isabella d'Este (by Irish River). The dam, placed once over 7f at 2 yrs in Ireland, subsequently won at 3 yrs in Canada and is closely related to the French winner and 10.5f listed placed Didwana and a half-sister to 6 winners including the French listed 10f winner Droiture and the dam of the minor US stakes winner Polish Spring. The second dam, Diamond Spring (by Vaguely Noble), won once in France and is a half-sister to 4 winners including the dams of the US Grade 1 winners No Review, Another Review and Urbane. *"A lovely, great big horse. I might well run him at Newmarket in April, he's straightforward in his work and I think he's a really class act".*
Significant sire/damsire crosses:- Endless Summer, Pacino.

752 - TWILIGHT BLUES (IRE) ** [79]   ch.c. Bluebird – Pretty Sharp (Interrex).
February 23. First foal. 140,000Y. Tattersalls October.
The dam, a modest 7f placed 2-y-o, is a half-sister to 5 winners including the quite useful 6f (at 2 yrs) to 10f winner Kings Assembly. The second dam, To The Point (by Sharpen Up), a fairly useful 2-y-o 5f winner and fourth in the Group 3 5f Molecomb Stakes, is a half-sister to 5 winners and to the dams of the Group winners Coquito's Friend, Ordinance and Muchea. *"A lovely, big, imposing Bluebird colt. He's definitely got Royal Ascot potential and despite the high purchase price I'd give it for him again. A real corker and I'd hope to get him on the racetrack sometime in May. One of my nicest, I'd say".*

753 - YAVARI (IRE) ** [79]   b.f. Alzao – Twin Island (Standaan).
April 16. Seventh foal. IR£300,000Y. Goffs Orby.
Half-sister to the unraced 2000 2-y-o Alcutain (by Indian Ridge), to the smart winner of the Group 1 6f Prix Morny, the Group 3 6f July Stakes and the Group 3 7f Supreme Stakes winner Tagula (by Taufan) and a winner in Japan by Wolfhound). The dam ran once unplaced and is a half-sister to the Group 3 C.L. Weld Park Stakes winner Jolly Saint (herself dam of the Breeders Cup Mile winner Da Hoss). The second dam, Jolly Widow (by Busted), was unraced. *"I've backed off her because although she looked like coming to hand quickly, she's just a little bit on the weak side. We bought her with the hope she'd be a Guineas filly so she'll be trained all this year with her 3-y-o career in mind".*

754 - UNNAMED * [92]   b.c. Revoque – Song Of The Glens (Horage).
March 26. Eighth foal. 75,000Y. Tattersalls October.
Half-brother to the very smart 2000 2-y-o Group 1 6f Prix Morny winner Bad As I Wanna Be, to the quite useful 8.5f winner Musical Heath (both by Common Grounds), the quite useful 2-y-o 6f and subsequent French dual 6f winner Sepoy, the fair 2-y-o 7f winner Syabas (by Northiam) and the modest 1m all-weather winner Glider (by Silver Kite). The dam is an unplaced half-sister to 2 minor winners. The second dam, Melodious Polly (by Tudor Melody), is a winning half-sister to the Two Thousand Guineas winner Right Tack. *"He's having a bit of a break, will take a bit of time and would be a colt for the back-end of the season. A very nice horse".*

755 - UNNAMED * [71]   b.c. Efisio – Thilda (Roi Danzig).
February 14. Second foal. 50,000Y. Doncaster St Leger.
Half-brother to 2 winners in Scandinavia by Mango Express and Lotus Pool. The dam is an unraced half-sister to 4 winners including the middle-distance listed-placed Yarn. The second dam, Domiciliate (by Kings Lake), is an unraced half-sister to 6 winners including the US Grade 3 winner Baylis. *"A big, imposing colt, he's a very nice horse that should be racing by the end of May or in early June".*

756 - UNNAMED * [75]   b.f. Honour and Glory – Gold Rule (Forty Niner).
April 5. Fourth foal. $190,000Y.
Half-sister to the minor US winner Golden Squall (by Summer Squall). The dam is a placed half-sister to the Japanese stakes winner Raise Suzuran. The second dam, Sintanius (by Danzig), is an unraced sister to the US Graded stakes winners Contredance, Shotiche and Skimble (herself dam of the US Grade 1 winner Skimming). *"A very nice filly – real quality. She's only just arrived so we're not rushing her".*

757 - UNNAMED [74]   ch.f. Tactical Advantage – Festive Mood (Bering).
April 3. Third foal. $92,000Y.
Half-sister to the minor US winner of 3 races Santa Battista (by Saint Ballado). The dam is a placed sister to the Group 1 1m Racing Post Trophy winner Peter Davies and a half-sister to the dam of the US Grade 3 winner Cinemine. The second dam, French Flick (by Silent Screen), won 5 races in the USA including the Fairway Fun Stakes. *"She's a nice filly – a scopey sort and will probably take a bit of time to get ready"*.

758 - UNNAMED * [77]   b.c. Forest Wildcat – French Lake (Lac Ouimet).
March 11. First foal. $77,000Y.
The dam won 2 minor races at 3 yrs in the USA and is a half-sister to 6 winners including the stakes winner Alisha's Favorite (herself the dam of a stakes winner). The second dam, Blue Herb (by Herbager), a minor winner in the USA, is a half-sister to 2 winners. *"Another very nice, early sort that we bought in America as 2-y-o's this year. We need to get them used to grass because they've been brought up on dirt. This strategy worked last year because of the five we got only one was no good"*.

759 - UNNAMED ** [82]   b.br.c. Wild Again – Rhythm of Life (Deputy Minister).
March 2. Second foal. $250,000Y.
Half-brother to the minor 2000 US 2-y-o winner Wild Rocket (by Deputy Minister). The dam is an unraced half-sister to 5 winners including the Grade 1 Spinster Stakes and Grade 2 Molly Pitcher Handicap winner Wilderness Song (by Wild Again) and the US stakes winner Sound The Fanfare (herself the dam of 2 stakes winners). The second dam, Nalee's Rhythm (by Nalees Man), was a Canadian stakes winner of 6 races. *"He is an out-and-out dirt bred horse, so we're taking a bit of a chance but we can always go back and race in the States. We won't be in a major hurry with him – and you never know he could end up a Kentucky Derby horse. That would wind up the Boys In Blue!"*.

760 - UNNAMED * [64]   b.f. Desert King – Urgent Liaison (High Estate).
April 25. Second foal.
Half-sister to the French-trained 3-y-o Cappadoce (by General Monash). The dam is an unraced half-sister to the very smart Group 2 9f Budweiser International Stakes winner Great Dane and to the fairly useful 2-y-o 6f winner Witching Hour. The second dam, Itching (by Thatching), is an unraced half-sister to Croco Rouge and to the outstanding broodmare Alidiva (the dam of Sleepytime, Ali Royal and Taipan). *"A lovely Desert King filly and it's great to have one by that sire. I think she'll be ready by the end of May"*.

761 - UNNAMED ** [80]   b.f. Indian Ridge – Please Believe Me (Try My Best).
March 28. Fifth foal.
Sister to the useful 2000 2-y-o 5f Windsor Castle Stakes winner Autumnal and to the useful 5.2f (at 2 yrs) to 7f winner Lord Pacal and half-sister to the fairly useful 5f and 6f winner Storyteller (by Thatching). The dam, a fairly useful 2-y-o 5f winner, is out of the Group 3 12f Princess Royal Stakes winner Believer. *"A full-sister to Autumnal, she's a lovely filly that won't come to hand as quickly as her sister did. I'll probably start her off in mid-season but she's certainly worth a mention"*.

R MILLMAN

762 - ADANTINO * [75]   b.c. Glory Of Dancer – Sweet Whisper (Petong).
April 14. Third foal. 13,000Y. Doncaster St Leger.
Half-brother to the fairly useful 5f (at 2 yrs) and 6f winner Blue Velvet (by Formidable) and to the fair 3-y-o 6f all-weather winner So Willing (by Keen). The dam, a modest 2-y-o 5f and 6f winner, is a half-sister to three other 2-y-o winners. The second dam, Softly Spoken (by Mummy's Pet), a quite useful sprint winner of 7 races from 2 to 5 yrs, was a half-sister to 3 winners. (Tarka Racing Two). *"A very strong, muscular colt bought by the people who own Factual Lad, he'll be out in May but will stay much further than five furlongs in time. His aim would be the Doncaster sales race"*.

763 - FIELLA (IRE) * [66]   b.c. Petorius – Creggan Vale Lass (Simply Great).
April 22. 15,000Y. Doncaster St Leger.
Brother to the unraced 2000 2-y-o Room To Room Value and to the quite useful 2000 3-y-o dual 1m winner Keltech Gold and half-brother to a winner in Turkey by Ile de Chypre. The dam is an unplaced

half-sister to 7 minor winners here and abroad. The second dam, Silk Trade (by Auction Ring), is an unraced half-sister to 2 minor winners. (Mrs G Dormer). *"A nice, strong colt. He'll start over five furlongs in May and will probably get seven later on. I've got 23 2-y-o's this year and they're a better quality lot than previously".*

---

764 - MAKTAVISH ** [72]
b.c. Makbul – La Belle Vie (Indian King).
February 12. Fifth foal.

Half-brother to the fair 2000 1m placed 2-y-o Flamme de la Vie (by Blushing Flame) and to the fairly useful 3-y-o dual 5f winner Paradise Lane (by Alnasr Alwasheek). The dam, a fair 6f and 7f winner, is a half-sister to several winners out of the Irish 5f to 1m winner Engage (by Whistling Wind). (Mr Robin Lawson). *"A very strong colt, he's already won his maiden and I'm aiming him at the National Stakes at Sandown and then hopefully the Norfolk Stakes at Royal Ascot. His brother Paradise Lane was fast but highly strung and this colt won't get further than six furlongs".*

---

765 - PRINCE ATRAF ** [70]
b.c. Atraf – Forest Fantasy (Rambo Dancer).
March 8. First foal. 30,000Y. Doncaster St Leger.

The dam, a modest 8.2f and 9f winner, is a half-sister to 4 winners including the US Grade 3 winner Imperial Star. The second dam, Another Treat (by Derring-Do), a fairly useful middle-distance winner of 2 races, is a half-sister to 2 winners. (Mr H Gooding). *"A really nice colt, he's big and strong and although he made hard work of his win at Nottingham I'm aiming him at a six furlong conditions event and then hopefully the Coventry Stakes".*

---

766 - WHITBARROW (IRE) * [69]
b.c. Royal Abjar – Danccini (Dancing Dissident).
February 25. First foal. IR32,000Y. Tattersalls Fairyhouse.

The dam, a minor Irish 2-y-o 5f winner, is a half-sister to 2 minor winners. The second dam, Fantoccini (by Taufan), is a placed half-sister to 5 winners in Ireland and abroad. *"A really compact, nice-looking horse, he's well-balanced and would suit somewhere like Chester or Epsom. He'll start off over five furlongs in early May and wouldn't stay beyond six".*

T MILLS

---

767 - FOOLS RUSH IN (IRE) [79]
b.c. Entrepreneur – Blinding (High Top).
January 30. Fifth foal. 200,000Y. Tattersalls Houghton.

Half-brother to the fairly useful 1995 2-y-o 5f winner and listed-placed High Priority (by Marju) and to a winner in Denmark (by Caerleon). The dam, unplaced on both her efforts at 3 yrs, is a half-sister to the Group 3 7.3f Hungerford Stakes, Group 3 7f Kiveton Park Stakes and Group 3 7f Beeswing Stakes winner Hadeer. The second dam, Glinting (by Crepello), won over 6f at 2 yrs, was placed in the Nell Gwyn Stakes and is a half-sister to the dams and grandams of numerous good winners including Bassenthwaite, Braashee, Ghariba and Keen Hunter. (Mrs B B Mills). *"A lovely horse, he's matured very well and I think he's going to make up into a lovely 3-y-o although he'll probably have a run or two this year".*

---

768 - FRANKIES DREAM (IRE) [93]
b.c. Grand Lodge – Galyph (Lyphard).
March 16. Third foal. IR£80,000Y. Goffs Orby.

Half-brother to the 3-y-o Echo Canyon (by Lahib). The dam, a modest Irish 10f winner at 4 yrs, is a half-sister to 2 minor winners. The second dam, Galexcel (by Exceller), is a placed half-sister to the US Grade 3 winner Oilfield, the French listed winner Beaconaire (herself dam of the US Grade 1 winner Sabin and the Musidora Stakes winner Fatah Flare) and the US Grade 2 winner Kittiwake (dam of the champion US filly Miss Oceana, the Prix Jean-Prat winner Kitwood and the US Grade 2 winner Larida). *"Developing all the time, he's coming on nicely and will want seven furlongs this year".*

---

769 - INCLINE (IRE) * [89]
b.c. Danehill – Shalwar Kameez (Sadler's Wells).
March 22. First foal. IR£90,000Y. Goffs Orby.

The dam is an unraced sister to the useful 7f to 14f winner and Group 1 Prix Marcel Boussac third Family Tradition. The second dam, Sequel (by Law Society), was third over 1m and fourth over 12f in Ireland as a 3-y-o. She is a half-sister to I Will Follow (the dam of Rainbow Quest), Slightly Dangerous (the dam of Commander in Chief, Warning, Dushyantor, Deploy and Yashmak) and Idyllic (the dam of Scenic). (Mrs P Merrick). *"He'll make a 2-y-o alright as he's a sharp sort and he's pleasing us in his work. He'll start off in May over five furlongs but might stay seven later on".*

770 - LEWIS ISLAND (IRE) * [89]   b.c. Turtle Island – Phyllode (Pharly).
February 27. Third foal. IR£60,000Y. Goffs Orby.
Brother to the quite useful 2000 2-y-o dual 1m winner Leatherback and half-brother to the fair 1998 2-y-o 6f winner College Dean (by College Chapel). The dam, placed once over 14f from 3 runs, is a half-sister to 8 winners including the useful 10.5f winner Catawba (dam of the Group 1 12f Yorkshire Oaks winner Catchascatchcan) and the Ribblesdale Stakes winner Strigida. The third dam, Catalpa (by Reform), also won the Ribblesdale. *"A big, strapping horse that will be suited by seven furlongs with cut in the ground".*

771 - LONG AGO * [92]   b.c. Exit To Nowhere – Shy Minstrel (The Minstrel).
March 3. Fifth foal. 100,000Y. Tattersalls October.
Half-brother to the 2000 2-y-o Group 3 1m Prix d'Aumale winner Green Minstrel (by Green Tune) and to 2 minor 3-y-o winners in Italy (by Highest Honor) and France (by Houston). The dam, a dual winner in the USA and Grade 2 placed, is a half-sister to 2 minor winners. The second dam, Shy Bride (by Blushing Groom), won 5 races including a minor stakes in the USA, is a half-sister to the Somerville Tattersall Stakes winner Imperial Frontier and is out of the French Group 3 winner Hartebeest (herself a half-sister to the US Grade 1 winners Musical Lark and Spark Of Life). *"He's maturing steadily and no buttons have been pressed yet but he should make a 2-y-o over six furlongs or more".*

772 - MOPPY MAY (IRE) ** [73]   b.f. Alhaarth – Lacinia (Groom Dancer).
April 28. Second foal. IR£42,000Y. Goffs Challenge.
The dam, an Irish 6f (at 2 yrs) and 11f winner, was fourth in the listed Leopardstown One Thousand Guineas Trial and is a half-sister to one winner. The second dam, Pretty Lady (by High Top), won the listed 6f Cock Of The North Stakes and is a half-sister to the listed 10f Sir Charles Clore Memorial Stakes winner Pilot Bird and the listed winner and Group 1 1m Racing Post Trophy second Mack The Knife. (Mr J E Harley). *"She's very sharp indeed. We've just let her grow up and develop a bit but she'll be a sharp 2-y-o over five furlongs, maybe six furlongs at the most".*

773 - WHERE OR WHEN (IRE) * [71]   ch.c. Danehill Dancer – Future Past (Super Concorde).
January 27. Seventh foal. 26,000Y. Tattersalls October.
Half-brother to the 3-y-o Lime Hill Honey (by Topanoora), to the smart 10f and 12f winner and Group 1 St Leger fourth All The Way (by Shirley Heights), the useful triple 10f winner Just In Time (by Night Shift), the 1997 French 3-y-o 1m winner Fluorescence (by Alzao) and the Spanish winner Kubrick (by Mt. Livermore). The dam, a winner of 4 races at up to 9f in the USA, is a half-sister to 8 winners including the dam of the Group 1 10f Prix Saint-Alary winner Air de Rien. The second dam, Afasheen (by Sheshoon), is a placed sister to the Prix de Minerve winner Flaming Heart (herself dam of the Prix Jean Prat winner Maroun) and a half-sister to dam of Blushing Groom. *"A lovely horse that will have a career over seven furlongs or further. He's a big, strapping colt".*

774 - WHITE LEDGER (IRE) ** [70]   ch.c. Ali-Royal – Boranwood (Exhibitioner).
March 14. Fourth foal. 30,000Y. Tattersalls October.
Half-brother to the useful 2000 2-y-o 6f winner and Group 2 6f Richmond Stakes third Ceepio (by Pennekamp) and to the quite useful 1999 2-y-o 5f winner Pegasus Star (by Lycius). The dam, a 2-y-o 6f winner at the Curragh, is a sister to the Group 3 5f Ballyogan Stakes winner Wicked Folly. The second dam, Glencoe Lights (by Laser Light), won 7 races including the listed 5f Goffs Stakes and is a sister to the listed winner Lucinda Light (herself dam of the US Grade 1 winner Granacus). (Mrs C Stephens). *"A medium-sized horse, he's quite sharp and doing some pleasing work at the moment. He should be racing sometime in May and looks a five to six furlong type 2-y-o".*

W MUIR

775 - BARBOUSATE NADIA ** [72]   b.f. Wolfhound – Sarabah (Ela-Mana-Mou).
April 28. Sixth foal.
Closely related to the useful 5f to 6f winner Cryhavoc, to the useful 7f to 9f winner Ice, a 7f winner in Germany (all by Polar Falcon) and the fairly useful 2000 2-y-o 7f winner Saratov (by Rudimentary) and half-sister to the German 1m and 9f winner Manguista (by Shareef Dancer). The dam, a quite useful 10f winner, is a half-sister to 3 winners including the very smart triple Group 2 1m winner Gothenburg. The second dam, Be Discreet (by Junius), won 5 races in France at up to 7f and is a half-sister to 9

winners including the US Grade 3 winner Kirov Premiere and the French Group 2 placed Theatre Critic. (Sheikh Al Dahlawi). *"A home-bred and a half-sister to lots of winners, she's a very sharp filly and could be pretty smart".*

776 - DOMINION ROSE (USA) [59]　　　　b.br.f. Spinning World – Louju (Silver Hawk).
January 12. First foal. IR£110,000Y. Goffs Orby.
The dam is an unraced half-sister to 8 winners including the US stakes winner At Full Feather and the Group 2 Beresford Stakes fourth Thameen. The second dam, Secretarial Queen (by Secretariat), won 3 races including a stakes event in the USA and was second in the Grade 1 Hollywood Oaks. She is a half-sister to 4 winners including the US Graded stakes winners Nicosia, Rastafarian and Tisab. (Mr C L A Edginton). *"A filly we bought for middle-distances although her pedigree suggests she may be more of a miler. She would take time so I won't rush her as we want a nice filly for the paddocks. She goes well, moves well but despite her early foaling date she's not mature and we'll just give her one or two runs this year".*

777 - GLOBAL POWER (IRE) [64]　　　　ch.c. Spinning World – Petroleuse (Habitat).
April 10. Twelfth foal. FF1,400,000. Deauville August.
Half-brother to the Grade 2 12f Long Island Handicap and listed 10f Prix Charles Laffitte winner Peinture Bleue (by Alydar and herself dam of the Prix de l'Arc de Triomphe winner Peintre Celebre), to the US Grade 3 1m William P Kyne Handicap winner Provins (by Chief's Crown), the Irish 2-y-o winner and Group 3 Gladness Stakes second Chateau Royal (by Personal Hope) and the Group 3 11f Andre Baboin winner Parme (by Blushing Groom). The dam won the Group 3 8.5f Princess Elizabeth Stakes and the 6f Blue Seal Stakes and is a half-sister to Pawneese (winner of the King George VI and Queen Elizabeth Stakes, the Oaks and the Prix de Diane). The second dam, Plencia (by Le Haar), won the listed Prix de l'Elevage and is a half-sister to the King George winner Montaval. (Mr M J Caddy). *"Like the Spinning World filly, this colt will want time. He moves beautifully and has a fantastic pedigree. I would think he could be a hell of a horse but not until the back-end and next year".*

778 - IMPELLER (IRE) * [87]　　　　ch.c. Polish Precedent – Almaaseh (Dancing Brave).
May 14. Sixth foal. 21,000Y. Tattersalls October.
Half-brother to the unraced 2000 2-y-o Trillium (by Sadler's Wells), the very useful Group 3 5f Curragh Stakes and Group 3 5f Molecomb Stakes winner Almaty (by Dancing Dissident), the useful 10f winner and listed-placed Salee (by Caerleon) and the fair 6f winner Sarah Stokes (by Brief Truce). The dam, placed once over 6f at 3 yrs, is a half-sister to 5 winners including the very useful listed 1m Garnet Stakes winner and Coronation Stakes second Hasbah. The second dam, Al Bahathri (by Blushing Groom), won the Irish One Thousand Guineas and is a half-sister to the US Grade 2 winner Geraldine's Store. (Mr D G Clarke). *"Despite his late foaling date and the fact that he's by a sire not known for producing 2-y-o's, you can tell already he has natural ability. I'll take my time with him and introduce him at the back-end of the season. A horse with a huge amount of talent".*

779 - JAHANGIR ** [66]　　　　b.c. Zamindar – Imperial Jade (Lochnager).
March 31. Twelfth foal. IR£32,000Y. Tattersalls October.
Half-brother to the modest 2000 5f placed 2-y-o Copy-Cat (by Lion Cavern) and to 7 winners including the very useful Averti, winner of the Group 3 5f King George Stakes, the German listed winner Indian Lake (by Kings Lake) and the fairly useful 7f winners My Valentina, Hawaash (both by Royal Academy) and Royal Jade (by Last Tycoon). The dam, a useful sprint winner of 4 races and second in the Group 2 Lowther Stakes, is a sister to the Greenlands Stakes, Palace House Stakes and Temple Stakes winner Reesh and a half-sister to the useful listed winner Tadwin (herself dam of the Queen Mary Stakes winner Nadwah). The second dam, Songs Jest (by Song), is an unraced half-sister to the dams of the smart sprinters Jester and Fayruz. (Percipatious Punters Racing Club). *"I think he's the best from this family since Averti. I've trained most of them and I know not to rush him but he does everything perfect. He also has lucky owners – so that's always a good sign! In common with my two other Zamindar's this fellow has got speed".*

780 - JUST THE TRICK (USA) ** [65]　　　　b.br.f. Phone Trick – Tammi's Pal (Lear Fan).
February 27. Third reported foal. 34,000Y. Tattersalls October.
Closely related to a minor winner in the USA by Clever Trick and half-sister to another by Manila. The dam won 5 races in the USA including 2 minor stakes events and is a half-sister to 5 winners including the minor US stakes winner Majestic Nasr. The second dam, Debrah (by Dactylographer), is an

unplaced half-sister to 7 minor winners. (Mr C L A Edginton). *"She's very strong and moves well. An early type, she's shown she's got plenty of speed and I think a lot of her at the moment".*

781 - MOUNTSORRELL (IRE) ** [62]   b.c. Charnwood Forest – Play The Queen (King Of Clubs).
March 18. Sixth foal. 32,000Y. Doncaster St Leger.

Half-brother to the fairly useful 6f (at 2 yrs) to 1m winner Salty Jack (by Salt Dome), to the quite useful 1998 2-y-o 5f winner Franco Mina (by Lahib), the fair 1997 2-y-o 6f all-weather winner Oh Never Again and the Swedish winner Windy Walkie (both by Ballad Rock). The dam, a winner over 7f in Ireland at 3 yrs, is out of the Group 2 1m Coronation Stakes and Group 3 7f Athasi Stakes winner Orchestration (by Welsh Pageant), herself a half-sister to the Group 2 Prix d'Harcourt winner Welsh Term and to the dam of the French Two Thousand Guineas winner Victory Note. (Delemere Partnership). *"A strong 2-y-o type, he will certainly be a 2-y-o and is a fantastic individual to look at. Strong and robust, I haven't tried him highly yet but I love him and he could be anything".*

782 - NIGHTWATCHMAN (IRE) * [86]   b.c. Hector Protector – Nightlark (Night Shift).
January 19. First foal. IR£75,000Y. Goffs Orby.

The dam, a quite useful 12.3f winner, is a half-sister to 6 winners including the Grade 2 American Derby winner Overbury. The second dam, Overcall (by Bustino), a winning Irish middle-distance stayer, is a half-sister to 9 winners including the dam of the Melbourne Cup winner Vintage Crop. (Troublefree Partnership). *"The loveliest horse you'll ever wish to see – a gorgeous old-fashioned type of horse. He should be ready for the mid-summer onwards and I do think he's a seriously nice colt. Big, strong and robust with fantastic bone. He has a similar head to Henry Cecil's good filly Bosra Sham and is a very strong, bold horse for later in the year and as a 3-y-o".*

783 - ZAKAT (FR) * [60]   b.c. Zamindar – Rose Douceur (Polish Precedent).
January 26. Third foal. FF220,000. Deauville August.

The dam won once in France at 3 yrs and is a half-sister to 2 winners. The second dam, Indian Rose (by General Holme), won the Group 1 12f Prix Vermeille and is a half-sister to the Group 1 Prix Ganay winner Vert Amande, the Group 1 Grand Prix de Paris winner Le Nain Jaune, to two other good winners in Mulberry and Woolskin and to the French middle-distance winner Featherhill - herself dam of the top-class Group 1 10.5f Prix Lupin winner Groom Dancer. *"A bigger type than my other two Zamindar's, he's shown me plenty and goes up the gallops as well as anything but he's a big horse that moves well and has a tough attitude. He'll need a bit of time so I won't rush him".*

784 - ZARGUS ** [62]   b.c. Zamindar – My First Romance (Danehill).
January 11. Third foal. 110,000Y. Tattersalls October.

Half-brother to the 2000 2-y-o Group 3 5f Queen Mary Stakes winner Romantic Myth (by Mind Games) and the useful 2-y-o 5f winner Power Packed (by Puissance). The dam ran twice unplaced and is a half-sister to 3 minor winners. The second dam, Front Line Romance (by Caerleon), won once and was Group 3 placed over 1m at 2 yrs in Ireland and is a sister to the triple Italian Group 3 winner Knight Line Dancer. (Mrs M Bruce-Copp). *"A strong colt that shows a lot of speed, he's had a very slight setback but that won't detract from him. A pretty smart chap, he will run and do well this year and I have quite high hopes for him".*

785 - ZYZANIA [70]   b.f. Zafonic – Moneefa (Darshaan).
May 6. Third foal. 26,000Y. Tattersalls October.

Half-sister to the 3-y-o Dandoun (by Halling). The dam, a fair 10f winner, is a half-sister to 6 winners including the Group 3 5f Duke Of York Stakes second Garah. The second dam, Abha (by Thatching), a very smart 5f and 6f winner of 4 races, was fourth in the Group 1 5f Kings Stand Stakes and is a half-sister to the listed Princess Margaret Stakes winner Sarissa. (Dr & Mrs J Wilson). *"A late foal, she's done exceptionally well since we bought her. She's had a little break and is only just back in training although there are no plans to rush her at all".*

786 - UNNAMED * [86]   ch.f. Selkirk – Surfing (Grundy).
March 14. Eighth foal. IR£135,000Y. Goffs Orby.

Half-sister to the useful 6f to 9.4f all-weather winner and subsequent US Grade 3 All American Handicap winner Mister Fire Eyes (by Petorius), to the very useful 12f French winner and listed placed Abou Eltawarek, the hurdles winner Sea Breaker (both by Glow), the Hong Kong listed winner Bumper Storm (by Great Commotion) and a winner in Sweden by Lake Coniston. The dam, a fair 7f placed maiden, is a sister to the Group 3 Prix d'Arenberg winner Glancing and a half-sister to the Group 1 Middle Park Stakes winner Bassenthwaite. The second dam, Splashing (by Petingo), won the Group 3 5f Cornwallis Stakes and is a half-sister to the dams of the Group winners Hadeer, Bay Street and Rose Of Montreaux. (Mr M J Caddy). *"She's really nice and goes exceptionally well. I call her my Queen Mary filly so I obviously think a lot of her. She's a really nice, striking filly and her movement is fantastic – she just glides. I haven't tried her out but I just know she'll have speed – she's just one of those that tells you. She oozes class, has a grand body on her and is a strong filly. You could mistake her for being a colt she's so strong. Definitely a 2-y-o".*

J NOSEDA

787 - DISTANT MIST (USA) * [80]

ch.c. Distant View – Sage Mist (Capote).
April 4. Third foal. 82,000Y. Tattersalls October.

The dam, a minor winner in the USA at 3 yrs, is a half-sister to 3 winners and to the unraced dam of 3 US stakes winners. The second dam, Reckoning (by Olden Times), is a placed sister to the US Grade 1 Norfolk Stakes winner Roving Boy and a half-sister to the dam of the US Grade 1 winner A Wild Ride. *"Already a winner at Lingfield on the all-weather, he's grown a little bit now and the plan is to run him sometime in the middle of May and move on from there".*

788 - EARTH STAR (IRE) ** [80]

b.c. Entrepreneur – Well Bought (Auction Ring).
March 28. Fifth foal. 100,000Y. Tattersalls October.

Half-brother to the smart 2000 2-y-o Tamburlaine (by Royal Academy), winner of a 1m maiden and second in the Group 1 1m Racing Post Trophy. The dam, a poor 7f and 1m placed maiden, is a half-sister to 6 winners including the Group 2 12f King Edward VII Stakes winner Open Day and the Group 3 1m Prix La Rochette winner River Knight. The second dam, Knighton House (by Pall Mall), won the Prix de la Calonne, was second in the Coronation Stakes and is a half-sister to the Champion Stakes winner Reform. *"A big, quite backward horse, he's going to take a bit of time but has all the attributes to make a racehorse. He moves well and I like him".*

789 - GOLD ACE (USA) ** [85]

ch.c. Gulch – Najecam (Trempolino).
March 13. First foal. $155,000Y. Keeneland September.

The dam won 6 races in the USA from 2 to 5 yrs, was placed in both the Grade 2 Princess Stakes and the Grade 2 San Clemente Handicap and is a sister to the French winner and listed-placed Lady Ilsley. The second dam, Sue Warner (by Forli), is an unraced half-sister to the Group 2 Prix Maurice de Gheest winner Beaudelaire out of the champion 2-y-o filly Bitty Girl (by Habitat). *"He's done a few bits of work, is a good, solid type and he'll make a 2-y-o over six or seven furlongs".*

790 - GOLDEN SONATA (USA) * [83]

b.f. Mr Prospector – Elissa Beethoven (Royal Academy).
February 16. Second foal. $300,000Y (NOT SOLD) Keeneland September.

The dam is an unplaced half-sister to the Group 3 7f C L Weld Park Stakes winner Shy Ninski (dam of the US stakes winner and dual Grade 2 placed Vinista) and to the grandam of the Group 1 winners Hernando and Johann Quatz. The second dam, Pass A Glance (by Buckpasser), a smart middle-distance performer, was placed in three Grade 1 events in the USA. *"This filly has changed a lot since the sales where she was rather 'blocky'. She's now got some length and has grown a bit. One for the late summer and early autumn. When we spoke at this time last year I was very despondent about my 2-y-o's because I felt they lacked quality. This year I believe they're a different proposition".*

791 - HIGH ROCK HENRY (IRE) * [88]

ch.c. Pennekamp – Belsay (Belmez).
February 1. First foal. 42,000Y. Tattersalls October.

The dam ran unplaced twice and is a half-sister to 4 winners including the Group 3 7f Nell Gwyn Stakes winner and One Thousand Guineas third Crystal Gazing. The second dam, Crystal Bright (by Bold Lad, Ire), won once in the USA and is a half-sister to 4 minor winners. *"A strong individual and a good mover, he should be on the track in early June. I think he's a solid horse that will do a job as a 2-y-o. I actually bought this horse because he reminded me a bit of my good 2-y-o of last year, Hurricane Floyd. He's a nice, athletic type".*

792 - INDIAN COUNTRY * [105]**   ch.c. Indian Ridge – Arethusa (Primo Dominie).
February 18. First foal. 88,000Y. Tattersalls October.
The dam was a useful winner of the listed 6f Sirenia Stakes at 2 yrs and was second in the Group 2 6f Lowther Stakes. The second dam, Downeaster Alexa (by Red Ryder), won 2 races at 2 yrs over 5f, was second in the Group 3 Shernazar 5f Curragh Stakes and is a half-sister to 3 winners. *"Quite a backward individual but he moves well and has a bit of quality. A July/August type 2-y-o with potential"*.

793 - JACK THE TRACK (IRE) * [92]   b.c. Barathea – Babushka (Dance Of Life).
February 6. Fourth foal. 42,000Y. Tattersalls October.
Half-brother to the fairly useful 2000 10f to 12.3f winner Julius (by Persian Bold) and to the fair 1997 2-y-o 5f winner Dancing Icon (by Mujtahid). The dam, an Irish 2-y-o 1m winner, is a half-sister to 4 winners including the Irish listed-placed St Ame. The second dam, Warm December (by He Loves Me), won once at 3 yrs and is a half-sister to the Queen Anne Stakes and Lockinge Stakes winner Then Again. *"A nice mover but quite backward and one for the second half of the season"*.

794 - JUST JAMES * [78]   b.c. Spectrum – Fairy Flight (Fairy King).
March 30. First foal. 80,000Y. Tattersalls October.
The dam, a 2-y-o 6f winner in Ireland, was listed-placed and is a sister to the useful dual 6f winner King Of The East and a half-sister to the French listed 10.5f winner Titled Ascent and the Irish listed winning sprinter Northern Tide. The second dam, Rising Tide (by Red Alert), was a useful 2-y-o 5f winner and a half-sister to 5 winners including the Group 1 Heinz "57" Phoenix Stakes winner King Persian. *"A backward 2-y-o at present but he moves well"*.

795 - LASCOMBES ** [85]   b.c. Bluebird – Arinaga (Warning).
March 6. First foal. 110,000Y. Tattersalls October.
The dam, a winner at 2 yrs in Norway, is a half-sister to 6 winners here and abroad. The second dam, Brillante (by Green Dancer), won the listed 11f Prix de la Seine, was second in the Group 3 10.5f Prix de Royaumont and is a half-sister to 7 winners including Bellman (Group 2 Prix Eugene Adam), Bellypha (Group 3 Prix Daphnis) and the Peruvian Grade 1 winner Run And Deliver. *"Quite a lazy horse but he definitely has ability and is a possible Royal Ascot 2-y-o. He's a strong, hardy colt that will be effective at five and six furlongs"*.

796 - LEGGY LOU (IRE) ** [78]   b.f. Mujadil – Alzeam (Alzao).
February 19. Fourth foal. IR£50,000Y. Goffs Orby.
Sister to the fairly useful 1999 2-y-o 6f winner Dashing Duke and half-sister to the poor 2000 6f placed 2-y-o Rachel Green and the Italian 3-y-o winner Armaren (both by Case Law). The dam, a poor middle-distance placed maiden, is a half-sister to 2 minor winners. The second dam, Classic Beam (by Cut Above), is a placed half-sister to Welsh Flame (grandam of numerous Group winners including Flame of Tara - herself dam of the top-class pair Salsabil and Marju) and to the dam of the Graded stakes winners Bourbon Boy and Electric Society. *"My plan was to run her early but because of the bad spring she hasn't come to herself yet. She's a nice, athletic, scopey filly and hopefully she'll be ready for action in early May. Six furlongs would probably be her ideal trip"*.

797 - LOUIS GEORGIO ** [74]   b.c. Royal Applause – Swellegant (Midyan).
March 21. Fifth foal. 80,000Y. Tattersalls October.
Half-brother to the fairly useful 2000 2-y-o 6f winner Racina (by Bluebird), to the useful 5f and 6f (including all-weather) winner Dil (by Primo Dominie) and a winner over hurdles by Pursuit Of Love. The dam, a quite useful 2-y-o 5f winner, is a half-sister to 5 winners including the Group 2 5f Prix du Gros-Chene winner Millyant, the Group 2 5f Flying Childers Stakes winner Prince Sabo and the Irish listed 2-y-o winner Bold Jessie (herself dam of the Gimcrack Stakes winner Abou Zouz). The second dam, Jubilee Song (by Song), a fair 3-y-o 5f winner, is a half-sister to 7 winners including the listed-placed Band On The Run and Shark Song. *"He was a colt I planned to have an early campaign with, but he didn't quite come to hand early on. He should start working in May and looks a 2-y-o sprint prospect"*.

798 - MELLOW PARK (IRE) *** [80]
b.f. In The Wings – Park Special (Relkino).
January 28.

Sister to the Group 1 12f Italian Derby, Group 2 7f Lanson Champagne Stakes and German Group 2 12f winner Central Park and half-sister to the very useful Group 2 6f Lowther Stakes and 3-y-o listed 10f winner Velvet Moon (by Shaadi) and the quite useful 2-y-o 7.5f winner Majal (by Caerleon). The dam won over 10f at 3 yrs in Ireland and is a half-sister to the useful 2-y-o winners Careafolie and Gouriev and the smart French 2-y-o winner Pantile. The second dam, Balilla (by Balidar), won over 5f at 2 yrs and is a half-sister to the useful 6f and 1m winning filly Leipzig and to Krakow - herself dam of the good winners Braashee and Ghariba. *"A filly I'm being patient with at present. I like her and she definitely has ability. I'll kick on with her when she tells me she's ready to go. She's a very nice filly".* Significant sire/damsire crosses:- Central Park.

799 - MONTEX (USA) ** [87]
ch.c. Royal Academy – Omara (Storm Cat).
April 1. First foal. 180,000Y. Tattersalls Houghton.

The dam, a quite useful 9.7f and 10f winner, is closely related to the US Grade 3 winner Trafalger and a half-sister to the listed 6f Sirenia Stakes winner Santolina and the listed Atalanta Stakes winner Etizaaz. The second dam, Alamosa (by Alydar), is an unraced half-sister to the top-class middle-distance colt Swain and to the Group 3 Prix de Conde winner Thief Of Hearts. *"A good, strong type that moves well and I like him. He's a July type 2-y-o that seems to take more after the damsire Storm Cat than Royal Academy. He just seems to have those typical Storm Cat attributes of a great top line and plenty of strength. One to follow".*

800 - PRAIRIE DUNES (IRE) *** [89]
br.c. Indian Ridge – Ceide Dancer (Alzao).
February 4. Third foal. IRE80,000Y. Goffs Orby.

Brother to the 2000 Italian placed 2-y-o Indiana Max. The dam, a winner over 8.5f in Ireland at 3 yrs, is a half-sister to the very smart sprinter Lavinia Fontana (by Sharpo), winner of the Group 1 6f Haydock Sprint Cup. The second dam, Belle Origine (by Exclusive Native), a minor winner over 9.5f at 3 yrs in France, is a half-sister to the French listed stakes winners Bel Sorel and My Volga Boatman. *"A strong, athletic type and I think he's a solid individual and a July type 2-y-o. He has the make and shape to be a decent type".*

801 - PRISA (USA) ** [83]
b.f. Danehill – Cantonese (Easy Goer).
April 11.

The dam, a fair 2-y-o 7f winner, is a sister to 2 winners and a half-sister to the useful 10.2f winner Private Song. The second dam, Queen Of Song (by His Majesty), won 14 races in the USA including the Grade 2 8.5f Shuvee Handicap and the Grade 3 8.5f Sixty Sails Handicap (twice), was third in the Grade 1 Apple Blossom Handicap and is a sister to the Grade 1 Jersey Derby winner Cormorant. *"A small filly that lacks a bit of scope, she should be ready to run in May and is quite capable of winning".*

802 - PROCRASTINATOR (IRE) [92]
b.c. Zafonic – Salvora (Spectacular Bid).
April 4.

Half-brother to the Grade 1 Yellow Ribbon Invitational winner Aube Indienne (by Bluebird), to the French listed 10.5f winner Raissonable, the minor French winner Spenderella (both by Common Grounds), the modest 2-y-o 6f and subsequent Brazilian listed winner Special Gallery, the minor French winner Valsora (both by Tate Gallery) and the French winner of 13 minor races Fuente Mayor (by Ti King). The dam won over 10f in France and is a half-sister to the US stakes winner Smackover Creek and to the dams of the Australian triple Grade 1 winner Flying Spur and the US Grade 2 winner Fit To Lead. The second dam, Grand Luxe (by Sir Ivor), is a stakes winner of 10 races in Canada and the USA and a half-sister to the Grade 1 winners L'Enjoleur, La Voyageuse and Medaille d'Or. (Niarchos Family). *"A very backward colt. The plan would just be to give him one run at the back-end of the season".*

803 - RISTRA (USA) ** [78]
b.f. Kingmambo – Rhetorical Lass (Capote).
January 30. Second foal. $100,000Y. Keeneland September.

The dam is a half-sister to 7 winners including the smart Reloy, winner of the Group 3 10.5f Prix de Royaumont and two Grade 1 events in the USA, the French Group 2 Prix du Conseil de Paris winner En Calcat, the smart French 1m winner Reine Imperiale and the French Group 2 placed Roi Guillaume. The third dam, the top-class filly Rescousse (by Emerson), won the 10.5f Prix de Diane and was second in the Prix de l'Arc de Triomphe behind San San. *"A very athletic filly, the plan would be to run her when the six furlong races start after mid-May. I think she's a nice prospect".*

804 - SEFTON LODGE * [95]   b.c. Barathea – Pine Needle (Kris).
February 17. Second foal. 65,000Y. Tattersalls October.
Half-brother to Dumaran (by Be My Chief), unplaced in one start at 2 yrs in 2000. The dam, a fairly useful 8.2f (at 2 yrs) to 14f winner, is a half-sister to 7 winners including the listed 12f Galtres Stakes winner Nibbs Point (herself dam of the Two Thousand Guineas and Derby third Border Arrow). The second dam, Fanny's Cove (by Mill Reef), a fairly useful 10f winner, is a half-sister to 3 winners including the Galtres Stakes winner Hymettus. *"A very nice colt I'm delighted with. He had a setback which has put him behind schedule so the plans no longer include Royal Ascot, but he's a good mover and is a June type 2-y-o".*

805 - SILENT CRYSTAL (USA) * ** [82]   ch.f. Diesis – Starlight Way (Green Dancer).
March 21. Third foal. $160,000Y. Keeneland September.
The dam, a stakes-placed winner of 6 races in the USA at 3 and 5 yrs, is a half-sister to the champion sprinter Moorestyle, winner of the July Cup, the Prix de la Foret and the Prix de l'Abbaye. The second dam, Guiding Star (by Reliance II), won at 4 yrs in England and is a half-sister to 2 winners. *"A typical Diesis, she's quite a narrow, athletic filly. I like her and she'll be an August type 2-y-o over seven furlongs".*
Significant sire/damsire crosses:- Halling.

806 - STAR OF NORMANDIE (USA) * [88]   b.f. Gulch – Depaze (Deputy Minister).
February 12. Fourth foal. FF400,000Y. Deauville August.
The dam is an unraced half-sister to 4 winners including the French Two Thousand Guineas and 10.5f Prix Lupin winner Fast Topaze. The second dam, Pink Topaze (by Djakao), is an unplaced half-sister to the French 2,000 Guineas winner Blue Tom, the Champion sprinter Amber Rama and the Prix Eugene Adam winner Timmy My Boy. *"A tall, lengthy filly that moves well. She's got a lot of scope and is a July type 2-y-o. I'm happy with her progress".*

807 - TAINWELL * [64]   ch.c. Most Welcome – Mountain Lodge (Blakeney).
May 27. Fourteenth foal. 75,000Y. Tattersalls October.
Half-brother to the quite useful 2000 2-y-o 7f winner Mayville Thunder (by Zilzal), to the 1999 Group 3 12f Gordon Stakes winner Compton Ace (by Pharly), the Belgian listed winner Turbine Blade (by Kings Lake), the useful 12f and hurdles winner Uluru (by Kris), the modest 2m winner Mountain Willow (by Doyoun) and a winner in Italy by Shirley Heights. The dam won 5 races including the Irish St Leger and the Cesarewitch Handicap and is a half-sister to 3 winners. The second dam, Fiddledee (by Eyewash), won once at 3 yrs, was third in the Park Hill Stakes and was a half-sister to 10 winners including the Park Hill Stakes winner Collyria and the Fred Darling Stakes winner Sijui. *"He's quite an active individual and has pleasantly surprised me how well he's done for a late foal. He'll run this year and looks the type of horse that would be capable of winning a mile maiden in the latter part of the year".*

808 - TAROUDANT (IRE) [86]   b.f. Danehill – Taibhseach (Secreto).
April 12. Third foal. IR£130,000Y. Goffs Orby.
Half-sister to the unraced 2000 2-y-o Theorique (by Theatrical) and to the US 3-y-o winner Woodseach (by Woodman). The dam, an Irish 2-y-o listed 7f winner, was fourth in the Group 2 10f Gallinule Stakes and is a half-sister to 5 winners including the US 10f and 12f Grade 1 winner Mi Selecto and the US Grade 2 13f Gallant Fox Handicap winner Bar Dexter. The second dam, Ribonette (by Ribot), won once at 3 yrs in the USA. *"A backward filly, she's going to be an autumn type 2-y-o".*

809 - WESTERN APPLAUSE * [72]   b.f. Royal Applause – Western Sal (Salse).
February 11. Third foal. 40,000Y. Tattersalls October.
Half-sister to the unraced 2000 2-y-o Due West (by Inchinor) and to the 1999 Italian 2-y-o winner Pemba (by First Trump). The dam, a fair 10f and 12f winner, is a half-sister to 4 winners including the smart 5f (at 2 yrs) and 7f winner Granny's Pet. The second dam, Patsy Western (by Precocious), a quite useful 3-y-o 6f winner, is a half-sister to the Queen Anne Stakes winner Mr Fluorocarbon, the Cornwallis Stakes winner Western Jewel and the dam of the Galtres Stakes winner Startino. *"I'm happy with her, although she's a little bit more backward than I expected. She should be a prospect for late June or early July".*

810 - WOODLYON (USA) * [87]** b.br.c. Woodman – Cloelia (Lyphard).
April 18. Fifth foal. 90,000Y. Tattersalls Houghton.
Brother to the Henry Cecil trained 3-y-o Wood Dalling (by Woodman), closely related to the 1999 French 2-y-o winner and Group 2 Prix Robert Papin third Finnan (by Mr Prospector) and half-brother to the 1999 French 3-y-o listed winner Passineti (by Slew O'Gold) and the 1998 French 3-y-o winner French Partner (by Seattle Song). The dam is a placed half-sister to 11 winners including the Italian Group 2 winner Proskona, the French Group 3 winner Keos and the outstanding broodmare Korveya (dam of the classic winners Bosra Sham, Hector Protector and Shanghai). The second dam, Konafa (by Damascus), won over 7f at 2 yrs, was second in the One Thousand Guineas and is a half-sister to the Yorkshire Oaks winner Awaasif (dam of the Oaks winner Snow Bride and thus grandam of Lammtarra). *"A small, active individual. He got sore shins so his introduction has been delayed until late May at the earliest. He'll do his job over six or seven furlongs this year".*
Significant sire/damsire crosses:- Fleur de Nuit (Gr 3).

811 - UNNAMED ** [75] b.c. Glitterman – Alieria (Lomond).
March 10. Fourth foal. IR£75,000Y. Goffs Orby.
Half-brother to a 3-y-o winner in South America by Affirmed. The dam, a winner at 2 yrs in France and second in the listed Prix Coronation, also won two minor races in the USA. She is a half-sister to 4 winners in Japan out of the Irish listed winner Welsh Charm (by Caerleon) - herself a half-sister to the Cheveley Park Stakes winner Woodstream and the Irish Two Thousand Guineas and Sussex Stakes winner Jaazeiro. *"He's just had a minor setback which put him a little behind schedule, but I would hope he'd be in action by mid-summer. He looks the type to do a job as a 2-y-o. Glitterman is a good solid sire of plenty of winners in America".*

812 - UNNAMED [84] b.c. Spinning World – Araadh (Blushing Groom).
May 1. Fifth foal. IR£110,000Y. Goffs Orby.
Closely related to a winner in Japan at 3 and 4 yrs by Nureyev. The dam is a placed half-sister to the listed 1m Premio Nearco winner Idle Son and to the dam of the US Grade 3 winner Solvig. The second dam, Idle Gossip (by Lyphard), a stakes winner of 5 races in the USA, is a half-sister to the US Grade 1 winners Plugged Nickle and Christiecat. *"Quite backward at the moment but a nice type of horse that moves well. One for the second half of the season".*

813 - UNNAMED ** [93] b.c. Alhaarth – Crystal City (Kris).
February 8. Fifth foal. 92,000Y. Tattersalls October.
Half-brother to the unplaced 2000 2-y-o Stoli (by Spectrum) and to the fairly useful 1998 2-y-o 5f and 6f winner Acicula (by Night Shift). The dam, a minor 10f winner at 3 yrs in France, is out of the Group 1 12f Yorkshire Oaks and Group 3 Hoover Fillies Mile winner Untold (by Final Straw) - herself a half-sister to the Yorkshire Oaks winner Sally Brown, the Group 3 Waterford Candelabra Stakes winner Shoot Clear and the dual listed winner Mohican Girl. *"A hardy colt that should win as a 2-y-o".*

814 - UNNAMED ** [83] b.c. Spinning World – Desert Jewel (Caerleon).
February 9. First foal.
The dam is an unraced sister to the Group 2 Prix Robert Papin winner and French Two Thousand Guineas third Psychobabble and a half-sister to 6 winners including the US Grade 1 Mervyn Leroy Handicap winner and Group 1 Criterium de Saint-Cloud second Louis Cyphre. The second dam, Princesse Timide (by Blushing Groom), won twice in France and was listed placed four times. *"A strong, racy colt and he'll make a 2-y-o in the latter part of May or early June".*

A O'BRIEN

815 - CENTURY CITY (IRE) * [107] b.c. Danzig – Alywow (Alysheba).
February 17. Third foal. IR£2,000,000. Goffs Orby.
Half-brother to the 3-y-o Suitably Discreet (by Mr Prospector). The dam, a champion filly in Canada, won 7 races including the Grade 3 8.5f Nijana Stakes and was second in the Grade 1 Rothmans International and the Grade 1 Flower Bowl Invitational. The second dam, Triple Wow (by Coastal), won 14 races including the Grade 3 9.5f Next Move Handicap and is a half-sister to the Ormonde Stakes winner Zilzal Zamaan.

816 - SAHARA DESERT [88]　　　　　　　　b.c. Green Desert – Apache Star (Arazi).

April 12. First foal. 140,000Y. Tattersalls Houghton.

The dam, a fairly useful 7f (at 2 yrs) to 9f winner, was listed placed twice at up to 11.4f. She is a half-sister to 3 winners including the US Grade 3 placed Duke Of Geen. The second dam, Wild Pavane (by Dancing Brave), is an unraced half-sister to 6 winners including the listed winner Nuryana (dam of the Group 1 Coronation Stakes winner Rebecca Sharp).

817 - DIAGHILEV (IRE) [82]　　　　　　　　b.c. Sadler's Wells – Darara (Top Ville).

May 5. Ninth foal. 3,400,000Y. Tattersalls Houghton.

Brother to the Group 2 12.5f Prix Maurice de Neiuil and subsequent Australian Grade 1 winner Darazari and to the winner and French Derby third Rhagaas, closely related to the minor French winner Dardjini (by Nijinsky) and half-brother to 4 winners including the listed 10.5f and 12f winner Dariyoun (by Shahrastani) and the smart 2-y-o 1m winner and Group 2 12f King Edward VII Stakes second Kilimanjaro (by Shirley Heights). The dam, a top-class filly, won the Group 1 12f Prix Vermeille and the Group 3 10f Prix de Psyche and is a half-sister to the Prix du Jockey Club winner Darshaan and the Group 2 Prix de Royallieu winner Dalara. The second dam, Delsy (by Abdos), won over 12f and was third in the Prix de Pomone.

Significant sire/damsire crosses:- Montjeu, Darazari.

818 - LINE RIDER (USA) * [106]　　　　　　　　b.c. Danzig – Freewheel (Arctic Tern).

April 6. Fourth foal. $650,000Y. Keeneland September.

Half-brother to a minor winner in the USA by Gulch. The dam, a fairly useful 6f (at 2 yrs) and 7f winner here, subsequently won 4 races in the USA including the Grade 3 9f Bewitch Stakes and is a half-sister to 6 winners. The second dam, Dinner Surprise (by Lyphard), is a placed half-sister to 11 winners including the dams of the Group/Grade 1 winners Belle Chanson, Legal Case and Malevic.

819 - MANUS MIGALUS (USA) [94]　　　　　　b.c. Boundary – Harbor Flag (Hoist The Flag).

May 25. Fifteenth foal. $625,000Y. Keeneland September.

Closely related to the US stakes winner Packet (by Polish Navy) and half-brother to 7 winners including the Grade 3 Louisiana Derby winner Country Light and the stakes-placed Vue (herself dam of the Grade 1 6f Spinaway Stakes winner Oath). The dam won once at 2 yrs in the USA. The second dam, Bayou Blue (by Bold Ruler), won at 3 yrs and is a sister to the Santa Barbara Handicap winner Batteur out of the champion 3-y-o filly Bayou.

820 - UNNAMED [90]　　　　　　　　b.br.c. Saint Ballado – Hey Janie (Seattle Slew).

May 9. Seventh foal. $525,000Y. Keeneland September.

Half-brother to 5 winners including 3 minor US winners by Concern, Ferdinand and Sovereign Dancer. The dam is an unraced half-sister to 8 winners including Broad Brush, winner of the Santa Anita Handicap, the Meadowlands Cup and the Suburban Handicap (all Grade 1 events) and the dam of the Gimcrack Stakes winner Mull Of Kintyre. The second dam, Hay Patcher (by Hoist The Flag), a stakes winner of 5 races, was third in the Grade 2 Cotillion Stakes.

821 - UNNAMED [98]　　　　　　　　b.c. Gone West – Honfleur (Sadler's Wells).

April 30. Third foal. $700,000Y. Keeneland September.

Closely related to the fairly useful 2000 3-y-o 1m winner Argentan (by Gulch) and half-brother to the modest 2000 7f placed 2-y-o St Florent (by Thunder Gulch). The dam, a useful winner of 2 races including a listed event in France over 13.5f, is a sister to the Prix de l'Arc de Triomphe winner Carnegie, closely related to the Group 2 Prix Guillaume d'Ornano winner Antisaar and a half-sister to the Group 3 St Simon Stakes winner Lake Erie. The second dam, Detroit (by Riverman), won the Prix de l'Arc de Triomphe and is a half-sister to the Cheveley Park Stakes winner Durtal (herself dam of the Ascot Gold Cup winner Gildoran).

822 - TASMANIAN TIGER (USA) * [103]　　　　　　ch.c. Storm Cat – Hum Along (Fappiano).

June 2. Seventh foal. $6,800,000Y. Keeneland September.

Closely related to the Grade 1 Breeders Cup Juvenile Fillies and Grade 1 Frizette Stakes winner Storm Song and to the minor US 2-y-o winner Hugsie (both by Summer Squall). The dam was placed at 2 yrs in the USA and is a half-sister to 7 winners. The second dam, Minstress (by The Minstrel), a stakes winner of 5 races, was Grade 3 placed and is out of the dual US Grade 3 winner Fleet Victress.

823 - DESERT EAGLE [69]   b.c. Desert King – In Full Cry (Seattle Slew).
February 5. Seventh foal. 230,000Y. Tattersalls Houghton.
Half-brother to the US stakes-placed winner of 3 races Private Seductress (by Private Account) and to a minor winner in the USA by Easy Goer. The dam, a winner of 2 races in the USA and second in the Grade 2 6f Adirondack Stakes, is a half-sister to the top-class miler Posse, to the US Grade 3 winner Late As Usual, the German Group 3 winner Hot Rodder and the dam of the Italian Group 2 winner Lonely Bird. The second dam, In Hot Pursuit (by Bold Ruler), a top 2-y-o filly in the USA in 1973 and winner of the Grade 3 Fashion Stakes at Belmont Park, is a half-sister to the top-class broodmare Bold Example (ancestress of the Group/Grade 1 winners Awe Inspiring, Culture Vulture, Polish Precedent and Zilzal).

824 - UNNAMED [95]   b.c. Sadler's Wells – Kasora (Darshaan).
March 11. Second foal. 270,000Y. Tattersalls Houghton.
The dam is an unraced sister to the Irish winner and listed-placed Korasoun and a half-sister to 6 winners including the Irish One Thousand Guineas Trial winners Kotama and Khanata and the Group 1 National Stakes, Group 1 Premio Parioli and Grade 1 Oak Tree Turf Championship placed Khoraz. The second dam, Kozana (by Kris), won the Group 2 10f Prix de Malleret and the Group 3 1m Prix de Sandringham, was third in the Prix de l'Arc de Triomphe and is a half-sister to the Prix du Cadran winner Karkour and to the dam of the Cumberland Lodge Stakes winner Kazaroun.
Significant sire/damsire crosses:- Crimson Tide, Ebadiyla, Greek Dance.

825 - UNNAMED [94]   b.c. Polish Precedent – Knight's Baroness (Rainbow Quest).
April 7. Seventh foal. 340,000Y. Tattersalls Houghton.
Brother to the high-class Riyadian, winner of the Group 3 12f Cumberland Lodge Stakes and the Group 3 12f Jockey Club Stakes and to the fairly useful 1m and 10.2f winner Idolize and half-brother to the useful 1m (at 2 yrs) and 12f winner Wales (by Caerleon). The dam, a smart filly, won over 7f (at 2 yrs) and the Irish Oaks and was placed in the Oaks, the Lingfield Oaks Trial, the Park Hill Stakes and the May Hill Stakes. The second dam, Knight's Beauty (by True Knight), won 12 races, including three stakes events, from 6.5f to 8.5f.
Significant sire/damsire crosses:- Riyadian, Shuwaib,

826 - UNNAMED [95]   b.c. Gone West – Lady Carla (Caerleon).
January 26. First foal. 775,000Y. Tattersalls Houghton.
The dam, a high-class filly, won over 1m (at 2 yrs) and the Group 1 12f Oaks and is a half-sister to a minor winner. The second dam, Shirley Superstar (by Shirley Heights), a fairly useful 2-y-o 7f winner, is a half-sister to the Duke Of York Stakes third Si Signor and the Hungerford Stakes third Moviegoer.

827 - SORCEROUS * [110]   b.c. Sadler's Wells – La Papagena (Habitat).
February 5. Ninth foal. 2,000,000Y. Tattersalls Houghton.
 Half-brother to the champion 1993 2-y-o Grand Lodge, winner of the Group 1 7f Dewhurst Stakes and the Group 1 1m St James's Palace Stakes, to the useful 1m listed winner Papabile (both by Chief's Crown) and the minor 11.5f winner Rose Noble (by Vaguely Noble). The dam is an unraced half-sister to the very useful 3-y-o 7f and 1m winner Pamina, the very useful 11f and 12.5f winner Lost Chord and the useful 11f Scottish Derby winner Eagling. The second dam, Magic Flute (by Tudor Melody), won the Cheveley Park Stakes and the Coronation Stakes and was very smart at up to 1m.

828 - BLACK MAMBO (USA) [94]   b.c. Kingmambo – Lassie's Lady (Alydar).
March 27. Twelfth foal. $1,100,000Y. Keeneland September.
Half-brother to 5 winners including the Grade 2 Sanford Stakes winner Bite The Bullet (by Spectacular Bid) and the listed Winter Hill Stakes winner Shuailaan (by Roberto) and to the unraced dam of the Grade 3 Comely Stakes winner Madison's Charm. The dam, a stakes-placed winner in the USA, is a half-sister to 10 winners including the dual US Grade 3 winner Weekend Surprise, the high-class sprinter Wolfhound, the US stakes winner Spectacular Spy and the French Group 3 placed Foxhound. The second dam, Lassie Dear (by Buckpasser), won the Grade 3 Villager Stakes and is a half-sister to the Grand Prix de Saint-Cloud winner Gay Mecene.

829 - GUNS OF NAVARONE (IRE) [99]　　　　　　　b.c. Barathea – Litani River (Irish River).
February 19. Seventh foal. 340,000Y. Tattersalls Houghton.
Half-brother to the very useful 1m winner The Editor (by Alzao), subsequently a stakes-placed winner over 8.5f in the USA. The dam was placed 4 times in France including a listed event and is a sister to the French 5.5f and 7f winner Or Vision (herself dam of the Group/Grade 1 winners Dolphin Street, Insight and Saffron Walden) and a half-sister to 7 winners. The second dam, Luv Luvin' (by Raise a Native), won 2 races in the USA and was stakes-placed.

830 - SEEINGISBELIEVING [74]　　　　　　　b.c. Polish Precedent – Nibbs Point (Sure Blade).
March 12. Fifth foal. 150,000Y. Tattersalls Houghton.
Half-brother to the very smart 1m (at 2 yrs) and 9f winner and Two Thousand Guineas and Derby third Border Arrow (by Selkirk), to the fairly useful 10f winner Baldaquin (by Barathea), the quite useful 1m winner Ermine (by Cadeaux Genereux) and the moderate dual 2m winner Pen Friend (by Robellino). The dam, a useful winner of the listed 12f Galtres Stakes, was second in the Group 2 Park Hill Stakes and is a half-sister to 6 winners including the Beresford Stakes second Prince Ibrahim. The second dam, Fanny's Cove (by Mill Reef), a fairly useful 10f winner on her only start, is a half-sister to 3 winners including the Galtres Stakes winner Hymettus.

831 - KINGOFTHEPIRATES (USA) [99]　　　　　　　b.c. Storm Cat – Pirate's Revenge (Pirate's Bounty).
February 15. Second foal. $250,000Y. Keeneland September.
The dam won 9 races including the Grade 1 8.5f Milady Handicap and the Grade 2 Bayakoa Handicap and is a half-sister to 3 US stakes winners including the Grade 1 placed Sweet Life. The second dam, Symbolically (by Flying Paster), was a stakes-placed winner of 6 races in the USA.

832 - TOREADOR (IRE) [82]　　　　　　　b.c. Danehill – Purchasepaperchase (Young Generation).
May 7. Ninth foal. 250,000Y. Tattersalls Houghton.
Brother to the useful listed Leopardstown One Thousand Guineas Trial winner and Group 3 1m Matron Stakes second Carambola and to the fair 7f to 8.3f and hurdles winner Purchasing Power. Half-brother to the 7f (at 2 yrs) and smart Irish One Thousand Guineas winner Matiya (by Alzao), to the useful 8.5f winner Mattiocco (by Last Tycoon), the German winner of 3 races Sandanista (by Pharly), the Irish 1m winner Al Naayy (by Tate Gallery) and the fair 10f winner Never Explain (by Fairy King). The dam was a useful winner of three races including the listed 1m Atalanta Stakes and was second in the Group 1 Prix Saint-Alary. The second dam, Tin Goddess (by Petingo), placed once at 3 yrs, is a half-sister to 5 winners.

833 - LANDSEER [88]　　　　　　　b.c. Danehill – Sabria (Miswaki).
·　April 28. Third foal. 260,000Y. Tattersalls Houghton.
Half-brother to the quite useful 10.2f winner (awarded race) Sabreon (by Caerleon) and to the French 1m winner Ghita (by Zilzal). The dam is an unraced half-sister to 3 winners including the very useful Grand Criterium third King Sound. The second dam, Flood (by Riverman), won over 6f in the USA and is a half-sister to the US Grade 1 Californian Stakes winner Sabona. The third dam, Hail Maggie, is a half-sister to the top-class racemare Trillion (the dam of Triptych) and to the dam of Generous. Significant sire/damsire crosses:- Danehurst.

834 - KASPAROV (USA) [94]　　　　　　　b.c. Mr Prospector – Sovereign Kitty (Sovereign Dancer).
March 11. Third foal. $1,500,000Y. Keeneland September.
The dam won 6 races including the Grade 2 Cotillion Handicap and the Grade 3 Tempted Stakes in the USA and was Grade 1 placed on five occasions. The second dam, I'm No Pussycat (by Valdez), is an unplaced half-sister to Family Style (four Grade 1 wins in the USA) and Lost Kitty (Grade 1 Del Mar Futurity winner).

J OXX

835 - ANCESTOR (IRE) **　　　　　　　ch.c. Polish Precedent – Anna Of Saxony (Ela-Mana-Mou).
March 23. Fourth foal.
Half-brother to the 2000 David Loder trained 2-y-o Al Montahaa (by Sadler's Wells) and to the smart French 2-y-o Group 3 1m Prix d'Aumale winner Anna Palariva (by Caerleon). The dam, a very useful winner of the Group 2 14.6f Park Hill Stakes, is a half-sister to the very smart Group 2 12.5f Prix de

Royallieu and Group 2 12f Prix du Conseil de Paris winner Annaba. The second dam, Anna Matrushka (by Mill Reef), is an unraced half-sister to the German Group 3 winner Anno Luce and to the dam of the very smart middle-distance colt Annus Mirabilis. The third dam, Anna Paola (by Prince Ippi), won the German Oaks. (Sheikh Mohammed). *"He's a lovely colt – a really beautiful looking horse, a good mover and he has a good nature. The family tend to take some time but he hasn't missed any work and he should make a 2-y-o later on. A well-balanced, well-made horse, he doesn't look backward but the family do take a bit of time".*

836 - BEHZAD (IRE)
b.c. Kahyasi – Behriya (Kenmare).
April 22. First foal.

The dam is a half-sister to the very useful Group 3 15.5f Prix Berteaux winner Bayrika (by Kahyasi). The second dam, Behera (by Mill Reef), won the Group 1 10f Prix Saint-Alary and the Group 3 10.5f Prix Penelope and was second in the Prix de l'Arc de Triomphe. The third dam, Borushka (by Bustino), won the Park Hill Stakes. (H H Aga Khan). *"A small horse but a good sort and well-made. Kahyasi's don't do much at 2 yrs in general but he's well put together and barring accidents he'll certainly be able to run this year".*

837 - BLATANT *
ch.c. Machiavellian – Negligent (Ahonoora).
February 24.

Closely related to the useful 7f (at 2 yrs) and 1m winner Asad (by Lion Cavern) and half-brother to the useful 2-y-o 7f winner Shawanni (by Shareef Dancer). The dam, a champion 2-y-o filly, won the 7f Rockfel Stakes at 2 yrs and was third in the One Thousand Guineas behind Salsabil on the first of her three outings at 3 yrs. She is a sister to the dual 2-y-o 6f winner and One Thousand Guineas fourth Ala Mahlik and a half-sister to the very useful Queen Alexandra Stakes winner Ala Hounak and the useful 1m and 10f winner Zalon. The second dam, Negligence (by Roan Rocket), was placed once over 10f at 3 yrs and is a half-sister to the dams of the very useful sprinter Governor General and the smart French 10f performer Galunpe. (Sheikh Mohammed). *"A biggish horse but very nice. He's a good-looking colt with a good temperament and he's a good mover. He doesn't look particularly precocious but the pedigree suggests he'll make a 2-y-o alright in the second half of the season".*

838 - CALORANDO (IRE) *
b.c. Green Desert – Key Change (Darshaan).
February 25. First foal.

The dam, a winner of 4 races including the Group 1 12f Yorkshire Oaks, is a full or half-sister to numerous minor winners. The second dam, Kashka (by The Minstrel), a winner over 12f at 3 yrs in France, is a half-sister to the Italian Group 3 winner Karkisiya and to the dams of the Derby winner Kahyasi and the Group 3 winners Kaliana and Kalajana and Kithanga. (Lady Clague). *"He takes more after the dam rather than Green Desert so we may not see much of him this year. He's having a break at the moment but he's a very nice horse".*
Significant sire/damsire crosses:- Desert Story.

839 - CLOUSEAU *
b.c. Selkirk – Mystery Play (Sadler's Wells).
March 15. Sixth foal.

Half-brother to the 2000 2-y-o Conceal (by Cadeaux Genereux), to the useful 1m winner Playacting (by Forty Niner) and the fairly useful 1m winner Crown Of Thorns (by Diesis). The dam, a useful 7f (at 2 yrs) and 11.5f winner, is a half-sister to numerous winners including the Queen's Vase winner Arden, the French listed winner Kerulen and the dam of the US Grade 1 winner Kiri's Clown. The second dam, Kereolle (by Riverman), is a placed half-sister to the top-class broodmare Miss Manon - dam of 5 stakes winners including the Group winners Mot D'Or, Lydian and Ballinderry (herself dam of the French Derby winner Sanglamore). (Sheikh Mohammed). *"He's had a trouble-free winter and has done plenty of ground work. He's a nice horse and I'd be surprised if he didn't make some sort of mark at 2 yrs".*

840 - CRISTALITA (IRE) **
ch.f. Entrepreneur – Strutting (Ela-Mana-Mou).
March 15. Third foal. 50,000Y. Tattersalls October.

Half-sister to Chiming (by Danehill), unplaced in two starts at 2 yrs in Ireland in 2000. The dam, a fairly useful 7f (at 2 yrs) and 10.2f winner, is a half-sister to 4 minor winners here and abroad. The second dam, Taking Steps (by Gay Fandango), won once at 3 yrs and was third in the Irish One Thousand Guineas and is a half-sister to 3 winners including the Gimcrack Stakes third Dee-Jay-Ess. (Mr T Wilson). *"She's a good sort and you'd be hoping she'd make her mark at 2 yrs. Certainly when we bought her she looked like she'd make a 2-y-o".*

841 - CROOKED WOOD (USA) **　　　　　　　ch.f. Woodman – Crockadore (Nijinsky).

Sister to the 1996 Irish 3-y-o 6f winner Shunaire and closely related to the unraced Irish trained 2000 2-y-o Gulch King (by Gulch) and the minor Irish 2-y-o 6f winner and subsequent US winner Mynador (by Forty Niner). Also, half-sister to the fair Irish 14f winner Circus Maximus (by Pleasant Colony). The dam won 7 races in Ireland and the USA including the Grade 2 12f Orchid Handicap and the Grade 3 11f Sheepshead Bay Handicap (both on turf). She is closely related to the Group 3 Flying Five winner Flowing out of Flo Russell (by Round Table), herself a placed half-sister to 3 stakes winners including the dam of the US Grade 1 Sword Dancer Handicap winner Dr Root. (Ballylinch Stud). *"A very correct, good-looking filly, she's not been here long and is a biggish 2-y-o that won't be ready to run until later this year".*
Significant sire/damsire crosses:- Bahhare, Ciro, Way Of Light.

---

842 - DEMINI (IRE) ***　　　　　　　b.c. Alzao – My Potters (Irish River).
　　　　　　　　　　　　　　　　　　　　　　　　　March 31.

Brother to the very smart 7f (at 2yrs) and Group 1 12f Irish Oaks winner Winona (by Alzao) and half-brother to Carlisle Bay, a winner over 6f in Ireland at 2 yrs in 1996 and third in the Group 3 7f Killavullan Stakes, the fairly useful 11.5f winner Gold Quest (by Rainbow Quest) and the minor Irish 2-y-o 1m winner Western Seas (by Caerleon). The dam, an Irish 3-y-o 1m handicap winner, is a half-sister to numerous winners including the champion US sprinter My Juliet, the good middle-distance colt Lyphard's Special and the 2-y-o 6f Blue Seal Stakes winner New Trends. The second dam, My Bupers (by Bupers), was placed at 3 yrs. (Lady Clague). *"A grand horse and he might well make a 2-y-o. He's going well and is a full brother to Winona. She wasn't bad at 2 yrs – we fancied her for the Moyglare and she disappointed but obviously she improved a lot the next year".*
Significant sire/damsire crosses:- Winona.

---

843 - EBARIYA (IRE) ***　　　　　　　b.f. Sadler's Wells – Ebaziya (Darshaan).
　　　　　　　　　　　　　　　　　　　　　　　　　May 13.

Sister to the J Oxx trained 3-y-o Elapour and to the high-class Irish Oaks and Prix Royal-Oak winner Ebadiyla and half-sister to the smart Group 1 7f Moyglare Stud Stakes winner Edabiya (by Rainbow Quest) and the high-class Ascot Gold Cup winner Enzeli (by Kahyasi). The dam won from 7f (at 2 yrs) to 12f including three listed races and was third in the Group 2 12f Blandford Stakes. The second dam, Ezana (by Ela-Mana-Mou), won over an exended 11f in France and is a half-sister to the French dual Group 3 winner Demia. (H H Aga Khan). *"A very nice filly, she's beautiful and probably the best-looking one out of the mare so far. Despite her fairly stout pedigree, I'd say she should show something at 2 yrs".*
Significant sire/damsire crosses:- Crimson Tide, Ebadiyla, Greek Dance,

---

844 - EGYPTIAN (USA) **　　　　　　　b.c. Green Desert – Link River (Gone West).
　　　　　　　　　　　　　　　　　　　　　　March 28. Second foal.

The dam won the Grade 1 9f John A Morris Handicap in the USA. The second dam, Connecting Link (by Linkage), was placed once in the USA, is a half-sister to the US stakes winner Spectacular Bev (herself dam of a stakes winner) and to the dam of the Queens Vase winner Stelvio. The third dam, Bev Bev (by Nijinsky), won twice at 2 yrs in France and is a full or half-sister to 7 winners, notably Formidable, Flying Partner, Ajdal (all Group 1 winners) and the grandam of Arazi. (Sheikh Mohammed). *"A very nice, sharp-looking colt. Quite well-forward, he looks like making a speedy 2-y-o".*

---

845 - ESTERLINA (IRE) *　　　　　　　ch.f. Highest Honor – Shaquick (Shadeed).
　　　　　　　　　　　　　　　　　　　March 7. Fourth foal. IR£90,000Y. Goffs Orby.

Sister to the French winner of 4 races Fneidik and to a minor winner in France by Bering. The dam won once at 3 yrs in France and is a half-sister to 8 winners including the Group 3 Hoover Fillies Mile winner Leap Lively (dam of the Irish One Thousand Guineas winner Forest Flower and grandam of the triple US Grade 1 winner High Yield) and the dam of the US Grade 2 winner Miss Golden Circle. The second dam, Quilloquick (by Graustark), won once in the USA and is a half-sister to the Grade 2 American Derby winner Fifth Marine. (Mr T Wilson). *"A big, good-looking filly, she doesn't look too precocious but the family would indicate that there's a chance of her showing a bit at 2 yrs. She's very nice".*

846 - FORTUNE (IRE) ***   b.f. Night Shift – Happy Landing (Homing).

March 10.

Sister to the US 2-y-o Grade 1 8.5f Starlet Stakes winner Creaking Board (herself dam of the US Grade 3 winner Crowd Pleaser) and to the Group 3 6f Prix de Seine-et-Oise and German Group 3 6f Benazet-Rennen winner Dyhim Diamond, closely related to the Italian listed-placed winner Mary The Best (by Be My Guest) and half-sister to 3 winners including the German listed winner Santenay (by Alzao) and the French listed-placed winner Three Greens (by Niniski). The dam was placed twice in France and is a half-sister to 4 minor winners. The second dam, Laughing Goddess (by Green God), won 3 races and was listed-placed over 1m at 2 yrs. (Sheikh Mohammed). *"She's a little bit backward but I'd hope she'd make a 2-y-o. A fine looking filly – you'd like her – and she's bred to have speed. Having said that, they can be bred to have speed but not be particularly precocious! But she's very correct and straightforward. A nice filly".*

Significant sire/damsire crosses:- Creaking Board, Dyhim Diamond.

847 - GALLETA *   b.f. Hernando – Fatah Flare (Alydar).

February 14. Eleventh foal. 22,000Y. Tattersalls October.

Half-sister to the 3-y-o Protagonist (by In The Wings), to the useful triple 7f winner Mata Cara (by Storm Bird and herself dam of a French listed winner), the fairly useful 6f (at 2 yrs) and 7f winner Flavian (by Catrail), the fairly useful 10f winner Refugio (by Reference Point), the fair 2-y-o 6f winner Fire and Shade (by Shadeed) and a winner in Dubai by Night Shift. The dam, a 2-y-o 6f winner, was placed in both the Princess Margaret Stakes and the Waterford Candelabra Stakes before winning the Group 3 10.5f Musidora Stakes at 3 yrs. She is a half-sister to Sabin, a dual US Grade 1 winner over 9f and 10f and to the dam of the Group 3 Desmond Stakes winner Asema. The second dam, Beaconaire (by Vaguely Noble), a winner of 3 races at up to 10f in France including a listed event, is a half-sister to the Grade 2 winner Kittiwake (dam of the multiple Grade 1 winner Miss Oceana, the Prix Jean Prat winner Kitwood and the Grade 2 winner Larida - herself dam of the Coronation Stakes winner Magic of Life). (Mr T Wilson). *"A nice filly and not too backward looking. Although Hernando's don't do a lot as 2-y-o's I'd hope she'd be a back-end filly and she's done nothing wrong so far".*

848 - GRAFITTI GIRL (IRE) *   b.f. Sadler's Wells – Maharani (Red Ransom).

March 18. Second foal. IR£110,000Y. Goffs Orby.

Half-sister to the quite useful 2000 7f placed 2-y-o Lucefer (by Lycius). The dam, placed once in Germany, is a half-sister to 7 winners including the Group 2 Laurent-Perrier Champagne Stakes winner Sri Pekan and the Group 3 Railway Stakes winner Daylight In Dubai. The second dam, Lady Godolphin (by Son Ange), won in the USA and is a half-sister to the US stakes winner Need A Dime. (Mr T Wilson). *"Quite a nice filly and not too big for a Sadler's Wells, she goes well and might just make a 2-y-o – especially as there's precocity on the dam's side".*

849 - KENYANE (IRE) *   b.f. Kahyasi – Siwana (Dom Racine).

April 24. Sixth foal. IR£21,000Y. Goffs Challenge.

Half-sister to the modest 2000 6f and 7f placed 2-y-o Ceralbi (by Goldmark) and to the modest 5f and 6f winner Skyers Flyer (by Magical Wonder). The dam, a winning Irish sprinter, is a half-sister to 3 minor winners. The second dam, Sharya (by Lord Gayle), won at 3 yrs in France and is a half-sister to 9 winners. (Lady O'Reilly). *"She's a nice, lengthy filly and has done well since the sales. She could be a back-end 2-y-o".*

850 - LOLITA'S GOLD (USA) ***   b.f. Royal Academy – Shamisen (Diesis).

March 14. Fourth foal. 32,000Y. Tattersalls October.

Half-sister to the French trained 2000 2-y-o Acid Jazz (by Danehill) and to the useful 3-y-o 6f and 7f winner Lone Piper (by Warning). The dam, a fairly useful 2-y-o 7f winner and second in the Group 2 6f Lowther Stakes, is a sister to the Group 3 8.5f Diomed Stakes winner Enharmonic and a half-sister to the listed 1m Atalanta Stakes winner Soprano. The second dam, Contralto (by Busted), a useful 2-y-o 6f and 7f winner, is closely related to the smart Group 3 Brigadier Gerard Stakes second Rhyme Royal and a half-sister to the Group 2 7f Lockinge Stakes and Group 3 8.5f Diomed Stakes winner Noalto. (Mr T Wilson). *"A nice filly, she's a good sort and fairly well forward – all being well she should make a 2-y-o".*

Significant sire/damsire crosses:- Carmine Lake (Gr 1).

851 - MISS GRIMM (USA) **

ch.f. Irish River – Gretel (Hansel).
February 28. First foal.

The dam, a useful 2-y-o 7f winner and third in the Group 3 1m May Hill Stakes, is a half-sister to the useful French 2-y-o and 3-y-o 1m winner Queen Catherine. The second dam, Russian Royal (by Nureyev), was a useful winner over 6f at 2 yrs and 7f at 3 yrs and was placed in the Jersey Stakes, the Fred Darling Stakes, the Supreme Stakes and the Beeswing Stakes. She is a half-sister to numerous winners here and in the USA including the very useful, though lightly raced, 9f winner Incinderator (by Northern Dancer). The third dam, Princess Karenda (by Gummo), won 6 races including the Grade 1 9f Hollywood Oaks and the Grade 1 9f Santa Margarita Invitational Handicap. (Sheikh Mohammed). *"A nice, sharp little filly. She certainly looks like a 2-y-o and may make it to the races by June or July".*

852 - MISS HONORINE (IRE)

b.f. Highest Honor – Nini Princesse (Niniski).
April 25. Fifth foal. 22,000Y. Tattersalls October.

Sister to the French winner of 3 races Princesse Baie and half-sister to the French trained 3-y-o Blue Canyon (by Bering) and the minor 1998 French 3-y-o winner Prince Shaan (by Darshaan). The dam won 6 races from 2 to 4 yrs in France, is a sister to the US Grade 1 Mervyn Leroy Handicap winner and Group 1 Criterium de Saint-Cloud second Louis Cyphre and a half-sister to the Group 2 Prix Robert Papin winner and French Two Thousand Guineas third Psychobabble. The second dam, Princesse Timide (by Blushing Groom), won twice in France and was listed placed four times. (Mr T Wilson). *"She's OK but she's had a little setback and I wouldn't think she'd be very precocious. She's a nice filly though and she could do something towards the back-end".*

853 - MUSICAL (IRE)

ch.f. In The Wings – Morn Of Song (Blushing Groom).
February 22. Fifth living foal.

The dam, a quite useful 3-y-o 7.6f winner, is a sister to the very useful Grade 2 Bel Air Handicap winner Rahy and a half-sister to the top-class middle-distance colt Singspiel, winner of the Japan Cup, the Dubai World Cup, the Juddmonte International etc., and the useful 9f and 10.2f winner Rakeen (by Northern Dancer) - subsequently a Grade 2 winner in South Africa. The second dam, Glorious Song (by Halo), won 17 races including four Grade 1 events and is a sister to the Champion 2-y-o colt Devils Bag and to the Grade 2 Arlington Classic winner Saint Ballado. (Sheikh Mohammed). *"A good-looker, she's not too backward looking but on pedigree I'd expect her to take a bit of time".*

854 - OREGON TRAIL (USA) **

b.f. Gone West – Oscillate (Seattle Slew).

Sister to Takesmybreathaway, unplaced in two starts at 2 yrs in 2000 and closely related to the fairly useful 1999 2-y-o 6f winner Quaestio, to the listed 7f John Of Gaunt Stakes winner and Group 2 placed Mutakkdim (both by Seeking The Gold) and a winner in Japan by Mr Prospector and half-sister to the US winner and Grade 1 Shuvee Handicap second Smooth Charmer (by Easy Goer). The dam, a sprint winner of one race in the USA, is a half-sister to the Grade 1 8.5f Breeders Cup Juvenile winner Rhythm, to the US Grade 3 Affectionately Handicap winner Get Lucky and the US winner and Grade 1 placed Offbeat. The second dam, Dance Number (by Northern Dancer), won 8 races including the Grade 1 Beldame Stakes and the Grade 2 Shuvee Handicap and is a half-sister to the high-class racehorse and sire Private Account and to the dam of the Group winners Assatis and Warrshan. (Mr L Neil Jones). *"Quite a nice filly and it looks like she'll make a 2-y-o. She's bred for it and hasn't had any setbacks so far".*

855 - PACIFIC (USA) ***

b.c. Gulch – Wedding Of The Sea (Blushing Groom).
May 9. Sixth foal.

Half-brother to the 2000 Irish 2-y-o 7f winner Pacific Union (by Seeking The Gold) and to the 1999 3-y-o stakes winner Neptune's Bride (by Bering). The dam, a very useful filly, won the Group 3 6f Prix de Ris-Orangis. The second dam, Sweet Mover (by Nijinsky), a fairly useful 10f winner, is a half-sister to the US stakes winners Hail Hilarious and Countess Fager. (Sheikh Mohammed). *"A lovely horse this fellow, he's very well-forward and I like him. I had his half-brother last year and this is a better-looking horse. Hopefully he won't start to grow because at the moment he's going well and it looks like we can press on with him".*
Significant sire/damsire crosses:- Catch A Glimpse (Gr 1 placed).

856 - QUEEN CONSORT **　　　　　　　　　b.f. Diesis – Queen Sceptre (Fairy King).

February 8. First foal. 96,000Y. Tattersalls October.
The dam, a useful 2-y-o winner of 2 races including the listed 6f Firth of Clyde Stakes, subsequently won a small stakes event in the USA. The second dam, Happy Smile (by Royal Match), a fairly useful Irish middle-distance winner of 4 races, is a sister to the Group 2 10f Pretty Polly Stakes and US Grade 2 winner Happy Bride and a half-sister to the Group 2 12f Blandford Stakes winner Topanoora. (Miss A H Marshall). *"A small, sharp little filly, she's quite well-forward and we'll be cracking on with her"*.

857 - RELISH (IRE) *　　　　　　　　　　　b.f. Sadler's Wells – Reloy (Liloy).

March 24.
Closely related to the useful 1994 2-y-o listed 6f Firth of Clyde Stakes winner Loyalize (by Nureyev) and half-sister to the 1999 Irish 3-y-o listed 10f winner Remuria (by Theatrical), the 2000 unraced 2-y-o Tannoy (by Southern Halo), the useful 1996 2-y-o 6f winner Reliquary (by Zilzal), the minor American winner Periscopic (by Secreto) and the fair French 10f winner Dimakya (by Dayjur). The dam was a smart winner of the Group 3 10.5f Prix de Royaumont, was second in the Group 1 12f Prix Vermeille and went on to win two Grade 1 events in the USA. She is a half-sister to the very useful French performers En Calcat and Roi Guillaume and to the smart French 1m winner Reine Imperiale. The second dam, the top-class filly Rescousse (by Emerson), won the 10.5f Prix de Diane and was second in the Prix de l'Arc de Triomphe behind San San. (Sheikh Mohammed). *"A good-looking filly, she's very nice and will obviously take time but she's well-made and is doing enough so hopefully we'll see her in the autumn"*.

858 - SALSA SADIE (IRE)　　　　　　　　　　b.f. Alzao – Priyanka (Last Tycoon).

March 6. Third foal. IR£20,000Y. Goffs Orby.
Half-sister to the 3-y-o Port Royal (by Night Shift). The dam is an unraced half-sister to 3 winners including the listed stakes winner Nordica - herself dam of the Group 3 Gainsborough Stud Fred Darling Stakes winner Sueboog. The second dam, Princess Arabella (by Crowned Prince), won at 3 yrs and is a half-sister to the Oaks and Irish Oaks winner Fair Salinia (herself the dam of 3 listed winners) and to the fairly useful sire Rambo Dancer. (Mr T Wilson). *"A fine, big, strong filly that didn't cost a lot of money. She's a really good sort, a bit behind some of the others but she's well-made and she might make a 2-y-o later on in the year"*.

859 - SAXE ***　　　　　　　　　　　　　ch.c. Zafonic – Blue Lustre (Nureyev).

March 7. First foal.
The dam is an unraced half-sister to the smart Group 1 6f Middle Park Stakes and Group 2 7f Challenge Stakes winner Zieten, the Group 1 6f Cheveley Park Stakes and Group 3 5f Queen Mary Stakes winner Blue Duster and the French listed 1m winner Slow Jazz. The second dam, Blue Note (by Habitat), won 5 races from 5f to 7f in France including the Group 2 Prix Maurice de Gheest and the Group 3 Prix de la Porte Maillot. (Sheikh Mohammed). *"A very nice, sharp-looking horse, he looks like he'll make a 2-y-o and he's quite well-forward"*.
Significant sire/damsire crosses:- Kareymah.

860 - SINNARIYA (IRE) *　　　　　　　　　b.f. Persian Bold – Sinntara (Lashkari).

March 14. Fifth foal.
Half-sister to the 2000 7f placed 2-y-o Sindapour (by Priolo), to the top-class middle-distance colt Sinndar (by Grand Lodge), winner of the Derby, the Irish Derby and the Prix de l'Arc de Triomphe, the modest 2m winner Sirinndi (by Shahrastani) and the minor Irish 12f winner Sinndiya (by Pharly). The dam won 4 races in Ireland at up to 2m. The second dam, Sidama (by Top Ville), won over 12f in France and is a half-sister to the high-class middle-distance colt Sadjiyd. (H H Aga Khan). *"She's a very nice filly and looks a bit like her half-brother Sinndar. The dam breeds them all medium-sized and with a very good action. She has a very good temperament and has a lot of quality about her"*.

861 - SPEECHLESS　　　　　　　　　　　　b.f. Desert King – Excellent Alibi (Exceller).

February 20. Eleventh foal. 70,000Y. Tattersalls October.
Half-sister to the very useful middle distance stayer Witness Box (by Lyphard), a winner of 6 races including the Northumberland Plate and placed in the Doncaster Cup and Goodwood Cup, to the useful 10f to 12.3f winner Arabian Moon (by Barathea), the fairly useful 7f and 1m winner Efharisto (by

Dominion), the quite useful 12f to 18f winner Xcellance (by Be My Guest) and a winner in Germany by Suave Dancer. The dam won three races from 10f to 12f in France and is closely related to the outstanding filly Dahlia (twice winner of the 'King George' and herself dam of three Grade 1 winners). The second dam, Charming Alibi (by Honey's Alibi), won 16 of 21 races in the USA including four stakes events. (Miss A H Marshall). *"A very nice filly, she'll take some time as she's grown quite a bit. She's gone home for a break but I like her".*

---

862 - TAKARNA (IRE) **　　　　　　　　　　b.f. Mark Of Esteem – Takarouna (Green Dancer).
　　　　　　　　　　　　　　　　　　　　　　　　　　　　　　　April 7. Fourth foal.
Half-sister to the smart 2000 Irish 10f and 12f winner Takali (by Kris), to the 1998 Group 3 12f Meld Stakes winner Takarian (by Doyoun), subsequently winner of the Bay Meadows Derby in the USA and the 1998 Irish 2-y-o 6f winner Takariya (by Arazi). The dam, a very useful winner of the Group 2 12f Pretty Polly Stakes at the Curragh, is a sister to the smart Group 2 Dante Stakes winner Torjoun and a half-sister to the quite useful 2m Northumberland Plate winner Tamarpour (by Sir Ivor). The second dam, Tarsila (by High Top), won over 1m and 9f and is a sister to Top Ville. The third dam, Sega Ville (by Charlottown), won the Group 3 10.5f Prix de Flore. (H H Aga Khan). *"A good sort, she's well-forward and is going well. Not a particularly precocious family but she looks earlier than some of them".*

---

863 - TEMPESTUOUS **　　　　　　　　　　　b.c. Zafonic – Air Distingue (Sir Ivor).
　　　　　　　　　　　　　　　　　　　　　　　　　　　　　　　　　　March 26.
Half-brother to the very smart French Two Thousand Guineas winner Vettori (by Machiavellian), to the French 9f to 10f winner Stage Manner (by In the Wings), the 10f winners Lodestar (by Rainbow Quest) and Decided Air (by Sure Blade) and the minor 9f winner Livonian (by Kris). The dam won the Group 3 1m Prix d'Aumale, was second in the Nassau Stakes and third in the 10.5f Prix de Diane and is a half-sister to the US Grade 2 winner Barkerville and the Prix d'Aumale winner Eastern Dawn. The second dam, Euryanthe (by Nijinsky), an unraced sister to the Irish St Leger and dual US Grade 1 winner Caucasus, is closely related to the champion Canadian turf horse One For All and a half-sister to both the Musidora Stakes winner Last Feather and the dam of Run the Gantlet. (Sheikh Mohammed). *"A nice, good-looking, slightly backward horse. He's a good mover with a good temperament but he'll take a bit of time".*
Significant sire/damsire crosses:- Xaar.

---

864 - TERESITA *　　　　　　　　　　　　　ch.f. Rainbow Quest – Strike Alight (Gulch).
　　　　　　　　　　　　　　　　　　　March 8. Fourth foal. 26,000Y. Tattersalls October.
Half-sister to the fairly useful 1m winner Cyber World (by Robin des Pins). The dam, a winner at up to 9f in the USA, is a sister to the listed 10f winner, Sun Chariot Stakes third and E P Taylor Stakes second Flame Valley and a half-sister to the US Grade 2 winner Beyrouth. The second dam, Lightning (by Kris), won the listed 7f Prix Imprudence, was placed in three Group 3 events and is a sister to the Prix de la Salamandre winner Common Grounds and a half-sister to the Prix de Psyche winner Angel In My Heart. (Mr T Wilson). *"This is a nice filly and despite being by Rainbow Quest she's fairly well-forward, so she might do something this year – I like her".*

---

865 - TIMAWARI (IRE) *　　　　　　　　　　gr.c. Sadler's Wells – Timarida (Kalaglow).
　　　　　　　　　　　　　　　　　　　　　　　　　　　　　　　April 8. Second foal.
Half-brother to the unraced 2000 Irish 2-y-o Tilimsana (by Darshaan). The dam, a high-class 10f filly, won the Group 1 Irish Champion Stakes, the Group 1 Dallymayr-Preis and the Grade 1 Beverly D Stakes and is a half-sister to numerous winners and to the dam of the listed winners Miss Sacha and Pinta. The dam, a fairly useful 7.6f winner, is a half-sister to the Group 1 Benson and Hedges Gold Cup winner Relkino. The second dam, Pugnacity (by Pampered King), was a smart winner of 8 races including the Lowther Stakes, the Falmouth Stakes and the King George Stakes. (H H Aga Khan). *"A lovely horse, he's very good-looking but backward. He may run at the tail-end of the season and he's a lovely mover. He's got his dam's colour but probably has more of his sire's shape".*

---

866 - TINTERA (IRE) **　　　　　　　　　　b.f. King's Theatre – Fluella (Welsh Pageant).
　　　　　　　　　　　　　　　　　　　April 30. Tenth living foal. IR£50,000Y. Goffs Orby.
Half-sister to the Irish winner of 12 races including a 7f listed event, Pre-Eminent (by Local Suitor), the Irish 6f (at 2 yrs) winner Flame Flicker, the minor Italian winner of 10 races Help Me (both by Doulab), the poor dual 2m winner Zola (by Indian Ridge) and the hurdles winner Jubail (by Sandhurst Prince). The dam, a fair 3-y-o 7f winner, is a half-sister to the Prince Of Wales's Stakes second Fluellen. The

second dam, Ya Ya (by Primera), a quite useful staying half-sister to the Park Hill Stakes winner African Dancer, won at 3 yrs. (Mr T Wilson). *"A lovely looker, she's quite well-forward and she may be out in June".*

867 - VIVIENTE (USA)

ch.f. Honor Grades – Bimbo (Bustino).
April 21. Fourth foal. IR£20,000Y. Goffs Orby.

Half-sister to a minor winner in the USA by Aksar. The dam won at 2 yrs in the USA, was stakes-placed twice and is a half-sister to 8 winners including the listed St Hugh's Stakes winner Easy Option and the dam of the Irish One Thousand Guineas winner Classic Park. The second dam, Brazen Faced (by Bold And Free), a quite useful 2-y-o 5f winner, is a half-sister to 8 winners including the Musidora Stakes winner Lovers Lane and the City And Suburban Handicap winner Belper. (Mr T Wilson). *"She's quite a nice filly that didn't cost a lot – I hope she'll make a 2-y-o".*

868 - ZAFARANIYA (IRE) *

b.f. Doyoun – Zafzala (Kahyasi).
May 25. Second foal.

Half-sister to the unraced 2000 2-y-o Zafayana (by Mark Of Esteem). The dam, a winner over 6f at 2 yrs and the listed 12f Ballyroan Stakes at 3 yrs, was second in the Group 2 10f Pretty Polly Stakes and third in the Group 2 12.5f Prix de Royallieu. The second dam, Zerzaya (by Beldale Flutter), a fairly useful 10f winner, is a half-sister to the smart 7f Greenham Stakes winner and Group 2 12f King Edward VII Stakes second Zayyani. (H H Aga Khan). *"A bit backward, she's a bit behind the others but she's a good-looking filly alright".*

PIP PAYNE

869 - ASHEER ** [60]

ch.c. Inchinor – Shoshone (Be My Chief).
April 13. Second foal. 105,000Y. Tattersalls October.

Half-brother to Snake Goddess (by Primo Dominie), unplaced in one start at 2 yrs in 2000. The dam is an unplaced half-sister to 5 winners including the Group 1 7f National Stakes and Grade 1 Hollywood Derby second Lockton and the dam of the Group 3 Sagaro Stakes winner Orchestra Stall. The second dam, Bridestones (by Jan Ekels), won 4 races and is a half-sister to 6 winners including the Group 3 Doncaster Cup winner Crash Course. (Mr C Cotran). *"A big horse with a lot of potential, I'm sure he'll be running by mid-season and I see him starting off at six furlongs".*

870 - BAROSSA (IRE) * [75]

b.f. Barathea – Ichnusa (Bay Express).
March 25. Fifth foal. 30,000Y. Tattersalls October.

Half-sister to the modest Maid O'Cannie, a winner of 3 races over 6f and to the modest 6f to 1m winner Sartigila (both by Efisio). The dam, a quite useful 3-y-o 7f winner, is a half-sister to 7 winners including the Ribblesdale Stakes second Rollrights (herself dam of the US Grade 2 winner Yestday's Kisses). The second dam, Skiboule (by Boulou), won 5 races in Belgium. (Mr Raymond Tooth). *"A really nice filly with very good conformation, she's a good mover and my only concern is that the dam hasn't yet bred a 2-y-o winner, but this is a nice filly".*

871 - JAWWALA (USA) [72]

b.f. Green Dancer – Fetch N Carry (Alleged).
March 28. Ninth foal. 100,000Y. Keeneland September.

Half-sister to 6 winners in the USA from 3 yrs and upwards, four of them by Woodman, including the stakes-placed Mojave Gold. The dam is a placed half-sister to 6 winners including the US stakes winners Libanon and Flaming Leaves (Grade 2 placed and herself dam of 2 stakes winners in the USA). The second dam, Distaff Decider (by Khaled), was unraced. (Mr C Cotran). *"A big, but very nice filly, she's a good mover and will take a bit of time – probably until the back-end of the season".*

872 - WAYYAK (USA) * [66]

ch.c. Gold Fever – My Testarossa (Black Tie Affair).
February 25. First foal. $90,000Y. Keeneland September.

The dam was placed at 3 yrs and is a half-sister to 6 winners including the US stakes winners Easter Mary (Grade 2 and Grade 3 placed) and Sortofa Lady. The second dam, Mary L (by Needles), was a stakes winner of 12 races from 2 to 5 yrs in the USA. (Mr C Cotran). *"Very much a sharp, early sort. He's well-forward and looks a nice horse".*

MISS L A PERRATT

873 - CAMEO COOLER ** [70]

ch.c. Inchinor – Mystique Smile (Music Boy).
March 9. First foal. 18,000Y. Doncaster October.

The dam, a fair 2-y-o 5f winner, is a half-sister to several winners including the useful dual 6f winner Friar Tuck (by Inchinor) and the quite useful 2-y-o 6f and 7f winner Kaibo. The second dam, Jay Gee Ell (by Vaigly Great), was a fair 2-y-o 5f and 6f winner, stayed 10f and is a half-sister to 4 winners here and abroad. (Ollard Westcombe 2000 Ltd). *"He was broken-in a little bit later than the other ones but he's coming on. A nice colt, he'll hopefully be out by the end of June. He looks a typical sprinter, strong and compact with a big backside on him".*

874 - GUMLAYLOY * [82]

ch.c. Indian Ridge – Candide (Miswaki).
April 21. Second foal. IR£55,000Y. Goffs Orby.

Half-brother to the 2000 placed 2-y-o Corneille (by Marju). The dam, a minor Irish 3-y-o 7f winner, is a half-sister to 5 winners including the US stakes-placed Beyond The Sun. The second dam, Carnet Solaire (by Sharpen Up), won at 2 yrs in France and subsequently won a stakes event winner in the USA. She is a half-sister to the top-class broodmare Korveya (dam of the classic winners Bosra Sham, Hector Protector and Shanghai) and to the Group 2 Premio Umbria winners Proskona and Keos. *"He's grown a lot and is huge but he's starting to fill out now. He's a gorgeous horse, moves very well and is a little bit excitable. A colt with a lovely stride on him and he's active in his work. He should make a 2-y-o later in the season".*

875 - HO CHOI ** [72]

b.c. Pivotal – Witch Of Fife (Lear Fan).
February 13. First living foal. 20,000Y. Doncaster St Leger.

The dam was a fairly useful 2-y-o 6f and 7f winner and was listed placed. She is a half-sister to 5 winners out of the fairly useful 1m winner Fife (by Lomond), also a half-sister to 5 winners including the Goodwood Cup second El Conquistador and the dam of the Grade 1 Hollywood Turf Handicap winner Frenchpark. *"A big colt but strong with it, he's a quality-looking individual by a sire who has done very well and we hope he can carry on the same way. Again, he's got a big, long stride on him and I'd say he'll make a 2-y-o later in the year over six or seven furlongs".*

MRS A PERRETT

876 - ASHKELON [70]

ch.c. Ashkalani – Subtle Blush (Nashwan).
February 6. Fourth foal. 20,000Y. Tattersalls October.

Brother to the unraced 2000 2-y-o Kelsen. The dam was placed once over 1m at 3 yrs from 2 starts and is a half-sister to 9 winners including the high-class Group 1 1m Prix du Moulin and Group 1 7f Prix de la Foret winner Indian Lodge, the high-class Group 2 10f Prix Eugene Adam winner Sarhoob and the very useful Group 3 10f Prix la Force winner Sifting Gold. The second dam, Repetitious (by Northfields), won 5 races including the listed 6f Stewards Cup, was second in the Group 2 7f Moyglare Stud Stakes and is a sister to the Ribblesdale Stakes winner Nanticious. (Mr Seymour Cohn). *"A nice, athletic colt, the second dam produced Indian Lodge. He's going to take a bit of time to come to hand and is a back-end type of 2-y-o".*

877 - AVERY ISLAND (USA) * [74]

ch.c. Tabasco Cat – Princess Harriet (Mt Livermore).
April 8. Second foal. $100,000Y. Keeneland September.

The dam was placed once in the USA and is a half-sister to the US Grade 3 stakes winner and Grade 2 placed Autobot and to the US stakes winner of 19 races Greg At Bat. The second dam, Nearly A Princess (by Prince John), is an unraced half-sister to numerous winners including the US stakes winner Near The Limit. (Mr Michael Watt). *"A nice colt, he's rangy and is doing everything right".*

878 - BARBERA [75]

b.f. Barathea – Premiere Cuvee (Formidable).
February 12.

Closely related to the Italian Group 3 1m Premio Bagutta winner She Bat (by Batshoof) and half-sister to the useful 1m listed and subsequent US winner Cask (by Be My Chief), the fair 1m winner Mapengo (by Salse) and a winner in Germany by Petoski. The dam won the Group 3 6f Goldene Peitsche, was second in the Group 2 5f Prix du Gros-Chene and is a half-sister to the listed 1m winner Fizzed. The second dam, Clicquot (by Bold Lad, Ire), a useful sprinter, won 4 races and is a half-sister to the dams of the Group winners River Falls and Deep Finesse. (Mr D Hicks). *"A nice, rangy filly, there's plenty of speed on the dam's side but I haven't done a lot with her yet. Hopefully she'll make a 2-y-o later on".*

---

879 - BRAZEN [66]
b.c. Singspiel – Bulaxie (Bustino).
May 29. Fourth foal.
Half-brother to the very useful Group 2 10f Premio Lydia Tesio winner Claxon (by Caerleon). The dam, a very useful winner of the Group 3 7.3f Fred Darling Stakes and the listed 10f Lupe Stakes, is a half-sister to the Group 3 10f Prix de la Nonette winner Dust Dancer and to the Grand Prix de Saint-Cloud third Zimzalabim. The second dam, Galaxie Dust (by Blushing Groom) was a quite useful 2-y-o 6f winner. (Hesmonds Stud). *"Given his pedigree I don't think we're going to see a lot of action before the back-end of the season, but I like what I see".*

---

880 - CHIVITE (IRE) ** [71]
b.c. Alhaarth – Laura Margaret (Persian Bold).
April 4. Seventh foal. IRE£290,000Y. Goffs Orby.
Half-brother to the champion Scandinavian 2-y-o colt and the winner of 10 races Account Express (by Roi Danzig) and to minor winners in Japan (by Namaqualand) and Italy (by Hamas). The dam, a 2-y-o winner in Italy, is a half-sister to 5 winners including the Group 2 1m Falmouth Stakes second Lovealoch and the US Grade 3 placed Civilynn. The second dam, Civility (by Shirley Heights), a very useful 12f winner and Park Hill Stakes fourth, is a half-sister to the smart 1976 2-y-o Piney Ridge. (Lady Harrison). *"He'll hopefully be a nice 2-y-o and will probably start off at six furlongs. He looks like he can run a bit at the moment".*

---

881 - CHRISTALENI * [68]
ch.f. Zilzal – El Jazirah (Kris).
February 20. Second foal. 42,000Y. Tattersalls October.
Half-sister to the 3-y-o Mount Elbrus (by Barathea). The dam is an unraced sister to the very smart Group 1 10.5f Prix de Diane winner Rafha (herself dam of the dual Group 3 winner Sadian and the listed winner Invincible Spirit). The second dam, Eljazzi (by Artaius), a fairly useful 2-y-o 7f winner, is a half-sister to the high-class miler Pitcairn (the sire of Ela-Mana-Mou), to the 12f Blandford Stakes winner Valley Forge and the Irish 1m and 10f winner Dingle Bay - herself dam of the high-class stayer Assessor. (Mr Athos Christodoulou). *"A lovely filly, she's very active and I imagine she'll start off at seven furlongs in mid-season".*

---

882 - DESERT ALCHEMY (IRE) * [81]
b.f. Green Desert – Waffle On (Chief Singer).
January 29. Third foal. 60,000Y. Tattersalls Houghton.
Half-sister to the French 9.5f and subsequent US winner La Frou Frou (by Night Shift). The dam, a quite useful 3-y-o 6f winner here, subsequently won in France and is a half-sister to the Group 3 Premio Omenoni winner Leap For Joy. The second dam, Humble Pie (by Known Fact), a fairly useful 2-y-o 6f winner, is a half-sister to the Group 2 Prix Maurice de Gheest winner College Chapel. (Mr R Grossman). *"A big, rangy filly, she'll be seen out over six or seven furlongs from the mid-season onwards".*

---

883 - DOLORES * [72]
b.f. Danehill – Agnus (In The Wings).
February 14. Second foal.
Half-sister to the unraced 2000 2-y-o Silvernus (by Machiavellian). The dam, a winner twice in Belgium, is a half-sister to 4 other winners abroad including Wavy Run, a winner of 13 races in Spain, France and the USA including the US Grade 2 San Francisco Mile Handicap. The second dam, Wavy Reef (by Kris), ran once unplaced and is a half-sister to 7 winners including Talented, winner of the Group 2 Sun Chariot Stakes. (Normandie Stud). *"A lovely, tall, rangy filly, she's was an early foal and she'll certainly make a 2-y-o – probably starting off at six furlongs".*

---

884 - FOREST RIDGE [68]
b.br.c. Charnwood Forest – Away To Me (Exit To Nowhere).
March 8. First foal. 62,000Y. Tattersalls October.
The dam is an unraced half-sister to 3 winners including the Group 2 1m Falmouth Stakes third Reason To Dance. The second dam, La Nureyeva (by Nureyev), is a placed half-sister to 6 winners including the South African Grade 1 winner Icona and the Group 1 William Hill Futurity Stakes second Cock Robin. (Mrs R C O'Hare). *"By a sire who did very well with his 2-y-o's last year, he's a big colt who'll take a bit of time and will probably be a better 3-y-o".*

885 - GOLD BULLION * [69]   b.c. Polar Falcon – National Treasure (Shirley Heights).

April 7. Second foal.

Half-brother to the unraced 2000 2-y-o Precious (by Danehill). The dam was placed fourth once over 10f from 3 starts. She is a sister to the listed Somerville Tattersall Stakes and Grade 3 8.5f Countess Fager Handicap winner Free At Last (herself dam of the US Grade 2 winner Coretta) and a half-sister to the high-class miler Barathea (winner of the Breeders Cup Mile and the Irish Two Thousand Guineas) and the French and German Group 3 winner Zabar. The second dam, Brocade (by Habitat), was a high-class filly at up to 1m, winning five races including the Group 1 7f Prix de la Foret and the Group 3 7f Bisquit Cognac Challenge Stakes and is a half-sister to 7 winners including the dam of the dual Irish Group 3 winner Desert Style. (Cheveley Park Stud). *"Yes, he's a nice, speedy colt and is developing the right way at the moment".*

886 - INDIAN SOLITAIRE (IRE) * [67]   b.c. Bigstone – Terama Sioux (Relkino).

March 26. Eighth foal. 30,000Y. Tattersalls October.

Half-brother to the modest 12f all-weather winner Dakota Brave (by Exactly Sharp), to a hurdles winner by Be My Native and winners abroad by Astronef, Exactly Sharp and Fourstars Allstar. The dam is an unraced half-sister to 3 minor winners. The second dam, Emmuska (by Roberto), is a placed half-sister to 7 winners including the Acomb Stakes winner Elusive. (Mr B Hinge). *"Quite a forward colt, he'll certainly be one of our earlier 2-y-o's".*

887 - IT'S THE LIMIT (USA) [72]   b.c. Boundary – Beside (Sportin' Life).

March 29. Sixth foal. $80,000Y. Keeneland September.

Half-brother to 3 winners including the US stakes winner and Grade 3 placed Warside (by Lord At War). The dam is an unraced sister to the minor US stakes winner Sportin Phil. The second dam, Raise A Ten (by Raise a Native), is an unplaced half-sister to the US Graded stakes winners Pretty Perfect and Wicked Park. (Mr John E Bodie). *"His sire's been doing very well but this is a big colt that won't be seen before September over seven furlongs".*

888 - LAISSEZALLER (USA) [70]   gr.c. End Sweep – Laissez Faire (Talinum).

March 26. Second foal. $77,000Y. Keeneland September.

The dam, a minor 3-y-o winner in the USA, is a half-sister to the US winner and Grade 3 placed Lets Get Cozzy. The second dam, Sweet Lassie (by Posse), won 4 races in France and is a half-sister to 4 winners including the US Grade 2 third and French Group 3 third Kalgrey. (Mr Seymour Cohn). *"A nice colt but very immature at the moment. His sire's doing incredibly well in America and I don't see any reason why this shouldn't be a nice horse, but you probably won't see a tremendous amount of him this year".*

889 - MARCH ALONE * [67]   b.f. Alzao – I Will Lead (Seattle Slew).

April 1. Second foal.

Half-sister to Stay Behind (by Elmaamul), a very promising third over 1m on her only start at 2 yrs in 2000. The dam is an unraced half-sister to 3 winners including the top-class racehorse and sire Rainbow Quest. The second dam, I Will Follow (by Herbager), was a smart middle-distance winner of the Group 3 12f Prix de Minerve and is a half-sister to the outstanding broodmare Slightly Dangerous (dam of Commander in Chief, Warning, Deploy, Dushyantor and Yashmak) and to the unraced dam of the Dewhurst Stakes dead-heater Scenic. (Khalid Abdulla). *"A half-sister to a 3-y-o I have called Stay Behind, she's a nice filly and will make a 2-y-o".*

890 - OUR IMPERIAL BAY (USA) * [76]   b.c. Smart Strike – Heat Lightning (Summer Squall).

March 15. Second foal. $50,000Y. Keeneland September.

The dam is a US placed half-sister to the Group 2 Pacemaker International Stakes winner and Group 1 Sussex Stakes fourth Fair Judgement. The second dam, Mystical Mood (by Roberto), won the Group 3 Schuylerville Stakes, was second in the Grade 1 Frizette Stakes and is a half-sister to 7 winners including the dam of the St Leger third Istidaad. (Mr A Jones). *"He'll make a 2-y-o and I like his sire who is a son of Mr Prospector. Hopefully he'll be out in mid-season and I would imagine, looking at the stride on him, that he'd start at seven furlongs".*

891 - PAGAN DANCE (IRE) * [69]

b.c. Revoque – Ballade d'Ainhoa (Al Nasr).
April 30. First foal. 32,000Y. Tattersalls October.

The dam won 2 minor races at 4 yrs in France and is a half-sister to the Group 3 Prix d'Hedouville winner Oa Baldixe. The second dam, Bal d'Oa (by Noir Et Or), is an unplaced half-sister to the Group 2 Prix Hocquart winner Top Waltz. (The Gap Partnership). *"A nice colt, he's going to take a bit of time but he does everything nicely and looks very much like his father. One for the seven furlong and mile races later on this season".*

892 - ROYAL STORM (IRE) * [71]

b.c. Royal Applause – Wakayi (Persian Bold).
April 23. Eighth foal. IR£50,000Y. Goffs Orby.

Half-brother to the unplaced 2000 2-y-o Encyclopedia (by So Factual), to the quite useful 5f (at 2 yrs) and 7f winner Arruhan (by Mujtahid), the fair 6f winner Fata (by Machiavellian) and a winner in Hong Kong by Marju. The dam, a quite useful 2-y-o 5f winner, was fourth in the Group 3 Queen Mary Stakes and is a half-sister to Reesh (a winner of three Group 3 sprints) and to the dams of the Group 3 winning sprinters Averti and Nadwah. The second dam, Songs Jest (by Song), is an unraced half-sister to the dams of the smart sprinters Jester and Fayruz. (The Cloran Family). *"A fine, big, strapping horse, he'll take a bit of time and will be more of a miler than a six furlong I horse I think".*

893 - SARI (USA) * [72]

gr.f. Cozzene – Yamuna (Forty Niner).
March 30. First foal.

The dam, a useful 8.3f winner, is a half-sister to numerous winners including the 2-y-o 7f Lanson Champagne Stakes and 1m Royal Lodge Stakes winner Eltish, the useful 5f and 6f winner Forest Gazelle and the French listed 10f winner Souplesse. The second dam, Nimble Feet (by Danzig),a quite useful 2-y-o 5f winner, is a sister to the Grade 1 Washington Lassie Stakes winner Contredance and to the listed Roses Stakes winner Old Alliance and a half-sister to the Group winners Shotiche and Skimble and to the dam of the One Thousand Guineas winner Wince. (Khalid Abdulla). *"A sharp filly, she's ready to run but will be better suited by six furlongs than five".*

894 - THE GAIKWAR (IRE) * [79]

b.c. Indian Ridge – Broadmara (Thatching).
February 22. Third foal. 55,000Y. Tattersalls October.

Half-brother to the modest 1m winner Grub Street (by Barathea). The dam won 2 races at 2 yrs including the Group 3 1m Killavullan Stakes at Leopardstown and is a half-sister to 3 winners including the Gimcrack Stakes third Headhunter. The second dam, Erzsi (by Caerleon), a quite useful Irish 3-y-o 10f winner, is a half-sister to the very smart 2-y-o Salieri, a winner of 6 races including the Group 2 Mill Reef Stakes. (Mr John E Bodie). *"A big, rangy colt and one you'll see later on in the year".*

895 - TREETOPS HOTEL (IRE) * [84]

ch.c. Grand Lodge – Rousinette (Rousillon).
April 10. Fifth foal. FF1,000,000. Deauville August.

Half-brother to 2 minor winners by Priolo and Rainbows For Life. The dam ran unplaced twice and is a half-sister to 8 winners including the Group 1 1m Premio Regina Elena winner Rosananti, the Swedish Group 2 winner Claddagh, the Group 3 Prix Berteux winner Sharnfold and the dam of the Group 2 Jockey Club Stakes winner Sapience. The second dam, Clarina (by Klairon), won twice. (Mr Seymour Cohn). *"A compact, racy type and one of our more forward 2-y-o's".*

K PRENDERGAST

896 - ARKAGA (IRE) *

b.c. Key Of Luck – Miss Kelly (Pitskelly).
April 6. IR31,000Y. Tattersalls Fairyhouse.

Half-brother to the quite useful all-weather 10f and 12f winner Frankie Ferrari (by Common Grounds) and to the modest 1m and all-weather 10f winner Total Rach (by Nordico). The dam was placed once in Ireland at 3 yrs and is a half-sister to 8 winners including the Irish listed sprint winner Back Bailey. The second dam, Beau Darling (by Darling Buoy), won at 2 yrs and is a half-sister to 4 winners. *"A very nice horse that should be out in May. I think he'll be grand when he gets over six or seven furlongs".*

897 - BALI BREEZE (IRE) *

b.f. Common Grounds – Bahia Laura (Bellypha).
May 13. Ninth foal. IR36,000Y. Tattersalls Fairyhouse.

Sister to the fairly useful 2000 6f and 7f placed 2-y-o Amicable and half-sister to 2 minor winners in France and Italy by Akarad and Exit To Nowhere. The dam, a minor winner over 10.5f at 4 yrs in France, is a sister to the Group 3 10.5f Prix de Flore winner Benicia and a half-sister to 6 other winners. The second dam, Bashi (by Stupendous), won 3 times in France and was listed-placed over 9f. *"A nice filly and she goes well. Despite being a May foal she'll be an early type and isn't very robust but very correct. She'll get seven furlongs easily in time".*

898 - HIAWATHA (IRE) **

b.c. Danehill – Hi Bettina (Henbit).
May 24. Tenth foal. IR£190,000Y. Goffs Orby.

Brother to the useful Group 2 6f Premio Melton Memorial Tudini winner Fred Bongusto and to the useful 5f and 6f winner Atlantic Viking and half-brother to the unplaced 2000 2-y-o Royal Enclosure, the Irish 3-y-o 7f and subsequent US winner La Serina (both by Royal Academy), the Irish 2-y-o 5f winner and Group 3 Anglesey Stakes third High Charger – subsequently a winner in the USA, the 1999 Italian 2-y-o winner Luisa Demon (by Barathea) and the German 2-y-o 6f winner Dolour (both by Last Tycoon) and the modest 6f (at 2 yrs) to 1m winner Legal Flair (by Law Society). The dam, a fairly useful Irish sprinter, won twice, was second in the Group 3 Debutante Stakes in Ireland and is a half-sister to the Group 3 Norfolk Stakes winner Marouble and the Irish Oaks second Kitza. The second dam, Pitmarie (by Pitskelly), won four sprint races (including two listed events) in Ireland. *"He's a late foal so it'll be June or July before he runs, but he's a nice horse. If he's not a 2-y-o I'll be surprised and six furlongs should be his trip".*

899 - HOT TROTTER *

b.c. Halling – Born To Glamour (Ajdal).
May 7.

Half-brother to the useful 1998 2-y-o 5f winner and Group 2 6f Gimcrack Stakes second Sailing Shoes (by Lahib) and to the fairly useful Irish 10f winner Tarbaan (by Nashwan). The dam, a winner over 6f at Leopardstown at 2 yrs, is a half-sister to 9 winners including the French listed winner North Haneena. The second dam, the French winner Haneena (by Habitat), was fourth in the Cheveley Park Stakes and is a half-sister to the Jersey Stakes winner Gwent. (Hamdan Al-Maktoum). *"A late May foal and a backward kind of 2-y-o".*

900 - IBTIHAL (IRE)

b.f. Marju – Taqreem (Nashwan).
May 8. Fourth foal.

Half-sister to the unraced 2000 2-y-o Jayed (by Marju) and to the useful 7f winner and 1m listed second Ma-Arif (by Alzao). The dam was second four times over middle-distances and is a half-sister to the high class middle distance colt Ibn Bey, winner of 4 Group 1 events including the Irish St Leger and second in the Breeders Cup Classic and to the very smart Group 1 Yorkshire Oaks winner Roseate Tern. The second dam, Rosia Bay (by High Top), a useful 7.5f and 1m winner, is a half-sister to the top class Queen Elizabeth II Stakes and Budweiser Arlington Million winner Teleprompter and to the Group 3 Brigadier Gerard Stakes winner Chatoyant. (Hamdan Al-Maktoum). *"Still in Dubai until the end of April".*

901 - JIDIYA (IRE) **

b.c. Lahib – Yaqatha (Sadler's Wells).
March 28.

Brother to the Irish 7f (at 2 yrs) to 12f winner Rasin (by Lahib) and half-brother to the Irish 2-y-o 7f winner Khasib (by Machiavellian). The dam, a winner over 10f at 3 yrs in Ireland, is closely related to the top-class Champion Stakes winner Northern Baby and a half-sister to the champion Canadian 2-y-o colt Baylord. The second dam, Two Rings (by Round Table), won 9 races at up to 1m including a small stakes race. (Hamdan Al-Maktoum). *"Still in Dubai until the end of April but he's a full-brother to a colt I had called Rasin who was backward enough as a 2-y-o but still won twice at that age".*

902 - KHOZA'AH *

b.f. Darshaan – Alajyal (Kris).
April 22.

The dam is an unplaced half-sister to the numerous winners including the useful 10.2f to 12f winner Estimraar and the quite useful 3-y-o dual 7f winner Anam. The second dam, Yaqut (by Northern Dancer), was a fair 2-y-o 7f winner. (Hamdan Al-Maktoum). *"Still in Dubai until the end of April. Apparently she's a nice, big filly but backward".*

Significant sire/damsire crosses:- Sayarshan (Gr 2).

903 - MISS BEABEA (IRE) **   ch.f. Catrail – Lady Ellen (Horage).

March 5.

Half-sister to the very useful 5f winner Ellen's Lad (by Polish Patriot) and to the quite useful 6f winner Ellen's Academy (by Royal Academy). The dam was a modest 5f placed 2-y-o. *"She could be really smart, I like her a lot and she looks more like a colt than a filly. She'll definitely make a 2-y-o".*

904 - MUGHAS (IRE) *   b.c. Sadler's Wells – Quest Of Passion (Saumarez).

April 1. First foal. IR£380,000Y. Goffs Orby.

The dam was placed four times in France at 3 yrs, is a sister to the listed Prix Isonomy winner Supreme Commander and a half-sister to 6 winners including the Group 2 10f Tattersalls Rogers Gold Cup winner Fair Of The Furze (herself dam of the Italian Derby winner White Muzzle). The second dam, Autocratic (by Tyrant), won over 5f at 2 yrs in Ireland. (Hamdan Al-Maktoum). *"A very, very nice horse. Not a great big colt, he has plenty of quality and looks like a horse that will pay his way from seven furlongs onwards".*

905 - OCTOMONE (USA)   b.f. Hennessy – Style N'Elegance (Alysheba).

January 24. Third foal.

Half-sister to 2 placed horses in Ireland by Affirmed (at 2 yrs) and Thunder Gulch. The dam was placed once in the USA and is a half-sister to 10 winners including the Irish One Thousand Guineas winner Trusted Partner and the Group 2 12f Premio Legnano winner Easy To Copy (herself the dam of 3 stakes winners). The second dam, Talking Picture (by Speak John), won 6 races in the USA at up to 7f including the Grade 1 Spinaway Stakes and the Grade 1 Matron Stakes. *"We haven't had her long, she's backward in her coat and so although she'll definitely make a 2-y-o she'll take a bit of time".*

906 - SA'ED (IRE) *   b.c. Flying Spur – Day Is Dawning (Green Forest).

March 17. Second foal. IR£38,000Y. Goffs Challenge.

The dam is an unraced half-sister to a listed-placed winner in Ireland. The second dam, Grand Morning (by King Of Clubs), won the listed Marble Hill Stakes. (Hamdan Al-Maktoum). *"A big horse, quite tall but he's goes nicely and will definitely want six furlongs plus. A nice colt".*

907 - SAMER (USA) *   b.c. Spinning World – Margaree Mary (Seeking The Gold).

January 28. First foal. IR£170,000Y. Goffs Orby.

The dam, a minor stakes-placed winner at 3 yrs in the USA, is out of the unplaced Valadina (by Lomond), herself a half-sister to 6 winners including the Irish St Leger winner Dark Lomond, the Blandford Stakes winner South Atlantic and the Silken Glider Stakes winner Forlene. (Hamdan Al-Maktoum). *"Of all the horses coming to me from Dubai, this is the one talked of as being particularly nice".*

908 - SANDFORD PARK (IRE)   ch.c. Fumo di Londra – Haysong (Ballad Rock).

March 25. Second foal. IR41,000Y. Tattersalls Fairyhouse.

Half-brother to the poor 2000 6f placed 2-y-o Missing A Bit (by Petorius). The dam is an unraced half-sister to 3 minor winners. The second dam, Hay Knot (by Main Reef), is an unraced half-sister to the Group 3 Molecomb Stakes winner Hayloft (herself dam of the Irish Two Thousand Guineas winner Wassl). *"He's an early sort. He shows quite a bit but I wouldn't want to run him on brick-hard ground".*

909 - SEIFI *   b.c. Hector Protector – Garconiere (Gay Mecene).

February 15. Tenth foal. 55,000Y. Tattersalls October.

Half-brother to the Italian 2-y-o listed 7f winner Giselle Penn (by Cozzene) and to 3 minor winners in France and Italy by Ballad Rock, Stalwart and Trempolino. The dam ran twice unplaced in France and is a half-sister to 9 winners including the Group 1 1m Gran Criterium winner Grease (herself dam of the Group 3 Prix Perth winner Susurration). The second dam, Greedy Of Gain (by Habitat), won 4 races in Italy including a listed event. (Hamdan Al-Maktoum). *"Still in Dubai until the end of April".*

910 - SIDE WITH ME (USA) **   b.c. West By West – Grand Slew Lady (Houston).

April 28. Second foal. IR£37,000Y. Goffs Orby.

The dam is an unplaced half-sister to 5 winners including the Grade 2 Arlington-Washington Futurity and Grade 2 Saratoga Special Stakes winner Caller I.D. The second dam, Plagiarizing (by Ramsinga), is an unplaced half-sister to 2 winners in the USA. *"A lovely horse, I like him a lot and he'll be a firm ground horse from six furlongs to a mile".*

911 - SOLID APPROACH (IRE) * ch.c. Definite Article – Dawn Chorus (Mukaddamah).
April 17. First foal. IR£24,000Y. Goffs Challenge.
The dam is an unraced half-sister to Barrier Reef, a winner of 5 races and second in the Group 3 Beresford Stakes. The second dam, Singing Millie (by Millfontaine), won twice in Ireland and is a half-sister to 7 winners including the dam of the Group 1 Racing Post Trophy winner Seattle Rhyme. *"A nice, quality colt, he's not over-big and he'll start over six furlongs in June. The Goffs Challenge race will be his target".*

912 - UNNAMED ** ch.c. Miswaki – Water Course (Irish River).
April 25. Seventh living foal. IR£110,000Y. Goffs Orby.
Half-brother to the fairly useful 1999 2-y-o 1m winner Paradise Garden (by Septieme Ciel), to the Irish 1m (at 2 yrs) and 10f winner King Of The Wire (by Danzig Connection), the fairly useful winner of 6 races at around 12f Star Of The Course (by Theatrical) and the smart hurdler Deep Water (by Diesis). The dam is an unraced half-sister to 10 winners including the US Grade 3 winner Flama Ardiente (herself dam of the Prix Jean Prat winner Magical Wonder and the US Grade 2 Carter Handicap winner and sire Mt Livermore) and the dam of the US Grade 2 winner and sire Salt Dome. The second dam, Royal Rafale (by Reneged), won 6 races in the West Indies and is a half-sister to the dam of the Derby and Irish Derby third Star Of Gdansk. (Hamdan Al-Maktoum). *"A nice horse and a real 2-y-o type from six furlongs plus. A well-coupled, sprint-type looking colt".*

SIR M PRESCOTT

913 - ADEPT [68] b.f. Efisio – Prancing (Prince Sabo).
February 18. Second foal.
Half-sister to the quite useful 2000 5f and 6f placed 2-y-o Firework (by Primo Dominie). The dam, a useful 2-y-o 5f winner, stayed 1m and is a sister to one winner in Australia and a half-sister to 3 winners including the Group 1 6f Middle Park Stakes, Group 2 6f Richmond Stakes and Group 3 6f July Stakes winner First Trump. The second dam, Valika (by Valiyar), was placed three times from 1m to 12f at 3 yrs and is a half-sister to the high-class sprinter Mr Brooks and to the smart 3-y-o dual 7f winner Larionov.

914 - ALBANOVA [82] gr.f. Alzao – Alouette (Darshaan).
February 16.
Sister to the high-class Champion Stakes, Nassau Stakes and Pretty Polly Stakes winner Alborada (by Alzao) and half-sister to the fair 2000 7f placed 2-y-o Alakananda (by Hernando). The dam, a useful 1m (at 2 yrs) and listed 12f winner, is a sister to the listed winner and Irish Oaks third Arrikala and a half-sister to the Nassau Stakes and Sun Chariot Stakes winner Last Second. The second dam, Alruccaba (by Crystal Palace), was a quite useful 2-y-o 6f winner. (Miss K Rausing).

915 - DESERTION (IRE) [85] b.f. Danehill – Sabaah (Nureyev).
May 22. Sixth foal. IR£650,000Y. Goffs Orby.
Sister to the useful 2000 2-y-o 6f and 7f winner and Group 2 7f Champagne Stakes third Chianti and to the top-class colt Desert King, winner of the National Stakes, the Irish Two Thousand Guineas and the Irish Derby and half-sister to the useful 7f winner of 4 races Wahj (by Indian Ridge) and a winner in Japan by Catrail. The dam, a modest 8.2f placed maiden, is a full or half-sister to 6 winners including the Group 1 1m Queen Elizabeth II Stakes winner Maroof and the useful 2-y-o 7f winners Mawwal and Arrasas. The second dam, Dish Dash (by Nureyev), a smart filly and winner of the Group 2 12f Ribblesdale Stakes at Royal Ascot, is a half-sister to 6 winners including Feliciano, Canterbury Tale, Silk and Satin and Smuggly - all at least very useful.
Significant sire/damsire crosses:- Desert King.

916 - ICE KING [78] ch.c. Polar Falcon – Fearless Revival (Cozzene).
February 9. Eighth foal.
Sister to the unraced 2000 2-y-o Resurgence and to the high-class sprinter Pivotal, winner of the Group 1 5f Nunthorpe Stakes and the Group 2 5f Kings Stand Stakes and half-brother to the fairly useful dual 1m winner Brave Revival (by Dancing Brave) and the fairly useful 10f winner Revival (by Sadler's

Wells). The dam, a useful winner of the 7f listed Rockfel Stakes at 2 yrs, was listed placed over 10f at 3 yrs. The second dam, Stufida (by Bustino), won the 10f Premio Lydia Tesio. (Cheveley Park Stud). Significant sire/damsire crosses:- Pivotal.

917 - INSOMNIE (USA) [76]

b.f. Seattle Slew – Wood Of Binn (Woodman). April 16. Third foal. $330,000Y. Keeneland September.

Half-sister to a minor winner at 2 and 3 yrs in the USA by Storm Cat. The dam won the Group 3 6.5f Prix Eclipse and is out of the US stakes winner and Grade 2 placed The Way It's Binn (by Peterhof).

918 - KEW [79]

b.c. Royal Applause – Cutleaf (Kris). January 26. Fifth foal. IR£100,000Y. Goffs Orby.

Half-brother to the quite useful 1999 2-y-o 1m winner High Cheviot (by Shirley Heights), to the German 3-y-o 11f winner Cheba (by Royal Academy) and the modest 2-y-o 7f and 3-y-o all-weather 12f winner Goodwood Lass (by Alzao). The dam, a quite useful 10.6f winner, is a sister to the useful middle-distance winners Knifeboard and Kenanga and a half-sister to the Group 2 12f Ribblesdale Stakes winner Strigida and the useful 10.5f winner Catawba (dam of the Yorkshire Oaks winner Catchascatchcan). The second dam, Catalpa (by Reform), won the Ribblesdale Stakes.

919 - NIGHT CAP (IRE) [74]

ch.c. Night Shift – Classic Design (Busted). February 28. Ninth foal. 52,000Y. Tattersalls Houghton.

Brother to to the very smart Eveningperformance, a winner of 7 races including the Group 3 Flying Five and second in the Group 1 Nunthorpe Stakes and half-brother to the unraced 2000 2-y-o Hays Mews (by Lion Cavern) and the quite useful 1m all-weather winner Well Drawn (by Dowsing). The dam is an unraced half-sister to the Two Thousand Guineas winner Tirol and to the unraced dams of the Group 1 Phoenix Stakes winner Lavery and the listed winners Sharp Point and High Target. The second dam, Alpine Niece (by Great Nephew), was quite useful and was placed over 6f (at 2 yrs) and 12f. She is a sister to the Observer Gold Cup third Alpine Nephew and a half-sister to the Group 3 9f Prix de Conde winner Minatzin.

920 - PENNY PASS (IRE) [83]

b.c. Pennekamp – Belle Etoile (Lead On Time). February 10. Second foal. 85,000Y. Tattersalls Houghton.

Half-brother to the placed 2000 2-y-o Starlight Venture (by Hernando). The dam, a winner at 3 yrs in France, is a half-sister to 4 winners including the listed 12f Prix de Nantes winner and Group 3 second Zaydiya. The second dam, Zarzaya (by Caro), is an unraced half-sister to the dams of Zainta (Group 1 Prix Saint-Alary), Zayyani (Group 3 Greenham Stakes) and the listed winners Zafzala, Zaranda and Zafadola.

921 - POLISH BELLE [73]

b.f. Polish Precedent – Miswaki Belle (Miswaki). March 8. Third foal.

Closely related to the very useful 2000 2-y-o Danehurst (by Danehill), winner of all 3 of her races including the Group 3 5f Cornwallis Stakes. The dam, second over 7f on her only start, is closely related to the smart Group 3 6f Cherry Hinton Stakes winner and One Thousand Guineas third Dazzle. The second dam, Belle et Deluree (by The Minstrel), won over 1m (at 2 yrs) and 10f in France and is a half-sister to the very useful 6f and 1m winner and Cheveley Park Stakes second Dancing Tribute (herself dam of the Lowther Stakes winner Dance Sequence).

922 - SHEER BLISS (IRE) [82]

b.f. Sadler's Wells – Sheer Audacity (Troy). February 20.

Closely related to the 1999 Derby winner Oath (by Fairy King), to the Group 1 1m Gran Criterium, Group 1 1m Premio Parioli and Group 1 10.5f Prix Ganay winner Pelder (by Be My Guest) and the 1997 Irish 12f winner Night Raider (by Night Shift) and half-sister to the fairly useful 1m to 10.4f winner Sheer Danzig (by Roi Danzig), the quite useful 12f winner Sheer Spirit (by Caerleon) and the Italian seven-time winner El Rashid (by Jareer). The dam, placed twice in Italy, is closely related to the Ribblesdale Stakes winner Miss Petard - herself dam of 9 winners including the Park Hill Stakes winner Rejuvenate. The second dam, Miss Upward (by Alcide), won at 10f. Significant sire/damsire crosses:- Helen Of Spain (Gr 2).

923 - SHOWDOWN [78]   gr.f. Darshaan – Last Second (Alzao).
January 19. First foal.
The dam, winner of the 10f Nassau Stakes and the 10f Sun Chariot Stakes, is a half-sister to several winners including the Irish Oaks third Arrikala and the Moyglare Stud Stakes third Alouette (herself dam of the Champion Stakes winner Alborada). The second dam, Alruccaba (by Crystal Palace), a quite useful 2-y-o 6f winner, is out of a half-sister to the dams of Aliysa and Nishapour.

924 - SNIP SNAP [71]   b.f. Revoque – Snap Crackle Pop (Statoblest).
January 31. First foal. 26,000Y. Tattersalls October.
The dam, a quite useful 2-y-o 5f listed winner, is a half-sister to 3 minor winners. The second dam, Spinelle (by Great Nephew), a quite useful 11f winner, was second in the Group 3 Oaks Trial and is a daughter of the champion 2-y-o and One Thousand Guineas second Jacinth.

925 - UNLEASH (USA) [78]   ch.c. Benny the Dip – Lemhi Go (Lemhi Gold).
February 16.
The dam won the Grade 2 La Prevoyante Handicap in the USA. The second dam, Midnight Rapture (by Giboulee), won at 2 yrs in the USA, was third in the Grade 1 6f Spinaway Stakes and is a half-sister to the US Grade 3 winner Refinish. (Cheveley Park Stud).

MRS J R RAMSDEN

926 - CAST THE NET (USA) [72]   b.c. Marlin – Carsona (Carson City).
May 9. Second foal. $32,000Y. Keeneland September.
The dam won 4 races in the USA, was third in the Grade 1 Hollywood Oaks and is a half-sister to 8 minor winners and to the dam of a champion filly in Panama. The second dam, Askmysecretary (by Secretariat), is an unraced half-sister to 4 winners. *"A horse that will make a back-end 2-y-o and he's probably going to need at least seven furlongs. We like him, he's very athletic and he was bought by James Delahooke in America".*

927 - FLY BACK ** [66]   ch.c. Fraam – The Fernhill Flyer (Red Sunset).
February 15. Third foal. 17,500Y. Doncaster October.
The dam was a fair 5f and 6f winner at 2 yrs. The second dam, Stradey Lynn (by Derrylin), was a modest maiden. *"This colt, by Fraam who has done very well with limited opportunities, is a good sort and is quite forward. Five or six furlongs will suit him and the omens are good for his 2-y-o career".*

928 - LINGO (IRE) * [70]   b.c. Poliglote – Sea Ring (Bering).
March 23. Third foal. FF300,000. Deauville August.
Closely related to a minor French winner by In The Wings. The dam, a winner of 2 races in France and listed-placed, is a half-sister to 7 winners including the listed winner Rayon Bleu. The second dam, Blue River (by Riverman), won once in France, was third in the Group 3 1m Prix d'Aumale and is a half-sister to the Group 3 12f Prix de Minerve winner Anitra's Dance. *"A colt by a son of Sadler's Wells that was second in the French Derby, this is a very good sort and he moves very nicely. He'll obviously need seven furlongs but at the moment we like him a lot".*

929 - THE COUNT (FR) * [64]   b.c. Sillery – Dear Countess (Fabulous Dancer).
April 5. Second foal. FF180,000Y. Deauville August.
The dam is a placed half-sister to 5 minor winners in France. The second dam, Dear Princess (by Prince Mab), is a placed half-sister to one winner. *"He hasn't got the greatest pedigree in the world but we do like him. He'll need seven furlongs and is a good sort".*

930 - WORDS AND DEEDS (USA) * [75]   ch.c. Shadeed – Millfit (Blushing Groom).
March 22. Sixth foal. 53,000Y. Tattersalls October.
Half-brother to the 3-y-o Blushing American, to the quite useful 9f winner Quiet Millfit (both by Quiet American), the smart 7f Bunbury Cup and 6f Stewards Cup winner Tayseer and the fairly useful 2-y-o 6f (all-weather) and 1m winner Shouf Al Badou (both by Sheikh Albadou). The dam, a modest 7f winner, is a half-sister to 2 minor winners. The second dam, Musique Royale (by Northern Dancer), won over 7f in Ireland at 2 yrs and is a half-sister to the Jersey Stakes and Waterford Crystal Mile

winner Gay Fandango and to the US stakes winners Happy Strings and Cellist. *"We like him and there's no reason why he shouldn't make a nice mid-season 2-y-o over six or seven furlongs".*

B SMART

931 - BOND DOMINGO ** [71]
b.c. Mind Games – Antonia's Folly (Music Boy). January 21. Fourth foal. 36,000Y. Doncaster St Leger.

Half-brother to the fair 2-y-o 5f winners Antonia's Dilemma (by Primo Dominie) and Zaragossa (by Paris House). The dam, a modest 2-y-o 5f winner, stayed 6f and is a half-sister to 2 minor winners. The second dam, Royal Agnes (by Royal Palace), was a fair 14f winner and a half-sister to the smart two-year-old All Systems Go. (Mr R C Bond). *"A lovely colt, he's been out already and will be racing again before your book is published. He'll improve with age and is a five furlong sprinter pure and simple. I'd like to think he has a really nice race in him somewhere. He's in the Doncaster Sales race and the Newbury Super Sprint".*

932 - BOND JOVI (IRE) * [63]
b.c. Danehill Dancer – Vieux Carre (Pas de Seul). March 9. 18,000Y. Doncaster St Leger.

Half-brother to the fair 2-y-o 6f winner Vintage Pride (by Pip's Pride), to the modest 2-y-o 5f to 7f all-weather winner Contravene, the German 3-y-o winner John's Law (both by Contract Law) and the modest 1m all-weather winner Amelia Jess (by Mac's Imp). The dam is an unplaced half-sister to 6 winners out of the French listed winner Two's Company (by Sheshoon). (Mr R C Bond). *"A nice colt and I thought he'd be my first 2-y-o runner until he started growing. He's just starting to level out now and I'll bring him along quietly.*

933 - DIVA MARIA * [65]
b.f. Kris – May Light (Midyan). March 12. Fourth foal.

Half-sister to the poor 2000 2-y-o Light Of Fashion (by Common Grounds) and to the fairly useful 1998 2-y-o 1m winner Trio (by Cyrano de Bergerac). The dam, a modest 7f placed maiden, is a half-sister to 10 winners including the Group 3 Prix de Flore winner Lighted Glory (herself the dam of 3 Group winners), the Group 2 Prix Kergorlay winner King Luthier and the dams of the US Grade 1 winner Cool, the Yorkshire Cup winner Mountain Kingdom, the smart Dr Massini and the US Grade 3 winner No Send No Glow. The second dam, Lighted Lamp (by Sir Gaylord), was placed in the USA and is a half-sister to the Middle Park Stakes winner Crocket. (Dr J Hobby). *"A very nice Kris filly, she'll be more of a seven furlong/mile filly at the back-end. She has a beautiful action and I can hardly believe she's by Kris because she's so relaxed. I couldn't be more pleased with her".*

934 - UNNAMED * [56]
ch.c. Beveled – Pretty Pollyanna (General Assembly). March 19. Fifth foal. 21,000Y. Doncaster St Leger.

Half-brother to the useful Peculiarity (by Perpendicular), a winner of 2 races and listed-placed at around 1m, to the modest 7f all-weather winner Exclusive Assembly (by Weldnaas) and the modest 7.5f to 10f winner Polly Peculiar (by Squill). The dam is an unraced half-sister to 2 minor winners. The second dam, Midaan (by Sallust), is an unplaced half-sister to the Group 3 Prix des Reservoirs winner Light Of Realm. (Mr Paul Darling). *"A very nice colt – I'm thrilled to bits with him. His long term objective would be the Doncaster Sales race, he goes nicely and I'm in no rush with him".*

T STACK

935 - FLOWER CHILD (IRE) *
b.f. Alzao – Schlefalora (Mas Media). May 10. Fourth foal. IR£80,000Y. Goffs Orby.

Half-sister to the smart 1998 2-y-o Group 2 5f Flying Childers Stakes winner Sheer Viking (by Danehill) and to the useful 1999 2-y-o 6f winner and Group 2 6f Princess Margaret Stakes second Journalist (by Night Shift). The dam won 6 races in Sweden and is a half-sister to 4 winners including the One Thousand Guineas winner and Irish One Thousand Guineas second Las Meninas. The second dam, Spanish Habit (by Habitat), is an unraced half-sister to 5 winners out of the Irish Group 2 Player-Wills Stakes winner Donna Cressida. *"A May foal and a bit backward at the moment, we'll probably wait until August with her. She's quite a strong filly though".*

936 - GRIMALDI * gr.c. Rainbow Quest – Flo Russell (Round Table).

May 28. Fourteenth foal. 47,000Y. Tattersalls Houghton.

Half-brother to the Grade 2 12f Orchid Handicap and Grade 3 11f Sheepshead Bay Handicap winner Crockadore (by Nijinsky), to the Group 3 5f Meadow Meats Flying Five winner Flowing (by El Gran Senor), the useful 7f and 1m winner Florazi (by Arazi), the fairly useful dual 1m winner Double Encore (by Nodouble), the modest 12f all-weather winner Flow Back (by Royal Academy) and 6 minor winners in the USA (by Damascus and Affirmed) and Japan (by Danehill, Lammtarra and Suave Dancer). The second dam, Flo Russell (by Round Table), was placed in the USA and is a half-sister to 10 winners including the Grade 3 winner Embassy Row and the stakes winner Knightly Belle - herself dam of the Grade 1 Sword Dancer Handicap winner Dr Root. *"He's a late May foal but he looks more forward than you'd expect. Quite a strong colt, he may well be out in mid-summer over seven furlongs".*

937 - ROYAL ULAY (FR) * br.f. Selkirk – Beaming (Mtoto).

March 4. Fourth foal. 55,000Y. Tattersalls Houghton.

Half-sister to the 3-y-o Cashelmara (by Sadler's Wells) and to the minor 2000 French 3-y-o winner Tunnel Topics (by Sri Pekan). The dam, a fairly useful 6f and 1m winner, was listed-placed and is a half-sister to 9 winners. The second dam, Glancing (by Grundy), a very useful 2-y-o 5f to 6f winner (including the Prix d'Arenberg), is a half-sister to the Middle Park Stakes winner Bassenthwaite and to the dam of the Prix de l'Abbaye winner Keen Hunter. *"I'd expect her to start off at six furlongs in June or July. She's a strong filly and quite forward in her coat".*

938 - SERIOUS PLAY (IRE) * b.c. Brief Truce – Zing Ping (Thatching).

February 5. Third foal. IR£24,000Y. Goffs Challenge.

Brother to the useful 1998 Irish 2-y-o 6f winner and Group 1 7f Moyglare Stud Stakes second Fear And Greed. The dam, a quite useful 2-y-o placed maiden, is a half-sister to 4 winners here and abroad. The second dam, Shebasis (by General Holme), is an unraced half-sister to 5 minor winners. *"He'll be earlyish unless he starts to grow a bit. We'll just have to see how he gets on".*

939 - SPECULATOR (IRE) * b.c. Spectrum – Pirouette (Sadler's Wells).

April 4. 50,000Y. Tattersalls Houghton.

Half-brother to the 3-y-o Isle Of Palms (by Caerleon) and to 2 winners in Japan by Woodman and Dehere. The dam, winner of the listed 7f Athasi Stakes in Ireland, is a half-sister to 8 winners including the Irish listed 6f Greenlands Stakes winner and very useful sire Ballad Rock. The second dam, True Rocket (by Roan Rocket), was a smart 2-y-o winner of 5 races in Ireland. *"A very good-looking horse, he's more of a back-end 2-y-o as he's quite a big colt".*

940 - TIN QUEST b.f. Rainbow Quest – Tizona (Pharly).

March 31. Fifth foal. IR£62,000Y. Goffs Orby.

Half-sister to the unplaced 2000 2-y-o Taffrail, to a 2-y-o 6f winner in Turkey (both by Slip Anchor), the quite useful 1998 10f winner La Tiziana (by Rudimentary) and the fair 7f (at 2 yrs) and 9f winner Striffolino (by Robellino). The dam is an unraced half-sister to 4 winners including the useful 12f, 14f and hurdles winner Valedictory (by Slip Anchor). The second dam, Khandjar (by Kris), a fair 9f winner, is a sister to the Group 1 1m St James's Palace Stakes winner Shavian and a half-sister to the Group 1 Ascot Gold Cup winner Paean. *"She's not over-big and should be ready to start off over seven furlongs this year".*

A STEWART

**941 - AMBER'S BLUFF ** ** [76] b.f. Mind Games – Amber Mill (Doulab).

February 7. Sixth foal. 35,000Y. Doncaster St Leger.

Closely related to the fair 5f to 7f placed 2-y-o Compton Amber (by Puissance) and half-sister to the moderate 2000 5f placed 2-y-o Mr Pertemps (by Primo Dominie) and the quite useful 1997 2-y-o dual 5f winner Salamanca (by Paris House). The dam, a useful winner over 5f (twice) and 6f, is a half-sister to 4 winners including the listed Cock of the North Stakes third Tenacity. The second dam, Millaine (by Formidable), a half-sister to the Italian dual Group 1 winner Svelt and to the dam of the Italian Group 1 winner Shulich, was placed once at 4 yrs and stayed 12f. (Racing For Gold). *"She looks very forward. A big filly, mature and I would think she'll be quite early. Goes quite nicely".*

942 - COLISAY ** [62] b.c. Entrepreneur – La Sorrela (Cadeaux Genereux).
April 9. Second foal. 42,000Y. Tattersalls October.
The dam is an unraced half-sister to 5 winners including the smart Group 3 6f Prix de Seine-et-Oise winner Central City and the fairly useful 1997 2-y-o 6f winner and Group 3 Princess Margaret Stakes second Miss Zafonic. The second dam, Miss Silca Key (by Welsh Saint), won the Group 3 7f Jersey Stakes and is a half-sister to 7 minor winners including the dam of the Group 3 July Stakes winner Fallow. (Mr M Hawkes & Mrs M E Domvile). *"A lovely colt bred by Pat Eddery, I really like him and he goes nicely. He won't be an early type but I'm sure he'll make a 2-y-o".*

943 - FOURTH DIMENSION (IRE) * [66] b.c. Entrepreneur – Isle Of Spice (Diesis).
April 27. Second foal. 38,000Y. Tattersalls October.
Half-brother to the quite useful 2000 1m and 8.5f placed Zanzibar (by In The Wings). The dam, a fair 3-y-o 9.7f winner, is a half-sister to 5 winners including the minor US 2-y-o stakes winner Crown Silver and the dam of the Kentucky Oaks third Sneaky Quiet. The second dam, Gold Treasure (by Northern Dancer), won 6 races in the USA including minor stakes events over 6f and 1m at 4 yrs and is a half-sister to the Group 3 8.5f Princess Elizabeth Stakes winner Kanz and to the dams of the Group 1 winners Ensconse, Diamond Shoal and Glint of Gold. (Mrs M Whelton). *"A nice colt, he's just a bit small and a late foal. I expect him to do well and be a late season 2-y-o. I like him".*

944 - ISA'AF (IRE) * [75] b.c. Darshaan – Shauna's Honey (Danehill).
February 2. First foal. 200,000Y. Tattersalls Houghton.
The dam, a 3-y-o 7f winner at Leopardstown, is a half-sister to 5 winners including the smart Ahohoney, a winner over 6f and 1m here at 2 yrs and the Group 3 10.5f Prix Fille de l'Aire and fourth in the Group 1 Prix Saint-Alary. The second dam, Honey Buzzard (by Sea Hawk II), was a placed daughter of the Italian Oaks winner Dolina. (Hamdan Al-Maktoum). *"Out in Dubai until late April and I'm told that they do like him. They think he'll make a back-end 2-y-o".*

945 - LAFI (IRE) * [79] ch.c. Indian Ridge – Petal Girl (Caerleon).
April 28. Fourth foal. 180,000Y. Tattersalls October.
Half-brother to the useful 2000 Scandinivian 2-y-o winner (at up to 6f) and 7f Tattersalls Houghton Sales Stakes second Pretty Girl (by Polish Precedent) and to Mutamam (by Darshaan), winner of the Rose Of Lancaster Stakes, Select Stakes, September Stakes and Cumberland Lodge Stakes (all Group 3 events at up to 12f). The dam, a fairly useful 3-y-o dual 1m winner, is a sister to the very useful Group 3 10.5f Prix Fille de l'Air winner Savoureuse Lady and a half-sister to no less than 13 winners, notably the top-class colt Mtoto, winner of the King George VI and Queen Elizabeth Diamond Stakes and the Coral Eclipse Stakes (twice), the French Group-placed winners Astonished and Button Up (both dams of stakes winners) and also the unraced Safe Haven, dam of the Group 3 Duke of York Stakes winner Lugana Beach. The second dam, Amazer (by Mincio), won once over 6f at 2 yrs in France and is a half-sister to the French Group 3 winner Silver Zara and to the dam of the Ebor Handicap winner Crazy. (Hamdan Al-Maktoum). *"Small, very attractive and a late foal, he's in Dubai and has had a slight setback and is going to be a back-end 2-y-o".*

946 - LAUD KARELIA ** [70] b.c. Royal Applause – Finlandaise (Arctic Tern).
March 5. Twelfth foal. 40,000Y. Tattersalls October.
Half-brother to the very useful German Group 3 12f winner Flying Dream, to the quite useful 2-y-o 6f winner Hyphen (both by Most Welcome), the useful 12f winner Dream Of Nurmi (by Pursuit Of Love), the fair 2-y-o 6f winner Aedean (by Risk Me), the modest 10f winner Madam Gymcrak (by Celestial Storm) and minor winners abroad by Seymour Hicks (3) and Be My Chief. The dam, a winner in France over 1m and 9f, is a half-sister to 6 winners. The second dam, Ferazza (by Hawaii), won twice in France and is a half-sister to the Canadian Grade 2 winner Flightish and to the dam of the Tattersalls Rogers Gold Cup winner Fair Of The Furze (herself dam of the Italian Derby winner White Muzzle). (Mrs M E Domvile & Mr M Hawkes). *"He's a good-looking son of Royal Applause but he's had a little setback and won't be that early".*

947 - MURGHOB * [76]   b.c. Lycius – Jamrat Samya (Sadler's Wells).
January 31. First foal.
The dam, unplaced over 6f on her only start at 2 yrs, is a sister to the quite useful 12f winner Raneen Alwatar. The second dam, Samya's Flame (by Artaius), a useful 3-y-o 9f and 10f winner, is a sister to the very smart filly Flame of Tara (herself dam of the top class filly Salsabil and the St James's Palace Stakes winner Marju) and a half-sister to the dams of the Breeders Cup Turf winner Northern Spur, the Doncaster Cup winners Kneller and Great Marquess and the 1m Grand Criterium winner Second Empire. (Sheikh Ahmed Al-Maktoum). *"For a first foal he's well grown, leggy and fairly mature. Not a great actioned horse, he doesn't look to be an early type and his pedigree suggests the same"* Significant sire/damsire crosses:- Hello.

948 - SEIHALI (IRE) * [72]   b.c. Alzao – Edwina (Caerleon).
March 28. Third foal. IR£180,000Y. Goffs Orby.
Half-brother to the 3-y-o Glenburn (by Dr Devious) and the quite useful dual 1m winner Your the Lady (by Indian Ridge). The dam, placed once over 6f at 2 yrs, is a half-sister to the useful listed sprint winner Roger The Butler. The second dam, Indian Jubilee (by Indian King), was a quite useful sprint winner of 6 races. *"A very attractive colt but he had a problem and has been back home. He's back with me now but he doesn't look that forward".*

949 - SELECTIVE ** [84]   b.c. Selkirk – Portelet (Night Shift).
January 25. Second foal. 60,000Y. Tattersalls October.
Half-brother to the useful 2000 2-y-o 6f (in Italy) and 7f winner Overspect (by Spectrum). The dam, a fairly useful winner of 4 races over 5f, is a half-sister to 3 minor winners. The second dam, Noirmont (by Dominion), is an unraced half-sister to the smart Prix Royal-Oak, Yorkshire Cup and Ormonde Stakes winner Braashee, the US Grade 3 winner Adam Smith and the Nell Gwyn Stakes winner Ghariba - both very useful. (Mr B Corman). *"A nice colt, very strong and robust-looking. I like him, he's an early foal and doesn't look as though he'll grow very much. One for June onwards I'd say and he's already showing me that he has ability".*

950 - SOLTAAT * [67]   b.c. Royal Applause – About Face (Midyan).
April 26. Third foal. 60,000Y. Tattersalls October.
Half-brother to Indian Giver (by Cadeaux Genereux), unplaced in 2 starts at 2 yrs in 2000. The dam is an unraced half-sister to 8 winners including the Group 1 1m St James's Palace Stakes winner Bijou d'Inde. The second dam, Pushkar (by Northfields), is an unraced half-sister to the Group 3 1m Brownstown Stakes winner Red Chip. (Sheikh Ahmed Al-Maktoum). *"Quite a late foal and he doesn't look precocious, but he's a nice sort of horse, a good mover and good-bodied. But I wouldn't think he'd be that early".*

951 - ZAWRAK (IRE) * [90]   ch.c. Zafonic – Gharam (Green Dancer).
February 25.
Brother to the fairly useful 2-y-o 7f winner and Group 3 Prestige Stakes third Elshamms and half-brother to the very useful 10f winner Shaya, the quite useful 10.5f winner Naazeq and the quite useful 2-y-o 1m winner Fatina (all by Nashwan). The dam, a very useful 2-y-o 6f winner, was third in the French 1,000 Guineas and is a half-sister to the US Grade 1 9f winner Talinum and the smart French middle-distance performer First Prayer. The second dam, Water Lily (by Riverman), was a very useful French 2-y-o and subsequently winner of the Grade 3 Next Move Handicap in the USA. (Hamdan Al-Maktoum). *"He's out in Dubai at the moment and is a little bit temperamental. He goes quite nicely and should make a 2-y-o".*

952 - ZUBAYRR (IRE) * [75]   gr.c. Darshaan – High Mare (Highest Honor).
May 17. Second foal. IR£200,000Y. Goffs Orby.
Half-brother to Caposo (by Common Grounds), unplaced in 2 starts at 2 yrs in 2000. The dam, a dual French 2-y-o winner at around 7f, was fourth in the Group 3 5f Prix du Bois and is a half-sister to 2 winners. The second dam, Belle et Chere (by Lyphard), is a placed half-sister to Ma Biche, a winner of four Group 1 events including the Cheveley Park Stakes and the One Thousand Guineas. (Sheikh Ahmed Al-Maktoum). *"A lovely colt. I very much like him but he's a late foal by Darshaan so he's*

certainly not going to be early. He's a very good mover though and a really good goer. A real quality horse and I like him a lot".

SIR M STOUTE

953 - AKEED MALIK (USA) [86]   ch.c. Diesis – Bella Ballerina (Sadler's Wells).
February 6. Second reported foal. 200,000Y. Tattersalls Houghton.
The dam, a quite useful 3-y-o 9f winner, is a sister to the high-class Group 2 10f Prince of Wales's Stakes and Group 3 10f Brigadier Gerard Stakes winner Stagecraft and the useful listed 9f winner Balalaika and a half-sister to the very useful dual 1m listed stakes winner Hyabella. The second dam, Bella Colora (by Bellypha), won four races including the Group 2, 9.2f Prix de l'Opera and the Group 3, 7f Waterford Candelabra Stakes and was a very close third in the One Thousand Guineas. She is a half-sister to the Irish Oaks winner Colorspin (herself dam of Opera House and Kayf Tara), to the Irish Champion Stakes winner Cezanne and the very useful filly Rappa Tap Tap. (Mohammed Jaber).

954 - BOLD AIM [84]   b.c. Indian Ridge – Baldemosa (Lead On Time).
April 22. Second foal.
Half-brother to the useful 2000 2-y-o dual 6f winner Caustic Wit (by Cadeaux Genereux). The dam won over 1m at Evry at 3 yrs and is a half-sister to 4 winners including the Group 1 5.5f Prix Robert Papin winner Balbonella (herself dam of the top-class sprinter Anabaa and the French One Thousand Guineas winner Always Loyal) and the French listed 12f winner Bamwhite. The second dam, Bamieres (by Riverman), was placed fourth twice in France and is out of the French middle-distance winner Bergamasque (by Kashmir II). (Maktoum Al-Maktoum).

955 - CASTANET [79]   b.f. Pennekamp – Addaya (Persian Bold).
April 1. Third foal. 85,000Y. Tattersalls October.
Half-sister to the promising 2000 2-y-o 7f winner Priors Lodge (by Grand Lodge). The dam ran once unplaced and is a half-sister to 4 winners in Japan. The second dam, Night Of Stars (by Sadler's Wells), won a listed event in Germany over 1m and is a half-sister to the Beeswing, Hungerford and Kiveton Park Stakes winner Hadeer.

956 - COMFY (USA) [83]   b.c. Lear Fan – Souplesse (Majestic Light).
January 26.
The dam, a listed 10f winner in France, is a half-sister to the very smart Eltish, winner of the 7f Lanson Champagne Stakes and the 1m Royal Lodge Stakes and runner-up in the Grade 1 8.5f Breeders Cup Juvenile and to the useful 5f and 6f winner Forest Gazelle. The second dam, Nimble Feet (by Danzig), is a sister to the Grade 1 Washington Lassie Stakes winner Contredance and to the listed Roses Stakes winner Old Alliance and a half-sister to the Group winners Shotiche and Skimble and to the dam of the One Thousand Guineas winner Wince. (Khaled Abdulla).

957 - CONTRACT [86]   b.c. Entrepreneur – Ispahan (Rusticaro).
March 13. Eleventh foal. FF1,500,000. Deauville August.
Closely related to the Group 1 10.5f Prix Lupin winner Cloudings (by Sadler's Wells) and half-sister to 6 winners including the French listed 1m winner Lady Wishing Well (by Hero's Honor). The dam, a quite useful 2-y-o 6f and 3-y-o 1m winner, is a half-sister to the Gallinule Stakes winner Bog Road, the Prix du Gros Chene winner Royal Hobbit and the dam of the Italian Oaks winner Ivor's Image. The second dam, Royal Danseuse, won the Irish One Thousand Guineas.

958 - EXCLUSIVITY [83]   b.f. Sadler's Wells – Exclusive Virtue (Shadeed).
April 7. Fifth foal.
Half-brother to the fairly useful 2-y-o 1m winner and listed 11.5f Oaks Trial third Virtuous, to the fair 12f all-weather winner Exclusion Zone (both by Exit To Nowhere) and the German winner Nulli Secundus (by Polar Falcon). The dam, a fairly useful 2-y-o 7f winner, stayed 12f and is a half-sister to 8 winners including the 1997 Two Thousand Guineas winner and Derby fourth Entrepreneur, the smart Group 1 1m Coronation Stakes winner Exclusive, the smart Cheshire Oaks winner and Epsom Oaks second Dance a Dream and the very useful middle-distance listed winner Sadler's Image. The second dam, Exclusive Order (by Exclusive Native), won the Group 2 6.5f Prix Maurice de Gheest and the Group 3 7f Prix de la Porte Maillot.

959 - FIRST CHARTER [79]   b.c. Polish Precedent – By Charter (Shirley Heights).
March 10. Seventh foal. 160,000Y. Tattersalls Houghton.
Half-brother to the fairly useful 2000 2-y-o 6f winner Ridge Runner (by Indian Ridge), to the fairly useful 12f winner and listed placed Careful Timing (by Caerleon), the quite useful 2-y-o 7f all-weather winner Magna Carta (by Royal Academy) and the fair 2-y-o 7f winner Green Charter (by Green Desert). The dam, a useful 2-y-o 7f winner and second in two listed events over middle-distances, is a sister to Zinaad and a half-sister to Time Allowed, both winners of the Group 2 12f Jockey Club Stakes. The second dam, Time Charter (by Saritamer), was an exceptionally talented filly and winner of the Oaks, the King George VI and Queen Elizabeth Diamond Stakes, the Champion Stakes, Coronation Cup, Prix Foy and Sun Chariot Stakes. (Saeed Suhail).
Significant sire/damsire crosses:- Her Ladyship.

---

960 - FUNFAIR [84]   b.c. Singspiel – Red Carnival (Mr Prospector).
January 28. Second foal.
The dam, winner of the Group 2 6f Cherry Hinton Stakes, stayed 1m at 3 yrs and is a half-sister to the US Grade 1 winners Golden Attraction and Cape Town. The second dam, Seaside Attraction (by Seattle Slew), won the Grade 1 Kentucky Oaks and is a half-sister to the triple US Grade 1 winner Gorgeous, the Canadian dual Grade 3 winner Key to the Moon and the Group 3 Princess Margaret Stakes winner Hiamm. The third dam, Kamar (by Key to the Mint), was a champion Canadian 3-y-o filly and is a sister to the Grade 1 winner Love Smitten (dam of the top-class colt Swain) and a half-sister to the US stakes winners Dancing on a Cloud and Stellarette (dam of the Grade 1 winner Cuddles).

---

961 - GALLANT HERO [81]   b.c. Rainbow Quest – Gay Gallanta (Woodman).
February 14. Third foal.
Half-brother to Gay Heroine (by Woodman), a promising second over 1m on her only outing at 2 yrs in 2000. The dam was a very smart winner of the Group 1 6f Cheveley Park Stakes and the Group 3 5f Queen Mary Stakes and was second in the 1m Falmouth Stakes. She is closely related to the useful 10.4f John Smiths Cup winner Porto Foricos and to the useful 6f (at 2 yrs) and 7f winner Sundance Kid and a half-sister to the smart Group 2 10f Gallinule Stakes winner Sportsworld. The second dam, Gallanta (by Nureyev), was a useful winner of 3 races from 5.5f to 1m including the Prix de Coburg, was second in the Group 1 Prix Morny and is a half-sister to the top-class French middle-distance colt Gay Mecene, to the Grade 3 winner Lassie Dear (dam of the high-class sprinter Wolfhound) and the French 10f winner Dry Fly (dam of the useful 2-y-o's Fotitieng and Grey Duster).

---

962 - GRAIN OF GOLD [85]   b.f. Mr Prospector – Pure Grain (Polish Precedent).
February 4. Second foal.
Closely related to the quite useful 2000 2-y-o 7f winner Goncharova (by Gone West). The dam won 5 races including the Group 1 12f Irish Oaks and the Group 1 12f Yorkshire Oaks and is a half-sister to 2 winners. The second dam, Mill Line (by Mill Reef), a fair 14.6f winner at 3 yrs and a half-sister to 6 winners, is out of the Group 2 Park Hill Stakes winner Quay Line - herself a sister to the Group 2 Premio Dormello winner Ancholia, the listed stakes winners High Finale and Trade Line and the dam of the dual Lockinge Stakes winner Soviet Line.

---

963 - JOLAN'S WISH [74]   ch.f. Woodman – Jumilla (El Gran Senor).
April 5. Second foal. 120,000Y. Tattersalls Houghton.
The dam, a quite useful 2-y-o 6f winner, is a half-sister to the fairly useful 2-y-o 7f winner Spurned (dam of the stakes winners Hidden Meadow, Kingsclere and Scorned) and to the German champion 2-y-o and subsequent US Grade 2 placed Winter Quarters. The second dam, Refill (by Mill Reef), placed fourth in the Group 3 6f Cherry Hinton Stakes at 2 yrs, subsequently won 4 races at up to 11f in the USA and is a half-sister to 9 winners including the dam of the Group 2 5f Kings Stand Stakes winner Don't Worry Me.

---

964 - KING OF HAPPINESS (USA) [76]   ch.c. Spinning World – Mystery Rays (Nijinsky).
April 11. Ninth foal. 220,000Y. Tattersalls Houghton.
Half-brother to the very promising 2000 7f and 1m placed 2-y-o King's Secret (by Kingmambo), to the French 2-y-o 1m winner and 3-y-o listed 1m placed Metaphor (by Woodman), the minor US winner John Irving (by Mr Prospector) and minor winners in Belgium (by Devil's Bag) and France (by Bering).

The dam won 3 races in France including the Group 3 12f Prix Minerve and Group 3 10.5f Prix Fille de l'Air, is closely related to the German Group 2 6f winner Robin des Pins and a half-sister 4 winners including the Group 3 1m Beresford Stakes winner Ahkaam. The second dam, Rare Mint (by Key To The Mint), was unplaced. (Saeed Suhail).

965 - LAYA'S WONDER (USA) [84]   ch.f. Woodman – Lyric Fantasy (Tate Gallery). February 5. Third foal. 360,000Y. Tattersalls Houghton.

Half-sister to the fairly useful 6f anf 7f placed Moon God (by Thunder Gulch). The dam was the champion European 2-y-o of 1992 and won 6 races including the Group 1 Keeneland Nunthorpe Stakes and the Group 3 Queen Mary Stakes. She is closely related to the Group 1 Dewhurst Stakes winner In Command and a half-sister to the Group 1 Middle Park Stakes and Group 1 Haydock Sprint Cup winner Royal Applause. The second dam, Flying Melody (by Auction Ring), was a sprint winner of 2 races in France and is a half-sister to the listed winners Pearl Star, Portese and Seadiver.

966 - LIGHT SCENT (USA) [92]   ch.c. Silver Hawk – Music Lane (Miswaki). April 19. Third foal. $300,000. Keeneland September.

The dam, a minor winner at 4 yrs in the USA, is a half-sister to 8 winners including Hawkster (winner of three US Grade 1 events), the French listed winner Silver Kite and the Group 3 Prix de la Grotte winner and Irish Oaks third Silver Lane (all by Silver Hawk - the sire of this colt). The second dam, Strait Lane (by Chieftain), is an unraced half-sister to 2 stakes winners in the USA. (Saeed Suhail).

967 - MEDALLIST [79]   b.c. Danehill – Obsessive (Seeking The Gold). February 7. Second foal.

Closely related to the quite useful 2000 2-y-o 6f winner Spy Master (by Green Desert). The dam, a useful 2-y-o 6f winner and third in the Group 3 10.4f Musidora Stakes, is a half-sister to several winners. The second dam, Secret Obsession (by Secretariat), a fairly useful 10f winner, is a half-sister to numerous winners including the Group 2 12f King Edward VII Stakes winner Beyton. The third dam, Ann Stuart (by Lyphard), is an unraced half-sister to the Champion US filly Chris Evert (dam of the Grade 1 winner Six Crowns), the US stakes winner All Rainbows (dam of the Kentucky Derby winner Winning Colors) and to the dams of Two Timing (winner of the Prince Of Wales's Stakes) and Missed The Storm (winner of the Grade 1 Test Stakes).

968 - PRINCELY VENTURE (IRE) [72]   ch.c. Entrepreneur – Sun Princess (English Prince). April 2.

Closely related to the high-class Group 1 7f Dewhurst Stakes dead-heater Prince of Dance, to the useful middle-distance winners Ballet Prince and Golden Ball and the quite useful 12f winner Stage Struck (all by Sadler's Wells). The dam was a top-class winner of the Oaks, the St Leger and the Yorkshire Oaks and was placed in both the Prix de l'Arc de Triomphe and the King George. She is a half-sister to the high-class middle-distance colt Saddlers Hall and to the Sean Graham Fillies Stakes winner Dancing Shadow - herself dam of the very useful fillies Dancing Bloom and River Dancer and thus grandam of the Champion Stakes winner Spectrum.

969 - PROCESSION [76]   b.f. Zafonic – Applaud (Rahy). March 23. Second foal.

Closely related to the fair 2000 7f placed 2-y-o Pagliacci (by Gone West). The dam, a smart 2-y-o winner of the Group 2 6f Cherry Hinton Stakes, is a sister to the useful 2-y-o 7f winner Houston Time. The second dam, Band (by Northern Dancer), is a placed half-sister to 5 winners including the US Grade 3 9f New Orleans Handicap winner Festive.

970 - RADIANT [88]   ch.f. Machiavellian – Brave Revival (Dancing Brave). February 3. Third foal.

Half-sister to the very useful 2000 2-y-o 6f winner Bravado (by Zafonic) and to the fairly useful 1999 2-y-o 7f winner Vigour (by Lion Cavern). The dam, a fairly useful dual 1m winner, was listed-placed over 8.5f and is a half-sister to the high-class Group 1 6f Nunthorpe Stakes winner Pivotal. The second dam, Fearless Revival (by Cozzene), was a useful 2-y-o 6f and 7f winner and was listed-placed over 10f at 3 yrs. (Cheveley Park Stud).

971 - SEQUENTIAL [88]   b.c. Rainbow Quest – Dance Sequence (Mr Prospector).
April 23. Second foal.
Half-brother to the fairly useful 2000 2-y-o dual 5f winner Dance On (by Caerleon). The dam, a very useful winner of the Group 2 6f Lowther Stakes, is a sister to the Japanese Grade 2 1m winner Shake Hand and to the minor US sprint stakes winner Dance With Grace. The second dam, Dancing Tribute (by Nureyev), a very useful 6f and 1m winner and second in the Cheveley Park Stakes, is a sister to the US stakes-placed winners Private Interview and Proper Dance and is closely related to the dam of the Cherry Hinton Stakes winner Dazzle.

972 - SHAKRAN [95]   ch.c. Zafonic – Myself (Nashwan).
January 21. Second foal. 170,000Y. Tattersalls October.
Half-brother to the useful 2000 2-y-o 6f winner and Group 2 7f Champagne Stakes third Ghayth (by Sadler's Wells). The dam, a smart winner of the Group 3 7f Nell Gwyn Stakes, is a half-sister to numerous winners including the Group 3 Princess Margaret Stakes winner Bluebook, the useful 1m winner Phountzi and the dam of the Nell Gwyn Stakes winner Thrilling Day. The second dam, Pushy (by Sharpen Up), won the Queen Mary Stakes and the Cornwallis Stakes at 2 yrs and is a half-sister to numerous winners including the Japan Cup winner Jupiter Island and the high-class 2-y-o Precocious. (Hamdan Al-Maktoum).

973 - SILISTRA [88]   gr.c. Sadler's Wells – Dundel (Machiavellian).
February 21. First foal. 180,000Y. Tattersalls Houghton.
The dam, a quite useful 7f winner, is a half-sister to 6 winners including the Group 3 6f Prix de Seine-et-Oise winner Seltitude. The second dam, Dunoof (by Shirley Heights), a fairly useful 2-y-o 7f winner, is a sister to the Premio Roma, Park Hill Stakes and Ribblesdale Stakes winner High Hawk (dam of the 3 Group winners including the high-class racehorse and sire In the Wings) and to the winning dams of the Derby winner High-Rise and the Grade 1 Rothmans International winner Infamy. (Ahmed Ali).

974 - SOUND ASLEEP (USA) [75]   b.f. Woodman – Sleep Easy (Seattle Slew).
January 27. Second foal.
Closely related to the unraced 2000 2-y-o Received Wisdom (by Gone West). The dam, winner of the Grade 1 9f Hollywood Oaks, is closely related to the quite useful 2-y-o 7f winner Shoogle and a half-sister to the smart US 6f (at 2 yrs) to 8.5f winner Electrify. The second dam, Dokki (by Northern Dancer), is an unraced half-sister to the champion US colt Slew O'Gold - winner of seven Grade 1 events - and Coastal, winner of the Belmont Stakes. The second dam, Alluvial (by Buckpasser), is an unraced daughter of the champion US 3-y-o filly Bayou and a half-sister to the Santa Margarita Handicap winner Batteur. (Khalid Abdulla).
Significant sire/damsire crosses:- Hishi Akebono (Gr 1), Patience Game (Gr 3), Rey Seattle (Gr 3).

975 - STARRING (FR) [76]   b.f. Ashkalani – Sweeping (Indian King).
April 27. Seventh foal. 160,000Y. Tattersalls October.
Half-sister to the very smart dual listed 5f winner Watching (by Indian Ridge), to the quite useful 12f to 20f winner Puteri Wentworth (by Sadler's Wells), the fair 1996 3-y-o 6f winner Desert Lynx and the Italian winner Svampita (both by Green Desert). The dam was a useful 2-y-o 6f winner, was placed over 8.5f at 3 yrs and is a half-sister to 9 winners. The second dam, Glancing (by Grundy), a very useful 2-y-o winner of the Group 3 5f Prix d'Arenberg, is a half-sister to the Middle Park Stakes winner Bassenthwaite and to the dam of the Prix de l'Abbaye winner Keen Hunter.

976 - SUPREMACY [82]   ch.c. Vettori – High Tern (High Line).
April 27. Tenth foal. 125,000Y. Tattersalls Houghton.
Half-brother to the unplaced 2000 2-y-o Blind Spot (by Inchinor), to the 1998 Derby winner and King George VI and Queen Elizabeth Stakes second High Rise (by High Estate), the quite useful and tough winner of 19 races at up to 10f Sooty Tern (by Wassl), the poor 7f and 8.5f all-weather winner Hi Mujtahid (by Mujtahid), two winners abroad by Persian Heights and Shaadi and the placed dam of the Italian Oaks winner Zomaradah. The dam, a fairly useful winning stayer, is a half-sister to the Group 1 Premio Roma and Group 2 Ribblesdale Stakes winner High Hawk (herself dam of the Breeders Cup Turf and Coronation Cup winner In The Wings) and to Seriema (dam of the Rothmans International and

Sun Chariot Stakes winner Infamy). The second dam, Sunbittern (by Sea Hawk II), was a very useful 2-y-o 6f and 7f winner and was fourth in the Cheveley Park Stakes.

---

977 - TANTALIZE * [105]   b.f. Lion Cavern – Belle et Deluree (The Minstrel).
March 16.

Sister to the fairly useful 7f winner Enchant, closely related to the smart filly Dazzle (by Gone West) winner of the Group 3 6f Cherry Hinton Stakes and placed in both the Cheveley Park Stakes and the One Thousand Guineas and half-sister to the useful 1999 2-y-o dual 7f winner Hypnotize (by Machiavellian), the dual Italian winner Jinx Joke (by Miswaki), the dual US winner Paula Sue's Prince (by Cozzene) and a winner in Hungary by Tank's Prospect. The dam won over 1m (at 2 yrs) and 10f in France and is a half-sister to the very useful 6f and 1m winner and Cheveley Park Stakes second Dancing Tribute (herself dam of the Lowther Stakes winner Dance Sequence). The second dam, Sophisticated Girl (by Stop The Music), a very smart American 2-y-o, was second in the Grade 1 8.5f Oak Leaf Stakes.

---

978 - WISH [76]   b.f. Danehill – Dazzle (Gone West).
February 3. First foal.

The dam, a smart winner of the Group 3 6f Cherry Hinton Stakes and placed in both the Cheveley Park Stakes and the One Thousand Guineas, is a half-sister to the fairly useful 7f winners Hypnotize and Enchant. The second dam, Belle Et Deluree (by The Minstrel), won over 1m (at 2 yrs) and 10f in France and is a half-sister to the very useful 6f and 1m winner and Cheveley Park Stakes second Dancing Tribute (herself dam of the Lowther Stakes winner Dance Sequence).

---

979 - UNNAMED [84]   b.c. Alzao – Ballet Shoes (Ela-Mana-Mou).
May 21. Fifth foal. 230,000Y. Tattersalls Houghton.

Half-brother to the 3-y-o Colorado Falls (by Nashwan), to the high-class Irish Oaks, Yorkshire Oaks and Prix de l'Opera winner Petrushka and the Irish 7f winner and listed-placed Danse Classique (by Night Shift). The dam, a fair 3-y-o dual 5f winner, is a half-sister to the Irish Two Thousand Guineas and Dubai Champion Stakes winner Spectrum and the useful 1m winner Nash House. The second dam, River Dancer (by Irish River), was a smart French winner over 5f (at 2 yrs) and the 1m Prix de la Calonne and was third in the French One Thousand Guineas. (Hamdan Al-Maktoum).
Significant sire/damsire crosses:- Alcazar.

J TOLLER

---

980 - CAUGHT SHORT (IRE) ** [61]   ch.c. Night Shift – Sharp Deposit (Sharpo).
March 18. Fourth foal. 20,000Y. Tattersalls December.

Half-brother to the useful 1998 2-y-o 6f winner and Group 2 6f Cherry Hinton Stakes fourth Rose Of Mooncoin (by Brief Truce), to the quite useful 2-y-o 6f winner Fly Tip (by Bluebird) and the Italian 5f (at 2 yrs) and 1m winner Come Va Va (by Tenby). The dam is an unraced half-sister to 3 winners including the Ebor Handicap winner Deposki. The second dam, Deposit (by Thatch), was placed at 2 yrs before winning in the West Indies and is a half-sister to the Sweet Solera Stakes winner Lucayan Princess (herself dam of the Group winners Cloud Castle, Luso and Needle Gun). (Mr P C J Dalby). *"I'm pleased with him and would have thought he'd make a 2-y-o over six furlongs. He's a good, strong horse with a good attitude".*

---

981 - MONSAL DALE (IRE) ** [67]   ch.c. Desert King – Zanella (Nordico).
February 28. Second foal. IR£85,000Y. Goffs Orby.

Half-brother to the fair 2000 Irish 3-y-o 6.5f winner Paws (by Brief Truce). The dam won over 7.5f in Ireland at 2 yrs and was listed-placed. She is a sister to the Group 3 Anglesey Stakes winner and Group 1 National Stakes second Malvernico and a half-sister to the useful 11f winner Biennale. The second dam, Malvern Beauty (by Shirley Heights), was a useful 10.5f winner and a half-sister to 2 winners. (Duke of Devonshire). *"He's a good, tough type of colt, I like him and hopefully he'll be ready to race in June over six furlongs. A fairly hardy sort, he'll probably want plenty of work to stop him getting too above himself".*

982 - RIBEAUVILLE * [66]   ch.f. Vettori – Juvenilia (Masterclass).

January 23. First foal.

The dam showed modest form in maidens when placed twice over 7f at 3 yrs (her only starts), but was injured an unable to race again. She is a half-sister to the quite useful 2-y-o 6f winner Kingswell Prince out of the unraced Amtico (by Bairn). (G B Partnership). *"A medium-sized, quite strong and fairly precocious filly, she's going to be one of our earlier 2-y-o's".*

983 - SIMON'S SEAT (USA) [82]   ch.c. Woodman – Spire (Topsider).

May 30. Third foal. $100,000Y. Keeneland September.

The dam, a stakes winner and Grade 3 placed in the USA, is a half-sister to 2 winners. The second dam, Eaves (by Cox's Ridge), a stakes-placed winner of 3 races, is a half-sister to the US dual Grade 3 winner Boundary. (Duke of Devonshire). *"Quite a nice sort, but because he's such a late foal I haven't done anything with him yet. He's beginning to develop now and is a beautiful mover. It's early days and we'll be patient with him with a view to running him at the back-end".*

984 - TWENTY SEVEN (IRE) * [63]   b.f. Efisio – Naked Poser (Night Shift).

May 10. First foal. 21,000Y. Tattersalls December.

The dam, a quite useful 2-y-o 6f winner, is a half-sister to 4 winners including the useful sprinter Damalis. The second dam, Art Age (by Artaius), is an unraced half-sister to 9 winners including the listed Irish Cambridgeshire winner National Form. (Paul Smith). *"She's quite a late foal so I haven't done much with her yet, but she looks a speedy type and is a sprinter in the making from the mid-season onwards".*

M TOMPKINS

985 - ALBUNDY (IRE) * [72]   b.c. Alzao – Grove Daffodil (Salt Dome).

March 17.

The dam, a quite useful filly, won over 7f at 2 yrs and was fourth in the Group 3 10.4f Musidora Stakes. She is a half-sister to several winners including the 1m and 10f winner Shannon Express. The second dam, Tatisha (by Habitat), won over 1m in France and is a half-sister to the high-class sprinter Green God. (Mr P H Betts). *"I trained the mother and this is a lovely, strong horse. He won't be early but he's a grand sort and I like him a lot".*

986 - BARKBY (IRE) * [79]   b.c. Lahib – Portree (Slip Anchor).

April 28. Fifth foal. IR£28,000Y. Goffs Orby.

Half-brother to the 3-y-o Chitterman House (by Charnwood Forest), to the fair dual 1m winner Sovereign State (by Soviet Lad) and the 2m seller winner Best Port (by Be My Guest). The dam, a modest 7f (at 2 yrs) to 12.2f placed maiden, is a half-sister to 4 winners including the Park Hill Stakes winner Coigach, the Cheshire Oaks winner Kyle Rhea and the Park Hill Stakes second Applecross (herself dam of the very smart winners Craigsteel and Invermark). The second dam, Rynechra (by Blakeney), a useful dual 12f winner, is a half-sister to 6 winners. (Beryl Lockey). *"He's done very well and is a very strong horse. He had a bit of a problem just when we broke him in and he's now starting to get into the swing of it. A compact type, he moves very well and he'll be racing in May".*

987 - BIT OF LUCK ** [62]   ch.c. First Trump – Elle Reef (Shareef Dancer).

May 10. Fifth foal. 22,000Y. Tattersalls October.

Brother to the modest 7f (at 2 yrs) to 10.5f winner of 6 races Ace Of Trumps and half-brother to the winner of 8 races at up to 10.5f in Italy Barbanera (by Aragon). The dam is an unraced half-sister to to 3 minor winners. The second dam, Lovely Lagoon (by Mill Reef), won once at 4 yrs and is a half-sister to 7 winners including the dual French Group 3 placed Chine. (Mrs Beryl Lockey). *"A nice, strong colt, he's a little bit on the leg but he's an attractive horse, a good mover and I should think his ideal trip this year will be six or seven furlongs".*

988 - BERK THE JERK (IRE) ** [70]   b.c. Bahamian Bounty – Pocket Book (Reference Point).

February 10. First foal. 67,000Y. Tattersalls October.

The dam, placed once in Ireland at 3 yrs, is a half-sister to 9 winners including the high-class colts Indian Lodge (winner of the Group 1 1m Prix du Moulin and the Group 1 7f Prix de la Foret) and Sarhoob (winner of the Group 2 10f Prix Eugene Adam) and the very useful Group 3 10f Prix la Force winner Sifting Gold. The second dam, Repetitious (by Northfields), won 5 races including the listed 6f Stewards Cup, was second in the Group 2 7f Moyglare Stud Stakes and is a sister to the Ribblesdale Stakes winner Nanticious. (Mrs Angela Lovat). *"The most expensive Bahamian Bounty yearling last year, he's a real 2-y-o type. A strong horse with a good outlook and a lovely mover. We won't aim him too high to begin with, but I think he could be a grand horse. He'll probably start off over five furlongs sometime in April".*

**989 - CORUNDUM (USA) ** [70]   b.br.c. Benny The Dip – Santi Sana (Formidable).
January 30. Fourth foal. 62,000Y. Tattersalls October.
Half-brother to the fair 1998 2-y-o dual 7f winner Minnesota (by Danehill). The dam, a quite useful 3-y-o 7f winner, is a sister to the very smart Group 1 Premio Emilio Turati winner and good sire Efisio and a half-sister to 3 winners including the Grade 1 Santa Barbara Handicap and Grade 2 San Gorgonio Handicap winner Mountain Bear (by Welsh Pageant). The second dam, Eldoret (by High Top), was a useful 6f and 1m winner and was second in the listed Virginia Stakes. (Mrs Angela Lovat). *"He's a small colt and black – just like his sire in that respect. He'll probably want seven furlongs, is a good mover and has the right attitude".*

**990 - SOSUMI ** [58]   br.f. Be My Chief – Princess Deya (Be My Guest).
February 11. First foal.
The dam, unplaced in both her starts at 2 yrs, is a half-sister to the Group 1 10f Eclipse Stakes winner Compton Admiral. The second dam, Sumoto (by Mtoto), a useful 6f (at 2 yrs) and 7f winner, is a half-sister to 3 winners including the useful listed Princess Elizabeth Stakes third Sumonda. (P A & D G Sakal). *"She's a very nice filly, could be an early 2-y-o and goes well. A filly with the right attitude, she's strong and is one to follow I should think".*

**991 - TAHITIAN STORM (IRE) * [65]   b.c. Catrail – Razana (Kahyasi).
April 1. Second foal. 56,000Y. Tattersalls October.
Half-brother to the fair 2000 1m placed 2-y-o Ovambo (by Namaqualand). The dam, a fair 10f winner here, later won at up to 12f in France and is a half-sister to the Italian listed winner Raysiza. The second dam, Raysiya (by Cure The Blues), a fairly useful Irish 10f and 12f winner, is a half-sister to 5 winners including the Group 3 10f Royal Whip Stakes winner Rayseka and the listed James Seymour Stakes winner Riyda. (P A & D G Sakal). *"He's another attractive horse with a lovely outlook on life. A good mover, he'll be a 2-y-o and will train on too. He'll have the speed for five furlongs but will get seven I should think. I don't think there's much wrong with him at all".*

M TREGONING

**992 - ALRAYIHAH (IRE) ** [94]   ch.f. Nashwan – Irish Valley (Irish River).
March 28.
Sister to the unraced 2000 D Loder trained 2-y-o Morahib, closely related to the champion 2-y-o of 1995, Alhaarth (by Unfuwain), winner of the Dewhurst Stakes, the Laurent Perrier Champagne Stakes, the Prix Dollar, the Budweiser American Bowl International Stakes and the Prix du Rond-Point and half-sister to the very useful 1990 2-y-o Group 3 7f Prix du Calvados winner Green Pola, the useful Irish middle-distance winner Gaelic Myth (both by Nijinsky) and to Celtic Brave (by Shadeed), a winner of 8 minor races at up to 8.5f in the USA. The dam is an unplaced half-sister to 10 winners, notably the Observer Gold Cup, French Two Thousand Guineas and 10.5f Prix Lupin winner and good sire Green Dancer, the US Grade 3 winner Ercolano and the US Graded stakes winner Val Danseur. The second dam, Green Valley (by Val de Loir), was an unraced daughter of the Prix de l'Abbaye and Prix Robert Papin winner Sly Pola. (Hamdan Al-Maktoum). *"By a Derby winner and out of a dam who's bred a champion 2-y-o. What more could you want? A beautiful mover, she's very, very nice and although she's a bit leggy she's furnishing all the time. She won't be necessarily an early one but if she's showing enough in mid-summer we might give her a go".*

**993 - ANOOF ** [68]   b.f. Marju – Waqood (Riverman).
March 19. Third foal.
Half-sister to Mutawaqed (by Zafonic), unplaced over 7f on his only start at 2 yrs in 2000. The dam, a fair middle-distance placed 3-y-o, is a half-sister to Harayir, a winner of six races from 6f to 1m including the One Thousand Guineas, the Tripleprint Celebration Mile, the Challenge Stakes and the Lowther Stakes and the useful 7f (at 2 yrs) and 10.2f winner Min Alhawa. The second dam, Saffaanh

(by Shareef Dancer), a quite useful 12.2f winner, is out of the high-class Irish Oaks, Lancashire Oaks and Musidora Stakes winner Give Thanks (by Relko). (Hamdan Al-Maktoum). *"Seemingly there's not much wrong with this filly and she's going OK. Also, she's not too big which is in her favour if she's going to do well as a 2-y-o".*

---

994 - ASAAFEER (USA) * [93]**   b.br.f. Dayjur – Mathkurh (Riverman).
May 15.
Sister to the 3-y-o Mufrah and to the very useful 1997 2-y-o Group 3 6f Cherry Hinton Stakes and listed 5f Windsor Castle Stakes winner Asfurah, closely related to the fairly useful 5.3f (at 2 yrs) and 6f winner Alumisiyah (by Danzig) and half-sister to the Dubai 10f winner Mutamanni (by Caerleon) and the quite useful 6f winner Istintaj (by Nureyev). The dam, a useful 5f (at 2 yrs) and 6f winner, is a half-sister to the Group 3 6f Princess Margaret Stakes winner Muhbubh. The second dam, Manal (by Luthier), is an unplaced sister to the good French horses Twig Moss and Tip Moss. (Hamdan Al-Maktoum). *"I had a good look at her in Dubai because the dam is interesting. She could be OK, but if she's going to be anything you'd think she'd be a 2-y-o. We'll have to see how we go with her when she arrives".*
Significant sire/damsire crosses:- Asfurah.

---

995 - ASHA'TH * [86]**   b.c. Barathea – Elrayahin (Riverman).
March 16. First foal.
The dam, a fair 7f and 1m placed 2-y-o, is out of the modest 6f to 10f placed Gracious Beauty (by Nijinsky), herself a sister to the dual US Grade 1 winner Maplejinsky (dam of the Grade 1 winner Sky Beauty) and closely related to the brilliant sprinter Dayjur. The third dam, Gold Beauty (by Mr Prospector), won 8 races including two Grade 2 stakes events and was a champion sprinter in the USA. (Hamdan Al-Maktoum). *"If he's anything he's a 2-y-o because he's not very big. He looked liked being very early but he's just on the easy list for the moment. He looks like being a 2-y-o runner later on".*

---

996 - BISHR * [74]**   b.c. Royal Applause – Hawayah (Shareef Dancer).
February 16, Fifth foal. 190,000Y. Tattersalls October.
Half-brother to the unraced 2000 2-y-o Showpiece, to the French 9f winner Nena Maka (both by Selkirk) and the fair 2000 3-y-o 7f winner Tee Cee (by Lion Cavern). The dam, a modest 2-y-o 7f winner, is a half-sister to 4 winners including the quite useful 6f winner and subsequent US stakes winner Promptly. The second dam, Ghariba (by Final Straw), a very useful winner of the Nell Gwyn Stakes, was fourth in the One Thousand Guineas and is a half-sister to the smart Yorkshire Cup winner Braashee and the very useful 1m to 12f winning colt Adam Smith. (Hamdan Al-Maktoum). *"A very good-looking horse, he hasn't grown too big and he's certainly athletic enough. He could well be a nice type".*

---

997 - CURATE (USA) * [84]   ch.c. Unfuwain – Carniola (Rainbow Quest).
April 9. Second foal.
Half-brother to the 2000 French trained 2-y-o Kranjska (by Caerleon). The dam was a French 10.5f listed winner at 3 yrs. The second dam, Carnival Spirit (by Kris), a fairly useful 3-y-o 1m winner, is a half-sister to the top-class Prix de l'Arc de Triomphe and Grand Prix de Paris winner Saumarez and to the very useful 2-y-o 8.2f winner and Italian Derby fourth Balliol Boy. (Sheikh Mohammed). *"Certainly on looks he's the nicest colt I've had sent to me by Sheikh Mohammed. It's about time we did some good for him and I hope this is the one. He's certainly a nice horse. His knees were a bit open earlier on but he seems to be a sound type, he's going quite well and I just like the way he moves. Despite his pedigree I'd still be hopeful of him being a 2-y-o".*

---

998 - ELUTRAH * [72]**   b.f. Darshaan – Balaabel (Sadler's Wells).
April 17. Third foal.
Sister to the very useful 2000 2-y-o Group 3 7f Rockfel Stakes winner Sayedah and half-sister to the quite useful 1999 3-y-o 7f winner Marasem (by Cadeaux Genereux). The dam, a quite useful 1m winneris a half-sister to 3 winners including the US Grade 2 7f winner Kayrawan. The second dam, Muhbubh (by Blushing Groom), won the Group 3 6f Princess Margaret Stakes and was second in the Group 2 6f Lowther Stakes. (Hamdan Al-Maktoum). *"A very good-looking filly. Her sister Sayedah is too, but in a way this filly seems to have even more scope. Anyone who bred a filly who looks like this would be absolutely thrilled – she's really nice and sensible just like her sister. She seems to be full of potential, is a nice mover and of all our fillies I'd pick her out – on looks anyway".*
Significant sire/damsire crosses:- Sayedah.

999 - ESLOOB (USA) * [81] b.f. Diesis – Roseate Tern (Blakeney).
January 29. Sixth foal.

Half-sister to the useful listed 10f winner Siyadah and to the fairly useful 1997 2-y-o 7f winner Fakhr (by Riverman). The dam, a very smart filly, won the Group 1 12f Yorkshire Oaks, the Group 2 12f Jockey Club Stakes and the Group 3 12f Lancashire Oaks, was second in the Epsom Oaks and third in the St Leger. She is a half-sister to several winners including Cerise Bouquet (dam of the smart 1996 2-y-o filly Red Camellia) and the high-class middle distance colt Ibn Bey, winner of the Irish St Leger, the Gran Premio d'Italia, two Group 1 events in Germany and second in the Breeders Cup Classic. The second dam, Rosia Bay (by High Top), a useful 7.5f and 1m winner, is a half-sister to the top class Queen Elizabeth II Stakes and Budweiser Arlington Million winner Teleprompter and to the Group 3 Brigadier Gerard Stakes winner Chatoyant. *"In Dubai at the moment and I haven't seen much of her".*

1000 - HASHID (USA) ** [83] b.c. Red Ransom – Hoh Flyer (Northern Flagship).
January 31. First foal. $400,000Y. Keeneland July.

The dam, a modest 2-y-o 6f winner, is a half-sister to 5 winners the smart Group 2 10f E P Taylor Stakes winner Wandering Star (by Red Ransom) and the US stakes winner Major Hero. The second dam, Beautiful Bedouin (by His Majesty), is an unraced half-sister to the Craven Stakes and Solario Stakes winner and Derby third Silver Hawk and to the dam of the US Grade 1 winner Papal Power. (Hamdan Al-Maktoum). *"I took a good look at him in Dubai because my good colt from last year, Ekraar, was also by Red Ransom. He certainly looks a nice type and he's big enough despite being a first foal. Of the ones I saw in Dubai, he was one of those I liked quite a lot".*

1001 - ISMAHAAN * [72] ch.f. Unfuwain – River Divine (Irish River).
March 6. Second foal. 150,000Y. Tattersalls October.

Half-sister to the unraced 2000 2-y-o Belleek Woods (by Charnwood Forest). The dam ran once unplaced and is a half-sister to 5 winners including the French dual listed 1m winner Bint Lariaaf. The second dam, Etoile d'Amour (by The Minstrel), a quite useful 3-y-o 7f winner, is a sister to the dam of the US Grade 2 winner Topicount and a half-sister to the German Group 3 6f Benazet-Rennen winner Elnawaagi. (Hamdan Al-Maktoum). *"This filly has gone very big and slightly upright at the moment so we've given her a break and we'll get her back later on".*
Significant sire/damsire crosses:- Alhaarth.

1002 - IZDIHAM (IRE) * [87] ch.c. Nashwan – Harayir (Gulch).
February 16. Third foal.

Brother to the unraced 2000 2-y-o Alqabas. The dam was a very smart filly and winner of the Lowther Stakes (at 2 yrs), the One Thousand Guineas, the Tripleprint Celebration Mile and the Hungerford Stakes. She is a sister to the quite useful 1998 2-y-o 10f winner Nasaayem and a half-sister to the useful 7f (at 2 yrs) to 10f winner Min Alhawa. The second dam, Saffaanh (by Shareef Dancer), a quite useful 12.2f winner, is out of the Irish Oaks winner Give Thanks. *"As he's beautifully bred I was slightly disappointed with him when I first saw him, but he's improving quite a bit as time goes on. It may have just been an immaturity thing. A liver chestnut, he looks nice, stands over a good bit of ground and I hope he can go because he's bred to".*

1003 - MANAWAR (IRE) ** [88] b.c. Darshaan – Dazzlingly Radiant (Try My Best).
March 27.

Brother to the useful dual 7f winner and Group 2 1m Falmouth Stakes fourth Bedazzling and half-brother to the quite useful 2-y-o 7f winner Bound For Pleasure (by Barathea), the fairly useful Irish 6f winner Alarme Belle and the fair 2-y-o dual 5f winner Rising Of The Moon (both by Warning). The dam, a quite useful winner of three races over 6f, is a half-sister to the dam of the French One Thousand Guineas winner Danseuse du Soir. The second dam, Elvina (by Dancer's Image), won over 6f and 10f in Ireland at 3 yrs and is a half-sister to 7 winners. (Hamdan Al-Maktoum). *"In Dubai at the moment, he's quite lean, tall and immature looking so we won't expect too much from him for a while".*
Significant sire/damsire crosses:- Josr Algarhoud.

1004 - MISSISSIPPI KING (USA) [89]　　　　　　　b.c. Dixieland Band – Fapany (Fappiano).
March 11. Sixth foal. $200,000Y. Keeneland September.
Brother to the US winner of 3 races and Grade 3 placed Mississippi Queen. The dam, a stakes-placed winner of 4 races in the USA, is a half-sister to 2 minor stakes winners in the USA. The second dam, Nany (by Great Above), won 14 races including two Grade 3 events in the USA. *"Still in Dubai at the moment".*

1005 - MISTERAH *** [67]　　　　　　　　　　b.f. Alhaarth – Jasarah (Green Desert).
April 11. Fifth foal.
Half-sister to the useful 1998 2-y-o 6f winner Muqtarb and to the fair 2000 10f all-weather winner Lahaay (by Lahib). The dam, a fair 7f placed maiden, is out of the useful French 7f and 1m winner Raise A Memory (by Raise A Native), herself a daughter of a half-sister to the top-class middle-distance colt Celestial Storm. (Hamdan Al-Maktoum). *"When I first started on this filly I told Sheikh Hamdan that she'd be Alhaarth's first 2-y-o winner. She's just had one or two small hiccups since then but she's much better now. She's going to be speedy and for us will be an early 2-y-o – possibly late May. She's got the most marvellous, powerful quarters behind – she really pushes away well. We're really quite keen on her and hoping for the best".*
Significant sire/damsire crosses:- Land Of Dreams (Gr 2).

1006 - MOJAMIL * [84]　　　　　　　　　ch.c. Polar Falcon – Green Danube (Irish River).
February 15. Fourth living foal. 160,000Y. Tattersalls October.
Half-brother to 3 minor winners by Suave Dancer (in Japan), Kris (in Sweden) and Caerleon (in France). The dam, a fairly useful 7.6f and 10f winner, is a half-sister to the French listed winner and Group-placed Firm Friend. The second dam, a French 1m winner, is a half-sister to the dam of the Norfolk Stakes and Cornwallis Stakes winner Magic Ring. *"A nice horse with a wonderful temperament but he's just going through a growing stage – the 'ugly duckling' stage I call it. We'll give him a bit more time and have another look at him but certainly he's quite a correct horse. He's got a typical, slightly pretty, Polar Falcon head".*

1007 - MUQARRAH (IRE) ** [84]　　　　　　ch.c. Alhaarth – Narjis (Blushing Groom).
April 2.
Closely related to the useful Group 3 1m May Hill Stakes winner Mamlakah, to the fair 14f winner Shamel and the fairly useful 2-y-o 7f Chesham Stakes winner Shamikh (all by Unfuwain) and half-brother to the quite useful 2-y-o 7f and 8.5f winner Elakik (by Green Desert) and the modest 2-y-o 5f winner Tahasun (by Shareef Dancer). The dam, a quite useful 2-y-o 5f winner, is a half-sister to the very useful 2-y-o winners Cedilla and Foulaad out of the smart 6f and 7f stakes winner Mashteen (by Majestic Prince). (Hamdan Al-Maktoum). *"I'm very keen on the Alhaarth's as he seems to have stamped nice horses. A lot of people have said very complimentary things about the sire so let's hope he can pull it off. This colt is a nice type of horse for the mid-season onwards. He needs to furnish a bit, is a nice-moving colt that stands over a lot of ground and has a lot of scope".*

1008 - NAFHAH (IRE) [84]　　　　　　　　　b.f. Barathea – Masharik (Caerleon).
January 15. First foal.
The dam, a fairly useful 10f winner, is a half-sister to the high-class middle-distance colt Ibn Bey, to the smart Yorkshire Oaks winner Roseate Tern and the smart 1m and 14f winner Tabareeh. The second dam, Rosia Bay (by High Top), was a useful 7.5f and 1m winner and a half-sister to the top class Queen Elizabeth II Stakes and Budweiser Arlington Million winner Teleprompter. The second dam, Ouija (by Silly Season), was a useful dual 1m winner at 3 yrs. (Sheikh Hamdan Al-Maktoum). *"A very tall, very correct filly, she's one for the back-end of the season".*

1009 - PRISM * [75]　　　　　　　　　　　b.c. Spectrum – Seal Indigo (Glenstal).
April 11. Sixth foal. 14,000Y. Tattersalls October.
Half-brother to the quite useful 2000 6f placed 2-y-o Cielito Lindo (by Pursuit Of Love) and to the fair 1999 2-y-o 6f all-weather winner Bhutan Prince (by Robellino). The dam, a fairly useful winner of 5 races over middle-distances, is a half-sister to the Italian winner and Group 3 placed Campalto and to the winner and listed Oaks Trial fourth Gorgeous Dancer. The second dam, Simply Gorgeous, (by Hello Gorgeous), is an unraced half-sister to the Irish Oaks, Lancashire Oaks, Musidora Stakes and Lingfield

Oaks Trial winner Give Thanks. (Mr M Calvert & Mr C Lewis). *"I think we've done quite well buying this horse so cheaply. He did turn both his feet out at the sales but with a bit of careful shoeing he's straightened up nicely. He's a backward type but he's developing all the time and is turning into a nice-looking horse. We'll give him every chance".*

1010 - SASARAN (IRE) *** [80]

ch.c. Indian Ridge – Flaming June (Storm Bird).
March 18. Second foal. 190,000Y. Tattersalls October.

Half-brother to Colour's Red (by Red Ransom), unplaced in one start at 2 yrs in Ireland in 2000. The dam was placed once over 7f at 2 yrs and is a half-sister to 5 winners including the useful Group 3 1m May Hill Stakes winner Majmu (herself dam of the Prix Jacques le Marois winner Muhtathir). The second dam, Affirmative Fable (by Affirmed), a minor US 4-y-o winner at around 1m, is a half-sister to the Grade 3 Palomar Handicap winner Northern Fable. The second dam, Fairway Fable (by Never Bend), won 3 races including a minor stakes and was placed in two Grade 3 events. (Sheikh Ahmed Al-Maktoum). *"I liked him very much at the sales where it was hard to fault him and he's definitely shaping up nicely now. He's got a great length to his quarters and stands over a nice bit of ground. He moves extremely well, is quite a tall horse with an awful lot to like about him. I'm certainly looking forward to seeing him run, everyone who rides him likes him and I think he's certain to be a nice horse".*

1011 - SEA LANE ** [88]

b.f. Zafonic – Yawl (Rainbow Quest).
April 11. Fourth foal.

Sister to the fairly useful 11.5f winner Genoa and half-sister to the useful 2-y-o 1m winner and 10f placed Clipper (by Salse). The dam, a very useful winner of 2 races over 7f at 2 yrs including the listed Rockfel Stakes, was second in the 10f Lupe Stakes at 3 yrs before injuring herself in the Oaks. She is a half-sister to several winners including the fairly useful 2-y-o 7f winner Trireme. The second dam, Bireme (by Grundy), a top-class though lightly raced middle-distance filly, won the 1980 Oaks and Musidora Stakes and is a half-sister to numerous good horses including the Coronation Cup winner Buoy. (Mr R D Hollingsworth). *"She's enormous – at seventeen hands the tallest 2-y-o I've ever had. But there's a lot to like about her and everything is in proportion. I'm determined we're going to give her every chance a bit later on".*
Significant sire/damsire crosses:- Zarfoot (listed winner, Gr 2 placed).

1012 - SHADOW DANCING [81]

b.f. Unfuwain – Salchow (Niniski).
March 6. Tenth foal.

Half-sister to the fair 7.5f winner Kalko (by Kalaglow), the fair 11.5f and jumps winner Meltemison (by Charmer), the modest 1m winner Carousella (by Rousillon) and minor winners over hurdles or abroad by Mystiko (2) and Terimon. The dam, a smart winner of the listed Cheshire Oaks, was second in the Group 2 Park Hill Stakes and is a half-sister to 6 winners including Gulland, winner of the Group 3 Chester Vase. The second dam, Spin (by High Top), was an unraced half-sister to 3 winners. (Mrs Hugh Dalgety, Dick Hern & Willie Carson). *"I was with Dick Hern when he trained Salchow who wasn't very big but won the Cheshire Oaks. She was out of a twin who was tiny and she threw this Salchow who we were all crazy about because she was so brave. Unfortunately she's spent much of her time going to very moderate sires and hasn't had much of a chance. This filly is quite tall but well-furnished and I think she stands out when you see her out with the string. Hopefully they'll have some fun with her".*

1013 - SMOOTH PASSAGE * [88]

b.c. Suave Dancer – Flagship (Rainbow Quest).
March 3. First foal. 40,000Y. Tattersalls October.

The dam, a quite useful 10f winner, is a sister to the Group 3 Rockfel Stakes and listed Lupe Stakes winner Yawl and a half-sister to 6 winners including the fairly useful 2-y-o 7f winner Trireme. The second dam, Bireme (by Grundy), a top-class though lightly raced middle-distance filly, won the 1980 Oaks and Musidora Stakes and is a half-sister to numerous good horses including the Coronation Cup winner Buoy. *"This is a colt we ought to say a bit about. Most of the good horses out of this family were trained by Dick Hern and owned and bred by the late Dick Hollingsworth. This is a very nice colt and definitely the nicest I've had from this stud. He obviously has a lot of stamina in his pedigree but is certainly not backward and I should think he'll be out in mid-summer. We'll have to wait and see how he can gallop but he's definitely very nice and has a strong, powerful action. He's done nothing wrong and I do like him".*

1014 - TARAFAH * [100]**   ch.c. Machiavellian – Elfaslah (Green Desert).
April 26.

Brother to the 2001 UAE One Thousand Guineas winner Muwakleh and to the high-class Dubai World Cup and Prix Jean Prat winner Almutawakel and half-brother to the smart 10f winner Inaaq (by Lammtarra) and the fairly useful 7f (at 2 yrs) and 10f Dubai winner Mawjud (by Mujtahid). The dam, a useful winner of three races from 10f to 10.4f at 3 yrs including a listed event at the Curragh, is a half-sister to the Group 1 12f Italian Derby winner and 'King George' second White Muzzle. The second dam, Fair of the Furze (by Ela-Mana-Mou), a very useful winner of four races including the Group 2 10f Tattersalls Rogers Gold Cup, was second in the Pretty Polly Stakes and is a half-sister to the listed stakes winners Majestic Role (in Ireland), Norman Style (in Germany) and Proconsular (in France). *"They all talk highly of his sister Muwakleh. This is quite a big colt and will be a back-end type but he has a very good temperament, is very sensible and has no problems as yet".*
Significant sire/damsire crosses:- Almutawakel, Kahal.

1015 - THEME SONG (IRE) ** [87]   b.c. Singspiel – Glatisant (Rainbow Quest).
February 13. Third reported foal. 140,000Y. Tattersalls Houghton.

Half-brother to the 3-y-o Margot (by Sadler's Wells) and to the fairly useful 1998 2-y-o 6f winner Frappe (by Inchinor). The dam, a very useful winner of the Group 3 7f Prestige Stakes at 2 yrs, is a half-sister to numerous winners including the very useful triple 10f winner Gai Bulga and to the dam of the very smart 2000 2-y-o Superstar Leo. The second dam, Dancing Rocks (by Green Dancer), won over 5f and 6f at 2 yrs and the Group 2 10f Nassau Stakes at 3 yrs and is a half-sister to the very useful 7f winner Cragador. *"He's developed quite nicely, but could do with growing just an inch I suppose. Certainly athletic, I'm very keen on Singspiel's progeny generally. If I could bet on one of the Darley stallions I think he is one that will make it. He seems to throw good hind quarters to his horses, they've got really good length and I like that. Even this smaller colt is typical and he has a really good, deep girth. I'm hopeful for him".*

1016 - THOLJANAH (IRE) ** [82]   b.c. Darshaan – Alkaffeyah (Sadler's Wells).
May 7.

Half-brother to the quite useful 2000 1m to 12f placed 3-y-o Ambry, to the useful Irish-trained 3-y-o winner Mudaa-Eb and the quite useful 1996 2-y-o 6f winner Kharir (all by Machiavellian). The dam is an unraced sister to the listed 12f Galtres Stakes winner and Group 1 12f Prix Vermeille third Larrocha and a half-sister to the outstanding middle-distance stayer Ardross and the Pretty Polly Stakes winner Gesedeh. The second dam, Le Melody (by Levmoss), won both her starts, over 7f and 10f, and is a half-sister to the Irish One Thousand Guineas winner Arctique Royale (herself dam of the Group winners Modhish and Russian Snows), to the Irish Oaks third Racquette (dam of the smart French colts Grand Chelem and Splendid Moment) and to the dam of the Queen Anne Stakes winner Alflora. (Hamdan Al-Maktoum). *"I know Sheikh Hamdan is pretty keen on Darshaan and this is a very good-looking colt. He's level, not too big and seems to go quite nicely. He was a little bit tricky to begin with and a bit spirited but he's pretty straightforward now".*
Significant sire/damsire crosses:- Sayedah.

1017 - TOHFAH (IRE) [84]   ch.f. Nashwan – Bintalshaati (Kris).
March 12. Third foal.

Sister to the quite useful 2000 1m placed 2-y-o Munadil. The dam, a fairly useful dual 1m winner, is out of the fair staying maiden Minifah (by Nureyev), herself a half-sister to the Kentucky Derby winner Winning Colors. *"Very tall like her sister, she's gone away for a holiday and I wouldn't expect her to be ready until the late summer or early autumn".*

1018 - TRAMONTO ** [70]   b.f. Sri Pekan – Manhattan Sunset (El Gran Senor).
February 28. Third foal. 34,000Y. Tattersalls October.

Sister to the unplaced 2000 2-y-o Twilight Dancer and half-sister to a winner of 5 races in Turkey by Primo Dominie and to the listed Cheshire Oaks third Pinnacle (by Shirley Heights). The dam, a fair 2-y-o 7f winner, is a half-sister to 2 minor winners in the USA. The second dam, Mezimica (by Dewan), won the Grade 3 Falls City Handicap and is a half-sister to 4 winners including the listed 10f Pretty Polly Stakes winner Spiranthes. (Mr Rupert Villers). *"She's done nothing but improve and we bought her hoping she'd do exactly that. She's good-looking and I remember Dick Hern saying when she first arrived that you can't help but like her. I always liked her at the sales, she's done very well and she hasn't missed much. So hopefully she'll be a 2-y-o".*

1019 - MOJALID * [93]　　　　　　　　br.c. Zafonic – Affair Of State (Tate Gallery).
February 8. Sixth foal. 150,000Y. Tattersalls October.
Half-brother to the fair 2000 2-y-o 5f winner Ice Maiden (by Polar Falcon), to the fairly useful 6f winner Diplomat (by Deploy), the fair 5f (at 2 yrs) and 6f winner Stately Princess (by Robellino) and the German and Swedish 5f to 1m winner Statesman (by Doyoun). The dam, a very useful Irish 2-y-o winner of the listed 6f Tattersalls Breeders Stakes, is a half-sister to 2 winners. The second dam, All Hat (by Double Form), won over 5f at 3 yrs and is a half-sister to 5 winners including the Cherry Hinton and Musidora Stakes winner Everything Nice - herself dam of the Irish One Thousand Guineas winner Nicer. *"He was a big horse when he was bought at the sales although he's levelled out now and hasn't grown any more. A nice horse that I like, he goes very nicely and I'm pleased with him. He seems to be a pretty sound horse but he is big so I'd be thinking of starting him around mid-summer, just to be fair on him".*

1020 - UNNAMED * [89]　　　　　　　　　　b.f. Danzig – Ajfan (Woodman).
January 9. Fourth foal.
Half-sister to the useful 1998 2-y-o 6f winner Mutamayyaz (by Nureyev) and the quite useful 1997 2-y-o 7f winner Elsurur (by Storm Cat). The dam was a very useful winner of 3 races from 7f (at 2 yrs) to 1m and was third in the One Thousand Guineas. She is a half-sister to several winners including Space Cruiser, winner of the Windsor Castle Stakes. The second dam, Misinskie (by Nijinsky), was placed over 6f and 7f at 2 yrs and is a half-sister to the high-class sprinter/miler Clever Trick. (Hamdan Al-Maktoum). *"This filly is in Dubai and I haven't seen enough of her to make an evaluation. I've only seen her canter steadily but it's nice to have a Danzig filly obviously. She could be alright".*

1021 - UNNAMED * [82]　　　　　　　　　b.f. Gone West – Elrafa Ah (Storm Cat).
March 20. Fourth foal.
Closely related to the unraced 2000 2-y-o Raajiya (by Gulch) and half-sister to the high-class 1998 2-y-o Mujahid (by Danzig), winner of the Group 1 7f Dewhurst Stakes and subsequently third in the Two Thousand Guineas. The dam was a useful winner of 3 races over 5f and 6f including the listed Bentinck Stakes. The second dam, Bubbles Darlene (by Fappiano), won twice at up to 1m. *"Still in Dubai at the moment".* (Hamdan Al-Maktoum).

C WALL

1022 - ACE OF HEARTS [62]　　　　　　　b.c. Magic Ring – Lonely Heart (Midyan).
January 30. First foal. 34,000Y. Tattersalls October.
The dam, a useful dual 10f winner, was listed-placed and is out of the quite useful 7f to 10f winner Take Heart (by Electric), herself a half-sister to 3 minor winners. (Lady Stuttaford & Mr W G Bovill). *"A nice horse, he's done quite a bit of growing this spring and although he's by Magic Ring, the dam stayed 10f. He doesn't look like a sprinter but perhaps over 7f or a mile later on this year he might be able to do something. A nice, easy-moving horse, he does everything well and I like him".*

1023 - PERFECT PUNCH * [65]　　　　　　b.c. Reprimand – Aliuska (Fijar Tango).
February 17. Third foal. 20,000Y. Tattersalls Autumn.
Half-brother to the fairly useful 2000 dual 6f winner Goodie Twosues (by Fraam) and to the fair 8.5f and 10f winner Altay (by Erin's Isle). The dam, a minor dual 5f winner in Ireland at 2 yrs, is a half-sister to 2 minor winners including one in Germany. The second dam, Ukraine's Affair (by The Minstrel), is an unraced half-sister to 3 minor winners. (Induna Racing Partners Two). *"His half-sister Goodie Twosues won the Tattersalls Autumn Stakes last year and this colt was bought to complete a family double. A well-grown colt so he won't be out early, but we hope that by the second half of the season we can get him on the track".*

1024 - SEEKING THE SUN (IRE) * [61]　　　b.br.c. Petardia – Femme Savante (Glenstal).
February 5. Second foal. 32,000Y. Tattersalls Autumn.
Half-brother to the fair 2000 5f placed 2-y-o So Sober (by Common Grounds). The dam, a quite useful 2-y-o 6f winner, is a half-sister to 3 winners including the dam of the useful Group 2 6f Mill Reef Stakes winner Bouncing Bowdler. The second dam, Femme Formidable (by Formidable), is an unplaced half-

sister to one winner. (The Boardroom Syndicate). *"Not as precocious as you'd think from his breeding, but that said I think he's a sprinting type and we hope he'll make his mark".*

1025 - STREET MUSIC ** [84]

ch.c. Barathea – Three Piece (Jaazeiro).
May 6. Eighth foal.

Half-brother to the 1997 2-y-o 6f and subsequent French Two Thousand Guineas winner Victory Note (by Fairy King), to the unraced 2000 2-y-o Ashkasi (by Sheikh Albadou), the Irish 2-y-o 6f and 7f winner Treble Hook (by Ballad Rock) and the useful middle-distance gelding Dance So Suite (by Shareef Dancer), a winner of 5 races on the flat and 4 races over hurdles. *"He looks a promising sort and I like the way he does everything. He'll be a late maturing horse and perhaps from the middle of the summer onwards we might be able to think of racing him".*

D WELD

1026 - AYMAN (IRE) **

b.c. Be My Guest – Chloe (Green Desert).
January 18. First foal. IR£60,000Y. Goffs Challenge.

The dam was placed twice at up to 8.5f in Ireland and is a half-sister to 2 winners. The second dam, Eileen Jenny (by Kris), was a very useful 3-y-o winner of a 12f listed event in Milan and a 12f Curragh maiden and was third in the Irish Oaks. She is a half-sister to the 3-y-o 12f listed winner Kasmayo, the Lingfield Oaks Trial winner Bahamian (dam of the high-class filly Wemyss Bight), the Irish miler Captivator, the Irish 7f winner Klarifi and the middle-distance stayer West China - all at least useful. (Hamdan Al-Maktoum). *"A nice colt, he's due to run before your book is published. He's pretty forward and he's been bought to win the Goffs Challenge race".*

1027 - BALSAM (IRE) *

b.f. Cadeaux Genereux – Diali (Dayjur).
April 21. First foal.

The dam is a half-sister to the Prix du Moulin and Prix Jacques le Marois winner and smart sire Polish Precedent. The second dam, Past Example (by Buckpasser), is an unraced half-sister to the Grade 2 Del Mar Oaks winner French Charmer (dam of the top-class miler Zilzal), to the US stakes winner Highest Regard (dam of the US Grade 1 winner Awe Inspiring) and to the unraced dam of the Fillies Mile, Prix Marcel Boussac and French One Thousand Guineas winner Culture Vulture. (Hamdan Al-Maktoum). *"A backward filly that's due in from Dubai soon".*

1028 - BUSHIDO (IRE) *

br.c. Brief Truce – Pheopotstown (Henbit).
March 29. Sixth foal. IR£72,000Y. Goffs Orby.

Half-brother to the unplaced 2000 2-y-o Stracomer Urania (by Paris House), to the dual winner and 2-y-o Group 1 7f National Stakes second Murawwi (by Perugino), the 8.5f to 10f winner Moonbi Range (by Nordico), the 10f and 14f winner Sunless (by Bluebird) and the minor winner Gold Chaser (by Imperial Frontier) – all in Ireland. The dam won 3 races in Ireland and is a half-sister to 4 minor winners. The second dam, Starduster (by Lucifer), won the Irish listed November Handicap and is a half-sister to 4 winners including the Great Voltigeur third Solar Wind. *"A very correct horse, he'll make a seven furlong 2-y-o".*

1029 - CATCH A SMILE (USA) **

b.f. Silver Hawk – Catch A Glimpse (Gulch).
May 14.

The dam won over 6f at 2 yrs in Ireland and is a half-sister to 2 winners. The second dam, Spring To Light (by Blushing Groom), won over 6f and 7f in Ireland. (Moyglare Stud Farm). *"A medium-sized filly that will make a nice 2-y-o".*

1030 - CHURCH CROSS (IRE) ***

b.c. Cadeaux Genereux – Watch Me (Green Desert).
March 8. First foal. IR27,000Y. Tattersalls Fairyhouse.

The dam, a useful 3-y-o 6f winner and third in the Group 3 6f Cork And Orrery Stakes, is a half-sister to 3 winners here and abroad. The second dam, Fenny Rough (by Home Guard), a very useful winner of 6 races from 5f to 7f here including the listed Oak Tree Stakes, subsequently won in the USA and was Grade 1 placed. (Mr F Sheehy). *"A winner of a £16,000 2-y-o maiden at Cork this week. He won easily and I bought him as a yearling because I thought he looked sharp and had stakes potential. He'll be heading for the Marble Hill Stakes next which is the first black-type 2-y-o race at the Curragh. Then he'll go for the Fairyhouse Sales race".*
Significant sire/damsire crosses:- Land Of Dreams (Gr 2).

1031 - DE LAROCHE (IRE)　　　　　　　　　　b.f. Danehill – Sea Port (Averof).

March 17. Twelfth foal. IR£110,000Y. Goffs Orby.

Half-sister to 7 winners including the very smart Hong Kong International Vase winner and Japan Cup second Indigenous (by Marju), the fair 11f, 14f and 2m Tote Cesarewitch winner Old Red, the useful 1m winner Wassl Port (by Wassl) and the modest 12f winner Medway (by Shernazar). The dam was fourth on her only start and is a half-sister to the King Edward VII Stakes winner Sea Anchor and the dam of the Australian Grade 1 winner Water Boatman. The second dam, Anchor (by Major Portion), won the Nell Gwyn Stakes and is a half-sister to the Coronation Cup winner Buoy and the Oaks winner Bireme. (Mr John Magnier). *"A fine, big filly. More of a 3-y-o type".*

1032 - DRESS TO THRILL (IRE) *　　　　　b.f. Danehill – Trusted Partner (Affirmed).

February 19.

Half-sister to the Irish 2-y-o 6f winner Act Of Defiance, the Irish 7f winner Trust In Luck and the Irish 3-y-o 9f winner Brave Raider. The dam was a very useful winner of both her 2-y-o races including the Group 3 7f C.L. Weld Park Stakes and next season won the Irish One Thousand Guineas. She is a sister to the useful middle distance performers Easy to Copy and Epicure's Garden and to the useful Irish 7f listed and US Grade 3 winner Low Key Affair. (Moyglare Stud Farm). *"A very nice Danehill filly but more one for next year".*

1033 - EASY SUNSHINE (IRE) **　　　b.f. Sadler's Wells – Desert Ease (Green Desert).

February 4. First foal.

The dam, an Irish 2-y-o listed 6f winner, is a half-sister to several winners including the Group 3 Tetrarch Stakes and Group 3 7f Concorde Stakes winner Two-Twenty-Two. The second dam, Easy To Copy (by Affirmed), was a useful winner of 5 races from 1m to 12f in Ireland and Italy including the Group 2 Premio Legnano and subsequently performed well in Graded stakes company in America. She is a sister to the Irish One Thousand Guineas winner Trusted Partner (dam of several winners), to the useful Irish listed 2-y-o 6f winner Low Key Affair and the useful 7f and 9f winner Epicure's Garden. (Moyglare Stud Farm). *"A nice filly, she's small but is a quality 2-y-o and she'll start off over six furlongs in June or July".*

1034 - GILDED VANITY (IRE) **　　　b.br.f. Indian Ridge – Searching Star (Rainbow Quest).

February 13. Fifth foal. IR£430,000Y. Goffs Orby.

Sister to the smart listed 1m winner and Irish Two Thousand Guineas second Fa-Eq and half-sister to the smart listed 7.3f and 1m winner Corinium (by Turtle Island), the useful dual 5f winner (including at 2 yrs) Ellway Star (by Night Shift) and the fairly useful Irish 2-y-o dual 5f winner Hartstown House (by Primo Dominie). The dam, a modest 6f (at 2 yrs) to 11.3f placed maiden, is a half-sister to 8 winners including the smart listed Blue Riband Trial winner Beldale Star and the listed winner Moon Drop (dam of several winners including the Group placed Moon King). The second dam, Little White Star (by Mill Reef), is an unplaced half-sister to 5 winners here and abroad. (Mrs T V Ryan). *"I would see her running in early June, she's very correct and goes very well".*

1035 - HASHEEMA (IRE)　　　　　　b.f. Darshaan – Dance Ahead (Shareef Dancer).

March 17. Sixth foal. IR£220,000Y. Goffs Orby.

Half-sister to the fair 2000 6f and 7f placed 2-y-o Atamana (by Lahib), to the Italian 7.5f and 9f winner Lycius Lord (by Lycius) and the Irish 1995 2-y-o 6f winner and Group 3 7f Killavullen Stakes third Dance Clear (by Marju) - subsequently a winner of 4 races and Grade 3 placed in the USA. The dam, a quite useful 2-y-o 7f winner, is a half-sister to 6 winners including the useful 12f winner Shoot Ahead. The second dam, Shoot Clear (by Bay Express), a smart 5f to 7f winner at 2 yrs including the Group 3 Waterford Candelabra Stakes, was fourth in the One Thousand Guineas and is a half-sister to the Yorkshire Oaks winners Untold and the Sally Brown. (Hamdan Al-Maktoum). *"Still in Dubai until the end of April".*

1036 - HATHLOOL (IRE) **　　　　　ch.c. Alhaarth – Cartier Bijoux (Ahonoora).

April 14. Fifth foal. IR£110,000Y. Goffs Orby.

Half-brother to the very useful 1995 2-y-o Fallow, winner of the Group 3 6f July Stakes and placed in the Group 1 Middle Park Stakes and to the modest 5f and 6f winner Muzz (by Gallic League). The dam, a fairly useful 2-y-o 5f winner, is a half-sister to 7 winners including the Group 3 Jersey Stakes winner

Miss Silca Key (herself dam of the Group 3 winner Central City). The second dam, Tremiti (by Sun Prince), won over 5f and 6f at 2 yrs and is a half-sister to 5 winners. (Hamdan Al-Maktoum). *"Not the strongest of colts but I like him, he'll make a 2-y-o and he'll be ready to run by about June".*

1037 - IRRESTIBLE JEWEL (IRE) *

b.f. Danehill – In Anticipation (Sadler's Wells). May 3.

Half-sister to the unraced 2000 2-y-o Diamond Trim (by Highest Honor) and to the useful Irish 2000 3-y-o 1m winner Legal Jousting (by Indian Ridge). The dam won over 12f and 14f in Ireland. The second dam, Aptostar (by Fappiano), won 6 races in the USA including the Grade 1 Acorn Stakes and the Grade 2 Bed O'Roses Handicap and is a half-sister to the US Grade 2 winner Man Alright. (Moyglare Stud Farm). *"She a very nice filly and definitely a 2-y-o type".*

1038 - JASSAS (IRE) **

b.c. Desert Style – Common Bond (Common Grounds). April 21. Third foal. IR£40,000Y. Goffs Challenge.

Half-brother to the 2000 Irish 2-y-o 5f winner Millenium Love (by Great Commotion). The dam, a winner at 2 yrs in Ireland, is out of the unraced Rinkamire (by Gay fandango), herself a half-sister to 8 winners. (Hamdan Al-Maktoum). *"A good sort, he's well-forward and I like him. He goes well and will be racing sometime in May over six furlongs".*

1039 - LUMINOUS BEAUTY (USA) **

b.f. A P Indy – Caerlina (Caerleon). February 11. Fifth foal. $2,000,000Y. Keeneland September.

Half-sister to La Nuit Rose (by Rainbow Quest), a winner over 7f at 2 yrs and placed in both the French and Irish One Thousand Guineas and to a winner in Japan by Bering. The dam, a very smart filly, won over 5.5f (at 2 yrs), the Group 1 10.5f Prix de Diane and the Group 3 10f Prix de la Nonette, is a sister to the French winner and Group 2 placed Leonila and a half-sister to 6 winners including the French listed winner Swalina. The second dam, Dinalina (by Top Ville), a French 2-y-o 10f winner, is a half-sister to the Doncaster Cup winner Karadar and to the dams of the Group 1 winners Kartajana and Khariyda. *"A beautiful filly, she's a very nice 2-y-o type that you should look out for".*

1040 - MOAYED

b.c. Selkirk – Song Of Years (Shareef Dancer). May 4. Second reported foal. 120,000Y. Tattersalls October.

The dam, a fairly useful 7f placed 2-y-o, later stayed 12f and is a half-sister to 4 minor winners here and abroad. The second dam, Seattle Serenade (by Seattle Slew), a quite useful 6f placed 2-y-o, is a half-sister to 5 minor winners. (Hamdan Al-Maktoum). *"Yet to arrive from Dubai, I've seen him and he's a nice horse but more of a 3-y-o".*

1041 - MOLLY ELLEN (IRE) ***

b.f. Fayruz – Magic Melody (Petong). February 14. First foal. IR£43,000Y. Goffs Challenge.

The dam, a modest 6f placed 2-y-o, is a half-sister to 6 winners including the Group 3 5f Norfolk Stakes winner Rosselli and the Irish listed sprint winner Dancing Music. The second dam, Miss Rossi (by Artaius), is an unraced half-sister to 6 winners here and abroad including the Japanese £1M earner Prest Symboli. (Mrs Julie Mitchell). *"She looks a precocious 2-y-o that should be racing by the end of May".*

1042 - MUAKAD (IRE) **

b.c. Spectrum – Danse Royale (Caerleon). April 14. Fifth foal. IR£900,000Y. Goffs Orby.

Half-brother to the Irish 4-y-o winner and Group 3 10f Gallinule Stakes fourth Twickenham (by Woodman) and to the 1998 2-y-o 7f winner Ballet Master (by Kingmambo). The dam, a very useful filly, won 3 races including the Group 3 10f Prix de Psyche and the listed 7f Derrinstown One Thousand Guineas Trial and was third in the Irish One Thousand Guineas. She is closely related to the Group 3 6f Railway Stakes winner Flame of Athens and a half-sister to numerous winners including the brilliant filly Salsabil, winner of the One Thousand Guineas, Oaks, Irish Derby and Prix Vermeille, the high-class St James's Palace Stakes winner Marju, the smart 12f winner Song of Tara and the very useful middle-distance filly Nearctic Flame (herself dam of the Group 3 winner Blushing Flame). The second dam, Flame of Tara (by Artaius), won 8 races including the Group 2 1m Coronation Stakes and the Group 2 Pretty Polly Stakes, was second in the Champion Stakes and is a half-sister to Fruition - dam of both the Breeders Cup Turf winner Northern Spur and the high-class stayer Kneller. (Hamdan Al-Maktoum). *"He's due in from Dubai soon. I've seen him and was very impressed. A very nice colt and come September I hope he'll make a good horse".*

1043 - MUSICAL FUSION **   b.c. Sadler's Wells – Spring To Light (Blushing Groom).
May 10. Seventh foal.
Sister to the fair Irish 8.5f winner Initial Figure and to the Irish 1997 2-y-o 7f winner Screen Idol and half-sister to the useful Irish 1995 2-y-o 6f winner Catch A Glimpse (by Gulch). The dam won over 6f and 7f in Ireland. (Moyglare Stud Farm). *"A medium-sized Sadler's Wells colt, I like him and he's a quality horse from a good family".*

1044 - PEACH SORBET (IRE) *   ch.f. Spectrum – Tootling (Pennine Walk).
April 2. Sixth living foal. IR£110,000Y. Goffs Orby.
Half-sister to the fairly useful 2000 Irish 2-y-o 6f winner and Group 3 5f Queen Mary Stakes third Little Firefly (by Danehill), to the very useful 5f (at 2 yrs) and listed 6f Cecil Frail Stakes winner Antinnaz (by Thatching) and a winner over 11f in Belgium by Tirol. The dam ran once unplaced and is a half-sister to 5 winners here and abroad and to the unraced dam of the 2-y-o Group 3 Futurity Stakes winner Jural. The second dam, Tootens (by Northfields), won the Group 1 Prix Saint-Alary and is a half-sister to the One Thousand Guineas winner Nocturnal Spree and the dam of the St Leger winner Moonax. (B R Firestone). *"A backward filly but she's really nice and she goes very well".*

1045 - REVUE (IRE) *   b.c. Sadler's Wells – Gold Tear (Tejano).
March 20. Fourth foal. IR£240,000Y. Goffs Orby.
Half-brother to the Irish trained 3-y-o Lunardi (by Indian Ridge), to the minor US 4-y-o winner England's Rose (by Alzao) and a winner of 5 races in Japan by Caerleon. The dam, a winner of 2 races in France at 3 yrs, is a half-sister to the Prix Lupin winner Galetto, the Prix de la Foret winner Gabina and to the dam of the Grand Criterium winner Goldmark. The second dam, Gold Bird (by Rheingold), won a listed event in France over 10.5f and is a half-sister to the Prix Chloe winner Gaelic Bird. (Michael J Smurfit). *"A very nice colt and although he's a big horse I can see him racing by June or July".*

1046 - ROWAN FLOWER (IRE)   b.f. Ashkalani – Forest Lair (Habitat).
April 21. Tenth foal. IR£110,000Y. Goffs Orby.
Half-sister to the modest 2000 7f placed 2-y-o Foxes Lair, to the smart Irish 10f winner Muakaad (both by Muhtarram), the very useful listed 12f winner Suhaad, the useful Irish 12f winner Rajjaaf (both by Unfuwain), the useful middle-distance winner Munif (by Caerleon), the minor Irish 12f winner Kuwah (both by Be My Guest), the Irish 12f winner Manarah (by Marju) and a winner in Germany by Doyoun. The dam won over 1m at 2 yrs in Ireland and is a half-sister to Pampabird, a winner of three Group 3 events in France. The second dam, Wood Grouse (by Celtic Ash), is an unplaced half-sister to the Jersey Stakes winner Pitskelly. *"A quality filly but more of a 3-y-o type".*

1047 - RUM CHARGER (IRE) **   b.f. Spectrum – Park Charger (Tirol).
April 28. Third foal. IR£130,000Y. Goffs Orby.
Half-sister to the 3-y-o Stage Presence (by Selkirk) and to the quite useful 1999 2-y-o 6f winner Alpine Park (by Barathea). The dam, a useful winner over 1m and 10f at 3 yrs in Ireland, was listed-placed several times and is a half-sister to 5 winners including the useful 6f (at 2 yrs) and 12f winner Indian Missile. The second dam, Haitienne (by Green Dancer), won once in France and ia a half-sister to 6 winners including the Prix Robert Papin third Harifa. (B R Firestone). *"Yes, she looks like she'll make a nice 2-y-o by June or July".*

1048 - SAVILE'S DELIGHT (IRE) **   b.c. Cadeaux Genereux – Across The Ice (General Holme).
April 28. Fourth living foal. 80,000Y. Tattersalls Houghton.
Half-brother to the fair 2000 Irish 2-y-o 7f winner Georgia Peach (by Pennekamp), to the 1999 listed 5f Rockingham Handicap winner and Group 3 Flying Five second Timote (by Indian Ridge) and the 1998 French 3-y-o winner Glissando (by In The Wings). The dam, a minor French 3-y-o winner, is a half-sister to 7 winners including Northern Premier (Group 3 1m Prix de la Grotte and Group 3 7f Prix de la Porte Maillot). The second dam, Madame Premier (by Raja Baba), won 4 races in the USA including a minor stakes and was fourth in the Grade 1 6f Spinaway Stakes. (Michael J Smurfit). *"A nice, strong colt and he should be running sometime during May".*

1049 - SHARP DON (IRE) * b.c. College Chapel – Cresalin (Coquelin).
April 22. Fifth foal. IR£38,000Y. Goffs Challenge.

Brother to the Italian 8.5f and 10f winner Cheap And Chic and half-brother to the poor 2000 5f placed 2-y-o Festino (by Lake Coniston). The dam, an Irish 10f and 11f winner, is a half-sister to 4 winners and to the unraced dam of the One Thousand Guineas winner Las Meninas. The second dam, Donna Cressida (by Don), won the Group 2 Player-Wills Stakes and two listed events in Ireland. (Mr David Prentice). *"A nice colt that goes well, he should make a 2-y-o by mid-season".*

1050 - SUN SEASONS (IRE) ** ch.f. Salse – Epicure's Garden (Affirmed).
March 3.

Half-sister to the useful Irish 11f and 12f winner Lisieux Rose (by Generous), to the fairly useful Irish 10f winner Among Equals (by Sadler's Wells) and the Irish 2-y-o 1m winner Creative Bloom (by Dixieland Band). The dam, a useful Irish 7f (at 2 yrs) to 9f winner, is a sister to the Irish One Thousand Guineas winner Trusted Partner, to the useful 1m to 12f winner Easy To Copy and the 7f listed winner and Moyglare Stud Stakes third Low Key Affair. The second dam, Talking Picture (by Speak John), was the champion US filly of 1973 and won at up to 7f. (Moyglare Stud Farm). *"An extra nice filly, she's big but will make a very nice 2-y-o in September".*

1051 - TEN TWENTY TWO (IRE) * b.br.c. Green Desert – Aptostar (Fappiano).
May 15.

Half-brother to the unraced Irish-trained 2000 2-y-o Sweet Retreat (by Indian Ridge) and to the Irish 12f and 14f winner In Anticipation (by Sadler's Wells). The dam won 6 races in the USA including the Grade 1 1m Acorn Stakes and the Grade 2 1m Bed O'Roses Handicap and is a half-sister to the US Grade 2 winner Man Alright. (Moyglare Stud Farm). *"A small, reasonably sharp colt. He's a sprint-type 2-y-o and he'll be racing around May or June time".*

1052 - TURN OF PHRASE (IRE) *** b.c. Cadeaux Genereux – Token Gesture (Alzao).
January 23. First foal.

The dam, a smart winner of the Group 3 7f C L Weld Park Stakes, is a half-sister to the US Grade 2 9f winner Wait Till Monday, to the useful Irish 10f to 12.3f winner Blazing Spectacle and the useful Irish middle-distance stayer and Triumph Hurdle winner Rare Holiday (by Caerleon). The second dam, Temporary Lull (by Super Concorde), is an unraced sister to the Nell Gwyn Stakes winner Martha Stevens. The second dam, Magazine (by Prince John), won the Grade 1 12f Coaching Club American Oaks. (Moyglare Stud Farm). *"A good, strong horse and I see him running at the end of May or early June. He takes more after his sire than his dam I'd say".*
Significant sire/damsire crosses:- Embassy (Gr 1).

1053 - WHISTLE DOWN (IRE) * b.c. Danehill – Trust In Luck (Nashwan).
March 13.

Half-brother to the unraced 2000 2-y-o Helpful Hint (by Cadeaux Genereux). The dam, an Irish 7f winner, is a half-sister to the Irish 2-y-o 6f winner Act Of Defiance and the Irish 3-y-o 9f winner Brave Raider. The second dam, Trusted Partner (by Affirmed), was a very useful winner of both her 2-y-o races including the Group 3 7f C.L. Weld Park Stakes and next season won the Irish One Thousand Guineas. She is a sister to the useful middle distance performers Easy to Copy and Epicure's Garden and to the useful Irish 7f listed and US Grade 3 winner Low Key Affair. (Moyglare Stud Farm). *"Quite a sharp, medium-sized colt, he'll be racing by mid-summer".*

1054 - UNNAMED * b.c. Danehill – Cruise Line (Rainbow Quest).
May 21. First foal. $175,000Y. Keeneland September.

The dam is an unraced sister to the Cheshire Oaks winner and Yorkshire Oaks and St Leger second High And Low. The second dam, Cruising Height (by Shirley Heights), a very useful 10.6f and 12.2f winner, was second in the Group 3 Lancashire Oaks and is a half-sister to the Park Hill Stakes winner Trampship. (Mr H Liang). *"He'll make a 2-y-o alright. Watch for him in June or July".*

1055 - ASHDOWN EXPRESS (IRE) * [74] ch.c. Ashkalani – Indian Express (Indian Ridge).
February 4. Third foal. IR£50,000Y. Goffs Orby.
Half-brother to a 4-y-o winner in Germany by College Chapel. The dam, a modest 8.5f and 10f winner, is a sister to the useful listed 6f winner Cheyenne Spirit and a half-sister to 3 winners. The second dam, Bazaar Promise (by Native Bazaar), is an unplaced sister to the smart sprinter Crofthall. (Mr W J P Jackson). *"A horse that we like a lot and he's got a very lucky owner. I'd like to think he'll do well, he looks quite forward and the Ashkalani's have been well-touted".*

1056 - GREEN CRYSTAL [91] b.f. Green Dancer – Dunkellin (Irish River).
May 13.
Sister to the smart Green Card, a winner from 1m to 10.3f from 3 to 6 yrs, closely related to a winner in the USA by Seattle Dancer and half-sister to a winner in the USA by Herat. The dam, a winner in the USA, is a half-sister to the Criterium des Pouliches winner Oak Hill. (Mr Arashan Ali). *"Very interesting. She moves well and does everything nicely. We'll probably start to do a bit with her around June time and we'll go from there. We hope she'll be a nice broodmare for us one day".*

1057 - IN SPACE (USA) ** [80] ch.c. Sky Classic – Thrilling Day (Groom Dancer).
January 26. First foal.
The dam, a winner of 6 races in England, Ireland and the USA including the Group 3 7f Nell Gwyn Stakes and a Grade 3 event at Keeneland, is a half-sister to one winner. The second dam, Pushoff (by Sauce Boat), a quite useful 3-y-o 5f winner, is a half-sister to 10 winners including the Nell Gwyn Stakes winner Myself and the Group 3 Princess Margaret Stakes winner Bluebook. The third dam, Pushy (by Sharpen Up), won the Queen Mary Stakes and the Cornwallis Stakes at 2 yrs and is a half-sister to numerous winners including the Japan Cup winner Jupiter Island and the high-class 2-y-o Precocious. (Lucayan Stud). *"I was delighted with his first run (at Newmarket) and he'll be very good at six furlongs. You could be seeing him in either the Coventry or the July Stakes".*

1058 - RICHEST VEIN (IRE) * [70] b.c. Ali-Royal – Antapoura (Bustino).
March 9. First foal. IR£20,000Y. Goffs Orby.
The dam won 6 races (including 2 over hurdles) in Ireland and is a half-sister to 5 winners including the French listed winner and Group 3 placed Aneysar. The second dam, Aneyza (by Blushing Groom), won once in France and is a half-sister to 6 winners. (Mr Arashan Ali). *"Not a big 2-y-o, he'll be an early sort but will be better suited to six or seven furlongs. A nice colt".*

1059 - TROJAN (IRE) ** [91] ch.c. Up And At 'Em – Fantasise (General Assembly).
April 30. Eighth foal. IR£62,000Y. Goffs Challenge.
Brother to the the modest 1998 2-y-o 6f winner Tampa Lady and half-brother to the fair 5f (at 2 yrs) to 1m winner Means Business (by Imp Society), the fair 2-y-o 6f winner Papita (by Law Society), the fair 2-y-o 5f all-weather winner Murtagh Hill Lad (by Cyrano de Bergerac) and winners abroad by Nordance and Pennine Walk. The dam was placed once over 7f at 2yrs in Ireland and is a half-sister to the dam of the Group 2 Prix Robert Papin winner Black Amber. The second dam, Flying Fantasy (by Habitat), is an unplaced sister to the One Thousand Guineas winner Flying Water. (R Hine, R Dawson & A Duke). *"He's going to lengthen and keep doing well and he's an extremely attractive colt. He's one I have a lot of time for and he's a seven furlongs plus horse".*

1060 - WIXOE EXPRESS (IRE) *** [92] b.c. Anabaa – Esquiline (Gone West).
February 11. First foal. 90,000Y. Tattersalls October.
The dam is an unplaced half-sister to 3 minor winners in France. The second dam, Ville Eternelle (by Slew O'Gold), won 3 races in France and is a half-sister to Mill Native (winner of the Grade 1 10f Arlington Million), the dual French Group 3 winner French Stress, the Group 3 10.5f Prix de Flore winner Sporades and the 2-y-o 5f Prix du Bois winner American Stress. (Mr P Pottinger). *"A big horse but he'll run this year over seven furlongs or a mile and I like him a lot. He oozes a bit of class, I'm very happy with him and he seems to be coming on all the time".*

1061 - UNNAMED * [96] b.c. Turtle Island – Blue Kestrel (Bluebird).
April 2. Third foal. IR£180,000Y. Goffs Orby.

The dam, an Irish 7f to 9f winner at 2 and 3 yrs, is a sister to the fairly useful sprint winner Kunucu and a half-sister to 4 winners. The second dam, Kunuz (by Ela-Mana-Mou), ran twice unplaced and is a full or half-sister to 5 minor winners. (Mr P K L Chu). *"An extremely good-moving horse, he'll want seven furlongs but is a very classy individual".*

1062 - UNNAMED * [88] b.c. Persian Bold – Catherinofaragon (Chief's Crown).
February 12. Second foal. IR£130,000Y. Goffs Orby.

Half-brother to Catstreet (by Catrail), unplaced in one start over 6f at 2 yrs in 2000. The dam is an unraced half-sister to 3 winners including the Canadian Grade 3 8.5f and 10f winner Gold Alert. The second dam, Croquis (by Arts And Letters), won 6 races in the USA including a stakes event, was placed in the Grade 1 CCA Oaks and the Grade 1 Delaware Handicap and is a half-sister to the Grade 1 winner Linkage. (Lucayan Stud). *"A little bit heavy-topped, he's a very good moving horse and a good, strong type. A nice type of horse for when the seven furlong races start".*

1063 - UNNAMED [71] b.c. Emperor Jones – Fakhira (Jareer).
February 27. Third foal. IR£26,000Y. Goffs Challenge.

Brother to Dakhira, unplaced in one start at 2 yrs in 2000 and to the modest dual 7f placed Akhira. The dam, a winner over 5f at the Curragh at 2 yrs, is a half-sister to the Group 1 National Stakes and Group 1 Heinz 57 Phoenix Stakes winner and Dewhurst Stakes second Danehill Dancer. The second dam, Mira Adonde (by Sharpen Up), ran once unplaced and is a half-sister to the listed John Of Gaunt Stakes winner Swordsmith. (Mr G Roberts). *"He looks a nice type and I think he'll make a 2-y-o by June or July".*

1064 - UNNAMED [91] br.gr.f. Danehill – Miss Toot (Ardross).
May 11.

Half-sister to the unraced 2000 2-y-o Dr Charlie (by Dr Devious), to the smart 8.3f (at 2yrs) and Group 3 10.4f Musidora Stakes winner and Oaks second Kalypso Katie, the Grade 2 E P Taylor Stakes winner and Grade 1 Gamely Handicap second Kool Kat Katie (both by Fairy King) and to a minor winner by Scenic. The dam, a fair 10f and 15f winner on her only starts, is out of the unraced Blue Stack (by Roberto), herself a half-sister to 6 winners including the Group 3 6f Railway Stakes winner Misty Bend. (Lucayan Stud). *"A filly with an especially nice pedigree, she's quite weak and backward and may only run once this year. She's a very, very good-moving horse and is one for the future. Hopefully a Guineas or Oaks runner next year".*

1065 - UNNAMED ** [84] b.c. Danzig Connection – Nonpareil (Pharly).
May 1.

Half-brother to the quite useful 2-y-o 5.8f winner Access Leisure, to the quite useful 2-y-o triple 5f and subsequent hurdles winner Mister Lawson, the moderate 15f to 16.5f winner Marathia (all by Blushing Scribe) and a winner in Hong Kong by Salse. The dam was a quite useful 7f placed 2-y-o. The second dam, Norme (by Dark Tiger), was a French listed 1m winner and a half-sister to the Prix Saint-Alary winner Scala III. (Mr Charles Lam Leung Seng). *"Quite forward, he should be seen out around June/July time and he's a very nice type of colt you shouldn't leave out. Danzig Connection is a stallion I like".*

1066 - UNNAMED * [80] b.c. Efisio – Triple Joy (Most Welcome).
May 8. Fourth foal. 28,000Y. Tattersalls October.

Half-brother to the unraced 2000 2-y-o Joy Of Norway (by Halling) and to the very useful 6f (at 2 yrs) and 1m winner Triple Dash (by Nashwan). The dam, a useful 6f and 7f winner and second in the listed Abernant Stakes, is a half-sister to 6 winners including the Sun Chariot Stakes winner Talented and to the unplaced dam of the US Grade 3 winner Wavy Run. The second dam, Triple Reef (by Mill Reef), is an unraced half-sister to 13 winners including the One Thousand Guineas and Oaks placed Maysoon, the Ribblesdale Stakes winner Third Watch, the Prix Foy winner Richard of York and the Premio Dormello winner Three Tails (herself dam of the high-class middle-distance colts Tamure and Three Cheers). (Tweenhills Racing. May Hill Syndicate). *"A bonny horse, he's done very well since he's been with us. You'll see him out over six or seven furlongs around July time".*

G WRAGG

1067 - AIAIE [88]   ch.f. Zafonic – Circe's Isle (Be My Guest).
January 28. Seventh foal.

Half-sister to the quite useful 2000 7f placed 2-y-o Steinitz (by Nashwan), to the very useful Don Micheletto, a winner over 7f (at 2 yrs) and the listed 10f Predominate Stakes and fourth in the French Derby (by Machiavellian), the 1998 French 3-y-o winner Circe's Symbol (by Soviet Star) and the useful 1m and 10f winner Flint Knapper (by Kris). The unraced dam is closely related to the useful Schweppes Golden Mile Handicap winner Little Bean and a half-sister to 12 winners including the high-class 7f Jersey Stakes and Challenge Stakes winner Sally Rous (by Rousillon), the Welsh Derby winner Assemblyman (by General Assembly) and the very smart Group 1 9.3f Prix d'Ispahan winner Sasuru. The second dam, Sassalya (by Sassafras), a useful 7f and 10f winner in Ireland, was a half-sister to the smart colts Beau Sham and Lafontaine. (Mr A E Oppenheimer).

1068 - BLUESTONE [81]   ch.c. Bluebird – Romoosh (Formidable).
February 18. Second foal. 190,000Y. Tattersalls October.

The dam, a fair 10f winner, is a half-sister to 6 winners including the Group 2 7f Laurent Perrier Champagne Stakes winner Unblest and the dam of the German Group 3 and listed Woodcote Stakes winner Silca Blanka. The second dam, Missed Blessing (by So Blessed), a smart 6f and 1m winner, was second in the Group 3 7.3f Hungerford Stakes and is a half-sister to the good hurdler Mysilv. (Mollers Racing).

1069 - CERTAINLY BRAVE [87]   b.f. Indian Ridge – Dead Certain (Absalom).
March 15. Seventh foal. 130,000Y. Tattersalls October.

Half-sister to the very useful 1998 2-y-o 5f and 6f winner and Cornwallis Stakes second Deadly Nightshade, to the quite useful 2000 3-y-o 6f winner True Night (both by Night Shift), the useful Irish 7f and 10f winner Hamad (by Sadler's Wells) and the very smart winner of the Group 1 6f Cheveley Park Stakes, the Queen Mary Stakes, the Lowther Stakes (all at 2 yrs) and the Group 2 6.5f Prix Maurice de Gheest, is a half-sister to 6 winners including the fairly useful 10f handicapper Fire Top. The second dam, the French 1m to 10f winner Sirnelta (by Sir Tor) is a daughter of a half-sister to the French Derby winner Sanctus II. (Mr T Stewart).

1070 - ELEGY (USA) [92]   b.f. Diesis – Affirmative Fable (Affirmed).
May 16. Tenth foal. 57,000Y. Tattersalls October.

Sister to the useful 10f winner Aesops and half-sister to 4 winners including the useful 1990 2-y-o Group 3 1m May Hill Stakes winner Majmu (herself dam of the Prix Jacques le Marois winner Muhtathir) and the modest 9.4f winner Lyphard's Fable (both by Al Nasr). The dam, a minor US 4-y-o winner at around 1m, is a half-sister to the Grade 3 Palomar Handicap winner Northern Fable. The second dam, Fairway Fable (by Never Bend), won 3 races including a minor stakes and was placed in two Grade 3 events. (Mr T Stewart).

1071 - FRANCIS OF ASSISI * [104]   b.c. Sadler's Wells – Miss Rinjani (Shirley Heights).
May 1. Fourth foal.

Brother to the smart 10f winner St Expedit and half-brother to the very promising 2000 2-y-o 7f winner Asian Heights (by Hernando) and the fairly useful 1998 2-y-o 7f winner Miss Amanpuri (by Alzao). The dam, a fair 2-y-o 7f winner, was placed over 12f at 3 yrs and is a half-sister to several winners. The second dam, Miss Kuta Beach (by Bold Lad, Ire), a fairly useful 6f and 10f winner, is a half-sister to numerous winners including the very useful Bali Dancer and Bali Magic. (Mr J L C Pearce).
Significant sire/damsire crosses:- In The Wings, Hawker's News, Hunting Hawk, Legend Maker, Subtle Power.

1072 - ISLAND DESTINY [90]   ch.f. Kris – Balnaha (Lomond).
February 20. Fifth foal.

Sister to the 1999 Group 1 1m Coronation Stakes winner Balisada and half-sister to the quite useful 12f winner Talk To Mojo (by Deploy). The dam, a modest 3-y-o 1m winner, is a sister to Inchmurrin (a very useful winner of the Child Stakes and herself dam of the very smart and tough colt Inchinor), closely related to the very useful 1m winner Guest Artiste and a half-sister to the Mill Reef Stakes winner

Welney. The second dam, On Show (by Welsh Pageant), won over 10f and was second in the November Handicap. (The Eclipse Partnership 2).
Significant sire/damsire crosses:- Balisada, Ultimately Lucky.

1073 - JERPAHNI [74] b.f. Distant Relative – Oublier L'Ennui (Bellman).
April 27. Sixth foal. 26,000Y. Tattersalls October.
Sister to the fairly useful 6f winner of 3 races and Group 3 5.5f Prix d'Arenberg second Shudder (by Distant Relative) and half-sister to the modest 2000 6f and 7f placed 2-y-o Troubleshooter (by Ezzoud). The dam, a winner over hurdles and fences, is a half-sister to 11 winners. The second dam, Cassowary (by Kashmir II), is a placed half-sister to 5 winners. (Mrs Claude Lilley).

1074 - MISS PINKERTON [85] b.f. Danehill – Rebecca Sharp (Machiavellian).
March 28. First foal.
The dam, a high-class winner of the Group 1 1m Coronation Stakes, is a half-sister to numerous winners including the smart Group 3 11.5f Lingfield Derby Trial winner Mystic Knight, the useful 10f winner Mayo and the quite useful 2-y-o 6f winner Nuryandra. The second dam, Nuryana (by Nureyev), was a useful winner of 2 races over 1m including the listed Grand Metropolitan Stakes and is a half-sister to 5 winners including the dam of the useful Laurent-Perrier Champagne Stakes, Gimcrack Stakes and July Stakes placed Take A Left. (Mr A E Oppenheimer).

1075 - MONTURANI (IRE) [79] b.f. Indian Ridge – Mezzogiorno (Unfuwain).
March 9. Second foal.
The dam, a very useful 7f (at 2 yrs) and 10f listed winner and third in the Oaks is a half-sister to the fairly useful 10f and 10.5f winner Rainbow Top. The second dam, Aigue (by High Top), a fairly useful 4-y-o dual 1m winner, is a sister to the listed middle-distance winner Torchon and a half-sister to 2 winners. (Mrs R Philipps).

STALLION
REFERENCE

Mind Games (top) and Tagula both had highly successful first crops in 2000

This section deals with the sires of the two-year-olds in the book. The reference numbers given with each stallion are the numbers of their chosen two-year-old representatives. Please take note of the fascinating statistical information provided in tabular form by Timeform in this book. These tables can be of great value when evaluating a stallion's ability to sire winners.

Amongst the stallions listed in this section are the best stallions of America and Europe. Horses like the American sires Danzig, Diesis, Gone West, Mr Prospector, Nureyev, Seeking The Gold, Silver Hawk, Storm Cat and Woodman. The top European sires include Cadeaux Genereux, Danehill, Darshaan, Green Desert, Indian Ridge, Machiavellian, Nashwan, Rainbow Quest, Sadler's Wells and Zafonic.

Each year we see a new batch of sires with their first runners. This season, the exciting young stallions with offspring racing for the first time include Alhaarth, Ali-Royal, Benny The Dip, Danehill Dancer, Desert King, Entrepreneur, Revoque, Royal Applause, Singspiel and Spinning World.

AFFIRMED   1975 Exclusive Native – Won't Tell You (Crafty Admiral).
(576)

Racing record: 22 wins in the USA, notably the Triple Crown (Kentucky Derby, Preakness Stakes and Belmont Stakes) and eleven other Grade 1 races. Horse of the Year and Champion at 2, 3 and 4 yrs. Stud record: Best winners include Affidavit, Affirmed Success (Vosburgh Stakes, Cigar Mile), Bint Pasha (Prix Vermeille, Yorkshire Oaks), Charlie Barley, Claude Monet, Flawlessly (Matriarch Stakes, Beverly Hills Handicap, Ramona Handicap, Beverly D Stakes, etc), Buy The Firm (Top Flight Handicap), Easy to Copy, Firm Stance (Top Flight Handicap), Mossflower (Hampstead Handicap), Low Key Affair, One From Heaven (Selene Stakes, Canadian Oaks), Peteski (Breeders Stakes, Queens Plate, Prince of Wales Stakes - Canada), Quiet Resolve (Atto Mile), Regal State (Prix Morny), Tibullo (Gran Criterium), Trusted Partner (Irish 1,000 Guineas) and Zoman (Budweiser International, Prix d'Ispahan). Died 2001.

ALHAARTH   1993 Unfuwain – Irish Valley (Irish River)
(4, 44, 60, 150, 187, 193, 321, 443, 495, 574, 580, 721, 729, 772, 813, 880, 1005, 1007, 1036)

Racing record: Champion 2-y-o of 1995 when winner of 4 group races, notably Dewhurst Stakes. Showed very smart form up to 1¼m at 3/4 yrs, winning three Group 2 events. Stud record: First crop now two-year-olds. Standing at Derrinstown Stud, Ireland. 2001 fee: IR7,000 gns.

ALI-ROYAL   1993 Royal Academy – Alidiva (Chief Singer)
(3, 153, 382, 633, 733, 774, 1058)

Racing record: Winner of 7 races, notably Sussex Stakes at 4 yrs. Stud record: First crop now two-year-olds. Died 2001.

ALZAO   1980 Lyphard – Lady Rebecca (Sir Ivor).
(31, 351, 575, 598, 620, 712, 743, 753, 842, 858, 889, 914, 935, 948, 979, 985)

Racing record: 3 wins from 1m to 9f. Stud record: Best winners include Alborada (Champion Stakes twice), Alcando (Beverly Hills Handicap), Alpride (Yellow Ribbon Invitational), Bobzao, Capricciosa (Cheveley Park Stakes), Lady Upstage, Last Second, Matiya (Irish 1,000 Guineas), Pass The Peace (Cheveley Park Stakes), Second Set (Sussex Stakes), Shahtoush (Oaks), Unblest, Wind In Her Hair (Aral-Pokal) and Winona (Irish Oaks). Standing at Coolmore Stud in Ireland. 2001 fee: IR15,000 gns (Oct 1st).

ANABAA   1992 Danzig – Balbonella (Gay Mecene).
(221, 402, 556, 642, 1060)

Racing record: Won 8 races including the July Cup and the Prix Maurice de Gheest. Stud record: First crop now three-year-olds. Sire of Prix Marcel Boussac winner Amonita and Champagne Stakes third Shaard. Standing at Haras du Quesnay in France. 2001 fee: 150,000FF (Oct 1st).

A P INDY   1989 Seattle Slew – Weekend Surprise (Secretariat).
(34, 1039)

Racing record: 8 wins from 6.5f (at 2 yrs) to 12f, notably the Belmont Stakes, the Breeders Cup Classic, the Santa Anita Derby and the Hollywood Futurity. Horse Of The Year. Champion 3-y-o colt. Stud record: First runners in 1996. Sire of the Grade 1 winners Golden Missile (Pimlico Special Handicap), Secret Status (Kentucky Oaks, Mother Goose Stakes), A P Valentine (Champagne Stakes), Symboli Indy (Japanese Group 1), Tomisue's Delight (Personal Ensign Handicap, Ruffian Handicap), Run Up The Colors (Alabama Stakes), Royal Indy (Gazelle Handicap) and Stephen Got Even (Donn Handicap), the US Grade 2 winners Let, Lu Ravi, Pulpit, A P Assay and Old Trieste, numerous Grade 3 winners and Kentucky Derby/Belmont Stakes second Aptitude. A P Indy is a half-brother to another American classic winner in Summer Squall (Preakness Stakes). He is inbred 4x3 to Bold Ruler and represents a complete outcross for the preponderance of Northern Dancer line mares. Standing at Lane's End Farm, Kentucky. 2001 fee: private.

ASHKALANI   1993 Soviet Star – Ashtarka (Dalsaan).
(90, 384, 539, 876, 975, 1046, 1055)

Racing record: Won 5 races including the French Two Thousand Guineas and the Prix du Moulin. Stud record: First crop now three-year-olds. Sire of French listed winner Lunaska, Italian listed winner Gabriellina Giof and fairly useful winners Ashlinn and There's Two. Standing at the Irish National Stud. 2001 fee: IR£12,500 (Oct 1st).

ATRAF   1993 Clantime – Flitteriss Park (Beldale Flutter)
(178, 765)

Racing record: Winner of 6 races, including Cork And Orrery Stakes at 3 yrs and US Grade 3 7f event at 4. Stud record: First crop now two-year-olds. Standing at Tweenhills Farm, Gloucs. 2001 fee: £2,000.

ATTICUS   1992 Nureyev – Athyka (Secretariat)
(242, 291)

Racing record: Won 7 races in France and USA, notably Grade 1 9f Oaklawn Handicap at 5 yrs. Second in Poule d'Essai des Poulains at 3 yrs. Stud record: His first crop are now two-year-olds. Standing at Three Chimneys Farm, Kentucky. 2001 fee: $20,000

BAHAMIAN BOUNTY   1994 Cadeaux Genereux – Clarentia (Ballad Rock)
(48, 70, 138, 319, 481, 491, 988)

Racing Record: Winner of 3 races at 2 yrs, notably Prix Morny and Middle Park: fourth in July Cup at 3 yrs. Stud record: First crop now two-year-olds. Standing at National Stud, Newmarket. 2001 fee: £4,500.

BAHRI   1992 Riverman – Wasnah (Nijinsky).
(133, 261, 301, 315, 365)

Racing record: 3 wins including the Queen Elizabeth II Stakes and the St James's Palace Stakes. Stud record: First runners in 1998. Sire of high-class Dante winner and Derby second Sakhee, Falmouth Stakes winner Alshakr, useful sprinter May Contessa and useful Lowther Stakes second Khulan. 2001 fee: $25,000.

BARATHEA   1990 Sadler's Wells – Brocade (Habitat).
(168, 170, 286, 309, 370, 467, 507, 519, 532, 793, 804, 829, 870, 878, 995, 1008, 1025)

Racing record: 5 wins from 7f to 1m, notably the Breeders Cup Mile and the Irish 2000 Guineas. Stud record: First runners in 1998. Sire of Prix de la Salamandre/Dewhurst winner Tobougg and Group 3 winners Barafamy, Barathea Guest, Enrique, Hidalguia, La Sylphide and Red Sea. Standing at Rathbarry Stud, Ireland. 2001 fee: IR25,000 gns (Oct 1st).

BEAU GENIUS   1985 Bold Ruckus – Royal Colleen (Viceregal)
(30)

Racing record: Won Grade 1 Philip H. Iselin Handicap at 5 yrs. Stud record: Best winners include Belle Genius (Moyglare Stud Stakes), Bo Cheryl (Canadian Grade 1 event) and Gentleman Beau (Grade 3 event). Standing at Ballena Vista Farm, California. 2001 fee: $6,000 (live foal).

BE MY CHIEF　　　　　　　　　　1987 Chief's Crown – Lady Be Mine (Sir Ivor).
(990)

Racing record: Won 6 races at 2 yrs from 6f to 1m notably the Racing Post Trophy. Stud record: Best performers include Donna Viola (Yellow Ribbon Handicap, Gamely Handicap), Cask, Dances With Dreams, Flying Squaw, Indian Light, Shigeru Summit, Thomire, Magongo.

BE MY GUEST　　　　　　　　1974 Northern Dancer – What a Treat (Tudor Minstrel).
(43, 431, 509, 1026)

Racing record: 4 wins from 6f to 8.5f including the Waterford Crystal Mile and the Blue Riband Trial. Stud record: Best performers include the Group winners Anfield, Assert, Astronef, Double Bed, Free Guest, Go and Go, Invited Guest, Intimate Guest, Luth Enchantee, Most Welcome, Media Starguest, Northern Treat, On The House, Pelder, Pentire, Salford Express and Valentine Waltz. Standing at Coolmore Stud in Ireland. 2001 fee: IR6,000 gns (Oct 1st).

BENNY THE DIP　　　　　　　1994 Silver Hawk – Rascal Rascal (Ack Ack)
(390, 413, 438, 925, 989)

Racing record: Winner of Derby and Dante at 3 yrs when also placed in Eclipse and Juddmonte International; won 3 times at 2 yrs, notably Royal Lodge Stakes. Stud record: First crop (conceived in USA) now two-year-olds. Standing at Cheveley Park Stud, Newmarket. 2001 fee: £8,000.

BERING　　　　　　　　　　1983 Arctic Tern – Beaune (Lyphard).
(24, 546)

Racing record: 5 wins from 8.5f to 12f notably the Prix du Jockey Club, the Group 2 Prix Hocquart and the Group 2 Prix Noailles. Stud record: Best winners include Matiara (French 1,000 Guineas), Glorosia (Fillies Mile), Pennekamp (2,000 Guineas), Peter Davies (Racing Post Trophy), Steamer Duck (Gran Criterium) and the Group/Graded Stakes winners Break Bread, Beau Sultan, Miss Berbere, Moiava, Salmon Ladder, Signe Divin, Serrant, Special Price, Three Points, Urban Ocean and Vertical Speed. Standing at the Haras du Quesnay. 2001 fee: 150,000 FF. (Oct 1st).

BEVELED　　　　　　　　　1982 Sharpen Up – Sans Arc (High Echelon)
(934)

Racing record: 6f/7f winner in USA, including in minor stakes: also second in Grade 3 event. Stud record: Best performers include Bold Edge (Prix Maurice de Gheest), Mantles Star (US Grade 3 event), and smart performers Chewit and Dancing Mystery. Died 1999.

BIGSTONE　　　　　　　　1990 Last Tycoon – Batave (Posse)
(886)

Racing record: Won Sussex Stakes and Queen Elizabeth II Stakes at 3 yrs and Prix d'Ispahan and Prix de la Foret at 4. Stud record: Best performers are Japan Cup runner-up Meisho Doto and useful performers Big Future (7f) and London Bank (up to 1¾m in Italy). Exported 1999.

BISHOP OF CASHEL　　　1992 Warning – Ballet Classique (Sadler's Wells).
(378)

Racing record: Won 4 races including the Group 2 7f Criterium de Maisons-Laffitte and the Group 3 7f Park Stakes at Doncaster (twice). Stud record: First crop now three-year-olds. Standing at Cheveley Park Stud, Newmarket. 2001 fee: £3,000 (Oct 1st).

BLUEBIRD　　　　　　　　1984 Storm Bird – Ivory Dawn (Sir Ivor).
(120, 188, 264, 273, 339, 406, 427, 469, 497, 538, 653, 752, 795, 1068)

Racing record: 4 wins from 5f to 6f including the Group 1 Kings Stand Stakes. Stud record: Best performers include Dolphin Street (Prix de la Foret), Lake Coniston (July Cup), Aube Indienne (Yellow Ribbon Invitational), Blue Siren, Delilah, Fly To The Stars (Lockinge Stakes), Harbour Master, Ronda, Swallow Flight and the Australasian Grade 1 winners Azzurro, Race Master, Flitter, Happiness, Lady of the Pines and Singing The Blues. 2001 fee: IR10,000 gns (Oct 1st).

BLUEGRASS PRINCE
1991 Bluebird – Amata (Nodouble)
(86, 682)

Racing record: Winner of 6 races from 2 to 4 yrs, including Group 3 Diomed Stakes and Grade 3 All American Stakes. Stud record: First crop are now two-year-olds. Standing at Benham Stud, Wiltshire. 2001 fee: £2,000

BLUES TRAVELLER
1990 Bluebird – Natuschka (Authi).
(422)

Won 6 races including the Grade 2 American Handicap, the Grade 2 Bay Meadows Handicap and the Grade 3 Rolling Green Handicap, also third in Derby. Stud record: Sire of useful Irish sprinter Romanylei and useful 1m/1¼m performer Blusienka.

BOUNDARY
1990 Danzig – Edge (Damascus)
(600, 605, 746, 819, 887)

Racing record: Winner of 8 races in USA, notably Grade 3 6f events A Phenomenon Handicap and Roseben Handicap at 4 yrs. Stud record: Sire of Middle Park winner Minardi, US 2-y-o Grade 1 7f/8.5f placed-performer She's Classy, and smart US graded event winners Conserve and Roxelana. Standing at Claiborne Farm, Kentucky. 2001 fee: $20,000.

BRIEF TRUCE
1989 Irish River – Falafel (Northern Dancer).
(938, 1028)

Racing record: 4 wins from 6f to 10f notably the St James's Palace Stakes and the Group 2 Gallinule Stakes and placed in the Breeders Cup Mile, the Irish 2,000 Guineas, the Prix du Moulin and the Queen Elizabeth II Stakes. Rated the top 3-y-o colt over a mile, three pounds below the filly Marling, in the International Classifications. Stud record: Sire of the Group 3 Railway Stakes winner Camargo and the listed winners Ella and Hopping Higgins.

CADEAUX GENEREUX
1985 Young Generation – Smarten Up (Sharpen Up).
(81, 202, 254, 268, 412, 591, 595, 655, 673, 699, 1027, 1030, 1048, 1052)

Racing record: 7 wins from 5f to 7f notably the July Cup, the William Hill Sprint Championship, the Group 3 Van Geest Criterion Stakes and the Group 3 Diadem Stakes. Champion sprinter. Stud record: Best winners include Bahamian Bounty (Middle Park Stakes), Barrow Creek, Bijou d'Inde (St James's Palace Stakes), Embassy (Cheveley Park Stakes), Hoh Magic (Prix Morny), Inglenook, Land of Dreams, Monaassib and Warning Shadows. Standing at Whitsbury Manor Stud in Hampshire. 2001 fee: £20,000 (live foal).

CARSON CITY
1987 Mr Prospector – Blushing Promise (Blushing Groom).
(652)

Racing record: Won the Grade 2 Sapling Stakes. Stud record: Best winners include City Band (Oak Leaf Stakes), City Zip (Hopeful Stakes), Flying Chevron (NYRC Mile Handicap), Pearl City (Ballerina Handicap) and the US Grade 2 winners Good And Tough, Imperfect World, Lord Carson, Ormsby and Gastown, Paved In Gold. 2001 fee: $35,000 (live foal).

CATRAIL
1990 Storm Cat – Tough As Nails (Majestic Light).
(474, 903, 991)

Racing record: 6 wins from 6f to 7f including the Group 2 Challenge Stakes, the Group 2 Prix Maurice de Gheest and the Group 3 Diadem Stakes. Stud record: Fourth crop now two-year-olds. Sire of US Grade 3 winner Storm Dream, Australian Group 3 winner, Catatonic, Prix de Sandringham winner Zarkiya, Prix Eclipse winner Potaro and smart performers Touch 'N' Fly (miler) and Lionhearted (sprinter). Standing at Wafare Farm, Midway, Kentucky. 2001 fee: $7,500.

CELTIC SWING
1992 Damister – Celtic Ring (Welsh Pageant).
(343, 656)

Racing record: Champion 2-y-o. Won 5 races including the Racing Post Trophy and the French Derby. Stud record: First crop now three-year-olds. Sire of Chesham Stakes winner Celtic Silence. Standing at Irish National Stud. 2001 fee: IR7,000 (Oct 1st).

CHARNWOOD FOREST 1992 Warning – Dance Of Leaves (Sadler's Wells).
(12, 78, 128, 615, 644, 781, 884)
Racing record: Won the Group 2 1m Queen Anne Stakes and the Group 2 7f Challenge Stakes. Stud record: First crop now three-year-olds. Standing at Rathbarry Stud in Ireland. 2001 fee: IR5,000 gns (Oct 1st).

CITIDANCER 1987 Dixieland Band – Willamae (Tentam)
(235)
Racing record: Won 3 6f races at 3 yrs and runner-up in Grade 1 1m Jerome Handicap (all his starts). Stud record: His best runners include Urbane (Grade 1 x2) and the Grade 3 winners Hookedonthefeelin, Latin Dancer and Disco Rico. Standing at Country Life Farm, Maryland. 2001 fee: $12,500.

COLLEGE CHAPEL 1990 Sharpo – Scarcely Blessed (So Blessed)
(245, 1049)
Racing record: Won Cork And Orrery Stakes, Prix Maurice de Gheest, Tetrarch Stakes and Greenlands Stakes (twice): also placed in July Cup and Nunthorpe Stakes. Stud record: Sire of smart 2000 2-y-o sprinter Superstar Leo, Prix Robert Papin winner Black Amber, Prix de Cabourg winner Hunan and useful handicappers Final Exam and Kathology. Exported to Italy in 2001.

COMMON GROUNDS 1985 Kris – Sweetly (Lyphard).
(206, 330, 336, 496, 533, 562, 728, 897)
Racing record: 2 wins including the Group 1 6f Prix de la Salamandre. Stud record: Best performers include Earl Of Barking (Hollywood Turf Handicap), Artema, Astudillo, Bad As I Wanna Be (Prix Morny), Clapham Common, Crisos II Monaco, Epitre, Fallow, Flanders, Golden Arches, Goombayland, Murghem, Riddlesdown, Rich Ground and Three For Fantasy.

COZZENE 1980 Caro – Ride The Trails (Prince John).
(215, 392, 454, 893)
Racing record: 10 wins from 6f to 9f including the Breeders Cup Mile. Stud record: Best performers include Alphabet Soup (Breeders Cup Classic), Environment Friend (Eclipse Stakes), Gaviola (US Grade 1 9f event), Hasten To Add (Grade 3 Laurel Turf Cup), Tikkanen (Breeders' Cup Turf), Star Of Cozzene (Man O'War Stakes), Running Stag (US Grade 2) and Rhythm Band (Group 3 Dubai Duty Free). Standing at Gainesway Farm, Lexington, Kentucky. 2001 fee: $60,000 (live foal).

DANEHILL 1986 Danzig – Razyana (His Majesty).
(95, 119, 123, 134, 184, 270, 314, 397, 409, 429, 448, 522, 526, 535, 560, 563, 601, 769, 801, 808, 832, 833, 883, 898, 915, 967, 978, 1032, 1037, 1053, 1054, 1064, 1074)
Racing record: Won the Ladbroke Sprint Cup and third in the Two Thousand Guineas. Stud record: Best winners (in Europe) include Clever Cliche, Danehill Dancer, Dansili, Desert King, Indian Danehill, Kissing Cousin, Regal Rose, Tiger Hill and Wannabe Grand. Also sire of numerous Grade 1 winners in Australia. Standing at Coolmore Stud in Ireland.

DANEHILL DANCER 1993 Danehill – Mira Adonde (Sharpen Up)
(6, 122, 124, 230, 473, 498, 618, 749, 773, 932)
Racing Record: Winner of 4 races, including Heinz 57 Phoenix Stakes and National Stakes at 2 yrs and Greenham at 3. Stud record: First crop now two-year-olds. Standing at Kilsheelan Stud, Ireland. 2001 fee: IR4,000 gns.

DANZIG 1977 Northern Dancer – Pas de Nom (Admiral's Voyage).
(135, 137, 394, 549, 666, 696, 716, 815, 818, 1020)
Racing record: 3 wins from 3 starts in the USA from 5.5f to 6f. Stud record: Best winners in the US include the Grade 1 winners Adjudicating, Chief's Crown, Contredance, Dance Smartly, Danzig Connection, Langfuhr, Military, Pine Bluff, Polish Navy, Stephan's Odyssey, Versailles Treaty and War Chant. In Europe, his best include the Group 1 winners Agnes World, Anabaa, Danehill, Dayjur, Elnadim, Green Desert, Hamas, Maroof, Mujahid, Pas de Reponse, Petit Loup, Polish Patriot, Polish Precedent, Polonia and Shaadi.

DANZIG CONNECTION 1983 Danzig – Gdynia (Sir Ivor)
(480, 540, 1065)
Racing record: Won Belmont Stakes and 9f Peter Pan Stakes, also minor stakes winner at 2 yrs. Stud record: Sire of Haydock Park Sprint Cup winner Iktamal, Irish 2000 Guineas runner-up Star of Gdansk, and Mill Reef Stakes winner Polish Laughter. First British-conceived crop now two-year-olds. Standing at Collin Stud, Newmarket. 2001 fee: £4,500.

DARSHAAN 1981 Shirley Heights – Delsy (Abdos).
(241, 324, 628, 732, 902, 923, 944, 952, 998, 1003, 1016, 1035)
Racing record: 5 wins from 1m to 12f, notably the Prix du Jockey Club, the Group 2 Criterium de Saint-Cloud, the Group 2 Prix Hocquart and the Group 2 Prix Greffulhe. Stud record: Best winners include Aliysa, Arzanni, Dilshaan (Racing Post Trophy), Grand Plaisir, Hellenic (Yorkshire Oaks), Josr Algharoud, Key Change (Yorkshire Oaks), Kotashaan (multiple Grade 1 wins including the Breeders Cup Turf), Mark Of Esteem (2,000 Guineas, Queen Elizabeth II Stakes), Mutamam, Sayarshan and Zayyani. Standing at the Gilltown Stud in County Kildare. 2001 fee: private.

DAYJUR 1987 Danzig – Gold Beauty (Mr Prospector).
(504, 739, 994)
Racing record: 7 wins from 5f to 6f notably the Keeneland Nunthorpe Stakes, the Ladbroke Sprint Cup and the Ciga Prix de l'Abbaye. Champion European Racehorse. Stud record: Best performers include Hayil (Middle Park Stakes) and the Group/Graded winners Asfurah, In Conference, Millstream, New Advantage, Tipsy Creek and With Fascination. Standing at Shadwell Farm, Lexington, Kentucky. 2001 fee: $10,000 (live foal).

DEFINITE ARTICLE 1992 Indian Ridge – Summer Fashion (Moorestyle).
(223, 371, 489, 911)
Racing record: Won the National Stakes and the Group 2 Tattersalls Gold Cup. Second in the Irish Derby and the Irish Champion Stakes. Stud record: First crop now three-year-olds. Sire of useful winners La Vita E Bella, Sixty Seconds and Vinnie Roe. Standing at Morristown Lattin Stud in Ireland. 2001 fee: IR£5,000 (Oct 1st).

DEPUTY MINISTER 1979 Vice Regent – Mint Copy (Bunty's Flight)
(705)
Racing record: Champion 2-y-o colt in North America when winning Young American Stakes and Laurel Futurity; won between 6f and 9f at 3/4 yrs, including 2 Grade 2 events. Stud record: Sire of numerous Grade 1 winners, including champion fillies Open Mind and Go For Wand, champion 2-y-o colt Dehere, Breeders' Cup Classic winner Awesome Again, Belmont winner Touch Gold and Kentucky Oaks winner Keeper Hill. Standing at Brookdale Farm, Kentucky. 2001 fee: $150,000 (live foal).

DESERT KING 1994 Danehill – Sabaah (Nureyev)
(51, 61, 165, 176, 207, 224, 420, 468, 476, 512, 514, 555, 622, 760, 823, 861, 981)
Racing record: Won National Stakes at 2 yrs and Irish 2000 Guineas/Derby at 3; also runner-up in Juddmonte International and Irish Champion Stakes. Stud record: First crop now two-year-olds. Standing at Coolmore Stud, Ireland. 2001 fee: IR15,000 gns.

DESERT STYLE 1992 Green Desert – Organza (High Top).
(742, 1038)
Racing record: Won the Tetrarch Stakes, Ballycorus Stakes and Phoenix Sprint Stakes (all Group 3). Stud record: His third crop are now two-year-olds. Sire of Poule d'Essai des Poulains/Irish 2000 Guineas winner Bachir and smart Free Handicap winner Cape Town. Standing at Morristown Lattin Stud, Ireland. 2001 fee: IR£12,500 (Oct 1st).

DEVIL'S BAG 1981 Halo – Ballade (Herbager).
(657)
Racing record: 8 wins in the USA including the Champagne Stakes, Laurel Futurity and the Cowdin Stakes. Stud record: Best winners include Taiki Shuttle (Prix Jacques le Marois), Devil His Due (Suburban Handicap), Devil's Orchid (Santa Monica Handicap) and Twilight Agenda (Meadowlands Cup Handicap). Standing at Claiborne Farm, Kentucky. 2001 fee: $15,000.

DIESIS 1980 Sharpen Up – Doubly Sure (Reliance II).
(38, 136, 149, 290, 320, 419, 449, 577, 614, 663, 805, 856, 953, 999, 1070)
Racing record: Champion 2-y-o in 1982. Winner of 3 races notably the Dewhurst Stakes and the Middle Park Stakes. Stud record: Best winners include Love Divine (Oaks), Diminuendo (Oaks, Irish Oaks, Yorkshire Oaks), Elmaamul (Coral-Eclipse Stakes, Phoenix Champion Stakes), Halling (Coral-Eclipse Stakes (twice), International Stakes (twice), Prix d'Ispahan), Husband (Rothmans International), Keen Hunter (Prix de l'Abbaye), Knifebox (Premio Roma), Daggers Drawn, Docksider, Marathon, Marillette, Rootentootenwooten (Demoiselle Stakes), Ramruma (Oaks, Irish Oaks and Yorkshire Oaks), Sabrehill and Sacred Song. Standing at Mill Ridge Farm, Lexington, Kentucky. 2001 fee: $30,000 (live foal, Sept 1st).

DISTANT RELATIVE 1986 Habitat – Royal Sister II (Claude).
(645, 1073)
Racing record: 8 wins from 6f to 1m including the Prix du Moulin and the Sussex Stakes. Stud record: Best winners include the Group winners Bin Rosie, Germane, Iftiraas and Star Of Akkar, the listed winner My Branch, the Grade 3 winner De Puntillas and the useful handicapper Wildwood Flower.

DISTANT VIEW 1991 Mr Prospector – Seven Springs (Irish River).
(158, 249, 414, 440, 557, 584, 623, 787)
Racing record: Won the Sussex Stakes. Stud record: His third crop are two-year-olds in 2001. Sire of Dewhurst winner Distant Music and top-class miler Observatory. 2001 fee: $20,000.

DIXIELAND BAND 1980 Northern Dancer – Mississippi Mud (Delta Judge).
(15, 277, 285, 1004)
Racing record: 8 wins including the Grade 2 9f Pennsylvania Derby and the Grade 2 9f Massachusetts Handicap. Stud record: Best winners include Bedeviled (Grade 2 Razorback Handicap), Cotton Carnival (Grade 3 Martha Washington Stakes), Del Mar Dennis (Grade 2 San Bernardino Handicap), Devoted Brass (Grade 2 Swaps Stakes), Didyme (Group 2 Prix Robert Papin), Dixie Brass (Metropolitan Handicap), Dixieland Brass (Grade 2 Fountain Of Youth Stakes), Dixie Union (Haskell Invitational Handicap, Malibu Stakes), Drum Taps (Ascot Gold Cup), Egyptband (Prix de Diane), Mutaahab (Group 2 Royal Lodge Stakes) and Spinning Round (Ballerina Stakes). Standing at Lane's End Farm, Lexington, Kentucky. 2001 fee: $75,000 (live foal, Sept 1st).

DOYOUN 1985 Mill Reef – Dumka (Kashmir II).
(96, 868)
Racing record: Won the 2,000 Guineas and the Craven Stakes. Stud record: Best winners include Daylami (multiple Group/Grade 1 winner), Manntari (National Stakes), Dalara, Kalanisi (dual Group 1 winner), Manndar (dual Grade 1 winner), Takarian and Rafayda.

DR DEVIOUS 1989 Ahonoora – Rose Of Jericho (Alleged).
(103, 231, 544, 631, 664, 730)
Racing record: Won 6 races including the Derby, Irish Champion Stakes and Dewhurst Stakes. Stud record: Retired to stud in Japan and sire of 3 stakes winners there. Now standing at Coolmore Stud in Ireland. 2001 fee: IR10,000 gns.

DYNAFORMER 1985 Roberto – Andover Way (His Majesty).
(240, 318, 478)
Racing record: 7 wins from 7f to 12f including the Grade 2 Florida Derby and the Grade 2 Discovery Handicap. Stud record: Best winners include Derby third Beat All, Vergennes (Hollywood Derby) and the US Grade 3 winners Blumin' Affair, Old Chapel and Rabiadella. Standing at Three Chimneys Farm, Lexington, Kentucky. 2001 fee: $30,000 (live foal, Sept 1st).

EAGLE EYED 1991 Danzig – Razyana (His Majesty).
(259, 461, 477)
Racing record: Won the Grade 2 9f Arlington Classic. Stud record: A full brother to Danehill, his second crop are now three-year-olds. Sire of useful performers Full Flow, Goggles and Royal Eagle.

EFISIO   1982 Formidable – Eldoret (High Top).
(161, 222, 226, 233, 353, 470, 755, 913, 984, 1066)

Racing record: 8 wins from 6f to 1m including the Group 1 Premio Emilio Turati, the Group 2 Premio Chiusura, the Group 3 Challenge Stakes and the Group 3 Horris Hill Stakes. Stud record: Best winners include Hever Golf Rose (Prix de l'Abbaye), Pips Pride (Phoenix Stakes), Casteddu, Tomba (Prix de la Foret) and Young Ern. Standing at Highclere Stud. 2001 fee: £9,000 (Oct 1st).

ELMAAMUL   1987 Diesis – Modena (Roberto)
(55, 57)

Racing record: 5 wins from 7f to 1¼m, including Eclipse Stakes and Irish Champion Stakes. Stud record: Best winners include Muhtathir (Prix Jacques le Marois) Dankeston (German Group 3) and the useful performers Ashbal, Blue Mountain, Mac Black and Mawwal. Exported to Italy in 1999.

EL PRADO   1989 Sadler's Wells – Lady Capulet (Sir Ivor).
(403)

Racing record: Won the National Stakes at the Curragh. Stud record: With 4 crops racing, sire of the US Grade 3 winners Nite Dreamer, Shires Ende and Chindi.

EMARATI   1986 Danzig – Bold Example (Bold Lad)
(250)

Racing record: Placed twice at 1m. Stud record: Best performers include Danielle's Lad, Emerging Market, Emma Peel, Golden Rule, Patsy's Double, Refuse To Lose and Westcourt Magic.

EMPEROR JONES   1990 Danzig – Qui Royalty (Native Royalty).
(1063)

Racing record: Won the Group 2 Lockinge Stakes and the Group 3 Craven Stakes. Stud record: Second crop are now three-year-olds. Standing at Haras du Quesnay. 2001 fee: 30,000 FF.

END SWEEP   1991 Forty Niner – Broom Dance (Dance Spell)
(888)

Racing record: Winner of 6 races in USA at 6f/7f, including a Grade 3 event. Stud record: Sire of Grade 1 7f winners Trippi (Vosburgh Stakes) and Nany's Sweep (Santa Monica Handicap).

ENTREPRENEUR   1994 Sadler's Wells – Exclusive Order (Exclusive Native)
(27, 109, 121, 199, 219, 350, 483, 488, 521, 568, 572, 599, 708, 767, 788, 840, 942, 943, 957, 968)

Racing record: Won 3 races, notably 2000 Guineas. Stud record: First crop now two-year-olds. Standing at Coolmore Stud, Ireland. 2001 fee: IR15,000 gns.

ERIN'S ISLE   1978 Busted – Chemise (Shantung).
(93)

Racing record: Won the Group 2 Ballymoss Stakes and the Group 2 Gallinule Stakes in Ireland prior to several Grade 1 wins in the USA including the California Stakes and the San Juan Capistrano Handicap. Stud career: Sire of numerous winners here and in the USA including useful Irish 2000 2-y-o 7f performer Affianced. Standing at Redmondstown Stud, Ireland. 2001 fee: IR£5,000 gns.

EXIT TO NOWHERE   1988 Irish River – Coup de Folie (Halo)
(486, 771)

Racing record: 4 wins including the Prix Jacques le Marois, the Group 3 Prix Thomas Bryon, Prix du Muguet and the Group 3 Prix Edmond Blanc. Stud record: Sire of Shaka (Criterium de Saint-Cloud), French Derby second Nowhere To Exit and Prix Daphnis winner Boutron. Standing at Haras de Fresnay-le-Buffard. 2001 fee: 50,000 FF (Oct 1st).

FAYRUZ   1984 Song – Friendly Jester (Be Friendly).
(194, 479, 1041)

Racing record: Won 7 races over five furlongs and Group 3 placed in the Cornwallis Stakes. Stud record: Best winners include the listed winners Farhana, Master Fay and Monkston Point. Standing at Rossenarra Stud in Ireland. 2001 fee: Ir£3,000 (NFNF)

FIRST TRUMP   1991 Primo Dominie – Valika (Valiyar).
                                                              (380, 516, 720, 987)
Racing record: 5 wins over 6f including the Middle Park Stakes and the Group 2 Richmond Stakes. Stud record: Sire of Group 2 Flying Childers winner Mrs P, listed winner Two Clubs, July Stakes runner-up Media Mogul and smart miler Bahamian Bandit. Standing at The National Stud. 2000 fee: £4,000 (Oct 1st).

FLYING SPUR   1992 Danehill – Rolls (Mr Prospector)
                                                                          (510, 906)
Racing record: Won 6 races in Australia at 2/3 yrs from 5f to 1m, including 3 Group 1 events. Stud record: First European-conceived crop now three-year-olds. Sire of fairly useful performers Denise Margaret, Flying Millie, Up Tempo and Volata.

FOREST WILDCAT   1991 Storm Cat – Victoria Beauty (Bold Native)
                                                                                (758)
Racing record: Won 9 races in USA, including two Grade 3 6f events at 5 yrs. Stud record: Had first 2-y-o crop in 2000. Standing at Brookdale Farm, Kentucky. 2001 fee: $25,000.

FORZANDO   1981 Formidable – Princely Maid (King's Troop)
                                                                          (1, 518, 738)
Racing record: Won seven 6f races at 2/3 yrs and US Grade 1 1m event at 4. Stud record: Sire of Cork And Orrery winner Superior Premium, Richmond/Flying Childers/Cornwallis Stakes winner Easycall, Group 3 winners Great Deeds and Up And At 'Em and listed winners Philidor, Pool Music and Zanay. Standing at Throckmorton Court Stud, Worcestershire. 2001 fee: £2,000.

FOXHOUND   1991 Danzig – Lassie Dear (Buckpasser).
                                                                                (416)
Racing record: Won 3 races from 5.5f to 6f and placed in three Group 3 races in France. Stud record: His first crop are now three-year-olds. They include Group 3 Cornwallis winner Kier Park and listed winners Mount Abu and Scarteen Fox. Standing at Castle Hyde Stud, Ireland. 2000 fee: IR5,000 Gns.

FRAAM   1989 Lead On Time – Majestic Kahala (Majestic Prince)
                                                                          (181, 927)
Racing record: Won 5 races, notably Schweppes Golden Mile and listed race at 5 yrs: in frame in pattern races 4 times at 6 yrs. Stud record: Third crop now two-year-olds. Best winners include useful performers Chagall (German listed winner), Dayglow Dancer and Lady Lahar (Group 3 Futurity Stakes). Standing at Tweenhills Stud, Gloucester. 2001 fee: £3,000.

FUMO DI LONDRA   1991 Indian Ridge – Fettle (Relkino)
                                                                                (908)
Racing record: Won 2 races at 2 yrs, including Italian listed event: also in frame in 3 pattern races. Stud record: His first crop are now three-year-olds. Standing at Benham Stud, Berks. 2001 fee: £2,500.

GENERAL MONASH   1992 Thorn Dance – Zummerudd (Habitat).
                                                                          (340, 354)
Racing record: Won the Group 2 5.5f Prix Robert Papin. Stud record: First crop are now three-year-olds. Sire of useful 5f/6f performer General Monash. Standing at Ballyhane Stud in Ireland. 2001 fee: IR£4,500.

GILDED TIME   1990 Timeless Moment – Gilded Lilly (What a Pleasure).
                                                                                (564)
Racing record: Champion US 2-y-o colt. Won the Breeders Cup Juvenile. Stud record: From three crops racing, sire of the US Grade 2 winners Added Gold, Elaborate and Time Limit, Grade 3 winner Old Topper and Prix de Cabourg winner Crystal Castle. 2001 fee: $20,000.

GLITTERMAN 1985 Dewan – Moon Glitter (In Reality)
(811)

Racing record: Won 9 races in USA, including a Grade 3 6f event. Stud record: Best winners include Grade 1 8.5f Ashland Stakes winner Glitter Woman and Grade 2 6f/7f winner J J's Dream. Standing at Wafare Farm, Kentucky. 2001 fee: $15,000.

GLORY OF DANCER 1993 Shareef Dancer – Glory of Hera (Formidable)
(762)

Racing record: Won Group 1 Gran Criterium at 2 yrs and Group 2 Dante Stakes at 3 yrs. Stud record: First crop now three-year-olds. Exported 1999.

GOLD FEVER 1993 Forty Niner – Lead Kindly Light (Majestic Light)
(872)

Racing record: Won 7 races in USA, notably Grade 1 NYRA Mile Handicap. Stud record: Sire of Grade 2 winner Gold Mover in first 2-y-o crop in 2000. Standing at Lane's End Farm, Kentucky. 2001 fee: $20,000.

GONE WEST 1970 Mr Prospector – Secrettame (Secretariat).
(160, 218, 298, 718, 821, 826, 854, 1021)

Racing record: 6 wins notably the Grade 1 9f Dwyer Stakes, the Grade 2 1m Gotham Stakes and the Grade 2 1m Withers Stakes. Stud record: Best winners include the champion 2-y-o and 3-y-o Zafonic (2,000 Guineas, Prix Morny, Prix de la Salamandre and Dewhurst Stakes), Da Hoss (Breeders Cup Mile), West by West (Nassau County Handicap), Link River (John A. Morris Handicap), Commendable (Belmont Stakes), the European Group winners Aboline, Dance Parade, Dazzle, Lassigny, Muqtarib, Raah Algharb, Royal Abjar, Tamayaz, West Man and Zamindar and the US Graded Stakes winners Mr Greeley, Old Tascosa and Supremo. Standing at Mill Ridge Farm in Lexington, Kentucky. $125,000.

GRAND LODGE 1991 Chief's Crown – La Papagena (Habitat).
(64, 92, 174, 186, 213, 217, 234, 236, 304, 434, 484, 529, 695, 768, 895)

Racing record: Won 4 races from 6f to 1m including the Dewhurst Stakes and the St James's Palace Stakes. Champion European Two-Year-Old of 1993. Stud record: Fourth crop are two-year-olds in 2001. Best winners include Derby/Irish Derby/Arc winner Sinndar, Prix du Moulin/Prix de la Foret winner Indian Lodge and Group 3 winners Chelsea Manor and Raise A Grand. Standing at Coolmore Stud. 2001 fee: IR35,000 gns (Oct 1st).

GREAT COMMOTION 1986 Nureyev – Alathea (Lorenzaccio)
(735)

Racing record: Won Cork And Orrery Stakes and Beeswing Stakes and runner-up in 5 pattern races, notably Irish 2000 Guineas and July Cup. Stud record: Sire of Gran Criterium/Duke of York Stakes winner Lend A Hand, Group 2 winner Deadly Dudley and US Grade 3 winner Blending Element. Standing at Damastown Stud, Ireland. 2001 fee: IR2,000.

GREEN DANCER 1972 Nijinsky – Green Valley (Val de Loir)
(232, 871, 1056)

Racing record: Won Observer Gold Cup at 2 yrs and Poule d'Essai des Poulains and Prix Lupin at 3 yrs. Stud record: Best winners include Group/Grade 1 winners Greinton, Fantastic Look, Vilzak, Northern Emerald, Senor Pete, Suave Dancer, Green Tune, Aryenne, First Waltz, Maximova and Market Booster. Died in 2000.

GREEN DESERT 1983 Danzig – Foreign Courier (Sir Ivor)
(91, 115, 118, 164, 197, 266, 292, 296, 447, 525, 630, 662, 734, 816, 838, 844, 882, 1051)

Racing record: 5 wins from 5f to 7f including the July Cup, the Vernons Sprint Cup and the Flying Childers Stakes. Stud record: Best winners include Bint Allayl (champion 2-y-o filly), Cape Cross (Lockinge Stakes), Desert Prince (Irish 2,000 Guineas, Prix du Moulin and Queen Elizabeth II Stakes), Owington (July Cup), Sheikh Albadou (Breeders Cup Sprint, Keeneland Nunthorpe Stakes, Haydock Park Sprint), White Heart (US Grade 1 winner), Greenlander (Group 2 Prix Robert Papin), Gabr (Group 2 Sandown Mile), Redden Burn (Group 2 Grosser Preis von Dusseldorf), Tamarisk (Haydock Park Sprint Cup) and numerous Group 3 winners including Absurde, Ardkinglass, Christmas Gift (in the USA),

Desert Shot, Desert Style, Magic Ring, Mint Crisp, Mojave, Shahid and Tropical. Standing at the Shadwell Stud, Norfolk. 2001 fee: £40,000 (live foal).

GULCH
1984 Mr Prospector – Jameela (Rambunctious).
(52, 274, 282, 391, 425, 593, 789, 806, 855)

Racing record: 13 wins (including seven Grade 1 stakes) from 5f to 9f, notably the Breeders Cup Sprint, the Metropolitan Handicap (twice) and the Wood Memorial. Champion sprinter at 4 yrs in the USA. Stud record: Best winners include the Group/Grade 1 winners Great Navigator (Hopeful Stakes), Harayir (1,000 Guineas), Thunder Gulch (Kentucky Derby, Belmont Stakes, Travers Stakes and Florida Derby), Torrential (Prix Jean Prat) and Wallenda (Super Derby) and very smart 2000 2-y-o Nayef. Standing at Lane's End Farm, Kentucky. 2001 fee: $60,000 (live foal, Sept 1st).

HALLING
1991 Diesis – Dance Machine (Green Dancer).
(28, 45, 107, 147, 643, 647, 689, 899)

Racing record: Won 12 races including the Coral-Eclipse Stakes (twice), the Juddmonte International (twice) and the Prix d'Ispahan. Stud record: First crop now three-year-olds. Sire of useful winners Arameen (in Ireland) and Baaridd. Standing at Dalham Hall Stud in Newmarket. 2001 fee: £15,000 (SLF).

HAMAS
1989 Danzig – Fall Aspen (Pretense).
(79, 442, 578)

Racing record: 5 wins from 5f to 1m including the July Cup and the Group 3 Duke of York Stakes. Stud record: With four crops racing, Hamas has sired Group 2 King's Stand Stakes winner Mitcham and several listed winners including Regal Revolution (Firth of Clyde Stakes). Standing at Station d'Etalons. 2001 fee: 30,000 FF.

HANSEL
1988 Woodman – Count On Bonnie (Dancing Count)
(552)

Racing record: Champion 3-y-o colt, winning Preakness Stakes and Belmont Stakes. Stud record: Best winners include dual Hardwicke Stakes winner Fruits of Love and Prix Marcel Boussac winner Loving Claim. He now stands in Japan.

HECTOR PROTECTOR
1988 Woodman – Korveya (Riverman)
(39, 156, 280, 373, 375, 433, 465, 485, 610, 782, 909)

Racing record: Brother to Bosra Sham. Won Prix Morny, Prix de la Salamandre and Grand Criterium at 2 yrs, and Poule d'Essai des Poulains and Prix Jacques le Marois at 3. Stud record: Sire of Limnos (Group 2 Prix Foy and Prix Jean de Chaudenay) and Shiva (Tattersalls Gold Cup). His first British-conceived crop are now two-year-olds.

HENNESSY
1993 Storm Cat – Island Kitty (Hawaii).
(302, 905)

Racing record: Won 4 races in the USA including the Hopeful Stakes, the Grade 2 Sapling Stakes and the Grade 2 Hollywood Juvenile Championship. Stud record: First crop now three-year-olds. Sire of useful irish 2-y-o's Keats and Perigee Moon

HERNANDO
1990 Niniski – Whakilyric (Miswaki).
(603, 847)

Racing record: Won 7 races including the Prix Lupin and the Prix du Jockey Club. Stud record: Third crop now two-year-olds. Sire of Prix du Jockey Club winner Holding Court, useful performers Bien Entendu and Miss Riviera Golf and promising 2000 2-y-o Autumn Rhythm. 2001 fee: 8,000 gns (Oct 1st).

HIGHEST HONOR
1983 Kenmare – High River (Riverman).
(326, 524, 692, 845, 852)

Racing record: 4 wins from 7f to 9f 55yds including the Prix d'Ispahan. Stud record: Best progeny include Medaaly (Racing Post Trophy), Admise (Oak Tree Turf Club Championship), Sagacity (Criterium de Saint-Cloud), Reve d'Oscar (Prix Saint-Alary), the Group 2 winners Erminius, Gothland and Dadarissime and the Group 3 winners Baroud d'Honneur, Saperlipoupette, Verglas, Perugina, Take Risks and Go Between. Standing at Haras du Quesnay. 2001 fee: 100,000 FF. (Oct 1st).

HONOR GRADES 1988 Danzig – Weekend Surprise (Secretariat)
(867)

Racing record: Won 5 races in USA at 6f to 8.5f and placed in Grade 3 events. Stud record: sire of Grade 1 10f Secretariat Stakes and 12f Sword Dancer Handicap winner Honor Glide. Standing at Darby Dan Farm, Kentucky. 2001 fee: $15,000.

HONOUR AND GLORY 1993 Relaunch – Fair To All (Al Nasr)
(756)

Racing record: Won 4 graded events, including Grade 1 Metropolitan Handicap, and third in Breeders' Cup Sprint. Stud record: Sire of Breeders' Cup Juvenile Fillies winner Caressing from first 2-y-o crop in 2000. Standing at Ashford Stud, Kentucky. 2001 fee: $40,000.

INCHINOR 1990 Ahonoora – Inchmurrin (Lomond).
(88, 590, 869, 873)

Racing record: Won 5 races from 6f to 7.5f including the Hungerford, Greenham and Van Geest Criterion Stakes (all Group 3 events). Stud record: From four crops racing, sire of smart performers at up to 1m Golden Silca, Umistim and Summoner, and Gimcrack winner Bannister. 2001 fee: £9,000 (Oct 1st).

INDIAN RIDGE 1985 Ahonoora – Hillbrow (Swing Easy).
(18, 49, 550, 710, 737, 761, 792, 800, 874, 894, 945, 954, 1010, 1034, 1069, 1075)

Racing record: 5 wins from 5f to 7f notably the Group 2 Kings Stand Stakes, the Group 3 Duke Of York Stakes and the Group 3 Jersey Stakes. Stud record: Best winners include Compton Place (July Cup), Ridgewood Pearl (Irish 1,000 Guineas, Coronation Stakes, Prix du Moulin, Breeders Cup Mile), Definite Article (National Stakes), Namid (Prix de l'Abbaye) and the Group winners Indian Rocket, Blomberg, Handsome Ridge, Ridgewood Ben, Tumbleweed Ridge, Fumo de Londra, St Clair Ridge, Cassandra Go and Island Magic. Standing at the Irish National Stud. 2001 fee: IR35,000 gns (Oct 1st).

IN THE WINGS 1986 Sadler's Wells – High Hawk (Shirley Heights).
(58, 209, 255, 747, 798, 853)

Racing record: 7 wins from 6f to 12f notably the Breeders Cup Turf, the Coronation Cup and the Grand Prix de Saint-Cloud. Stud record: Best winners include Singspiel (Japan Cup, Canadian International Stakes), Central Park (Italian Derby and Premio Presidente della Repubblica), Winged Love (Irish Derby), Air Marshall (Group 2 Great Voltigeur), Annaba (Group 2 Prix de Royallieu), Kutub (Group 2 Prix Noailles), Davide Umbro (Group 2 Premio Parioli), the Group/Grade 3 winners Apprehension, Cloud Castle, Irish Wings, Just in Fun, Right Wing, Thief Of Hearts and very smart Tillerman. Standing at Kildangan Stud, Kildare, Ireland. 2001 fee: IR£15,000 (SLF).

IRISH RIVER 1976 Riverman – Irish Star (Klairon).
(851)

Racing record: A top-class miler and winner of 7 Group 1 races in France – the Grand Criterium, the Prix de la Salamandre, the Prix Morny (all at 2 yrs), the French 2,000 Guineas, the Prix d'Ispahan, the Prix Jacques le Marois and the Prix du Moulin. Stud record: His Group or Grade 1 winners are Brief Truce (St James's Palace Stakes), Exit to Nowhere (Prix Jacques le Marois), Hatoof (1,000 Guineas and Beverly D Stakes), Leariva (Budweiser International), Mashkour (San Juan Capistrano Handicap), Natalie Too (Clasico Pamplona), Navarone (Oak Tree Invitational), Navarone (Oak Tree Invitational), Orban (Premio Roma), Paradise Creek (Arlington Million, Manhattan Stakes and Hollywood Derby), River Bay (Hollywood Turf Handicap) and Seven Springs (Prix Morny and Prix Robert Papin). Standing Gainesway Farm, Lexington, Kentucky. 2001 fee: $25,000.

KAHYASI 1986 Ile de Bourbon – Kadissya (Blushing Groom).
(836, 849)

Racing record: Won 5 races including the Derby and the Irish Derby. Stud record: Best winners include Vereva (Prix de Diane), Zainta (Prix de Diane), Enzeli (Ascot Gold Cup) and the Group 2 winners Shamadara, Shemaran, Massyar and Mouramara. Standing at Haras de Bonneval, France. 2001 fee: 40,000 FF (Oct 1st).

KALDOUN   1975 Caro – Katana (Le Haar)
                                                                                    (369)

Race record: Won 5 races in France, including a listed event: placed in Prix du Palais Royal, Prix Perth, Prix Edmond Blanc and Prix du Muguet (all Group 3 races). Stud record: Best winners include La Koumia (Gamely Handicap), Mercalle (Prix du Cadran), Occupandiste (Prix de la Foret, Prix Maurice de Gheest), See You Soon (Ramona Handicap) and Spadoun (Criterium de Saint-Cloud)

KENDOR   1986 Kenmare – Belle Mecene (Gay Mecene)
                                                                                    (104)

Racing record: Winner of Grand Criterium at 2 yrs and Poule d'Essai des Poulains at 3. Stud record: Best winners include Prix Morny winner Charge d'Affaires, US Grade 2 winner Bonapartiste and French Group 3 winners Grey Risk, Joyeuse Entree, Marie de Ken, Nec Plus Ultra and Nombre Premier. Standing at Haras de la Reboursiere et de Montaigu, France. 2001 fee: 70,000 FF.

KEY OF LUCK   1991 Chief's Crown – Balbonella (Gay Mecene)
                                                                (632, 648, 658, 704, 896)

Racing record: Winner of Prix d'Arenberg at 2 yrs and Dubai Duty Free at 5 yrs, when also runner-up in US Grade 1 9.5f event. Stud record: First crop now two-year-olds. Standing at Tara Stud, Ireland. 2001 fee: IR£3,500.

KINGMAMBO   1990 Mr Prospector – Miesque (Nureyev).
                                                           (166, 551, 592, 627, 687, 803, 828)

Racing record: 5 wins from 6f to 1m notably the French 2,000 Guineas, the Prix du Moulin and the St James's Palace Stakes. Stud record: A son of an outstanding sire and of the great racemare Miesque, Kingmambo's best winners to date are the 2000 Guineas winner King's Best, Japan Cup and Grand Prix de Saint-Cloud winner El Condor Pasa, multiple US Grade 1 winner Lemon Drop Kid, the Grand Criterium winner Okawango and the Poule d'Essai des Pouliches winner Bluemamba. Standing at Lane's End Farm, Kentucky. 2001 fee: private.

KING'S THEATRE   1991 Sadler's Wells – Regal Beauty (Princely Native).
                                                                       (225, 276, 359, 866)

Racing record: Won the King George VI and Queen Elizabeth Diamond Stakes and the Racing Post Trophy. Second in the Derby and the Irish Derby. Stud record: First crop now three-year-olds. Sire of Solario Stakes winner King's Ironbridge. Standing at Ballylinch Stud in Ireland. 2001 fee: IR7,000 gns.

KNOWN FACT   1977 In Reality – Tamerett (Tim Tam).
                                                                                     (50)

Racing record: Won the 2,000 Guineas (upon the disqualification of Nureyev), the Middle Park Stakes and the Queen Elizabeth II Stakes. Stud record: Best winners include the outstanding miler Warning, So Factual (Nunthorpe Stakes), the high class miler Markofdistinction, the Group 3 Prix de Porte Maillot winner Nidd, the dual Sagaro Stakes winner Teamster, the July Stakes winner Bold Fact, the Grade 2 Delaware Handicap winner Night Fax and the Breeders Cup Juvenile second Itsali'lknownfact. Died in 2000.

KRIS   1976 Sharpen Up – Doubly Sure (Reliance II).
                                                                 (89, 360, 494, 639, 933, 1072)

Racing record: 14 wins from 6f to 1m notably the 2,000 Guineas, the Sussex Stakes and the St James's Palace Stakes. Twice Champion European Miler. Stud record: Best winners include Balisada (Coronation Stakes), Common Grounds (Prix de la Salamandre), Fitnah (Prix Saint-Alary), Flash of Steel (Irish 2,000 Guineas), Oh So Sharp (1,000 Guineas, Oaks, St Leger), Rafha (Prix de Diane), Riviera (Atto Mile), Shamshir (Brent Walker Fillies Mile), Shavian (St James's Palace Stakes), Sudden Love (E P Taylor Stakes), Unite (Oaks, Irish Oaks), Single Empire (Italian Derby and San Juan Capistrano Handicap) and numerous Group 2 winners including Sure Blade. Standing at the Plantation Stud, Newmarket. 2001 fee: £15,000 (Oct 1st).

KRIS S 1977 Roberto – Sharp Queen (Princequillo).
(20, 398, 542, 570, 701, 726)

Racing record: Minor stakes winner in the USA. Stud record: Best winners include Dr Fong (St James's Palace Stakes), Hollywood Wildcat (Breeders Cup Distaff), Prized (Breeders Cup Turf), Kissin Kris (Haskell Invitational), Brocco (Breeders Cup Juvenile), Soaring Softly (Flower Bowl Handicap, Breeders' Cup Filly And Mare Turf) and You and I (Metropolitan Handicap). Standing at Winstar Farm, Kentucky. 2001 fee: $150,000.

KYLIAN 1989 Sadler's Wells – Stormette (Assert)
(337)

Racing record: Unraced half-brother to US Grade 1 winner Storm Trooper from family of Storm Bird. Stud record: Sire of Group 2 Sun Chariot Stakes winner Lady In Waiting. Standing at Kirtlington Stud, Oxfordshire. 2001 fee: £2,500 (live foal).

LAHIB 1988 Riverman – Lady Cutlass (Cutlass).
(629, 901, 986)

Racing record: 3 wins, notably the Queen Elizabeth II Stakes and the Group 2 Queen Anne Stakes. He was also second in the Dubai Champion Stakes and the Prix Jacques le Marois. Stud record: His best winners to date include the National Stakes winner Mus-If, the Group 2 Challenge Stakes winner Last Resort, the Group 3 Horris Hill Stakes winner La-faah and Ebor handicap winner Vicious Circle. Standing at Derrinstown Stud in Ireland. 2001 fee: IR5,000 gns.

LAKE CONISTON 1991 Bluebird – Persian Polly (Persian Bold)
(271, 362, 613, 723)

Racing record: Winner of 4 pattern races, notably July Cup at 4 yrs. Stud record: his third crop are now two-year-olds. Sire of May Hill winner Karasta and useful handicapper Capricho. Standing at Castlehyde Stud, Ireland. 2001 fee: IR 4,000 gns.

LAMMTARRA 1992 Nijinsky – Snow Bride (Blushing Groom)
(547)

Racing record: An outstanding colt, winner of the Derby, the King George and the Prix de l'Arc de Triomphe. Stud record: Best winners are Melikah, placed in Oaks and Irish Oaks, and Inaaq, third in Princess Royal Stakes. He now stands in Japan.

LEAR FAN 1981 Roberto – Wac (Lt. Stevens).
(17, 466, 571, 649, 956)

Racing record: 5 wins from 7f to 1m notably the Prix Jacques le Marois and the Group 2 Laurent Perrier Champagne Stakes. Stud record: Best winners include Casual Lies, Corrupt, Fanmore, Fantastic Fellow, Glaieul (Criterium de Saint-Cloud), Labeeb (Hollywood Derby and Woodbine Mile), Lear Spear, Loup Solitaire (Grand Criterium), Ryafan (Prix Marcel Boussac and three US Grade 1 wins), Run Don't Fly, Sikeston (Gran Criterium, Premio Ribot, Premio Parioli, etc), Tiraaz (Prix Royal-Oak), Verveine and Windsharp (San Luis Rey Stakes). Standing at Gainesway Farm, Lexington, Kentucky. 2001 fee: $25,000 (live foal).

LINAMIX 1987 Mendez – Lunadix (Breton)
(368)

Racing record: Won 4 races in France, notably Poule d'Essai des Poulains; also second in Prix Jacques Le Marios, Prix du Moulin and Champion Stakes. Stud record: Best winners include Sagamix (Prix de l'Arc de Triomphe), Fragrant Mix (Grand Prix de Saint-Cloud), Amilynx (Prix Royal-Oak), Goldamix (Criterium de Saint-Cloud), Slickly (Grand Prix de Paris), Miss Satamixa (Prix Jacques le Marois) and Group 2 winners Diamond Mix, Walk On Mix, Housamix, Clodora and Sage Et Jolie. Standing at Haras du Val Henry, France. 2001 fee: FF 250,000.

LION CAVERN 1989 Mr Prospector – Secrettame (Secretariat).
(53, 65, 189, 265, 361, 456, 736, 977)

Racing record: 5 wins from 6f to 7f including the Grade 2 True North Handicap, the Group 3 Horris Hill Stakes and the Group 3 Greenham Stakes. Stud record: A full brother to the highly successful stallion Gone West, Lion Cavern's best winners include very smart 1m/1¼m performer Crimplene, the listed

Oak Tree Stakes winner Beraysim, Stewards' Cup winner Harmonic Way. Standing at Wimbledon Farm, Kentucky. 2001 fee: $15,000.

LURE
1989 Danzig – Endear (Alydar).
(237)

Racing record: Won 14 races including the Breeders Cup Mile (twice) and the Caesars International Handicap. Stud record: Sire of Prix Morny winner Orpen, smart French miler Memory Maker and several useful performers. Standing at Ashford Stud, Kentucky. 2001 fee: $15,000 (live foal).

LYCIUS
1988 Mr Prospector – Lypatia (Lyphard).
(196, 947)

Racing record: 2 wins over 6f and 7f including the Middle Park Stakes and placed in six other Group 1 races. Stud record: His best winners include the Group/Graded winners Athlumney Lady, Hello (Gran Criterium), Aylesbury, Media Nox and Ivan Luis, the smart US performer up to 1¼m Self Feeder and the useful performers Miss Universal, Coney Kitty and Khasayl. Standing at Stoneriggs Farm, Florida. 2001 fee: $12,500.

MACHIAVELLIAN
1987 Mr Prospector – Coup de Folie (Halo).
(108, 200, 238, 247, 310, 325, 399, 400, 418, 452, 597, 617, 688, 837, 970, 1014)

Racing record: 4 wins from 6f to 7f notably the Prix de la Salamandre and the Prix Morny. Stud record: His best winners have been Almutawakel (Dubai World Cup and Prix Jean Prat), Invermark (Prix du Cadran), Vettori (French 2,000 Guineas), Rebecca Sharp (Coronation Stakes), Phantom Gold (Group 2 Ribblesdale Stakes and Geoffrey Freer Stakes), Kahal (Group 2 Challenge Stakes), Majorien (Group 2 Prix du Conseil de Paris), Medicean (Group 2 Celebration Mile), Best Of The Bests (Group 2 Prix Guillaume d'Ornano), Susu (Group 2 Challenge Stakes), and the Group 3 winners Sinyar, Titus Livius, Whitewater Affair, No Excuse Needed, Morning Pride and Kokuto Julian. Standing at Dalham Hall Stud, Newmarket. 2001 fee: £60,000.

MAGIC RING (IRE)
1989 Green Desert – Emaline (Empery)
(10, 129, 579, 1022)

Racing record: Won Norfolk Stakes and Cornwallis Stakes at 2 yrs, when also third in Prix de l'Abbaye. Stud record: Sire of Jersey Stakes winner Lots of Magic, Prix Eclipse winner Merlin's Ring and Cheveley Park runner-up Crazee Mental. Standing at Whitsbury Manor Stud, Hampshire. 2001 fee: £3,000.

MAKBUL
1987 Fairy King – Royaltess (Royal And Regal)
(764)

Racing record: Won 2 6f events at 2 yrs: lightly-raced and below best at 3/4. Stud record: Best performer is listed winner Lord Kintyre. Standing at Longdon Stud, Staffs. 2001 fee: £1,250.

MARJU
1988 Last Tycoon – Flame of Tara (Artaius).
(228, 423, 451, 537, 700, 731, 900, 993)

Racing record: 3 wins including the St James's Palace Stakes and the Group 3 Craven Stakes and placed second in the Derby. Stud record: Sire of My Emma (Prix Vermeille), Sil Sila (Prix de Diane), Oriental Fashion (Group 2 Premio Ribot), Miletrian (Group 2 Ribblesdale Stakes) and smart sprinter Munjiz. Standing at Derrinstown Stud in Ireland. 2001 fee: IR10,000 gns.

MARK OF ESTEEM
1987 Darshaan – Homage (Ajdal).
(98, 116, 159, 267, 508, 625, 654, 740, 862)

Racing record: Outstanding miler, winning 2000 Guineas and Queen Elizabeth II Stakes. Stud record: First crop now three-year-olds. Sire of useful May Hill second Ameerat. Standing at Dalham Hall Stud, Newmarket. 2001 fee: £20,000 (SLF).

MARLIN
Sword Dance – Syrian Summer (Damascus)
(926)

Racing record: Winner of 6 graded stakes on turf, including 10f Arlington Million, 11f Man o'War Stakes and 14f San Juan Capistrano Handicap. Stud record: First crop now two-year-olds. Standing at Airdrie Stud, Kentucky. 2001 fee: $7,500 (live foal).

MILLKOM   1991 Cyrano de Bergerac – Good Game (Mummy's Game)
(493)

Racing record: Winner of 5 pattern/graded events, notably Prix Jean Prat, Grand Prix de Paris and Man o'War Stakes. Stud record: First crop now two-year-olds. Standing at Egerton Stud, Newmarket. 2001 fee: £3,000.

MIND GAMES   1992 Puissance – Aryaf (Vice Regent).
(59, 71, 346, 444, 931, 941)

Racing record: Sprint winner of 7 races including the Group 2 Temple Stakes (twice), the Group 3 Palace House Stakes and the Group 3 Norfolk Stakes. Stud record: First crop now three-year-olds. Sire of Queen Mary winner Romantic Myth. Standing at Bearstone Stud. 2001 fee: £5,000.

MISTER BAILEYS   1991 Robellino – Thimblerigger (Sharpen Up).
(8, 214)

Racing record: Won the 2,000 Guineas, the Group 2 Royal Lodge Stakes and the Group 3 Lanson Champagne Vintage Stakes. Stud record: His first crop are three-year-olds of 2000. 2001 fee: $7,500 (live foal).

MISWAKI   1978 Mr Prospector – Hopespringseternal (Buckpasser).
(201, 417, 460, 912)

Racing record: 6 wins notably the Prix de la Salamandre and placed in the Prix Morny and the Dewhurst Stakes. Stud record: Best winners include Black Tie Affair (Breeders Cup Classic), Kistena (Prix de l'Abbaye), Misil (Premio Roma), Papal Power (Hopeful Stakes), Playlist (Canadian Oaks), Urban Sea (Prix de l'Arc de Triomphe), Waki River (Criterium de Saint-Cloud), the Australian Grade 1 winner Umatilla and numerous other Group/Graded stakes winners including Abou Zouz, Allied Forces, Balawaki, Diligence, Hurricane State, Le Belvedere, Magellano, Midyan, Miswaki Tern, Rossini, Tertullian and Whakilyric (the dam of Hernando). Standing at Walmac International Farm in Kentucky. 2001 fee: $35,000 (live foal).

MOST WELCOME   1984 Be My Guest – Topsy (Habitat).
(21, 807)

Racing record: Won the Group 2 Lockinge Stakes and the Group 2 Select Stakes. Placed in 6 Group/Grade 1 events, including Derby and Breeders' Cup Mile. Stud record: Best winners include Sasuru (Prix d'Ispahan), Arctic Owl (Irish St Leger), Suances (Prix Jean Prat), Prize Giving (US Grade 2 event), Flying Dream (German Group 3 event) and the listed winners Arriving and Croeso Cariad. Standing at Barton Stud, Bury St Edmonds. 2001 fee: £3,000

MR PROSPECTOR   1970 Raise a Native – Gold Digger (Nashua).
(143, 144, 691, 790, 834, 962)

Racing record: 7 wins notably the 6f Whirlaway Stakes and the 6f Gravesend Handicap. Stud record: His multitude of Group/Grade 1 winners include Chester House (Arlington Million) Distant View (Sussex Stakes), Ravinella (1,000 Guineas, French 1,000 Guineas), Rhythm (Breeders Cup Juvenile Stakes, Travers Stakes), It's in the Air (Vanity Handicap, Alabama Stakes), Eillo (Breeders Cup Sprint), Fusaichi Pegasus (Kentucky Derby), Kingmambo (French 2,000 Guineas, St James's Palace Stakes), Tank's Prospect (Preakness Stakes) and Ta Rib (French 1,000 Guineas). He has also proved an exceptional sire of sires, particularly through his sons, Fappiano, Forty Niner, Gone West, Gulch, Jade Hunter, Kingmambo, Machiavellian, Miswaki, Seeking the Gold and Woodman.

MT LIVERMORE   1981 Blushing Groom – Flama Ardiente (Crimson Satan).
(205, 220, 243, 694, 713)

Racing record: 11 wins from 6f to 1m including the Grade 2 Carter Handicap and Grade 2 Fall Highweight Handicap. Stud record: Best winners include Housebuster (three US Grade 1 wins), Eliza (Champion US 2-y-o filly), the US Grade 1 winners Mt Sassafras, Peaks And Valleys and Subordination, the Canadian Grade 1 winner Humpty's Hoedown and the US Grade 2 winners Blushing Julian, Greek Costume, More Royal and Parlay. Standing at Gainesway Farm, Lexington, Kentucky. 2001 fee: $50,000 (live foal).

MTOTO   1983 Busted – Amazer (Mincio).
(204, 295, 581, 702)

Racing record: 8 wins notably the King George VI and Queen Elizabeth Diamond Stakes, the Coral-Eclipse Stakes (twice) and the Group 2 Prince of Wales's Stakes (twice). He was also placed twice in the Prix de l'Arc de Triomphe. Stud record: Best winners include Shaamit (Derby), Celeric (Ascot Gold Cup), Presenting (Group 2 Geoffrey Freer Stakes), Arbatax (Group 2 Prix Hocquart), Mousse Glacee (Group 3 Prix des Reservoirs), Maylane (Group 3 September Stakes), Cap Juluca (Cambridgeshire Handicap) and the Classic placed Book At Bedtime and Crown Of Light. Standing at the Aston Upthorpe Stud in Oxfordshire. 2001 fee: £5,000 (SLF).

MUJADIL   1988 Storm Bird – Vallee Secrete (Secretariat).
(75, 83, 513, 569, 585, 796)

Racing record: 3 wins including the Group 3 Cornwallis Stakes. Stud record: His best winners include Bouncing Bowdler (Group 2 Mill Reef Stakes), Show Me The Money (Group 3 Cornwallis Stakes), Daunting Lady (Group 3 Fred Darling Stakes), the listed winners Bay Prince and Craigievar, the Molecomb Stakes second Connemara and the useful Irish staying handicapper Barba Papa. Standing at Rathasker Stud, Naas, Ireland. 2001 fee: IR10,000 gns.

NASHWAN   1986 Blushing Groom – Height of Fashion (Bustino).
(35, 37, 281, 284, 287, 308, 401, 410, 589, 992, 1002, 1017)

Racing record: 6 wins from 7f to 12f notably the 2,000 Guineas, the Derby, the Coral-Eclipse Stakes and the King George VI and Queen Elizabeth Diamond Stakes. Champion 3-y-o colt. Stud record: Best winners include Aqaarid (Fillies Mile), One So Wonderful (Juddmonte International), Swain (King George VI and Queen Elizabeth Diamond Stakes (twice), Coronation Cup etc), Wandesta (Santa Barbara Handicap and Santa Ana Handicap), the US Grade 2 winners Didina and Elhayq and the Group 3 winners Bint Salsabil, Bint Shadayid, Haami, Mistle Song, Myself, Rabah and Silent Warrior. Standing at the Nunnery Stud in Norfolk. 2001 fee: £35,000.

NICHOLAS   1986 Danzig – Lulu Mon Amour (Tom Rolfe)
(621)

Racing record: Won from 5f to 7f in USA before developing into a smart sprinter in Europe, winning Group 2 Jacobs Goldene Peitsche. Stud record: Winners include smart Irish sprinter Lidanna. Standing at Calumet Farm, Kentucky. 2001 fee: $3,000

NIGHT SHIFT   1980 Northern Dancer – Ciboulette (Chop Chop).
(85, 125, 175, 260, 328, 356, 463, 511, 561, 582, 583, 607, 846, 919, 980)

Racing record: Minor winner over 6f in the USA. Stud record: Best winners include Creaking Board (Starlet Stakes), Daryaba (Prix de Diane, Prix Vermeille), In The Groove (Juddmonte International, Champion Stakes, Irish 1,000 Guineas and Coronation Stakes), Listening (Hollywood Oaks), Lochangel (Nunthorpe Stakes), Nicolotte (Premio Vittorio di Capua and Group 2 Queen Anne Stakes), the Group winners Ascension, Eveningperformance, Just Happy, Lady Alexander, Northern Goddess, Struggler and Time Gentlemen, Vision of Night and the smart Midnight Legend. Standing at Coolmore Stud in Ireland. 2001 fee: IR20,000 gns.

NUMEROUS   1991 Mr Prospector – Number (Nijinsky)
(724)

Racing record: Won 4 races in the USA, including Grade 3 1m Derby Trial and Grade 2 7f Malibu Stakes. Stud record: First crop of US 2-y-o's in 1999. Standing at Hill 'n' Dale Farms, Kentucky. 2001 fee: $7,500.

NUREYEV   1977 Northern Dancer – Special (Forli).
(393, 405, 430, 446, 744)

Racing record: Ran three times. Won the 7f Prix Djebel and the 7.5f Prix Thomas Bryon and was disqualified from first place in the 2,000 Guineas. Stud record: His Group/Grade 1 winners include Alwuhush, Annoconnor, Atticus, Crystal Music, Fasliyev, Flagbird, Kitwood, Mehthaaf, Miesque, Pattern Step, Peintre Celebre, Polar Falcon, Reams of Verse, Sonic Lady, Soviet Star, Spinning World,

Stately Don, Stravinsky, Theatrical, Vilikaia, Wolfhound and Zilzal. Standing at Walmac International Farm in Lexington, Kentucky. 2001 fee: private.

OCTAGONAL
1992 Zabeel – Eight Carat (Pieces of Eight)
(432, 500, 671, 741)

Racing record: Winner of 10 Group 1 races in Australia from 2 to 4 yrs at up to 1½m. Stud record: First French-conceived crop now two-year-olds. Standing at Haras du Quesnay. 2001 fee: 80,000 FF.

PENNEKAMP
1992 Bering – Coral Dance (Green Dancer).
(283, 502, 554, 606, 791, 920, 955)

Racing record: Won 6 races including the Two Thousand Guineas, the Dewhurst Stakes and the Prix de la Salamandre. Stud record: First crop now three-year-olds. Sire of useful 6f winners Ceepio, Hurricane Floyd and Polyandry. Standing at Kildangan Stud in Ireland. 2001 fee: IR£12,500 (SLF).

PERSIAN BOLD
1975 Bold Lad (Ire) – Relkarunner (Relko).
(127, 860, 1062)

Racing record: Won the Group 2 6f Richmond Stakes, the Group 3 Horris Hill Stakes and the listed John Of Gaunt Stakes. Stud record: Best winners include Kooyonga (Irish One Thousand Guineas), Persian Heights (St James's Palace Stakes), Kings Island (Sunset Handicap), King Persian (Phoenix Stakes) and smart stayers Travelmate and Romantic Affair. Died in 1998.

PETARDIA
1990 Petong – What A Pet (Mummy's Pet)
(506, 636, 719, 1024)

Racing record: Won Coventry Stakes and Champagne Stakes at 2 yrs, best effort when fourth in 2000 Guineas. Stud record: Sire of Santa Anita Derby winner The Deputy, Rockfel Stakes winner Name Of Love and Cornwallis Stakes winner Halmahera. Standing at Tally-Ho Stud, Ireland. 2001 fee: IR£3,000.

PETONG
1980 Mansingh – Iridium (Linacre).
(640)

Racing record: 10 wins including the Group 2 Vernons Sprint Cup. Stud record: Best winners include the Group 2 winners Paris House, Son Pardo and Petardia. Standing at Red House Stud, Newmarket. 2001 fee: £2,500.

PETORIUS
1981 Mummy's Pet – The Stork (Club House)
(763)

Racing record: Won Cornwallis Stakes at 2 yrs and dead-heated in Temple Stakes at 3. Stud record: Best performers include Group 2 winner Kill The Crab, Group 3 winners Eastern Purple, Nautical Pet and Sapieha and Grade 3 winner Mister Fire Eyes. Standing at Tara Stud, Co Meath, Ireland. 2001 fee: IR£1,500.

PHONE TRICK
1982 Clever Trick – Over The Phone (Finnegan)
(229, 459, 780)

Racing record: Winner of 3 Grade 2 events at 6f/7f. Stud record: Best winners include champion US 2-y-o colt Favorite Trick, champion US 2-y-o filly Phone Chatter, the Grade 2 winners Bella Chiarra, Intidab, Caller One, Mazel Trick, Speed Dialer and Caller I.D. and smart European performer up to 1¼m Calling Collect. Standing at Walmac International, Kentucky. 2001 fee: $30,000 (live foal).

PICCOLO
1991 Warning – Woodwind (Whistling Wind).
(84, 167, 172, 183, 344, 604, 638)

Racing record: 4 wins including the Keeneland Nunthorpe Stakes and the Group 2 Kings Stand Stakes. Stud record: His third crop are now two-year-olds. Sire of smart performer up to 7f Hunting Lion, and useful 2y-o sprinters Don Puccini and Piccolo Player. 2001 fee: £4,000 (Oct 1st).

PINE BLUFF
1989 Danzig – Rowdy Angel (Halo)
(114)

Racing record: Won 5 graded events at 2/3 yrs, notably Preakness Stakes. Stud record: Sire of I Ain't Bluffing (Grade 1 x2) and the Grade 2/3 winners Middlesex Drive, Lil's Lad, Pine Dance, Megans Bluff and Follow The Money. Standing at Lane's End Farm, Kentucky. 2001 fee: $15,000

PIVOTAL   1993 Polar Falcon – Fearless Revival (Cozzene).
(42, 383, 457, 727, 875)

Racing record: Four wins over 5f and 6f including the Nunthorpe Stakes and the Group 2 King's Stand Stakes. Stud record: First crop now three-year-olds. Sire of smart Middle Park third Red Carpet and useful Italian Group 3 winner Low Pivot. Standing at Cheveley Park Stud, Newmarket. 2001 fee: £5,000 (Oct 1st).

PLEASANT COLONY   1978 His Majesty – Sun Colony (Sunrise Flight).
(140)

Racing record: 6 wins notably the Kentucky Derby, the Preakness Stakes, the Wood Memorial Stakes and the Woodward Stakes. Stud record: His US Grade 1 winners include Behrens, Colonial Affair, Colonial Waters, Pleasant Tap, Pleasant Stage, Pleasant Variety, Roanoke, Shared Interest and Sir Beaufort, whilst in Europe his outstanding performer is the Irish Derby and King George VI and Queen Elizabeth Diamond Stakes winner St Jovite

POLAR FALCON   1987 Nureyev – Marie d'Argonne (Jefferson).
(19, 47, 74, 531, 619, 624, 660, 885, 916, 1006)

Racing record: 5 wins notably the Group 1 6f Haydock Park Sprint Cup, the Group 2 1m Lockinge Stakes and the Group 3 1m Prix Edmond Blanc. Stud record: The sire of Pivotal (Nunthorpe Stakes and Group 2 Kings Stand Stakes), Exclusive (Coronation Stakes), Red Camellia (Group 3 Prestige Stakes), Icicle (Group 3 Prestige Stakes), Italian Group 3 winner Poseidon, the listed winners Arctic Char, Merry Merlin, Falkenham, Sand Falcon, Just Ice and Bomb Alaska and the smart handicapper John Ferneley. Standing at the Cheveley Park Stud, Newmarket. 2001 fee: £8,000 (Oct 1st).

POLIGLOTE   1992 Sadler's Wells – Alexandrie (Val de L'Orne).
(928)

Racing record: Won Group 1 Criterium de Saint-Cloud at 2 yrs and Group 2 Grand Prix d'Evry at 4 yrs: runner-up in Prix du Jockey Club at 3 yrs. Stud record: His first crop are now two-year-olds. Standing at Haras d'Etreham, France. 2001 fee: FF25,000.

POLISH PRECEDENT   1986 Danzig – Past Example (Buckpasser).
(602, 685, 778, 825, 830, 835, 921, 959)

Racing record: 7 wins notably the Prix Jacques le Marois and the Prix du Moulin. Stud record: Best winners include Nouskey, Pilsudski (Breeders Cup Turf, Eclipse Stakes, Champion Stakes and Grosser Preis von Baden), Predappio, Pure Grain (Irish Oaks and Yorkshire Oaks), Red Route, Riyadian, Sobieski and Social Harmony. Standing at Dalham Hall Stud, Newmarket. 2001 fee: £15,000 (SLF).

PRIMO DOMINIE   1982 Dominion – Swan Ann (My Swanee).
(56, 141, 185, 198, 305, 464, 505, 527)

Racing record: 6 wins including the Group 2 Richmond Stakes, the King George Stakes, the Coventry Stakes and the July Stakes (all Group 3 events). Stud record: Best winners include First Trump (Middle Park Stakes), Le Magister (Grade 1 Highlander Stakes, Woodbine), Primo Valentino (Middle Park Stakes), the Group 2 winners Arranvanna, Lara's Idea, Millyant and Perryston View and the Peruvian Grade 1 winner Dalnamein. Standing at Cheveley Park Stud in Newmarket. 2001 fee: £7,000 (Oct 1st).

PRINCE SABO   1982 Young Generation – Jubilee Song (Song)
(40, 363)

Racing record: Won the Group 2 Flying Childers Stakes and the Group 3 Palace House Stakes. Stud record: Best winners include Princely Hush (Group 2 Mill Reef Stakes), Tippitt Boy (Group 3 Norfolk Stakes) and the listed winners Cathedral, Easy Option, Jolis Princess, Marweh, Sea Gazer, Sipsi Fach and Vita Spericolata. Standing at Cheveley Park Stud, Newmarket. 2001 fee: £3,000.

PUISSANCE   1986 Thatching – Girton (Balidar).
(2, 11, 72)

Racing record: 3 wins over 6f including the Group 3 Greenlands Stakes. Stud record: Sire of the winners of over 144 races, including the high-class Group 2 Temple Stakes winner Mind Games and the Group 3 Norfolk Stakes winner Rosselli. Standing at Bearstone Stud. 2001 fee: £2,500 (Oct 1st FFR).

PULPIT 1994 A P Indy – Preach (Mr Prospector)
(389)
Racing record: Won Grade 2 8.5f/9f events and second in Grade 1 9f Florida Derby at 3 yrs. Stud record: His first crop are now two-year-olds. Standing at Claiborne Farm, Kentucky. 2001 fee: $40,000

PURSUIT OF LOVE 1989 Groom Dancer – Dance Quest (Green Dancer).
(126, 146, 347)
Racing record: 4 wins including the Group 2 6.5f Prix Maurice de Gheest and the Group 3 7f Kiveton Park Stakes and placed in the July Cup, the 2,000 Guineas and the Dewhurst Stakes. Stud record: Sire of Catchascatchcan (Yorkshire Oaks), the listed winners Basse Besogne, Ippon, Head Over Heels, Courting and Embraced, the Dewhurst Stakes second Musical Pursuit and smart handicapper For Your Eyes Only. Standing at the Plantation Stud, Newmarket. 2001 fee: £5,000 (Oct 1st).

QUEST FOR FAME 1987 Rainbow Quest – Aryenne (Green Dancer).
(558)
Racing record: Won the Epsom Derby. Stud record: His best winners are Famous Digger (Del Mar Oaks), the US Grade 2 winner Sagasious, the Australian Grade 2 winner Hockney and the smart French/UAE performer Sibling Rival.

RAINBOW QUEST 1981 Blushing Groom – I Will Follow (Herbager).
(132, 142, 253, 278, 307, 523, 594, 680, 684, 714, 864, 936, 940, 961, 971)
Racing record: 6 wins from 7f to 12f including the Prix de l'Arc de Triomphe and the Coronation Cup. Placed in six other Group 1 races. Stud record: A leading British-based sire, Rainbow Quest's Group 1 winners are Armiger (Racing Post Trophy), Bright Generation (Italian Oaks), Croco Rouge (Prix Lupin and Prix d'Ispahan), Edabiya (Moyglare Stud Stakes), Fiji (Gamely Handicap and Yellow Ribbon Stakes), Knight's Baroness (Irish Oaks), Millenary (St Leger), Nedawi (St Leger), Quest For Fame (Derby, Hollywood Turf Handicap), Raintrap (San Juan Capistrano Handicap), Rothmans International, Prix Royal-Oak), Sakura Laurel (Tenno Sho, Japan), Saumarez (Prix de l'Arc de Triomphe, Grand Prix de Paris), Sought Out (Prix du Cadran), Spectrum (Champion Stakes and Irish 1,000 Guineas), Sunshack (Coronation Cup, Prix Royal-Oak and Criterium de Saint-Cloud) and Urgent Request (Santa Anita Handicap). Standing at Banstead Manor Stud, Newmarket. 2001 fee: £50,000 (SLF).

RED RANSOM 1987 Roberto – Arabia (Damascus).
(112, 239, 248, 272, 1000)
Racing record: 2 wins, over 5f and 6f, from three outings. Stud record: Best performers include Bail Out Becky (Del Mar Oaks), Perfect Sting (Queen Elizabeth II Challenge Cup and BC Filly and Mare Turf), the Group/Grade 2 winners Intikhab, Sri Pekan, Trail City and Wandering Star, and the Group/Grade 3 winners Comic Strip, Ekraar, Petrouchka, Shining Hour and Upper Noosh. Standing at the Vinery Stud in Kentucky. 2001 fee: $75,000 (live foal).

REPRIMAND 1985 Mummy's Pet – Just You Wait (Nonoalco).
(1023)
Racing record: Won Gimcrack Stakes at 2 yrs and Earl of Sefton Stakes and Trusthouse Forte Mile at 4 yrs. Stud record: Sire of Fard (Middle Park Stakes), Deep Finesse (Palace House Stakes), smart sprinter Now Look Here and useful performers Honesty Fair, React, Reprehend and State of Caution. Standing at Lismacue Stud, Co Tipperary, Ireland.

REVOQUE 1994 Fairy King – La Bella Fontana (Lafontaine)
(46, 67, 105, 169, 263, 289, 352, 357, 503, 541, 674, 675, 748, 754, 891, 924)
Racing record: Won 4 races, notably Prix de la Salamandre and Grand Criterium at 2 yrs; runner-up in 2000 Guineas and Greenham Stakes at 3. Stud record: First crop now two-year-olds. Standing at Morristown Lattin Stud, Ireland. 2001 fee: IR £7,500.

ROBELLINO 1978 Roberto – Isobelline (Pronto).
(5, 23, 63, 130, 323, 646, 670)
Racing record: 5 wins including the Group 2 Royal Lodge Stakes and the Group 3 Seaton Delaval Stakes. Stud record: Best winners include Mister Baileys (2,000 Guineas), Classic Park (Irish 1,000 Guineas), Robertico (German Derby), Diamond White (Group 2 Prix de l'Opera), Royal Rebel (Group 2

Goodwood Cup),Tot Ou Tard (Group 2 Grand Prix d'Evry), Street Rebel (Group 3 Greenlands Stakes), Holly Golightly (Group 3 Prix Chloe), Faustus (Group 3 Greenham Stakes) and Local Herbert (Premio Lazio). Standing at Littleton Stud in Hampshire. 2001 fee: £6,000 (Oct 1st.).

ROYAL ABJAR
1991 Gone West – Encorelle (Arctic Tern).
(766)

Racing record: Won 6 races from 7f to 8.5f including the Group 2 Mehl-Mulhens Rennen and the Group 3 Oettingen-Rennen. Stud record: First crop now three-year-olds.

ROYAL ACADEMY
1987 Nijinsky – Crimson Saint (Crimson Satan).
(69, 80, 275, 372, 407, 462, 471, 659, 672, 799, 850)

Racing record: Won the Breeders Cup Mile and the July Cup and second in the Irish Two Thousand Guineas and the Haydock Park Sprint Cup. Stud record: Best winners include Zalaiyka (French One Thousand Guineas), Lavery (Phoenix Stakes), Oscar Schindler (Irish St Leger, twice), Carmine Lake (Prix de l'Abbaye), Sleepytime (One Thousand Guineas) and Ali Royal (Sussex Stakes). Standing at Ashford Stud, Kentucky. 2001 fee: $25,000 (1st Sept).

ROYAL APPLAUSE
1993 Waajib – Flying Melody (Auction Ring)
(66, 171, 179, 182, 299, 374, 376, 472, 492, 499, 515, 559, 565, 586, 588, 612, 634, 711, 797, 809, 892, 918, 946, 950, 996)

Racing record: Winner of 9 races, including Coventry, Gimcrack and Middle Park at 2 yrs and Duke of York, Cork And Orrery and Haydock Park Sprint Cup at 4. Stud record: First crop now two-year-olds. Standing at The Royal Studs, Norfolk. 2001 fee: £6,500.

SABREHILL
1990 Diesis – Gypsy Talk (Alleged)
(212)

Racing record: Won 1 race at 1¼m and second in Juddmonte International from only 3 starts. Stud record: Best winners include Eco Friendly (Group 3 Prix Saint-Roman), the listed winners Alboostan and Iridanos and the smart 1m to 1½m performer Gargalhada Final. Exported to France in 1999.

SADLER'S WELLS
1981 Northern Dancer – Fairy Bridge (Bold Reason).
(94, 99, 100, 157, 251, 256, 258, 262, 288, 293, 294, 300, 313, 317, 329, 331, 334, 366, 367, 381, 395, 404, 415, 421, 424, 445, 528, 553, 567, 609, 626, 665, 679, 709, 717, 817, 824, 827, 843, 848, 857, 865, 904, 922, 958, 973, 1033, 1043, 1045, 1071)

Racing record: Winner of the Irish 2,000 Guineas, the Phoenix Champion Stakes and the Coral-Eclipse. Placed in the French Derby and the King George. Stud record: Group or Grade 1 winners include Barathea, Beat Hollow, Carnegie, Commander Collins, Daliapour, Dance Design, Dream Well, Entrepreneur, In The Wings, Intrepidity, Kayf Tara, King Of Kings, King's Theatre, Leggera, Montjeu Moonshell, Northern Spur, Old Vic, Opera House, Saffron Walden and Salsabil. Standing at Coolmore Stud in Ireland. 2001 fee: private.

SAINT BALLADO
1989 Halo – Ballade (Herbager)
(820)

Racing record: Brother to Devil's Bag and Grade 1-winning dam of Rahy and Singspiel. Won 4 races at 3 yrs in USA, including Grade 2 9f event and Grade 3 1m event. Stud record: Best winners include Captain Bodgit (Florida Derby), Sister Act (Hempstead Handicap), Yankee Victor (Metropolitan Handicap), and Grade 2 winners Flame Thrower and Straight Man. Standing at Taylor Made Farm, Kentucky. 2001 fee: $125,000 (live foal).

SALSE
1985 Topsider – Carnival Princess (Prince John).
(152, 1050)

Racing record: 8 wins including the Group 1 Prix de la Foret, the Group 2 Bisquit Cognac Stakes and three Group 3 races. Stud record: Best winners include Air Express (Queen Elizabeth II Stakes), Bianca Nera (Moyglare Stud Stakes), Classic Cliche (St Leger), Lemon Souffle (Moyglare Stud Stakes), Luso (Italian Derby, Aral Pokal, Hong Kong International Vase), Timboroa (Premio Presidente della Repubblica) and Spout (Group 3 Lancashire Oaks and Group 3 John Porter Stakes). Standing at Side Hill Stud in Newmarket. 2001 fee: £2,500 (Oct 1st).

SEATTLE SLEW   1974 Bold Reasoning – My Charmer (Poker).
(36, 548, 917)

Racing record: Triple Crown winner in the USA. Stud record: Best performers include the Grade/Group 1 winners Slew O'Gold, A.P.Indy, Swale, Capote, Landaluce, Slew City Slew, Life At The Top, Tsunami Slew, Adored, Slewpy, Lakeway, Seattle Song, Septieme Ciel, Honest Lady and Surfside. 2001 fee: $150,000.

SEEKING THE GOLD   1985 Mr Prospector – Con Game (Buckpasser).
(450, 543, 690, 707)

Racing record: 8 wins from 6f to 10f, notably the Grade 1 Dwyer Stakes and the Grade 1 Super Derby. Stud record: Best winners include Group/Grade 1 winners Dubai Millennium, Heavenly Prize, Flanders, Seeking The Pearl, Cash Run, Cape Town, Dream Supreme, Oh What A Windfall and Lujain. Standing at Claiborne Farm in Kentucky. 2001 fee: private.

SELKIRK   1988 Sharpen Up – Annie Edge (Nebbiolo).
(13, 14, 106, 162, 177, 211, 252, 322, 385, 428, 534, 678, 786, 839, 937, 949, 1040)

Racing record: 6 wins including the Queen Elizabeth II Stakes, the Lockinge Stakes, the Beefeater Gin Celebration Mile and the Challenge Stakes. Stud record: His best winners include Field of Hope (Prix de la Foret), Wince (1,000 Guineas), Kirkwall (Group 2 Prix Eugene Adam), Sign of Hope (Grade 2 Oak Tree Derby), Squeak (Group 3 Lancashire Oaks and dual US Grade 1 winner), Orford Ness (Group 3 Prix de Sandringham), Hidden Meadow (Group 3 Prix du Palais-Royal), Trans Island (Diomed Stakes), the 2000 Guineas and Derby placed Border Arrow and the listed winners Entice and Pawn Broker. Standing at Lanwades Stud in Newmarket. 2001 fee: £30,000 (Oct 1st).

SHADEED   1982 Nijinsky – Continual (Damascus).
(930)

Racing record: 4 wins notably the 2,000 Guineas and the Queen Elizabeth II Stakes. Stud record: Best winners include Sayyedati (1,000 Guineas, Prix Jacques le Marois, Sussex Stakes, Cheveley Park Stakes and Moyglare Stud Stakes), Shadayid (1,000 Guineas and Prix Marcel Boussac), the Canadian and US Grade 1 winner Alydeed, the Brazilian Grade 1 winner Indian Hope, the very useful English winners Nadwah (Queen Mary Stakes), Satin Flower (Jersey Stakes) and Splendent (Gimcrack Stakes) and the US Graded Stakes winners Citadeed and Infamous Deed. Standing at Gainesborough Farm in Kentucky. 2001 fee: $5,000 (Oct 1st).

SHAMBO   1987 Lafontaine – Lucky Appeal (Star Appeal)
(113)

Racing record: Won 8 races from 3 to 7 yrs, including Group 2 Geoffrey Freer Stakes and Group 3 Ormonde Stakes (twice). Stud record: Second crop are now two-year-olds. Sire of fairly useful 2-y-o 5f/6f winner Shush. Standing at The Elms Stud, Northants. 2001 fee: £750.

SHAREEF DANCER   1980 Northern Dancer – Sweet Alliance (Sir Ivor).
(7, 41, 111)

Racing record: 3 wins including the Irish Derby. Stud record: Best winners include Glory Of Dancer (Gran Criterium and Group 2 Dante Stakes), Possessive Dancer (Irish and Italian Oaks), Dancer Mitral (Group 2 Premio Parioli), Rock Hopper (seven Group wins including the Group 2 Hardwicke Stakes), Shaima (Grade 2 Long Island Handicap), Kazoo (Group 2 German 1,000 Guineas), Colorado Dancer (Group 2 Prix de Pomone), Danceabout (Sun Chariot Stakes) and Spartan Shareef (Group 3 September Stakes).

SILLERY   1988 Blushing Groom – Silvermine (Bellypha).
(929)

Racing record: 7 wins including the Group 2 Prix Dollar and placed in several Group 1 events. Stud record: From 4 crops racing, best winners include Breeders' Cup Mile winner Silic and German Group winner Indikator. Standing at Haras du Quesnay, France. 2001 fee: 50,000 FF (Oct 1st).

SILVER HAWK 1979 Ribot – Gris Vitesse (Amerigo).
(279, 358, 426, 616, 966, 1029)

Racing record: 3 wins including the Group 3 Craven Stakes and the Intercraft Solario Stakes and placed in both the Derby and the Irish Derby. Stud record: His best performers include the 1997 Derby winner Benny The Dip, 1999 St Leger winner Mutafaweq, the Group or Grade 1 winners Lady in Silver (Prix de Diane), Magnificent Star (Yorkshire Oaks), Memories of Silver (Queen Elizabeth II Invitational), Hawkster (Secretariat Stakes, Oak Tree Invitational and Norfolk Stakes), Silver Ending (Pegasus Handicap), Hawk Attack (Secretariat Stakes), Red Bishop (San Juan Capistrano Handicap), Platinum Blonde (Natalma Stakes) and Zoonaqua (Oak Leaf Stakes). Standing at the Airdrie Stud in Kentucky. 2001 fee: private.

SINGSPIEL 1992 In The Wings – Glorious Sing (Halo)
(203, 312, 327, 332, 342, 377, 487, 703, 879, 960, 1015)

Racing record: Winner of 9 races, notably Canadian International and Japan Cup at 4 yrs and Dubai World Cup, Coronation Cup and Juddmonte International at 5. Stud record: First crop now two-year-olds. Standing at Dalham Hall Stud, Newmarket. 2001 fee: £20,000 (SLF).

SKY CLASSIC 1987 Nijinsky – No Class (Nodouble).
(1057)

Racing record: Stakes winner of $3.3 million including the Rothmans International. Stud record: Sire of Canadian horse of the year Thornfield and the Grade 3 winners Daylight Savings, Idle Rich and Certainly Classic. Standing Pin Oak Stud, Kentucky. 2001 fee: $20,000.

SLIP ANCHOR 1982 Shirley Heights – Sayonara (Birkhahn).
(62)

Racing record: 4 wins including the Derby, the Group 3 Lingfield Derby Trial and the listed Heathorn Stakes. Second in the Champion Stakes, the Group 2 Jockey Club Stakes and the Group 3 September Stakes. Stud record: Best winners include User Friendly (Oaks, Irish Oaks and St Leger), L'Hermine (Sword Dancer Handicap), Posidonas (Gran Premio d'Italia, Hardwicke Stakes and John Porter Stakes), Slicious (Premio Roma), the Group 2 Great Voltigeur Stakes winner Stowaway, the Group 2 Ribblesdale Stakes winner Third Watch and the Group 3 winners Give The Slip, Kaliana, Khamaseen, Safety in Numbers, Three Cheers and Up Anchor. Standing at Newmarket's Plantation Stud. 2001 fee: £4,000.

SMART STRIKE 1992 Mr Prospector – Classy 'n Smart (Smarten)
(890)

Racing record: Winner of 6 races in North America, including Grade 1 8.5f Philip H. Iselin Handicap. Stud record: First 2-y-o crop in 2000 included 6f winner Strike The Green in Britain. Standing at Lane's End Farm, Kentucky. 2001 fee: $30,000.

SO FACTUAL 1990 Known Fact – Sookera (Roberto)
(345)

Racing record: Won 4 races, notably Nunthorpe Stakes at 5 yrs. Stud record: First crop now three-year-olds. Standing at Littleton Stud, Hampshire. 2001 fee: £3,000.

SOUTHERN HALO 1983 Halo – Northern Sea (Northern Dancer).
(437)

Racing record: Stakes-placed winner in the USA, second in the Grade 1 Super Derby. Stud record: Leading sire twice in Argentina (sire of numerous Grade 1 winners there). Also sire of US Grade 1 winner More Than Ready and Princess Margaret Stakes winner Saintly Speech. Standing at Ashford Stud, Kentucky. 2001 fee: £40,000 (live foal).

SPECTRUM 1992 Rainbow Quest – River Dancer (Irish River).
(54, 97, 101, 163, 379, 482, 530, 686, 794, 939, 1009, 1042, 1044, 1047)

Racing record: Won four races including the Irish Two Thousand Guineas and the Champion Stakes. Stud record: First crop now three-year-olds. Sire of smart listed winner Hemingway, useful Italian listed winner Blu Air Gun and promising 7f winner Golan. Standing at Coolmore Stud in Ireland. 2001 fee: IR15,000 gns (Oct 1st).

SPINNING WORLD 1993 Nureyev – Imperfect Circle (Riverman)
(33, 131, 439, 776, 777, 812, 814, 907, 964)

Racing record: Winner of 8 races, notably Irish 2000 Guineas and Prix Jacques le Marois at 3 yrs and Prix du Moulin, Prix Jacques le Marois and Breeders' Cup Mile at 4. Stud record: First crop now two-year-olds. Standing at Ashford Stud, Kentucky. 2001 fee: $35,000 (live foal).

SRI PEKAN 1992 Red Ransom – Lady Godolphin (Son Ange).
(227, 475, 490, 725, 1018)

Racing record: Won 5 races from 5f to 7f including the Group 2 Laurent-Perrier Champagne Stakes, the Group 2 Richmond Stakes and the Group 3 Coventry Stakes. Stud career: His third crop are now two-year-olds. Sire of Cherry Hinton winner Dora Carrington, smart French 6f/7f performer Blu Air Force and Canadian Grade 3 winner Hoh Dear. Standing at Castle Hyde Stud, Ireland. 2001 fee: IR7,000 gns.

STORM BIRD 1978 Northern Dancer – South Ocean (New Providence).
(661, 669)

Racing record: Champion 2-y-o, winner of the Dewhurst Stakes. Stud record: Best winners include Indian Skimmer (French Oaks, Champion Stakes, Irish Champion Stakes etc,), Balanchine (Irish Derby), Prince Of Birds (Irish 2,000 Guineas), Bluebird (Kings Stand Stakes), Magical Wonder (Prix Jean-Prat), Storm Cat (Young America Stakes) and Summer Squall (Preakness Stakes).

STORM CAT 1983 Storm Bird – Terlingua (Secretariat).
(154, 411, 545, 822, 831)

Racing record: 4 wins from 6f to 8.5f notably the Grade 1 Young America Stakes. Stud record: His best winners include Group/Grade 1 winners Tabasco Cat, Cat Thief, Giant's Causeway, Sharp Cat, High Yield, Sardula, Catinca, Desert Stormer, Aljabr, Hennessy and Forestry. Storm Cat stands at Overbrook Farm in Lexington, Kentucky. 2001 fee: $400,000.

SUAVE DANCER 1988 Green Dancer – Suavite (Alleged).
(1013)

Racing record: Winner of five of his nine starts, including the Prix de l'Arc de Triomphe, the Irish Champion Stakes and the French Derby. Stud record: Best winners include Compton Admiral (Eclipse Stakes), Volvoreta (Prix Vermeille), Craigsteel (Group 2 Princess of Wales's Stakes) and Dust Dancer (Group 3 Prix de la Nonette). Died 1998.

SUNDAY SILENCE 1986 Halo – Wishing Well (Understanding)
(693, 715)

Racing record: Horse of The Year in USA at 3 yrs, winning 6 Grade 1 events, notably Kentucky Derby, Preakness Stakes and Breeders' Cup Classic. Stud record: The outstanding sire in Japan. Best winners include Japan Cup winner Special Week and Dubai Sheema Classic winner Stay Gold.

TABASCO CAT 1991 Storm Cat – Barbicue Sauce (Sauce Boat)
(877)

Racing record: Winner of Belmont Stakes and Preakness Stakes. Stud record: Sire of several minor stakes winners in USA and Irish 2-y-o 5f winner Tribal Drum. Standing at Overbrook Farm, Kentucky.

TACTICAL ADVANTAGE 1990 Forty Niner – Twitchet (Roberto)
(757)

Racing record: Won 3 races, notably Grade 2 6f Saratoga Special Stakes at 2 yrs. Stud record: Sire of Grade 2 winners Forty One Carats and Prime Directive. Standing at Marablue Farm, Florida. 2001 fee: $12,500.

TAGULA 1993 Taufan – Twin Island (Standaan).
(22, 32, 68, 73, 195, 501, 750)

Racing record: Won 4 races including the Prix Morny, the Group 3 Supreme Stakes and the Group 3 July Stakes. Stud record: First crop now three-year-olds. Sire of Royal Lodge winner Atlantis Prince, German Group 2 winner Tagshira and useful 5f performer Red Millennium. Standing at Rathbarry Stud in Ireland. 2001 fee: IR6,000 gns (Oct 1st).

THATCHING
1975 Thatch – Abella (Abernant)
(190, 338)

Racing record: Won Duke of York Stakes, Cork And Orrery Stakes and July Cup at 4 yrs when also first past post in William Hill Sprint Championship. Stud record: Best winners include Tirol (2000 Guineas/Irish 2000 Guineas), Danseuse du Soir (Poule d'Essai des Pouliches, Prix de la Foret), very smart 6f/7f performer Shalford and smart performers Archway, Fitzwilliam Place, Hot Tin Roof, Mistertopogigo, Puissance, Revelation and Sugarfoot. Died in 1999.

THEATRICAL
1982 Nureyev – Tree of Knowledge (Sassafras).
(408)

Racing record: 10 wins from 8.5f to 12f – including six Grade 1 races in the USA – notably the Breeders Cup Turf, the Turf Classic and the Man O'War Stakes. Stud record: Best winners include the Group/Grade 1 winners Broadway Flyer (Sword Dancer Invitational), Dahlia's Dreamer (Flower Bowl Invitational), Duda (Matrirach Stakes), Geri (Oaklawn Handicap), Golden Treat (Santa Anita Oaks), Hishi Amazon (Champion Japanese 2-y-o filly), Madeleine's Dream (French 1,000 Guineas), Marchand de Sable (Criterium de Saint-Cloud), Pharma (Santa Ana Handicap), Portland Player (Victoria Derby), Royal Anthem (Canadian International/Juddmonte International/Gulfstream Park Breeders' Cup Handicap), Vaudeville (Secretariat Stakes) and Zagreb (Irish Derby). Standing at Diamond A Farms, Kentucky. 2001 fee: $80,000.

THUNDER GULCH
1992 Gulch – Line Of Thunder (Storm Bird).
(387, 677, 681)

Racing record: Won the Kentucky Derby, the Belmont Stakes, the Travers Stakes and the Florida Derby. Stud record: From three crops of racing age his best winners include Spain (Breeders' Cup Distaff), Point Given (Hollywood Futurity), and the Grade 2/3 winners C'est l'Amour and Thunder Bertie. Standing at Ashford Stud, Kentucky. 2001 fee: $30,000 (live foal).

TINNERS WAY
1990 Secretariat – Devon Diva (The Minstrel)
(348)

Racing record: Won 7 races in Britain and USA, notably Grade 1 1¼m Pacific Classic at 4/5 yrs and Grade 1 9f Californian Stakes at 6 yrs. Stud record: First crop are now three-year-olds. Standing at Harris Farms, California. 2001 fee: $3,500 (live foal).

TORRENTIAL
1992 Gulch – Killaloe (Dr Fager).
(26)

Racing record: Won the Prix Jean-Prat and second in the Grade 2 American Derby. Stud record: First crop now two-year-olds. Standing at Gainsborough Stud, Kentucky. 2001 fee: $10,000.

TREMPOLINO
1984 Sharpen Up – Trephine (Viceregal).
(192)

Racing record: Winner of four races including the Prix Lupin, the Prix Niel and most notably the Prix de l'Arc de Triomphe. Stud record: Best winners include Dernier Empereur (Champion Stakes), Germany (Grosser Preis von Baden), Juvenia (Prix Marcel Boussac), Snow Polina (Beverly D Stakes), very smart Cesarewitch winner Spirit of Love, the Group/Grade 2 winners Arkadian Hero, Hidden Trick, Talloires and Trampoli, the European Group 3 winners For Valour, Neuilly and Triarius and the US Graded Stakes winners Cox Orange and Summer Ensign. Trempolino stands at Haras du Mezeray in France. 2001 fee: 80,000 FF.

TURTLE ISLAND
1991 Fairy King – Sisania (High Top).
(244, 566, 770, 1061)

Racing record: 6 wins from 5f to 1m including the Irish 2,000 Guineas, the Heinz "57" Phoenix Stakes and the Group 2 Gimcrack Stakes. Stud record: Sire of 2,000 Guineas winner Island Sands and smart performers Lincoln Dancer (6f) Corinium (1m), Island Sound (1¼m) and King O' The Mana (up to 15f). Standing at Castle Hyde Stud in Ireland. 2001 fee: IR6,000 gns.

TWINING   1990 Forty Niner – Courtly Dee (Never Bend).
                                                                              (341)
Racing record: Stakes winner of 5 races in the USA including the Grade 2 Peter Pan Stakes. Stud record: From 2 crops racing, sire of numerous winners including the Grade 3 placed Exact.

UNBRIDLED'S SONG   1993 Unbridled – Trolley Song (Caro)
                                                                              (745)
Racing record: Won 5 races in the USA, notably the Breeders' Cup Juvenile and the Florida Derby. Stud record: Had first 2-y-o crop in 2000 and sire of Fountain of Youth Stakes winner Songandaprayer. Standing at Taylor Made Farm, Kentucky. 2001 fee: $40,000.

UNFUWAIN   1985 Northern Dancer – Height of Fashion (Bustino).
                                     (25, 155, 216, 311, 573, 997, 1001, 1012)
Racing record: Won 6 races including the Group 2 Princess of Wales's Stakes and the Group 3 Jockey Club Stakes. Stud record: Best performers include the champion 1995 2-y-o Alhaarth (winner of the Dewhurst Stakes), Petrushka (Irish Oaks), Bolas (Irish Oaks), Lahan (1,000 Guineas), Zahrat Dubai (Nassau Stakes), Mamlakah (Group 3 May Hill Stakes), Gulland (Group 3 Chester Vase), the German Group 3 winner Alpha City, the Oaks second Mezzogiorno and the Chesham Stakes winner Shamikh. Standing at the Nunnery Stud in Norfolk. 2001 fee: £25,000.

UP AND AT 'EM   1990 Forzando – Ergo (Song)
                                                                             (1059)
Racing record: Won Cornwallis Stakes at 2 yrs and listed 5f event at 4 yrs. Stud record: Sire of useful performers Electrum, James Stark and Rich Vein. Standing at Blakeley Stud, Shropshire.

VETTORI   1992 Machiavellian – Air Distingue (Sir Ivor)
                                                      (87, 173, 520, 976, 982)
Racing Record: Won Poule d'Essai des Poulains and third in St James's Palace Stakes. Stud record: From 3 crops of racing age, sire of Group 3 winners Hightori and Lady Vettori. Standing at New England Stud, Newmarket. 2001 fee: £5,500.

WEST BY WEST   1989 Gone West – West Turn (Cox's Ridge)
                                                                              (910)
Racing record: Winner of 10 races in USA, notably Grade 1 9f Nassau County Handicap. Stud record: Best runners include Grade 3 2-y-o 6f winner Appealing Phylly and Grade 1 8.5f Frizette Stakes third Western Justice. Standing at Walmac International, Kentucky. 2001 fee: $12,500.

WHITTINGHAM   1989 Fayruz – Bohemian Rhapsody (On Your Mark)
                                                                           (191, 335)
Racing record: Won three listed sprint races in Italy at 2 yrs. Stud record: Best runners include Inya Lake (Molecomb Stakes) and useful performers up to 7f Blue Star and Patriot. Standing at Holly Bush Farm, Gloucestershire. 2001 fee: £2,000.

WILD AGAIN   1980 Icecapade – Bushel-n-Peck (Khaled)
                                                                              (759)
Racing record: Won 8 races in USA, notably Breeders' Cup Classic. Stud record: Best winners include Breeders' Cup Sprint winner Elmhurst, Florida Derby winner Vicar, and other Grade 1 winners Wild Rush, Wild Event and A Wild Ride. Standing at Three Chimneys Farm, Kentucky. 2001 fee: $60,000

WOLFHOUND   1989 Nureyev – Lassie Dear (Buckpasser).
                                                                           (82, 210, 775)
Racing record: Won 6 races from 5f to 7f, notably the Hazlewood Foods Sprint Cup at Haydock Park, the Prix de la Foret and the Group 3 Diadem Stakes. Stud record: Sire of the listed 5f winner Sakha, Lancashire Oaks third Chez Cherie and useful 2-y-o 7f/1m performer Attache. Standing at Longholes Stud in Newmarket. 2001 fee: £3,000.

WOODBOROUGH 1993 Woodman – Performing Arts (The Minstrel)
(453, 635, 722)

Racing record: Won 2 races at 2 yrs, including Anglesey Stakes, and placed in Prix de la Salamandre and Middle Park. In frame in 3 pattern-race sprints at 3 yrs. Stud record: First crop now two-year-olds. Standing at Ballyhane Stud, Ireland. 2001 fee: IR£3,000.

WOODMAN 1983 Mr Prospector – Playmate (Buckpasser).
(9, 117, 151, 208, 269, 306, 333, 364, 396, 455, 596, 608, 611, 650, 651, 668, 676, 697, 698, 810, 841, 963, 965, 974, 983)

Racing record: A high class Irish 2-y-o in 1985, Woodman won two Group 3 races – the 6.3f Anglesey Stakes and the 1m Ferrans Futurity Stakes – but failed to train on. Stud record: Best winners include Bosra Sham (champion filly and winner of the Fillies Mile, 1,000 Guineas and Champion Stakes), Gay Gallanta (Cheveley Park Stakes), Hansel (Belmont Stakes and Preakness Stakes), Hector Protector (champion 2-y-o and winner of the French 2,000 Guineas, the Prix Jacques le Marois, etc.), Ciro (Grand Criterium, Prix Lupin and Secretariat Stakes), Hula Angel (Irish 1,000 Guineas), Mahogany Hall (Whitney Handicap), Timber Country (champion 2-y-o and winner of the Breeders Cup Juvenile, the Preakness Stakes etc.), Way Of Light (Grand Criterium), Andromaque (Group 2 Prix de l'Opera), Bahhare (Group 2 Laurent Perrier Champagne Stakes), Kathie's Colleen (Grade 2 Monmouth Oaks) and Mujtahid (Group 2 Gimcrack Stakes and Group 3 July Stakes). Standing at the Ashford Stud in Kentucky. 2001 fee: $45,000 (live foal).

ZAFONIC 1990 Gone West – Zaizafon (The Minstrel).
(110, 139, 145, 148, 257, 297, 303, 316, 355, 386, 388, 435, 441, 458, 517, 641, 667, 706, 751, 785, 802, 859, 863, 951, 969, 972, 1011, 1019, 1067)

Racing record: Won 5 races from 6f to 1m notably the 2,000 Guineas, the Dewhurst Stakes, the Prix de la Salamandre and the Prix Morny. European Champion 2-y-o and 3-y-o. Stud record: Sire of champion 2-y-o Xaar, Italian 1000 Guineas winner Shenck, Gran Criterium winner Count Dubois, German 2000 Guineas winner Pacino, Richmond Stakes winner Endless Summer, Budweiser International winner Alrassaam and the Group 3 winners Clearing, Kareymah and Ozone Layer. Standing at Banstead Manor Stud, Cheveley, Newmarket. 2001 fee: £20,000 (SLF).

ZAMINDAR 1994 Gone West – Zaizafon (The Minstrel)
(16, 76, 77, 102, 180, 436, 587, 683, 779, 783, 784)

Racing record: Brother to Zafonic. Won Prix de Cabourg at 2 yrs when also placed in Prix Morny and Prix de la Salamandre. Best effort at 3 when fifth in 2000 Guineas. Stud record: First crop now two-year-olds.

ZILZAL 1986 Nureyev – French Charmer (Le Fabuleux).
(29, 246, 349, 536, 637, 881)

Racing record: 5 wins from 6 races notably the Sussex Stakes, the Queen Elizabeth II Stakes, the Group 3 Jersey Stakes and the Group 3 Criterion Stakes. Champion European 3-y-o miler. Stud record: Best winners include Always Loyal (French 1,000 Guineas), Among Men (Sussex Stakes), Faithful Son (Group 2 Prince of Wales's Stakes), Nero Zilzal (Group 3 Prix Exbury), Ocean Queen (Grade 3 Bay Meadows Breeders Cup Derby), Shaanxi (Group 2 Prix du Rond-Point) and Zilzal Zamaan (Group 3 Ormonde Stakes). Standing at Lanwades Stud, Newmarket. 2001 fee: £7,000 (SLF).

RACING TRENDS

Beckett (top) will be trying to follow in the footsteps of three of the last four National Stakes winners—Desert King, King of Kings and Sinndar—by adding a classic victory to his record; Tobougg completed the Salamandre-Dewhurst (pictured) double which went to subsequent Guineas winners Zafonic and Pennekamp in the 'nineties

This section is my attempt to predict some of the three year old stars of 2001. I have focused on a certain number of two-year-old races that seem to have the knack of producing the type of horse that improves as a three-year-old. Although some of these races will come as no surprise to many racing fans (the Dewhurst Stakes for instance), there are others that should raise a few eyebrows. I feel that this type of statistical analysis can enable one to select a good number of the very best of this year's classic generation.

Just as important, there are some two-year-old Group races which should be avoided when compiling lists of horses to follow. I hope that regular readers will forgive me for repeating the astonishingly abysmal record of the Mill Reef Stakes and the Beresford Stakes. The last twelve winners of the Group 2 Mill Reef Stakes have won just one race between them as three-year-olds, whilst the Group 3 Beresford Stakes has fared only one better! The Richmond Stakes had an equally poor record until last year when finally it came good with the victories of Bachir in both the French and Irish Two Thousand Guineas. From the previous eleven winners however, only one had managed to win a race as a three-year-old.

Over the past few years, the following selected races have thrown up the classic winners King Of Kings, Pennekamp, Mister Baileys, Rodrigo de Triano and Zafonic (all 2,000 Guineas), Bosra Sham, Cape Verdi, Harayir, Sayyedati (1,000 Guineas), Marling (Irish 1,000 Guineas), Culture Vulture (French 1,000 Guineas), Dr Devious (Derby), Lammtarra, Sinndar (Derby and 'Arc'), Desert King, (Irish 2,000 Guineas and Irish Derby), Reams Of Verse (Oaks), Celtic Swing (French Derby), Silver Patriarch and Bob's Return (St Leger), along with a multitude of other Group race winners.

In the tables, the figure in the third column indicates the number of wins recorded as a three-year-old, with GW signifying a Group race winner at that age.

The horses listed below are the winners of the featured races in 2000. Anyone looking for horses to follow in the Group and Classic events of this season might well want to bear them in mind. Those in bold text are, I feel, particularly worthy of attention.

Beckett	Enthused	Malhub	Regal Rose
C D Europe	Fair Question	**Nayef**	Tarfshi
Crystal Music	Ghayth	No Excuse Needed	**Tobougg**
Demophilos	**Karasta**	Noverre	Worthily
Dilshaan	**King Charlemagne**	Palatial	
Dora Carrington	Lunar Crystal	Prizeman	

Lowther Stakes
York, 6 furlongs, August

1981 Circus Ring	0	
1982 Habibti	4 GW	
1983 Prickle	0	
1984 Al Bahathri	3 GW	
1985 Kingscote	0	
1986 Polonia	3 GW	
1987 Ela Romara	1 GW	
1988 Miss Demure	0	
1989 Dead Certain	1 GW	
1990 Only Yours	2 GW	
1991 Culture Vulture	2 GW	
1992 Niche	2 GW	
1993 Velvet Moon	1	
1994 Harayir	4 GW	

1995 Dance Sequence	0
1996 Bianca Nera	0
1997 Cape Verdi	1 GW
1998 Bint Allayl	Non-runner
1999 Jemima	0
2000 Enthused	

This race has turned up the 1,000 Guineas heroines Harayir and Cape Verdi, the respective French and Irish 1,000 Guineas winners Culture Vulture and Al Bahathri, and the top-class sprinters Habibti and Polonia. Bint Allayl would surely have been favourite to win a classic herself had she not come to an untimely end. A filly by Seeking The Gold (the sire of Dubai Millennium) out of the Coronation Stakes winner Magic of Life, Enthused will win another nice race or two this year – probably at distances of up to seven furlongs.

Coventry Stakes
Royal Ascot, 6 furlongs, June

1981	Red Sunset	0
1982	Horage	1 GW
1983	Chief Singer	3 GW
1984	Primo Dominie	1 GW
1985	Sure Blade	3 GW
1986	Cutting Blade	1
1987	Always Fair	1 GW
1988	High Estate	1
1989	Rock City	2 GW
1990	Mac's Imp	0
1991	Dilum	2 GW
1992	Petardia	1
1993	Stonehatch	Non-runner
1994	Sri Pekan	Non-runner
1995	Royal Applause	1
1996	Verglas	0
1997	Harbour Master	Non-runner
1998	Red Sea	0
1999	Fasliyev	Non-runner
2000	C D Europe	

This race has proved disappointing in the past few years, particularly as four recent winners have failed to reappear as 3-y-o's. My personal favourite amongst those listed above was Jeff Smith's sprinter/miler Chief Singer. C D Europe has good, solid form to his name, but he may struggle to win again this year if campaigned in the top races.

Dewhurst Stakes
Newmarket, 7 furlongs, October

1981	Wind and Wuthering	0 (2,000 Gns 2nd)
1982	Diesis	0
1983	El Gran Senor	2 GW
1984	Kala Dancer	0
1985	Huntingdale	0
1986	Ajdal	4 GW
1987	ABANDONED	
1988	Prince of Dance &	1 (DISQ)
	Scenic (dead-heat)	1
1989	Dashing Blade	2 GW
1990	Generous	3 GW
1991	Dr Devious	2 GW
1992	Zafonic	1 GW
1993	Grand Lodge	1 GW
1994	Pennekamp	2 GW
1995	Alhaarth	1 GW
1996	In Command	0
1997	Xaar	1 GW
1998	Mujahid	0
1999	Distant Music	1 GW
2000	Tobougg	

The list of colts here is impressive, with Derby winners Generous and Dr Devious, champion sprinter Ajdal and the Guineas winners Pennekamp, Zafonic and El Gran Senor outstanding. Will Tobougg end this season with a record as impressive as any of those top colts? Maybe not, but I still expect him to pick up another Group 1 prize – quite possibly the Two Thousand Guineas.

Zetland Stakes
Newmarket, 10 furlongs, November

1981	Paternoster Row	0
1982	John French	1 GW
1983	High Debate	0
1984	Ulterior Motive	2 GW
1985	Highland Chieftain	2 GW
1986	Grand Tour	0
1987	Upper Strata	Non-runner
1988	Mamaluna	1 GW
1989	Rock Hopper	1 GW
1990	Matahif	0
1991	Bonny Scot	2 GW
1992	Bob's Return	3 GW
1993	Double Trigger	1 GW
1994	Double Eclipse	1
1995	Gentilhomme	0
1996	Silver Patriarch	2 GW
1997	Trigger Happy	0
1998	Adnaan	1
1999	Monte Carlo	0
2000	Worthily	

Previous winners of this race include the St Leger and Coronation Cup winner Silver Patriarch, the good four-year-olds Double Eclipse and Rock Hopper, Bob's Return (the second St Leger winner in this list) and the Ascot Gold Cup winner Double Trigger - surely the most notable of them all. Worthily was one of Mick Channon's many good 2-y-o's last season and he can win more races where stamina is at a premium.

Champagne Stakes (formerly the Laurent Perrier Champagne Stakes)
Doncaster, 7 furlongs, September

1981	Achieved	1 GW
1982	Gorytus	0
1983	Lear Fan	2 GW
1984	Young Runaway	2 GW
1985	Sure Blade	3 GW
1986	Don't Forget Me	2 GW
1987	Warning	3 GW
1988	Prince of Dance	0
1989	ABANDONED	
1990	Bog Trotter	2 GW
1991	Rodrigo de Triano	4 GW
1992	Petardia	1

1993 Unblest   1 GW
1994 Sri Pekan   Non-runner
1995 Alhaarth   1 GW
1996 Bahhare   0
1997 Daggers Drawn   0
1998 Auction House   0
1999 Distant Music   1 GW
2000 Noverre

Despite a disappointing period of late, this race continues to be of major importance as far as the following season's big 3-y-o races are concerned. Rodrigo de Triano and Don't Forget Me won both the English and Irish 2,000 Guineas and Warning was arguably the most talented of them all. Noverre was easily the most successful of the Godolphin 2-y-o's last season and his 3-y-o career will depend upon his preference for either dirt or turf surfaces. A tough and genuine colt, if he's brought back to Europe his adversaries will certainly know they've had a race whenever they take him on.

Cheveley Park Stakes
Newmarket, 6 furlongs, October

1981 Woodstream   0
1982 Ma Biche   3 GW
1983 Desirable   0
1984 Park Appeal   0
1985 Embla   1
1986 Forest Flower (Disq)   1 GW
1987 Ravinella   4 GW
1988 Pass the Peace   0
1989 Dead Certain   1 GW
1990 Capricciosa   Non-runner
1991 Marling   3 GW
1992 Sayyedati   2 GW
1993 Prophecy   0
1994 Gay Gallanta   0
1995 Blue Duster   1
1996 Pas de Reponse   2 GW
1997 Embassy NR
1998 Wannabe Grand   1
1999 Seazun   0
2000 Regal Rose

A number of these fillies have gone on to further Group race success, although it is some years now since a classic winner emerged. This year's Cheveley Park was a slowly-run affair, but that shouldn't put you off Regal Rose. Her trainer, Sir Michael Stoute, has two other strong contenders for the 1,000 Guineas. Regal Rose misses Newmarket through injury but if she returns fit and well later in the season she should win good races.

Cherry Hinton Stakes
Newmarket, 6 furlongs, July

1981 Travel On   0
1982 Crime of Passion   0
1983 Chapel Cottage   0
1984 Top Socialite   1 GW
1985 Storm Star   0
1986 Forest Flower   1 GW
1987 Diminuendo   4 GW
1988 Kerrera   1
1989 Chimes of Freedom   2 GW
1990 Chicarica   0
1991 Musicale   1 GW
1992 Sayyedati   2 GW
1993 Lemon Souffle   1 GW
1994 Red Carnival   0
1995 Applaud   0
1996 Dazzle   1
1997 Asfurah   0
1998 Wannabe Grand   1
1999 Torgau   0
2000 Dora Carrington

There have been some top-notch winners of this event in the period under review, notably the 3-y-o Group 1 winners Forest Flower, Diminuendo, Chimes of Freedom and Sayyedati. The race has been a disappointment of late, but there should be more races for Dora Carrington to win, provided she isn't over-tried in Group 1 events.

Washington Singer Stakes
Newbury, 6 furlongs, August

1981 Custer   0
1982 Horage   1 GW
1983 Trojan Fen   2 GW
1984 Khozaam   0
1985 Faustus   2 GW
1986 Deputy Governor   0
1987 Emmson   0
1988 Prince of Dance   1 (DISQ)
1989 Karinga Bay   1 GW
1990 Heart of Darkness   0
1991 Rodrigo de Triano   4 GW
1992 Tenby   2 GW
1993 Colonel Collins   0
1994 Lammtarra   3 GW
1995 Mons   0
1996 State Fair   0
1997 Bahr   2 GW
1998 Valentine Girl   0
1999 Mana-Mou-Bay   0
2000 Prizeman

As can be seen from the table, this race quite often provides us with Group or Classic pointers and in that regard Lammtarra and Rodrigo de Triano were outstanding. Prizeman does not seem up to proving himself a classic contender, but he can win more races at distances of around a mile.

Champagne Lanson Vintage Stakes
Goodwood, 7 furlongs, July

1981 Treboro	0
1982 All Systems Go	0
1983 Trojan Fen	2 GW
1984 Petoski	2 GW
1985 Faustus	2 GW
1986 Don't Forget Me	2 GW
1987 Undercut	0
1988 High Estate	1
1989 Be My Chief	0
1990 Mukaddamah	1 GW
1991 Dr Devious	2 GW
1992 Maroof	1
1993 Mister Baileys	1 GW
1994 Eltish	0
1995 Alhaarth	1 GW
1996 Putra	0
1997 Central Park	2 GW
1998 Aljabr	1 GW
1999 Ekraar	3 GW
2000 No Excuse Needed	

All in all, this race is very informative in terms of sorting out future stars, with the classic winners Don't Forget Me, Dr Devious and Mister Baileys and the King George winner Petoski standing out. Aljabr was another Group 1 winner as a 3-y-o – he picked up the Sussex Stakes. No Excuse Needed will have to improve to figure prominently in Group 1 events but he is certainly capable of winning more races at around 1m.

National Stakes
Curragh, 7 furlongs, September

1981 Day Is Done	0
1982 Glenstal	1 GW
1983 El Gran Senor	3 GW
1984 Law Society	2 GW
1985 Tate Gallery	0
1986 Lockton	3
1987 Caerwent	2
1988 Classic Fame	1 GW
1989 Dashing Blade	2 GW
1990 Heart Of Darkness	0
1991 El Prado	0
1992 Fatherland	0
1993 Manntari	1
1994 Definite Article	1
1995 Danehill Dancer	1 GW
1996 Desert King	3 GW
1997 King Of Kings	1 GW
1998 Mus-If	0
1999 Sinndar	5 GW

2000 Beckett

As one can see by the list of recent winners, Sinndar crowned a superb run for this race last year when capturing the Derby, the Irish Derby and the Arc. I feel that Beckett, a son of Fairy King and trained by Aidan O'Brien, has the ability to win more good races this season at distances of a mile or more.

Racing Post Trophy
Doncaster, 8 furlongs, October

1981 Count Pahlen	1 GW
1982 Dunbeath	0
1983 Alphabatim	3 GW
1984 Lanfranco	2 GW
1985 Bakharoff	1 GW
1986 Reference Point	5 GW
1987 Emmson	0
1988 Al Hareb	0
1989 Be My Chief	0
1990 Peter Davies	0
1991 Seattle Rhyme	0
1992 Armiger	1 GW
1993 King's Theatre	2 GW
1994 Celtic Swing	2 GW
1995 Beauchamp King	1 GW
1996 Medaaly	0
1997 Saratoga Springs	1 GW
1998 Commander Collins	0
1999 Aristotle	0
2000 Dilshaan	

Despite two disappointing periods (including over the last few years), during this review, the Racing Post Trophy still retains its status as an important classic pointer. Dilshaan, a son of Darshaan whose stock invariably improve with age, will no doubt be aimed at the Derby and probably the St Leger too. I doubt him being able to win a Derby, but if he stays the trip then the Doncaster race will surely be his best chance for classic success.

betonsports.co.uk Conditions Stakes
Sandown, 8 furlongs, September

1981 ABANDONED	
1982 Magic Rarity	Non-runner
1983 Forest of Dean	2
1984 Lord Grundy	1
1985 Dancing Brave	6 GW
1986 Reference Point	5 GW
1987 Albadr	1
1988 Mired	0
1989 Elmaamul	3 GW
1990 Generous	3 GW
1991 King's Loch	1
1992 Geisway	1
1993 Overbury	1 GW
1994 Dreamer	0

1995 Inchrory	Raced abroad
1996 Barnum Sands	1
1997 Setteen	NR
1998 Bathwick	3
1999 Sakhee	2 GW
2000 Tarfshi	

Most of these previous winners managed to win as a 3-y-o and four of them (Dancing Brave, Reference Point, Elmaamul and Generous) were top-class. Being by Mtoto, the very promising Tarfshi will no doubt stay further than her dam, Pass The Peace, managed. According to my interpretation, that means she can win more races from a mile to twelve furlongs and a Group race win is certainly not out of the question.

European Trainers' Federation Conditions Stakes (formerly the Mornington Stakes)
Ascot, 7 furlongs, September

1981 General Anders	0
1982 By Decree	0
1983 Donzel	0
1984 Tour d'Or	0
1985 Zahdam	1 GW
1986 Ajdal	4 GW
1987 Sheriff's Star	2 GW
1988 Shaadi	3 GW
1989 Shavian	2 GW
1990 Big Blow	Non runner
1991 Assessor	2 GW
1992 Inchinor	3 GW
1993 Mutakddim	3
1994 Wijara	1
1995 Story Line	0
1996 Kahal	2 GW
1997 Mudeer	0
1998 Mukhalif	1 GW
1999 Bogus Dreams	0
2000 Lunar Crystal	

As a precursor to better things, this event has an exceptional record for a non-pattern race. Previous winners include the champion sprinter Ajdal and the high-class colts Inchinor, Sheriff's Star, Shaadi and Shavian. Kahal too, was a very smart colt and Mukhalif continued the good record of this race last year when winning the Italian Derby. Lunar Crystal has a middle-distance pedigree and I would expect her to win again this year over twelve furlongs or thereabouts.

May Hill Stakes
Doncaster, 8 furlongs, September

1981 Height of Fashion	2 GW
1982 Bright Crocus	Non runner
1983 Satinette	0
1984 Ever Genial	2 GW

1985 Midway Lady	2 GW
1986 Laluche	0
1987 Intimate Guest	1
1988 Tessla	0
1989 Rafha	3 GW
1990 Majmu	0
1991 Midnight Air	0
1992 Marillette	1 GW
1993 Hawajiss	2 GW
1994 Mamlakah	0
1995 Solar Crystal	0
1996 Reams of Verse	2 GW
1997 Midnight Line	1
1998 Calando	0
1999 Teggiano	0
2000 Karasta	

There are plenty of high-class fillies on this list and Karasta can be another one. A big, but easy-moving filly, she would appear to have the scope to train on and become a serious contender for further Group race glory over a mile or perhaps ten furlongs.

Fillies Conditions Race
Newbury, 7 furlongs, September

1981 NO RACE	
1982 Salvinia	1
1983 Mahogany	1 GW
1984 Dubian	1
1985 Mill On The Floss	1
1986 Milligram	3 GW
1987 Andaleeb	1 GW
1988 Samaza	0
1989 Free At Last	1 (In USA)
1990 Fragrant Hill	1
1991 Freewheel	1
1992 Sueboog	1 GW
1993 Balanchine	2 GW
1994 Musetta	1
1995 Wild Rumour	0
1996 Etoile	0
1997 Amabel	NR
1998 Fragrant Oasis	1
1999 Veil Of Avalon	1
2000 Palatial	

The brilliant fillies Balanchine and Milligram stand out in this group and although the race has thrown up a few disappointments of late, I'm prepared to stick with it. Palatial ran six times as a 2-y-o, winning the last three. Although her form is seemingly exposed, she can still pick up another race or two – maybe even a listed event.

Haynes, Hanson and Clark Stakes
Newbury, 8 furlongs, September

1981 Super Sunrise	1 GW
1982 Polished Silver	0

1983 Rainbow Quest	1 GW
1984 Northern River	0
1985 My Ton Ton	0
1986 Thameen	1
1987 Unfuwain	3 GW
1988 Star Shareef	0
1989 Tanfith	0
1990 Prince Russanor	1
1991 Zinaad	1
1992 Pembroke	1
1993 King's Theatre	2 GW
1994 Munwar	2 GW
1995 Mick's Love	1
1996 King Sound	1
1997 Duck Row	0
1998 Boatman	0
1999 Ethmaar	0
2000 Nayef	

Rainbow Quest, Unfuwain and King's Theatre are an impressive testament to the record of this race and Shergar was another previous winner (in 1980). It will come as a major disappointment if Nayef does not prove himself out of the top drawer. The Two Thousand Guineas may be a bit sharp for him and the Derby could well be more his race. Hopefully he can go on to become as successful as his illustrious half-brother, Nashwan.

Fillies Mile
Ascot, 8 furlongs, September

1981 Height of Fashion	2 GW
1982 Acclimatise	1 GW
1983 Nepula	0
1984 Oh So Sharp	4 GW
1985 Untold	1 GW
1986 Invited Guest	1 GW
1987 Diminuendo	4 GW
1988 Tessla	0
1989 Silk Slippers	0
1990 Shamshir	0
1991 Midnight Air	0
1992 Ivanka	0
1993 Fairy Heights	0
1994 Aqaarid	1 GW
1995 Bosra Sham	3 GW
1996 Reams of Verse	2 GW
1997 Glorosia	0
1998 Sunspangled	0
1999 Teggiano	0
2000 Crystal Music	

Aqaarid, who won the Fred Darling Stakes and was then placed in the 1,000 Guineas, halted a desperately poor run for this race. Bosra Sham and Reams of Verse did much more than that. In fact Bosra Sham's performances were outstanding and certainly bear comparison with that of the Fillies Triple Crown heroine Oh So

Sharp. The last three fillies failed to win at 3 yrs, but it would be surprising if Crystal Music failed to add more Group race successes this year.

She will probably stay twelve furlongs and has a major chance in both the One Thousand Guineas and the Oaks.

Moorestyle Convivial Stakes
York, 6 furlongs, August

1981 Rebollino	0
1982 Diana's Pet	0
1983 Double Schwartz	2
1984 Local Suitor	0
1985 Sit This One Out	0
1986 Bali Magic	1
1987 Brilliant Bay	0
1988 Danehill	3 GW
1989 In The Groove	4 GW
1990 Jallad	0
1991 Great Palm	1 GW
1992 Revelation	1 GW
1993 Owington	3 GW
1994 Green Perfume	0
1995 Desert Boy	0
1996 Indiscreet	1
1997 Bintang	0
1998 Stravinsky	2 GW
1999 Fath	1
2000 Ghayth	

Since 1988 the winners of this race have included the high-class sprinters Stravinsky, Double Schwartz and Owington, the very smart ten furlong colt Great Palm and the cracking eight to twelve furlong filly In The Groove. Ghayth may prove something of a rarity by being a son of Sadler's Wells that doesn't stay a mile. He is decidedly useful though and will win more races.

Girton Maiden
Newmarket, 7 furlongs, August

1981 Hayakaze	1
1982 Alligatrix	0
1983 Rainbow Quest	1 GW
1984 Koffi	0
1985 Stage Hand	0
1986 Roman Gunner	1
1987 Sheriff's Star	2 GW
1988 Lady Shipley	1
1989 Marienski	0
1990 Shamshir	0
1991 First Century	1
1992 Emperor Jones	1 GW
1993 Innishowen	0
1994 Classic Cliché	2 GW
1995 Even Top	1 GW
1996 Yalaietanee	1 GW

1997	Fantasy Island	NR
1998	Sossus Vlei	1
1999	Merry Merlin	1
2000	Fair Question	

An intriguing maiden this, with the four-year-old dual Group 1 winners Rainbow Quest and Sheriff's Star, the St Leger and Gold Cup winner Classic Cliche and the smart colts Emperor Jones and Even Top catching the eye. A son of Rainbow Quest out of an Ela-Mana-Mou mare, Fair Question will win more races once he's upped in trip and twelve furlongs should suit admirably. He'll be a smart colt this year.

Somerville Tattersall Stakes
Newmarket, 7 furlongs, September/October

1981	Wind and Wuthering	0
1982	Polished Silver	0
1983	Round Hill	0
1984	Damister	3 GW
1985	Truely Nureyev	0
1986	Imperial Frontier	1
1987	Salse	5 GW
1988	Opening Verse	1
1989	Free At Last	1 (in USA)
1990	Peter Davies	0
1991	Tertian	0
1992	Nominator	0
1993	Grand Lodge	1 GW
1994	Annus Mirabilis	1
1995	Even Top	1 GW
1996	Grapeshot	1
1997	Haami	1
1998	Enrique	1 GW
1999	Scarteen Fox	0
2000	King Charlemagne	

The bare figures in this table don't really tell the whole story, for there are some very good horses here. The Group winners speak for themselves but Opening Verse, Free At Last and Annus Mirabilis all went on to win good races abroad and Haami was certainly a smart colt too. A son of Nureyev, King Charlemagne is a very interesting candidate for the Group races at up to a mile.

Westley Maiden Stakes
Newmarket, 7 furlongs, September

1981	Simply Great	1 GW
1982	DIV 1 Tolomeo	1 GW
	DIV 2 Mandelstam	0
1983	Chelkov	0
1984	Profess	0
1985	DIV 1 Cromwell Park	1
	DIV 2 Illumineux	0
1986	DIV1 Pollenate	0
	DIV 2 Tweeter	0
1987	DIV 1 Doyoun	2 GW
	DIV 2 Charmer	0
1988	DIV 1 Pirate Army	1
	DIV 2 Observation Post	0
1989	DIV 1 Mukddaam	1
	DIV 2 Cutting Note	0
1990	DIV 1 Environment Friend	2 GW
	DIV 2 Sapieha	0
1991	DIV 1 Modernise	0
	DIV 2 Pursuit of Love	3 GW
1992	DIV 1 Placerville	2 GW
	DIV 2 Barathea	1 GW
1993	Darnay	0
1994	DIV 1 Painter's Row	1 GW
	DIV 2 Smart Alec	Non-runner
1995	Astor Place	1
1996	Mashhaer	0
1997	Quiet Assurance	0
1998	Easaar	0
1999	DIV 1 Zentsov Street	NR
	DIV 2 Qamoos	0
2000	DIV 1 Demophilos	
	DIV 2 Malhub	

The stand-outs in this list are the 2,000 Guineas winner Doyoun, Eclipse winner Environment Friend, Prince of Wales's Stakes winner Placerville, the July Cup second Pursuit of Love and, best of all, the Breeders Cup Mile winner Barathea. The race has been very disappointing lately, but I'll be surprised if at least one of these latest winners doesn't prove successful this year. Malhub is a very promising colt and will win more races at up to a mile. Demophilos is bred to stay further and can also win again this year.

Autumn Stakes
Ascot, 8 furlongs, October

1988	Nashwan	4 GW
1989	Noble Patriarch	1
1990	Sea Level	0
1991	Ninja Dancer	0
1992	Taos	0
1993	NO RACE	
1994	Presenting	4 GW
1995	Beauchamp King	1 GW
1996	High Roller	NR
1997	Dr Fong	2 GW
1998	Daliapour	1
1999	French Fellow	1
2000	Nayef	

This race took over from the seven furlong Hyperion Stakes in 1988 and has produced plenty of good horses, notably the outstanding colt Nashwan, the top-class miler Dr Fong, the very smart middle-distance horse Presenting and the Derby second Daliapour – subsequently a high-class 4-y-o. Of all last year's good two-year-olds, Nayef is the one most pundits envisage being a classic winner this year. That could be the Two Thousand Guineas or more likely the Derby – hopefully both. Follow him this year and enjoy watching his beautiful action (reminiscent of his half-brother Nashwan). The biggest doubt regarding Nayef's Derby prospects is whether a son of Gulch can show top-class form at a mile and a half. The plain truth is we won't know until Derby day itself, but racing needs its heroes so let's hope Nayef is the latest.

TIMEFORM
STATISTICAL REVIEW

The following tables are extracted from the 'Timeform Statistical Review' which provides detailed and innovative statistics on hundreds of trainers and sires, including a written analysis of about a hundred top performers by Timeform's team of experts. The tables selected here relate only to achievements with two-year-olds.

The 'Timeform Statistical Review' includes an important development on the mass of previous racing statistics in its extensive use of Timeform Ratings which are internationally renowned as the most accurate measure of a horse's racing merit. The median Timeform Ratings are a measure of average ability.

Summary ...
Races won 143   Rated 100+ 9   Win prize ......
Leading earner: CLASSY CLEO (IRE) £54,085
Individual Median Rating All Horses: 73

	2-y-o	3-y-o	Older	All
	85	63	27	108
Individual Horses	46	30	15	67
Winning Horses	85	63	35	183
Horses by Season	74	44	25	143
Number of Wins	498	502	344	1344
Number of Runs	71	69	65	73
Individual Median	71	69	65	69
Median by Season	5.8	7.8	8.7	6.9
Avg Winning Distance				

Horses rated 100+ Barba Papa, Bouncing Bowdler, Classy Cleo, Connemara, Cotton House, Craigievar, Daunting Lady, Show Me The Money, Sir Ferbet

Mujadil was the surprise leader by number of wins in Britain in 2000, his sixty-one wins more than the combined totals of his 1998 and 1999 seasons. What made his achievement more remarkable was that he had fewer runners (considerably fewer in most cases) than any of the other top dozen or so sires in that list. That improved total was due in part to a larger number of runners, but more importantly to a much-improved percentage of winning horses compared to earlier seasons. Two-year-olds account for the bulk of Mujadil's success, and whilst not a high-quality group (only two out of eighty-five juveniles rated 100+ in the last four years), they've won more races than any other sire's youngsters, both in 2000 and in the last four years combined. Only two sires have a better winning horse percentage than Mujadil at two. Most of Mujadil's runners are best up to a mile, though a notable exception (out of a staying mare) in the latest season was his useful two-and-a-half-mile Ascot Stakes winner Barba Papa

*An extract from
Timeform Statistical Review*

Trainers by strike rate with two-year-olds in Britain 1998-2000

		Strike rate %	Wins-Runs	Strike rate % first time	Wins-Runs	Strike rate % second time	Wins-Runs	Stable 2-y-o median rtg
1	Saeed bin Suroor	53	9-17	56	5-9	57	4-7	94
2	H. R. A. Cecil	29	35-120	25	18-72	44	12-27	83
3	P. F. I. Cole	21	68-331	19	22-114	26	23-89	78
4	D. J. G. Murray Smith	20	3-15	25	1-4	0	0-4	60
	J. Noseda	20	39-191	17	11-65	15	7-48	74
6	J. H. M. Gosden	19	60-323	14	19-139	31	26-84	78
	J. W. Payne	19	12-64	15	3-20	13	2-15	60
	Sir Mark Prescott	19	75-397	14	15-104	17	16-94	66
	Sir Michael Stoute	19	62-334	12	21-170	28	26-93	77
10	R. Charlton	18	25-141	11	6-57	37	15-41	77
	J. R. Fanshawe	18	25-139	13	7-56	24	9-38	73
	M. Johnston	18	92-524	11	15-139	16	19-119	75
	M. P. Tregoning	18	25-141	12	8-69	22	10-46	74
14	W. J. Haggas	17	27-163	5	3-55	19	7-37	69
	J. Neville	17	1-6	0	0-1	0	0-1	72
	S. P. C. Woods	17	24-144	7	3-42	29	10-35	78
17	J. L. Dunlop	16	108-659	11	24-224	22	43-199	75
	B. Hanbury	16	18-116	14	6-44	19	6-32	81
	P. J. Makin	16	14-90	17	6-36	13	3-24	75
20	M. L. W. Bell	15	59-395	8	8-103	17	15-89	64
	E. A. L. Dunlop	15	52-350	10	13-132	17	17-98	72
	B. W. Hills	15	99-665	11	25-221	18	29-165	79
	Andrew Turnell	15	7-46	0	0-14	15	2-13	71
24	M. R. Channon	14	129-907	11	20-183	16	26-166	74
	C. R. Egerton	14	1-7	0	0-3	33	1-3	45
	R. Hannon	14	179-1298	9	26-281	16	41-259	75
	T. G. Mills	14	15-109	12	4-34	22	6-27	73
	G. Wragg	14	12-85	10	4-39	16	4-25	75
29	T. D. Barron	13	21-163	17	6-35	3	1-32	64
	G. A. Butler	13	15-113	11	5-46	14	4-29	74

Trainers by 2-y-o's rated Timeform 100+ in Britain 1998-2000

	Trainer	No.						
1	R. Hannon	18	17	B. Hanbury	5		T. G. Mills	2
2	M. R. Channon	17	18	G. A. Butler	4		C. F. Wall	2
	Sir Michael Stoute	17		R. Charlton	4	37	D. W. P. Arbuthnot	1
4	J. H. M. Gosden	16		J. R. Fanshawe	4		G. C. Bravery	1
5	J. L. Dunlop	15		M. A. Jarvis	4		N. A. Callaghan	1
6	B. W. Hills	14		Sir Mark Prescott	4		C. A. Cyzer	1
7	P. F. I. Cole	12	23	C. E. Brittain	3		M. W. Easterby	1
8	B. J. Meehan	8		L. M. Cumani	3		R. Hollinshead	1
9	H. R. A. Cecil	7		P. W. Harris	3		W. Jarvis	1
	E. A. L. Dunlop	7		Saeed bin Suroor	3		N. P. Littmoden	1
	M. P. Tregoning	7		S. P. C. Woods	3		G. G. Margarson	1
12	M. L. W. Bell	6	28	I. A. Balding	2		W. McKeown	1
	T. D. Easterby	6		T. D. Barron	2		B. A. McMahon	1
	D. R. C. Elsworth	6		M. Blanshard	2		B. R. Millman	1
	M. Johnston	6		Mrs P. N. Dutfield	2		J. W. Payne	1
	J. Noseda	6		W. J. Haggas	2		M. Pitman	1
				J. W. Hills	2		B. Smart	1
				P. J. Makin	2		A. C. Stewart	1

Sires by Timeform 2-y-o median ratings in Britain 1997-2000
For sires with at least 15 two-year-old runners

		Median Rating	C & G Median	No. Colts & Geldings	Fillies Median	No. Fillies	No. Horses	Winners	Wins	Win Money
1	Danzig (USA)	97	98	20	96	8	28	18	22	£335,175
2	Storm Cat (USA)	93	93	6	90	4	10	5	7	£63,194
3	Nureyev (USA)	91	96	21	72	10	31	16	20	£262,485
4	Seeking The Gold (USA)	90	91	5	89	6	11	6	10	£170,205
5	Alleged (USA)	89	89	9	44	2	11	3	4	£15,643
	Dixieland Band (USA)	89	95	7	76	3	10	5	8	£112,500
7	El Gran Senor (USA)	86	86	11	79	6	17	6	7	£136,107
	Machiavellian (USA)	86	88	26	81	15	41	19	24	£151,900
9	Miswaki (USA)	84	84	13	89	4	17	8	10	£62,746
	Sadler's Wells (USA)	84	84	31	82	23	54	14	16	£294,972
	Silver Hawk (USA)	84	85	24	76	11	35	15	16	£85,798
	Zieten (USA)	84	83	11	86	8	19	10	14	£183,176
13	Gone West (USA)	82	89	19	78	20	39	15	20	£142,299
14	Danehill (USA)	81	82	32	76	38	70	22	32	£581,032
	Warning	81	84	38	74	32	70	28	36	£155,541
	Zafonic (USA)	81	88	38	72	22	60	26	35	£335,327
17	Barathea (IRE)	80	83	32	75	23	55	19	28	£284,680
	Nashwan (USA)	80	85	26	66	16	42	15	22	£272,655
19	Caerleon (USA)	79	82	37	76	36	73	27	32	£312,626
	Diesis	79	80	26	79	26	52	20	25	£220,355
	Gulch (USA)	79	79	17	72	7	24	8	12	£75,859
	Halling (USA)	79	78	7	79	5	12	5	6	£33,018
	Irish River (FR)	79	83	13	75	10	23	8	10	£80,544
	Kris S (USA)	79	81	6	78	5	11	4	7	£76,358
	Lear Fan (USA)	79	81	15	66	5	20	7	12	£55,963
	Riverman (USA)	79	77	7	81	7	14	4	6	£42,849
	Unblest	79	83	10	66	1	11	5	8	£23,175
28	Selkirk (USA)	78	84	32	74	29	61	24	32	£160,448
	Shirley Heights	78	82	23	72	11	34	7	7	£33,313
30	Dayjur (USA)	77	72	21	81	18	39	16	22	£191,211
	Rainbow Quest (USA)	77	77	25	76	19	44	9	10	£39,857
	Sheikh Albadou	77	70	5	82	12	17	7	10	£33,875
33	Indian Ridge	76	80	57	69	27	84	25	32	£157,325
	Mt Livermore (USA)	76	77	9	71	3	12	4	5	£20,736
	Red Ransom (USA)	76	80	20	68	11	31	11	12	£100,520
36	Chief's Crown (USA)	75	79	9	72	7	16	4	4	£17,327
	Darshaan	75	81	22	74	20	42	14	16	£288,499
	Generous (IRE)	75	75	17	69	17	34	8	11	£118,756
	Last Tycoon	75	75	13	75	11	24	9	10	£35,505
	Mister Baileys	75	64	5	81	6	11	4	5	£22,527
	Mr Prospector (USA)	75	93	9	74	12	21	7	8	£41,098
	Woodman (USA)	75	81	20	72	30	50	13	17	£103,483
43	Cozzene (USA)	74	73	5	78	6	11	2	2	£6,545
	Kris	74	79	22	69	18	40	11	13	£54,218
	Marju (IRE)	74	81	32	67	24	56	22	27	£125,191
	St Jovite (USA)	74	76	9	20	1	10	2	3	£15,375
	Storm Bird (CAN)	74	80	4	64	8	12	4	4	£14,448
	Unfuwain (USA)	74	74	16	72	33	49	11	12	£73,894
49	Affirmed (USA)	73	71	10	86	2	12	5	5	£45,795
	Bahri (USA)	73	89	3	70	8	11	5	6	£27,595
	Cadeaux Genereux	73	77	32	69	42	74	26	34	£254,092
	Dynaformer (USA)	73	72	10	75	4	14	2	2	£7,612

	Green Desert (USA)	73	80	34	71	40	74	26	37	£292,603
	In The Wings	73	74	15	71	10	25	5	7	£69,204
	Kingmambo (USA)	73	91	10	66	7	17	6	7	£45,050
	King's Theatre (IRE)	73	73	7	48	4	11	2	4	£29,779
	Mujtahid (USA)	73	73	38	74	35	73	26	39	£292,595
	Second Set (IRE)	73	73	14	57	11	25	6	7	£39,233
	Suave Dancer (USA)	73	75	15	66	12	27	7	11	£75,735
60	Arazi (USA)	72	74	14	70	16	30	7	11	£42,151
	Bering	72	80	11	68	8	19	6	9	£123,377
	Known Fact (USA)	72	72	9	58	2	11	4	5	£31,072
	Mtoto	72	76	24	65	21	45	8	9	£43,095
	Pursuit of Love	72	72	36	71	43	79	28	35	£124,892
	Royal Academy (USA)	72	74	35	69	32	67	19	24	£144,893
	Sri Pekan (USA)	72	72	17	71	21	38	9	13	£87,496
	Tenby	72	78	16	66	10	26	9	16	£87,859
	Turtle Island (IRE)	72	76	23	66	25	48	19	30	£160,211
69	Alzao (USA)	71	71	36	72	40	76	26	28	£123,620
	Brief Truce (USA)	71	73	35	67	46	81	21	24	£107,814
	Distant View (USA)	71	71	9	72	6	15	5	9	£207,886
	Ela-Mana-Mou	71	74	10	67	4	14	4	4	£27,005
	Exit To Nowhere (USA)	71	78	13	54	7	20	5	6	£19,218
	Fairy King (USA)	71	77	35	69	36	71	23	29	£217,456
	Grand Lodge (USA)	71	80	30	55	22	52	16	20	£91,644
	Hernando (FR)	71	66	14	72	6	20	4	4	£14,107
	Mujadil (USA)	71	71	35	69	50	85	46	74	£328,035
	Thunder Gulch (USA)	71	69	6	71	5	11	4	5	£23,079

Sires by 2-y-o's rated Timeform 100+ in Britain 1997-2000

	Sire	No.
	Sire	No.
1	Caerleon (USA)	12
	Danzig (USA)	12
	Zafonic (USA)	12
4	Sadler's Wells (USA)	11
5	Danehill (USA)	10
6	Diesis	9
	Fairy King (USA)	9
	Green Desert (USA)	9
	Nureyev (USA)	9
10	Barathea (IRE)	8
	Machiavellian (USA)	8
	Night Shift (USA)	8
	Royal Academy (USA)	8
14	Darshaan	6
	Dayjur (USA)	6
	Gone West (USA)	6
17	Marju (IRE)	5
	Nashwan (USA)	5
	Selkirk (USA)	5
20	Alzao (USA)	4
	Cadeaux Genereux	4
	Common Grounds	4
	Indian Ridge	4
	Mr Prospector (USA)	4
	Primo Dominie	4
	Rahy (USA)	4
	Seeking The Gold (USA)	4
	Silver Hawk (USA)	4
	Spectrum (IRE)	4
	Turtle Island (IRE)	4
	Warning	4
32	Affirmed (USA)	3
	College Chapel	3
	Fayruz	3
	Foxhound (USA)	3
	Gulch (USA)	3
	Inchinor	3
	Lear Fan (USA)	3
	Lion Cavern (USA)	3
	Miswaki (USA)	3
	Mujtahid (USA)	3
	Owington	3
	Perugino (USA)	3
	Petardia	3
	Polar Falcon (USA)	3
	Red Ransom (USA)	3
	Shirley Heights	3
	Sri Pekan (USA)	3
	Storm Cat (USA)	3
	Suave Dancer (USA)	3
	Unfuwain (USA)	3
	Woodman (USA)	3
	Zieten (USA)	3
54	Alleged (USA)	2
	Bahri (USA)	2
	Boundary (USA)	2
	Brief Truce (USA)	2
	Desert Style (IRE)	2
	Distinctly North (USA)	2
	Dolphin Street (FR)	2
	El Gran Senor (USA)	2
	Exbourne (USA)	2
	First Trump	2
	Generous (IRE)	2
	Grand Lodge (USA)	2
	In The Wings	2
	Kingmambo (USA)	2
	Kris S (USA)	2
	Lahib (USA)	2
	Lycius (USA)	2
	Magic Ring (IRE)	2
	Mujadil (USA)	2
	Pennekamp (USA)	2
	Piccolo	2
	Pips Pride	2
	Rainbow Quest (USA)	2
	Robellino (USA)	2
	Sabrehill (USA)	2
	Southern Halo (USA)	2
	Tenby	2
	Tirol	2
	Unblest	2
	Wolfhound (USA)	2

Sires by winning 2-y-o's percentage in Britain 1997-2000
For sires with at least 10 two-year-old winners

		Winning Horse %	Horses	Winners	Wins	Runs	Wins/Runs %	Median Rtg
1	Danzig (USA)	64	28	18	22	66	33	97
2	Ballad Rock	63	16	10	13	57	23	69
3	Mujadil (USA)	54	85	46	74	498	15	71
4	Zieten (USA)	53	19	10	14	83	17	84
5	Nureyev (USA)	52	31	16	20	70	29	91
6	Machiavellian (USA)	46	41	19	24	101	24	86
7	Komaite (USA)	45	65	29	36	337	11	61
8	Namaqualand (USA)	44	52	23	31	289	11	65
9	Silver Hawk (USA)	43	35	15	16	89	18	84
	Tagula (IRE)	43	23	10	20	109	18	64
	Zafonic (USA)	43	60	26	35	147	24	81
12	Dayjur (USA)	41	39	16	22	126	17	77
	Paris House	41	44	18	33	235	14	64
14	Case Law	40	35	14	21	238	9	64
	Mukaddamah (USA)	40	40	16	29	231	13	66
	Turtle Island (IRE)	40	48	19	30	232	13	72
	Warning	40	70	28	36	194	19	81
18	Distant Relative	39	62	24	39	232	17	68
	Marju (IRE)	39	56	22	27	189	14	74
	Persian Bold	39	51	20	24	238	10	59
	Pips Pride	39	61	24	34	294	12	67
	Selkirk (USA)	39	61	24	32	183	17	78
23	Diesis	38	52	20	25	100	25	79
	Gone West (USA)	38	39	15	20	95	21	82
	Piccolo	38	60	23	36	297	12	66
26	Blues Traveller (IRE)	37	38	14	18	185	10	56
	Caerleon (USA)	37	73	27	32	186	17	79
	Charnwood Forest (IRE)	37	27	10	12	99	12	65
	Spectrum (IRE)	37	30	11	13	78	17	70
30	Mujtahid (USA)	36	73	26	39	321	12	73
	Nashwan (USA)	36	42	15	22	98	22	80
32	Barathea (IRE)	35	55	19	28	162	17	80
	Cadeaux Genereux	35	74	26	34	215	16	73
	Distinctly North (USA)	35	72	25	30	382	8	59
	Efisio	35	83	29	41	345	12	66
	Forzando	35	43	15	22	212	10	66
	Green Desert (USA)	35	74	26	37	219	17	73
	Hamas (IRE)	35	37	13	21	159	13	69
	Mind Games	35	34	12	18	165	11	62
	Pursuit of Love	35	79	28	35	285	12	72
	Red Ransom (USA)	35	31	11	12	84	14	76
42	Alzao (USA)	34	76	26	28	226	12	71
	Cyrano de Bergerac	34	47	16	22	264	8	58
	Imp Society (USA)	34	32	11	15	145	10	49
	Rambo Dancer (CAN)	34	32	11	13	184	7	53
46	Darshaan	33	42	14	16	114	14	75
	Fayruz	33	55	18	30	298	10	67
	General Monash (USA)	33	33	11	19	199	10	50
	Muhtarram (USA)	33	30	10	12	121	10	64
	Night Shift (USA)	33	109	36	43	412	10	70
51	Fairy King (USA)	32	71	23	29	197	15	71
	Primo Dominie	32	94	30	43	360	12	70

53	College Chapel	31	68	21	33	345	10	67
	Danehill (USA)	31	70	22	32	217	15	81
	First Trump	31	74	23	39	332	12	64
	Grand Lodge (USA)	31	52	16	20	143	14	71
	Lahib (USA)	31	45	14	18	141	13	68
58	Common Grounds	30	110	33	55	469	12	65
	Indian Ridge	30	84	25	32	248	13	76
	Rudimentary (USA)	30	79	24	30	364	8	62
	Up And At 'em	30	40	12	17	213	8	60
62	Elmaamul (USA)	29	48	14	18	180	10	66
	Lion Cavern (USA)	29	58	17	21	164	13	70
64	Ezzoud (IRE)	28	43	12	14	163	9	67
	Kris	28	40	11	13	107	12	74
	Magic Ring (IRE)	28	78	22	27	377	7	63
	Most Welcome	28	43	12	15	138	11	54
	Polar Falcon (USA)	28	71	·20	28	246	11	69
	Royal Academy (USA)	28	67	19	24	183	13	72
70	Eagle Eyed (USA)	27	37	10	16	187	9	60
	Emarati (USA)	27	85	23	30	383	8	61
	Perugino (USA)	27	55	15	24	264	9	58
	Sabrehill (USA)	27	55	15	17	183	9	52
74	Brief Truce (USA)	26	81	21	24	335	7	71
	Inchinor	26	86	22	38	363	10	59
	Sadler's Wells (USA)	26	54	14	16	91	18	84
	Shalford (IRE)	26	54	14	14	243	6	55
	Woodman (USA)	26	50	13	17	128	13	75

Sires by number of wins in Britain 2000—Two-year-olds

Sire	Wins	Horses	Wnrs	2000 2-y-o Median Rating
1 Mujadil (USA)	32	29	19	76
2 Tagula (IRE)	20	23	10	64
3 General Monash (USA)	19	33	11	50
4 Mind Games	18	34	12	62
5 Piccolo	17	34	12	64
6 Common Grounds	16	26	10	61
Komaite (USA)	16	24	11	68
8 Eagle Eyed (USA)	14	30	8	59
First Trump	14	27	6	66
Inzar (USA)	14	22	8	60
11 Namaqualand (USA)	13	17	10	67
Spectrum (IRE)	13	30	11	70
13 Charnw'd Forest (IRE)	12	27	10	65
Danehill (USA)	12	23	8	84
Night Shift (USA)	12	20	10	75
16 Emarati (USA)	11	18	7	62
Mujtahid (USA)	11	11	7	74
Primo Dominie	11	31	9	71
19 Barathea (IRE)	10	21	7	80
Clantime	10	26	7	56
Definite Article	10	30	8	60
Timeless Times (USA)	10	22	6	51
Zafonic (USA)	10	14	6	81
24 Caerleon (USA)	9	21	8	78
Celtic Swing	9	17	7	63
Distinctly North (USA)	9	20	8	61
Imp Society (USA)	9	16	5	49
Paris House	9	5	4	81
Pivotal	9	20	7	67
Selkirk (USA)	9	16	6	79

Sires by number of wins in Britain 1997-2000—Two-year-olds

Sire	Wins	Horses	Wnrs	2-y-o Median Rating
1 Mujadil (USA)	74	85	46	71
2 Common Grounds	55	110	33	65
3 Night Shift (USA)	43	109	36	70
Primo Dominie	43	94	30	70
5 Efisio	41	83	29	66
6 Distant Relative	39	62	24	68
First Trump	39	74	23	64
Mujtahid (USA)	39	73	26	73
9 Inchinor	38	86	22	59
10 Green Desert (USA)	37	74	26	73
11 Komaite (USA)	36	65	29	61
Piccolo	36	60	23	66
Warning	36	70	28	81
14 Pursuit of Love	35	79	28	72
Zafonic (USA)	35	60	26	81
16 Cadeaux Genereux	34	74	26	73
Pips Pride	34	61	24	67
18 College Chapel	33	68	21	67
Paris House	33	44	18	64
Petardia	33	103	26	56
21 Caerleon (USA)	32	73	27	79
Danehill (USA)	32	70	22	81
Indian Ridge	32	84	25	76
Petong	32	116	24	54
Selkirk (USA)	32	61	24	78
26 Namaqualand (USA)	31	52	23	65
Timeless Times (USA)	31	88	21	52
28 Distinctly North (USA)	30	72	25	59
Emarati (USA)	30	85	23	61
Fayruz	30	55	18	67
Rudimentary (USA)	30	79	24	62
Turtle Island (IRE)	30	48	19	72
33 Fairy King (USA)	29	71	23	71
Mukaddamah (USA)	29	40	16	66
35 Alzao (USA)	28	76	26	71
Barathea (IRE)	28	55	19	80
Polar Falcon (USA)	28	71	20	69
38 Magic Ring (IRE)	27	78	22	63
Marju (IRE)	27	56	22	74
40 Prince Sabo	26	84	20	59
41 Diesis	25	52	20	79
42 Brief Truce (USA)	24	81	21	71
Machiavellian (USA)	24	41	19	86
Persian Bold	24	51	20	59
Perugino (USA)	24	55	15	58
Royal Academy (USA)	24	67	19	72

Sires by win prize money in Britain 2000—Two-year-olds

	Sire	£	Wins	Chief Earner	
1	Danehill (USA)	£367,498	12	Mozart	£229,200
2	Eagle Eyed (USA)	£201,466	14	Goggles	£163,133
3	Darshaan	£175,120	6	Dilshaan	£105,000
4	Barathea (IRE)	£165,824	10	Tobougg	£131,194
5	Tagula (IRE)	£159,043	20	Atlantis Prince	£95,398
6	Mujadil (USA)	£155,230	32	Bouncing Bowdler	£51,525
7	Nureyev (USA)	£149,669	5	Crystal Music	£126,151
8	College Chapel	£146,066	8	Superstar Leo	£138,515
9	Boundary (USA)	£104,810	3	Minardi	£89,320
10	Mind Games	£95,354	18	Romantic Myth	£45,136
11	General Monash (USA)	£90,014	19	Amelia	£23,515
12	Inchinor	£84,187	5	Bannister	£72,500
13	Repriced (USA)	£83,952	4	Dim Sums	£83,952
14	Zafonic (USA)	£83,319	10	Endless Summer	£33,992
15	Rahy (USA)	£80,300	2	Noverre	£80,300
16	Seeking The Gold (USA)	£78,044	4	Enthused	£75,314
17	Spectrum (IRE)	£75,961	13	Hemingway	£19,992
18	Common Grounds	£74,852	16	Taras Emperor	£15,334
19	Paris House	£66,432	9	Misty Eyed	£46,389
20	Fraam	£61,483	4	Goodie Twosues	£55,222
21	Komaite (USA)	£61,096	16	Proud Boast	£10,712
22	Piccolo	£60,921	17	Piccolo Player	£19,929
23	Green Desert (USA)	£60,009	8	Palatial	£34,618
24	Sri Pekan (USA)	£59,263	8	Dora Carrington	£34,142
25	Celtic Swing	£58,426	9	Celtic Silence	£27,300
26	Royal Academy (USA)	£57,977	7	Cd Europe	£40,427
27	Irish River (FR)	£57,162	5	Atmospheric	£50,109
28	Night Shift (USA)	£56,931	12	Ascension	£12,636
29	Primo Dominie	£52,031	11	Imperial Dancer	£14,706
30	Mujtahid (USA)	£49,015	11	Muja Farewell	£15,043
31	Emarati (USA)	£48,618	11	Patsy's Double	£22,405
32	Charnwood Forest (IRE)	£47,974	12	Forwood	£11,248
33	Machiavellian (USA)	£47,907	5	No Excuse Needed	£37,280
34	Timeless Times (USA)	£47,678	10	Vicious Dancer	£16,723
35	Caerleon (USA)	£46,675	9	Vacamonte	£12,818
36	First Trump	£46,459	14	Clarion	£15,652
37	Definite Article	£45,325	10	La Vita E Bella	£16,807
38	Distinctly North (USA)	£45,063	9	Innit	£26,852
39	Inzar (USA)	£44,999	14	Inzacure	£11,266
40	Pivotal	£44,394	9	Red Carpet	£20,570
41	Indian Ridge	£44,355	7	Autumnal	£23,826
42	Selkirk (USA)	£42,756	9	Quink	£14,741
43	Gone West (USA)	£42,130	8	West Order	£12,984
44	Whittingham (IRE)	£38,966	5	Blue Reigns	£30,559
45	French Deputy (USA)	£37,961	3	Freefourracing	£37,961
46	Lake Coniston (IRE)	£36,934	5	Karasta	£28,875
47	Namaqualand (USA)	£36,626	13	Uhoomagoo	£9,708
48	Imp Society (USA)	£36,375	9	Silver Jorden	£20,966
49	Sadler's Wells (USA)	£36,153	4	Ghayth	£14,755

50	Miswaki (USA)	£34,645	4	Rasoum	£26,520
51	Grand Lodge (USA)	£34,061	8	Lady Bear	£11,148
52	Clantime	£33,980	10	Appellation	£9,116
53	Turtle Island (IRE)	£33,826	7	Peaceful Paradise	£16,741
54	Rudimentary (USA)	£33,559	6	Saratov	£21,580
55	Halling (USA)	£33,018	6	Baaridd	£18,003
56	Danzig (USA)	£32,468	4	Alshadiyah	£15,917
57	Distant Relative	£32,465	7	Blushing Bride	£10,525
58	King's Theatre (IRE)	£29,779	4	King's Ironbridge	£23,148
59	Zieten (USA)	£28,799	3	Zietunzeen	£22,680
60	Pursuit of Love	£28,714	8	Borders Belle	£5,051
61	Northern Spur (IRE)	£28,712	3	Worthily	£28,712
62	Gulch (USA)	£27,207	3	Nayef	£22,927
63	Prince Sabo	£26,702	6	Shoeshine Boy	£17,663
64	Deputy Minister (CAN)	£25,000	1	Turnberry Isle	£25,000
65	So Factual (USA)	£24,765	8	Jack Spratt	£9,757
66	Kris	£24,217	5	Lil's Jessy	£17,986
67	Cadeaux Genereux	£23,768	5	Caustic Wit	£12,620
68	Anabaa (USA)	£23,567	4	Shaard	£16,195
69	Dilum (USA)	£23,250	6	Inspector General	£14,848
70	Efisio	£22,621	7	Silca Legend	£9,546
	Wolfhound (USA)	£22,621	5	Attache	£8,570
72	Dolphin Street (FR)	£22,426	7	Princess Emily	£6,698
73	Be My Chief (USA)	£21,671	3	Forever My Lord	£21,671
74	Woodman (USA)	£21,132	5	Down To The Woods	£10,368
75	Environment Friend	£20,525	3	Snowstorm	£18,558

Sires by win prize money in Britain 1997-2000—Two-year-olds

	Sire	£	Wins	Chief Earner	
1	Danehill (USA)	£581,032	32	Mozart	£229,200
2	Zafonic (USA)	£335,327	35	Xaar	£117,674
3	Danzig (USA)	£335,175	22	Mujahid	£142,823
4	Common Grounds	£333,517	55	Flanders	£101,402
5	Mujadil (USA)	£328,035	74	Bouncing Bowdler	£51,525
6	Caerleon (USA)	£312,626	32	Sunspangled	£103,550
7	Sadler's Wells (USA)	£294,972	16	Commander Collins	£107,407
8	Green Desert (USA)	£292,603	37	Bint Allayl	£84,767
9	Mujtahid (USA)	£292,595	39	Teggiano	£140,520
10	Darshaan	£288,499	16	Dilshaan	£105,000
11	Barathea (IRE)	£284,680	28	Tobougg	£131,194
12	Primo Dominie	£284,504	43	Primo Valentino	£120,861
13	Nashwan (USA)	£272,655	22	Inchlonaig	£166,850
14	Inchinor	£265,718	38	Bannister	£72,500
15	Nureyev (USA)	£262,485	20	Crystal Music	£126,151
16	Cadeaux Genereux	£254,092	34	Embassy	£99,552
17	Hamas (IRE)	£236,710	21	Sheer Hamas	£157,548
18	College Chapel	£231,141	33	Superstar Leo	£138,515
19	Diesis	£220,355	25	Daggers Drawn	£85,041
20	Fairy King (USA)	£217,456	29	Royal Kingdom	£71,250
21	Eagle Eyed (USA)	£208,485	16	Goggles	£163,133
22	Distant View (USA)	£207,886	9	Distant Music	£182,120

23	Pips Pride	£201,251	34	Pipalong	£90,867
24	Sure Blade (USA)	£197,228	7	Boomerang Blade	£182,162
25	Night Shift (USA)	£195,980	43	Lady Alexander	£24,025
26	Dayjur (USA)	£191,211	22	Hayil	£68,785
27	Piccolo	£189,161	36	Don Puccini	£76,876
28	Distant Relative	£186,935	39	Misty Miss	£45,011
29	Zieten (USA)	£183,176	14	Seazun	£81,326
30	Efisio	£177,718	41	Kalindi	£20,150
31	Seeking The Gold (USA)	£170,205	10	Lujain	£80,199
32	First Trump	£165,340	39	Mrs P	£30,234
33	Selkirk (USA)	£160,448	32	Quink	£14,741
34	Turtle Island (IRE)	£160,211	30	King O' The Mana	£32,982
35	Tagula (IRE)	£159,043	20	Atlantis Prince	£95,398
36	Indian Ridge	£157,325	32	Littlefeather	£27,832
37	Petardia	£155,622	33	Halmahera	£43,840
38	Warning	£155,541	36	Mudeer	£15,609
39	Lycius (USA)	£155,153	14	Khasayl	£118,285
40	Machiavellian (USA)	£151,900	24	No Excuse Needed	£37,280
41	Magic Ring (IRE)	£151,400	27	Magic of Love	£54,852
42	Royal Academy (USA)	£144,893	24	Cd Europe	£40,427
43	Paris House	£143,195	33	Misty Eyed	£46,389
44	Gone West (USA)	£142,299	20	Muqtarib	£30,748
45	El Gran Senor (USA)	£136,107	7	Saratoga Springs	£110,086
46	Polar Falcon (USA)	£133,814	28	Icicle	£26,360
47	Petong	£126,358	32	Ra Ra Rasputin	£18,555
48	Komaite (USA)	£125,685	36	Proud Boast	£10,712
49	Distinctly North (USA)	£125,233	30	Innit	£26,852
50	Marju (IRE)	£125,178	27	Qhazeenah	£24,303
51	Pursuit of Love	£124,892	35	Courting	£17,815
52	Rahy (USA)	£124,324	8	Noverre	£80,300
53	Mukaddamah (USA)	£123,958	29	Branston Berry	£21,378
54	Alzao (USA)	£123,620	28	Eurolink Raindance	£12,631
55	Bering	£123,377	9	Glorosia	£96,768
56	Timeless Times (USA)	£122,687	31	Vicious Dancer	£16,723
57	Perugino (USA)	£120,873	24	Hoh Steamer	£46,456
58	Rudimentary (USA)	£120,041	30	Saratov	£21,580
59	Generous (IRE)	£118,756	11	Teapot Row	£82,737
60	Prince Sabo	£118,038	26	Tippitt Boy	£28,528
61	Fayruz	£115,133	30	Master Fay	£18,491
62	Dixieland Band (USA)	£112,500	8	Mutaahab	£92,369
63	Puissance	£108,519	23	Rosselli	£42,918
64	Brief Truce (USA)	£107,814	24	Buy Or Sell	£27,078
65	Makbul	£105,530	4	Lord Kintyre	£77,930
66	Boundary (USA)	£104,810	3	Minardi	£89,320
67	Emarati (USA)	£104,257	30	Patsy's Double	£22,405
68	Woodman (USA)	£103,483	17	Hula Angel	£26,498
69	Exbourne (USA)	£103,146	9	Auction House	£78,642
70	Owington	£102,932	15	Jemima	£55,245
71	Lahib (USA)	£102,387	18	La-Faah	£33,974
72	Red Ransom (USA)	£100,520	12	Shining Hour	£36,403
73	Whittingham (IRE)	£99,059	13	Inya Lake	£32,496
74	Wolfhound (USA)	£98,918	23	Chez Cherie	£10,650
75	Mind Games	£95,354	18	Romantic Myth	£45,136

INDEX TO HORSES

Two Year Olds of 2001 – Index To Horses

Two Year Olds of 2001 – Index To Horses

Two Year Olds of 2001 – Index To Horses

Two Year Olds of 2001 – Index To Horses

Two Year Olds of 2001 – Index To Horses

Two Year Olds of 2001 – Index To Horses

INDEX TO DAMS

Two Year Olds of 2001 – Index To Dams

Two Year Olds of 2001 – Index To Dams

Two Year Olds of 2001 – Index To Dams

Two Year Olds of 2001 – Index To Dams